UNIVERSITY OF ALBERTA
QUAECUMQUE VERA
Ex Libris
Universitatis
Albertensis

"My imagination is rarely as active

as when I am writing to a friend!"

Edvard Grieg ca. 1900. (Troldhaugen)

Edvard Grieg

Letters to Colleagues and Friends

Edvard Grieg

Letters to Colleagues and Friends

SELECTED AND
EDITED BY

Finn Benestad

TRANSLATED BY

William H. Halverson

PEER GYNT PRESS / COLUMBUS

3700 Riverside Drive
Columbus, Ohio 43221-0845
Fax (614) 451-4750

Publication of this book was made possible by generous grants
from the following institutions and foundations:
Anders Jahre's Humanitarian Foundation / The Norwegian Academy of Science and Letters, Oslo
Centre for Advanced Study, Oslo
Edvard Grieg Committee / The Norwegian Cultural Council, Oslo
Grieg Forsk / Troldhaugen / Norsk Hydro ASA

Library of Congress Catalog Card Number:
99–74400

ISBN 0–9645238–2–5

Designed and typeset by Diane Gleba Hall.
Printed in the United States of America.
The paper in this book meets the guidelines for permanence and durability of the Committee on Production Guidelines for Book Longevity of the Council on Library Resources.

9 8 7 6 5 4 3 2 1

Preface

Edvard Grieg (1843–1907), who remains to this day Norway's foremost composer, did much more than write the music for which he is famous all over the world. He was also an excellent writer of prose, a man who had the ability to express his thoughts in striking and powerful ways in letters, articles and speeches. It is, therefore, an unusually interesting experience to read the many well-written letters that have come down to us from his hand. They are a virtually inexhaustible source of knowledge of the composer's life and work and constitute, in many ways, a kind of autobiography. They provide a fascinating insight into the workings of an alert, informed and active mind.

Moreover, Grieg's letters make an exceedingly important contribution to our understanding of Norwegian cultural history in the latter half of the nineteenth century—the very time when Norway was struggling to emerge from the cultural and political dependency that had been its lot for over five hundred years. Grieg's correspondence with colleagues and friends in Norway and other countries—prominent figures in Scandinavian cultural life as well as such composers as Johannes Brahms and Peter Tchaikovsky and the leading European conductors of his day—also bear witness to a deep insight into the art and culture of other countries and to a constantly recurring desire to immerse himself in the larger perspectives, to look beyond his homeland toward the wider horizons.

When Grieg acceded to requests from would-be biographers for information about his life and work, he always insisted that what he sent them must not be quoted verbatim but must be rewritten. He never explained, however, why he felt so strongly about this. During his lifetime he rarely allowed excerpts from his letters to be published. On September 3, 1903, he wrote to Gerhard Schjelderup, who at that time was putting the finishing touches on a Grieg biography written in connection with the composer's sixtieth birthday: "To write down or dictate memories from childhood and early youth would be poison for my poor shattered nerves. Given my present condition, you must not try to get from us any information beyond that which you have already received. My wife cannot report anything without a conference with me, and that is the very thing I absolutely cannot tolerate. I must still strongly insist that private letters except for the ones I have mentioned (the letters in *Samtiden* to my parents in Rome in 1870) must not be published."

Grieg was of course aware that he could not control the letters he had written to colleagues and friends—to people he knew as well as people in foreign countries, many of whom he had never met—but to Schjelderup he nonetheless expressed the following pious wish: "In general it is my unalterable position that my private letters must not be published before I am gone, and even then the selection should be made with the very greatest discretion."

One can raise a question whether Grieg himself always exercised "the very greatest discretion" in his correspondence. He was extremely sensitive about any criticism of his music or his actions and sometimes did not hesitate to lash out at someone who ventured to express a negative word. One finds instances of this, for example, in his letters to Iver Holter in connection with the Norwegian music festival held in Bergen, Norway, in the summer of 1898. On rare occasions he even managed to put his foot in his mouth—for example, in his first letter to Johannes Brahms, where he makes an unflattering comment about Brahms's friend, Eduard Hanslick. For the most part, however, Grieg maintained a dignified tone in his letters, both when he aired his displeasure and when he expressed his opinions about composers and other artists whose art was not entirely to his liking.

Most importantly, however, Grieg had a unique ability to write in a vivid and engaging manner. He seasoned his letters with copious quotations from and allusions to world literature, especially Norwegian and German masterworks. Also notable are his frequent references to biblical passages. A humorous element often found expression in connection with matters that were not inherently funny, not least in innumerable descriptions of his frequent struggles with influenza, bronchitis, pneumonia and gastric disorders.

Grieg was like a migratory bird. In late autumn he always longed to get away from the ice and snow of the Norwegian winter, to immerse himself in the flourishing cultural life of the great cities of Europe. But when spring was approaching he developed an equally intense longing for his homeland, especially for the mountains of West Norway. The magnificent scenery of his native country drew him homeward with irresistible power. His descriptions of summery, life-affirming stays on the shores of the Hardangerfjord, of oneness with nature and its inner life at Troldhaugen, of hikes in the wild, majestic Norwegian mountains—all bear witness not only to an open mind but to a special affinity and affection for his homeland, which he loved and on which he was dependent—in his art no less than in his life. In Grieg's letters we hear these sentiments expressed as if in his own voice.

The Grieg Collection in the Bergen Public Library—to which Edvard and

Nina Grieg bequeathed all of Grieg's manuscripts, music, books and letters—contains ca. 5,000 letters *to* Grieg as well as several hundred letters *from* Grieg. Most of the letters in Grieg's hand, however, are preserved in libraries, archives and private collections all over the globe. Over 3,000 of these have now been published (see Bibliography).

Most of the letters in the present volume have been taken from Finn Benestad (ed.), *Edvard Grieg: Brev i utvalg 1862–1907,* vols. I–II, Aschehoug & Co., Oslo 1998, which contains more than 1600 letters either in Grieg's original Norwegian or in Norwegian translations. Fifty letters have been translated from Finn Benestad & Bjarne Kortsen (eds.), *Edvard Grieg: Brev til Frants Beyer 1872–1907,* Oslo 1993. In selecting the letters for inclusion in *Edvard Grieg: Letters to Colleagues and Friends,* only a few of those readily available in modern editions in either English or German have been included. This step eliminated most of the Delius letters (available in English in Lionel Carley, *Grieg and Delius: A Chronicle of Their Friendship in Letters,* London & New York 1993), the Röntgen letters (available in German in Finn Benestad & Hanna de Vries Stavland, *Edvard Grieg und Julius Röntgen: Briefwechsel 1883–1907,* Amsterdam 1997), and the letters to the C. F. Peters Musikverlag (available in German in Finn Benestad & Hella Brock, *Edvard Grieg: Briefwechsel mit dem Musikverlag C. F. Peters 1863–1907,* Frankfurt am Main 1997).

Concerning the letters considered for inclusion in the present volume, the following questions were asked:

> Does the letter have to do with people or events of historical importance?
> Does it shed light on the outward circumstances of Grieg's life?
> Does it reveal something about Grieg's character, values, or innermost thoughts?
> Does it provide significant information about the creation of one or more of Grieg's compositions?
> Does it deal with other matters that can be presumed to be of general interest?

The letters eliciting an affirmative response to at least one of these questions have been included in *Edvard Grieg: Letters to Colleagues and Friends.* The result is a collection of some 500 letters, most of which are here presented in English translation for the first time. All except the few written in English by Grieg himself have been newly translated for this volume. In a few cases, passages judged to be of lesser interest and importance have been deleted. All such deletions are indicated by the symbol (. . .). Elliptical dots *not* enclosed in parentheses were in the source documents.

In three cases, because of their inherent interest, correspondence in both directions has been included: letters to and from Johannes Brahms, Henrik Ibsen and Peter Tchaikovsky. In the remaining letters, footnotes clarify the connection between Grieg's letters and those he received. The footnotes also provide brief comments on events, topics, names, literary allusions and the like that might otherwise be puzzling to some readers.

The letters have been arranged alphabetically by addressee, and multiple letters to a given recipient are ordered chronologically. The letters to each addressee constitute, in effect, a chapter in the book. Each chapter begins with an introduction indicating who the addressee was, his/her relationship to Grieg and, when known, where the originals of Grieg's letters to him/her are preserved.

To spare the reader the necessity of paging backward and forward to find needed information, facts stated in a footnote in one chapter are sometimes repeated in another. Dates, when known, are also provided the first time a person is mentioned in a given chapter.

Readers desiring to consult letters written during a certain period of Grieg's life are referred to the chronological list of Grieg's letters on pp. 687–692. Those interested in specific compositions are advised to consult the index of compositions on pp. 707–710. The general index is primarily an index of proper names, but topics that recur with great frequency in Grieg's letters—his love of nature, political and religious views, opinions of other composers etc.—are also indexed.

It might reasonably be asked whether Grieg's demand for discretion in the selection of letters for publication has been observed in the present collection. There are, for example, instances in which Grieg made intemperate remarks about various contemporaries who had incurred his wrath in one way or another, and there is one series of intimate letters to a young woman to whom he candidly confessed his infatuation. In the latter case it is clear from the letters themselves that Grieg wanted them to be destroyed, so it cannot be denied that his explicit wish is subverted by including them here. However: This episode in Grieg's life is by now common knowledge, the letters have been published previously in Norwegian and thus are in the public domain, and a decision *not* to include them could easily be construed as an attempt to whitewash the author of these letters. Indeed, neither letters nor portions of letters have been omitted out of concern that they might be regarded as unflattering to Grieg. The choices have been made in strict accordance with the criteria stated earlier. The result is a group of letters revealing Grieg as he presumably was: an exceptionally good but admittedly imperfect man whose basic decency and integrity are abundantly evident in the composite picture that he presents of himself.

It is unfortunate that very few letters from Grieg's youth are extant. The Bergen Public Library contains a substantial number of letters from Grieg's parents to their son, but none of the letters that Edvard is known to have sent to his parents or his siblings during his days as a student at the Leipzig Conservatory have been located. Hopefully they will turn up some day, for they would undoubtedly add immeasurably to the account of this period that Grieg himself has given in his autobiographical essay, *My First Success*. This essay, which will be printed in a new English translation in Finn Benestad & William H. Halverson (eds.), *Edvard Grieg: Diaries, Articles, Speeches* (Columbus, Ohio, 2001), was not written until 1903.

The form of the dating of the letters has been made uniform (month/date/year), and the division into paragraphs has often been altered to facilitate ease of reading. Grieg was a frugal man, and he made maximum use of the space available to him on a sheet of paper. Not infrequently, when he ran out of space before he had finished his letter, he wrote a "second layer" of text at a 90° angle over the "first layer"—a practice that sometimes has rendered it difficult to decipher the text, especially when the ink from one page has seeped through the porous paper and obscured the text on the other side.

Norway's capital city was called Christiania from 1624 to 1877, when the spelling was changed to Kristiania. Although Grieg uses both spellings, the former has been used throughout the book except when referring to proper names such as "Kristianiagade". Prior to 1624 and since 1925 the city has been called Oslo.

Titles of Grieg's compositions are given in English. Opus/EG numbers are added when the identity of the composition to which Grieg is referring is not immediately evident. The original—usually Norwegian or German—titles corresponding to the English ones will be found in the list of compositions on pp. 693–704. Works by other composers are referred to by English titles when such titles are in common use. Otherwise original titles are used and, when necessary, with English translations in brackets or in a footnote.

Grieg's quotations from world literature are given in English in the letter and in the original language in a footnote.

Nearly all of Grieg's letters to non-Scandinavian addressees were written in German, though on a very few occasions he used English or French. His German was excellent but, as he himself admitted, his command of both English and French was limited. In the present collection, the letters written by Grieg in English are presented just as they left their author's hand, grammatical errors and all. The letters written in Norwegian, German or French are presented in English translations that attempt to be completely faithful to the meaning and tone of Grieg's originals.

The task of gathering Grieg's letters from the four corners of the earth was begun in the mid-1960's in connection with the preparation of the 20-volume C. F. Peters edition of Grieg's complete works, the last volume of which was published in 1995. This task could not have succeeded without the willing cooperation of the librarians and private collectors in whose care the letters now reside, and I hereby express my most sincere thanks to both the institutions and their leaders. The institutions are: Bergen Offentlige Bibliotek (Bergen Public Library), Bergen; Cambridge University Library; 'collection Haags Gemeentemuseum, The Hague; Det kgl. Bibliotek (The Royal Library), Copenhagen; Gesellschaft der Musikfreunde, Vienna; Grainger Museum, University of Melbourne, Australia; Griegsamlingen, Bergen Offentlige Bibliotek (The Grieg Collection, Bergen Public Library), Bergen; Koninklijke Bibliotheek Albert I, Brussels; Kungliga Biblioteket (The Royal Library), Stockholm; Lincoln Center Library, New York; MacDowell Club of Music and Allied Arts, Los Angeles; Musikhistorisk Museum Carl Claudius Samling (Museum of Music History, Carl Claudius Collection), Copenhagen; National Library of Norway, Oslo Division, Oslo; New York Public Library; Norwegian Royal Archives, Oslo; Pierpont Morgan Library, Mary Flagler Cary Music Collection and The Frederick R. Koch Foundation, New York; Russian Institute of History of the Arts, St. Petersburg; Staatsbibliothek zu Berlin, Preussischer Kulturbesitz, Musikabteilung; Stiftelsen Musikkulturens Främjande (Society for the Promotion of Musical Culture), Stockholm; Tchaikovsky Museum, Klin (Russia); The British Library, London; Universitätsbibliothek Leipzig (University of Leipzig Library); Universitetsbiblioteket i Bergen (University of Bergen library).

Special thanks must be expressed to Karen Falch Johannessen, Curator of the Grieg Collection at the Bergen Public Library, for willing assistance.

I also wish to express my most sincere gratitude to the following institutions for the generous financial support without which it would have been impossible to complete this project: Anders Jahre's Humanitarian Foundation / The Norwegian Academy of Science and Letters, Oslo; Centre for Advanced Study, Oslo; Edvard Grieg Committee / The Norwegian Cultural Council, Oslo; Grieg Forsk, Troldhaugen / Norsk Hydro ASA.

• • •

It has been a great privilege to work with my dear colleague and friend, Professor Dr. William H. Halverson, during the translation process. Grieg's nineteenth-century Norwegian, with its often complex grammar and syntax, poses numerous challenges for a translator. With his deep insight into the Norwegian language and his lifelong affection for Grieg's music, Dr. Halverson has succeeded in producing a translation that presents Grieg's letters in modern English while at the same time preserving the flavor of the master's own style. He has worked closely with me in the preparation of the book since we began planning it together during an extended stay at the Centre for Advanced Study in Oslo in spring, 1998. I hereby express my profoundest gratitude for his invaluable contribution.

Finn Benestad
Oslo, Norway

Contents

---

[1] The number in brackets is the number of letters to the recipient included in the present collection. When the brackets contain two numbers, the first indicates the number of letters in this collection from Grieg to the recipient, the second the number from that individual to Grieg. Each recipient's nationality is indicated in accordance with the following scheme: (A) Australia, (Au) Austria, (B) Belgium, (C) Czechoslovakia, (D) Denmark, (E) England, (F) Finland, (Fr) France, (G) Germany, (H) Holland, (Hu) Hungary, (N) Norway, (P) Poland, (R) Russia, (S) Sweden, (Swi) Switzerland, (US) United States.

To Max Abraham

Max Abraham (1831–1900) had a doctorate in jurisprudence but got involved in the publishing business early in his career. In 1863 he became co-owner of the C. F. Peters Musikverlag, which had been founded in 1800, and he immediately wrote to Grieg asking permission to publish his op. 1, *Four Piano Pieces.* This was the beginning of what proved to be a lifelong collaboration and a lifelong friendship between publisher and composer.

The complete correspondence between Grieg and the owners of C. F. Peters—a total of 635 letters, which are preserved in Bergen Offentlige Bibliotek (Bergen Public Library)—has been published by Finn Benestad and Hella Brock in the original German in the book *Edvard Grieg. Briefwechsel mit dem Musikverlag C. F. Peters 1863–1907,* Frankfurt 1997. Many of these letters deal with business minutiae, others give information of great interest with respect to Grieg's biography, and not a few provide a glimpse of the friendship that existed between Grieg and Abraham. Two of these letters are given here in English translation as a sample of what will be found in the Benestad-Brock collection.

1

Bergen, May 23, 1883

Dear Doctor!
I really should be embarrassed at receiving your latest kind remittance after you had already "advanced" so much to me earlier. I honestly admit that the burden is beginning to get a bit heavy, but on the other hand the voluminous letter came as a rescuing angel at the last moment. Receive, therefore, my warmest thanks—also for the distribution of my works in France, where I quite definitely hope to spend next winter.[1]

And now for a word about Pegasus: He has been here all right, but I wouldn't call him "Presto", and he can't be called "Allegro". If I were to christen him the name would have to be "Andante quasi Lento".[2]

You have wanted three works from me. As the first of these, will you accept

[1] Grieg had jokingly written to Max Abraham on August 22, 1881, that if someone would pay him 1,000 German "Thalers" annually as a kind of advance on future compositions he would regard it as a matter of honor to produce the "required number of works." Abraham took him seriously and on September 7 answered that he would give him 3,000 marks for the coming year if Grieg would write for him a piano concerto, some piano pieces and a piece of chamber music. Grieg wrote on September 16 accepting the arrangement but requesting an additional half year to fulfill the commission and insisting, further, that he had to be somewhat free in his choice of the kind of works he would write. Abraham agreed to these conditions and the agreement was implemented. When Grieg thanks him in the letter of May 23 for a new remittance, the reason is that Abraham had sent him 1,000 marks above and beyond the honorarium he had already received for earlier works as part of the firm's profit for 1882. Abraham had also reported in his letter that Grieg's works were becoming very popular in France.

[2] Pegasus, in Greek mythology, was a winged horse that sprang from the blood of Medusa and eventually became a constellation and the servant of Zeus. In modern times Pegasus has been regarded as a symbol of poetic inspiration. Grieg's use of the musical expression has a double meaning, for two of Dr. Abraham's saddle horses were named "Presto" and "Allegro".

a cello sonata?[3] I have been more inclined to write this kind of work instead of a violin sonata. I started on a piano concerto, but Pegasus refused to budge, so I have not continued with it. Some piano pieces will also be finished soon, and then I hope to go with a relieved conscience to either little Paris or big Paris[4] in the fall.

I have indeed orchestrated op.14; yes, I heard those movements in Copenhagen many years ago. They sounded pretty good, but I would not for all the world publish the orchestral score now because it is altogether too clear that this composition belongs to a long-vanished Schumann period of my life.[5]

You have also expressed a desire to receive world-wide rights to all of my works that may be published in the future, and even though my situation unfortunately is such that I dare not make such a commitment I need not tell you that I infinitely prefer to be associated with the Peters firm and its amiable proprietor rather than with all kinds of French and English publishers.[6]

I hope to hear soon as to whether you intend to receive my *Cello Sonata* with *open* arms, with *folded* arms—or *not at all.*

Cordially yours,
EDVARD GRIEG

---

[3] *Cello Sonata* in A minor. The piano pieces to which Grieg refers are *Waltz Caprices* and *Lyric Pieces II* op. 38. Both were published by C. F. Peters Musikverlag in 1883. The piano concerto mentioned by Grieg was never finished. The sketches have been printed in *Edvard Grieg: Complete Works,* vol. 20.

[4] Grieg often called Leipzig "little Paris" (Klein-Paris) in contrast to Paris, France—"big Paris" (Groß–Paris).

[5] Grieg composed his only symphony (EG 119) in 1863–64. After portions of it had been played during the years 1864–67, Grieg wrote on the score the following words: "Must never be performed." In 1869, however, he arranged the two inner movements of the symphony for two pianos and had them published by Horneman & Erslev in Copenhagen under the title *Two Symphonic Pieces* (*Deux pièces symphoniques*) op. 14. Grieg's wish that the symphony not be performed was respected until 1980, when a copy was spirited to Russia and the work was performed there. Once this had happened, the Board of the Bergen Public Library made the work available for performance. It was played at the International Music Festival in Bergen in 1981 and in 1984 was printed in *Edvard Grieg: Complete Works,* vol. 11. Several CD recordings of the symphony have been made.

[6] In 1889 Grieg entered into a general contract with C. F. Peters Musikverlag giving the firm the exclusive right to publish all his future compositions. The text of the contract reads as follows: "The C. F. Peters firm, which has most of Mr. Edvard Grieg's compositions in its catalogue, commits itself to Mr. Grieg until his death—or to his wife Nina, nee Hagerup, if she outlives him, until her death—to pay an annual pension of DM 4,000—four thousand marks—which shall be paid quarterly in the amount of DM 1,000 per quarter beginning January 1, 1890. Mr. Grieg commits himself to first offer to the C. F. Peters firm, for a specified honorarium, the world-wide rights to all his future compositions. If the firm, within two weeks of having been apprised of the new work, does not accept the offer, this means that the firm has declined the work in question."

In 1901 the annual pension was increased to DM 6,000 with the provision for Grieg's widow remaining at DM 4,000. Thus Nina Grieg continued to receive an annual pension until she died in 1935. These were very large sums of money that Grieg and, later, Nina received from C. F. Peters in addition to an honorarium for each composition. By comparison, a teacher at the College of Music in Berlin received an annual salary of ca. DM 2,500 at that time. All of Grieg's subsequent compositions were accepted by the firm.

2

Voksenkollen Sanatorium, December 5, 1900

Dear Doctor!

Today I learned quite by chance of the celebration on December 1 of the centennial jubilee of Edition Peters. I need not tell you how greatly I regret that I did not have the privilege of expressing my deepest congratulations to you on this day that was so significant both for you and for me. Kindly tell your nephew[7] that I will *never* forgive him for failing to inform me about the jubilee. That was not nice of him. But I can assure you that my congratulations *post festum* come from the depths of my heart, and they are indeed as strong as my disappointment and annoyance over the apparent lack of interest are great.

I hope that you have been in tolerably good health[8] and that you have been able to take pleasure in the many proofs of your popularity and the many expressions of affection from all directions.

With respect to my personal relationship with Edition Peters, an overall picture rolls past my inner eye on this occasion, and this picture shows me anew the deep gratitude toward the firm C. F. Peters and its dear proprietor that will permeate my being until I draw my last breath.

Here each day is more splendid than the preceding one. An absolute fairy-tale world. I have no cold and my strength is coming back. We are thinking, therefore, of staying here for the time being. Presumably we will go to Denmark at the beginning of next year. And soon thereafter to Leipzig. We'll have to put away some "jubilee oysters" together![9] You really should have had a jubilee sonata —one that, like Beethoven's op. 22, "had washed itself, dear brother!"[10]

With the friendliest greetings, also from my wife, I am,

Faithfully yours,
EDVARD GRIEG

---

[7] Max Abraham's nephew Henri Hinrichsen (1868–1942) had become co-owner of C. F. Peters.

[8] The same day that Grieg wrote his letter, Abraham sent a farewell letter to his Norwegian friend. Sadly, neither would receive the other's letter before Abraham died. He had been very ill for some time, and just three days after he sent his letter to Grieg he took his own life. In his letter he mentioned that Grieg would be receiving a jubilee catalogue and added, "In this catalogue your name naturally plays a large role, for the firm owes infinitely much to you. Nearly forty years ago I received from you your op. 1, and since then I have been so fortunate as, with very few exceptions, to publish all of your splendid compositions. My gratitude for this will never cease." See also Grieg's letter to Henri Hinrichsen of December 9, 1900.

[9] Grieg was very fond of oysters. Wherever he went he tried to get hold of "the little animals", as he sometimes called them.

[10] "Dieser Sonate hat sich gewaschen, lieber Herr Bruder!" ("This sonata has washed itself, dear Mr. brother!") On January 15, 1801, Beethoven used these words in offering his *Septet in E-flat Major*, op. 20, to Franz Anton Hoffmeister (1754–1818) in Leipzig. Hoffmeister and Ambrosius Kühnel (1770–1813) had recently (1800) established the Bureau de Musique, which later became C. F. Peters Musikverlag.

To George Augener

George Augener (1830–1915) was born in Germany but moved to London in 1852 and in 1855 established a music publishing company bearing his name. In 1873 he became the general agent for the Leipzig firm C. F. Peters, in which capacity he collaborated in an effort to produce inexpensive editions of the works of the classical masters. Grieg had close contact with the Augener family during his visits to England and often stayed at their home in Clapham Common.

On February 13, 1902, Augener wrote to Grieg asking if he would write a coronation march for use in connection with the coronation of King Edward VII (1841–1910) and Queen Alexandra[1] (1844–1925) in June of that year. As a man who had no enthusiasm for monarchism, Grieg was not at all inclined to take on the assignment, and his reluctance was further strengthened by his declining health. Augener sent Grieg a reply on March 5 assuring him that he understood his Norwegian friend's honest scruples about undertaking the task.

The translation that follows is based on a draft of Grieg's letter (in German) that is preserved in Bergen Offentlige Bibliotek (Bergen Public Library).

[Copenhagen, February 1902]

Dear Mr. Augener!

I am very happy and grateful to you for thinking of me in connection with the composition of a coronation march, but in my opinion I am not the right man for such a task. I have, indeed, written an "Homage March" for *Sigurd Jorsalfar.* That was a matter of writing incidental music to a play that had inspired me. But to get enthused about the coronation festivities for a living royal couple—and a foreign one at that—would, to be candid, be totally impossible for me. The minimum of energy that my declining health has not yet sapped I would rather use on tasks that are more appealing to me.

However, the English royal couple have treated me so cordially and have made such a favorable impression that it would hardly have been possible for me to refuse the request if it had come from the highest level. Since it comes from you, however, it is a different matter. Our cordial relationship through many years hopefully allows me to express openly my views, which the higher-ranking people might have regarded as incomprehensible and insulting.

One more thing: What would the British—and especially the British musicians—say about using a foreigner on such a solemn occasion? All in all I think that after more careful consideration it would be more appropriate to drop the idea of my involvement in the festivities.

With hope that you will not take offense at my freely expressed remarks and with cordial greetings to the whole Augener family—and especially with the best wishes for William's improvement[2]—also from my wife, I remain

Yours truly,
EDVARD GRIEG

---

[1] Edward VII, English king 1901–10; Alexandra, daughter of Danish king Christian IX (1818–1906).

[2] William Augener (1854–1904), George Augener's son, had for many years been co-owner and director of operations of the firm founded by his father. He was now seriously ill and died in 1904 at the age of 50.

To Tor Aulin

The Swedish violinist, conductor and composer Tor Aulin (1866–1914) was an enthusiastic admirer of Grieg's music. His string quartet performed Grieg's *String Quartet* in G minor several times during the years 1888–90. He wrote his first letter to Grieg on December 29, 1891, after performing Grieg's *Violin Sonata No. 3* in C minor. Here he reported, "At our last chamber-music concert before Christmas I performed, for the first time in Stockholm, your C-minor piano-violin *Sonata*, and with a success for both composer and performer such as one seldom witnesses. The reviewers couldn't find expressions warm enough to convey their admiration, and the audience's applause can only be compared with that with which they greeted your *String Quartet* when we presented it for the first time—and the applause has been repeated each time your work has appeared on our program." This letter became the prelude to an extensive correspondence between the two artists and they soon developed a warm friendship.

Grieg's letters to Aulin were published (in Norwegian) in 1952 by Bo Wallner in an article entitled "Edvard Griegs brev till Tor Aulin" in the Swedish journal *Ord och Bild* (pp. 558–76). A follow-up article by Wallner with Aulin's letters to Grieg, which are preserved in Bergen Offentlige Bibliotek (Bergen Public Library), appeared in the same journal in 1955 (pp. 484–94).

1

Christiania, September 7, 1899

Dear Aulin!

Well, as we say in Norway, you have "made a Swede of yourself." In other words: You didn't come. I told everyone that you were coming with your quartet. I waited and waited through the whole of June, the whole of July, while I scanned all the newspapers and inquired at all the music stores. No. Nobody knew anything about you. So, very disappointed, I gave up hope and took a trip to the mountains with two friends (one of them being Julius Röntgen[1]).

About eight days ago I came here, where I have participated in the dedication of the new National Theater and where I met Messrs. Burén and Nordquist,[2] who have been so kind as to invite me to Stockholm this fall. Now above all I want to be sure that you will be home then, so you must send me a few lines. In general I would like so much to hear a little about you—how your plans and your hopes are coming along, whether you are still living in the period of *Sturm und Drang* or whether you have become more calm.

I have also met Mrs. Dagmar Möller.[3] She will be home only during the latter half of October, and I am so reluctant to miss both her and her beautiful singing. Burén and Nordquist, however, prefer that I come later. If I do, whom do you think I should get to replace Mrs. Möller? You must tell me that. Give Mr. Möller

---

[1] Grieg's close friend, the Dutch pianist, conductor and composer Julius Röntgen (1855–1932).

[2] Axel Burén (1842–1923) was administrative director of the Stockholm opera, Conrad Nordquist (1840–1920) was chief conductor at the same institution.

[3] The Norwegian-born singer Dagmar Möller (1866–1956), wife of Swedish architect Carl Möller (1857–1933), whose designs included Johanneskirken [St. John's Church] in Stockholm.

my warm greetings and thank him for the photo of his beautiful church—the photo his wife brought me.

Now we have finally gotten a good orchestra here. It's about time. You would have enjoyed yourself if you had been here during these days. I have rarely had an opportunity to work with such good horn players. The principal is a man by the name of Spohr and is a nephew of the famous Louis.[4] He has five ribbons on his chest and deserves ten, for he plays marvelously. Almost all the winds are Germans, so you can see how inconsistent the Norwegian chauvinists are—the ones who ran me down in the newspapers because I engaged the Dutch musicians for the music festival in Bergen last year.[5]

And with that I must close for today, dear friend. Hopefully we will see each other again soon.

Yours truly,
EDVARD GRIEG

P.S. We leave tomorrow to spend a few days with Bjørnsons[6] in Gausdal, then go on to Copenhagen. Address: Wilhelm Hansen.

Nina asks that I send warm greetings to a lion![7]

2

Troldhaugen at Bergen, July 21, 1904

Dear Aulin!
Thanks for both the postcard and the letter! As for your plan, I had something quite different in mind for the winter months. This fall I absolutely will go to Denmark and from there to Germany and perhaps elsewhere. And as for the financial arrangements: Since you have been so candid as to mention this, I will tell you with equal candor that I have reached the point where I will neither play nor conduct outside of Norway for an honorarium of less than 1,000 Norwegian crowns. The self-conquest and strenuous exertion, the tension and nervousness are *too* great. For this reason it is entirely natural that the smaller cities are excluded. And in the larger ones? Yes, there I am really "worn out"! My repertoire, as you know, is small. To sit down and practice thoroughly my more difficult compositions—the ones I have stayed away from because they exceed my technical abilities—for that I have neither strength nor time nor inclination.

---

4 German composer and violinist Louis Spohr (1784–1859).

5 Grieg is referring to the Norwegian music festival held in Bergen June 26–July 3, 1898. He was severely criticized by many Norwegian musicians for engaging the Concertgebouw orchestra of Amsterdam for the festival instead of a Norwegian orchestra.

6 Norwegian author Bjørnstjerne Bjørnson (1832–1910) and his wife Karoline (1835–1934).

7 Nina Grieg (1845–1935), nee Hagerup, married Edvard in 1867. Aulin's friends often called him "the lion" ("lejonet"), partly because of his appearance but partly also because of his somewhat brusque manner.

Last time it went well. Why? Especially, I think, because the weather was so absolutely marvelous.

You mention November. That, so far as the climate is concerned, is a poor month for an impossible person like me. In April I am supposed to go to Russia. But I will probably give up on that for political reasons. Let's talk further after Christmas. Perhaps you, too, will have concluded that your proposal with my conditions is not practicable.

The emperor[8] came out dressed like a tourist. He didn't look any more like an emperor than you or I. But he is an unusual man, that's for sure. A mixture of great energy, great self-confidence and great kindheartedness. I spoke with him alone for almost an hour after dinner at the home of the German consul. We talked about art, about religion, about socialism and God knows what. I also had to play for him. Then he had arranged for his whole orchestra (NB: with strings, thus a complete ensemble), consisting of about forty men, to perform. After coffee he took two chairs and placed them in front of the others. He sat down on one of them and motioned for me to sit in the other one, saying: "Please, orchestra seat!" And then I heard both *Sigurd Jorsalfar* [op. 56] and *Peer Gynt* [op. 46] and many other things. I told him as much as I could remember regarding the two dramas, which interested him greatly. When he especially liked something he conveyed his impression with gestures. In "Sigurd" an expression for "royal" dignity and, for example, in "Anitra's Dance" with the most irresistibly funny contortions mimicking a belly dancer. The next day the whole program was repeated on board the *Hohenzollern* in the most glorious summer evening Norway could ever have. When the ship was suddenly illuminated with thousands of electric candles, it created a fairytale atmosphere that was absolutely enchanting.

No, enough of this chatter about the emperor. More when we get together.

Warmest greetings to you and your wife from Nina and from

Yours truly,
EDVARD GRIEG

3

Troldhaugen, June 29, 1905

Dear friend!

Warm thanks both for the concerto "Der reine Tor!" and for the songs.[9] Believe me, I am enough of a gourmet to appreciate the fact that you are giving me

---

8 Grieg is telling here of two meetings in Bergen with German Keiser Wilhelm II (1859–1941), who for a number of years visited Norway with his yacht *Hohenzollern*.

9 Aulin's compositions included three violin concertos and a number of songs. In using the phrase "Der reine Tor" in his letter of thanks, Grieg is making a play on words. He often used this phrase from Wagner's *Parsifal* in the sense of "the innocent fool." In this case, however, he is alluding to his friend Tor and his

your manuscript as a gift. If only I could now send you something to demonstrate my gratitude. But manuscripts are my weak point, and to tell the truth I have not been healthy enough lately to be able to rummage through my papers. But since you really would like to own something by a "most highly esteemed old graybeard!"[10] (as a young German autograph-seeker dubbed me in a recent letter) you certainly will get it. Time begets wisdom. I hope that may also apply to political questions, about which you utter not a single word.[11] For me during these days—and I think the same is true for many other Norwegians—it is as if I have come closer to Sweden and to my Swedish friends now that the terrible quarrel about the union seems finally to have come to an end.

This is a great time for the Nordic countries, and it is no wonder that Norwegian and Swedish politics, which are rooted in completely different philosophies of life, finally had to collide. In Norway, the nation itself rules. In Sweden, only a reactionary minority. In Norway one feels politically *modern.* In Sweden the leading circles, which make the decisions there, are strictly Medieval. How, then, could it be possible for people in Sweden to understand the Norwegian motivation? We understand that clearly. That is why there is nothing in Norway that resembles hatred toward Sweden and the Swedes. To the contrary: We hold the people in high esteem and only pity the old king, for whom we have much sympathy. What is not mentioned in Sweden, but what is nonetheless the main point, is that he had acted in such a way that he was left without a government [in Norway]. For all practical purposes he was unable to enlist the services of a single Norwegian man. That is completely unique. But in that very moment he ceased to be Norway's king. He didn't have to be dethroned, for he had dethroned himself. A king without a government is an impossibility. We, therefore, had to choose another way: a government without a king. How easy it is to explain his first angry protest as he reacted with painful surprise—but how noble and beautiful has been his behavior since then. It takes a man of stature to exercise such self-conquest, a man who understands the demands of the times. If his wishes prevail—and I think a secret nudge of the great powers in the same direction is occurring—then a bright, new time is dawning over Scandinavia that will leave the vanished time of the union in its wake. May you and I still live to experience it!

And then, dear friend, this: When we get older a conflict arises in us that we—

---

violin concerto, which has given him the impression of being "pure Tor", i.e., exactly what he would expect from his friend Tor Aulin. The songs to which Grieg refers are Aulin's *Tannhäuser* songs to texts by Julius Wolff. The songs were dedicated to Grieg.

10 Grieg uses the German expression: "hochverehrter Greis".

11 Grieg is alluding to the conflict between Sweden and Norway concerning Norway's demand for complete independence. On June 7, 1905—i.e., just three weeks before this letter was written—the Norwegian Parliament (Stortinget) had passed a resolution declaring that the union with Sweden had ceased to exist and authorizing the Norwegian cabinet to remain in office and rule the country.

especially we artists—must struggle to come out of victorious. I know this tendency to apathy toward the world and toward people. But then one must say to oneself: Damn it all, now I'm on the verge of losing the fight. The best troops must go to battle to win the victory. And the troops—you have them. For they are called *energy* and *a belief in beauty.* Hurrah for these two greatest values. I could add a third: *belief in truth.* For we have need of that as well.

I, too, was born with energy, and in recent years under the pressure of life I have many times had the feeling that it had forsaken me. But that is just nonsense. If one has energy one has it for life. It's just a matter of taking the trouble to use it. Don't be discouraged. Illness among those one loves most takes its toll, and that is no less true when one is ill oneself. But you have within yourself so much with which Mother Nature has blessed you that you should just be thankful and "make the best out of it."[12] The affection you have for Nina and me is *completely mutual* and will continue to be so, even if a thousand Boströms[13] try to choke the Swedish democracy with their megalomania.

I am going into the city and must, therefore, close. Thank you once again for the beautiful music and beautiful thoughts, and warm greetings to you and your wife and children from Nina and from

Yours truly,
EDVARD GRIEG

P.S. I no longer remember your address. Please send it to me at your convenience.

4

Christiania, October 9, 1905
Hotel Westminster

Dear friend!
Finally, finally! You are right if you are thinking: What is the matter with the man? Has he become a chauvinist? Or what? However: Whatever I might become in my old days, I won't ever become that, for it is the worst thing I can think of.

Somebody told me a few days ago that your name had been included in an address having to do with a peaceful solution, and I thought: It is fate that is reminding me of my duties—and here you have me at your feet with: *Pater peccavi.*[14]

Something can be said in my defense, however. For I rummaged around Troldhaugen looking for a manuscript for you until in the end I looked like a

---

[12] Both the quotation marks and the English phrase enclosed by them are in Grieg's original letter.

[13] Erik Gustaf Bernhard Boström (1842–1907) was the Swedish prime minister in 1902–05 and was a leading figure in the union negotiations between Norway and Sweden.

[14] *Pater peccavi*: Father, I have sinned.

chimney sweep. Finally, the last day before my departure, I found the *Symphonic Dances* for piano four hands, which I performed in an orchestral version in Stockholm. If, for want of anything better, you will take them it will be a pleasure for me to know that they are in your possession. I will send them at the same time that I send this letter. But since I don't know or remember your present address I will address both to Abr. Lundquist's Music Store.

And how goes it with you now? Your wife? Your children? Your last letter was dated July 16, so I hope you can report good progress during the summer with respect to your health. Here things are status quo. I have been free of actual illness and perhaps, therefore, my resistance is slightly improved. But to write long letters, that I cannot manage. Everything tires me so quickly. And your letter invites me to give a very long answer. But the political situation has indeed had so many new phases, and has changed so drastically in every way during the past months, that much of what you say is no longer relevant.

As for the old king, he actually removed himself as Norway's king since he *couldn't* form a government and didn't want to come to Norway at the critical moment. For we could not be without a government. Without a king it is possible: History shows that. I think the old king acted and continues to act stupidly, but he is old and feels wounded so one shouldn't pay too much attention to him. And yet, it was *he* who first rejected the idea of war and demanded a peaceful settlement. That was a great and noble deed and it will not be forgotten. True, he unfortunately spoke later the incredible words that if Riksdagen[15] should nonetheless choose war, he would be obliged *loyally* to accept this decision. And after that I do not have another word to say about this man. I am done with him—and I pity him.

Still, there is one thing more: I can assure you that the offer to place a Bernadotte on Norway's throne was dictated solely by the desire for peace and good understanding with Sweden outside the union.[16] This offer has to this day—over four months after it was issued—not even been considered worthy of a reply. If such an insult is an act of personal vengeance, then it is completely misdirected and could in the future do Sweden and Norway irreparable harm. It is just a pity that in Sweden neither the king nor Riksdagen has been able to see the issue practically and impartially, without ulterior motives.

I am in complete agreement with what you say about the press. It incorporates, in my opinion, everything that is rotten and demoralized in society. That the press *could* be something else, yes, I have no doubt about that. And that is what is so exasperating, that this which it could be but is not is something that

---

[15] Riksdagen: the Swedish parliament.

[16] The invitation to King Oscar II (1829–1907) to allow a prince of the Bernadotte dynasty to ascend to the throne of Norway was adopted by the Norwegian Parliament at the same session at which it declared that the union with Sweden had ceased to exist.

it wears like a motto in good times and bad, and in so doing conceals the culprits. During the entire crisis the Swedish press has not hesitated to smear Norway and the Norwegians with all its filth, and as little as I think of our own press I must say that I am astonished at the crushing equanimity with which it has taken all this ignominy. And yet, this too has its deeper ground. What we did on June 7 was not an act of hate against a country and a people for whom, in fact, we harbor no feelings of hate. Our feeling has been merely the desire to have our constitution respected and to become masters in our own house. When a young man is "confirmed" he no longer wants guardianship. He wants at that time to free himself, and if he is not stupid it doesn't occur to him to be rude about it. For there is no reason to do so.

We had no reason to use abusive language toward Sweden just because we disagreed with its ruling politicians. Therefore we merely looked wide-eyed at the Swedish press and thought: No, that is not how one ought to act. This irritation only made us all the more calm, and that was our good fortune. The same held true when Sweden expelled peaceful men and women from the country as criminals. We stood there like "der reine Thor".[17] We didn't understand what was happening because we ourselves felt no similar urge. I maintain that the agitation of the Swedish press, which for a time has indeed succeeded in inciting the Swedish people against the Norwegians—that this agitation is an artificially fabricated movement that is grounded in ignorance of the realities and of the way of thinking of the Norwegian people. Because of that, the movement will also wane of its own accord. Yes, both for that reason and because there is no corresponding opposition movement here.

The unanimity of our press has unfortunately come to an abrupt end of late in that a fanatical little party refuses to accept the Karlstad agreement[18] and the republic. These loudmouths would probably drive us into anarchy if the government were not as able as it is. The governmental leaders as well as the Swedish delegates have, indeed, amply demonstrated this ability in the Karlstad agreement, which in my humble opinion is a *masterwork* and will become one of the pillars on which a spiritually forward-moving Scandinavia must build its future.

How stupid people become during a political agitation! When I think of the artistic enjoyment that I and many other Norwegians have experienced during our performances in Sweden, and then I read that for the time being Bjørnson's plays cannot be given and that my music is hissed by "the high society" in Strömstad—the same music they otherwise would be applauding! It makes you nauseous! But I believe that the mood will soon return toward that which is normal.

---

[17] Here Grieg is using the phrase "der reine Thor" from Wagner's music-drama *Parsifal* in the sense "the innocent fool."

[18] The agreement certifying Norway's independence from Sweden was signed at Karlstad, Sweden on September 23, 1905.

And I believe that in the fundamental concepts of both countries—concepts in the direction of honor and love of one's homeland—there is occurring in these days a powerful sense of "Forward!" that under peaceful conditions it would have required generations to achieve. The Swedish liberal elections, too, are of the greatest importance in this connection.

But now farewell to politics! Let us hope for "understanding". That is the main point.

I asked Halvorsen[19] if he would perform a symphony by Glass,[20] to which he replied that they can't buy any more music than that which he has already bought for the season and that the program is settled for this year. But he is interested in the idea and hopes to get acquainted with the work. Is it the symphony that Glass has dedicated to me or is it an earlier one? Has it been printed? Please write soon. Do not recompense my long silence according to my desserts!

Affectionate greetings from house to house.

Yours truly,
EDVARD GRIEG

P.S. I must just in all confidence report to you, as an illustration of the conditions, that I have had to decline two concerts in Helsinki in the middle of September because I do not dare to travel through Sweden. Shall we not drink to that? (So that the sort of thing that has occurred will not occur again!)

5

Christiania, February 5, 1906
Hotel Westminster

Dear friend!
This interminable illness! Except for it you would have heard from me long ago with thanks for your excellent violin pieces. They are fine and noble things. Beautiful and genuine music in all of them. Perhaps especially in "Märchen". Parenthetically, I also admire the ease with which you, the sophisticated violinist, get the piano to resound. Here you distinguish yourself from most of your composer colleagues, who always make the piano heavy and dry. Now you must write a violin sonata and it will be good, of that I am sure!

And congratulations on your—and your countrymen's—triumphs in Copenhagen.[21] But all three of you are too great artists to be used as political bait.

---

19 Norwegian composer and violinist Johan Halvorsen (1864–1939) was the first musical director of the National Theater in Christiania.

20 Danish composer Louis Glass (1864–1936).

21 Aulin had collaborated with his Swedish colleagues Wilhelm Stenhammar (1871–1927) and Hugo Alfvén (1872–1960) in giving an orchestral concert in Copenhagen.

Well, let that be as it may. Each *rapprochement* and each attempt at one is to the good. Therefore I also note with pleasure that Scholander[22] is giving an evening program here in Christiania in the middle of this month.

I am not blind to the fact that artists have a power to unite that it is important to use precisely in critical times. The situation here is such that I feel sure that every Swede will be received with the greatest kindness. How long the resentment in Sweden will last it is not easy to say. Naturally it will take time. And we understand its innermost root; therefore we cannot be angry about it but must simply regret it. Unfamiliarity with and ignorance of Norwegian political circumstances are responsible for the fact that you Swedes have no eye for the absolute shortsightedness and deceptive behavior that your politicians have exhibited in the union matter. When a proud people are subjected to such treatment, the steadily tightened knot finally has to break. When it finally is broken, it is indeed so very human that these gentlemen, instead of acknowledging their own guilt, throw it back at us. But such injustice cannot long survive. I think that everything will normalize itself as a matter of course, despite some fanatical loudmouths in the military and among the merchants.

As I may have told you, I am a republican and have been so since my youth. Nonetheless, I voted for the monarchy because I regarded it as the wisest course for us in the present European situation. Now I see that the popularity of the Bernadotte dynasty in Sweden appears to be so tenuous that it would not surprise me if Sweden were to be the first republic in Scandinavia! Yes, wouldn't that be something! I would greet it with exultation, and I don't think it would be many years before we would follow suit. Write many fifths and octaves! It prepares the mood!

And how are things going, dear friend? Are you beginning to recover from your great loss? It will go with you as it did with Nina and me: The memory will come to be like a beautiful dream. But it takes time for it to develop in this way.[23]

Warm greetings both from Nina and from

Yours truly,
EDVARD GRIEG

---

[22] Swedish singer Sven Scholander (1860–1936).

[23] In a letter dated January 1, 1906, Aulin had told Grieg of the death from tuberculosis of his little daughter Karin. The Griegs had also lost their only child—a daughter, Alexandra—in 1869, shortly after her first birthday. That is the background of Grieg's words of comfort to his friend.

To Fridtjof Backer-Grøndahl

The Norwegian pianist and composer Fridtjof Backer-Grøndahl (1885–1959) was the son of Agathe Backer Grøndahl (1847–1907) and Olaus Andreas Grøndahl (1847–1923), both of whom were professional musicians. Indeed, Agathe Backer Grøndahl is regarded to this day as the most important female composer Norway has produced. Fridtjof was still at the beginning of his career in 1907, having played his debut concert in Christiania in 1903. He eventually became one of the foremost interpreters of Grieg's music.

Grieg's letter to Fridtjof Backer-Grøndahl is privately owned.

Skodsborg,[1] *June 1, 1907*

Dear Fridtjof!
Your dear, serious letter stirred me mightily in the depths of my soul. I myself am so despondent at this time that I can hardly think, not to mention read or write. But I must nonetheless tell you that what you say about Dohnányi[2] I can also say about your mother: There are few people whom I regard so highly. Thus what you say about her suffering pains me. But I understand that it is the same nerves that are the common source of the greatest suffering and of art's most sublime revelations. She was an exceptionally finely tuned soul—and she has had to pay for the joy of being that! May she soon find peace! In this wish I include all that I would have liked to say to her in gratitude for everything that she, through her art and her noble personality, has meant for me ever since my youth.[3]

I was afraid that my letter might have reached her when she was so weak that it would have been impossible for her to read it. So I am all the happier to learn that she still cherished such heartfelt thoughts for Nina and me. Give her one last, sincere greeting from both of us if you have the opportunity. Tell her again—as I wrote to her—that you could not find a better friend than me. To be sure, I share the opinion that having an older artist friend is not overly important because young people always follow—and must follow—their own convictions. But if you should sometime need the support that life and experience can provide in many a case, then you may count on me as long as I am living.

I see in the newspapers that your father is taking his singers to the north of Norway.[4] It must be hard for him to perform his duties with all the sorrow that fills his heart. But there are people who would absolutely collapse if they did not have the opportunity to struggle through their sorrow by working. Each of us

---

1 Skodsborg Sanatorium near Copenhagen, where Grieg was a patient at this time.

2 Fridtjof Backer-Grøndahl was studying at this time—on Grieg's recommendation—with the Hungarian pianist Ernst (Ernö) von Dohnányi (1877–1960). See Grieg's letter to Dohnányi of January 8, 1906.

3 Fridtjof's mother, Agathe Backer Grøndahl, died on June 4. The letter from Fridtjof to which Grieg refers was a reply in behalf of his mother to a letter of May 15 from Grieg to her.

4 Fridtjof's father, Olaus Andreas Grøndahl, was one of Norway's foremost choral conductors. In 1878 he established his own choir ("Grøndahl's Choir"). He also served as conductor of the Norwegian Students' Chorus from 1888 to 1911 and of the Businessmen's Chorus from 1888 to 1905.

must handle it in our own way, and I understand that it is a heavy weight he has to bear. You must give him my most heartfelt greetings.

Outside my window I hear the whistling sound of the sea. It has helped me to write these few lines. But now it will also help to calm my nerves after the strain. It is unbelievable what power the sea has to calm the nerves. Remember that if the going ever gets rough.

We probably will not see each other in Christiania. I don't dare to stay there any longer than necessary en route [to Bergen]. As soon as I can manage it we will be heading north; I'm hoping it might still be this week or early next week. I long for peace and quiet at Troldhaugen. But in my present condition the trip from here to there is altogether too long for me in this strange winter-summer.

And now farewell, dear Fridtjof! Your good nature will help you bear all the sadness that you must live through. I know it well from days gone by, believe me. May God strengthen you!

Your devoted
EDVARD GRIEG

To Thomas Ball Barratt

Thomas Ball Barratt (1862–1940) was a clergyman. He was born in Cornwall, England, but moved to Norway as a boy of five when his father became foreman of a mining company in Hardanger. He studied in England from 1873 to 1878 but returned to Norway as a clergyman in about 1880. During the 1880's he took private instruction from Grieg in thoroughbass,[1] but in 1885 he abandoned the study of music to devote himself entirely to religious work. He was originally a Methodist, but during a visit to the USA in 1905–06 he was greatly influenced by the Pentecostal movement. Upon returning to Norway he became the leader of this revival movement both in Norway and in other European countries.

Grieg's letters to Barratt are preserved in Nasjonalbiblioteket, Oslo (National Library of Norway, Oslo Division). The one included here is of particular interest because of the insight it provides into some of Grieg's views on religion.

Copenhagen, May 17, 1905
Hotel Phoenix

Dear Pastor Barratt:

Only now have I reached the point where I can thank you for your so well-intentioned letter of January 23.[2] There is something inexpressibly moving about it that I deeply appreciate, but each of us must seek his understanding of the truth in his own way through his own nature. If someone says to me, "Believe that black is white!" I will answer, "No, in accordance with the abilities God has given me I cannot do that." By the same reasoning I cannot believe that a human being is a god. But I do believe, and I feel it, that there is something of God in all of us and that Christ was filled by God as no one else known to me, living or dead, in the family of man.

You say, "Just try Jesus!"[3] One can try a topcoat, but not Jesus. Our understanding of Jesus' personality, I repeat, is conditioned by our abilities. There is only one thing that we must *not* do: We must not play the hypocrite. The great

---

1 Also called "figured bass," "basso continuo" and, in the Germanic languages, "Generalbass."

2 Barratt's letter is preserved in the Bergen Public Library. Barratt had read in the newspapers that Grieg was sick and decided to write to his former teacher. "Ever since I studied 'thoroughbass' with you," he wrote, "I have felt personally linked to you notwithstanding the fact that you, occupied as you have been with your many and great works, obviously have rarely had occasion to think of me."

3 Barratt, in his letter, had reminded Grieg of a conversation they had had in Bergen: "What initiated it was my telling you that I couldn't have a lesson on the day after Easter because I had to preach. (. . .) I know on the basis of this conversation that you were tormented by *doubt* and found it difficult to commit yourself to *the simple way of salvation in Christ Jesus.* (. . .) I beg you, if you still have not accepted Jesus, accept him *now.* Händel, Bach, Haydn and many other great spirits bowed beneath the blessed stream of the gospel and in so doing were cleansed. *Do the same thing* yourself. *Just try Jesus!* He himself says, 'Him who comes to me I will not cast out'—and he never goes back on his word. (. . .) The Lord will fill your heart's chambers with an undreamed-of power, with *life*—and from this life will come still more wonderful and more beautiful music than ever. *Believe, and you will see God's wonder!*"

spirit—the world-soul that we call God—has breathed into each human being a desire to bow before him, and I, too, do that in full measure as I calmly entrust myself to His care when I shall depart this life.

This has more and more become my religion, which I feel can no longer be shaken. In this I am very close to the so-called Unitarians,[4] among whom I—especially in England—have met some of the noblest people I know.

I can only smile at you theologians who are out early and late hunting for the souls of men. That a great personality forces his own views on the little ones is logically correct. Otherwise there would be no progress. But when all the little ones engage in the same sport it is, to put it mildly, comical.

Still, I do not underestimate your good intention and I remain, with friendly greetings,

Respectfully yours,
EDVARD GRIEG

[4] Grieg first came in contact with the Unitarian movement in Birmingham, England, in 1888. Unitarianism was a neo-Protestant denomination that rejected the doctrine of the trinity, which the Unitarians considered inconsistent with pure monotheism. The name "Unitarians" was first used in reference to a congregation established in London in 1884. American Unitarianism developed within New England Congregationalism, partly as a reaction against the 18th-century revival movement.

To Otto Benzon

Grieg spent the winter of 1899–1900 in Denmark, and it was during this time that he met Otto Benzon (1856–1927), who was both a pharmacist and an author. He used Benzon's home as a work place for a time, and while there came upon some poems by Benzon that captured his fancy to such an extent that he resolved to set them to music. The result was opp. 69 and 70, both of which bear the title *Five Songs.* These proved to be Grieg's last compositions in this genre.

Grieg's letters to Benzon are taken from Benzon's article, "Nogle Breve fra Edvard Grieg" ("Some Letters from Edvard Grieg"), which appeared in *Gads Magasin,* Copenhagen, 1907–08, pp. 1–8.

1

Troldhaugen, Hop Station at Bergen, May 19, 1900

Dear Otto Benzon!

"As everyone knows, what appears in the newspapers is not always correct." No, you are absolutely right. What is correct is this: As I told you,[1] I set ten of the poems of which you so kindly gave me copies. I divided them into two volumes, as follows:

Dedicated to the author.
5 Poems
by Otto Benzon.
1) Summer Night. 2) At Mother's Grave. 3) Snail, Snail.
4) To My Son. 5) To a Devil.

Dedicated to N. J. Simonsen.
5 Poems
by Otto Benzon.
1) Eros. 2) A Life of Longing. 3) Dreams.
4) A Poet's Song. 5) A Boat on the Waves is Rocking.

These two volumes are here at Troldhaugen, and no step has yet been taken apropos their publication. In taking the liberty of dedicating one volume to you as an expression of my gratitude to you both as a person and as an author, in making my selection I have of course had in mind precisely the two poems that

[1] Benzon had read in the Copenhagen newspapers that Grieg had composed two collections of songs to his—Benzon's—poems and that these were now going to be published and dedicated to Danish singer Niels Juel Simonsen (1846–1906). Benzon then wrote to Grieg requesting that he not publish the songs inasmuch as two of them were completely private in character.

you mention as being "very private", namely "The Birthday Letter" and "The Grave Song".[2] Surely you wouldn't expect me to dedicate these to Simonsen?

I cannot share your feelings regarding the material. For me the most intimate things, when they have really been transformed into art—as is the case here—are elevated to a higher sphere in which the "private" becomes one with the universal. This must also have been the view of other poets when they, like you, wrote from the depths of their hearts about their sorrow at father's or mother's grave, about their joy on a child's birthday. Otherwise they would not have published what they wrote.

But even if I cannot understand your point of view here, fortunately I can nonetheless respect it—all the more easily in that I am favorably disposed both toward you and toward your poetry. Moreover, I am certain that you will try to be as flexible as possible so as not to "create snags".

Believe me, I think it is your excessive modesty that is playing a trick on you. This modesty is so vast that you even renounce the poem's right to be mentioned alongside the music! Whereas my goal (and that of many modern musicians) is *just* to let the poem come into its own. Only then does the music become what it is intended to be.

I have also suspected you of a certain caution and respect for the pettiness in Copenhagen. You imagine people saying, "What do Otto Benzon's mother and son have to do with us!" You think that's the way your fellow townsmen are. But remember what you say about yourself in "A Poet's Song": "But I—I was fashioned of different stuff; and though I should suffer scorn and rebuff, 'twould only increase my desire." Desire to what? To *defy* the narrow-mindedness, that's what I understand you to be saying. And are you perhaps not speaking just as intimately here as when you speak about your mother and your child? Where, precisely, is the boundary between the private and the artistic use of the material? "You have to feel it," you will reply. But I say: There is no boundary. All the material lies at our feet. We have only to raise it up in order to make it our own—and everyone's. Yes, precisely: Raise it to the level where there no longer is a "mine" or "thine". And that is what you have done, with or without your conscious will, because in the moment when you were gripped by a son's sorrow, a father's joy, you were an instrument of God's grace.

Forgive me. Here I sit and ramble on, forgetting that you could answer me like the dying man answered the clergyman who had pulled out all the stops to give him a proper send-off: "Is that all you have to say, Father? I knew all of that long before you were even born!"

---

[2] Set by Grieg as "To My Son" and "At Mother's Grave". The titles of most of the poems mentioned by Grieg in the Benzon letters correspond to the titles of his songs in opp. 69 and 70.

We should just have had an opportunity to talk together a little about this. It would soon have become evident that at root we are in agreement.

It seems to me that the fact that the poems (except for "Summer Night") are still in manuscript only gives our collaboration heightened interest. How many of Bjørnson's[3] poems were first published and translated with my music! Only good things have resulted from that. And you must not say that a translation is a nuisance. Good Lord! Now that you have been both so kind and so careless as to entrust your poetry to my music, you, too, must endure that purgatory. For you cannot deny, dear Benzon, that you have really done so. If you have "not thought of publishing" the poems, why did you give them to me as a possible basis for music? That I don't understand. You must not do what in Norwegian we call a "kuvending"—a bovine about-face. That would be a big, big disappointment for me and would put me in an awkward position.

It was outrageous that *you* had to leave and that *I* fell ill, with the result that you didn't get to hear the songs. If you had heard them, this whole matter would have taken care of itself. Yes, I am so immodest that I assume the possibility that in that case you would even have reconciled yourself to the publication of "Nielsemand's"[4] emergence from his *privatissimo!*

Still, who knows what value there may be in this exchange of letters? At least it adds to our collection of autographs! (Ow!)

I wish you weren't sitting down there in "Kristianiagade" with its graveyard atmosphere! It only begets pessimistic letters like the one you recently sent to me.

Here I sit with so much rheumatism in my mid-section that I could howl, and still I look at everything with confidence and optimism! Take a little trip up here! You'll get a good bed, and we'll take good care of you! Do it! It's not a bad idea. Both of us can win a little independence and quiet. I have my composer's hut and you can wander wherever you like, do what you want—also work in Drachmann's tower room![5]

Warm greetings from Nina and from

Yours truly,
Edvard Grieg

[3] Norwegian author Bjørnstjerne Bjørnson (1832–1910).

[4] Nielsemand was the name of the boy in the poem "To My Son".

[5] Danish poet Holger Drachmann (1846–1908) had stayed in the tower room at Troldhaugen during a visit there in the summer of 1886.

2

Troldhaugen, Hop Station at Bergen, June 4, 1900

Dear Otto Benzon!

We are *very* disappointed that we will not get to see you here! But I must be happy to know you are in the sunny south. For that, surely, is where you have thawed out! Yes, thank you for the beautiful modulation from minor to major! As a musician I value that doubly![6]

So: "Summer Night" is from *Anna Bryde*.[7] But with respect to the dedication you have certainly put me in a dilemma, for the *only* songs suitable for Simonsen are the ones I have dedicated to him. And especially "A Poet's Song". Couldn't we make one of those very useful compromises that are decried in Stortinget and Riksdagen?[8] Such that I would give you "A Boat on the Waves is Rocking"—and you would give me (for Simonsen) "A Poet's Song". Do it, please!

Unfortunately, it is possible that I will omit "To a Devil" (if it stays in, you will of course get the note regarding the original that you requested)[9] —because I am not happy with it. But a few days ago I wrote in its place, "Walk with care on the pathway of life" (from *Anna Bryde*). The division would then, with your anticipated most gracious permission, look like this:

a) *To you:*
1) Summer Night. 2) At Mother's Grave. 3) Snail, Snail.
4) To My Son. 5) A Boat on the Waves is Rocking.

b) *To Simonsen:*
1) Eros. 2) A Life of Longing. 3) Dreams. 4) Walk with care
on the pathway of life. 5) A Poet's Song.

You would, to say the least, be "endearing" if you would approve this arrangement.

My stomach is crying out for food. Therefore: enough for today.

Warm greetings and thanks!

Your devoted
EDVARD GRIEG

---

[6] Benzon had received Grieg's letter of May 19 in Paris. He accepted Grieg's urgent request that he be allowed to publish the songs but asked him to change the sequence.

[7] *Anna Bryde* was the name of a play written by Otto Benzon.

[8] Stortinget and Riksdagen were the parliaments in, respectively, Norway and Denmark. Riksdagen was renamed "Folketinget" in 1953.

[9] "To a Devil" was a little poem that Benzon had written in English and did not want translated into Danish or Norwegian. Grieg then omitted this song from op. 69, and it was not published during Grieg's lifetime. It was printed for the first time in 1991 (as EG 154) in *Edvard Grieg: Complete Works*, vol. 15, p. 266. The text is also given there in a German translation and the piece was given a Norwegian title, viz. "Til en hunndjevel".

3

Troldhaugen, August 22, 1900

Dear Otto Benzon!

Now it is obvious that you have been in the pharmacy and have swallowed a Schopenhauerian drug that has spoiled your good humor![10] Your letter, and not least the mistrustful pessimism of the thrice-underlined command in the manuscript—"They *shall* be included!"—sounds almost sinister![11] Yes, at this moment I am quite happy that there is an ocean between us! For you are being absolutely biting. And suppose, now, that you went crazy —then, of course, I, to avoid going crazy myself from your bite, would have to order you killed, *sans phrase*![12] Not like an "ordinary snail",[13] but like an ordinary dog. But—neither Denmark nor your friends, including the undersigned, can afford to lose you. I'd rather risk going mad!

But to the point: It was a damn misfortune that this dreadful copy should have fallen into your hands and absolutely heartless of Wilhelm Hansen[14] to let you get it. Still, I thank both you and the chance event itself, for the result was that I had an opportunity to right the wrong: I had forgotten to tell you about the two stanzas. I omitted them 1) because the *song* with all five stanzas would sound monotonous, 2) because I found that the three stanzas I chose to keep would give the impression of completeness, and 3) because the third and fourth stanzas do not come off so well with respect to declamation, i.e., rhythmically. But of course you are right: When the poem is not going to be published in any other way (which I did not know), then it ought to be presented in its entirety. That's as clear as the sun. I have now, as well as I could, placed the third and fourth stanzas beneath the melody along with the others and have merely resorted to the old household remedy that I have often used before of adding a note at the bottom of the page. For example: "If it is necessary to omit some stanzas at a public performance, for the sake of completeness stanzas 1, 2 and 5 should always be retained and the entire poem should be printed in the program." In this way I think that all the requirements are for the time being taken care of.

I have just come home from a trip to the majestic scenery of Sunnmøre (that you must see!) with impressions so powerful that if they don't some day transform themselves into art—well, then I must be all washed up. The unfortunate thing is that it takes time for nature to become art. And I have no time to waste, for I am slowly declining. There's no use denying it. My body tells me that.

---

10 German philosopher Arthur Schopenhauer (1788–1860) was often called "the philosopher of pessimism".

11 Benzon had discovered upon reading the proofs that Grieg had omitted two stanzas of "To My Son", and in a letter had demanded that they be restored.

12 "sans phrase": without circumlocution.

13 In the printed edition of the Benzon songs, "Snail, Snail!" is op. 69, no. 4.

14 The Benzon songs were published by Wilhelm Hansen in Copenhagen in 1900.

And the arrogance that would like to make the spirit into a person in its own right—it is able to wring out of me nothing more than a sad smile.

And with that, farewell for today. Warm greetings, also from my wife.

Your devoted
EDVARD GRIEG

4

Troldhaugen, September 1, 1900

Dear Otto Benzon!
Forgive me if I "ramble" today, for now we are colleagues. I am also a patient. Chills in the body. I spent Sunday in bed. (. . .)

When I wrote you one time that my principle as a composer was to let the poem come fully into its own—yes, this above all—what I meant was this: the *spirit* of the poem. It has happened that I have been unable to find the right form for poems of Bjørnson and Vinje without leaving something out. This might look like barbarism, but it isn't. What do you say about the old heroic ballads with 124 stanzas? The spirit of the poem is expressed in music in the first stanza, and it would be impossible to hear all 124 stanzas sung in a row.

In my opinion the poem about Nielsemand does not lend itself to through-composing—and five stanzas to the same melody could easily become monotonous. To be sure, a brilliant interpretation can compensate for this. In any case we are in complete agreement as soon as the poem in this volume of songs is printed in its original form. I should indeed have assured myself of this. But what can a person do except to say: *Pater peccavi!*[15]

Warm greetings!

Your devoted
EDVARD GRIEG

[15] *Pater peccavi:* Father, I have sinned.

To Francesco Berger

Francesco Berger (1834–1933) was secretary of The Royal Philharmonic Society of London during the years 1884–1911, and in this capacity had extensive correspondence with Grieg concerning his appearances with the Society's orchestra. Letter 1 was addressed to the Management of the Philharmonic Society, but thereafter all of Grieg's letters were addressed to Berger. Most of them deal only with details of various planned concerts—dates, honoraria, programs, soloists—and are not included here. Grieg's extant letters to Berger include forty-one in German, seven in English.[1] All of the letters are preserved in The British Library, London.

1

Copenhagen, January 4, 1880

Dear Sir:
As I intend to visit England this winter in order to perform my compositions, I take the liberty of asking the honored Management of the Philharmonic Society if it might be possible to engage me for one of the Society's concerts. The work I should like to play is my only piano concerto (op. 16 in A minor). But since I do not intend to come to England without firm engagements, I would be most grateful to the honored Management for a speedy reply with information concerning the financial arrangements.

Regarding my qualifications, I take the liberty of referring to a statement by Joseph Joachim to Mr. Cusins.[2]

Lastly, I must ask for your indulgence because of my faulty knowledge of the English language—a circumstance that has led me to avail myself of German, which I handle better.

Respectfully,
EDVARD GRIEG
Norwegian Musician

2

Copenhagen, January 16, 1880

Dear Sir:
In answer to your kind letter of January 13[3] I take the liberty of informing you that it was originally my intention to stay in England from the middle of February

---

[1] Also extant are contemporary versions of letters 1–3 in clumsy English, but they are not in Grieg's hand and are presumed to be faulty English translations of the German originals.

[2] Joseph Joachim (1831–1907) was one of the leading violinists of that time. William George Cusins (1833–93) was conductor of The Philharmonic Society from 1867 to 1883.

[3] In a reply from The Philharmonic Society dated January 13, 1880, Grieg had been asked if he might be available for an engagement on June 30 of that year.

to the end of April, but as it would be of great interest to me to play at "The Philharmonic Society" concerts I am prepared to delay my departure until the end of June, provided that in the interim I am offered other engagements—in the provinces, for example.

Since I am totally unfamiliar with the English practice, you would be doing me a great favor if you could let me know to what extent you personally could do this or that or, more generally, tell me how to proceed in order to secure engagements. So far as this year is concerned, I have written too late to Mr. Hallé,[4] so at present I do not know what to do.

If I could get engagements enabling me to prolong my stay in England, it would be an honor for me to alter my travel plans to some extent in order to play in "The Philharmonic Society" concert.

Hoping to hear further details from you soon, I am,

Most Sincerely Yours,
EDVARD GRIEG

P.S. Address: Hotel King of Denmark

Please tell me: Does the Philharmonic Society arrange chamber-music concerts? If so, would it be possible that I might have an opportunity to present some of my chamber music?[5]

3

London, May 21, 1888
5 The Cedars, Clapham Common

Dear Sir!

Unfortunately I cannot say for sure whether or not I will write a new piano concerto for next year. In October of this year, however, two orchestral scores will be published—a suite and a concert overture.[6] And when I return to England next year, as I hope to do, it would be a great pleasure for me to perform some completely new work or other with such an outstanding orchestra as "The Philharmonic Society".

Respectfully,
EDVARD GRIEG

P.S. I leave London tomorrow. My address as of July 1 will be Bergen, Norway.

---

[4] German-born English pianist and conductor Charles Hallé (1819–95) was the founder and conductor of the Hallé orchestra in Manchester.

[5] Francesco Berger's letter in response to Grieg's questions is not extant. In any case, Grieg did not play any engagements in London in 1880.

[6] Grieg is alluding to *Peer Gynt Suite No. 1* and the concert overture *In Autumn*.

4

Bergen, July 13, 1897

Dear Sir!
Permit me to write to you in German, which is easier for me than English, to express my thanks for your letter. I would be pleased to conduct on November 4 the three works that you suggested in your letter of April 14: the *Piano Concerto*, something for voices, and an orchestral work. For the orchestral work I choose, in accordance with your wish, the overture (*In Autumn* op. 11). As for the vocal piece, I would very much like to present *Before a Southern Convent* (soprano and alto solos, women's chorus, organ and orchestra) assuming that you can furnish a women's chorus for the occasion. The piece lasts only a quarter of an hour. If this is not possible, I take the liberty of recommending some songs with orchestra that I arranged recently: "From Monte Pincio", "Solveig's Cradle Song" and "A Swan" [EG 177 nos. 3, 4 and 2]. If you would prefer to have the songs with piano, I should like to accompany them myself; but the songs are especially effective with orchestral accompaniment and have been extremely successful everywhere they have been played.

An excellent interpreter of my songs is Miss Elisa Wiborg, royal court singer in Stuttgart. Anton Sistermans from Frankfurt am Main also sings my songs in a superb manner—he, too, with orchestra. For the *Piano Concerto* I take the liberty of suggesting Professor Arthur de Greef of Brussels. If this is not acceptable, since he may previously have played the same work in "The Philharmonic Society", I can strongly recommend the young German pianist Oscar Meyer, who lives in London. He is a fine, poetic pianist.[7]

And with that I think I have said enough about the matter for now.

In the hope that I will soon hear from you regarding this matter, I remain

Respectfully yours,
EDVARD GRIEG

---

7 The artists Grieg mentions in this letter often performed his works. Elisa Wiborg (1862–1938) was Norwegian, Anton Sistermans (1865–1920) Dutch, Arthur de Greef (1862–1940) Belgian and Oscar Meyer (1865–1935) German. For some reason, Grieg called Meyer "der Hofpianist"—the court pianist. However, none of the artists mentioned here participated in the concert in London on November 4. As a matter of fact, Grieg himself did not take part in that concert because of illness. The concert was given, however, with Frederick Dawson (1868–1940) as soloist in the *A-minor Concerto*. Grieg recovered in time to perform in Liverpool (November 20), London (November 22 and December 4, 13 and 15), Manchester (November 24), Birmingham (November 26), Edinburgh (November 30), Cheltenham (December 9) and Brighton (December 11). On December 6, the Dutch violinist Johannes Wolff (1863–?) joined Grieg and his wife Nina for a private concert for Queen Victoria (1819–1901) at Windsor castle. Nina and Wolff assisted in many of the other concerts as well.

To Frants Beyer

Frants Beyer (1851–1918), an attorney who was also a competent amateur pianist, was Grieg's closest friend and confidante for thirty-five years. Never did Grieg unburden himself more candidly than he did to his friend Frants. Of special interest in this connection are the letters from 1883, when Edvard, in agonizing uncertainty regarding the future of their marriage, left his wife Nina. It was largely through Beyer's mediation that the Griegs were eventually reconciled.

One of the most beautiful expressions of Grieg's deep affection for Beyer appears in a letter of March 2, 1901: "Until my final hour you will stand for me as representative of the very noblest and best that I met on my life's journey." On April 29 of the same year he wrote, "You are the sun, I am the earth."

It is regrettable that the most profoundly revealing letters between the two friends have been destroyed. Grieg himself burned many of the most personal ones, and Marie Beyer wrote (in an unpublished manuscript from 1925 preserved in the Royal Archives in Oslo) that her husband acted in the same spirit when, after working for several years on a planned edition of the correspondence, he "destroyed a large quantity of letters—strong and direct expressions of Edvard Grieg's spiritual suffering and inner struggles in intimate and personal relationships concerning which Frants was his only confidante."

Grieg and Beyer carried on a voluminous correspondence during the years 1872–1907. Of the 230 extant letters from Grieg to Beyer, nine are preserved in Nasjonalbiblioteket, Oslo (National Library of Norway, Oslo Division), the rest in Riksarkivet, Oslo (Royal Archives in Oslo). They have all been published in Norwegian in Finn Benestad & Bjarne Kortsen (eds.): *Edvard Grieg. Brev til Frants Beyer 1872–1907*, Oslo 1993. Sixty of these letters have also been published in English translation in Bjarne Kortsen (ed.): *Grieg the Writer II. Letters to Frants Beyer*, Bergen 1973.

1

Christiania, April 18, 1872

Noble Beyer!

It was good that you wrote, but think what it took: a greeting through Miss Smith![1] Moreover, I will now just tell you in advance that if you think I am stupid you are badly mistaken. Period. Or, more correctly, semicolon; for I must indeed add that Miss Smith is a sweet, lovable girl, that is increasingly clear to me. Your law studies must be extremely important to you when even such a being cannot entice you to come here.

Now, Beyer, hear this! If I don't go to Denmark this summer, we must take a trip to the mountains together. We ought to correspond about this. Then we would really have fun with *langeleik*[2] and fiddle. Since I am speaking of the

---

[1] Marie Smith (1852–1929), who later became Beyer's wife.

[2] The *langeleik* is an indigenous folk instrument still played in the Valdres region of Norway. It is a type of zither, having one fretted melody string and from three to seven drone strings.

Frants Beyer, Grieg's closest friend and confidante throughout his adult life. Grieg wrote to Beyer: "I rarely offer anyone my friendship, but you have won it unreservedly, and that is my final word." (Bergen Offentlige Bibliotek)

langeleik: *Pictures from Folk Life* was published several weeks ago. But my publisher[3] is a stingy pig, as a result of which I am as poor as a church mouse when it comes to copies. Otherwise you would be the first to get one.

One Saturday evening some time ago I played "Bridal Procession" for the students in the Association,[4] and wouldn't you know I got tears in my eyes. First I explained to them what I had had in mind and then I played—and their understanding of my intentions hit them like a bolt of lightning. They began shouting, "Play it again! Play it again!" How happy I was! For there was a mutual language of the heart.

I missed you greatly that evening. You would have fit right in there. And then you should have heard what happened afterwards. After I had played this and that for them I spoke a few words in memory of Nordraak, and then I asked

[3] Sophus A. E. Hagen (1842–1929), proprietor of the Horneman & Erslev music publishing company in Copenhagen.

[4] The Norwegian Students' Association.

the students to sing the National Anthem. I didn't have to ask twice. I rushed to the piano, and with bubbling enthusiasm they sang in such a way that no one could doubt their sincerity: "Yes, we love this land!"[5] There was a charged atmosphere shared by all. I could feel it. And when the song was finished, everyone wanted to be poets—some in verse, others in prose. It was wonderful!

Damn the luck, that you can't come here! We would have had such a splendid time. I have nothing but enemies here, and in you I know that I have a friend! Is that not true? Indeed, I do! I rarely offer anyone my friendship, but you have won it unreservedly, and that is my final word.

Write to me soon, and let us dispense with all ceremony.[6] Therefore, from this moment on I am

Sincerely yours,
EDVARD

P.S. My wife sends warm greetings.

2

The Gazebo,[7] August 27, 1874

Dear Frants!
Thank you for your letter. (. . .) My decision is now definite: I am not coming to Christiania this winter. I will leave here in the middle of next month for Copenhagen and in all probability will spend the winter in Leipzig or Dresden. No matter what the future may hold with respect to income, I must get away, must hear something and do something. Scoot down to us in Germany and we will take that much-discussed inexpensive 18-hour train trip together from Berlin to Rome. Yes, if you were to come I think it would happen—though it is my firm decision not to go to Italy this time.

The work on *Peer Gynt* is progressing very slowly, and there is no possibility that I can finish it by autumn. It is a terribly intractable subject with which to deal, except for a few places—for example, the scene where Solveig sings, all of which I have already finished. I have also written something for the scene in the hall of the Mountain King—something that I literally can't stand to listen to because it absolutely reeks of cow pies, ultra-Norwegianness and trollish self-sufficiency! But I also have a hunch that the irony will be discernible, especially

---

5 The Norwegian national anthem. The words are by Bjørnstjerne Bjørnson (1832–1910), the music by Rikard Nordraak (1842–66).

6 The meaning is: Let us dispense with the polite form of "you" and address each other as friends. All of Grieg's letters to Beyer from this point on are addressed to "Dear friend" or "Dear Frants".

7 Grieg is referring to the gazebo at "Elsero", a villa in Sandviken (on the northern edge of Bergen) owned by his friend Rasmus Rolfsen (1812–1903). Grieg wrote portions of both *Olav Trygvason* and *Peer Gynt* here. The gazebo is preserved at the "Gamle Bergen" ("Old Bergen") Museum.

afterwards when Peer Gynt, against his will, is obliged to say, "Both the dancing and playing—may the cat claw my tongue—were pure delight."

If you see Bull,[8] greet him. But first and foremost greet "Marie and Frants", then everyone else and especially your parents-in-law.

Sincerely yours,
EDVARD

P.S. Nina sends greetings! Have I thanked you for the telegram? You made me very happy! My address in Copenhagen until the middle of October is Wagner's Music Store, Østergade 4. After that time you will hear from me.

3

Børve, September 2, 1877

Dear Frants!
Do me a *big* favor: Under separate cover I am sending a "boot". Take it under your arm, go downtown and buy a pair of galoshes that fit it (not too large), charge them to my account until I come, and send them to me as soon as possible (i.e., on "Hardangeren"[9] on *Thursday* morning) along with the boot. If I don't get them I will have to go around in "stocking-feet".

Hearty thanks for your visit. I know perfectly well that I was not very pleasant company, but don't be angry with me. During these days I had many troubling things on my mind, but I shouldn't have let them show—especially in front of such dear friends.

Since you left me I have been working on something that has interested me, namely a free arrangement of folk songs for five solo voices.[10] What beauty lies hidden in these things. But one cannot credit Lindeman[11] with having made much of it evident. I have now arranged one tragic song, two humorous ones and two hymns, and I hope to be able to hear them in Bergen. I think I will be coming at the end of September.

Farewell for now! Greet your Marie.

Sincerely yours,
EDVARD

---

[8] The Norwegian virtuoso violinist Ole Bull (1810–80).

[9] "Hardangeren": a coastal steamer that went from Bergen to Lofthus and other communities on the shores of the Hardangerfjord. Børve is near Lofthus.

[10] *Album for Male Voices.*

[11] In 1867 Ludvig Mathias Lindeman (1812–87) had finished his edition of hundreds of Norwegian folk tunes, *Ældre og nyere norske Fjeldmelodier* [*Older and Newer Norwegian Mountain Melodies*], most of them in simple arrangements for piano.

4

Rudolstadt, July 29, 1883

Dear Frants!

How beautifully you think! Or is it instinct? In any case, your letters are like balm for my sick soul. I have just in this moment received your greeting of last Sunday. Why do your letters make me simultaneously sad and happy? Why do they affect me more deeply than those of anyone else in the world? It must be the power of friendship. For it certainly is not because we agree on all matters. It is the sympathetic understanding—born of a *mutual* love—of all views held by the other, even those one is unable to share. For love that is not reciprocated gives no feeling of closeness. Thank you for writing so often! That is the thought that I think is so beautiful—to write untiringly because you feel that in my present condition I need to know, and to be constantly reminded anew, that I have a complete and true friend.

You wonder how I am!! Yes, if only I could tell you! If I were to try, I would start writing twenty letters and would tear them all to shreds. I am too confused to be able to give my thoughts wings with my pen. So that is not why I am writing either. But your letter contains so much that I want to discuss with you.[12]

It is the questions about subjectivity and objectivity—or "individuality" as you call it—in relation to "the good" about which there is so much to say. You can understand that lately I have not been thinking less about these questions than I always have done, especially in recent years—but while I understand your thoughts, because I have had them myself, I must confess that my development has led me further and further away from them.

I have noticed that when I try to plumb the depths of these things I always get farthest by standing back from myself. When I now express my opinion you must remember that I am absolutely not thinking about my own little self and its experiences. I want to propose objectivity as a pattern for all discussion, and on that I know in advance that we are in agreement. You see, when I have read through what you write about the individuality that must be opposed, I find that it sounds nice—but I can't get to the bottom of it because the following question immediately thrusts itself upon me in all its infinite immensity: In which cases shall individuality be opposed and in which shall it not? For we are hopefully in agreement that it neither can nor should *always* be opposed. Fighting against individuality is one of Christianity's basic principles that in our time has become a stock phrase of the clergy—and it leads straight to the devil, away from all truth and spiritual freedom. You cannot require any human being to say

---

[12] Edvard and Nina were in the midst of a serious marital crisis at this time, and Beyer was doing his best to bring about a reconciliation. Unfortunately, all of Beyer's letters to Grieg from this period and several of Grieg's to Beyer are no longer extant. The ones that remain provide, however, a moving picture of Grieg's torment.

to himself or herself: In this case I will follow, and act in accordance with, what I feel is the truth, and in that case I won't. To be sure, one must test oneself before one acts, that is true, but if I demand that each individual shall act according to what *I* consider right, and if I judge people's actions in accordance with this principle, then I am committing an injustice—one, to be sure, that a majority of people commit but that is Medieval in origin and based on ignorance and narrow-mindedness.

Christ was a strange prophet. For what does it mean: "Judge not" etc. without giving individuality its right! Do you remember Vinje's words in the hymn: "He knows that if we murder our brother, it was for *his* sake that we did it."[13] I understand this line as follows: *He* knows that however the human race may condemn an act, it may nonetheless have been done out of innermost conviction. Thus for me the question comes down to this: Shall one do what others consider right or what one considers right oneself? And then the answer is obvious.

I will not elevate Bjørnson's change of signals[14] to the status of law, but I will say that there are happy natures and there are less happy natures. The happy ones—I think you are one of them and I know that my father was, for example—are natures that feel the same regarding life's big questions from age 20 to age 70. And the less happy ones are those that develop—whether through external influences and experiences or in accordance with their inner disposition I shall not decide. The clergymen will say that those who think that they develop are those of weak character, and those who stand where they stood as children are the strong ones, the "chosen." But what would this wretched and yet so divinely beautiful life on earth mean if it didn't teach us something? I cannot hear a Beethoven symphony now with the same feelings that I had when I was eighteen. I see much more deeply, more intensely. I immerse my whole individuality more fully into it, and I feel that it is that which earlier struck me as daring and new that grips me and makes it great—in direct contrast to the traditional, which is also there and before which I bow as before a perception that has achieved what it sought but whose power now is broken. So it is with life. I bow to the power of tradition, to all the past greatness that has led us forward. But if we were to act only according to convention, we would make no progress, and out of fear of a false personality we would end up with none.

Yes, I wish that I could live a thousand years in order to study history and, in so doing, to understand myself. I don't mean the history of kings and wielders

---

[13] Rolf Kr. Stang, to achieve a singable translation of this line, renders it as follows in *Edvard Grieg: Complete Works*, vol. 14: "He knows, in war, how brothers murder, done in His name, their sure mainstay." The quotation is from the poem "Faith" by the Norwegian poet Aasmund Olavsson Vinje (1818–70). Grieg set this poem in op. 33, no. 11.

[14] Grieg is alluding to the big "chastity" debate that followed the publication of Norwegian playwright Bjørnstjerne Bjørnson's play *En Hanske* [*A Glove*], where the main character, Sava, urges pre-marital chastity for both men and women. The play was ridiculed in radical circles as an example of "glove morality".

of power and wagers of war—the kind of history with which we are stuffed in the schools—but the history and development through the ages of the small, unnoticed people. In lieu of those thousand years, and since I can reasonably expect to live another ten to twenty years at most, my silent prayer to the great Unknown is always this: Let me *live*—really live life—in the time that I have left! I don't mean *enjoy*, but live in such a way that I feel that it is me, not a possibility of something or a ruin of something, that is living.

Now I am indeed stuck with myself again, but deliberately. For I must tell you that although a hike in the mountains with you sounds like a refreshing bath that would strengthen my soul, loneliness here is nonetheless of even greater importance for me.

I repeat: To come home now would be a disaster for me. It would be to go back to school, to tear myself out of my development—the fermentation that I can undergo only out here.

And with that, farewell, dear Frants.

Sincerely yours,
EDVARD

5

Leipzig, October 17, 1883

Dear Frants!

The confused letter that I sent you most recently[15] was no doubt even more confused than I am able to imagine at the present time. I was just about to leave for Weimar and was so preoccupied and filled with nervous tension. I have just written several pages to Nina and feel, therefore, a need to send you a few lines as well.

I came home again this afternoon and am feeling how much one can experience in a few days—and how great a power art has to liberate and ennoble. I was so grateful and as happy as a child. I embraced in thought that which is dearest to me—first and foremost you, dear Frants.

A few days ago John[16] sent me such a beautiful postcard that I will write to him and tell him about Weimar. You can hear the details of my memorable two days there from him. Never have I felt more strongly than I did yesterday that artist and man cannot be separated. If the artist gets sunshine, the best in the man awakens. The desire for the good and the true. Naturally this desire is always present in each striving individual, but there are moments when one makes a solemn vow to oneself to aim high and to renounce egoism. I am sure that you know such

---

[15] Presumably a letter that was destroyed by Marie Beyer.

[16] John Grieg (1840–1901), Edvard's brother.

moments. They are so beautiful and so true because the vow is voluntary—not coerced, as in all ecclesiastical ceremonies. In such moments it is as if one no longer had a body but hovered, blessedly enchanted, in space.

Oh, you should have heard "The Wounded Heart" and "Last Spring" last evening. It was absolutely wonderful to hear how they played it. Beautiful *crescendos, pianissimos* such as you don't dream of, and *fortissimos* like a world of sound. And then the fact that the German audience was caught up in it! In addition to the applause of the audience, at the best places I heard from the orchestra, "Bravo, bravo." And from the box to my left (I was conducting on the stage) I heard Liszt's grunt, this familiar sound that he makes only when something pleases him. Believe me, Dr. Abraham,[17] who had come from Leipzig during the afternoon, enjoyed the situation. I think he calculated the number of copies that were used, for it must have been an absolute delight for a publisher.

Liszt, by the way, has become incredibly old since I spoke with him in Rome.[18] It was sad to see him again. We talked about Ole Bull, and then it occurred to me to ask him about Ida G.,[19] who reportedly had made such a strong impression on him that he had kissed her on the cheek. But he remembered neither her name nor her playing, said only in his peculiar, mumbling *pianissimo* style: "There are so many who come"—to which he added a gesture that was anything but flattering to these "many".

Have I told you that *Land-sighting* and *The Mountain Thrall* are going to be played in "Euterpe"[20] on December 4? Unfortunately it is the same day I am playing in Cologne, so I will not be able to conduct the performance myself. Next week I am playing the *Cello Sonata* here in the Gewandhaus. (. . .)

Please write soon in any case. Greet Marie and hold in loving remembrance

Yours truly,
EDVARD

6

Leipzig, November 15, 1883

I am sending you just these few lines today to ask you to give Nina the enclosed letter on her birthday. It contains no jeremiads about life but a report about my experiences on the trip to Meiningen, from where I returned last evening. I know this report will interest you, too, and make you happy. I am sending some sheet

---

17 Max Abraham (1831–1900), proprietor of the C. F. Peters Musikverlag in Leipzig.

18 Grieg visited Franz Liszt (1811–86) in Rome in 1870. See his letters to his parents of February 17 and April 9, 1870.

19 Norwegian pianist Ida Christensen *nee* Geelmuyden (1863–?).

20 "Euterpe" was a concert association in Leipzig that featured contemporary music in deliberate competition with the well-established and more conservative Gewandhaus concerts.

music, also in care of your address. Let her receive the music on her birthday as well. I know from your last letter, of course, that you and Marie will do everything to make it a happy day for her.

You always write in a way that moves me very deeply. Dear, dear Frants, if only I could ever get you to feel the grateful joy at having a true friend that pervades my whole being when I read your letters. I think and think until I almost go crazy, but I won't even try to dig around in that anthill of feelings, moods and impressions that make me feel that it is best for me to be where I am. For I really could not give you a clear picture of my condition. Life must develop in its own way, and everything in the world comes in the fullness of time if one can wait for it and believe in it. But that is just what is often so hard to do.

I have asked Nergaard[21] to send Nina the interest income on December 11. Please deposit it afterwards to our account at Kreditbanken.

I am so stiff and tired after writing the long letter to Nina that I cannot move my fingers any more. I hope to have another letter from you soon, although I certainly do not deserve it.

A busy time for me will soon begin. On the 25th I go to Breslau, and from then on I will be on the road steadily until Christmas. If only I knew that I would find Norway again some day, and at the same time find joy in the thought of home, then, of course, all this traveling would be cause only for rejoicing. But for me, *happiness* is nowhere to be found unless I find it within myself.

Farewell, then, for today, and thank you for each line and for each thought.

Yours truly,
EDVARD

7

Leipzig, December 1, 1883

Dear Frants!
This one day in Leipzig shall be used for many things, first and foremost to thank you for your letters, which I received at the same time upon my return from Breslau this morning. I think I cannot defend canceling out of the artistic opportunities that are opening up for me and that perhaps will never occur again. Nothing, nothing other than this drives me to Paris. Everything else strongly holds me back from going there. One thing is certain: The stay will not be a long one if anything comes of it at all.

Tomorrow morning I leave for Cologne. From there I go to Karlsruhe, then to Frankfurt and then to Holland. If at that point I am feeling very exhausted it will be extremely tempting to use my health as a reason not to go to Paris—and

---

[21] The Bergen businessman Olaf Valdemar Rasch Nergaard (1835–87), who helped Grieg in financial matters.

to cover this eventuality, I already have a letter in French ready to send to Colonne[22] in which I withdraw from the engagement. But of course I don't dare to hope that this will really be the reason. Well, if the trip to Paris comes to nothing and I report this to you in a letter or telegram, the explanation that shall be given to everyone, even to Nina, is that it was done for reasons of *health.*

Ah, Frants, if only you knew what draws me most! Though, of course, you do know, for you say it in your latest letter. It is Norway with its scenery and with you. One thing that troubles me greatly is that you do not answer my question as to whether you can be ready by the end of January![23] Remember to do so immediately, for all of my plans are dependent on your answer.

Nina wrote recently that you are more serious than ever about your building plans. I, too, have more desire than ever and feel more than ever a need to build near you. But lately I have been studying the idea of Italy so much, it keeps popping up again and again—I wish so much that I could combine the two ideas. But what scares me the most is that you say: Either – Or. Give me an answer on this right away if you please. Could you be ready within fourteen days after making a decision if I inform you by telegram? Yes, yes, here I sit fantasizing and imagining everything being so nice. This much is certain: If the four of us could meet abroad now it would be even more beautiful than meeting at home, if that is possible. I wish we could meet *here,* listen to a little music together, and then head south!

Naturally I canceled the trip to London in the spring. I have not yet sent the final answer after having received word of the honorarium (it's a paltry 15 £ sterling), but I think the size of the honorarium is a good enough reason to say "No, thank you." I don't know how I must be constituted, for I hear that everyone else would most gratefully accept the offer, even at a loss. It must be a flaw in me, but I don't care in the least about the so-called honor. I suppose that is easier for me to say than it is for many others, since I have now become a big name in both England and Germany.

It is so strange to be writing a letter in Norwegian. I haven't done that for a long time. And I almost never hear Norwegian spoken. Tuesday the Old Norse poem[24] and *Land-sighting* are being performed in "Euterpe", and things worked out so well that this forenoon I got to hear the first rehearsal with solo, chorus and orchestra. It was strange to hear the German text, which unfortunately isn't too good in some parts of *Land-sighting.* The orchestra was excellent but the chorus, to be sure, was better when I myself conducted the piece in Norway.

---

22 French violinist and conductor Édouard Colonne (1838–1910), initiator of the so-called Colonne concerts in Paris.

23 Grieg is alluding to the possibility of a trip that he hoped he, Nina and the Beyers might take together to Italy.

24 *The Mountain Thrall.*

The soloist is an unmusical fool—unfortunately for the Old Norse piece. One good thing is the fact that the conductor, Dr. Klengel,[25] admires me greatly and will do his very best.

Tomorrow I begin a vagabond life so concentrated that I do not anticipate the possibility of time for letter-writing. I will send messages in bits and pieces now and then. God bless all three of you, and thank you, thank you, thank you, my dear friend, for everything!

Yours truly,
EDVARD

8

Amsterdam, December 29, 1883

Dear, dear friend!
I really must have a couple of words with you before the old year comes to an end. I cannot thank you for the year. I can only tell you that without you I probably would not have gotten through it, that you are my best friend, and that I will care for you in a different way than I care for all other people as long as this heart of mine continues to beat. I was so unhappy when I left, also later during the first part of the summer, and now I feel so much less unhappy—no, I simply would not have believed it possible!

Happy! That is something else. Why should I be happy? I am completely happy only in your friendship, for you are the only human being in the world who has never failed me. I *should* be completely happy in my art, but I am not—because I have not always gone straight forward and therefore have not achieved that which I was called to achieve. But—people! They are phantoms, subject to the eternal law of necessity. How, then, can one demand complete spiritual freedom? But the struggle for spiritual freedom, that is life! And life's most beautiful feeling! It's a pity that one is blind and weak and often—oh, so often!—mistakes the means and thus disappoints oneself. And now farewell, philosophy!

I open my arms to you, to the new year, to spring, the new spring of the spirit and of nature, to joy, to peace. I could embrace the whole of humankind in gratitude for the bright star that—despite everything, and through the fog—shines over my existence.

I wrote to Nina regarding the practicalities, so far as I could remember the details. Since neither of us is practical, Marie will have to handle the arrangements for all four of us!

I think we will choose the Fredrikshavn route. I don't think the route through Rotterdam would be any more expensive, but I believe the voyage would be

---

[25] German cellist, composer and conductor Julius Klengel (1859–1933).

longer. Rather than going via Christiania and Copenhagen, however, we will take our excursion in southern Europe. I will play my last concert on the 12th and leave on the 13th. Be sure to send me a telegram telling me the day of your departure as soon as it is definite. And farewell until we meet. God bless all three of you!

Yours truly,
EDVARD

P.S. I cannot visualize the day when I will meet all of you at the railway station in Leipzig! NB: Remember to find out the date of moving day next spring.

9

Rome, February 15, 1884

Dear Frants!
(...) Go to Lofthus[26] and you will see what is said about the performance of my quartet.[27] One of my fondest wishes was that you could have been present, for no one would have enjoyed it as much as you. The four Italians played exceptionally well; applause broke out already in the middle of the first movement, and it was so loud that it was no longer possible to hear what was being played.

I must explain myself a little more precisely. You know that in my larger works—in order to enhance the architectonic effect and to emphasize the contrast of the themes—I have the habit or weakness or whatever I should call it of concluding in the home key before the second theme is introduced rather than, like most composers, using a transitional passage that leads imperceptibly to that theme. The same pattern occurs again after the return of the first theme following the development section. But this procedure created a difficulty in that most of the audience, not understanding the larger context, thought the movement was finished! For a brief moment it was difficult for the players, who naturally could not even hear each other's playing. The situation was ludicrous, but everything went well. And when the movement was finished there was an ovation that absolutely would not cease.

Can you imagine such a thing? The Italians encountering such a piece! I didn't believe my own ears, but it continued until Ravnkilde[28] whispered, "You must stand up." At the same moment I also felt the necessity to do so, and just think! The whole audience had risen and turned toward me, and on the platform even the players joined in the applause. I remained standing and bowed to right and left, and the same thing occurred several times during the rest of the quartet

[26] Olav Lofthus (1847–94), editor of the Bergen newspaper *Bergens Tidende.*
[27] The Italian pianist and composer Giovanni Sgambati (1843–1914) had given a matinee concert in Grieg's honor on February 15. The *String Quartet* in G Minor was one of the works played at that concert.
[28] Grieg's Danish friend Niels Ravnkilde (1823–90), who lived in Rome.

—and twice as loud at the end. One's own inner life of the soul, expressed in the natural scenery of Hardanger—finding its way straight into those Italian hearts. It's incomprehensible! But this much I know, that I love Norway even more deeply after this experience. Not in the sense that I will *strive* for the Norwegian element in my art, but I will strive for *that which is great*, and it grows and flourishes up there in the great surroundings.

I have just finished writing a letter to Hans Utne[29] at Lofthus in which I ask whether, if I were to choose Hardanger as a place to spend the summer, I could count on getting the little house up on the hillside—where, as you know, I lived once before. It would be good to get this nailed down. But I hope this does not prevent you from looking into the possibilities in the vicinity of Nordåsvannet[30] and letting me know the result of your inquiry as soon as possible. If Gullachsen is not willing to give me a discount for another half year, then I have the advantage of not being committed to him for the autumn (I can terminate my lease on Midsummer's Day), which undeniably is also an advantage.

I should like to live in Bergen next winter, for I believe that I would find the greatest quiet for my work there and that you and I could get together as often as we might wish. Of course Nina and I wouldn't hesitate to head your way on a winter evening, use your silken blankets for the night, and then go about our business in the city again the next morning. Yes, thank God, I am still not too old to look forward to the future!

We are with Aubert[31] daily and talk about many things. He is more liberal than I first thought, but I still don't know him well. We fantasized recently about living in Sorrento or Capri this summer. It sounds beautiful, but going to the mountains with you sounds even more beautiful—and to embrace the wonders of Norwegian nature has never been a more beautiful dream for me than it is just now.

May you now come home and find everything in good shape! Greet Blytt[32] from me. I am actually very glad that I did not persuade you to stay. Now you have done your duty, and the awareness of having done it is not a bad thing. I will be happy when I hear that you have both gotten home safely, for it was a strenuous journey that you undertook.

Affectionate greetings to both of you from Nina and me.

Your best friend,
EDVARD

---

29 Hans Utne (1827–95), Grieg's sometime landlord in Ullensvang, Hardanger.

30 Nordåsvannet is the body of water a short distance south of Bergen on the shore of which Troldhaugen was erected in 1885.

31 Norwegian district governor Otto B. Andreas Aubert (1841–98).

32 Peter M. Blytt (1836–1928), a friend of Grieg who lived in Bergen.

P.S. (. . .) Nina's throat is sore, unfortunately, but we hope that today the crisis is past. This evening we will be playing whist at the Ravnkilde's and will drink a toast to both of you.

10

Rome, March 16, 1884

Dear Frants!

Thanks so much for your latest letter! Your many recommendations are right on target—and of course you knew that ahead of time, otherwise you wouldn't have made them. There are many of them, and they are all equally attractive to me.

I would have answered your letter the day I received it, but I couldn't get enough time because of concert preparations. Today I am finally finished with these and have your letter lying in front of me so that I will not forget anything.

So: When we come home in the middle of May (or hopefully also if it should be later), we will immediately take advantage of your hospitality while we gather our thoughts. Bravo! Recommendation accepted with strong approval. Then to Hardanger. Yes, that will certainly be the best option, and, as I told you, I wrote to Utne in that connection some time ago. Why he then wrote to *you* rather than to *me* I really don't understand. But the information was distressing. Now I have the idea that we should *live* at Utne's if I can rent for my own use the room that I have been thinking of. There is a new house up on the road to Helland where Eidnæs the shoemaker lives, and it has a spiral staircase on the outside that leads from the porch up to the second floor. In this second floor are two rooms with a view of the fjord. I would like to rent one of these, NB, if townspeople will not occupy the other one or any other part of the house.

Will you inquire whether, if I were to come to Hardanger this summer, I could rent this room on a monthly basis, and at what price? Just write to Utne and he will handle it in the best way. Whether or not I can find the quiet needed for work there certainly is a big question. This much is certain: I will come with the firm intention not to let myself be disturbed by others.

Then at last comes August with the mountain scenery! Yes, I am firmly committed to that arrangement. If you make the same commitment, it will be definite. Thereafter back to Hardanger, and then we will get together for the winter. (. . .)

It's nice that you are helping me to think: It makes me feel so happy and secure. And now I must tell you about yesterday. I sent a letter to Hagerups,[33] so I assume that you have heard the news. But I must tell you yourselves how I missed you and how happy I think you would have been in this strange, grandiose

[33] Nina's parents, Herman Hagerup (1816–1900) and Adeline Hagerup (1813–1907), who had lived in Bergen since 1870.

situation. Just think of sitting on the Capitoline Hill on a sunny afternoon and making Norwegian music to the delight of a multinational audience![34]

As you will see from the program, it was just Nina and I who performed. I decided for several reasons not to include the Romans, and it was a good thing, for at the last moment an orchestra rehearsal was scheduled for the very hour that I had my concert. You will of course see at a glance that the program could not have any artistic interest for me personally. It was a program for Englishmen and Americans—and it was correctly planned, for it was exclusively "vox populi" that "rang the bell" best. What interested me was the uniqueness of the situation—and the money for the trip to Naples. This presumably will take place the first of April. With whom is still undecided.

Here things are getting more marvelous each day, but so warm that one can hardly survive in the middle of the day. I am beginning to long for Norwegian nature more than I dare to admit, and I feel more than ever that I could never leave it for good.

Lucky you, who have been able to place the wreath on your own house![35] Yes, what I wouldn't give for a wreath like that! Ten thousand laurel wreaths! District governor Aubert says that up in Nordland the most marvelous little properties are for sale dirt cheap—but of course that is *too* far away. (. . .)

Recently I had the pleasure of being with Holger Drachmann.[36] He is an amiable, forthright fellow, rather self-confident, but childlike and true. We became good friends in an evening. Unfortunately he returned the next day to Nice, where he lives. He said—and it is true—that what is lacking in Scandinavia is a center. But if it is going to come, it must be born out of the circumstances now prevailing in Norway. Where shall one go if one does not want to live amidst hate and personal dissension? Those of free intelligence must unite. Men of intellect shall serve neither farmers nor reactionaries; they shall serve good ideas. And fortunately men of good ideas are to be found among both Liberals and Conservatives.

I am so weak and tired today, otherwise I would have written both later in the evening and better.

Warm greetings,
EDVARD

P.S. Please send me your route over St. Gotthard if you still have it.

---

[34] On March 15 Grieg gave a concert in the German ambassador's residence, which was situated on the Capitoline Hill in Rome.

[35] Beyer was in process of building his villa "Næsset" at Nordåsvannet. "Placing the wreath" is an allusion to *kranselaget*, "the topping-out ceremony", a celebration for workers given by a building owner when the ridgepole is installed.

[36] Danish author Holger Drachmann (1846–1908).

March 19, 1884

Unfortunately the letter was not mailed during all this time. (. . .) Last evening we attended a party at Ross's where Ibsen was also present.[37] Nina sang many songs, including nearly all of my songs to texts by Ibsen, and just think, after "Little Haakon" ["Margaret's Cradle Song"] and especially after "I christened you joy's harbinger" ["Album Lines"] and "A Swan" the icy exterior melted, and with *tears* in his eyes he came over to the piano where we were and pressed our hands, almost unable to speak. He mumbled something to the effect that this was true understanding, and I don't need to tell you that on this occasion Nina did not sing with *less* understanding than she customarily does. And with that the letter can be mailed.

Affectionate greetings.

Yours truly,
EDVARD

11

Copenhagen, January 5, 1886

Dear Frants!
It's 11 P.M. and I am so tired, so tired. But still, I will not deny myself the pleasure of sending you a few lines even if they do not prove to be inspired. But inasmuch as friendship includes a bit of inspiration there will be no lack of it in my letters.

Well, so we really must now write 1886! May it bring the two of us some of that which we love so much and which binds us so firmly together. Not a day goes by when I do not say in my heart of hearts, "Hail to thee, bosom of Norway!"[38] And you are indeed included in the thought! But just as often I think, "Hail to thee, Frants!"—and then Norway is included! For in my consciousness the two of you are absolutely inseparable!

Believe me, I am floundering these days. My main failing is that I get up late, but unfortunately life here requires it. I emerge from the blankets at 8:30. By 9:00 I have done my exercises and am sitting down in the café having breakfast. Then Nina and I take a morning walk, from which we return home at about 11:00. Only then do I get down to work. But then I keep on without a break until 6:00, and thank goodness I can tolerate it because otherwise I don't know what would happen.

---

37 Norwegian painter Christian Meyer Ross (1843–1909) and Norwegian dramatist Henrik Ibsen (1828–1906), both of whom were living in Rome at this time.

38 This is a quotation from the poem "Bergens Stift" ["The County of Bergen"] by Norwegian poet J. S. Welhaven (1807–73).

First I have to practice the piano (I am to perform at Svendsen's[39] philharmonic concert at the end of January), and then I dig into *Peer Gynt*, many parts of which I have completely re-orchestrated. But now I am working on the last of these—fortunately, for time is very short.

In the café I am bombarded by copyists and musical directors who grab each page from me as soon as I am finished with it. In this way we rehearse a little at a time. Two pieces gave me much satisfaction at the first rehearsal. They were the introduction to the second act and the scene with the herd girls. The latter you wouldn't even recognize. When I first conceived it I felt something, but now I *know* something; that is the difference. It has acquired life, color and devilry—which really were not there before because the orchestration was so defective.

Enormous preparations are being made for the performance, which will certainly be something totally different from the one in Christiania so far as the stage set and the music are concerned.

Now Nina is winding her watch—which means, in other words: Good night and affectionate greetings to both of you!

Yours truly,
EDVARD

12

Copenhagen, April 26, 1886

Dear Frants!
Spring is spring and birdsong is birdsong. I have a goodly measure of both down here—and still it seems to me as if I had none of either. And friends are friends, and I have many of them here, too, but none of them understand as you do what is drawing me toward scenes of home—and for that reason I also have the feeling that all the others more or less disappear into the fog for me at this time. How about a quiet forenoon in the boat or out between skerries and cliffs!

The other day I got so full of this longing that it took the form of a gentle tune of thanksgiving. There is nothing new in it, but it is genuine. And since in essence it is nothing but a letter to you, I will include it here *[see page 44]*.[40]

If Næsset's and Troldhaugen's surroundings had been grander, the music would have been different. But I am glad they are as they are, and this quiet joy about the fact that everything up there is as it is was the sentiment that found expression in some music. The colors are the soft hues of West Norway, but the heart of the piece was beating for you, old friend, when I wrote them down.

---

[39] Norwegian composer and conductor Johan Svendsen (1840–1911), who was musical director of the Royal Theater Orchestra in Copenhagen.

[40] "In My Native Country" op. 43 no. 3.

Wasn't there something else I was going to tell you? Damn my Karlsbad[41] memory that has made me forget what it was. Ah well, I don't think it was important. Keep an eye on Troldhaugen (so the old man doesn't throw chunks of manure from the flower beds onto the road. Now I have to laugh when I remember last year!), but above all watch out for your health. It's not just a matter of the food, but also clothing and above all the feet. Moreover, in order to have a normal bowel movement in the morning I hear it enthusiastically recommended down here that one should drink a glass of warm boiled water on a fasting heart.

Unfortunately I likely will not be home for your birthday. If a *good* ship leaves on Wednesday eight days from now (May 5), and if the weather then is really good, then I won't swear that I won't cut things short and take the direct route. But if we have to go by land, we *must* wait. It's sad to have property in the country and not be able to be home in early spring, for that is when one gets all one's ideas. And what about the birds' nests that I have forgotten! It's annoying, for now it is too late. If only some of the small birds could come and take up residence amongst us! For believe me—I need surroundings that can breathe a little life into the daily drudgery! Yes, indeed! I can't write any music about this privation, for it just tinkles without giving wings to the longing. I expect and hope that something good will come of Marie's lecturing on moral philosophy. You must tell her that, for Nina believes in her! You see, I am an optimist after all!

And now, farewell to both of you for today. Loving greetings!

Yours truly,
EDVARD

---

[41] Karlsbad was a health spa in Germany. The town of Karlsbad now lies in the Czech Republic and has been renamed Karlovy Vary.

13

Troldhaugen, August 27, 1886

Dear Frants!

The situation is fairly classic: Nisk and I have had grouse for dinner with Majsen[42] (when the cat's away, "Rockemauren"[43] dances on the table), and at coffee time we received a visit from two nondescript women, whereupon I, with *Morgenbladet*[44] in hand, fled up into your guest room, where I had a marvelous siesta on the sofa—without sleeping. (. . .)

It is a beautiful sunny day at Troldhaugen, and in comes Majsen—beaming even more than usual, for she has received a letter! Nina was in the city, and like a gallant Don Juan I invited her on the spot out to the veranda, which fortunately was not covered with leaves. Here she handed me the letter, and now you must imagine me reading it aloud to Majsen—every single word, even all the *crescendos* in the prelude to *Tristan.* I read it more or less as I would have performed the prelude, so you can easily imagine that the effect was irresistible. But the reward was also beautiful, for when I looked up from the paper again and let my glance fall on Majsen, I saw two big tears glistening in her eyes. Yes, that prelude certainly can evoke tears from both men and women. It was just yesterday that I had it in my hands. I am so glad that I own the score so that I can also enjoy the marvelous orchestration.

I have made a happy discovery, namely that the selfishness I first felt at the thought of not being present at the Wagner performances has totally vanished into thin air and has been replaced by a completely impersonal, sincere joy over the fact that you really have been granted the opportunity to experience this. For you are not only one of the chosen few who understand—yes, perhaps the only chosen one in our city—but it will greatly enrich the life that you still have left to live. And it has brought the two of us—yes, in truth this is no longer *impersonal*—this has brought the two of us closer to each other, if this can be thought possible.

You will now be able to understand why I many times go about and stare up at the clouds as if I could find there the Norwegian drama in Norwegian music that I have dreamt of, that I have indeed always believed that I could some day create, but that I am now beginning to believe has been decreed by fate to come from the hand of another. But come it will. And if it comes profound and great like the Wagner music-dramas, perhaps after our time—well, if only there are then minds like yours to welcome it, I will go to my grave as happy as if I had written it myself. For man's aspirations do indeed have an insatiable desire to

---

[42] "Nisk" and "Nisken" were pet names for Nina, "Majs" and "Majsen" pet names for Marie Beyer.

[43] A brand of red wine.

[44] The conservative Christiania newspaper *Morgenbladet.*

encompass everything, and I must remember—ah! I say it with sadness—that the circumstances of my life have induced me to sing out the innermost feelings of my soul in lyrical music.

But apart from this, and however that may be, I have still never seen a text that was capable of setting my musical soul afire. And if I don't get such a text, I know very well who would prefer to leave the music-drama unwritten rather than to write a piece of trash. (. . .)

How strange that art is so aristocratic that in the whole human race there are so infinitesimally few who manage to understand these mysteries! Just think if *everyone* could feel these beauties! That would certainly be "the new heaven and the new earth, where blessedness dwells!"[45] No! That would be only an *earth*, for we would all embrace one another out of sheer joy! And that is not allowed! Thus the whole idea is wrong, no matter how one twists and turns it. I suppose it is most practical for us artists, in any case, as it is: that we who love so much and would like to love still more, that we live in asceticism—in relation to our longings, I mean—for otherwise there would be no art, art really being the surplus of longing that cannot find expression in life or in any other way. (. . .)

Now off to Majsen and Nina down in the living room. No one has come, so now we are going back to Næsset to play Saint-Saëns's *Variations*.[46]

Affectionate Greetings!

Your old
EDVARD

14

Karlsbad, October 8, 1887

Dear Frants!

Thank you for your dear letter! (. . .) Believe me, I have regretted that I shared with you so much of the sad mood that found expression in my last letter.[47] But as it says in the proverb: As the Lord is, so also are his servants. Similarly: As the stomach is, so also are the letters!

And praise be to God! It is decreed that after rain there follows sunshine. It is a long time since life has been as bright and good for me as it is at this time. I am healthy again—yes, healthier than I have ever been here in Karlsbad—and many friendly letters full of goodness and understanding make it easier for me to face the future than it has been for a long time. And what obviously makes such an infinite difference: Nina is healthier and more lighthearted than she is at

---

[45] Cf. Revelation 21:1.

[46] French composer Camille Saint-Saëns (1835–1921). Grieg probably is referring to Saint-Saëns's *Variations on a Chorus from Handel's "Judas Maccabaeus"* for piano four hands (1850).

[47] This letter is not extant.

home. Karlsbad clearly is good for her, even though each day before breakfast she feels wiped out and exhausted from the effects of the water cure. The best proof of the extent to which she has improved is that each day she goes for long walks with me in the lovely, autumn-brown forests—and instead of getting tired, the farther she goes the spryer she feels. If Majsen could achieve the same result from a Karlsbad cure, we could once again be ready for a trip together to the Jotunheimen mountains, all four of us!

Yes, Norway! Norway! Let Ibsen say a hundred times that it is best to belong to a big nation: I can perhaps agree with him from a practical point of view, but I will not go a step further. For ideally viewed, I would not want to belong to any other nation in the world! The older I get the more I feel that I love Norway precisely because it is so poor, precisely because we are such damned idiots in practical respects. Good Lord! A nation can always become rich and practical—but *profound*, no, and *introspective*, no! And it certainly is these two characteristics that determine the future for our people. These characteristics seem to grow so surprisingly (in my mind) when I am abroad. Therefore it is doubly nice to get away. (. . .)

I have now gotten—or, more correctly, I am busy these days getting—the Autumn Overture ready for the copyist. Dr. Abraham is publishing the score of the overture and of the *Peer Gynt* music [op. 46]. Hopefully I will get an opportunity to hear the Autumn Overture in Leipzig. And now that I have heard an orchestra again I have begun to believe that it will sound all right.

It's a good thing that I am not at home coaxing you to take long walks, for after the disastrous trip to the mountains you certainly need rest more than anything else. If you concentrate seriously and exclusively on this for now, the time will certainly come when we will revel together between the mountain peaks while the clear air echoes with the unforgettable [G][48]

Yours truly,
EDVARD

15

Leipzig, November 22, 1887
10 P.M.

Dear, dear Frants!
(. . .) You should know how strangely the sad impression of your letter intermingles with my own joy and grateful mood at this moment. I have just returned

[48] The note "G" had a completely concrete significance in Grieg and Beyer's friendship. It refers to an experience that they shared on a hike in the Jotunheimen mountains in August, 1887, when a milkmaid played a simple tune on a *bukkehorn* (a primitive folk instrument made from a ram's horn) that ended with a sustained G that echoed in the mountains. See Grieg's letter of October 17, 1887, to the Danish composer Niels Ravnkilde for a detailed description of the event.

from the home of Professor Brodsky,[49] Halvorsen's[50] teacher, with whom I have played the new *Violin Sonata* of which you got such a poor impression last summer.[51] I was as disappointed then as you were, but tonight (albeit after changing the shortcomings) I experienced a joy that is seldom granted to an artist. Brodsky played *absolutely incomparably*, and was himself completely enthusiastic about my work. I assure you, I didn't recognize it. It was indeed what I had intended, but I just didn't think my intentions could be made real. He definitely wants to perform it at one of his *soirees*, and hopefully I will then have the pleasure of playing it with him. On December 10 he and his incomparable colleagues are playing my *String Quartet*, and judging from the way they played Beethoven recently it should be "above all criticism".

Apropos: I mentioned Halvorsen. A fine fellow, I like him more and more. The other evening he was up here and played through the sonata with me, and he did it with so much warmth and genuine artistry that I felt a wave of pride over the fact that he was my countryman. And then Sinding[52] is here too. You wouldn't believe what a strange man he is.

We four—Mr. and Mrs. Grieg, Sinding and Halvorsen—spend an hour after dinner almost every day playing nine-pins bowling. It is an absolutely first-rate pastime after the meal, and the fun we have defies description. The first time we did it I shouted: No, Frants should have been here for this! You are hereby invited to bowling at Troldhaugen next year!!!

My walks consist of—exercises in the bedroom! But I am not complaining. Am just grateful, because I feel healthier than I have felt for a long time. Weighed myself the other day: 47½ kilograms! Lighter than ever! No, but let me not forget to tell you that recently I *privatissimo* got to conduct the *Autumn Overture* with a military orchestra. Most of it sounded wonderful. A few passages must still be changed. That was a stone removed from my heart. I recently received an invitation from Birmingham to conduct a composition there at the music festival in August. I still don't know what will come of it. But our meeting is written in the stars—as sure as the fact that we are standing on our feet!

Affectionate greetings to both of you from Nina and me.

Yours truly,
EDVARD

---

49 Russian violinist Adolf Brodsky (1851–1929).

50 Norwegian violinist, conductor and composer Johan Halvorsen (1864–1935).

51 Grieg is referring to his *Violin Sonata No. 3* in C minor. Grieg and the German-born amateur violinist, music publisher Carl Rabe (1829–97), had played the sonata for Frants Beyer in the summer of 1887.

52 Norwegian composer Christian Sinding (1856–1941).

16

Leipzig, December 25, 1887

Dear Frants!

I'm not really in a mood conducive to letter-writing, but the day after tomorrow we leave for four days in Berlin—and when I come home from that trip there will be so many new impressions that will also be demanding attention that the earlier ones will be obscured. (. . .)

Is not the desire to maintain one's spiritual "I" a case of justified egoism? And you, who *should* have become an artist but who, in the absence of an artistic career, have nonetheless had the good fortune to have the main thing—a wife whom you love and who loves you, and who has not saddled you with a flock of children who would have inhibited your love of nature which, as the years have passed, has nonetheless, in the best sense of the word, preserved the *artist* in you.

You are now beginning of your own free will to take detours from the path that your lucky star until now has so beautifully illumined! Yes, yes, I understand that what you are doing is Christian and nice, and of course, as you say, it can also convey many joys. But, but—you are not cut out for the kind of struggle that you, out of a feeling of friendship, are now taking upon yourself. And this certainly is an easy question to answer: whether someone can act *contrary* to his nature without being punished for it!

My reasoning may seem cold and selfish, I admit it. But for me, the individual is number one. The human being must *first* take care of himself—of the best that is in him, just as he has received it from the hand of the Creator. Everything else—yes, excuse once again the cold words—is what I call public assistance, and this is a practical matter to be arranged without your whole life and its obligations being shaken to their very foundation. I know that I am expressing myself poorly, but I'll be damned if there isn't something in my thought that is so high and contains so much truth—not aesthetic but moral truth—that I have a right to demand understanding from *you.*[53] (. . .)

But back to the doorbell, which has been ringing steadily and bringing communication after communication, flowers and cards from acquaintances and strangers and finally my guests, so that I as quick as lightning must climb up on the piano and light the candles. Everyone in a happy mood. Thereupon distribution of presents. And then a festive meal, for which Dr. Abraham had sent a whole basket of the most delicious things to eat and drink.

---

[53] Beyer had written that he and his wife were considering an action that Grieg regarded as ill-advised. A friend of the Beyers—a widower by the name of Waldemar Solberg—had died leaving several young children. The Beyers, who were childless, took 8-year-old Sverre into their home and were considering doing the same for some of the other Solberg children. They eventually decided not to do so, but Sverre remained with them until he was grown.

As we popped the cork from the champagne we also remembered you, dear friend, and many things were said that it is better for you not to hear. Just this much: that next summer you run the risk of being visited by the whole group. Delius[54] is "Norway crazy". He has been to Norway four times, spends fourteen days by himself up on the Hardanger Plateau and so on. After the meal we were all without exception more or less plastered, but the show had to go on—so there was music, music and more music!

What a Christmas Eve! Yes, if you had been there you would have said that you will never experience a more beautiful or interesting one!

First Halvorsen played hallings and springars,[55] then Sinding and Halvorsen played a suite by Sinding in the old style[56]—i.e., in the spirit of Bach. It was so profound and full and rich, and it rendered so authentically the atmosphere of Bach's time that I do not hesitate to call it a masterwork. It brought me, among other things, an observation of interest regarding my own *Holberg Suite*, which, alongside Sinding's piece, shows such a strong French influence—which is just as it should be. But Sinding's work lays claim to quite a different kind of depth—and, in truth, has it. Then Halvorsen and I played my *Violin Sonata No. 2* and Nina sang songs by Sinding and me, then Mr. Delius gave an absolutely brilliant performance of a piano piece that he calls "Norwegische Schlittenfahrt" ["Norwegian Sled Tour"]. Thereafter Sinding and Halvorsen again joined forces in a *Suite* in the old style by F. Ries,[57] whereupon Sinding's *Suite* was played again. By then it was past 1 a.m. But Nina began anew, this time singing the Vinje songs [op. 33], songs by Elling[58] and three of the new songs by Frants Beyer. You can be proud of both the performance and the reception. Sinding said, "Yes, by George, I'm going to have to go there and see Bergen and Frants Beyer and Jotunheimen and all those things!"

We parted at 2:30 A.M. Today a big hangover—but never mind, it'll pass. Let me now have a similarly detailed account of your Christmas Eve. And with that, thanks to you and to Majs for the old year! As nice as we have had it together, I nonetheless have the definite feeling that the best is yet to come in another year! That's true, isn't it! Yes, it *is!*

God bless both of you.

Yours truly,
EDVARD

---

54 English composer Frederick Delius (1862–1934).
55 "Halling" and "springar": two types of indigenous Norwegian folk-dance tunes.
56 Later published as *Suite im alten Stil.*
57 German violinist and composer Franz Ries (1846–1932).
58 Norwegian composer Catharinus Elling (1858–1942).

17

Leipzig, January 29, 1888

Dear Frants!

That was a heart-rending letter![59] I wept bitterly! But thank you, nonetheless, for telling me about your circumstances! That was also necessary in order for me to understand the situation—for I had no idea things were like this. The secretary position[60] was indeed wonderful, but to purchase it with Næsset! No, it just cannot be allowed to happen! For here I sit and I am saying, "O my Sulamit! All that I have is also yours!"[61] And at this moment I have more than I need. Must I tell you, dear Frants, that everything I own is at your disposal! I would be unhappy if you did not take me up on this—indeed, I'm afraid I could no longer love you in the same way as before. You yourself know best *what* more is required and how you want to arrange things. Just tell me what you need and it would be very strange if I couldn't help you deal with the problems. (. . .)

If you finally decide that you absolutely must sell Næsset—well, then one of two things will happen: Either I will also sell Troldhaugen or else I will be at the auction when Næsset is sold! Above all, don't do anything without informing me in advance. Promise me that! And then you will see that for many more summers—if we live—you will be able to shout "Tra-o-ho" from Næsset to Troldhaugen. (. . .)

I have just come from Brodsky's, where we have been to dinner along with Tchaikovsky, who is still here with a young and *wonderfully brilliant* Russian pianist, Sapelnikov.[62] Sinding and Halvorsen were also present, and we made music all the time. First, at Tchaikovsky's request, Brodsky and I played my new sonata. Then Sinding's quintet was tried out, with Sapelnikov at the piano, and lastly my *String Quartet.* Those fellows can really play! My God, what a sound! Sinding's quintet is a large-scale work—at times too garish, even brutal (which Sinding considers a virtue!), but of great, rare power.

In Tchaikovsky I have gained a warm friend for my music. He is as favorably disposed toward me as I am toward him, both as an artist and as a human being. You will learn to know him because he undoubtedly will be coming to Troldhaugen.[63]

Just think that d'Albert[64] has promised to play my *Concerto* at the music festival [in Copenhagen] this summer! I wrote of it to Svendsen yesterday, and if

---

59 Beyer had just informed Grieg that he had fallen into serious financial difficulty and was in danger of losing his home, Næsset.

60 See Grieg's letter to Beyer of December 25, 1887.

61 This is a quotation from the hymn "How Fair is Thy Face" by Danish hymn-writer Hans Adolf Brorson (1694–1764), set by Grieg in *Four Psalms.*

62 Russian pianist Vasilij Sapelnikov (1868–?).

63 Grieg's prediction was not fulfilled: Tchaikovsky never visited Troldhaugen.

64 The British-born German pianist and composer Eugène d'Albert (1864–1932).

foreign artists are going to be allowed to participate at all I hope his offer will be accepted with pleasure. He is a wonderfully gifted artist. Yes, the young ones, and especially the non-Germans—the future belongs to them. To hell with the academicians and the professors!

Now I must get ready for my concert tour to England, which is scheduled for the middle of March. I am doing this very reluctantly, but I'll just have to take the plunge! Fortunately my health is pretty good, thanks to the exercising. Each morning I devote 25 minutes to it! You should do the same! On the 18th my quartet is being played in the Gewandhaus. Think of me and of it on that day. It is related to the deepest recesses of our hearts, isn't it!

And with that, my dear, only and best friend—farewell! Loving greetings to both of you from Nina and me.

Yours truly,
EDVARD

18

Leipzig, February 13, 1888

Dear Frants!
It has been an extremely great joy for me to read your last two letters and your telegram. That the circumstances could improve so quickly and so much exceeded my wildest expectations. I can well understand, of course, that for now you are abandoning plans for both Copenhagen and Bayreuth, but that my miserable offer of material assistance could move you so much really pains me. As if it weren't the only thing to do. We will *always* share joy and sorrow—indeed, everything—with each other, will we not? Let us take this opportunity to say this to each other, for we both feel it as if it were a law of nature.

I have just returned home from a long afternoon walk in lovely spring weather together with Sinding and the "Hardangervidda Man",[65] and I look forward to a quiet evening by myself—which is something that has not come my way for a long time. Time passes—no, it runs, at full speed as a matter of fact—and before I know what is happening it will be time to pack up and say farewell to Leipzig, where we have had it *so* nice with respect to both health and company.

Since the first of February I have been a conservatory student, i.e., I practice the piano for several hours so that I will not make a complete fool of myself in London. I regret terribly that I have promised to play my *Piano Concerto*, but now it is decided and I cannot pull out. Unfortunately, there is no possibility of doing anything here in the way of composition. The afternoon must be used to get fresh air, and in the evening I nearly always go to a concert or to the theater.

But now you must hear about some frivolity that took place a few days ago.

---

[65] The "Hardangervidda" is the vast mountain plateau in Hardanger county where Delius enjoyed going on long, solitary hikes that sometimes lasted for several days at a time.

We came home and found a telegram from Madame Désirée Artôt[66] in Berlin inviting us to an elegant evening meal at her house the next day together with Tchaikovsky. Without hesitation I accepted with pleasure, and the following day we chugged off to Berlin carrying plenty of chicken and red wine. It was a most original evening. Big party, scads of the musical elite.

The worst part was that a large number of pupils marched in, all of whom made a stab at singing songs by Grieg—which yours truly had to accompany. It was not enjoyable, and I don't understand how it can be that Madame Artôt has nothing better to offer. Unfortunately, Madame Artôt presumably knew nothing about Nina's singing. During the dinner (10–12 P.M.), however, she got wind of it, and fortunately Nina had one of her "good" days, so believe me there was tremendous applause. It really was a triumph for her, and I am extremely happy about that.

Later there was dancing, and when Madame Artôt suddenly took hold of me and dragged me out onto the dance floor, you can certainly understand that there was a carnival atmosphere! But it didn't work at all. She wanted to dance the polka and I the galop, so the result was nothing but ridiculous and impossible movements. Her figure defies any attempt at description. She reminds one very much of Mrs. Sars[67] in Christiania and is above all infinitely natural and likable. She sang some poor music—in an absolutely charming and beautiful way. The next evening we attended Tchaikovsky's concert and thereafter were at a big evening meal with him in a restaurant. Then the following morning we returned here and had the feeling of having read a fairytale. (. . .)

But anyway, you can be sure that not a day goes by when I do not long for home. Troldhaugen and Næsset are such lovely thoughts to me, and then there is this: rest, rest! According to what I hear, the [Copenhagen] music festival will be in May—and that is good, for then I can come home all the earlier. I shall be in London only briefly.

And then I shall expect something from my little hut down in the valley.[68] Tchaikovsky also lives in a villa some seven miles from Moscow, and he won't see *anyone* when he is working. He has his servant say that he has gone into the city. That's not such a bad idea.

Well now, dear Frants, let me conclude, for I am not in the mood for writing. The beginning of my letter contains what I wanted to say. The rest is trash.

Loving greetings to both of you! Also from Nisk.

Yours truly,
EDVARD

---

[66] Belgian singer Désirée Artôt (1835–1907).

[67] Maren Sars (1811–98), a sister of the Norwegian poet J. S. Welhaven, was married to Michael Sars (1805–69), a zoologist.

[68] Grieg is referring to the composer's hut that he was planning to build in Trolddalen (the "Troll Valley"), close to the water and just a short distance away from his villa (Troldhaugen).

19

London, May 4, 1888
5 The Cedars, Clapham Common

Dear Frants!
These lines must and shall reach you by the 9th.[69] God bless you because "you are along" as it said in the telegram, and warm thanks to all of you, both for the Leipzig telegram and for the one yesterday.

It is actually difficult for me to tell about last evening. You cannot imagine how it was. When I was conducting "Last Spring" [op. 34 no. 2], and it sounded as if the whole of nature there at home wanted to embrace me, then I was indeed proud and glad to be a Norwegian. I really think that the appreciation of the English for my art must come from their appreciation for Norway, for I cannot explain the ovations yesterday in any other way. I was reminded of the old days when Ole Bull appeared with his fiddle in front of the people of Bergen. Except that the ovations lasted much longer here. When I appeared in the doorway that leads on stage, the audience that filled every last seat in the huge auditorium (St. James's Hall) began applauding so intensely and so endlessly—I think it lasted over three minutes—that I didn't know what to do. I continued to bow in all directions, but it wouldn't stop. Isn't that strange? In a foreign country.

Yes, art certainly is a mystery! "More I received than I ever have deserved"[70] —that is true and certain. But then, in my dear homeland, more than once I have received *less.* Thus everything balances out in this world.

No doubt you think it is not much like me to speak so much about all this outward stuff instead of getting right to the event itself, the performance. But the impression of the reception was altogether too overwhelming because it was so unexpected. I was aware, of course, that I was well known, but I was not aware that my art was held in such high regard here. I played on a splendid Steinway piano, and the *A-minor Concerto,* as far as I am concerned, went well enough. To be sure, my performance did not come close to satisfying me, but it was passable. And the best part was that my playing improved as I went along.

Cowen,[71] the conductor (the one who has written the so-called *Scandinavian Symphony*), was a *blockhead,* so in the concerto the orchestra left much to be desired. But believe me, I made up for it when I myself conducted the string orchestra. And what an orchestra: about sixty string players of absolutely top quality! I have never heard a sound like that in Germany. No, it's too bad you didn't hear "The Wounded Heart" and "Last Spring"![72] How my thoughts were with you.

---

[69] May 9 was Beyer's birthday.

[70] Grieg often cited these words from A. O. Vinje's poem "Last Spring", which he set for voice and piano in op. 33 no. 2.

[71] English composer, pianist and conductor Frederic Hymen Cowen (1852–1935).

[72] *Two Elegiac Melodies.*

There were passages that sounded so wonderful as to move me to tears. I had rehearsed it in every detail, and all the musicians vied with one another to do their best, so the effect was absolutely captivating. There were *fortissimos* and *pianissimos*, accents and passages that soared. It was like a song of harmonies in ethereal heights which, as you know, we musicians always strive for but so rarely achieve.

An English singer, a Miss Elliot, sang "The First Meeting" in German and then—believe it or not—"Farewell to Tvindehaugen" in English. And she sang well! You alone will understand how the word "Tvindehaugen" resounded for me! When she was called back for an encore she sang "Good Morning" (in German).

I still do not know how long we will stay here and whether I will give a concert (with Nina and Mrs. Norman-Neruda[73]). I will write again soon. Loving greetings from both of us and *good luck on the 9th!* Give my warmest greetings also to Majsen.

Yours truly,
EDVARD

P.S. Thanks for the letter. It was so good to get it!!! No one can write about nature there at home as you can! It is as if I were with you.

20

London, March 16, 1889
5 The Cedars, Clapham Common

Dear Frants!
I have waited to write until I could give you the culminating treat at the same time. And now I can: the visit to Miss Brooke's. It was yesterday afternoon that we strolled over to Manchester Square No. 1. A quiet, stately square with equally stately, aristocratic buildings. We were led up a stairway, after which the door was opened and the estimable Miss Honor Brooke welcomed us in person. She looked beaming and noble and, I thought, almost prettier than before. She led us into the commodious living room where a large group of women was assembled. I didn't like this and remained standing somewhat hesitantly by the door until Miss Brooke made the introduction: "My sisters!" I stumbled backwards a step: "What do you say? All these your sisters? Impossible." "Yes, indeed, they are all my sisters!" I clasped my hands together. General delight.

That set the tone, and I don't need to tell you that we found ourselves among a group of noble, amiable, pretty and cheerful young women. The father, who has an injured foot, could not come down, so after a while we went up the three

[73] Czech violinist Wilhelmina Norman-Neruda (1838–1911).

flights of stairs to his study. He received us outside the door—like an old acquaintance. What a man! Nina said, and it is true: How much there is that reminds one of Bjørnson! A big, splendid, sparkling personality full of fire and power. We talked about this and that: about Unitarianism and socialism, about Ibsen and Bjørnson, also a little about politics (the Parnell story[74]), and I daresay he felt just as I do. Only once did we disagree: He maintained that art and science have nothing to do with each other and that a person who cultivated both of them could never accomplish anything. And that, for a Unitarian, is to be pretty illiberal. But I think that here, too, we would have come to an understanding if I had been able to express myself in English as I wished. He must be a splendid public speaker. I may go over to hear him tomorrow forenoon.

Nothing in this world is without some disappointment. So also here: There was no feeling for music in this home. I certainly can draw this conclusion, since no one in the whole family has heard a single tone of ours in spite of our many performances here. I had looked forward specifically to hearing what they thought of the *Peer Gynt Suite* [op. 46], which I had conducted the previous evening, and even while I was still in Berlin I had mentioned the date, for I thought that Miss Brooke, with her interest in Ibsen and in us, would want to hear it. Yes, I more or less assumed it. But there was not a word either about it or about music in general. Well, so much for that. This much is certain: I left happy and enriched in spirit as never before here in London! Still, that doesn't mean much in London. For God knows, the talk here is about everything but ideal matters. If only you knew how I long for ideal air!!!

Oh, believe me, there was excitement the day before yesterday! Every single movement of the suite received thunderous applause, but I just let them clap and went on. At the end the noise was like the howling of animals. Well, you understand me: those primitive sounds that occur only in moments of great enthusiasm. I had to make three curtain calls, and then I had to repeat the troll stuff ["In the Hall of the Mountain King"]. The performance was absolutely splendid. Nina was also in excellent form and scored a big success. She had three curtain calls. One of the songs she sang was "Last Spring", where I had to sit and play the whole postlude while the audience clapped loudly.

Our entire visit here has been a singular success. May it continue! On Wednesday I am giving a concert (which Chappel[75] has "bought" from me for 80 £!) in which I will play my last *Violin Sonata* with Johannes Wolff.[76] We had

---

[74] In 1875 the Irish politician Charles Stewart Parnell (1856–91), who was the leader of the struggle for Irish Home Rule, was elected to the British Parliament. He opposed the direct use of force in support of independence but advocated sabotage and boycott. In 1881 he was arrested and imprisoned but reached an agreement with Prime Minister William Ewart Gladstone (1809–98) that led to his release. Shortly thereafter, however, the chief secretary and the permanent undersecretary for Irish affairs were murdered, and although Parnell was not involved in these acts of violence they led to a break between him and Gladstone.

[75] English impresario Thomas Chappel (1819–1902).

[76] Dutch violinist Johannes Wolff (1863–?). The sonata was *Violin Sonata No. 3* in C minor.

a rehearsal today. He is absolutely brilliant. On the 28th I will conduct the piano concerto with Agathe Grøndahl.[77] On the 31st I will again play the *Third Sonata*, this time with Madame Neruda. And what will happen after that the gods only know. I am still uncertain whether it will be Paris or Leipzig (just between us).

We have indeed heard about all your anxiety for Gabriel[78] and of your trip to Ålesund. May God grant that you will not lose him. Send him a warm greeting when you write.

It is late in the evening and I am so tired, so tired. I feel that I won't be good for anything without sleeping. Therefore, farewell! Loving greetings to both of you!

Yours truly,
EDVARD

P.S. Harding[79] and his wife visited us here one day. They were amiable as before and asked that we greet you most warmly from them.[80] They love you! So also does Miss Brooke—well, I mean she asks us to *greet* you, for as for the rest I have not examined her heart and kidneys thoroughly enough to make a decision. (. . .)

21

Christiania, October 31, 1889

Dear Frants!

God bless you for your letter. It brought me to tears, and I wanted to send a telegram, but then I was called away to another part of the city, and with that the plan I had improvised went down the drain. It seems to me that I had so much, so very much, to write to you today, but I don't have the time. You must read what only the heart of a friend can read between the lines. You will understand better than anyone else what I have gone through during these days. I have lived in a bright light—and in a dark shadow. For Nina's condition has in truth been a shadow!

But why dwell on this? I must just admire nature, which never forgets the proportionate distribution of opposites! Still—not to be bitter! The artistic joy as a result of *Olav Trygvason* has been incomparably great. It sounded more beautiful and impressive than I had dared to hope.[81]

---

[77] Norwegian pianist and composer Agathe Backer Grøndahl (1847–1907).

[78] Norwegian engineer Gabriel Smith (1853–1934), brother of Marie Beyer.

[79] English attorney Charles Harding, who was vice president of the Birmingham Music Festival.

[80] Beyer had been in England with Grieg in 1888.

[81] During the years 1873–76 Grieg and Bjørnson had collaborated on what both had hoped would be a great national opera based on the exploits of the legendary Norwegian king, Olav Trygvason. Problems arose, however, leading in 1876 to an end to the collaboration as well as a rupture in their friendship that was to

And then the meeting with Bjørnson! I wrote to him from here requesting that I be allowed to dedicate my music to him, for I thought it was such a beautiful thought that the very work that at one time divided us should again bring us together. And then I concluded like this: "So blot out all the little things!" For several days I waited in suspense. But then I got a letter! Yes, you can read it when we see each other again. Just this passage you must have right away, for it is so characteristically Bjørnsonian: "When you write, 'Blot out all the little things,' I reply: They shall be blotted out! But I do it only out of obedience, for nothing of the sort was needed!" And farther down in the letter he says of Nina, "And then you know that we love your wife, Karoline[82] and I: We think she is the sweetest person whom one can embrace and address as *du*."[83] You should see how remarkably nice and amiable he has become. I suddenly feel as if I had become 16 years younger! For that is how long it has been since we last spoke! How much I have deprived myself of! But of course it had to be!

Well, dear Frants, that was just a little puff of air, but it comes from your best friend in Norway—this wonderland to which tomorrow evening I will bid farewell more wistfully than ever before.

Loving greetings to both of you!

Yours truly,
EDVARD

P.S. No doubt you have followed the official festivities through the newspapers. Bjørnson's speech at the dinner last evening was marvelous, and Rolfsen's[84] song was beautiful.

22

Paris, December 14, 1889
Hotel de Sêze, 16 rue de Sêze

Dear Frants!
I sent you a telegram from Brussels on the afternoon of the 8th. But according to a letter just received from the Hagerups,[85] they still knew nothing as of the 9th. (. . .) That you have received the telegram without telling the Hagerups is

---

last for thirteen years. In 1888–89 Grieg resurrected the fragments of the uncompleted opera (music for three scenes from Act 1) and orchestrated them. The premiere of *Scenes from Olav Trygvason* op. 50 took place at a concert of the Music Association in Christiania on October 19, 1889. Grieg and Bjørnson also reconciled at this time, and the composer dedicated op. 50 to his old friend. See Grieg's letters to Bjørnson from 1873–76 and 1889 for further details.

[82] Karoline Bjørnson (1835–1934), wife of Bjørnstjerne Bjørnson.

[83] Address as *du*: use the familiar rather than the formal word for "you".

[84] Norwegian author and educator Nordahl Rolfsen (1848–1928).

[85] Nina Grieg's parents, Herman and Adeline Hagerup, who lived in Bergen.

impossible as it said explicitly, "Make it known among friends."[86] So much for that.

By the time you receive this you will long since have heard about the concerts, and especially about the last one.[87] The effect was singular and magnificent in every respect. The orchestra was assembled on the stage, which had been transformed into a splendid salon. The theater, illumined by electric lights, was filled to the rafters. It was completely sold out, and since we had been unable to have a rehearsal in the theater itself I was a bit nervous when I made my entrance. I was very warmly received, but when I was ready to start conducting there was no baton. Orchestra assistants are idiots everywhere—so after waiting for a moment I had to step down from the podium again. Finally the dunce came with a baton about as long as I am tall, but fortunately it was as thin as a reed. I did what you would also have done: Despite the assistant's angry look and energetic protest, I broke a piece of it off and threw the rest over in a corner, whereupon I again mounted the podium and gave the signal to start the *Autumn Overture*. You won't find this in any review, so you shall have this private account of the episode.

As you can see, I am so weak and exhausted from the illness—influenza—that is going around Europe now that I can hardly move a pen, and my thinking is so unclear that I can't pull anything together (I have been in bed for three days and today received permission to be up). But you must and shall have a few lines at Christmas from which you will see that I am the old

(...)

Believe me, I have had my hands full, and this, I think, I ought to keep to myself. I could not give a half-way account to you—that would be worse than nothing at all. But now that time is past. Come what may, my sole wish is more than ever to go home again! Yes, home, home!

Oh, that last quiet stroll around the Hop[88] neighborhood the afternoon before I left! May it just be granted to us to be together for a few more years when both nature and our friendship are as beautiful as on that day. For the friendship is indeed the loveliest because it is the most profound. "The first love." Yes, it is the decisive moment in the life of each human being, but he to whom it is granted, with his life behind him, to feel the greater love that hovers over art and life—art is indeed the model—for him the first love is merely like a tiny flower in relation to the whole of nature. In the years that still remain to us in which to walk together through nature, it will appear to us still lovelier. (...)

---

[86] Grieg wrote this in French: "Fait communiquer aux amis."

[87] Grieg gave concerts in Paris on December 22 and 29, 1889, and on January 4, 1890.

[88] Hop is the region south of Bergen where both Troldhaugen and Næsset are located.

Today is Saturday, and on Thursday there is an orchestra rehearsal. God grant that I may be well enough to handle it! I am depending on fresh air and exercise. Tonight I hope to be able to sleep without medication—I have had a high fever—and if this goes well, tomorrow I will walk until I get bone tired.

From Majs's letter received today we learned that you have been on a long hike in the mountains and were *just a little unwell* afterward. Good Lord! It depends on the length of the hike!

Now I can't tolerate any more writing. Farewell, then, dear friend. Greet Majs, and merry Christmas to both of you!

Yours truly,
EDVARD

23

Paris, January 11, 1890
Hotel de Sèze, 16 rue de Sèze

Dear Frants!
Let me seize the moment and send you what I think are the first lines of the new decade. May it often lead us together in happy quietude and joy in the splendor of the mountain scenery.

If only you knew how this nervous life pains and torments me and with what longing I look forward to the time when I can breathe the fresh air of Norway and not feel as weakened and enervated as I do now. For it cannot be denied that I have gone downhill of late. My brain can indeed tolerate a bit, but not my stomach. And it is just a matter of nerves. Now, when I no longer have concerts here, I have the feeling that I am killing time. Perhaps you cannot understand this, but I have neither the serenity nor the health to see Paris and I cannot leave for Stuttgart until the end of the month. What occupies me to a certain degree is trying to keep all would-be visitors and invitations off my neck. It's really a worthwhile existence!

Perhaps by the time you receive this you will have seen the reviews of the concert on the 4th. It was an absolutely unique success. It was like nothing else of the kind that I have ever experienced before. Already during the C-minor *Violin Sonata*, with which the program began, I sensed these odd sounds that are characteristic of the French—but, to be sure, only when they are enchanted. Namely: "Ah! Charmant! Ravivante! Superbe!" etc. etc. even during the performance. I played the introduction to the second movement—the passage in E major for piano only—very beautifully (I had an absolutely superb piano), and just as the violin was about to come in the bravos and applause began and grew in intensity throughout the entire remainder of the concert. I had to play two encores after many curtain calls following "Bridal Procession". And then Nina! Believe me, it was a pleasure for both of us that she was able to participate! And she scored a great success as evidenced by both the wild applause and the insistence that she repeat a song. She is healthier than me and is absolutely healthier than at home. (...)

These are not long letters that you are getting, and unfortunately they contain very little that goes beneath the surface! I am annoyed at that, but *que faire?*[89] We are strongly influenced by our surroundings. I don't think I could ever compose a note here. I will be happy when I can write to you from Germany.

Loving greetings to both of you from Nina and me.

Yours truly,
EDVARD

24

Leipzig, March 10, 1890

Dear Frants!

It seemed like an eternity since I had heard from you, and then I received your welcome letter, which I am taking the first opportunity of answering. One would think that I should have plenty of time at my disposal, but that is not the case. I have a slew of proofs to read, and I must also play a little, because I will be performing the G-major *Violin Sonata* at the Gewandhaus with Brodsky on the 21st—and then I have no study, so as a result I am not certain of being uninterrupted for a single moment.

Believe me, I thought about you on February 27 when I conducted *Olav Trygvason*. And believe me, it was a strange feeling to mount *this* podium for the first time to conduct *this* composition. Since I don't want to be unreasonable I must say that the performance was good. Sinding thought there had been more enthusiasm in Christiania, and perhaps he is right. But the language, the language! That makes such a difference. The choruses were very impressive, and the *vølve*[90] sang her parts very confidently and with verve. (...)

Thank you for writing to Bjørnson.[91] But I don't think he has the stomach or the inclination to take hold. He is occupied with totally different subjects now. I will not complain, either, as there are so many other things I want to do.

If only you knew how I look forward to coming home again! No, you can't have the slightest concept of that. Just today we talked about the fact that perhaps you are already at Næsset. I can't say that I hope for that, for I am so afraid that you won't be able to tolerate it. This is the very worst time of the year—albeit also the most beautiful. This certainly is the season when one relives one's youth each year! Youth! One evening we were together with your sister and her fiancé,

---

[89] What can I do?

[90] In Old Norse mythology, on which the text of *Scenes from "Olav Trygvason"* was based, the "vølve" was a woman who practiced witchcraft and had the ability to foresee the future.

[91] Beyer had written to Bjørnson asking him to renew the collaboration on *Olav Trygvason*.

and this incipient poetry of life together—indeed, how infinitely moving it is. What kind of a demon is it that prevents the perpetuation of this happiness!

It is good that youth knows of nothing and believes in nothing other than itself! But isn't it true that although youth slips away from us, we believe equally firmly—indeed, more firmly—in the good, the beautiful, the pure! And in this there is eternal youth. The younger generation can boast all they please that *they* have a monopoly on the truth. You understand that I am referring to the Bohemian movement against Bjørnson, whose sandals they are not worthy to untie. Can't those people understand that there is no *absolute* truth? When each one seeks the truth in his own way, then everything is fine. One-sidedness is certainly forgivable in a great mind, and I should think Bjørnson has a right to be so regarded.

I am sad this evening, having just received the news of Johannes Brun's[92] death. It is true! But how the feeling forces itself upon me that we have lost not just a talent but a genius! How empty Norway is becoming! Soon we will have to be content to embrace trees and stones, for in them lies the whole of nature's genius. I say "be content to." But to embrace Norway is for me the highest act, and I do it each day in my thoughts. There is no great mind that one can love so completely and purely as one can love nature! Long may it live! But not without you!

Loving greetings to both of you!

Yours truly,
EDVARD

25

Copenhagen, February 9, 1891

Dear Frants!

During the past 10–12 days I have been "pregnant" with an answer to your last welcome letter, but I have put off the birth of the fetus from day to day because I thought I couldn't make the answer good enough, i.e., such as I feel it. But if you are going to wait until I find a suitable form for what I feel, then you will be waiting a long time. So to the point. You console me in my dispirited mood as only you can do—and only contribute to a heightening of my longing for home. These winter months abroad have taught me that I am no longer young. I need home in order to do creative work, and when I travel it must be either to make music or to breath fresh air and gather impressions. You speak so alluringly about next winter. Yes, indeed, we will talk about that. It is certain that the urge to be with you becomes stronger and stronger each time I go away. May there still

92 Norwegian actor Johannes Brun (1832–90), who had played the title role in the premiere performance of Bjørnson's play *Sigurd Jorsalfar* in 1872.

be some happy times in store for us in the world of nature. In this life and this togetherness lies all the music of which some gets written down—but most of it, and the best of it, unfortunately does not.

Still, the music inspired by this singular mixture of nature and friendship tends to be good. It is different down here in the foreign country. The music that I come up with one day I tear out of my heart the next—because it isn't genuine. My ideas are bloodless just like me, and I am beginning to lose faith in myself. In view of this, it helps little when Dr. Abraham writes that my compositions—the *Peer Gynt Suite*, for example—are being performed in Europe, Asia, Africa, America and Australia! Therefore: to the mountains, to the mountains! There alone is the cure.

Drachmann is now in Vienna, but I will tell his wife that you are enjoying his Edith;[93] she will pass it on to him and I know it will please him. Yes, there are some marvelous things in that book—especially, perhaps, the descriptive passages. For even Edith seems to me to lack a—yes, what shall I call it—a child?! In any case there is something there, something cold, that I don't really believe in.

You ask about the trip home. I am thinking of going to Christiania for 8–14 days in early April, because I promised Eilif Peterssen[94] that I would pose for a portrait. Otto Aubert, district governor[95] in Skien, has invited us down to his home, but we will stay there a couple of days at most if we go there at all. And then we head home. Have still heard nothing from Moltke Moe.[96] But he presumably is managing the affair on his own. I think it is highly unlikely that he is just letting it lie. (...)

Your brother-in-law's death put me in a most serious mood, even though I never knew him.

I will not say that I fear either life or death, but there is one thing I do fear: noticing that I myself am growing old—that the ideas of the younger generation will sail out on expeditions the meaning of which I do not fully comprehend. In short, I fear the possibility of losing the capacity to feel what is true and great in the intellectual avant garde, which moves steadily forward the longer we live. For that reason I have—more now than ever before—an instinctive need to know all the nuances that are stirring in the intellectual life of our time. If one allows anything of significance to glide by without having assimilated it—before one knows what is happening it will become a power that one doesn't understand, because one hasn't followed that which is new from the very beginning. To be left lying

---

93 A character in the Drachman novel *Forskrevet* (*Pledged*) from 1890.

94 Norwegian painter Eilif Peterssen (1852–1928).

95 Otto Aubert (1841–98) was a *stiftamtmann*, i.e., chief administrative officer having jurisdiction over a prescribed area under a system of regional governance that was in effect in Norway from 1692 to 1918.

96 Norwegian folklorist Moltke Moe (1859–1913). Grieg had asked Moe to support an application for a grant for Beyer to enable him to use the summer months to gather folk tunes from West Norway. Moe supported the application, but the Norwegian Parliament did not give Beyer the requested funds.

half forgotten on the road as time marches over my wretched cadaver—that seems to me the greatest misery that can befall a person. And with how countless many does this not happen? Perhaps with most—but they do not know it, and thus they do not care. It is different with the artist: When he becomes one of the reactionaries he is lost.

Yesterday we had ourselves vaccinated, thereby doing our bit to make it possible to see old Norway again. Yes, that will be a delight! This steady *crescendo* of joy at the sight of home—that, thank God, makes up for a lot of things.

Yours truly,
EDVARD

P.S. Did Majs get the book by Zola?[97]

26

London, May 6, 1894

Dear Frants and Majs!
Now you are at Næsset and here we sit—with *only* the ocean between us! We came here late last evening, and I swore in Paris that the first thing I would do in London would be to send you a letter. First to congratulate you on being together again, and secondly to tell you a little about the triumph in Paris on April 22. For it was a triumph for Norway, one of the few that I shall not forget.

Naturally, since it does not have to do with literature you get only idiotic reports in Norway. And the press itself has now sunk so low that one absolutely must be present oneself if one does not wish to be misled by untruthful or bought reviews. I was told that I absolutely had to—at the very least!—make visits to the leading critics in Paris. You can surely understand who did *not* do it. The result was that *Figaro*—the famous, or more correctly the infamous Jewish paper—killed the whole Châtelet concert by *silence*. For this newspaper is accustomed not only to visits but to something else called money! Other papers treated the whole event humorously, and still others wrote that the huge success was due to the Scandinavians (of whom among over 3,000 living in Paris there were ca. 150–200 at the concert) or the muted strings in "Solveig's Song" [EG 177 no.1] or on the fact that I was a "ladies' man" etc.

But to speak of the event itself, I especially wished that you had heard *The Mountain Thrall*—*Le Solitaire*—and "A Swan" [EG 177 no. 4], which I had orchestrated. The latter was sung *da capo* and the rendition was absolutely splendid. The same must be said of the interpretation of *The Mountain Thrall*, and that is significant. That all the orchestral pieces sounded good goes without saying, and

[97] French author Émile Zola (1840–1902).

Raoul Pugno[98] played the *Piano Concerto* with a furious fire and speed, breadth and enormous power. When we returned to the green room I of course embraced the sweating pianist and said, "Mais Vous êtes le Rubinstein français!"

Listen now to the French style of advertising: A few days later I had to attend a concert given by the same Pugno in which he presented only his own piano works. As an overture to the concert he had gotten a poet, who went so far as to proclaim himself a friend, to give a lecture that bulged with words of praise for the man giving the concert. He concluded thus: "At the last big concert in Châtelet he scored a unique triumph with Grieg's *Concerto*, a triumph after which the master (who is present here in the auditorium!) embraced him and shouted, 'You are the French Rubinstein!'" Great applause. Tableau! Alexander Bull[99] and I were sitting alone in a box. He coughed and cleared his throat more than he normally does, I made myself even smaller than usual and disappeared into a dark corner. Well, what do you say about not disdaining undisguised means of that sort! Then, indeed, the hidden ones—financial pay-offs, etc.—count as nothing in comparison. It is quite true that Paris is a splendid city, but the demoralization in art is enormous and I am happy to be gone.

Home looms before my mind's eye more enticingly than ever. May it not disappoint me! But before I shall have the joy of treading the soil of old Norway, which I certainly will do in the manner of Chilian,[100] I still have some unpleasant things to endure. On Thursday (the 10th) I will play a comic role in Cambridge. Costume: blue and white surplice, Medieval cap. Scene: a festively decorated street. Action: procession through the town![101]

That is how Saint-Saëns described it to me in Paris, and he took part in the same thing last year. How one views such things evidently depends on one's nationality. When I said to Saint-Saëns, "Basically the whole thing must be regarded as comedy," he replied passionately, "No, not at all; on the contrary, the whole thing is 'serieux' in the highest degree." That sort of public display means something to a Frenchman.

Moreover, believe me, it was a pleasure to meet Saint-Saëns. To my surprise, one day I found his calling card at the hotel before I had let him hear from me, and I wasted no time before returning the visit. He of course embraced me in the French manner and kissed me "left and right". And when I, to also be pleasant in my own way, thanked him for everything I had learned from his art, he answered as we were parting: "One does not learn from others when one is oneself!" He always has wittiness at the tip of his tongue!

---

[98] French pianist and composer Raoul Pugno (1852–1914).

[99] Norwegian impresario Alexander Bull (1839–1914), who lived in Paris.

[100] Chilian was a comical figure in the German comedy tradition, a kind of harlequin. In *Ulysses von Ithacia*, a 1723 comedy by Norwegian author Ludvig Holberg (1684–1754), Chilian is Ulysses' servant.

[101] Grieg was to receive an honorary doctorate at Cambridge University.

I conduct on the 24th, rest on the 25th, and on the 26th we rush homeward as fast as we can. Would that we dared to go by sea! But—I simply don't dare! The first steamship from Aberdeen doesn't leave until June 7, and I won't wait that long. Yes, if only you had been along! That would have been a different matter.

Majs, we are very anxious to know something about your trip home, how you found Næsset, the garden, Frants—not Frants [first] and [then] the garden!—etc. etc. It is a long time indeed since I have heard from you now, Frants. Well, on Wednesday you will get a telegram anyway![102] And then we will empty a glass of good old Bordeaux to your health! May we just meet in tolerably good health! I think the winter has taken a lot out of me and that is *not* going to happen again—not next year, at any rate. I hope to stretch out the autumn as long as possible at home—with the concerts that have long been under discussion.

And now farewell, dear friends! Write soon! Most loving greetings from both of us.

Your old
EDVARD

P.S. Greet the Giertsens![103]

27

Copenhagen, December 29, 1894

Dear Frants!
I am having trouble with my stomach, am weak and exhausted after an altogether too long-lasting emptying out. Nonetheless: The old year must not end before I thank you for your welcome letter. I missed a bit of the sunshine that I usually find in your letters—but how can it be otherwise than that as the years go by the oppressive Bergen winter darkness must take its toll. Still, your reserve of sunshine is so great that you have more than enough to last you as long as you live. And then it is strange with our getting older: It is as if we are preoccupied more and more with illness and death and everything around us that is sad and serious.

The question of transitoriness is beginning to dominate my thoughts more and more. It was also a painful surprise for us down here to learn of Didrik Smit's[104] death. He was so infinitely amiable on the trip, and we felt so very close to him. I know this, that in one respect he was in a category that perhaps contains no more than seven or eight people in Bergen: He was a true lover of music. And when such a person passes away, for me it leaves a gaping hole there at home.

---

[102] Beyer's birthday was May 9.
[103] Bergen shipowner Børre Giertsen (1851–1905) and his wife Nancy (1859–1911).
[104] Grieg's friend Didrik Smit (1849–1894), an attorney in Bergen, had died of tuberculosis on December 13.

When you, on the occasion of a death like this that hits you so closely, think you should say to yourself: "I will be nice. We will be nice to one another, we human beings, while we are puttering about"—it is as moving as it is strange that it is precisely you who entertain such thoughts. For you of all people do not need to. You have every reason to say it to the rest of us—to me, for example. But *you*, in my opinion, are so nice—yes, so excessively nice—that just in order to be so you sometimes seem almost to renounce something that I wish your strong feeling of justice could keep a secure hold on. So: To myself I say, "Be nice." But to you I say, "Do *not* be too nice. Not nicer than the best elements of your nature can endorse." I am constituted in such a way that I have the best intention to be nice, but there is something in my own nature that now and again says "No!" I am often indignant at all this niceness. The fact is, I think, that I often get the impression that *I benefit from* being nice—and for that reason, from an ideal standpoint it is not where I ought to be. And this irritates me in such a way that the whole idea of "niceness" declines in value for me.

You want to hear something about myself. Well, you see, although Copenhagen is replete with life and amusements and good will and friendly people, my own "self" is anything but cheerful. I am now quite aware of the fact that the reason for this is my stomach, for if my stomach happens to be relatively good for one day out of 30 or 40, then I am immediately a different person. A brighter outlook and a desire to work and imagination and everything that is good suddenly come knocking at my door. Then I say to myself: Continue tomorrow in order to seize the mood while it is there—and then tomorrow comes and I am once again back in the old condition, melancholy and depressed, without the ability to continue what I have begun.

And you see, this feeling that my life's work is essentially over—to date I have not been able to accept it. I think there is so much that I should do, so much for which I feel both the ability and the desire—in the fleeting good moments. But now I realize that I should recognize the situation, capitulate, and be happy for all that good Mother Nature has bestowed on me. In other words, I must say to myself: "Relax and be content!" But I can't do it. For the desire to work and my ambitions are by no means extinct in me. And this hurts. It hurts more than I can say. It is like an endless nightmare. It is as if I were nearly choking or that some other horrible accident were about to occur.

Lately, dark thoughts of this sort have disturbed my mind even more than before. And there are times when I become terrified about what is going to happen. I really know of only one medicine. But thank God I do know of it, and it is mentioned in your letter, for it is also your medicine. "A little mouse hole to hide in, or a solitary hut up in the mountains." I will supply a few more details and say: life in the Norwegian (western Norwegian) mountain terrain in general. And as long as you feel as I do about this matter, a balm descends upon my soul each time I, in a dark moment, am able to evoke this happy thought. How strange it is, though, that in this respect nature is superior to the human being. For the human being—even the one for whom one has infinite affection—can disappoint. Nature, never. One never takes refuge in its bosom in vain, come what may. The thought of Norway: That is what I live on when I am away—and when I am home. So: I'll see you in the Norwegian summer, dear Frants, and thank you for everything you contributed to this, our glorious shared vision of all its beauty!

Happy New Year to you, to Majs and all of you!

Yours truly,
EDVARD

P.S. Presumably you did not forget to get some toys for Salomon's[105] children for Christmas Eve?

The picture you sent made me very happy: Næsset as seen from Troldhaugen. How many memories it contains! Warm thanks to both of you!

(Don't forget to greet Børre and Nancy!!)

28

Leipzig, October 27, 1895
Addr. C. F. Peters, Thalstrasse 10

Dear Frants!
What an eternity since we parted! And what a great, great disappointment that I didn't get to see you in Christiania! I waited and waited, and then we heard that Majs was sick. Thereupon, of course, we gave up both hope and expectation. Hopefully she is now well again, and we will look forward to summer and to seeing you again. For me these things loom more beautifully than ever—thank God!

It is not pleasant here. It is lonely and sad, and my tendency to melancholy thrives only too well. Worst of all is the fact that my fatherly old friend, Dr. Abraham, is so sick that I almost never see him. I would certainly have stayed in Copenhagen, where I feel well, had I not received the invitation from Dr. Abraham. As matters now stand I don't think I will be here long, for I have become so inflexible that I can no longer find my true self down here in all this Germanness and so-called musical life, which now strikes me as so worm-eaten in many respects. And in addition: There is neither sea nor mountain, just coal dust and swampy fog. No: Long live Scandinavia! Yes, I will gladly be so liberal as to include Sweden![106]

---

105 Salomon Monsen Hop (1846–1927) was the farmer from whom Grieg purchased the property on which Troldhaugen was built.

106 There was considerable tension between Norway and Sweden at this time because of Norway's demand for independence from Sweden.

But now a little biography. You have heard from Tonny,[107] of course, that we had a splendid trip across the country from Bergen to Christiania and also that the concert went well.[108] The string piece[109] sounded good, I think, but it is not what one would technically call a *da capo number*. The songs, on the other hand, deserve such an appellation. Both "Monte Pincio" and "A Swan" [EG 177 nos. 3 and 4] had to be repeated. Then we went to Copenhagen, where I was sick when I arrived (too much champagne on the departure from Christiania). And by the time I was well, Nina got a fever and was completely wretched for a couple of days.

The result was that our departure from Copenhagen was delayed, and we didn't get here until Sunday, eight days ago today. I have secured a study and wanted to get to work on *The Mountain Maid*. But—all of that lies hundreds of miles away. I can no longer revive the former moods. Yes, indeed, one's surroundings are a delicate spider web, more delicate than one realizes oneself. During Christmas I hope to go north again and get to work in Copenhagen. Provided I don't go to Vienna, which is still undecided.

Believe me, it was thrilling to hear the big orchestra sound again in the Gewandhaus—and especially now with the brilliant new conductor, Arthur Nikisch, a Hungarian.[110] And then Tchaikovsky's posthumous *Symphony Pathétique*. A remarkable piece. Strangely differing from the traditional forms, it is pervaded by a subdued undercurrent of premonitions of death.

At the same concert a Miss Ternina,[111] a royal court singer from Munich, sang several songs including "Solveig's Song" [EG 177 no. 1]. And I can only say: To hell with all female singers. Now that Nina no longer sings I understand for the first time how fortunate I have been in this respect. But now the time is also coming when I, like Diogenes, must look high and low for a person who knows how to continue where she is leaving off. I won't find her in Germany. It absolutely must be in Scandinavia. For it has been demonstrated in both London and Paris that the public prefers to hear the original Norwegian text sung with understanding by a Scandinavian rather than to hear a poor translation sung by one of their own singers. But in Norway, unfortunately, all these little maidens have little or no knowledge of their own musical heritage. But it will all come eventually—that and the railroad to Christiania—when I have found the rest that in agonizing moments I often desire. And yet, at other moments I feel such an immensely strong, pulsating urge to live! Strange contradictions.

Yes, dear Frants, life is mysterious and complex—and perhaps most of all for a person who lives in my skin. Therefore I must also go home again and be with

---

107 Tonny (Antonie) Hagerup (1844–1939), Nina Grieg's sister.

108 Grieg had given a concert in Christiania on October 12 with the Music Association orchestra.

109 "In Folk Style", *Two Nordic Melodies* op. 63 no. 1.

110 Austro-Hungarian conductor Arthur Nikisch (1855–1922) was appointed musical director of both the Leipzig Gewandhaus Orchestra and the Berlin Philharmonic Orchestra in 1895. He held both positions until the end of his life.

111 Croatian soprano Milka Ternina (1863–1941).

you, with whom I can always learn anew the simple, uncomplex joy of existence! That is not the smallest part of all the beauty that your friendship has represented for me—and will continue to represent until my final hour.

Most loving greetings to both of you, also from Nina. Write soon!

Yours truly,
EDVARD

29

Leipzig, January 24, 1896

Dear Frants!
Thank you for the New Year's letter and telegram. As for the former, it was as good as hearing a beloved old melody that always revives the purest and best memories. Thank you, dear friend! The same thing is happening between me and you as between me and nature and art: The relationship gets firmer and grows in depth with each day that passes.

And if I can say this about three different things in this enigmatic world, I am simply rich—a fact that I should never get tired of repeating to myself.

I had to laugh at the telegram. It was so outlandish that I found it most advisable to reply in German. Salomon certainly is right. Besides, I would like to ask you for advice and help in this matter. But you must be patient, for the story on which I must fill you in is a complicated one.

The main point is that the new well (assuming that it contains good water) will do what I have spoken to him about. Couldn't you and Børre Giertsen saunter over to the place some Sunday and hatch something brilliant? Do it, and write and tell me what you—i.e., in association with Salomon—have decided. Now as I sit here I absolutely cannot understand how, last summer, I could many a time have toyed with the idea of selling Troldhaugen. For at this moment it gives me the mental peace and quiet that I so desperately need. It is possible that I might find a place that would be more practical in several respects, but then I would not have you nearby—and then to hell with all the splendor!

Last night, I am ashamed to say, I went on a spree. We sat with Sängers[112] drinking copious quantities of Moselle wine until 1 A.M. So I'm under the weather, but for some unknown reason I don't have a real hangover. We four are accustomed to getting together at a tavern after the Gewandhaus concerts.

Last evening I was asked to get together with Siegfried Wagner,[113] who is staying at our hotel and will be conducting in the Liszt Society tomorrow. But I am not convinced of his talent as a conductor in the first place—and besides, I much preferred my own likable company.

---

[112] The German physician Max Sänger (1853–1903)and his Norwegian-born wife Helga (nee Waagaard) (1854–1931).

[113] Siegfried Wagner (1869–1930), Richard Wagner's son.

Last evening we heard *Vyšehrad*, a symphonic poem by Smetana[114]—a piece that in many respects is brilliant and that was composed by a man who died without receiving the recognition he deserved. He has written a string quartet, "From My Life", which you should get Halvorsen to play.[115] Smetana became deaf, but suddenly he heard a blaring high

This is illustrated in the last part of the quartet.

Röntgen's[116] friend, the brilliant Dutch singer Messchaert,[117] also sang last evening. Among the pieces he sang were Brahms's "Feldeinsamkeit" ("Mountain Loneliness") and my "Cradle Song" to Munch's poem, "Sleep, my son".[118] Both were sung in an exquisite manner with exactly the right coloring and sublime calmness. Just this choice of my song, this recklessness, are characteristic of the artist. Believe me, it was strange to sit here and listen to this 35-year-old reminder of my youth. I could hardly comprehend that I had written it. It was really almost like the words in Brahms's song, "Mir ist, als wenn ich längst gestorben wäre!"[119] But I had a deep inner feeling of joy and gratitude toward the artist, who did not destroy my deepest intentions but understood them precisely and knew how to communicate them to others. I daresay that I almost never experience this when I am just a member of the audience.

Last week we were frequently with Brahms in Leipzig, where he was visiting for a few days, and we enjoyed his company immensely. I don't understand how a one-sided person like Brahms—one-sided in his greatness, that is—can have such a positive opinion of my music, which, as far as I can see, goes in a very different direction from his. But, taciturn though he is, he nonetheless showed me that he does. His *Symphony No. 4* in E Minor was performed in the Gewandhaus. The first movement of that work, which I had never heard before, is one of his most beautiful creations. And then the performance under Nikisch! I wish you could hear this orchestra under this conductor. (. . .)

Accept my most loving greetings, and also greet Majs warmly from me and congratulate her on her birthday. Also greet the Giertsens.

Yours truly,
EDVARD

---

[114] Czech composer Bedřich Smetana (1824–84). *Vyšehrad* was no. 1 in the cycle of six symphonic poems called *Má vlast* (My Fatherland).

[115] Johan Halvorsen was at that time musical director of the National Stage in Bergen.

[116] Dutch pianist, conductor and composer Julius Röntgen (1855–1932).

[117] Dutch baritone Johannes Messchaert (1857–1927).

[118] *Songs and Ballads* op. 9 no. 2, text by Norwegian poet Andreas Munch (1811–84).

[119] "It seems to me that I have been dead for a long time!"

30

Christiania, November 5, 1896

Dear Frants!

I have just returned home from Lysaker, where I had a lovely dinner at Werenskiold's with Munthe, Skredsvig, Lammers and Nansen and their wives.[120] And now you shall have a few lines, primarily to thank you for last summer and to tell you how many thoughts I have sent your way since we parted.

You, who are happier than anyone when things are going well for me, will also understand what it has meant to me just at this time to be healthier than I have been for—yes, I daresay for many years. For that reason I was also youthful and flexible in Stockholm and was able to give my best both as an artist and as a person. It would have gone exactly the same for you as it did for me. You wouldn't have been able to resist all this courtesy either but would have been taken by storm. Naturally there is a certain portion of the press and the aristocracy that can be excepted, but otherwise it is my impression that Norway and its artistic life are admired and held in high regard.

Presumably you have read in the newspapers what a unique success I have scored.[121] And how the orchestra played! In the end it sounded as if I were just improvising. The finest, most subtle nuances found expression. The orchestra loved me, there were no annoyances—that is the reason for the good result. And what a male chorus! I never dreamt that *Land-sighting* could sound like that. And the solo singing! Lundqvist was powerful and imposing in "Henrik Wergeland", for example.[122] And Mrs. Dagmar Möller,[123] nee Bosse (Norwegian), was sweet and charming and sang with the finest intelligence and understanding. Her voice is not beautiful, but it didn't matter to me or to the audience either, for she scored a big success.

The king[124] and his family were present at two concerts, and at one of them I was called into the lion's den. I admit that he is an amiable man (he was absolutely effusive in his enthusiasm), the very opposite of [Crown Prince] Gustav, who stood glaring at me as if I were an enemy. But he also has another son, the painter Eugen, who came to the party at the Grand Hotel. You surely have read about this. He is a fine, warm and straightforward person. Another person who attended the party was Nordenskjöld,[125] who gave the impression of being a fat professor who likes to hear himself talk. (...)

Believe me, it was strange at the orchestra rehearsal yesterday to hear the

---

120 Norwegian painters Erik Werenskiold (1855–1938), Gerhard Munthe (1849–1929) and Christian Skredsvig (1854–1924), baritone Thorvald Lammers (1841–1922), polar explorer Fridtjof Nansen (1861–1930).

121 Grieg gave concerts in Stockholm on October 24, 29 and 31, 1896.

122 Swedish baritone Carl Fredrik Lundqvist (1841–1920) in "Henrik Wergeland" EG 177 no. 6.

123 Norwegian-born soprano Dagmar Möller (1866–1956).

124 Oscar II (1829–1907), at that time king of Sweden and Norway.

125 Swedish geologist and polar explorer Adolf Erik Nordenskjöld (1832–1902).

coarse sound on the same pieces that were still ringing in my ears from Stockholm. I struggled for over two hours and got the worst rough spots taken care of. We'll find out tomorrow if it helped. I hope so, for 1,200 people will be sitting there (at the dress rehearsal) listening. Lammers will sing *The Mountain Thrall* and "Henrik Wergeland". Believe me, it made me happy that the latter was one of the pieces that most gripped everyone in Sweden.

So: Saturday evening is the Music Association concert, and at the beginning of next week we leave for Vienna via Copenhagen. How far Nina will accompany me on the trip I do not know. It depends on her health. Upon my return from Stockholm she was like a new person: red cheeks, healthy and happy. Yes, that's the way it is: You are right, separation stimulates love! And just between us, I don't think it would have gone as well for me in Stockholm if I had not been a free man. I was able to arrange matters as I thought best for my art. That was the secret. I didn't want anyone to be talking about Norwegian discourtesy, so I daresay that never in my life have I made so many visits. I know the city of Stockholm primarily as viewed from taxicabs. That I should acquire Swedish friends—both male and female—is something I had considered an impossibility. But now I have them and I am genuinely fond of them.

Well, dear Frants, now you have gotten some biographical snatches. You will read between the lines that I have experienced a bit of joy on which I will feast for a long time. Greet your dear Majs, and accept the most loving greetings from me yourself.

Faithfully yours,
EDVARD

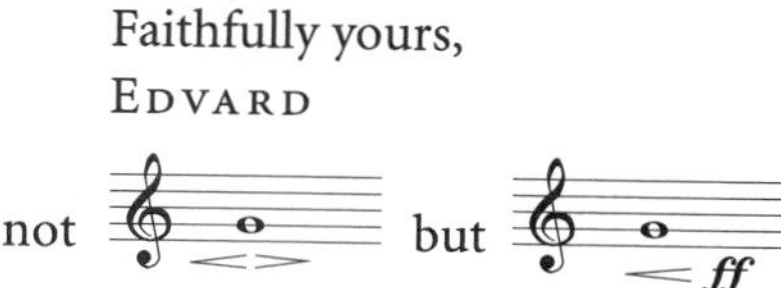

31

Semmering at Vienna, December 27, 1896

Dear Frants!
Your welcome letter and the book arrived today! Thank you for both of them. If only you yourself had come along! (. . .)

We are a group of five people up here who left Vienna together on Christmas Day: court music dealer Gutmann, Professor Neovius from Helsinki and his wife[126] (nee Hammerich, you certainly remember them from Hop) and the two of us. We are enjoying ourselves very much here, with a level of comfort that rivals that of both Stalheim and Voss. The weak point is all the rich Jews from Vienna

---

[126] Austrian music dealer and concert agent Albert Gutmann (1862–1915), Finnish mathematician and politician Edvard Rudolf Neovius (1851–1917) and his wife, Thyra Hammerich Neovius.

who come here at Christmas time. Wherever I go they surround me like wolves. Today a whole bunch of them who are art enthusiasts invited all of us to dinner and were, we all had to admit, exceptionally cordial. But New Year's Eve will be more fun. Then we will be at Gutmann's in Vienna along with Brahms, Joachim[127] and other interesting people. Yesterday I sent Brahms the following telegram:

Auf des Jahres letzte Stunde
freut sich Edvard und Kunigunde.[128]

He has—ill as he is, poor fellow—been exceptionally cordial toward us. During my illness he inquired personally three times about my condition, and at the orchestra concert he stayed for the whole program from beginning to end—which is something he never does these days. Yes, he even came to an informal party at the hotel after the concert. This, for me, is what gives my stay in Vienna its greatest value, for although I am not such a great admirer of the later Brahms I am all the more so regarding his earlier compositions. Above all, he is Germany's leading—yes, unfortunately, perhaps its only—truly great personage living today.

Perhaps you have heard about the great pleasure I had from the concerts[129] —yes, even from my modest attempt at playing the piano! But popularity can be unpleasant at times. I found that out at mealtime yesterday when a zither-player suddenly lit into "Solveig's Song". And still more today when an enthusiastic, dark-eyed Jewish beauty administered the following dose: "Grieg! You know, your music—oh, it is certainly an insult to say it, for you are indeed much greater, but your music reminds me a little of Chopin! And also—but it is certainly an even greater insult—of Liszt!" What do you say to that? Can you swallow it? One should keep enough in reserve to be able to vomit right in the face of people like that. (. . .)

This afternoon we went for a marvelous hike, just Nina and I. We left the road and crawled up through the snowdrifts that were hard enough to bear our weight, and we had the most beautiful view in the evening light. We will stay here for another 2–3 days. After dinner we moved here to Hotel Panhaus from a little annex villa, where we had stayed for lack of a better place. Now we think we have it like petty kings. Gutmann has gone back to Vienna, and the four of us plan to play whist together this evening.

I wish I could stay here for a whole week, as my evening program of songs with Sistermans[130] is not until the 6th of January, but since I am going to be the

---

127 Hungarian virtuoso violinist Joseph Joachim (1831–1907).

128 "In the last hour of the year Edvard and Kunigunde [Nina] are enjoying themselves."

129 During his stay in Vienna Grieg gave three concerts: December 16 and 19, 1896, and January 6, 1897.

130 Dutch baritone Anton Sistermans (1865–1920).

pianist I have to go down to Vienna to get my fingers limbered up a few days ahead of time. Sistermans is Dutch and an excellent singer. A magnificent bass-baritone who nonetheless does not hesitate to sing a G—in "Prologue" and "Outward Bound", for example. I am almost glad that I got sick so that I didn't have my songs ruined by Mrs. Gulbranson.[131] He is so musical and his singing so unaffected. You should have heard him sing "Henrik Wergeland" [EG 177 no. 6] with orchestra. It was absolutely masterful and made a strong impression. I am so happy, because this song has qualities that elevate it above local patriotism. I dare to say what Bjørnson said of his play, *Mellem Slagene* [*Between the Battles*]: "Yes, God knows that it was written with reverence!" And it is well translated and sounds good in German. A critic who does not like the song as well as the rest of the audience appeared to do—and who, fortunately, is patently unmusical—writes the most hilarious slander in one of the Vienna newspapers. I couldn't help but wonder what you would say of it and am enclosing it herewith.

Apropos critics: The worst thing is that I have—in some degree, anyway—found favor in the ears of the famous Hanslick.[132] As you know, he is a conservative so-and-so, and fortunately he regards my *String Quartet* as an absolutely impossible piece of music. But his discussion of me is creating quite a stir, and people are guessing that there is something behind it. But what is it? He discusses approvingly my Schumann article that appeared in *The Century Magazine*[133] and my indignation over the Wagnerites' contemptuous judgment of Schumann—which they inherited from Wagner. I am therefore identified as anti-Wagnerian, and he deliberately leaves out everything in the article wherein I express admiration for Wagner. Since my article is unknown [in Vienna], it is to be expected that the Wagnerites will now attack me. Is this what Hanslick was trying to accomplish? It will be fun to see. If I get hold of a copy of *Neue Freie Presse* I will send it to you when I get to Vienna.

The piece that Sistermans sang splendidly and that, to my pleasure, also won the hearts of the German audience, was "The Youth", which has been fairly well translated.

Before I conclude I must, however, tell you what a beast I am. Three weeks ago I read in the newspapers about *Die versunkene Glocke*, a new play by Gerhart Hauptmann[134] that had been performed in Berlin and been very well received. By damn, I thought, that would be a good present for Frants. So I bought a copy of the book, but it piqued my curiosity to such an extent that I read it and never

---

[131] Swedish-born soprano Ellen Nordgren Gulbranson (1863–1947). Because of illness, Grieg was unable to accompany Mrs. Gulbranson at a concert on December 23 in which she sang a number of his songs.

[132] Austrian musicologist and music critic Eduard Hanslick (1825–1904).

[133] This article will be printed in full in Benestad & Halverson (eds.), *Edvard Grieg: Diaries, Articles, Speeches* (Columbus, Ohio, 2001).

[134] *The Sunken Bell*, a fairy play in five acts by German author Gerhart Hauptmann (1862–1946).

sent it. In my defense I could perhaps mention both illness and other difficulties, but the truth is that I must say with Brewer Jacobsen:[135] "I'm a dirty dog!" The book is yours, though, and you will get it sooner or later. It contains some surpassingly beautiful things. That we modern people have our roots in both fairytale and mysticism—that is what so many of the younger writers, perhaps influenced by Ibsen, have gotten hold of.

And Borkman![136] It is praised in glowing terms in newspapers here. The old man certainly knew what he was doing when he reverted to his youthful poem about "the miner".[137] It is just the thing for him to dig into.

Now, dear friend, the old year is ebbing away! Yes, thanks for everything to both you and Majs! I feel a sense of peace when I know that you are sitting up there thinking lovingly of me—despite the fact that I realize more and more that I am related in many ways to the aforementioned Brewer Jacobsen. Thank you for the old year—and best wishes to both of you for the new one!

Faithfully yours,
EDVARD

P.S. Nisk sends her love!

32

Amsterdam, March 4, 1897

Dear Frants!
We just came home from The Hague and have eaten our 6 P.M. dinner. I am tired and sleepy and have gone upstairs while Röntgen is in the city giving the lessons that he had postponed. (He had gone along to The Hague.)

Thanks for your telegram! Yes, you should have been along there. It was absolutely not "Amsterdamesque", for it was fine—what the Germans call *hoffähig*.[138] We stayed at the home of some friends of Röntgen, an attorney (future minister of justice?) by the name of Hartogh who is now a member of the Dutch Parliament. Noble people—like all liberals! (Hm!) Then quickly off to a choir rehearsal at 12:00, then orchestra and choir rehearsal in front of a full house at 1:00, then home to rest for an hour, eat oysters and beef steak, then getting dressed and conducting a concert for ca. 2,000 people.[139]

Everything went absolutely splendidly. But there were two queens present, so the festivity was marked by a certain solemnity. Nonetheless, the place exploded

---

135 Brewer Jacobsen is one of the leading characters in Bjørnstjerne Bjørnson's play *The Bankrupt*.
136 Henrik Ibsen's play, *John Gabriel Borkman* (1896).
137 Ibsen's poem "Miner" ("Bjergmanden") was written in 1850, revised in 1863 and 1871.
138 *hoffähig*: good enough for use at the royal court (German).
139 Grieg's concert in The Hague took place on March 3.

with fanfares the moment I strode in. The laurel wreath (undeserved!!) lay in its place, and in the middle of the concert a general came forward, gave a speech, and handed me a diploma declaring me an honorary member of the "Diligentia" Society.[140] Warm applause. (Utterly comical!)

The queens did something that it is said they never do: They stayed until the end of the concert. And then they sent a general into the green room to report, with great solemnity, that the queens sent greetings, to thank me, and to say that they had made me an Officer (in Norwegian we would say "Commander") of—yes, what was it? I have already forgotten it. But it was Dutch.[141] Congratulations from everyone. Champagne with snacks, big reception with large quantities of nonsense. (. . .)

Then we came home for dinner: tough ox tongues and tougher wild duck. Miss Reuter[142] is no genius. But stop. The day before yesterday, just before the trip to The Hague, was a wonderful evening: The Bechstein grand piano had just arrived at a time when Röntgen was not home. (You recall that I told you it was bought with money left over from concerts.) We expected him at about 6 P.M.—Miss Reuter, the children, Tiefenthals and the trolls.[143] And sure enough: At just about 6:00 he came storming up the stairs, tired and worn out from lessons and rehearsals. I sat at the piano, and as he came into the room I let loose with

at full volume. But he just stood there and didn't understand anything. So I switched over and began playing his *Ballade* in B-flat minor

but NB: in B-flat major. Then he went over to the other piano (which previously had been a Blüthner instrument, but it had been removed and his own old Bechstein was standing there instead) and wanted to play together with me. And only when he observed that the name Bechstein was on the piano instead of Blüthner did he understand. But then you could have knocked him over with a feather. I tell you, it was a Christmas-like atmosphere such as I remember from my

140 "Diligentia" is the name of both a concert hall in The Hague and a concert series presented under the auspices of *Maatschappij voor Natuur en Letterkunde*, which dates back to 1793.
141 It was the Orange-Nassau Order.
142 Röntgens' maid.
143 "The trolls": residents of Troldhaugen, i.e., Edvard and Nina. Benno (Benjamin) Tiefenthal (1851–1906) and his wife Nanni were friends of Röntgen and Grieg.

childhood. Thereafter we went down to dinner, which in honor of the occasion included oysters and champagne. A big celebration with tears of joy. (. . .)

Farewell, dear friend!

Yours truly,

33

London, December 10, 1897
47 North Side, Clapham Common

Dear Frants!
The letter I was going to write—well, it *must* wait. Thank you for your letters! "We're a-comin'—but it may take awhile."[144] Now I have seven concerts behind me, and they were even brilliant! On the 15th I perform (with Nisk) for the last time.

Yesterday we visited Queen Victoria in Windsor Castle and made music for over an hour. She would have liked even more. It was *very* interesting compared with other court affairs. She is a *woman*, one who is interested and interesting to talk with. She speaks brilliant German. Nina sang her best, I played my best—and Johannes Wolff his. She gave me her jubilee medallion, and Nisk received a brooch inscribed with her name.

Our plan is to go to the Brodsky's in Manchester for a couple of days on the 17th. On the 21st or 22nd we will leave for Berlin or Leipzig (wherever Dr. Abraham is), and beyond that I don't know.

Italy is inviting me to go there and conduct six concerts. The desire is very strong, but I have not ventured to respond affirmatively yet. I probably *should* give up the idea. And the music festival?[145] It appears that people are acting in accordance with the words of the Mountain King: "Cool your blood!"[146] But that would be to misunderstand one's classics!

Most loving greetings to all three of you!

Yours truly,
EDVARD

---

144 A quotation from the poem "Dei vil alltid klaga og kyta" ("They will always grumble and boast") by Norwegian author Ivar Aasen (1813–96).

145 Grieg is referring to the Norwegian music festival being planned for Bergen in the summer of 1898.

146 The quotation is from Ibsen's *Peer Gynt*, Act 2, Scene 6.

34

Leipzig, February 4, 1898
Hotel Hauffe

Dear Frants!

I had to smile when I read in your last letter that the music festival "has created plenty of thoughts and sleepless nights for both you and me, *and now we will lay them aside in the hope that everything will work out.*" Yes, that is easy for you to say. But now begins my real work, which seems so in danger of overwhelming me that from now on I will not get a moment's peace until the festival is over. Virtually the whole day is filled with writing letters and sending telegrams. I have now reached an agreement regarding the artistic content of the festival and to date have also been involved with the practical dimension. To mention just one example: I have written to Tiefenthal almost every day in order, through his good offices, to get the best possible consideration from Olaf Kyrre's shipping company in Rotterdam.[147] There seems to be some trouble brewing, and to send telegrams between Leipzig, Bergen and Rotterdam was hopelessly time-consuming. Today, through Tiefenthal, I finally got results. He is incomparable. I can say the same about Joachim Grieg,[148] despite his unfortunate dispositions, because he has exhibited the one quality that is most important and that certain people in Christiania seem to be lacking: nobility. And I have the impression that Grieg the book publisher[149] is also as noble a man as you can find.

Since you mention it, I have not doubted for a moment that you have acted in accordance with your conviction. But now that I see the whole picture better than I did before, insofar as it is possible to do so from a distance, I cannot get over being surprised that it was on the advice of the smaller committee—you, [Johan] Halvorsen and John[150]—that Joachim Grieg, without my knowledge, engaged the Norwegian orchestra when you all knew that I was negotiating with the Dutch orchestra and that it was my fondest wish to bring these negotiations to a successful conclusion. To you—the three of you plus Joachim Grieg—I had confided my plan, so what happened? Well, it was what in politics is called a *coup d'etat.* But, as you say, you must have misunderstood the connection. So: Let us say no more about that time that was so painful for me—yes, so painful that whatever may await me in the way of meanness and smears in connection with the music festival, I will accept it with tranquility in the knowledge that I suffered the biggest blow in advance.

---

147 Grieg was making arrangements for the Concertgebouw Orchestra of Amsterdam to play at the music festival in Bergen and wanted to transport the orchestra to and from Norway as economically as possible. He was severely criticized by many people in Norway for insisting that the Amsterdam orchestra be engaged for the festival rather than a Norwegian one. The controversy also put a strain on Grieg and Beyer's friendship, but both men valued it too highly to allow it to be destroyed.

148 Bergen ship broker Joachim Grieg (1849–1932), Edvard's second cousin.

149 Bergen book publisher John Grieg (1856–1905), Edvard's second cousin.

150 John Grieg (1840–1901), Edvard's brother.

But I wish so very much that you could share my view, for which I will fight tooth and nail and which I can briefly formulate like this: A Norwegian music festival is one in which Norwegian compositions are given the best performance possible—and the best performance is especially important in this case, because it is a matter of an international exhibition in Bergen, one in which all Europe will be represented. I regard everything that lies outside this view as 1) chauvinism or 2) fear for the opinion of others or 3) pettiness. The first and third certainly do not apply to you, but I wonder if there may not be a little trace of the second?

It is your best quality—the desire not to hurt anyone—that is at play here. But there are times when even the best is not—the "very best"! Yes, with you I can indeed sit here and let my pen run. Is that not so? I claim this right as a right of friendship. I fully agree with the decision of the old committee—that it had to withdraw.[151] There was nothing else to do. But what do you think of the resolution of the musicians' meeting in Christiania? According to Joachim Grieg's telegram—or, more correctly, according to Holter's[152] telegram to Joachim Grieg—it went like this: "All the musicians here assembled express their regret and disapproval of the use of a foreign orchestra at a Norwegian music festival when a Norwegian one is available." Note well that the resolution states clearly: "the use of a foreign orchestra... when a Norwegian one is available." It does not say "when an equally good" or even just "when a good Norwegian one is available." To me this represents such a contemptible standard—call it chauvinism or whatever you will—that I will fight against it tooth and nail both privately and publicly if necessary.

I would almost like to write an article to be called, "What is Norwegian?" When Norwegian music, by virtue of a sublime performance, makes an impression such that love for the homeland is enhanced and the people are drawn closer to Norwegian art, then the effort to achieve this result is dictated by Norwegianness—that I say from the bottom of my heart. Who complained when Holter engaged German woodwinds for the Christiania orchestra? Nobody. And I am convinced that if the Dutchmen had been engaged without the unfortunate prior hog-tying of the Christiania orchestra, the incipient chauvinism would immediately have been nipped in the bud. But now, indeed, efforts are being made in every quarter to evoke it—subconsciously in Bergen, but in Christiania? Yes, ask the Bagler bishops' lackey there.[153] He knows what is going on. Now I

---

[151] The committee planning the music festival had, without Grieg's knowledge and contrary to his wishes, engaged the Christiania Music Association Orchestra to play at the festival. Grieg resigned in protest, and knowing that they could not proceed without his support the committee disbanded. A new committee was formed immediately which gave Grieg a free hand to do as he wished. Thereupon he proceeded to engage the Concertgebouw Orchestra.

[152] Iver Holter (1850–1941), conductor of the Music Association Orchestra in Christiania.

[153] The *baglers* were a 13th-century political party founded by the bishops in opposition to King Sverre Sigurdson (1150–1202), who had reaffirmed the supremacy of the king over the church. Grieg presumably is

am on the verge of writing myself into a fit of anger, but the fact is that when something good is about to happen among us the cow and its cow-pies and the bull with its mead enter the scene and make it distasteful from the very first moment. (. . .)

Nina has now been indoors for a whole week because of her influenza, so we have had to take our meals at the hotel. Yesterday, for the same reason, I had to go alone to the Gewandhaus, where I had the pleasure of hearing Paderewski[154] for the first time. He played *Chopin's Piano Concerto No. 2* in F Minor so marvelously beautifully and with such a genuinely Chopinesque spirit that I had to go in and hug him and shout, "Thank God, Chopin's spirit is still alive!"

But what happens: Today *all* the newspapers tear him to shreds. Naturally: His was not this wretched, bourgeois, correct German interpretation of Chopin. Those stuck-up bastards! There should be a thorough house-cleaning among those descendants of Balaam,[155] that gang called the press. And it should occur everywhere, all over Europe at the same time. Is not the whole Dreyfus scandal perhaps the work of the press in the deepest sense? But the old God lives! This time he is called Zola.[156] Thus it always is: In the midst of the deepest darkness there suddenly shines a clear, pure light of a kind that cannot be extinguished. Yes, long live optimism!

And with that, good night, good night!

Now to bed, but there won't be much sleep, unfortunately. Ow! There the pessimist in me again raises his ugly head.

Most loving greetings.

Yours truly,
EDVARD

P.S. Loving greetings also to Majs! Greet Salomon's family! Greet the Giertsens!

---

referring to the organist, composer and music critic Johannes Haarklou (1847–1925), who was one of his most outspoken critics.

154 Polish pianist, composer and statesman Ignaz Paderewski (1860–1941).

155 The allusion is to Numbers 22:4ff., where the story is told of Balaam, the Mesopotamian diviner who tempted the Israelites to disobedience. In the New Testament (II Peter 2:15 and elsewhere) Balaam is depicted as an example of one who uses his position to lead God's people astray.

156 The "Dreyfus scandal" had to do with Captain Alfred Dreyfus (1859–1935), a French Jew who had been convicted of high treason on what virtually everyone knew to be false evidence. French author Émile Zola (1840–1902) incurred the wrath of his countrymen and the admiration of Grieg and other lovers of justice when he came to Dreyfus's defence in his famous article "J'accuse" ("I accuse"), which was published in the newspaper *L'Aurore* in 1888. For further details see Grieg's letters of September 14 and October 2, 1899, to Bjørnstjerne Bjørnson and that of October 4, 1899, to Édouard Colonne.

35

Leipzig, March 27, 1898
Hotel Hauffe

Dear Frants! But not dear committee member!
You do indeed need some new blood in your peculiarly one-sided understanding of the orchestra matter. First of all, it won't do to say to me that "The committee, including you, has felt obliged to respect the negotiations undertaken with the Christiania orchestra through Holter." That sounds nice enough, but what will you do, then, about my negotiations—undertaken with the committee's knowledge—with the Dutchmen? You apparently do not feel obliged to respect them! Truly a strange "sense of justice", and an equally strange "logic". No, that is precisely what you have not done, and in any case this would be the height of thoughtlessness toward me. But given my relationship to the matter, it is more than that. It is nothing less than a colossal insult. I have exercised leadership in this undertaking. The committee wants to use my name but not my artistic arrangements. Indeed, on the main issue it acts in conscious disagreement with me and completely on its own authority.

No! *One* will must decide how this matter is to be resolved. And in this case that *one* will must be mine. We can, or at least we should, agree on that. The entire artistic responsibility lies with me, so I must also make the artistic arrangements. It is incredible that such a thing has to be said and equally incredible that the committee regards me as such a blockhead that it expects me to be willing to accept the olive branch it has offered me.

Thus far, of course, I have treated this purely personal slight as if I did not notice it—but believe me, it has hurt. But *you* shall indeed be told—since you appear to be as blind as a bat—what a fateful blow you have joined in giving me. Whether the Dutchmen or the Norwegians had been engaged for the festival, it would soon no longer have been a topic of discussion. But after the committee's two grievous errors—first stupidity No. 1: the untimely engaging of the Norwegian orchestra, and then stupidity No. 2: thereafter to ask for freedom to act again. These two stupidities have made me so vulnerable to attack that my future has been determined in a manner that is deeply harmful both to me and to Norwegian art. For as long as I live it will never again be possible for me to assemble an orchestra in Christiania.

The committee has wanted to save itself, and in order to achieve this it has sacrificed me. For do you really think the Christiania orchestra cares a whit about the committee in Bergen? No, its desperate action is directed at me and no one else.

And since you emphasize so strongly the committee's "obligation", I will tell you what you absolutely were obliged to do: You—the "smaller music committee" plus Joachim Grieg and the whole horde—should have resigned *sooner*, before stupidity No. 1 and above all before stupidity No. 2. Even Holter understood

Some of Grieg's Norwegian colleagues and friends who gathered in Bergen for the music festival in 1898. L. to r. standing: composer Ole Olsen, baritone Thorvald Lammers, composer and organist Christian Cappelen, composer and conductor Johan Halvorsen, Nina Grieg, composer and conductor Johan Svendsen, composer Christian Sinding. L. to r. seated: soprano Amalie Gmür-Harloff, composer and pianist Agathe Backer Grøndahl, Grieg, composer Gerhard Schjelderup, pianist Erika Lie Nissen, composer and conductor Iver Holter. (Troldhaugen)

this, for as early as in a letter of January 12 he wrote to me, "*The committee could and should have found another and better solution. Since it—with every reason, in my opinion—feels itself committed, it could simply disband and let a new committee take up the matter, given the present situation. But the gentlemen will really have to work it out themselves.*"

But the committee continued to function, made bad into worse, and only after having squeezed me between shields in such a way that I was forced to withdraw—then, with a clear conscience, it could disband. It is sheer comedy.

And yet I do not doubt for a moment that the intention has been of the best and that no one, least of all you and Joachim Grieg, has had any clear understanding of how desperate you were making the situation for me. It reminds me of the relationship between king and government. When the men with whom the king surrounds himself do not agree with him, *they* are the ones who resign. I have never before heard of the *king* being the one who must do so. And since I have likened myself to a king, I hasten to add that it was not I who desired this authority to begin with: It was the committee that gave it to me. I had hoped for support, but it has turned out that I have to manage everything alone.

The experience has made me wiser, however, and I understand that, as conditions are in Norway, it cannot be otherwise. You are stubbornly silent in your letters about this one thing that in my opinion has been the decisive factor, so I will repeat it for the last time. You all were informed. You all knew my keen desire even before my departure, but even I did not know at that time whether the desire could be realized. If you [the committee] did not share my opinion, you could have said so. And if at that time you still had not dug deeply into the matter, you could, at a later stage, have conveyed your opinion to me *before* you acted. That would have been your duty instead of acting like petty kings. But since I, by virtue of the circumstances, have now become the festival's king, let me then be Harald Fairhair[157] himself and by the power of music conquer the petty kings at the great battle in Bergen June 26–July 3, 1898.[158] Such a triumph could never have been achieved if I had joined the petty kings and sacrificed my entire beautiful plan! (. . .)

Yes, Mr. committee member! With all respect for your logic and sense of justice as well—you know how highly I regard it!—I venture to say that in *this* instance you are not unaffected by the milieu in which you are living. I know a logic that strikes all other logic dead, and it is this: that the solitary individual is always wrong in relation to the compact majority, especially when this solitary individual—as I am in this case—is hundreds of miles away and cannot personally argue the justice of his own case. Never again will I create a committee, and still less will I put my best friend on it. As a committee member you will always be morally compromised. For if a committee does wrong, such a tiny portion of the blame falls on each member that it amounts to almost nothing. Thus the honored member can do as Mark Twain does with his conscience: He can cuff its ears good and proper until it no longer dares to object!

The fact is, as a committee member, as far as I am concerned you can be a you-know-what. I will easily get over that. But as a friend you must not make use of committee logic and committee consciousness. These concepts are like morality: They are the fruit of many factors and cannot claim a monopoly. I know that you have so much self-criticism, that you are such a severe judge of yourself, that you—completely independent of our friendship—purely out of respect for objective truth, will not be content with the viewpoint adopted earlier but will constantly seek to attain higher ground with more unobstructed views.

I owed *you* this explanation. NN and NN [both names are completely obliterated in the original] can think and believe what they will. To tell the truth, I am too proud to defend myself against them. Besides, nothing would come of it. But

---

[157] "Harald Fairhair" ("Harald Hårfager"), who gathered Norway into a single kingdom, was king of Norway ca. 900–940.

[158] June 26–July 8, 1898: the dates of the music festival.

in my relation to you I have no pride, only the desire for clarity and light. We should rather have spoken together, but time flies and my memory is faulty. So I must use the pen. Moreover, the music festival is drawing nearer, and we will soon have the realities to talk about—fortunately. May it be a joyful event for all of us!

Most loving greetings to both of you.

Your old
EDVARD

P.S. You should have heard Eugène d'Albert play the *Ballade* in G minor (an echo from 1876!) in the Gewandhaus last Thursday—so brilliantly that it took people by storm. Just think what that means! He had more or less *all* the qualifications: elegance and grand style, mighty *crescendos* culminating in utter fury. And then after this you should have heard the daringly long *fermata* on the deep

I think he held it for half a minute![159] But the effect was colossal. And then he concluded that old, sad song so slowly, quietly and simply that I myself was completely enthralled. Yes, it certainly was strange!

Now the two items—both the orchestra score of the *Symphonic Dances* and the *Mountain Maid* songs with German texts—have been sent to Peters for printing. I have worked very hard to improve the German translation, and I think the result is better than I had hoped for. I look forward to hearing Messchaert sing them. (. . .)

You talk about phlegm. Yes, I can join in on that subject as never before. The doctor says I should take a trip to southern Europe before I leave for home, and there is much to say for it. But, but. . .

Well, good-night now, dear Frants! It is midnight. Nina is already asleep.

Yours truly,
EDVARD

P.S. We leave for Copenhagen in a week. Address: Hotel King of Denmark.

---

[159] In an extant recording of Grieg's *Ballade*, Eugène d'Albert (1864–1933) holds the fermata for ca. seven seconds.

36

Copenhagen, November 25, 1899

Dear Frants!

A letter from Trondhjem? A big surprise. What a pity that I couldn't reach you by letter in Christiania! I was sure that you were still there, but I had no idea of your address. The day before yesterday when I told Röntgen (he and Messchaert are here) that you were in Christiania, he immediately exclaimed: "But then we must have him come here. We must have him here!" But that wouldn't have worked, as I also told him, for your vacation time was, of course, limited. Moreover, "vacation time" probably is a misleading expression, for you certainly have had more than enough to do. But we have thought about you and talked about you, and we have rejoiced in the fact that you had the opportunity to live for a time amidst the rich life that pulsates in Christiania just now.

Yes, it is wonderful—and it could be even more wonderful if only I agreed with our dear Bjørnson regarding the language controversy.[160] But I am in complete disagreement. Bjørnson's lecture and his actions are good as a warning to the *language fanatics*, and he does indeed say things that are so brilliant and noble that one must continue to love him and thus to forgive him for his point of view. But it is really hard to have *him* standing where he does. About Ibsen I will say nothing at all, which is only to say that one cannot demand that he be a party to destroying the very literature that he himself has helped to create. That is a weak reason—indeed, it is worse than weak. Bjørnson's and Ibsen's literature is no less great or good just because the people of the future will speak a more authentically Norwegian language.

How is it possible to take Bjørnson seriously when he reports that he, too, uses the language of the people when he wants to find a word to characterize something really *vulgar*! Every day when I read *Verdens Gang*[161] my fingers are itching to take up my pen. For I think there is so much that should be said on this matter that

---

160 The prevailing language in educated circles in Norway at this time was Dano-Norwegian, a form of Norwegian strongly influenced by the Danish language as a result of Norway's political and cultural subordination to Denmark for over 400 years prior to 1814, when Norway was ceded to Sweden. During the nineteenth century, as Norwegians began to aspire to independence in all spheres of their national life, a small but influential group of people led by Ivar Aasen began to agitate for a return to an indigenous Norwegian language. This language was presumed to exist in the dialects spoken by the farmers and other uneducated people of rural Norway—people whose language had not been "corrupted" by direct exposure to Danish influences. Aasen, drawing on these dialects, created a language that he and his followers proposed should take the place of Dano-Norwegian. They called this language *landsmål*, i.e., "rural language", later called *nynorsk*, "New Norwegian". The country soon found itself sharply divided over the issue. Bjørnson, whose writings were all in Dano-Norwegian, was a fierce opponent of *landsmål*. On October 23, 1899, he had given a lecture on the subject at the Freemasons' Lodge in Christiania and it had been widely discussed. In the weeks that followed he gave similar lectures in other places, including one in Bergen on December 17, 1899. Grieg, on the other hand, had a very positive view regarding *landsmål*, not least because of his love for the poems of Aasmund Olavsson Vinje (1818–70) and Arne Garborg (1851–1924). *Twelve Songs to Poems by A. O. Vinje* and *The Mountain Maid* are stellar works in Norwegian and international song literature. As time went on, however, Grieg's enthusiasm for *landsmål* waned somewhat because of what he perceived as fanaticism on the part of its advocates. See his letter to Bjørnson of May 16, 1907.

161 *Verdens Gang*: the leading liberal newspaper in Christiania.

remains unsaid. But since I am not a linguist I must, of course, be careful about what I say.

One thing I know: The language will evolve away from the Danish despite Bjørnson and Christiania for the simple reason that urban conservatism cannot stand against 4/5 of the population of the country. Look at my own experience. By a lucky stroke of fortune I was thrown into Hardanger not having the slightest inkling of the beauty and Norwegianness of the language—and I became so enthralled that I will never let go of it again. Had Bjørnson had this good fortune —and, in addition, had he been a *composer*—he would have had a different view, of that I am sure. For I dare to speak as a composer about the beauty and power of the language to express more than piggishness. (...)

I was in Stockholm again and enjoyed my stay there just as I did last time.[162] To be sure, I wasn't exactly well: The bronchitis began to bare its fangs, but I stifled it with strict abstinence, a steady temperature, potassium iodide and oatmeal soup. Please give me your approval, Mrs. Dr. Majsen!

Our old king [Oscar II] was extremely cordial, and I will tell you about our conversation when we are together. He was at three of the four concerts—namely, all three of those during which he was in Stockholm. I must tell you that I had been invited to conduct two concerts but that a couple days after my arrival—five or six days before the first concert—three concerts were sold out. I was told that if I were not returning to Copenhagen to prepare my concert there I could have continued for four more concerts in Stockholm. Yes, it is strange that of the three Scandinavian countries Sweden is the one where I am best known and, above all, most highly regarded—there where I have been the least and there where—etc.[163]

Perhaps you have heard about the concert here. It was very successful. The little mountain piece [op. 68 no. 4] sounded just the way I had imagined it. People continued to clap, but I did not do it *da capo*. Afterward I played one of the other *Lyric Pieces* in the same volume: "At the Cradle". That one they got to hear twice. One piece I wish you had heard: the Cecilia Society's rendition of two religious choruses *a cappella*.[164] You remember the first one as a song for solo voice and piano: "At the Grave of a Young Wife" (poem by O. P. Monrad). The other was "Ave Maris Stella". I have written for 8-voice chorus and in so doing have achieved a coloration which an ordinary choral piece—the four-part kind—cannot match. Would that we could hear both these and other things together in Christiania sometime.

In general I wish that now in your older years your work load could decrease and be arranged in such a way that you could spend a little more time in

---

[162] Grieg conducted his own works at concerts in Stockholm on November 4, 7 and 9, 1899.

[163] Grieg is alluding to the political tension between Norway and Sweden.

[164] *Two Religious Choral Songs*, an arrangement for 8-part mixed chorus *a cappella* of "At the Grave of a Young Wife" op. 39 no. 5 and "Ave Maris Stella" EG 150.

"Norway's head".[165] For Norway's heart—or, more correctly, "Norway's chest"—is and always will be our dear West Norway. I have thought about Christiania more than once with precisely the future in mind—the scrap of future that remains!—and if I could suppose that circumstances might lead you there more often than before, this would contribute mightily to the maturation of my plan.

For the time being I am still a wanderer and suffer greatly from that. This week I have spent every single forenoon running up and down stairways all over the city in my search for a study—but in vain. They are all terrible. If one day I finally have found a room that appeals to me and then say that I will be coming with a piano, I hear, "My God, are we going to have music! That will be nice! We will all look forward to that!" Whereupon I take my hat and, very crestfallen, say "adieu".[166] Yes, indeed, that is how it is: A home, a home, my kingdom for a home![167]

Then there is Harmonien.[168] Believe me, I am happy that both it and I have had fortune with us. But now it is also rumored that the "Music Society" is performing good things in Bergen. How is that possible? Is it because they have engaged one or two good players? Or have they also gotten a new orchestra? I am completely confused. But I know this, that both Christiania and Bergen can be grateful to that famous and infamous music festival. It has given a powerful push to artistic morale and stimulated the feeling for music quite explicitly.

Well, now I must close. Today Röntgen and Messchaert are in Århus but are giving a concert here on Monday. Then they go to Odense and will give their second concert here on Friday. Thus I am hoping to be with them a little. Yesterday I got a whole album of photographs from a man in Germany. He calls it *Auf dem Weg nach Troldhaugen* (*En route to Troldhaugen*). To my surprise I see there a scene on board a steamship where you are standing talking to an Italian (I remember him!) and Julius, Lulla[169] and I are engaged in intimate conversation. Naturally it is on board the "Jupiter". *Utterly comical*!

Most loving greetings to both of you, also from Nina. Thanks for the telegram yesterday! Write soon!

Yours truly,
EDVARD

---

165 Grieg means Norway's capital, Christiania.

166 Grieg needed complete seclusion for his work. He was never able to compose if he knew that people were listening to his playing.

167 An allusion to Shakespeare's *Richard III*: "A horse! A horse! My kingdom for a horse!"

168 The Music Society Harmonien, predecessor of the modern Bergen Philharmonic Orchestra. The "Music Society" (*Musikforeningen*) was another organization that had been established exclusively for amateur musicians, but it soon found itself in competition with Harmonien. See Grieg's article, "Our Musical Conditions", in Benestad & Halverson (eds.), *Edvard Grieg: Diaries, Articles, Speeches* (Columbus, Ohio, 2001).

169 Lulla: Julius Röntgen Jr. (1881–1951).

P.S. Thank God the sale of Næsset did not occur! Hip, Hip, Hurrah![170]

37

Copenhagen, March 10, 1900

Dear Frants!
As I wrote the other day to Bergh:[171] It is a pity that you, as busy as you are, must still be bothered with my testamentary matters. And after receiving your latest welcome letter, this feeling asserts itself all the more strongly. But I know that you understand me. I simply cannot rest until this matter is settled—especially now when all my alterations have threatened to render the document invalid.[172]

I have been in extremely poor health of late. The awful influenza and bronchitis have assumed new forms, the latest of which is dreadful nerve-induced pains in my head and throat that have totally disheartened me—with my resistance as weak as it has increasingly become. Just think of having to sit here at home this evening and having to miss Svendsen[173] and the Royal Theater Orchestra's performance of Strauss's[174] *Death and Transfiguration*, other interesting French and Russian novelties and the brilliant little Visanka[175] in Beethoven's G-major concerto. It's hard. I have to stay at home in the evening because of the air and the temperature. But I have indeed evened things up by attending three rehearsals, the last of which was this forenoon.

As we drove to the concert hall we saw the flags on the Royal Theater and many other buildings at half mast. It was for old Hartmann,[176] who had just died. It was with this impression in mind that we then heard *Death and Transfiguration*. It says a lot that this work of art could tolerate the stark reality. But it really is so. From the rehearsal we went to a floral shop and from there, with roses in hand, down to the old man's home, where all the children and grandchildren had gathered. It was solemn. There he lay, the 95-year-old, not yet cold but with the peace of death upon him.

So it is: to be or not to be. Now Gade[177]-Hartmann is a saga! But a beautiful one. And how it is interwoven into the mysteries of my own existence. It is as

---

170 Beyer had been having financial difficulties and was on the verge of selling his villa Næsset. See Grieg's letter to Beyer of January 29, 1888.

171 District Judge Karl Jakob Bergh (1841–1906) was a friend of Grieg's who helped him in business matters.

172 Grieg is referring to the legal instruments whereby he and Nina proposed to will his collection of manuscripts, music, books and letters to the library in his native city. See his letter to the Bergen Public Library of November 12, 1906, in Benestad & Halverson (eds.), *Edvard Grieg: Diaries, Articles, Speeches* (Columbus, Ohio, 2001).

173 Johan Svendsen (1840–1911) had been musical director of the Royal Theater Orchestra in Copenhagen since 1883.

174 German composer Richard Strauss (1864–1949).

175 Polish piano virtuoso?

176 Danish composer Johan Peter Emilius Hartmann (1805–1900).

177 Danish composer Niels W. Gade (1817–90).

if this beautiful old word "saga" acquires new and deeper meaning for me as my own life belongs more and more to the past. Soon everything will be saga, saga! (. . .)

Ah, how wonderful it will be to come home again. NB safe and sound and able to use our feet. Most loving greetings to both of you, also from Nisk.

Yours truly,
EDVARD

P.S. Greet Giertsens most warmly! Børre is indeed tough and persevering.

• • •

1. All our musical effects, including manuscripts as well as books having to do with music, shall go to the Bergen Public Library on the condition that they will maintain them.
2. The remainder of our property and effects shall be liquidated and the net proceeds shall be used to create a fund under the name "Edvard Grieg's Foundation". The income from this fund shall be used to further the music life of Bergen in ways specified more closely below.

The capital shall, so far as possible, be invested in top-rated secure mortgage bonds or, if necessary, in a bank, and one half of the annual interest income shall be remitted to the Music Society Harmonien as a contribution to the completion and expansion of its orchestra or, if this Society should be disbanded, to the same purpose as that stated below for the other half of the income.

The second half of the interest income shall, upon nomination by Harmonien's board of directors and orchestra conductor (or, in case Harmonien should cease to exist, by a committee from Bergen appointed for this purpose by the Ministry of Church and Education), be used for annual travel grants for training abroad of young music students from Bergen and the surrounding area. Preference is to be given to creative talents.

P.S. Dear Frants! As a postscript I must nonetheless ask: Isn't there a need for an additional petition to the Ministry seeking permission to obligate it as proposed here?

38

Copenhagen, March 1, 1902
10 P.M. Hotel Phoenix

Dear Frants!
Thanks for the letter today! I read it aloud for Nina, and when I was finished I added, "Yes, there is warmth in good old Frantsie!" I didn't *say* more than that, but I was thinking more. Thinking so strangely much all at the same time.

Can you believe that Arctander[178] has come to me! I told him that it had to be completely confidential and that you had no inkling that I had visited him. He must have forgotten that. Well, you understand that the intention was good.

And now you are there in Tigerville[179]—where there fortunately are animals other than just tigers—and are getting a new injection of life. Now you probably understand for the first time how absolutely essential it was for you to get away. You can't get around it: The machine must be lubricated. Otherwise it comes to a standstill at the wrong time.

And then you happen to come into town just as *Peer Gynt* is being performed! I realized immediately that the play had not been a great success, for then there would have been a telegram here already yesterday. And if *Peer* isn't up to par—well, so what? That's not my concern. So far as the music goes, I relied confidently on [Johan] Halvorsen, although despite his great ability he does not have what I would call flexibility—which is precisely what the *Peer Gynt* music requires. I deeply regret that I was not there to clarify my intentions so far as possible. There are places where the music needs to be coordinated almost to the second with what is transpiring on stage. And then of course there are other things that could have been improved with just a few strokes of the pen. But never mind. If I am granted a few more years of life I will perform *all* of this music as I have conceived it, and as I am capable of making it sound. Moreover, I had hoped to see and hear a performance around the first of May when I will be en route to Bergen. But unfortunately there is so much trouble brewing that the concert in Warsaw will perhaps be later than was first planned. In that case I must just be happy if I can get to Bergen in time for the silver wedding.[180] (. . .)

Did I write to you about the trip over the mountains? I simply became a new person en route. Yes, Norway is Norway. And I want to go back there. Take care that the future becomes what we both wish it to be. But in any case, what you say is true: The future will surely bring us what is best! I have not come as far as you: I do not *believe* that. But I *hope* for it. And in this hope I now go to bed and greet you both most affectionately. Also from Nina.

Yours truly,
EDVARD

P.S. If you see Hanssen,[181] greet him. And write soon, even if it be just a few lines.

---

178 Norwegian politician Sofus Arctander (1845–1924).

179 Tigerville: a derogatory name given to Christiania by Norwegian author Bjørnstjerne Bjørnson.

180 Marie and Frants Beyer were to celebrate their silver wedding anniversary on May 16, 1902.

181 Probably Norwegian physician and medical researcher Klaus Hanssen (1844–1914), Grieg's physician in Bergen.

39

Paris, April 21, 1903
Hotel de Sèze

Dear Frants!
Of course you should have heard from me long ago thanking you for your welcome letter from Voss, which affected me like a warm bath. But the rumbling and cramping these last days have been too great. Finally it went right down into the intestines with the result that I couldn't stand to ride in a carriage and was unable to retain food. But just as the concert[182] began it all went away, and now I am spryer than I have been for a long time—despite all the filth around me. What a strange people! But good Lord, they cannot be different from that which their history has made them.

Now you shall hear about the concert—before the news becomes too old. I have indeed experienced many things in my life, but never anything like this: [Édouard] Colonne, without saying a word to me, ran off to Spain—he who had written that he would stand guard over me!

If Jaurés's[183] dredging up of the Dreyfus affair and the passions associated therewith[184] had occurred *before* the invitation from Colonne, I would definitely have thought twice about accepting it. But now it would of course have appeared cowardly to back out, and the press would have come down hard on me nonetheless—so it was better to just go on with it. In the days preceding the concert the newspapers had contained articles urging demonstrations against me. Fortunately I didn't know this at the time. But my friends told me that *if* there should be heckling etc.—so there was an *if.* I am not aware of having been nervous about more than *one* thing: that they would prevent me from starting.

But I was composed. The theater was packed, and many had to be turned away. There were 3,500 in the audience, some say 4,000. I came in at 2:30 and was received with loud applause, which I had to acknowledge four times. But as this was going on we began to hear whistling and cat-calls that grew louder and louder. I quietly laid the baton, which I had already picked up, back on the conductor's stand, stepped down from the podium and stood waiting beside it as if nothing were amiss. By this time there was a real battle going on. Some shouted, *À la porte!*[185] Others sang rhythmically à la the Mountain King's daughter:[186]

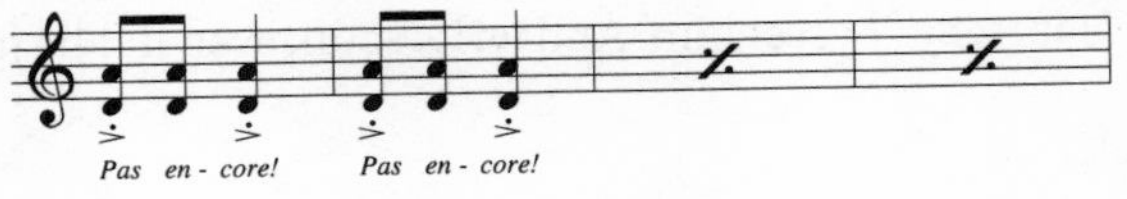

---

182 The concert in the Paris Châtelet Theater took place on April 19, 1903.

183 French politician Jean Jaurés (1859–1914).

184 Grieg is alluding to his involvement in the controversy surrounding the Dreyfus affair. See his letters of September 14 and October 2, 1899, to Bjørnstjerne Bjørnson and that of October 4, 1899, to Édouard Colonne.

185 *À la porte*: "Out with him!"

186 The Mountain King's daughter in *Peer Gynt*.

Still others shouted "Out with the whistlers!" The number of policemen had been *tripled*, and the worst rabble-rousers were literally carried out, whereupon the applause drowned out the rest of them. Then I mounted the podium again and picked up the baton, but God help me if they didn't start in anew. Luckily the overture *In Autumn* starts out *fortissimo*, and I didn't give the hecklers a moment's advantage. I gave the orchestra an energetic sign, so it was with great vigor that the big string orchestra played the first two measures.

Then it became quiet in the auditorium and the overture went *splendidly*. But it was not a fortunate choice for *that precise audience*. It was *too long* for the Parisians and quite especially for a few of them. Still I was given a warm curtain call. Next came Ellen Gulbranson, who with her wonderful voice sang "Solveig's Cradle Song", "From Monte Pincio", and "A Swan".[187] Then came Raoul Pugno with the *Piano Concerto*. He is the Parisians' darling. He had a colossal success and received thunderous applause. Now came both of the arrangements for strings of songs to Vinje's texts[188]—beautifully played, but so far as I can recall there was just *one* curtain call. Some years ago after playing these I was called out four times.

Then came *Before a Southern Convent*. Except for the orchestra, everything was mediocre: Ellen has none of the sensitivity that is required, the alto was abominable, the chorus tiny (20) and poor. Colonne dares to offer me this because he himself does not have the responsibility! Yes, even the organ was much too weak. In short, it was a performance that I would have been ashamed of *at home*. So that little piece, which is dear to me, scored only a meager *succes d'estime*. Now all that remained was the *Peer Gynt Suite No. 1*, but that has the same unfailing effect on every audience as oil on a hard stomach. (You will say "No, the same as an enema!")

Already after the first movement there was loud clapping. After "The Death of Åse", long applause. Ditto after "Anitra's Dance", interspersed with cries of "bis, bis!" ("Encore, encore!") to such an extent that I had to repeat it. After "In the Hall of the Mountain King" the audience went absolutely crazy. I made 4–5 curtain calls but the applause continued. So it, too, had to be repeated. And thereafter ovations such as—that's what they say here—no French composer has ever received. But now I was also dead tired in my poor hips. (. . .)

But now come the proudest moments. When we came out and were about to climb into our carriage, it was surrounded by a triple cordon of police! I felt like a king, emperor and pope—or why not like a criminal, you will say. No, you can swear to it: I had a feeling of triumph that was unmistakable.

The following day the press was, of course, furious. The scandal had turned

---

[187] EG 177 nos. 2, 3 and 4 respectively.

[188] *Two Elegiac Melodies*, arrangements for string orchestra of "Last Spring" op. 33 no. 2 and "The Wounded Heart" op. 33 no. 3.

into a triumph for me, not for the hecklers. There was only one noble review: that by the composer Fauré[189] in *Le Figaro.* All the others are nothing but vileness from beginning to end. Just think that in *Le Temps* a man by the name of Lalo[190] —a son of the late composer, who stole an entire episode from my "In the Mountains"—some years ago praised the very same works that he is now running down. He also says that my songs are stolen from folk melodies! And you know that of all my more than 100 songs there is only *one*—"Solveig's Song"—that borrows the mood, and nothing more. Another critic says that I am well paid and that this is why I have dared to come here, that I am leaving with my vest more richly lined than with all that fur I use in Norway!!!

It is wonderful here in Paris. Yesterday I saw Jonas Lie and consul Børs and his wife—dear old friends.[191] Now we are expecting Johannes Wolff, with whom we shall go out and have some oysters. *If only you two were along!* How often I think this: If only you two were along! How wonderful it would have been! We must still take a trip abroad together sometime!

Farewell, Farewell. Loving greetings to both of you!

Yours truly,
EDVARD

P.S. [Johannes] Wolff greets you most heartily. He loves you.

40

Christiania, November 17, 1904
Hotel Westminster

Dear Frants!
Two hours ago I sat down at my desk to answer your welcome letter. But of course: The door opened and in strode Hanchen Alme[192] and her daughter. You know, of course, that I love Hanchen. But I don't know what is wrong: Every time I start doing something that can't wait, she shows up. And then she is so amiable that she is very reluctant to leave. Now, however, she is gone. It is 8 P.M.—and here I am. After you it will be Julius Röntgen's turn.

During the past week I have been more negligent about letter-writing than usual, because in the evenings I have not been able to tear myself away from Ibsen's [published] letters. What a world! I do not hesitate to say that they are the most interesting thing I have read in decades. They have given me a better understanding of Ibsen and of the Norway whose progress I have followed from the

---

189 French composer Gabriel Fauré (1845–1924).
190 The conservative critic Pierre Lalo (1866–1943), son of composer Edouard Lalo (1823–92).
191 Norwegian author Jonas Lie (1833–1908) and Norwegian consul Christian Børs (1823–1905) and his wife, all of whom were living in Paris.
192 Mrs. Hanchen Waagaard Alme (1846–1936), a friend of Nina Grieg from youth.

1860's and 70's to the present, thereby also giving me a new and deeper view of my own life. I thought that as a letter-writer Ibsen would be totally aloof. And to be sure, one bumps into more than enough of that sort of thing. But there are also times when he practices restraint out of concern both for the judgement of his countrymen and for his view of the demands he places on us contemporaries. How much I have learned during these evenings! And what a pleasure to read the genuine Ibsenian style with its plastic formulation and its terseness of expression.

From the perspective of the wide world horizon expressed in these letters, Arne Garborg's *Knudehejbrev* (*Knudehej Letters*) are basically only rural impressions. Garborg seems no longer to be European—indeed, he hardly seems to be national in the broader sense. He has become more and more confined within trivialities and narrow-mindedness. With genuine peasant distrust he sees goblins in everything and everyone. What makes up for it, fortunately, is the marvelous descriptions of nature. They are truly felt and appear to reflect direct experience. But all too soon they are replaced by language fanaticism and cantankerousness. Both you and I, therefore, are "foreigners". So now you know. No, to tell the truth I claim to be as Norwegian—I mean to have as great a capacity to feel national—as Garborg. Whether or not my father has gone around and "farted in leather britches" doesn't mean a damn thing. (. . .)

Let me now switch to music for a moment in order to show you that the relationship to art is, as always, consistently implemented pettiness. The evening program of songs that I gave recently with Ellen Gulbranson has taught me that. You know that there really are not very many of my songs that are regularly sung, and those that are come almost entirely from my youth. At first people were reluctant to recognize anything of value here either, but as I began to acquire a name they wanted to get on the bandwagon—so they got acquainted with my songs from that period. Now they had done their duty. This was Grieg. But woe to that self-same Grieg if he later were to develop beyond this youthful level.

I had purposely chosen for this occasion those of my *best* later songs that were seldom, if ever, heard. And then I learned from the press that it was not *that Grieg* that people would take the trouble to hear. People simply don't *bother* to follow an artist's development—and then they brush him off without a trace of understanding that such a development has taken place. To put it bluntly, we are still not mature enough to have music around us—or, let me say, art in general. Political and local interests plus big words about things that people understand no better than a cat understands mustard—these are the things that are all-absorbing and that make life here at home impossible for one who wants to fight for a good cause.

I certainly have received "more than I have deserved"[193] in life, so I can cheerfully accept whatever people may wish to place upon my plate. But it pains

[193] Grieg often quotes this line from the poem by A. O. Vinje set as "Last Spring" op. 33 no. 2.

me on behalf of the young people who want to achieve something. See how mediocrity and envy conspire to attack Halvorsen at every opportunity. And he is so terribly sensitive on this point—incomprehensibly so, strong as he is otherwise. At heart he is really a fine fellow. I notice that each time I meet him and have an opportunity to talk something through with him.

Do you really think I should be congratulated for being able to accompany a few songs? But I don't want to be ungrateful. I have been getting along for almost a year, and it has happened because I have realized how I must treat myself. Then I can still live on the remnants for awhile. For remnants is what they are. Who knows? Maybe with these remnants we can still get an opportunity to travel together by train from Bergen to Christiania! (...)

You can't imagine how much I have to attend to! If only I could get certain orchestral things off my back. Today the score of "Gangar" went to the copyist. I will not leave here until I have heard all four pieces. I have now heard two of them: "Nocturne" and "March of the Dwarfs". "Gangar" and "Bell Ringing" remain. The latter is also ready for the copyist.[194] As you see, I am struggling with "the snows of yesteryear".[195] Ah, when shall I get a home with a study!

How wonderful that life is turning out so well for you! Yes, with *good will* one can go incredibly far. Now I shall conclude. If I were to wait until I ran out of things to write about I would be sitting here all night. Most loving greetings to both of you! Also from Nina.

Yours truly,
EDVARD

41

Troldhaugen, August 4, 1905

Dear Frants!
Thank you for the postcard! (...) You speak about "sadness". Consider: I believe that when I was your age (54) I did not yet feel, in relation to the towering mountain scenery, the sense of sadness that has since cast itself over my outlook. Your sadness is premature! Up with joyfulness! Yes, if only it could be commanded. But no, my opinion is: Just let the sadness come. It, too, has beauty. I can understand that for you the transition feels more abrupt because you have been so much more cheerful by nature than I. For me, mysticism has always prevented the jubilation from taking the upper hand. I could indeed rejoice inwardly over the free life. But nature itself? Face to face with nature I stood in silent reverence and

194 Grieg is referring to *Lyric Suite*, four pieces from op. 54 arranged for orchestra. "Bell Ringing" was later replaced by "Shepherd's Boy".

195 The quotation is from a line in *Ballade des Dames du Temps Jadis* by François Villon (1431–d. after 1463): "But where are the snows of yesteryear?"

awe as if before God himself. You did the same, it is true. But in me the awe extinguished all other feelings.

It is quite true: I love science's urge to clarity. But the mystical attracts me nonetheless—yes, even today. I don't think there is any contradiction in this. Life itself sees to it that science does not violate mysticism.

Majs was here yesterday. She says the same as I do: If only you could take it easy someplace—Turtagrø, for example. That would be the best for you. But then there is this matter of the referendum.[196] I understand very well that you will ruin your open-air life and your vacation by being forced to come home on the 13th. But then you must also regard it as a sacred duty to send an excuse for a legitimate absence. I am sure you do not doubt that for a moment. If you are not here, I will go to Næstun with Salomon. The referendum will take place at Birkeland Church in Midttun. So it says in Mr. Mohn's[197] advertisement.

I have not regretted for a moment that I didn't go with you. The main reason is that my physical condition has been wretched ever since you left. The reaction and the weather have worked together here. Indeed, I also retain a little fragment of the sense of duty. That is to say, I should finish this and that before the short time that remains to me up here is past.

Farewell now, dear Frants, and be careful about climbing and exertion! That advice sounds so boring—but you are going to get it anyway.

Loving greetings from all of us!

Yours truly,
EDVARD

42

Christiania, October 25, 1905
Hotel Westminster

Dear Frants!
Recently I had a lovely hour. It was owing to the letter from Gjendine.[198] To have the opportunity to feel tenderhearted, truly tenderhearted—yes, for that I will gladly give up much of what is generally regarded as desirable. Then I began to think of you, and suddenly I was overwhelmed with the realization of how it is that I want you to be. It is absolutely not as a Christiania person. I was happy when you were safely away from there. The awareness that you were here without my being able to get in touch with you seemed so unnatural to me and made

[196] The purpose of the referendum was to give the citizens an opportunity to decide whether an independent Norway should become a constitutional monarchy or a republic.
[197] Presumably the county clerk in Bergen.
[198] Gjendine Slaalien (1872–1971), a dairy maid from Lom whose beautiful, unaffected singing was the source of "Gjendine's Lullaby" and other folk melodies in op. 66.

me feel as out of sorts as if I had gotten lice and fleas on me. But you are present in Gjendine's letter, both when you are mentioned and when you are not. Your spirit hovers over—the waters.[199] Yes, I use this expression audaciously—or rather, honestly—for real water fell upon the letter. What she wrote was so beautiful and genuine. And then she included Nina as if she were an old friend. That was such a tender touch.

It's incredible that she thinks I am an actor. She relates that she has devoured every word she has read in the newspapers about the honors I have received for my good talents in the art of acting. That is even better than "Hochverehrter Greis".[200] This is a disappointment to me. She is so dear to me because of her association with memories of nature that I wish she knew that I am a musician. You can convey that to her when you have an opportunity.

Here life still goes on in a mood of high and interesting tension. But many dregs are dredged up at a time such as this. For that reason it ought not last too long. When you get this you will have known for a long time the result of this moment's significance. If the decision this forenoon is in favor of a referendum or the calling of a special meeting of the Norwegian Parliament, then I am a complete pessimist, for then Michelsen[201] is done for. That would be a shame. Here it is necessary to act quickly, decisively, and in certain respects recklessly.

That Denmark is also being boycotted by Sweden now is, indeed, absolutely hair-raising. Danish conductors at restaurants in Stockholm are thrown out and heckled, not only because they play "The Shepherd Girl's Sunday"[202] and "Solveig's Song" [op. 55 no. 4], but even for playing Danish music! It must be a proud politics that turns people into stupid hicks and idiots.

Here come the Halvorsens to fetch us for dinner.

Farewell to both of you. I hope that all is well with you. Most loving greetings.

Yours truly,
EDVARD

43

Christiania, December 12, 1905
Hotel Westminster

Dear Frants!
I have both wanted and intended to write to you for a long time. But it is usually the case that he who, strictly speaking, has nothing to do thinks he has the most of all. One thing is certain: I not only do not have time to be bored, I do

199 Cf. Genesis 1:2, ". . .and the Spirit of God hovered over the waters."

200 *Hochverehrter Greis*: "Most honored old graybeard". Grieg is alluding to the fact that a German autograph-seeker had recently written to him using this unflattering salutation. See his letter to Swedish composer Tor Aulin (1866–1914) of June 29, 1905.

201 Norwegian prime minister Christian Michelsen (1857–1925).

202 A piece by Norwegian composer Ole Bull (1810–80), text (written to fit the music) by Jørgen Moe (1813–82).

not have time to do what I have to do, even if this is just letter-writing. In front of me lies a pile of business letters that still have not been answered. Each day I attack the pile and write and write but I never get caught up. New letters are constantly arriving. (. . .)

There were tens of thousands of things about which I was going to write to you. I don't know where to begin and where to end, and of course I forget the main point. First and foremost, it is old Norway that has been saved.[203] Yes, indeed, we older folks can feel nothing but gratitude because it has been given to us to experience this. And then admiration. The more I think about the whole matter the more surprised I am that it is true. When I walk up Slottsbakken[204] I stand and indulge in daydreams about the royal banner that waves so gloriously up there on the royal palace, about the sentries, about the lively, cheerful activity in general. This really has become a warmer, friendlier place to live. I have indeed been a republican since my youth—and I think that at root you are the same—but I do not doubt for a moment that under the circumstances the right course was chosen here. And not only that but also that we have been so indescribably fortunate.

It's too bad the Swedes have to be so narrow-minded that they can feel only envy and the thirst for revenge that they tried to satisfy as best they could by demanding the border fortifications. It makes what was achieved in Karlstad all the greater.[205]

Personally I have not seen much of the royal couple. After the performance of *Sigurd Jorsalfar* (*Sigurd the Crusader*) Bjørnson and I were called up to the royal box, and I may say that the King and Queen[206] were the very soul of simplicity and courtesy. During a formal dinner at Michelsen's we sat more or less directly across the table from them. (. . .) Later the King came over to Nina and, without being introduced, said, "I have seen you often in Copenhagen. Indeed, we were neighbors." (We lived at Hotel Phoenix opposite his residence.) Nina: "Yes, Your Majesty certainly never thought then that we would meet under these circumstances." The King: "No, that's true. When I wake up in the morning I have to pinch my arm to make sure it really is me. But by the way, I think I will be the same person I was then and not otherwise." Nina: "Does Your Majesty know Professor Rovsing?"[207] The King: "Yes, I certainly do." Nina: "When he was appointed a professor he said that he hoped he would never let the professorship *change his personality*." The King: "So, you think that being His Majesty might change me! No, I promise you, that will never happen."

What do you say to that? A most modern king with no false dignity. And if

---

203 Grieg is alluding to the fact that Norway had at last won its independence from Sweden.

204 Slottsbakken: the gentle slope leading up to the royal palace in Christiania.

205 The agreement certifying Norway's independence from Sweden was signed at Karlstad, Sweden on September 23, 1905.

206 King Haakon VII (1872–1957) and Queen Maud (1869–1938).

207 Danish physician and professor of medicine Niels Thorkild Rovsing (1862–1927).

we don't corrupt him with importunity and snobbery, then in him we have indeed been incredibly fortunate. And his wife is equally unassuming. If you come here after Christmas—you did mention the possibility—you will be pleased with the whole milieu. There is something so new and at the same time so fine.

I had hoped to fill at least four pages, but now I am getting tired. It's 10:30 P.M. I'll write another letter soon! Loving greetings to both of you!

Yours truly,
EDVARD

44

Christiania, December 20, 1905
Hotel Westminster

Dear Frants!
I send these few lines just as a loving Christmas greeting and to accompany the book that I am mailing at the same time. The latter is by Finck,[208] an American. It is fragmentary, to be sure, but it has a chapter that will become very significant for the correct appraisal of the undersigned when he is gone. This chapter is entitled "Norwegian Folk Music – Grieg's Originality". It is exceptionally well written and finally makes amends in a way for the unjust and obtuse criticism to which I have been subjected by a number of German and English-American journalists. These criticisms have now been repeated for so many years that they were on the verge of becoming the accepted view. So I owe Finck all the more thanks for his bold correction of the record—even though I think, unfortunately, that he can hurt me with his altogether too outspoken praise. Wagner is supposed to have said, "In order to understand me one must love me." You have a warm affection for me, and for that reason you will also understand and like the book.

I hope things are better for you than they have been for me of late. Once again the days have come of which one says, "I have no pleasure in them."[209] A very strong depression of the gastric nerves, inability to tolerate food, declining strength etc. Tomorrow I will probably enter Lovisenberg Hospital and let Unger Vetlesen[210] pump me out and prescribe a strict diet. It will be sad for Nina, but it has to be. I don't dare to wait until after Christmas. She is brave and cheerful and loving. I see more and more the beautiful development that she has undergone in recent years. No wonder, then, that she is my comfort in difficult times.

---

208 American musicologist Henry T. Finck (1854–1926) published a biography of Grieg in 1905 entitled *Edvard Grieg*. In 1909 he published a second book on Grieg entitled *Edvard Grieg and His Music.* In preparation for writing the latter he asked Beyer to record some of his memories from Grieg's last days, and this material was included in the concluding chapter of the book.

209 An allusion to Ecclesiastes 12:1, "Remember also your Creator in the days of your youth, before the evil days come, and the years draw nigh, when you will say, 'I have no pleasure in them.'"

210 Norwegian physician Johan Carl Unger Vetlesen (1851–1914).

And now farewell. Most loving wishes to both of you for a merry Christmas from Patient, Graybeard, Autograph-writer, Quasi Idiot! But owner of the hearts of two true friends and hopeful of a happy reunion.

Yours truly,
EDVARD

45

Christiania, January 6, 1906
Hotel Westminster

Dear Frants!
So: New Year's greetings by letter! And thank you for the old year, for all the friendly thoughts and friendly deeds! Thanks, too, for the book! I have not read it yet. There is so much literature that I *must* read before I get around to leisure reading. During the evenings I am working my way through an English book: *Tchaikovsky's Life and Letters.* It grips me to the depths of my soul. Often it is as if I were looking at my own life. There is so much that reminds me of myself. He is a melancholiac, almost to the point of insanity. He is a wonderful and good person—but an unhappy one. I did not perceive him to be unhappy when I met him on one occasion. But such is life: Either one must fight against others or one must fight against oneself. One thing I wish for in the new year: that my optimism may thrive at the expense of my pessimism. It is indeed of no use: We were not put into this world to be pessimists. There must be a real counterbalance. (. . .)

I'm glad that you have taken note of the chapter [in Finck's book] on the folk song and my originality. The author has done a good job there and has done me a big favor as well. May the book just become as well known as it deserves to be. It is quite true that the author has praised me too highly. I have reproached him for that, but he does not think so. Otherwise, in my opinion, the worth of this book, by virtue of its concentration, is much greater than that of Schjelderup's,[211] which is filled with effusive statements of a subjective nature. I am indeed furious with Schjelderup, because he lets his wife tour Germany with a person who recites lines from *Peer Gynt* accompanied by my music played on a piano. If it weren't for the fact that it is being done for the sake of earning money to buy groceries I would protest. But I won't even mention it.

We are having the most glorious winter weather. Since yesterday we have had a little snow, and the temperature has been just a couple degrees below freezing. Notwithstanding the winter calm over Nordåsvannet, I am so impious that I have no desire to be there. But I will keep Troldhaugen as long as I live, that has been

---

[211] Norwegian composer and cellist Gerhard Schjelderup (1859–1933) had published a biography, *Edvard Grieg og hans Værker* (*Edvard Grieg and His Works*), Copenhagen 1903.

decided.[212] Circumstances have arisen that have made this definite—about which I shall write more at another time.

Now you must not overexert yourself. One must not turn the person with a strong sense of duty into an automaton! If that happens, life exacts a terrible revenge. Many affectionate greetings to both of you from both of us.

Yours truly,
EDVARD

46

Christiania, January 14, 1906
Hotel Westminster

Dear Frants!
It is a quiet Sunday forenoon with a glorious layer of snow covering all the trees in Wergeland Square. And there is something so strange about it. At times you and your—our—warm friendship stand out as such a great happiness for me in the midst of life's emptiness and superficiality that it has to be expressed. (. . .) How good it is that *something* is genuine. Nature and art never let one down, that I know. Other than that, I am not sure of anyone or anything. How marvelous, then, that there is something in addition that we have for ourselves, something that we *know* stands fast, even if I look at you with business eyes, and even if my stomach makes me bad-tempered.

Yesterday I received from Copenhagen a copy of *Det ny Aarhundre*, in which I have written about my childhood and early youth.[213] You certainly have not read it in its entirety, so I am sending it to you today. This article has give me more aggravation than I can tell you and certainly added a nail to you-know-what—as the press and its lackeys always do.

This morning I got a telegram from *Neue Freie Presse* in Vienna asking if I would write an article in honor of the 150th anniversary of Mozart's birthday on January 27. It's a damn big honor, but the article is supposed to be delivered eight days from today and the telegram, which was sent to Copenhagen, cost four crowns. I can say with Falstaff: What is honor? etc. etc. I have just phoned Gerhard Gran[214] requesting that he send me my Mozart article that appeared in *Samtiden* some years ago. Naturally I will steal as much from it as I can.[215]

---

212 Grieg had been considering selling Troldhaugen and moving permanently to Christiania because he could not tolerate the climate of West Norway.

213 Grieg is referring to the essay, "My First Success", which was first printed in Norwegian in *Det ny Aarhundre* (*The New Century*), Copenhagen 1905–06. It will appear in English translation in Benestad & Halverson (eds.), *Edvard Grieg: Diaries, Articles, Speeches* (Columbus, Ohio, 2001).

214 Norwegian professor of literature Gerhard Gran (1856–1925) was one of the founders of the monthly journal *Samtiden* (1880) and became its editor in 1892.

215 The German article, *Mozart und seine Bedeutung für die musikalische Gegenwart*, was printed in *Neue Freie Presse*, Vienna, on January 21, 1906. It was based on the *Samtiden* version of the article written for

What a peculiarly half-barbarian country we are still living in. There is no sign here of a deeper musical understanding. Yesterday afternoon Halvorsen performed Richard Strauss's *Death and Transfiguration* for the first time in Christiania, and there were empty seats throughout the auditorium. And what is even worse is that the critics' treatment of significant new works such as that is almost like that of the Cossacks toward the poor Russian peasants. They fire away and don't care in the least whom they hit. Yes, I'll say this, that if I were to *work* here I would go stark, raving mad. Now when it is a matter of spending my life's evening in my homeland in contemplative tranquility, however, Christiania is the only place to be.

A little bird told me that you will be coming to Christiania for a couple of days this month. If that happens, I won't let you go. I am drinking loads of black molasses in order to get strong enough to hold on to you.

Now Nina is coming home from church, where she went with Betten,[216] so I must close. Most loving greetings.

Yours truly,
EDVARD

47

Christiania, December 19, 1906
Hotel Westminster

Dear Frants!
These lines merely as an "accompaniment" to the enclosure. I had first thought of sending you some book or other for the Christmas table, but then it occurred to me that you certainly would rather have something from my own storehouse. So I made a copy of the last hymn I wrote.[217] I think it is going to sound good, and in my mind's eye I can see you sitting at the piano playing it on a quiet Christmas forenoon. I hope you will like it!

I think death is beginning to send us its calling card during these days. It is as if it wanted to say: "I am not far away. You can expect me soon." Troye's[218] death affected me deeply. But even more, dear [Benno] Tiefenthal's. That was a blow! And his poor widow! Yesterday Peter Bjørnson[219] died after a long illness and desperate struggle. (...)

I love Fridtjof Nansen[220] and his accomplishment, but it is certain that it is

---

The Century Illustrated Monthly Magazine in 1896. Both articles will appear in new English translations in Benestad & Halverson (eds.), *Edvard Grieg: Diaries, Articles, Speeches* (Columbus, Ohio, 2001).

216 "Betten" was a pet name for Edvard's sister Elisabeth (1845–1907).

217 From *Four Psalms*, Grieg's last composition.

218 Norwegian educator Vilhelm Theodor Troye (1851–1906), especially known for his book *Thomas Carlyle*, Bergen 1898.

219 Peter E. Bjørnson (1838–1906), Norwegian public registrar and notary public.

220 Norwegian polar explorer Fridtjof Nansen, who at this time was ambassador to Great Britain.

not understood by our people. It is the intrepid "physical laborer" upon whom Lady Luck has smiled that has made a big hit in this nation of barbarians. When people break their arms and legs up on the slopes of Frognersæteren it is said that the fault lies with the people who are out walking. Yes, it was even stated in *Aftenposten* yesterday that people should find places to walk where there isn't any sledding! And since there is now sledding everywhere, I had a notion to write a humorous article recommending the emigration of all walkers. Then Norway could belong to the sledders. Or, to speak with Ibsen, "give all walkers a *stipend*!" (Actually, Ibsen was even more radical, for he wanted everyone in Norway to have a stipend!)

This Christmas letter will arrive too early, but better that than too late! Many warm Christmas greetings to both of you!

Yours truly,
EDVARD

P.S. Nina and I talked about going to Fuglsang[221] for Christmas. Julius Röntgen will arrive there on the 25th. But we have abandoned that plan for reasons of health. I must conserve every ounce of strength for use in the spring.

48

Leipzig, April 19, 1907
Hotel Hauffe

Dear Frants!
I have just come home exhausted from a forenoon visit (my hip is paining me so much that I could scream!), and I have a moment of leisure—the first, I daresay, in a long time. So: Thank you, thank you for the letter and the telegram! Yes, now I really have five concerts behind me and only one to go. It's strange, but the concerts themselves are the things I handle best. Then my nerves and my hips and I myself are so highly stimulated that the pains are drowned out. And for that I must be so thankful. But the reaction that sets in later—now, for example, when I have a week free—is something that I would not wish on anyone. Both mind and body are so heavy that I could keel over. The only thing I want to do is go to bed and sleep. That is not good.

The day after tomorrow we go to Kiel, and I am greatly looking forward to the first rehearsal, which may shake me up a little and relieve me of some of the heaviness.

Believe me, many a time I have wished that you were near—most of all, I think, in Berlin, for that was indeed the high point. And how the Philharmonic

---

221 "Fuglsang" ("Birdsong") was the home of Danish businessman Rolf Viggo de Neergaard (1837–1916).

Orchestra played! It is so enormously disciplined that when something was said once it never had to be repeated. Not so in Munich, where at each rehearsal I had to repeat everything. After the concert Weingartner[222] came in. That made me very happy. Another person, one whom you know, came and asked me explicitly to greet you most warmly. It was Max Schillings.[223] He made an agreeable impression, but I felt somehow that he was remote.

Then whole families came in—a mother with two sons who, with tears in her eyes, told me what joy my music had created in their home and that I had no idea how much I had meant to them for many years. What could I say? God help me, I almost got tears in my eyes myself.

Yes, how things are piling up! Today a postcard from Constantinople with thanks for the *String Quartet*, which had been superbly played by a Czech ensemble. And in general, all the stacks of letters, of which many are so moving. Strange that I should experience this! A warm feeling of gratitude pervades me and makes me want to become a better person. That it has this effect on me is owing to the fact that I am approaching the age of 64. When I was younger it would not have affected me in this way. But I am glad about the 64 years in this connection—although the saying is hard to take: "Even the beautiful must die!" I mean, that all the beautiful feelings that are streaming in on me are so soon to die. The joy in existence is now a sad joy. This expresses it exactly: "More I received than I ever have deserved—and everything must vanish!"[224]

5 P.M.

I just came home from dinner at Hinrichsen's[225] (Peters), where I met one of the "famous"—yes, suddenly famous—German composers, Max Reger, who offers mashed rutabagas and sausages for the first course and plum pudding for the second. What is most remarkable is that Julius Röntgen is crazy about him. Julius can stomach an awful lot. As you know, I do indeed love his liberal and broad-minded views and am striving in the same direction myself. But here I throw in the towel.

This evening we will hear Richard Strauss's *Salome*, which we [once] heard at the Hofopera with the composer conducting. In that work you can indeed hear strange things. There is something of the "great harlot" of Revelation[226] in it. It is the gospel of decadence, despite a technique that is brilliant. I would still take my hat off to it if I knew that it was written with conviction. But this is where it

---

222 German-Swiss composer and conductor Felix Weingartner (1863–1942).

223 German composer and conductor Max Schillings (1868–1933).

224 Grieg often quotes this line from the poem by A. O. Vinje set as "Last Spring" op. 33 no. 2.

225 Henri Hinrichsen (1868–1942), who became proprietor of the C. F. Peters Musikverlag upon the death of his uncle, Max Abraham, in 1900. C. F. Peters published the music of Max Reger (1873–1916).

226 Cf. Revelation 17.

falls short. A doubt sneaks in to the effect that what is important above all is sensation. And the minute that happens, the crime has been committed. Where, indeed, is music heading? Wagner is a veritable Mozart in comparison with this. For the audience that fills the auditorium evening after evening it is like "The Emperor's New Clothes".[227] I don't understand what *they* are feeling when I, listening with two musical ears, am on the verge of going crazy—so much so that I want to run out as fast as I can.

I must rest a little before going to the theater, so farewell for now. This certainly is a letter without arms and legs, but I am experiencing so much these days that I can't put it all into proper form.

The day after tomorrow we leave for Kiel, where I will conduct on the 26th.[228] From there we probably will go to Copenhagen—Hotel Bristol—and then homeward. May we still have some time together!

Take good care of yourself! Most loving greetings to both of you!

Yours truly,
EDVARD

49

Copenhagen, May 3, 1907
Hotel Bristol

Dear Frants!
You speak about how different our lives are. True—and yet, when all is said and done they are the same. We have both happily completed "the evening meetings!" Yet, how strange: As long as one is fully engaged everything goes fine, but when the work is done the reaction sets in. I felt it as soon as I came here, and I realized that it didn't make sense to head home in this winter-like springtime without doing some repair work on myself. So I sought out a neurologist, and now I am taking Finsen electric light-baths.[229] It is an exhausting regimen. Yesterday was my first attempt, and today I began with twenty minutes followed by an hour's rest. And when I came home I went straight to bed. Now I am up again, have had dinner by myself (Nina is at the Henriques's[230]) and have to stay indoors. Fortunately the treatment is only twice a week, so on the other days I am free. But I will not be normal as long as the therapy continues. I feel a prickling and tingling sensation all over my skin. Now we will see if there is any help to be had for constricted breathing and for neuralgia. The secret is that little by little the blood

---

[227] Fairytale by Danish author Hans Christian Andersen (1805–75).

[228] This proved to be Grieg's last concert.

[229] Danish physician Niels R. Finsen (1860–1904), who won the Nobel prize for medicine in 1903, offered "electric light-baths" to patients at "Finsen's Medical Light Institute" in Copenhagen. Grieg was at first very hopeful that this experimental therapy would improve his steadily worsening health, but it did not.

[230] Danish banker and broker Martin R. Henriques (1825–1912).

is drawn out toward the skin, where it can circulate more freely, thereby relieving pressure on the body's more vital parts. The doctors don't know the reason for it, but they have observed the phenomenon—or, more correctly, Finsen has certainly observed it. You see, I had to try something, for both the hip pain and the breathing difficulty are increasing. If I could just get to the point where I can keep these evils in check, so they don't get even worse, I would be more than satisfied. I am scheduled to take ten baths, so the process will last until the end of May.

It will not be until the middle of June, then, that I can come home for our brief time together this summer. In July you go to the mountains, August goes by quickly, and in early September we must leave to prepare and rehearse for the Leeds Festival.

There will be no rest for me until my eternal rest. And that certainly will not be long in coming. The members of my family do not grow older than I am now, and a physical lightweight like me must accept the fact that my strength will soon be exhausted.

This trip has been strange. I have the public on my side. In Germany my art has been lauded as never before. But the critics in both Munich and Berlin have let me know that I am a dead man. That is the punishment for my lack of productivity in recent years, which is a consequence of my physical misery. It is a hard and undeserved punishment.

But I console myself with the fact that it is not the critics who rule the world. When a genius like Wagner could say, upon being attacked in the vilest manner in the press: "Yes, indeed, you honorable critics, you can say what you will, but I have the public on my side"—he understood what it signified, and I am in the very best company. Thus I am grateful and happy for everything that I have behind me.

But yet I am not happy. This inactivity pains me. If I were even at a sanatorium, where I could get totally away from the world—a spa or something like that. But this constant fatigue coupled with all kinds of demands on me from friends and acquaintances—that torments me. It's going to be a rough month, this beautiful month of May, which must nonetheless make its entry. But it will end. If only I could head for home breathing a little more easily and feeling a little more cheerful! Yes, indeed!

Would that I could remember well enough to be able to tell you about what I have experienced. Did I greet you from Max Schillings, who came to see me in the green room in Munich? So also did Felix Weingartner. In Berlin I got acquainted with Richard Strauss—and his opera *Salome!* That's the end of everything! The future of art, in any case. One can say, "Après Strauss le déluge!"[231]

---

[231] Après Strauss le déluge: "After Strauss comes the deluge!" A rewriting of the French saying attributed to Madame de Pompadour (1721–64), mistress of French King Louis XV (1710–74): "Après nous le déluge."

By the way, we are not stupid in Norway now either. Today in *Verdens Gang* I read Mr. Borgstrøm's[232] assessment of Tchaikovsky's *Symphony Pathétique*: It is the confession of a perverse nature. I consider it a duty to protest. And yet I cannot bring myself to do it. What purpose shall music not be made to serve in this artistic period that is so sated with megalomania? Why doesn't Mr. Borgstrøm depict [the text is crossed out at this point in the original]. Music should be able to do that too. Mr. Borgstrøm has probably heard some of the slander and lies being whispered about Tchaikovsky. Then he mixes these up and produces this! That is supposed to be interesting. And the unsuspecting Norwegian public shall be instructed! Ha, ha! Shame, shame!

Now the dolorous City Hall bells are ringing announcing that it is 8 P.M. It is dark and I must conclude. Kindest regards to both of you!

Yours truly,
EDVARD

50

Skodsborg,[233] *May 29, 1907*

Dear Frants!
It is a wretched friend that you have here. Since I last wrote, life has been and continues to be sheer misery. All my afflictions rage simultaneously as furiously as they can. But the ones that still upset me most are the hallucinations, the increasing breathing difficulty and insomnia.

I tried the Finsen electric light-baths but had to quit them. It was they that ruined my nerves, not the concerts. If I had gotten them at a clinic where I could have been alone, I think maybe they would have helped. But when the doctor allows me to live in a hotel and attend parties etc. during the period when the therapy is under way, he has destroyed me because he has not understood me.

In my despair I have moved out here, but I absolutely cannot tolerate the vegetarian fare in the combined form in which it is dished out here. The result has been a further weakening, so I think we will go back to Hotel Bristol tomorrow, and the next day we will leave for Christiania. Then, as soon as possible, homeward—homeward on the wings of longing!

Now I am to go out into a glassed-in veranda right next to Øresund,[234] where I will be laid out on a bed and bundled in blankets. (It is beastly cold!) If I manage to fall asleep, this soothes my nerves tremendously. But at this moment

---

232 Norwegian composer Hjalmar Borgstrøm (1864–1925) was music critic in the Christiania newspaper *Verdens Gang*.

233 Skodsborg Sanatorium near Copenhagen, where Grieg had gone in a desperate attempt to arrest the continuing decline of his health.

234 Øresund is the sound between Denmark and Sweden.

I am so weakened that I can't even tolerate writing any more. If I try to read I have to reread each sentence four times, and still I do not grasp it. My eyes close, all my muscles relax, and I suddenly jump up as if I were in a state of delirium. You understand that this is no joke.

The people out here are nice. They belong to a religious sect called "Adventists", whose difference from the Lutherans is not exactly clear to me. But it is a happy form of Christianity, for they sing cheerful hymns, and the people are equally cheerful.

Lucky the man now sailing into Bergensfjord! Do you really want to cancel the trip to Jotunheimen this year? If so, I know somebody who would be happy. But you must promise yourself, Majs and me that you will do what your body requires!

I have been thinking lately that I had so much to tell you. But my poor memory is gone. If I did not have my dear Nisk the outlook would be bleak. She is absolutely courageous and tireless, and so nice to me early and late. She, too, knows, of course, that my condition is serious.

May we still be together a little at home! Farewell, both of you dear ones! Many loving good wishes from Nina and me.

Your old
EDVARD

To Bjørn Bjørnson

Bjørn Bjørnson (1859–1942), the son of Grieg's close friend Bjørnstjerne Bjørnson (1832–1910), is considered one of Norway's foremost dramatic artists. In 1884, at the age of 25, he was appointed director of the Christiania Theater. He breathed new life into the somewhat stodgy old institution and cast himself in dramatic roles which he played with bold imagination and profound insight. In 1899 he became the first director of the newly established National Theater in the Norwegian capital, a position he held until 1907 and again in 1923–27. He produced and played the title role in *Peer Gynt* in both 1892 (Christiania Theater) and 1902 (The National Theater).

Grieg's letters to Bjørn Bjørnson are preserved in Nasjonalbiblioteket, Oslo (National Library of Norway, Oslo Division).

1

Troldhaugen, February 7, 1892

Dear Bjørn!
It's a stroke of good luck that I have made you go insane, for insanity is absolutely necessary for a good Peer Gynt! Can't you understand that when I cable, "Done with *Peer Gynt.* Remember *Olav Trygvason*," the meaning is that just as your father, after the passing of many years of our Lord, did not want to do more with *Olav Trygvason* because he was "done with" that period, so also I do not want to write any more music to *Peer Gynt* because I am "done with" that period!! I hope that with this spoon-feeding you have gotten the point! Hell's bells! To understand a telegram requires at least a nickel's worth of imagination. But of course you have used up all of yours studying the role, so you have my forgiveness! And now to the matter at hand.

Unfortunately I do not have any "suitable music preceding the grand monologue 'Castle upon castle' etc." The only possible surrogate is the *Norwegian Dances*[1] mentioned in my telegram (unfortunately I don't have them), of which you will play No. 4, the last piece in the book—and NB, play it well. Then there are possibilities for a proper mood.

I have sent "Solveig's Song" for Orchestra [op. 55 no. 4] to Leipzig, where just now it is in process of being printed, so with the best will in the world I couldn't provide that for you. But believe me, it wouldn't be good either. You are forgetting that "Solveig's Song" is already heard in the Prelude to Act I. It would destroy the effect of the song itself.

On the other hand, "Largo in B-flat Major"[2] can be played before the scene with Solveig on skis (hut in the forest, twilight), whereas the score incorrectly indicates that it should be played preceding Act III. That's some nonsense from the production in Copenhagen.

---

1 Three of the *Norwegian Dances* op. 35 as orchestrated by Danish composer Robert Henriques (1858–1914) had been used in the 1886 production of *Peer Gynt* at the Dagmar Theater in Copenhagen.

2 Grieg is referring to "Peer Gynt at the Statue of Memnon".

"The Death of Åse" shall be played preceding Act III (*be sure to remember this, which Hennum*[3] *must also know!*), and the same piece shall be played for the second time, off-stage, in the death scene—*starting* with Peer Gynt's line "Press on, Grane, my pacer!" and *ending* with the line "An end to this fuss and bother!" This is of great importance and of great effect. I have figured out that it can fit. You must see to it that it does. If the music ends a little early, that's no problem. (Åse can, of course, be dead a few seconds sooner.) But it must not for anything end later. And to cut it off would be a disaster, as the ending is just the thing to depict the moment of death. The piece must be played so far in the distance that it sounds indefinite. That's the only way to produce a realistic effect.[4]

Dear Bjørn, let all of this be important to you. And with that: Good luck! Warm greetings from both of us.

Yours truly,
EDVARD GRIEG

P.S. With that Boyg[5] you have made me insane! But as I said: I'm trying. It's a great pity that I won't be there before the performances begin. There is so much for which my presence would be of the greatest importance!!!

2

Copenhagen, [March 14, 1895]
Thursday

Dear Bjørn!

I am in bed and am miserable. It will go slowly. For that reason I don't want to wait to tell you that the reason "Hymn of the Fatherland" is unsuitable for concert use is not that it is a children's song but that it is a school song. You can see that from the fact that the many stanzas stand side by side [and are sung in succession] without any interlude. This would inevitably sound boring in a concert. And it is the only song in the set that is so simple.

Good lord, why must I lie here! I would like so much to come up and hear your wife sing all of them. The songs no one has yet chosen are the best ones. I mean: "The Ocean" and "Fisherman's Song".

Now I'm sweating profusely, so I'd better stop. Warm greetings to both of you!

Yours truly,
EDVARD GRIEG

---

[3] Johan Hennum (1836–94), conductor of the Christiania Theater orchestra.

[4] The score indicates that the music should be played "behind the stage".

[5] The "Great Boyg" is an enigmatic, disembodied voice that appears in Act II of *Peer Gynt*. Bjørnson had asked Grieg to write some additional music for this scene.

To Bjørnstjerne Bjørnson

Bjørnstjerne Bjørnson (1832–1910)—poet, dramatist, novelist, journalist, editor, theater director, public speaker—was one of the most prominent figures in Norwegian public life in the late nineteenth century. Drawing upon the sagas as well as his knowledge of rural life in Norway, he created an impressive number of poems, plays, novels and peasant tales that played an important role in awakening the national pride and aspirations of his countrymen and won him international fame. He was awarded the Nobel prize for literature in 1903.

Bjørnson exerted a very strong influence on Grieg both politically and as a close personal friend. Edvard and Nina were often guests in the hospitable home of Bjørnstjerne and Karoline Bjørnson (1835–1934). On June 15, 1903, in the course of the festivities celebrating his own sixtieth birthday, Grieg made an extemporaneous speech extolling his old friend as "the Norwegian who is closest to our hearts. And why? Because you are always our wakeful conscience. Because it is through you that we feel Norway's pulse."[1]

Grieg composed a number of works both large and small to texts by Bjørnson. Several of them are among his best and most dearly loved compositions.

Letters 1–7 and 26–28 are preserved in Nasjonalbiblioteket, Oslo (National Library of Norway, Oslo Division). Letters 8 and 10 are taken from Gunnar Hauch (ed.), *Breve fra Grieg* [*Letters from Grieg*], Copenhagen 1922. No. 25 was printed in the Christiania newspaper *Verdens Gang*. All of the remaining letters to Bjørnson included here are preserved in Bergen Offentlige Bibliotek (Bergen Public Library).

1

Bergen, June 17, 1873

Dear Bjørnson!
Thanks for the material you sent.[2] A matchless mystique hovers over it, and I look forward to getting to work on it. Rolfsen has offered me the use of a gazebo at Sandviken, and that's where I will get the project under way![3] But I would like to have known a bit more. Is this the last night's heathen sacrifice prior to Olav's coming? And what becomes of the antagonism later on?

In reading through it I realized that much of it should be treated as melodrama, and with regard to that you must give me complete freedom. I have now

---

1 The full text of this speech and other testimonials to Bjørnson by Grieg will be found in Benestad & Halverson (eds.), *Edvard Grieg: Diaries, Articles, Speeches* (Columbus, Ohio, 2001).

2 The reference is to Bjørnson's draft of a libretto for a projected national opera about Olav Trygvason, the Viking king credited with bringing Christianity to Norway ca. 997 AD. Bjørnson had written a poem called *Olav Trygvason* in 1862, and it had been set to music by Norwegian composer Rikard Nordraak (1842–66). Now it was Bjørnson's intention to further develop the material and adapt it to a new format. Grieg was enthusiastic about the idea, and the two men set to work in earnest to bring their common dream to reality. Little by little problems arose, however, leading in 1876 to a rupture in their friendship that was to last for thirteen years. The opera, unfortunately, was never finished; the completed fragment consists of just three scenes.

3 Rasmus Rolfsen (1812–1903), owner of a factory in Bergen, lived in a villa called "Elsero" in Sandviken, a community on the western edge of the city. Grieg also wrote much of the *Peer Gynt* music in this gazebo, which is preserved in the "Gamle Bergen" ("Old Bergen") Museum.

learned a lot that I can put to good use here. But above all, send the next installment as soon as possible.

I hope you are satisfied with my vote for Stortinget: red Sverdrupians![4]

The day before yesterday I gave a very successful concert to raise money for Håkonshallen.[5] Your *Land-sighting*[6] was very effective and had to be repeated. I have now changed the declamation and like the piece. But those Bergensians can sing, too—NB, when I am conducting! Through all the tones there surged one single, great tone—and that is not possible unless *everyone* is completely caught up. I'll send you the program so that you can see how it smells of *Bear* steak![7]

Farewell for now, and warm greetings to all of you from

Your devoted
EDVARD GRIEG

P.S. Special greetings from Tonny, Nina and John.[8]

2

Bergen, July 5, 1874

Dear Bjørnson!

Thanks for your letter. I enjoyed it tremendously. But I don't concede a particle of what you say about egoism—although my old father thought it was the best thing you ever said in your life. No, you see, in recent years I have been living suppressed, without being able to express myself, and under those circumstances much can appear to be egoism which isn't that at all.[9] I don't know what has come over me these days—a whiff of something that I can't explain. But it is of something nice.

---

[4] "Stortinget" is the Norwegian parliament. On July 10, 1873, Bjørnson had written to Grieg: "See to it that there is a good election in Bergen, you clumsy fool!" Grieg was a lifelong republican and a great admirer of Johan Sverdrup (1816–92), leader of the Liberal [Venstre] party, who was president of the Norwegian Parliament from 1871 to 1884.

[5] "Håkonshallen"—Håkon's Hall—is a splendid structure erected by King Håkon Håkonsson in 1247–61 as part of the royal compound in Bergen, the political center of Norway at that time. The building had fallen into disrepair, and Grieg joined Bjørnson and other cultural leaders in a successful effort to have it restored.

[6] *Land-Sighting*, a setting of a text by Bjørnson, was composed in 1872 for baritone, male chorus and harmonium but in 1881 was revised and re-scored for baritone, male chorus and orchestra.

[7] A play on words: "Bjørn" is the Norwegian word for "bear".

[8] Nina Grieg's sister Tonny Hagerup (1845–1935) and Edvard's brother John Grieg (1840–1901).

[9] On June 26 Bjørnson had written Grieg a long letter which started out as follows: "Dear Grieg, I send you my hearty congratulations on the composer's grant that you and Svendsen received! I think I played a part in this, which makes me all the happier. For the same reason I rather expected to hear a word from one of you now that it has happened. But you artists are the most egotistical creatures on earth. You expect the whole world to wait on you hand and foot. If it doesn't, to hell with it, and if it does—well, then it is only doing its duty. You are just like that thousands of times. Place your hand over your sinful heart, bow your head and say: *Pater peccavi* [Father, I have sinned]!"

Your battle hymn,[10] which I received this morning, is completed, and if it isn't democratic then nothing is. Moreover, it is a solid piece. It comes marching up like a whole battalion—the kind that takes its objective by storm. (. . .)

I thank you sincerely for the letter to Sverdrup. It wasn't published, since we preferred to prevent in every way the premature discussion of our case by the public.[11] That I did not answer you at that time was, naturally, because I was furious at you. And you may well ask, Why? Because now I'm sitting here composing music to *Peer Gynt* instead of to *Olav Trygvason*. That's the whole story. But how can I hold a grudge against anyone now when I am feeling so happy—and least of all against you, of whom I am so infinitely fond both because of what you are in yourself and because of what you awaken in me!

Unfortunately, we probably won't see each other in the near future, as I am spending the summer here in order to work in peace and quiet in the lovely gazebo in Sandviken. Then in September I will be going to Germany. If only we could meet in Denmark for a short time then!

Warm greetings to all of you from Nina and from

Your devoted
EDVARD GRIEG

3

[Kristiansand], September 12, 1874

Dear Bjørnson!

Your last letter was indeed highly original![12] Do you think that I willingly declined to go [to Italy] last winter? Since you had a part in securing the three hundred *spesidalers* that I received in Bergen,[13] I do thank you most sincerely; but with just those funds could I take my wife and go out into the world and devote myself exclusively to composing? And yet, I would have done it if I had gotten rid of my

---

[10] "Chorus for the Supporters of Freedom in Scandinavia" for male chorus *a cappella* was published for the first time in *Dansk Folketidende* on July 24, 1874 with the following inscription: "Dedicated by the author to Denmark's united Liberal Party."

[11] In 1874 Grieg and his fellow composer Johan Svendsen (1840–1911) jointly applied to the Norwegian Parliament [Stortinget] for an annual composers' grant. On June 1 of that year, when the matter came up for a final decision, Johan Sverdrup made an impassioned speech in support of the request. The speech had a decisive impact: The application was approved by a vote of 61 to 44. Both Grieg and Svendsen were awarded "until decided otherwise by the parliament" an annual artist's grant of 400 *spesidalers*—a very considerable sum of money. (1 *spesidaler* = 4 Norwegian crowns.)

[12] In a letter dated July 16 Bjørnson had suggested that Grieg had given up working on *Olav Trygvason* in order to devote his time to *Peer Gynt*: "Now you are working on *Peer Gynt*! Much good may it do you! It has *some* parts that lend themselves to poetic music, but the totality is a flight away from such music—a flight that often leads through comical and dry places that you will not conquer. Once again you are wasting your time and talents. This, my solemn warning, I will not neglect to send to you, even if it rubs you the wrong way. Possibly some day as an older man you will be able to master such material in its entirety, but you can't do it now."

[13] Grieg, with strong support from Bjørnson, had received a travel grant in Bergen.

Bjørnstjerne Bjørnson. In a letter to Iver Holter dated February 9, 1867, Grieg wrote: "It is a sacred duty for me to call attention to the great influence that my association with Bjørnson from the autumn of 1866 to the spring of 1873 had on my art. He formed my personality in countless ways—that is to say, he contributed mightily to that process. He made me a democrat, both artistically and politically. He gave me the courage to follow my own natural bent." (H. Aschehoug & Co., Oslo)

lodgings. No! It certainly was good that I stayed home, for otherwise the four hundred[14] would likely not have been forthcoming. It really is a fact that if I had gotten your text I would have said no to Ibsen and thus would have avoided *Peer Gynt* with its many perils. I hope to be finished with it this autumn (it is only a matter of a few fragments here and there), and then I am enthusiastically ready for *Olav Trygvason.* But—I must be in a place where I can hear good dramatic music, stay in touch with the times, and have frequent contact with art and artists in general. As much as I would like to first take a side trip to Italy to meet you and discuss everything that we need to discuss, I just can't afford it, even though I seriously hope to settle down and work undisturbed abroad. I feel that the moment that has come for me now will not come again, and it must not be wasted in traveling and pleasure. It must be used. So even if you were to send me the most tempting letter from Italy, I would have to be like stone and push all the feelings away.

---

[14] The composer's grant.

This has been about the eternally recurring *I*, but you write to me so honestly and forthrightly that I have to be completely open with you. Selmer[15] writes me that you are staying in Rome this winter! Just write away at *Olav*! Do it! If you have grand scenes they will be suitable for opera, that I know. You have now lived for so long with contemporary images that it will be a joy and an urge for you to get to work on the saga again.

Be sure to write to me about your building plans. Because I have become uneasy about what several people have said, and most recently now in a conversation with Mr. Fougner, the Bergen hatter, who reportedly was well-informed.[16]

I am sitting and writing these lines at the hotel in Kristiansand, where I am en route [to Denmark]. In a few days I will arrive in Copenhagen for a month's stay (Address: Music Dealer Wagner,[17] Østergade 4). I will hope to hear from you there that the outlook both for *Olav* and for the prospect of our meeting is more promising than I think. For example: next spring in Germany? Make some suggestions, in any case!

Now you have also made me into a political monster in Denmark! I get letters with regrets, requests for a retraction, about explanations in the newspapers regarding non-participation in the dedication,[18] etc.—all of which is water off the duck's back and inexpressibly funny to

Your devoted
EDVARD GRIEG

P.S. Many greetings to your wife and the children! Also from Nina!

4

Copenhagen, October 1, 1874

Dear Bjørnson!
Your letter was incredible![19] There is so much in it for which I thank you again and again! You open vistas for me of precisely the kind that I love! But listen: I will not be finished with the work I currently have under way[20] until Christmas. I have promised that the score will be delivered then, so I must work here, both for the sake of the work itself and, through it, to earn the money needed for travel.

---

15 Norwegian composer and conductor Johan Selmer (1844–1910).

16 Bjørnson had recently purchased "Aulestad", a farm in Gausdal—near Lillehammer—and had made arrangements for the construction of a new farmhouse. He wrote more about this in a letter to Grieg of September 17, 1874. Eilert Fougner (1838–1908) was a mutual friend.

17 Danish music dealer and publisher Eduard Wagner (1846–?).

18 Grieg is alluding to the dedication of "Chorus for the Supporters of Freedom in Scandinavia". See Grieg's letter to Bjørnson of July 5, 1874.

19 On September 17 Bjørnson had sent an unusually long letter to Grieg strongly urging him to come to Rome: "Until you are with me you will hear nothing from me."

20 Grieg was working on the incidental music to Henrik Ibsen's *Peer Gynt*.

And now I think that when I go south in January, the stay in Rome would be of too short duration to be productive, whereas spending the first months of next year in Germany and then meeting you next spring would enable me to make the best use of the winter.

Now the question is: Are you going to Tyrol in the spring, and will you be staying there for the summer? If so, I will meet you there early in the spring, maybe even in March, and we'll get to work! If, however, you are going back to Norway at that time it would be absurd for me to waste both time and money on a *short* visit to Rome. That's how it looks to me, and *I* cannot act otherwise. In a certain mood I could just walk away from everything here and head south—but no, that must not happen. If you will be away for a full year starting next spring, I will move heaven and earth to be with you in Italy the whole time—for that is what it will take. That is: It takes *ten* times as long to write an opera as it does to write a play, NB, a modern opera. I have almost laughed myself to death over your remark about Wagner,[21] and because of those two lines I hesitate to send your letter to Holmboe.[22] If I didn't get it back again I would hate him for the rest of my life.

If you delete two zeros from the sum you mention, then it comes close to describing my circumstances. If in fact I still have the 300 from last year, and I get another 200 for the *Peer Gynt* music plus another 150 that a publisher here owes me, I will leave happily with my head held high.[23]

Recently I was with H. C. Andersen,[24] who might now appropriately be called Babble Andersen. He's in his second childhood! But he speaks of you with the old admiration, whereas he loathes Ibsen and considers *Peer Gynt* the worst thing he has ever read. I can only marvel at how it is filled with witticism and invective from beginning to end, but it never engages my deepest emotions. Still, I think it is the best thing Ibsen has written. Don't you agree? Surely you don't think it was a voluntary choice on my part! I was approached by Ibsen in the spring,[25] and naturally I bridled at the idea of writing music for that most

---

[21] In his letter to Grieg of September 17, Bjørnson had written regarding Wagner: "Then I was in Munich and saw *Tannhäuser*; I liked it much better this time. But Wagner is sick; there are whole keyboards in the soul that in his case do not function. This autumn I saw *Tristan and Isolde*. It is the most enormous depravity I have ever seen or heard, but in its own crazy way it is so overwhelming that one is deadened by it as by a drug. Even more immoral and enervating than the plot is this seasick music that destroys all sense of structure in its quest for tonal color. In the end one becomes just a glob of slime on the ocean shore, something ejaculated by that masturbating pig in an opiate frenzy! My considered final impression is that *the melodrama* has a great future instead of the opera he has had in mind."

[22] Bergen physician Jens Andreas Holmboe (1827–76).

[23] In his letter of September 17 Bjørnson had given an account of his income. He expected to earn at least 24,000 *spesidalers* per year for the next several years—an enormous sum of money in those days.

[24] Hans Christian Andersen (1805–75), the Danish writer of children's stories. Two of Grieg's best-known songs are settings of his texts: "Two Brown Eyes" and "I Love But Thee".

[25] Ibsen had written to Grieg from Dresden on January 23, 1874, inviting his interest in composing incidental music for *Peer Gynt*. See pp. 441–442.

unmusical of subjects. But I thought about the 200, and about the trip—and I made the sacrifice. The whole thing hangs over me like a nightmare; if I could be done with it I would leave in a moment. If I had not had to write music for the unveiling of the monument to Kjerulf I would be done with it now.[26] It is awful to be in a certain way the only one, as I have sometimes been; one is used as the organ grinder of the day, and one has no time to write what is in one's heart—one is always doing something else. For that reason it is high time that I get away. I've had enough realism for now.

You *must* let me know whether or not you will be in Tyrol from spring and on, because that will determine my plan!

Warm greetings from Nina (if only she could come along) and from

Your devoted
EDVARD GRIEG

P.S. First of all, be sure to greet your wife! Then: the Borch family. Then: Bravo. Then: Ravnkilde.[27]

I must not forget to tell you: I have been in Italy twice and was sick almost continuously because I couldn't tolerate the climate. The memory of this also somewhat dampens my enthusiasm for Italy.

5

Solhejm by Brobyværk at Fyen
January 2, 1875

Dear Bjørnson!
Your last letter[28] was nice, but it did not give me an answer to the question that for me is so important: How long will you be staying in Italy? Please tell me this immediately. Address: E. W. Fritzsch,[29] *Musikalien-Verlagshandlung, Neumarkt,*

---

26 *At the Halfdan Kjerulf Statue,* text by Andreas Munch (1811–84). The cantata was written for male chorus with tenor solo for the unveiling of the monument in honor of Halfdan Kjerulf (1815–68). It was performed on September 23, 1874, in Christiania by the Norwegian Students' Chorus.

27 Norwegian sculptor Christopher Borch (1817–96). Bjørnson wrote a laudatory poem to Borch on the occasion of his fiftieth birthday in 1867. Bjørnson wanted among other things to honor Borch because for a number of years he had given free drawing lessons to talented prisoners in Christiania's Akershus fortress in the hope that after their incarceration they might find gainful employment.

Johan Bravo (1797–1876) was a Danish painter and art dealer who served in Rome as Danish consul beginning in 1847 and Swedish-Norwegian consul beginning in 1855.

Danish composer Niels Ravnkilde (1823–90) was a close friend of Grieg with whom he frequently associated in Rome in 1865–66.

28 Bjørnson's letter of December 8, 1874, in which he once again strongly urged Grieg to join him in Rome. He also hinted that during the following summer they could work together at Aulestad: "This is what I visualize: that I can write you text after text, and that it is the strongest desire I have. And that here is something we must do together about which I have hardly spoken to you, but which will no longer leave me in peace."

29 Leipzig music publisher E. W. Fritzsch (1840–1902) had published Grieg's *Piano Concerto* in 1872.

Leipzig. I leave for Leipzig tomorrow and will be there—how long? Well, that depends on your letter! I hear via a letter from Norway that you are expected home in the spring. Is this true? And if so, what shall I do in order to be able to work with you this summer? That is the question, and I know you won't let me down.

With *Peer Gynt* it has gone as you predicted: It hangs over me like a nightmare, and I can't possibly be done with it until spring. It was the need for money—or, more precisely, it was the offer of money—that drove me. Perhaps it should not have done so, but the prospect of travel and visions of great beauty loomed before me. I could now be so mean as to wish that your house would not be finished by summer, so that you would have to go abroad again; yes, in that case I would clear everything out of the way and follow you wherever you went—all summer and next winter as well. But if you are going to stay home, advise me: I will so gladly take your advice once the Gyntian crisis is over. By the way, the performance of *Peer Gynt* just now can do some good in Christiania, where materialism is trying to rise up and choke everything that we regard as high and holy. There is a need for a mirror, I think, wherein all the egotism can be seen, and *Peer Gynt* is such a mirror; then you will come home and rebuild. For it cannot be denied: The people must see their own ugliness before you can be of use, but once their eyes are opened you are just the man to lead the parade. I have this definite feeling, and I would be very surprised if I were mistaken. And then you will be followed by many who now fear for our homeland, including

Your faithful friend,
EDVARD GRIEG

P.S. Warm greetings, also from Nina, to all of you. Happy new year!!! My landlord and brother-in-law Dr. Nommels[30] sends you his warmest greeting!

6

Leipzig, February 21, 1875

Dear Bjørnson!

Thank you so much for your letter![31] I have received everything you have written to me, and as far as I can recall have not expressed any doubts about it either. And thanks for all your friendly suggestions. I can't tell you how nice it would be to go with you up to Gausdal and stay there for the summer. I can make the commitment to do that—but unfortunately, no more than that. To come to

---

[30] Danish physician Karl Nommels (1845–1912) was married to Nina Grieg's sister, Yelva Hagerup (1847–86).

[31] In a letter dated January 20, 1875, Bjørnson again encouraged Grieg to come to Italy: "The loveliest weather. The whole winter without an overcoat!"

Rome is out of the question. We will stay here until at least the middle of April, then we will go to Munich for a month. Thereafter I can be with you in Tyrol—NB, if you really will be there for at least a few months, for I need that much time to get anything done. If you are planning to go northward *as early as June*, I prefer to wait for you in Munich and then go on with you to Gausdal. What I need to know is how long you will be staying in Tyrol, but of course you can hardly decide that since it depends on when you finish your play.

The same is true regarding *Peer Gynt* and my stay in Leipzig: I can't decide how long it will last because I want to finish this job here. It was my intention to send it off the first of April, which is why I shall be working like a horse. But yesterday I heard how things stand with respect to music in the Christiania Theater, as a consequence of which I am today writing to both Ibsen and Josephson[32] that I consider it my duty not to deliver anything to the Christiania Theater so long as the orchestra is not fully staffed. It is absolutely scandalous, the worst that it has ever been, and [Johan] Svendsen says that if the situation continues we will in the course of a few years have no orchestra at all in Norway's capital city—a city of nearly 100,000 people. Old Mozart operas won't be destroyed, that we know, but to deliver a score with modern orchestration to the Christiania Theater *now* would be the same as wishing it to become a grand fiasco.

I must not forget to greet you from Neupert,[33] who played my *Piano Concerto* here last Tuesday with great success. Last evening Nina sang at the Conservatory's evening program. How strange the Norwegian words sounded in those very German halls! How closely the audience listened to "To Springtime My Song I'm Singing"—and then this jubilation afterward. If only you had been here! You have many friends here who have read your play *Halte-Hulda* [*Lame Hulda*], and one evening in a tavern recently I got hold of a cut-rate [German] edition of your play *De Nygifte* [*The Newlyweds*], which I immediately brought to my German friends—and when I met them again a few days later I was greeted with, "Ah, how wonderful, how enchanting!" By the way, the translation is stilted in some places. (. . .)

You talk about Protestantism's oratorios. I will just tell you that Germany has such marvelous ones that I cannot imagine anything more beautiful. They have been buried for centuries and only now are beginning to be noticed. The man who has plumbed the depths in this area is Bach. A person cannot ever conquer everything in the world, and I am drawn by other ideals. To depict Norwegian nature, Norwegian folk life, Norwegian history and Norwegian folk poetry in music stands for me as the area in which I think I can achieve something. What

32 Ludvig Oskar Josephson (1832–99), a Swede, was director of the Christiania Theater from 1873 to 1877 and was responsible for the production of *Peer Gynt* in 1876.

33 Norwegian pianist Edmund Neupert (1842–88), who had played the solo part in the premiere of Grieg's *Piano Concerto* in Copenhagen on April 3, 1869.

you are speaking of certainly has my full appreciation, but I am not the man for it—not in this period of my life in any case. For now, Romanticism in all its fullness still beckons me.

If you remain in Tyrol into the summer months and your wife goes home, then I intend to let Nina go home too so that the time together in Tyrol can be devoted entirely to *Olav Trygvason.* Tell me your opinion about this so far as possible. So:

1. Meeting in Tyrol in the middle of May if the stay can last at least two and a half months, thereafter to Gausdal until the end of the summer; or
2. Meeting in Munich—when? Surely not later than June.

Warm greetings to all of you from Nina and from

Your devoted
EDVARD GRIEG

P.S. Thank Ravnkilde most heartily for the letter!!

7

Leipzig, March 17, 1875

Dear Bjørnson!
I would certainly have expected to hear from you if I had not known that you, poor fellow, have had an eye infection. By the time you receive this letter presumably everything will be fine, and then you must tell me how long you will be in Tyrol, exactly when you are arriving there, and about your plans regarding Munich. I am leaving here for Munich on May 1, and I will either wait for you there or go to wherever you are—depending entirely on your letter!

But why am I writing today? Because I am so exceedingly happy, and because you are the first one who must know it. Last evening *Before a Southern Convent* was performed at "Euterpe"[34] and was very well received. I myself conducted. Nina sang. Many curtain calls. Emma Dahl's translation had to be abandoned, as many competent people here found it to be—terrible. The well-known librettist-composer Franz von Holstein[35] has now translated the poem to everyone's satisfaction—also to mine, and I hope—to yours. Emma Dahl, what shall I do with her? I better bite the bullet[36] and send her a letter describing the situation exactly as it is. Hopefully in this way the affront will be minimized, though I fear that after this Christiania will be even more cross with me than before.

---

34 "Euterpe" was a concert association in Leipzig that featured contemporary music in deliberate competition with the well-established and more conservative Gewandhaus concerts.

35 Emma Freyse Dahl (1819–96) was a German-born singer and composer who lived in Christiania. Franz von Holstein (1826–78) was a German composer and author.

36 Grieg's expression is *bide i det sure Æble*, literally "bite in the sour apple".

Are you aware that Ibsen is coming to Munich in May to take up residence there? If not, perhaps it is good that you learn of it. He wrote to me a short time ago that *Peer Gynt* is not going to be performed in the current season—to my great joy, for now I can relax and wind up my affairs here before I head south.[37]

To my great annoyance (I lose money because of it), a pirated edition of my songs from *Fiskerjenten* [*The Fisher Maiden*][38] has recently been published in Berlin. The texts are poorly translated into German. There is nothing I can do, as the original edition was published in Copenhagen, and it is legal to reprint all of the music that is published there. But if you as the author of the texts *can* intervene, you would be doing me and my German publisher an immense favor by doing so. I must hear your view of this matter as soon as possible.

Johan Selmer is here now—this strange, gifted person of whom you very rightly said that he is so cold and yet so infinitely passionate. He is continuing to work on his Victor Hugo.[39] Yes, there are many riddles!

Farewell for now. Greetings to all of you from Nina and from

Your devoted friend,
EDVARD GRIEG

P.S. Is it true, as I read in *Illustrierte Zeitung*, that your play *En Fallit* [*The Bankrupt*] is going to be staged in Munich? And when?

8

Bergen, May 2, 1876

Dear Bjørnson!
Yes, I really am still living, although it is only in these lovely spring days that I have awakened from a long, long stupor. Heavy waves have engulfed me since you last heard from me. Perhaps you have heard that last fall both of my parents were suddenly called away,[40] and I ended up spending the winter here. It has been dark and depressing, and I have been living cooped up within reflections of all kinds. What I have composed during this time reflects this as well.[41] But though I may have grown ten years older, it is as if the reflections just now have waned, the child in me has come to the fore again—and with it affection for all that is lovely in life. You had to put up with hearing all this, because the first thing that comes to

---

37 *Peer Gynt* had its premiere performance at Christiania Theater on February 24, 1876.
38 *Four Songs* op. 21 for voice and piano, texts from Bjørnson's novel *Fiskerjenten* [*The Fisher Maiden*].
39 Johan Selmer's great work *Tyrkerne gaar mod Athen* [*The Turks Approach Athens*] for baritone solo, chorus and orchestra, to a text by French author Victor Hugo (1802–85).
40 Grieg's father, Alexander, passed away on September 13 and his mother, Gesine, on October 23, 1875.
41 During the period in question Grieg wrote his *Ballade* in G minor, one of his most somber compositions.

mind when I once again see my goal is *you*! You who have shown me as no one else has that art and life must permeate one another. I come to you now and demand of you that you shall understand me, and I long to hear from your own lips that you do so.

If so, then also do not refuse what I now request: Give me a sketch of the course of the action in *Olav Trygvason*—but soon, yes, immediately. Good Lord, as I write this the longing grows to once again take hold, it becomes an absolute passion. And that this time has gone by is good, because I have become another person. I see things differently and more broadly. Dear friend, do it. Then I have thought of dropping in on you in Gausdal when I am on my way south in June. I will be en route to the performance in Bayreuth of Wagner's *The Ring of the Nibelung*, the most remarkable work of our cultural epoch—and doubly remarkable because it is miles ahead of our time.[42]

Then I have one more request: I'm crazy about the idea of restoring Håkonshallen and am thinking of inviting all of the singers from West Norway to a meeting here next summer. If it could be a big, popular festival, so much money would come in that the work could begin immediately. Just think: There already is a sum of 10,000 crowns. If you will write a kind of cantata or whatever we should call it—something nice, something over which the spirit of the saga hovers—I would enthusiastically write the music.

This is still between us. I must know what you are feeling. I can tell you that people here would endorse the undertaking with great enthusiasm. But you yourself would have to come and give the kind of speech that only you can give! You understand that we have to observe time limits if the project is to be carried out in an orderly fashion. I would not want eastern Norway involved; I don't think one can count on a warm interest from those quarters, and besides, chicaneries would make it impossible for me to unite the leading people over there. But it is also absolutely unbelievable how much easier I am finding it to get everyone to pull together here in West Norway. The people here relate to art differently and more closely than do those easterners.

And now—write, so that I can see that you are still the same old Bjørnson. If you have lost interest in me, I will only tell you that I do not deserve it. But I know that there are strange, "boyg"-like[43] things in me—unfortunately! But never has my desire to drive out this demon been greater than it is now.[44]

---

[42] During the visit to Bayreuth Grieg wrote eight long articles about the Wagner productions for *Bergensposten*, a Bergen newspaper. The articles will be found in translation in Benestad & Halverson (eds.), *Edvard Grieg: Diaries, Articles, Speeches* (Columbus, Ohio, 2001).

[43] The "Great Boyg" is an enigmatic, disembodied voice that appears in Act II of *Peer Gynt*.

[44] There is no evidence that Bjørnson ever answered this letter. The bad feelings that had developed between Grieg and Bjørnson were not dispelled until 1889.

I don't see anyone here except the Holmboes, these amiable people in whom you have warm friends. You must write to them.

Warm greetings to you and your dear ones both from Nina and from

Your friend,
EDVARD GRIEG

9

Christiania, October 6, 1889

Dear Bjørnson!
When I ask you for permission to dedicate to *you* the music for the completed scenes of *Olav Trygvason,* (which will soon be performed here in the Music Association under my leadership), you should see therein a proof that ever since we parted I have always loved you and what you are fighting for—and a fervent hope that this work, which was the cause of our losing each other, might also be the thing that brought us together again! So blot out all the little things, and let these dramatic sketches, which are the products of a full heart, also find their way to your great heart—which I loved in days gone by, and which I continue to love in the confidence that it has not changed in the intervening years!

Heartiest greetings to you and your wife both from Nina and from

Yours truly,
EDVARD GRIEG

10

Christiania, October 15, 1889

Dear Bjørnson!
Thank you again and again for your letter![45] You don't know how happy you have made me! If only we could come up to see you for a couple of days, but I'm stuck right in the middle of things here. I have this very moment just come home from the first orchestra rehearsal of the fragments of *Olav Trygvason.*

---

45 Bjørnson's reply of October 13 is very moving:

Dear friend:
There has been a lot of commotion here because of a wedding, which is the only reason that the answer has been delayed.

When you write, "blot out all the little things," I answer, "they are already blotted out!" But I do it only out of obedience, for nothing of the sort was necessary. You possess the greatest lyrical power of all the musicians living today, and it exceeds my ability to remember whatever else the problem might be. (...)

I am first and foremost a Norwegian, and your world renown has now and then made me both proud and moved. You also know that we love your wife, Karoline and I; we think she is the sweetest person, the kind whom one can call by her first name.

I am not coming down to hear *Olav Trygvason.* I'm afraid for the old text; I don't remember it any more. It would be better if you came up here; that way we could make decisions about one thing and another in quietude. Your warmest admirer, Bjørn, told me that you had heard that I didn't like your *Bergliot.*

I am exhausted, drenched in sweat—but it was marvelous! Man oh man, how it is going to sound! Regarding your not coming to Christiania, I had already resigned myself to that. I saw Erling[46] at a restaurant yesterday—practically bumped right into him—and learned that you won't be coming here until *after* Christmas. Well! That's hard to take. Because there is a vølve[47] here who is outstanding! The Swedish Miss Ellen Nordgren![48] That you are afraid for the text is touching. It's *brilliant.* That's a fact. But that neither you nor I could work further on it *now*—that I understand completely. Perhaps it is best just the way it is. Little but good, as the girl said—and now *you* have given me a boldness and a zeal that cannot be overestimated! What you say about my lyrical talent, however, is not true. On the other hand, I am not without dramatic talent—and *Olav T* proves it.

Nina sends heartiest greetings to both of you. So also does

Yours truly,
Edvard Grieg

11

Bergen, August 25, 1890

Dear Bjørnson!

I have just returned from a trip to the mountains in Sogn. I had hoped to continue all the way to Gausdal, but the weather willed otherwise. My mission unaccomplished, I had to interrupt the trip and head for home. We hadn't given a thought to having Nina come along. Unfortunately, she has been ill all summer. Nonetheless, we got a glimpse of you through Bjørn,[49] whom I told that I was about to send you a telegram saying, "Is Olav Trygvason not coming?"[50]

Nonsense. I didn't find the beginning on a level with the subject; but some things there were magnificent, and the conclusion is such that one could not listen to it and remain seated.

Here there are still so many people in the house following the wedding, also many letters to write. So: farewell for this time! Greet Nissen's and Holst's. And kiss your wife from both of us.

Your old friend,
Bjørnstjerne Bjørnson

...

The premiere of the first three scenes of *Olav Trygvason* took place at a concert of the Music Association in Christiania on October 19, 1889. Bjørnson did not attend the first performance, but he was present when the program was repeated a week later. The day after the concert the Christiania newspaper *Morgenbladet* reported that Grieg, after five or six curtain calls, shouted from the podium, "To this I have just one thing to say: Long live Bjørnstjerne Bjørnson!" Beaming with joy, Bjørnson responded by leading the audience in a ninefold "hurrah" for the composer.

46 Erling Bjørnson (1868–1959), son of Bjørnstjerne Bjørnson.

47 In Old Norse mythology a "vølve" was a woman who practiced witchcraft and had the ability to foresee the future. The "vølve" plays an important role in *Olav Trygvason.*

48 Swedish-born soprano Ellen Nordgren (1863–1947) went on to become an outstanding interpreter of large roles in Wagner's music-dramas. In 1890 she married Norwegian Lieutenant Hans P. J. F. Gulbranson (1860–1946), and thereafter used her married name.

49 Bjørn Bjørnson (1859–1942), actor and theater director, son of Bjørnstjerne Bjørnson.

50 A quotation from Bjørnson's poem, "Olav Trygvason".

Just think: It will soon be a year since we talked—and still no sign of further progress. I won't press the matter, for that sort of thing must come of itself. In the meantime, of course, your fragment is still in manuscript, whereas my score has now been published. You certainly will understand that I don't want to be the only one to receive a material benefit from our common labor. Permit me, therefore, in any case to send you the enclosed 1,000 crowns from the honorarium that I received. Whether you write more or not—well, the future will tell. If there is no more, let me just tell you how happy you made me when, some years ago, you sent me your fragment. Yes, when I think back on the moments of inspiration of which you have been the source! Accept my deepest thanks for what your writings as a whole have meant to me!

When I now read the literature of the young writers and see how they understand their relationship to the literature to which they owe their existence—well, then I bow out and am happy to have lived my youth at a time when the concept of reverence was a part of one's development. And certainly it is not just in the world where I am at home that all the great ones practically grew up on the concept of reverence, while it was reserved for the petty ones to bite the hand that fed them. I am angry and saddened by the situation nowadays. I assume that we know as well as the young people that we must move "Forward!"[51]—and I don't see art in the same way I did twenty-five years ago either. But this I see, that what is going on now walks on four legs instead of on two. And that, God damn it, is not the way it ought to be.

Dear Bjørnson! This was a rewriting of what I would call, "Now thanks for everything since we were young!"[52] Heartiest greetings to all!

Yours truly,
EDVARD GRIEG

12

Copenhagen, December 10, 1890
Hotel King of Denmark

Dear Bjørnson!
What do you think of the idea of taking thoughts of peace, to which music can give added richness and depth, and turning them into a Bjørnson poem—in a kind of cantata form, a work suitable for solo voices, chorus and orchestra?

It has been my fondest thought in recent years to write a requiem—a modern requiem, without dogmatism. But I have not found a text, though I

---

51 This is an allusion to Bjørnson's poem "Fremad!" ("Forward!"), which Bjørnson wrote to Grieg's "National Song" op. 12 no. 8.

52 Grieg is quoting the opening line of "Synnøve's Song" from Bjørnson's novel *Synnøve Solbakken* (published in English under several different titles: *Trust and Trial, Love and Life in Norway*, and *Sunny Hill*). "Synnøve's Song" had been set to music by Grieg's predecessor Halfdan Kjerulf.

have searched both in secular literature and in the Bible. But when I read the peace talk that you gave in the Labor Union hall, the idea immediately struck me: An apotheosis to peace, that is a requiem of quite another kind! There need be no lack of contrasts: the great light of peace against the horrors of war! I believe in this idea. Think it over, and if it interests you—then answer.[53]

Many greetings.

Yours truly,
EDVARD GRIEG

P.S. The old Latin requiem text contains many important things regarding the formal structure.

13

[Copenhagen], Christmas Day, 1890
Hotel King of Denmark

Dear Bjørnson!

Merry Christmas! Down here the feeling of Christmas is overshadowed by the deaths of Gade and Mrs. Heiberg.[54] This is all anyone thinks of where there is only a minimum of spirit. I haven't seen Mrs. Heiberg for a number of years, and I never liked her. Gade, on the other hand—a rough-hewn individual with farmer's blood in his veins who was not world-renowned by accident—had come to see us in the hotel café the same day he died. There was nothing wrong with him—the next morning I saw him as a corpse.

Whether one believes in God, Satan, Christ along with the Holy Ghost and the Virgin Mary, in Mohammed or in nothing, it still is the case—and Gade gave me new confirmation—that the mystery of death cannot be explained away. It is this mystery which I have thought of finding a way of expressing. The Old Testament has, in both content and style, passages of absolutely dazzling fervor and power—in the Psalms of David, for example—especially where they deal with the transitoriness of life. I am able to find less of what I am seeking regarding the complete abandonment to thoughts of death combined with a belief in

---

[53] Grieg is here for the first time proposing to Bjørnson the idea of a Peace Oratorio—an idea to which Bjørnson responded with enthusiasm. In a letter dated December 14, 1890, he told Grieg that he could start working on it immediately: "I for my part wished it thus (whatever it might be called, requiem or not): The children are going to school one fine day, workers out in the fields, factories in the distance—all of this is in the children's song. Then, as if from the abyss, there rise up the menacing tones of mankind's restless heritage of war that frightens away everything that is innocent and peace-loving. We hear the soldiers' unbridled propensity to boast, the kings' and warriors' ideal of manhood filled with lust."

The idea of such a work continued to occupy both Grieg and Bjørnson for many months. See also Grieg's letters to Bjørnson of December 24, 1890, and June 2 and November 6, 1891.

[54] Danish composer Niels W. Gade (1817–90) and Danish actress Johanne Luise Heiberg (1812–90) had both died on December 21.

universal love, whether or not there is a life after death. For the idea of "security at any price" does not interest me in the least. Atheists and dogmatic Christians are equally abhorrent to me.

Your vision of a paean of thanks to the benefactors of humanity is thoroughly captivating. It is marvelously conceived! I wish you would write it down just as you feel it. It seems to me that I could do several things in this connection. But the requiem I have dreamed of writing shall not be only about the great. I want to be able to think about father and mother and friend, about the great and the small, the poor and the rich, who have passed on.

You mention Ibsen's play![55] What is the underlying idea? The idiots can live but the others shall shoot themselves. A wonderful lesson for the coming generation! And on this all the cold, technical mastery is wasted! I haven't yet read Lie's book but—to use your own words—I wonder if milord sees phantoms in broad daylight?[56]

I am sure this blessed Christmas season will also place great demands on you until it is over. But then—it must come.

Warm greetings to all of you from Nina and from

Yours truly,
EDVARD GRIEG

14

Troldhaugen at Bergen, June 2, 1891

Dear Bjørnson!
Thanks for the corrections! I find them excellent. Only this: I will stumble over the expression "sacrificed *us* to stone gods" until I get used to it. But musically it makes no difference to me.

You stated in Christiania that your quotation, "This is the highest commandment" etc., in the context in which you used it, might be construed as trickery. You are certainly right about that. But why not introduce the idea through some words in the spirit of the original context? For example: "Love one another! This is the highest commandment," etc. Or perhaps even better, just: "Love!" (For this can apply to both God and man.)

I understand perfectly well that this is actually none of my business! And *musically,* of course, it is not. But I am sure there must be something in my suggestion. My common sense tells me that.

---

55 Grieg is alluding to Ibsen's new play, *Hedda Gabler*, in which two of the leading characters—Ejlert Løvborg and Hedda Gabler—shoot themselves. In a letter dated December 23, 1890, Bjørnson had written to Grieg regarding the play: "What a damnable thing—damned by improbability and witchcraft. In the end people will just laugh at it."

56 Grieg is alluding to Jonas Lie's recently published novel *Onde Magter* (*Evil Powers*), which Bjørnson discussed negatively in a letter to Grieg of December 23, 1890.

Still, I realize more and more what wonderful things there are in what you have written. But I am an idiot. I am like a cat going around a saucer of hot milk, and I can't get going. What I want now lies beyond my reach. When I try to touch it I shrink from it. I am too clumsy. But it will come. Send me some of your self-confidence. That's what I need. In former days, without knowing it, you have given it to me on more than one occasion.

Warmest greetings to all of you! From both of us!

Yours truly,
EDVARD GRIEG

15

Troldhaugen, July 23, 1891

Dear Bjørnson!
If you want to change the beginning, there is still time, because to date I have come no further than to "sniff" at your text.[57] I think I understand what you mean, but when you want "direct speech" I will answer that the indirect, the expository, just at this place is especially suitable for the music. Remember how much direct speech comes later!

I have just welcomed one of your guests to my home. The Englishman Delius,[58] a talented and modern musician, a man with the highest ideals. I am going with him to the Jotunheim mountains, where I will get the strength to throw myself into your "direct speech". Warmest greetings to all!

Yours truly,
EDVARD GRIEG

16

Christiania, November 6, 1891

Dear Bjørnson!
That I'm swindling you out of 500 crowns is divine![59] In the face of such arguments I yield immediately. So do as you wish, I will do my best. But—it will no longer be as I have conceived it. The text will lose for me that which is best, that

---

[57] On July 14, 1891, Bjørnson had written that he wanted to write a new beginning for the *Peace Oratorio*: "This is a great improvement, but just at the moment I don't have time to do it! Hurrah for the summer, the season of imagination."

[58] English composer Frederick Delius (1862–1934), a close friend of Grieg, was a great admirer of Norway and enjoyed hiking in the Norwegian mountains. Grieg called him the "Hardangervidda Man" because of his special love for the vast mountain plateau ("vidda") of Hardanger.

[59] On November 4, 1891, Bjørnson had written to Grieg that he (Bjørnson) could earn 500 crowns by publishing the text of the *Peace Oratorio*, so if Grieg opposed his doing so he would thereby "swindle" him out of this money. Bjørnson's text was published in the Christmas, 1891, issue of *Folkebladet*. Later it was printed in *Verdens Gang* and in a publication of the Danish Peace Association.

which is inexpressible, that which creates the trembling of enchantment (as it did in "Olav Trygvason"). Now I will be glad if ulterior motives do not prevent me from keeping up steam during my work. It seems as if you have no feeling for the fact that the big risk for me is that the publication of the text just *now* will paralyze my creative urge. But it has already happened anyway. And I will tell you this right now, that if I note a lack of enthusiasm I will go on strike and stop working. Still, you may be sure—I repeat—that I will do my best and will use all the energy I can muster.

You should have been in the Students' Association the other evening. The rest of us were just surrogates. And yet there was a triumph in this defeat. Thank you for your warm words![60]

Yours truly,
EDVARD GRIEG

17

Leipzig, March 5, 1896
Hotel Hauffe

Dear Bjørnson![61]

You to honor, you to cherish,
I myself would gladly perish.
I'll respond to your gibberish
with some verse that's—well, cleverish.
I think you are plain tigerish
to demand I deliverish
an "impromptu" so feverish
for Dodge City's Norwegerish.
Clearly, now, my "I" I'll nourish
with the peacock plumes that flourish

---

60 On May 13, 1891, the Norwegian Students' Association had decided that beginning on May 17 of that year the union insignia (symbolizing the union with Sweden) should be removed from the flag and the "pure Norwegian" flag be flown atop the Association building. That autumn, however, the Association received a proposal to reinstate the union flag. The issue was hotly debated at a meeting of the Association on October 31, and at one point Grieg asked for the floor and made an impassioned speech against the proposal and concluded by urging those present to join in singing the Norwegian national anthem. According to the report in *Verdens Gang* on November 2, the anthem was sung "with an enthusiasm and warmth such as it perhaps has never before been sung by Norwegian young people." In his letter of November 4, Bjørnson praised Grieg for his brave action: "Dear, dear Grieg, what you did there in the Association will live as long as your best songs. I have always said it: That little fellow has character so complete and courageous that he could nourish ten Ibsens. There is sympathy for and involvement in our national cause. Thank you so much! I have a right to express those thanks on behalf of thousands, for I know how Norway feels about such things. Thank you from those thousands!"

61 The Director of the Norwegian-American "Grieg Male Chorus" in Fort Dodge, Iowa, probably Olaf Martin Oleson (1849–1946?), had asked Grieg if he would kindly write a choral piece for them. Grieg shared the

'round you since you insisterish
that I do this task nightmarish.
You should know, my friend so bearish,[62]
your verse has this trait contrarish:
It gives unconventionarish
zeal that, wholly arbitrarish,
makes me spurn tasks customarish.
Your word, though't be antiquarish,
makes all else quite ancillarish,
sets me hopping coronarish,
lest I fail my friend so rare-ish.
Well, old bear (soon centenarish),
let us not be adversarish;
I will act disciplinarish
(I'm not revolutionarish)
and conclude this verse bugbearish:
You to honor, you to cherish!

P.S.

Just one question corollarish:
Is it true that in your parish
two young Bjørnsons (both so fairish)
soon shall wed? Extraordinarish!
We send love complimentarish.
All your children soon binarish!
Greetings warm and debonairish
Both to you and lady fairish,
From E.G. and his—Ninarish! (Ow!)

---

request with Bjørnson, who hastily wrote a little poem, "Norwegian tones", which he sent to Grieg on February 29, 1896, accompanied by the following rhymed letter:

> "You to honor, you to cherish,
> I myself would gladly perish.
> Quick as lightning wrote this down,
> Which I send—and don't you frown—
> With this note. You'll get no rest
> Till you send to his address
> Music—and some verse as well.
> Hi to Nina, your sweet belle!

Grieg, who very much enjoyed this sort of thing, responded in kind. He also immediately set Bjørnson's poem, calling the composition "Impromptu". A facsimile of the manuscript, which is preserved in the Bergen Public Library, was printed in the Bergen newspaper *Bergens Tidende* on November 24, 1959. The piece was first printed in *Edvard Grieg's Complete Works* vol. 17, 1985.

62 "Bjørn" is the Norwegian word for "bear".

18

Troldhaugen, July 1, 1896

Dear Bjørnson!
Some years ago I imagined that the *Peace Oratorio* lost its attraction for me when you allowed your poem to be published and the press got wind of the fact that I was going to compose it. There is *some* truth in this, for there is something of the mimosa in me. But the main cause lies deeper: I wasn't equal to the task. Partly because the text was more comprehensive than I had anticipated, and particularly because just at that time my health got the serious blow that shook my creative energy to its very roots. As proof I can cite the fact that the only things I have written since then have been short works. How I wait for the day when the body's leadenness will subside so that, forgetting myself, I can throw myself into one of the larger forms! Dear Bjørnson, if you feel a desire to see your poem set to music, do what you wish with it and don't worry about me! This is hard to bear, but it needs to be said.[63]

Bjørn once spoke to me about your plan for some Aulestad songs.[64] I told him then—when he mentioned the idea of setting them to music—the same thing I am now telling you: Remember that I am an incorrigible son of West Norway from head to toe. Is that the sort of person who should do this job? But—time will tell. One thing I know, that if I feel it is something appropriate for me, I will do it, preferably when no one asks me to—yes, even if someone asks me to keep hands off.

That you, the 65-year-old, want to be a lyricist for a whole year is splendid! All I can say is "Hurrah!" That's the way it ought to be. What is this damn nonsense about "growing out of" lyricism!

Warm greetings!

Yours truly,
EDVARD GRIEG

19

Troldhaugen at Bergen, July 15, 1896

Dear Bjørnson!
I can openly recommend that you choose Selmer, who seems to me to be just the man to write the interludes in *Kongen* [*The King*]. I look forward to reading the play again—am taking it along to the mountains. That will provide just the right wide horizon for it.[65]

---

[63] On July 7, 1896, Bjørnson replied, "Dear friend, of course I will wait for you. It will be best if *you* do it." Nothing more came of the planned collaboration, however. Grieg never resumed work on the oratorio. Only one song based on Bjørnson's oratorio text was completed: "I Loved Him", which probably was composed in 1896 but was first published posthumously in 1908.

[64] Grieg never wrote music for any Aulestad poems.

[65] The Christiania Theater had declined to stage Bjørnson's play *The King* (1877) because it was considered too tendentious. In 1896 Bjørnson had asked Grieg's counsel as to whom he ought to approach about

Since you haven't heard from Svendsen, the reason probably is that he isn't up to writing. I was told recently that he has been frightfully close to death, is visibly exhausted, and is trying to regain his strength at Holmenkollen.[66] He has the constitution of a horse. Otherwise he would have succumbed long ago with that "wild life" he leads. I weep inwardly when I think of what he is and what he should have been in view of his beautiful talent—one of the absolutely greatest of our time. One can say of the Norwegian national character what Peer Gynt said of our Lord: "He does many things well, but—an economist he is not!"[67] It is terrible what Norway loses because so many of its best people carry on like madmen. It is the uncontrollable force that falls short of its goal. But on the other hand we have something with which to make real men—something that one day, no doubt, we will gratefully try to develop. For what nation in Europe has amassed treasures of unused material like we have? There is our future, our viability, no matter how divided we may be. Philosophy? Hell and damnation!

Warm greetings to all!

Yours truly,
EDVARD GRIEG

20

Troldhaugen, July 10, 1897

Dear Bjørnson!

Thanks for your lines! I have unfortunately had to say no to the idea of participating in the St. Olaf's Day celebration.[68] You really didn't have to urge me, for I had plenty of desire, if for no other reason than to see you again. But it would be impossible for me to be along. I am wiped out by the winter's exertions and illness and am having, in general, a bad time of it. In a few days I am going to the mountains—the only medicine that helps me. Now it has become doubly painful to miss the festival, since *you* have asked me to come.[69] But I require of you, Løken,[70] Wexelsen[71] and the others that you respect my health concern, which is absolutely compelling.

Besides, from a national perspective, what purpose would be served by my

writing incidental music for the play. Notwithstanding Grieg's advice, it was not Johan Selmer (1844–1910) who wrote the music but Johan Halvorsen (1864–1935). The premiere performance of the play, with Halvorsen's music, took place at the National Theater in Christiania on September 11, 1902.

66 Holmenkollen sanatorium near Christiania.

67 Grieg is quoting—not quite accurately—some lines from *Peer Gynt* Act 4, scene 2.

68 The observance in Trondheim on July 29, 1897, of St. Olaf's Day, commemorating the death of King Olaf Haraldsson (St. Olaf) in 1030. Bjørnson had been pushing to get the day recognized as a national holiday on a par with Constitution Day (May 17). In 1897 he gave one of his great speeches at the festivities in Trondheim.

69 Bjørnson had written on July 7: "Just do it! Rent a room for yourself and Nina, let us meet there and have a happy time together."

70 Hjalmar Løken (1852–1932), who was editor of the Christiania newspaper *Norske Intelligenssedler* from 1890 to 1918.

71 Vilhelm Andreas Wexelsen (1849–1909), at that time school superintendent in the Trondheim diocese.

presence? Unlike you, I have no resources to work with up there. You yourself are the great chorus, the great orchestra that responds to your slightest gesture—precisely what I lack. For I would not have wanted to be along just "for meat and flesh." And then the Trondheim Cathedral, which refuses [permission for the concert]! It has been my dream to get *Land-sighting* grandly performed at precisely this place sometime. Orchestra from Christiania, many singers, the organ playing! It should be overwhelming, I think. I heard it last fall in Stockholm and had never dreamed that it could sound so powerful!

Ah, these Swedes! How they sang "Yes, we love this land"[72] at the station upon our departure from Stockholm! God help me, I began to believe it was true! It is as you say: We have nothing to fear from the people—the Swedish people, I mean. For our worst enemies are among ourselves. Everything, everything is divided. No, it's too crazy, the whole mess. And then this clergy that crushes every tender shoot that appears! There is just one thing that all of us should do: resign from the state church, this lizard that in view of its complete impotence has nothing to stab with but a poisonous stinger. There is something in me that could become a criminal if I didn't choose to avoid that repulsive creature.

You position yourself in the middle of the road in front of it and say, "Go ahead! Lash out! Stab!" I can't do that. But I admire you, who can. (. . .)

What do you say to the idea of meeting in Rome next spring? That would be something!

Warm greetings to both of you from Nina and from

Yours truly,
EDVARD GRIEG

21

Christiania, Thursday September 14, 1899
Victoria Hotel

Dear friend!
Never have I felt as I do today that I dare to call you my friend! I am glowing inwardly from all the wonderful memories when I think of those unforgettable days at Aulestad. It is as I said; I have, so to speak, gotten my life enclosed within a frame: the home in Piperviken[73] and the home at Aulestad, that is the frame. And this I know, that my life in sorrow and in joy would not have developed the way it did without this frame. If I am to imagine you and your great influence on me—and on my art—I must think of you at home. I had almost forgotten how I saw you that time that we were together in Piperviken. But now it is as clear

---

[72] The Norwegian national anthem.
[73] Piperviken was a run-down section of Christiania where the Bjørnsons lived in the 1860's when the young Edvard Grieg began his work there as a music teacher and orchestra conductor.

as a bell, as if it were yesterday. Your joy in life and your belief in it is as it was then, except that now it is permeated by a mildness and tolerance that have gripped me deeply and in double measure—because I myself have long sought in vain to acquire those qualities. But during these days you have shown me the way. Many small, casual remarks indicated this.

The Dreyfus battle[74] was hard, it is true, but up there with you I got rid of such a load of pessimistic ballast that I think I am now going to conquer the sterile self-criticism that for all too long has inhibited my art.

Yes, dear Bjørnson, I feel in this moment as if we were taking one of our glorious walks in the forest; the soughing of the wind in the spruce trees is mingled with thoughts and words.

Sigurd Hals[75] just came in and sends greetings. So: Thank you! Thanks to you, Karoline and the whole Bjørnson clan from Nina and from

Yours truly,
EDVARD GRIEG

22

Copenhagen, October 2, 1899
Hotel King of Denmark

Dear Bjørnson!
A small parenthesis in the midst of your "Beyond Human Power"[76] mood! Tell me how many hundreds of nasty letters you received in connection with your support of Dreyfus? Tell Langen[77] that after following his advice and allowing the publication of my answer to Colonne I have been pelted with libelous French communications, both signed and unsigned. At least two of these maintain that

---

[74] Edvard and Nina were guests of the Bjørnsons at Aulestad for a week in September, 1899. The event that overshadowed everything else during that week was a new development in the so-called Dreyfus affair—a development to which both the Griegs and the Bjørnsons reacted with deep indignation: A French court martial, despite widespread indications of trumped-up charges and falsified evidence, reaffirmed the guilt of Captain Alfred Dreyfus (1859–1935), a French Jew, who had been convicted of high treason.

Just at this time Grieg was considering an invitation from the French conductor Édouard Colonne (1838–1910) to give some concerts with the Colonne orchestra in Paris, and unable as he was to separate the artistic opportunity—which was very attractive to him—from the human-rights issue, he found himself in a moral dilemma. Emboldened by Bjørnson, on September 12 he sent a letter to Colonne declining the invitation. This letter was published in a German newspaper and was soon reprinted in newspapers all over Europe. Four years were to pass before Grieg would again set foot on French soil. See Grieg's letter to Colonne of October 4, 1899 and to Bjørnson of October 2, 1899. Dreyfus's conviction was reversed in 1906 by a civilian court of appeals, but the French military did not officially acknowledge its mistake until September 7, 1998, when General Jean-Louis Mourrut, head of the army's historical service, made a public statement on the matter to France's Central Consistory of Jews.

[75] Sigurd Hals (1859–1931), piano manufacturer and music publisher in Christiania.

[76] *Over Evne I* [*Beyond Human Power*] was a play by Bjørnson published in 1883. He wrote another play by the same title that was published in 1895.

[77] Albert Langen (1869–1910), who was married to Bjørnson's daughter Dagny, was at Aulestad when Grieg wrote his letter to Colonne.

I of all people should not speak of justice—I who am from a country whose king is a descendant of a traitor by the name of Bernadotte!!! And one is supposed to put up with such nonsense! Still, one thing is certain: The shameless and furious tone of these letters is typical. At the very least it only adds to the proof of Dreyfus's innocence. That I am advised not to come to France, from where I would be kicked out again—well, that I can tolerate. The world is bigger than France. (From Russia and elsewhere come enthusiastic paeans to me for the same reason.) But if I were to cast a horoscope for the forthcoming Zola trial, judging by the French letters to me the outlook is not good.[78]

Why has your beautiful poem[79] not been published in *Verdens Gang* so that our many friends here—yours and mine—can read it? Just let Thommessen[80] reprint it from *Ringeren*, where Bjørn tells me you plan to publish it.[81]

How wonderful it must be to share with the young people your most sublime thoughts! I wish I were up there!

Warm greetings to all of you!

Yours truly,
Edvard Grieg

23

Copenhagen, January 16, 1900
Hotel King of Denmark

Dear Bjørnson!

It is you who have been endearing toward us in the year just past—and we return your friendship tenfold! And that despite the fact that you stand where you do in the language controversy![82] How sad it is for me and many with me that *you*, with your rhetorical skills, stand where you do! I think that we who live in West Norway are more favorably disposed toward the rural language because it is so much more beautiful and often gives expression to that which is noble in the character of the people. If, like me, you had lived in Hardanger for a year and a half at an important point in your development, you would find it easier to understand me. But I do not doubt for a moment that your lecture has done some good in relation to the "language fanatics"—these narrow-minded people who

---

[78] The French author Émile Zola (1840–1902) was acclaimed by freedom-lovers throughout the world in 1898 when he published his famous article "J'accuse" ("I accuse") in the newspaper *L'Aurore*. He was convicted of libel and sentenced to a year in prison but escaped the punishment by fleeing to England.

[79] Grieg is alluding to a poem Bjørnson had written for Grieg during their time together at Aulestad in September, 1898.

[80] Olav Anton Thommessen (1851–1942), editor of the Christiania newspaper *Verdens Gang*.

[81] *Ringeren* was a literary and philosophical journal published in Christiania in 1898–99. It was founded and edited by Sigurd Ibsen (1859–1930), the son of Henrik Ibsen, who was married to Bjørnson's daughter Bergliot (1869–1953). Bjørnson often contributed material to *Ringeren*.

[82] See footnote 160 to Grieg's letter to Frants Beyer of November 25, 1899, for a detailed discussion of the language controversy and of Grieg's and Bjørnson's respective views regarding that controversy.

go so far as to look down on those of us who only love the language but cannot speak it!

You aren't coming to the Ole Bull unveiling! Would that I could say the same. For judging from what Sinding[83] did with you, Ibsen and, I am told, with Mrs. Gundersen, I am very worried about what he will perpetrate with Ole Bull. (...)

Listen to this: In April I am coming to Christiania, where I will conduct a concert at the National Theater. When this is over I will give a benefit concert for Rikard Nordraak's monument. Will you be in Norway then? And would you say a few words about Rikard? Or write a little prologue? Or would you prefer to be free from all tasks? I won't try to talk you into it, but you know very well that no one is more at home with this sort of thing than you and that the whole affair will be empty without you.[84]

While I think of it: Did you get my bust?[85] Sigurd Hals promised to send it.

Last week I had the pleasure of performing my three violin sonatas in collaboration with Lady Neruda-Hallé for the best Danish audience, which responded with the warmest understanding.[86] Believe me, we performed well, but the concert had a special significance for me in that these three works are among my best compositions and represent periods in my development: the first, naive, reflecting many antecedents; the second national; and the third with its wider horizons.

I visualize you sitting up there at your writing desk with the white valley in front of you! And all the thoughts bathed in light and peace and contemplation. Magnificent!

---

[83] The sculptor Stephan Sinding (1846–1922) created a statue of Norwegian violinist Ole Bull (1901) after having created some controversial statues of Bjørnson (1898) and Ibsen (1899) to stand in front of the National Theater in Christiania, and one of the actress Laura Gundersen (1832–98) to adorn the foyer. The Bull statue was unveiled on May 17, 1901, in an atmosphere of great festivity. Grieg had written a piece for male chorus for the occasion—"To Ole Bull"—a setting of a text by Norwegian poet J. S. Welhaven (1807–73). Bjørnson had planned to write the text but gave up on it.

[84] Grieg had taken the initiative in arranging for a monument to be erected to Rikard Nordraak in Christiania. To raise money for the project he gave a Nordraak concert in Christiania on April 28, 1900. In an open letter in *Verdens Gang* on May 1 he thanked the musicians who had participated and added, "I encourage the public to support, with the same enthusiasm it displayed during the concert, the request that will be published in a few days to make a contribution to the monument to Rikard Nordraak. I further request that the Norwegian singing societies, with the assistance of our artists, further the cause by giving Nordraak concerts. If this is done, the monument will soon be raised and the nation will have shown that it understands what it owes to the brilliant composer of 'Yes, we love this land' [the Norwegian national anthem]."

One thing that irritated Grieg enormously was that at the very time that he was trying to get his project off the ground, a committee in Christiania launched a separate effort to raise money for a "Nordraach Fund" to erect another monument in the composer's memory. The end result of the two efforts was two monuments, one at Nordraak's grave in Berlin and a huge statue of Nordraak designed by Gustav Vigeland (1869–1943) and erected in Nordraak Square in Christiania. Bjørnson spoke at the unveiling of the monument in Berlin on May 17, 1906. When Grieg came to Berlin to give a concert in April, 1907, he laid a wreath on his friend's grave. See Grieg's diary entry for April 13, 1907 in Benestad & Halverson (eds.), *Edvard Grieg: Diaries, Articles, Speeches* (Columbus, Ohio, 2001).

[85] Grieg is referring to a bust designed by the sculptor Mathias Skeibrok (1851–96).

[86] The concert took place on January 9, 1900. Czech violinist Wilhelmina Neruda (1838–1911) was married to Sir Charles Hallé (1819–95), founder of the Hallé Orchestra in Manchester, England, hence the name "Lady Hallé". Grieg had first performed with her in Christiania on October 15, 1866.

I also say "hurrah" for you and all who are at Aulestad and hope for a good meeting in the new year!

Warm greetings to all from Nina and from

Yours truly,
EDVARD GRIEG

24

Also an "open letter" to Bjørnstjerne Bjørnson[87]
[Printed in the Christiania newspaper Verdens Gang]
Christiania, December 7, 1904

Dear Bjørnson!
Hamsun's "open letter" to you has made me angry. Unfortunately, you will certainly see it and I want you to know, therefore, that many others share my anger. With this letter Hamsun has compensated for his lovely poem written in honor of your seventieth birthday. He begins by calling you "master", as if that could cover up the breadth of his accusations. I know this "master". If I myself were to have this title thrown in my face I would know that there is danger afoot.

Isn't it a relic of barbarism that prominent men in this society cannot think —not to mention act—without having ignoble motives ascribed to them? This is what I have witnessed again and again with great frequency in our dear city for a couple of months, and it is turning my stay here into a doubtful pleasure.

Whether the consular issue[88] could have been solved in the fullness of time through Blehr's[89] efforts I will not presume to decide. But my common sense tells me that any insinuation that you bought your Nobel prize with your so-called political about-face is totally disgraceful.

And as for the other insinuation—"Then you went to Stockholm." "It looked so bad."—the only thing to say about it is that it is as far-fetched as it is cheap to apply the expression "Stockholm-goers" from the Wergeland period[90] as an

[87] Grieg's open letter to Bjørnstjerne Bjørnson was occasioned by an open letter to Bjørnson from Norwegian author Knut Hamsun (1859–1952) that had appeared in the non-political Christiania newspaper *Forposten* on December 5, 1904. In the letter, Hamsun fiercely attacked Bjørnson for having gone to Stockholm to accept the Nobel prize in literature in 1903—an act that Hamsun construed as a betrayal of the Norwegians who were struggling for political independence from Sweden.

[88] The so-called "consular question" was a major bone of contention between Norway and Sweden during the years 1892–1905. In 1892 the Norwegian Parliament passed a resolution establishing an independent consular service, which they thought Norway had a right to do. But the Swedish king refused to approve the resolution on the grounds that Norway had no right to take such action without prior authorization from Sweden. The issue was very much alive in 1904 because of the failure at that time to find a compromise acceptable to both countries.

[89] Otto Albert Blehr (1847–1927), who was the highest-ranking representative of the Norwegian government in Stockholm in 1902–03, played an important role in the union negotiations.

[90] Norwegian poet Henrik Wergeland (1808–45) was a symbol of Norway's desire for independence during the first half of the nineteenth century.

insult to the men of our time. Hamsun knows this as well as we do, and the condemnation of this insinuation is, therefore, self-evident. And what shall one say about accusing a man like you who, with your life behind you, have reached the pinnacle of fame—accusing you of such reprehensible status-seeking! How psychologically unlikely! Why, it's an improbability that approaches impossibility!

I don't know what can be behind it, but it seems to me as if a prevailing majority of the younger talents that now feel impelled to take charge don't have the foggiest idea of what it was that inspired the men of the 60's and 70's and 80's with a sense of mission. They don't seem to have the foggiest idea of the belief in our cause—no, more than that: the belief in the future's cause, the homeland's cause—that absolutely filled our souls. This belief gave birth to a joy that caused us to approve and admire everything viable that sprang up around us. And now? What do people believe in now? Maybe in themselves, insofar as they sense within themselves the capacity to kick others out of the way? I surely know it from my own art. I see it around me in other arts, in literature, journalism, politics—everywhere. What persecution sickness! What insidious casting of suspicion! Here they lie as if in a well-concealed trench and aim with poisoned weapons at us whenever they find an opportunity.

Still, I do not want to be unfair to Hamsun. He, at least, does not hide. He speaks openly in his own name. That should be acknowledged. But otherwise he is no stranger to the art of crawling into hiding when he says, "Some of us younger ones travel around a little, we meet other people—at least as many as you—and from the younger age group we hear this and that." To this we may reply that there are also other people who travel around a little, meet people and hear this and that. What Hamsun has heard, however, is only the howling of a combination of hate, pettiness and slander.

It is unfortunate that Hamsun's style is so captivating that it hypnotizes the reader and paralyzes his sound judgment. That is why his assertions are dangerous. He is almost a virtuoso at the art of lying in wait behind his words. Listen, for example, to this: "It was an exceedingly malicious accident of fate that this trip (to Stockholm) had to follow so quickly after your change of tactics." It is absurd to allow himself to be misled by this happenstance into uttering a witticism such as: "The emperor shall not even provide an occasion for suspicion." To the contrary, in my opinion. He shall *precisely* give such occasion. It is only the bad conscience and the philistine caution that does not do so. Your entire life has been marked by scorn for suspicion. Hamsun surely should be able to see that if he wanted to. And your wonderful scorn for suspicion has never been expressed more forcibly than by your trip to Stockholm.

That you should have refused the Nobel prize? Ha! That makes me laugh. Why? Is it, perhaps, as I told you at Aulestad: "That damned Nobel prize! The first thing it will do is teach you, the great optimist, about people's deceitfulness!" Is the Nobel prize like the Rhine gold in Wagner's *Ring of the Nibelung*—which was accompanied by a curse?

There would, in any case, have been a reason if you, after such a premonition, had refused the Nobel prize. But what can one say about Hamsun's motivation? About his political—and human—casting of suspicion?

Believe me, Bjørnson, no clearsighted, independent-thinking person in Norway doubts for a moment that you have acted with integrity. Therefore: Glory to you and thank you—because you gave occasion for suspicion!

And now this stuff about age! Shall it, too, be dragged out? After I had read the first two acts of *Daglannet*[91] I thought, "My, how young and vigorous!" It's infuriating that all means shall be used when it is a matter of "elbowing one's way" —as Georg Brandes[92] once said specifically of Hamsun—through the men in Norway who make a difference because they are sitting in the driver's seat.

You said last year, "It is a great art to understand how to grow old." After Hamsun's article I say: It is a greater art to understand how to be young. To understand youth's and manhood's relationship to old age. To understand that it doesn't work to apply the ordinary measure of old age to extraordinary people.

I began these lines as a private letter to you. But as I wrote I began to realize: This sort of thing should be said aloud so that all can hear it. Unfortunately, it ought not to be my inexpert pen that takes on the task of replying to Hamsun's letter. But no one else is doing it. So the stones must speak.

I can conclude with Søren Kierkegaard: "This shall be said, so let it then be said."[93]

With heart-felt greetings,

Yours truly,
EDVARD GRIEG

25

Christiania, December 20, 1904
Hotel Westminster

Dear Bjørnson!
I don't have a lot of courage. It's just a tiny reflection of yours! But I always have had a sense of justice and a strong indignation when it is violated—and that I still have as strongly as ever.

For half a year I have written to you almost every day in my thoughts. Then came Hamsun's garbage and I swore: Today I will do it! And then it went just as I wrote: I started writing a private letter to you and midway through it I stopped:

---

91 *Daglannet*, a play by Bjørnson published in 1904. It was dedicated to "The Swedish Academy in gratitude". The name of the play is taken from the estate where the action takes place.

92 Georg Brandes (1842–1927), Danish aesthete and man of letters.

93 The quotation is from Søren Kierkegaard (1813–55): *Samlede Værker* vol. 14, p. 83.

Damn it all, this could be said publicly! But I was afraid of doing you a disservice, while my intention was to do both you and the truth a service. Therefore it was only after a conference with Thommessen and Collin[94] that I ventured to leap out into the dirty flood that is called the press.

In your letter[95]—thank you for it!—you do not say a word about Hamsun. That is very beautiful of you. But I would have liked to have gotten a little taste of the psychological "herring salad"[96] that could motivate his altered attitude toward you. Collin said that a few weeks ago Hamsun perpetrated a singularly bruising critique of Ibsen's letters. Why does such a talented man act like this?

You know how much we would like to see you in March. But it depends on a lot of things that are still beyond my control. This winter I have more or less just been keeping my head above water, and between Christmas and New Year's we are going to Copenhagen. Up here the air is stifling—both the political and the economic air. We must indeed be a childish people, not yet mature enough to govern ourselves. We lack a feeling for moderation in all its forms—yes, even for social morality. We are as a nation what Dagny said of Erling:[97] a creature of pleasure! Never before have I understood this as clearly as I do now! And in our enjoyment of pleasure we are without a goal. If this is true, a day of judgment must come upon us. That is the inexorable law of logic.

What a strange Christmas letter! Shame on me! The lower level is out of order, that's the reason for it. Wish Karoline good luck with her lower level: I'm glad that it is in working order again. For old friendship's sake I request of her that she do some repair work on mine when we meet again!

And with that I send the most heartfelt greetings to you old, dear, blessed people from Nina and from

Yours truly,
EDVARD GRIEG

26

Copenhagen, February 22, 1905
Hotel Phoenix

Dear Bjørnson!
To my great sorrow we must give up on South Europe this time. Immediately when I came here I got bronchitis and influenza, and I have still not regained my strength after being sick in bed for almost two months. The doctor forbids me to undertake the travel—which also forbids itself. I'll have to be content if I am

---

[94] Christen Collin (1857–1927), a literature historian who in 1902 had written the first biography of Bjørnson.
[95] This letter from Bjørnson is not extant.
[96] "Herring salad" ("sildesalaten") was a nickname for the Swedish-Norwegian union flag, the only flag authorized for use in Norway at this time. In radical Norwegian circles "herring salad" was used as a term of contempt in the struggle for the right to fly the pure Norwegian flag, i.e., the flag *sans* the union insignia.
[97] Dagny Bjørnson (1876–1974) and her brother Erling (1868–1959), children of Bjørnstjerne Bjørnson.

able to crawl home again—and fight with all "the united". A splendid unity, where even the government is split! I hope and believe that you will not regard me as a poor patriot when I say now as I did before: *Not one drop of blood for the sake of the consular issue.*[98] I find that this view harbors more human self-respect than the one that is now playing so strongly on the strings of national honor there in Norway. We seem to be surprised by the trickery of the Swedish union policy. God knows why. Ever since 1814[99] it has never been any different. It is true: What the Swedes have offered us this time goes beyond everything that happened earlier. But that does not justify us in acting unwisely. I know from conversations with informed Norwegians that if we now unilaterally implement the consular act, the Swedes will triumph. For this matter is more intimately connected to and entangled with the ministry of foreign affairs than most people realize—yes, so intimately that despite a Norwegian law, when it comes right down to it we couldn't do a thing without the Swedes if the law is to be carried out. And then, after nine years of increasing divisions, we will once again be in the middle of an even worse impasse. No. "The transformation of the union into a defense pact," that is the question before us. To place this on the agenda of the day is "to act". The other alternative is merely a brief respite. And I would be surprised if this wasn't the meaning behind Hagerup's[100] brave words to Boström.[101]

But now to something else. You remember my Dutch friend Julius Röntgen, who is equally distinguished as a person and as a musician. He will turn fifty on May 9 and will be presented with an album containing bits of poetry, music and paintings from all the important men and women he has met in his life. I exact a promise from you that you, in a spare moment, will jot down a couple of lines and send them to me. That will crown the work, for he is one of your very greatest admirers.

Thank you, thank you for the New Year's Day letter. Yes, that day began gloriously: Right at breakfast time a letter came from "King Bjørnson", a half hour later a telegram from "Kaiser Wilhelm II", and after another half hour I of course expected a telegram from—the pope in Rome. But it didn't come. A great disappointment that depressed me to such an extent that the influenza bacillus had an easy time getting me down.

Yes, dear Bjørnson: Your profound words, "It is a great art to understand how to grow old," constitute one of life's greatest *leitmotifs*. For the moment all I

---

[98] See footnote 88.

[99] Norway became subject to the Swedish crown in 1814.

[100] Francis Hagerup (1853–1921), a Norwegian politician who played a prominent role in the process leading up to the dissolution of the union with Sweden. He was a member of the Conservative party and served as prime minister from autumn 1903 to March, 1905. He was succeeded by Christian Michelsen (1857–1925), who successfully negotiated the final separation from Sweden.

[101] Erik Gustaf Bernhard Boström was the Swedish prime minister 1891–1900 and 1902–05. In November, 1904, he made a proposal to Norway which prime minister Hagerup rejected on grounds that it would "place upon Norway a stamp of dependency." On April 13, 1905, Boström stepped down.

understand is that I shall not press your hand in Rome, and I won't get over that right away!

Warm greetings to both of you from Nina and from

Yours truly,
EDVARD GRIEG

27

Copenhagen, March 6, 1905
Hotel Phoenix

Dear Bjørnson!
It is indeed strange: Since sending my latest letter to you I see in *Verdens Gang* that my opinion regarding our political crisis is also yours. And may it not also be Hagerup's? I cannot get it through my head that people do not see that the sick point is the union as it now is. To dig in here, that is the politics of the future. Hagerup sees logically and far; if he can stand by his words he will surely take the helm again.

The crown prince's[102] letter seems to be a disaster. But it has contributed mightily to the unification of Norway. This crown-prince regent is becoming our worst enemy, and there is no hope for Norway until we get rid of him. Yes, watch out that our people don't start to think like this: "Stang—Gunnar Heiberg!"[103] There are ugly forces on the loose, brutal and negative forces! We must detest both of them. To incite the young people to war and to scorn is a disgrace in times like these. It is the old Norse contentiousness and desire for revenge that is rampant once again.

You would be doing me a great favor if you enlighten me about one matter. Until—I think the mid-80's—foreign affairs, including the consular question, were under the king. He ruled alone. But then he handed these matters over to the Swedish ministry of foreign affairs without consulting Norway, whose affairs thus came under the Swedish civil authorities, who were not responsible to Norway. Where was Norway when this monstrosity occurred? Why was there no angry opposition to this colossal act of tyranny? I was in Christiania at that time but didn't hear a word about it. There, then, *we* have failed to intervene and in so doing have laid the foundation for all the discord that has followed. Is this not correct? And how does it all hang together?

You totally forgot the Röntgen matter in your last letter. Dear Bjørnson, take a piece of paper as you read this and send it off immediately.

---

102 Swedish crown prince Gustav, later King Gustav V (1858–1950).

103 Georg Stang (1858–1907) was the Norwegian defense minister in 1900–03, and he thought Norway had to be heavily armed and to risk war with Sweden in order to end the union. Norwegian writer Gunnar Heiberg (1857–1929) was known for his extremely radical opinions regarding both moral and political questions.

You tempt me! If you knew how things really are for me you wouldn't do so. It is absolutely out of the question—unfortunately. If I could improve a little, yes; but with my weakness, my asthma, my nights! No, no, "it is a great art to understand how to grow old."[104]

Warm greetings to both of you from both of us!

Yours truly,
EDVARD GRIEG

28

Copenhagen, May 13, 1905
Hotel Phoenix

Dear Bjørnson!

Illness, illness and always illness! Otherwise you would have heard from me long, long ago with thanks for your dear letter containing your contribution to Röntgen's fiftieth birthday and because you wish you could see us in Rome. But now just listen to this: I go every single day to a specialist in digestive illnesses to be pumped out and have a rectal washout, and Nina is in the Øresund hospital with an infection in her arm—so you understand that we can't travel. Nina's attack is indeed a light one, so I hope that within a fortnight we can head for home.

Down here people are celebrating Help-the-children Day, the hundredth anniversary of J. P. E. Hartmann's birth,[105] and in addition they know how to enjoy themselves in the characteristically harmless Danish manner. What a glaring contrast to life back home!

Whatever happens up there, I think now as before that the opinions that led to Hagerup's resignation will eventually win the day. It is possible, of course, that what they want to push through right away will succeed. There is something moving in the childlike determination that currently prevails. That is the sort of thing—childlikeness—that often has luck on its side. If only it could succeed!

If anyone down here asks me, I make no secret of the fact that my opinion is different from that of the majority—but I constantly add that it goes without saying that I bow before the now seriously united Norway, which indeed wants only what is our right. What the result will be clearly depends on how the chessmen stand on Europe's chessboard on the day of decision.[106]

---

[104] See Grieg's "open letter to Bjørnson" of December 7, 1904.

[105] Danish composer J. P. E. Hartmann (1805–1900), whom Grieg greatly admired.

[106] Both Bjørnson and Grieg opposed the use of force in the conflict with Sweden. They thought that a negotiated solution was the only way out of the impasse. On September 9, 1904, Bjørnson had expressed his view of the matter in *Verdens Gang* as follows: "Do not force any matter in which one thinks one has the king against one, because he is also the king of another and bigger country which he must take into account. And if we, under such circumstances, absolutely cannot achieve what is our right, then rather dissolve the union. The Swedes cannot withstand a Norwegian wish for this that wins two-thirds of the voters. Their own interest tells them that there are other forms of association that would be more useful and more secure than the union. This is what I mean when I say that in our conflict with our sister nation we should negotiate, 'just negotiate'."

I have thought so much about you, who now stand as an observer there where a generation and a half ago you were the movement's vital center. But—faithful to your conviction, and elevated high above the day's commotion, you can be a witness to a patriotic enthusiasm that in the end is a fruit of your own work, even if you at the moment might have wished that it were being expressed differently. It is springing up all around you. That is something you must view with gratitude!

I sincerely hope that we may still meet! Maybe at the end of May en route through Christiania if, as rumor has it, you intend to come home. Or in September.

Goodbye for now, then, dear Bjørnson! Affectionate greetings to you and Karoline from Nina and from

Yours truly,
EDVARD GRIEG

29

Copenhagen, May 16, 1907
Hotel Bristol

Dear Bjørnson!
Sigrid Wolf-Schøller came up to us yesterday to ask me to write to you. She didn't want to do it herself, because she is her mother's daughter. The fact is that Asta Nørregaard has painted a portrait of Mrs. Lucie Wolf that many people in Christiania wish might be purchased for display in the foyer of the National Theater.[107] Some ladies had started to take the matter into their own hands but in Mrs. Schøller's opinion had botched it. She says the only way to rescue it now is for you to write four lines proposing that friends of Mrs. Wolf's art acquire the picture. Mrs. Schøller also wanted me to sign the proposal. But that is nonsense. It is best that it come from you alone. I have now given her the following suggestion, with which she concurred and which I hope you will also approve: no public advertising, newspaper articles or other outward hullabaloo that looks good but accomplishes nothing. No, with your lines, which you will please send to me, I will get Sigurd Hals to assign a man to the job of collecting contributions (minimum ten crowns) from a list of potential contributors. In that way the required 2,000 crowns will soon be gathered. Still, this shall not be done now, when everyone is leaving the city, but the first of September. But *your four golden lines shall be written now!* As you can see, I'm not so stupid yet!

Dear Bjørnson, I have admired and embraced you for your statement regarding the language controversy.[108] I probably would not have done that earlier on.

---

107 Norwegian soprano Sigrid Wolf-Schøller (1863–1927) was the daughter of Lucie Wolf (1833–1902), an actress from Bergen whose career included stints at The National Stage in Bergen and the Christiania Theater and the National Theater in the capital. The portrait of Lucie Wolf by Danish painter Asta Nørregaard (1853–1933) hangs to this day in the foyer of the National Theater.

108 See also Grieg's letter to Bjørnson of January 16, 1900.

But since the language issue has become a matter of political power, I have distanced myself from it. I will continue to love the rural language as before, but all this stuff about forcing it on people is against nature. A language forms and develops not by coercion but according to very different laws of nature.

I have had wonderful concerts in Germany,[109] and I think I succeeded in speaking on behalf of Norway's position. The jubilation was tremendous. Of course *you* were there as the grand chieftain. The sound of your mighty wings resounded through the auditorium in *Bergliot*, in *Sigurd Jorsalfar*, in *Landsighting*, in *Before a Southern Convent*, in many lyrical songs!

Yes, dear Bjørnson, I daresay that the thanks I send you today are more sincere than ever before. The gratitude growing out of the mood of youth has evolved more and more into the gratitude of acknowledgment, of conviction. The years have ripened it, deepened it, enriched its content. May you feel that everything in me that is good joins in expressing this gratitude!

We will be here the rest of the month, and then I will use Finsen's electric light-bath to repair my nerves and my shortness of breath.

It's beautiful here! At your place it is certainly even more beautiful!

Warm greetings to you and Karoline from Nina and from

Yours truly,
EDVARD GRIEG

---

109 Grieg conducted concerts in Munich (April 6), Berlin (April 12) and Kiel (April 26). The concert in Kiel proved to be his last public performance.

To Hakon Børresen

During his lifetime, the Danish composer Hakon Børresen (1876–1954) was regarded as an outstanding orchestra virtuoso. He was strongly influenced by Grieg's friend, Norwegian composer and conductor Johan Svendsen, who was his teacher. Grieg became acquainted with Børresen in Copenhagen and invited him to the Norwegian music festival held in Bergen in 1898.

Grieg's letters to Børresen are preserved in Det kgl. Bibliotek (The Royal Library, Copenhagen).

1

Christiania, November 16, 1903
Hotel Westminster

Dear Mr. Børresen!

Thank you so much for your sextet![1] When I received it I was sick, as is altogether too often the case these days, so the music just had to wait. During the last few days, however, I have started to perk up a little, and yesterday I had the pleasure of reading through your composition. I congratulate you wholeheartedly. You have a quite impressive mastery of the material; how solidly built, clear, transparent and sonorous it is from beginning to end!

In addition to your own significant talent, I admire in the highest degree the ability Svendsen must have to impress upon others the importance of the characteristics of artistic technique that have contributed so much to his own greatness. I admire also your capacity to be influenced by that which is excellent in so brilliant a nature as that of Svendsen. But you must not be blind to the fact that in this capacity to receive influences there may lie a danger. But you surely know this as well as I, and I will therefore just restrict myself to expressing the joy that I have had in getting acquainted with so well-crafted a composition.

I really don't know which movement I like best. All of them must sound wonderful. When I get to Copenhagen I'm going to order an evening in your home with the *Sextet* and Svendsen! So now you know. But when shall it be? That I don't know myself. I have now been fussing with doctors and pharmacists for four weeks for the sake of my damned bronchitis. There is no possibility of my leaving Norway until after Christmas.

In a few days we will be going to Voksenkollen[2] for three or four weeks, and we will spend Christmas with Bjørnson at Aulestad[3]. By then I hope to be strong enough to travel southward. It will be fun to meet again. NB: for me. Because for

---

[1] *Sextet for Strings*, op. 5, from 1901.

[2] Voksenkollen Sanatorium was located on the outskirts of Christiania, near Holmenkollen.

[3] Aulestad was the name of the estate of Norwegian author Bjørnstjerne Bjørnson (1832–1910). It was located in Gausdal, not far from Lillehammer.

a high-spirited young man like you it can't any longer be particularly alluring to spend much time with

One who is strongly afflicted with the seriousness of old age,
EDVARD GRIEG

P.S. Warm greetings to everyone! Also from my wife.

2

Troldhaugen, August 5, 1907

Dear Børresen!
(. . .) Although my health does not allow me to work, I have nonetheless had a marvelous time recently, thanks first to Röntgen and more recently to Percy Grainger, who left yesterday.[4] What an artist and what a person! What a high level and what a child! The words apply to him: "Aus Mitleid wissend, der reine Thor."[5] You presumably are familiar with his piano-playing. It comes very close to perfection. How he plays Bach! And Chopin! And how he handles the English folk song! And then there is this, that it is always the art that concerns him, not himself. In my youth that was something we took for granted, but now the advertising business has turned it upside down. Yes, he is one of the few. And his knowledge of and enthusiasm for the Scandinavian sagas, languages and music can be of great value to all of us. I hope that you will get to know him well. You have the advantage of youth, the opportunity to be influenced and developed by so important and serious a mind. In his presence I feel doubly how far I have been left behind, but the mutual affection nonetheless makes time spent with him a joy. He is now in Jutland with his mother at a place bearing the beautiful name "Svinkløv" ["Pig's gulch"]. In October he will play my *Piano Concerto* in Leeds, where I am also "supposed" to appear.[6]

In any case, I hope that we will see each other this fall. For no matter what happens, I'm leaving this place. Warm greetings, first and foremost to the Børresen household, then to the Svendsens and Hansens[7] etc.

Your devoted
EDVARD GRIEG

---

[4] Grieg's Dutch friend, the composer and pianist Julius Röntgen (1855–1932), and the Australian-born pianist Percy Grainger (1882–1961) had just visited Troldhaugen. See Grieg's diary entries for July 27 and August 5, 1907, in Benestad & Halverson (eds.), *Edvard Grieg: Diaries, Articles, Speeches* (Columbus, Ohio, 2001).

[5] Grieg is quoting from Wagner's opera *Parsifal*: "Knowing through compassion, the innocent fool." According to Wagner—and Grieg as well—it is only through compassion, shared suffering, empathy that one can achieve real insight and understanding.

[6] Grieg was scheduled to participate in the music festival at Leeds in September, 1907, but had to give up the trip at the last minute because of illness. He died in Bergen on September 4—after having packed his bags and actually started out for Leeds the day before!

[7] The reference is to Norwegian composer and conductor Johan Svendsen (1840–1911) and Copenhagen music publisher Alfred Wilhelm Hansen (1854–1923).

To Hans Lien Brækstad

The Norwegian writer Hans Lien Brækstad (1845–1915) operated a book and paper business in Trondheim during the years 1866–77, then moved to London, where he became a publicist for Norwegian art and culture. In 1905 he played a prominent role in the English press as a spokesman for the Norwegian side of the union controversy between Norway and Sweden. In 1906 he was appointed Norwegian vice-consul in London. Grieg made extensive use of his connection with Brækstad during his visits to England.

Grieg's letters to Brækstad are preserved in Nasjonalbiblioteket, Oslo (National Library of Norway, Oslo Division).

1

London, Friday evening, March 22, 1889
5 The Cedars, Clapham Common

Dear Mr. Brækstad!
8 P.M. Just came home, tired and wiped out! Excuse me for not being up to going out again to send a telegram.

I do not have a portrait of my wife from Norway or Germany. But Elliot & Fry's[1] half-length picture of her certainly is good and is already in the shop windows. They have not sent any to us yet.

I am furious over the interview in the *Pall Mall Gazette.*[2] I thought you knew the facts, otherwise I would never have subjected myself to such treatment. As recommended, I have even sent the editor a song in manuscript, for which he not only has not thanked me but has allowed his music critic to say unkind things about my *Piano Concerto*, which is one of my best works. How can I get the truth out? By speaking with him personally? If you will be in the city at the concert tomorrow, perhaps we can meet immediately thereafter.

Sincerely yours,
EDVARD GRIEG

2

London S. W., March 23, 1889
5 The Cedars, Clapham Common

Dear Brækstad!
Thank you for yesterday! It was a damned nuisance from beginning to end! But that isn't what I wanted to say. It was the letter we talked about to the editor of *Pall Mall Gazette* that I wanted you to take a look at. I hope you will understand

---

[1] Elliot & Fry, a London firm dealing in photographs.

[2] The March 20, 1889, issue of the *Pall Mall Gazette* contained an interview with Grieg concerning his artistic development. He was so displeased with it that he felt compelled to correct its many errors, not least out of concern for the German press.

my wretched English, correct it where necessary, and send the corrected copy back to me with instructions as to the address to which I should send it and what I should say in the cover letter to the editor.[3]

Sincerely yours,
EDVARD GRIEG

3

Paris, April 12, 1889
Grand Hotel

Dear Brækstad!
Please do me the big favor, *immediately* upon receiving this, of securing a copy of the issue of *Pall Mall Gazette* in which my answer appears and sending it on my behalf to the editor of *Berliner Tageblatt*, Berlin. For the very thing I feared has happened. I have learned via letters received from Germany today that people in Berlin have attacked me because of the interview article. *Berliner Tageblatt* has carried it, other papers have reprinted it, and the music journals have added their own comments. A Berlin friend writes that people are furious and that I must defend myself. It's scandalous that they haven't also carried my reply, but the fact is that the interview has fallen into the hands of my enemies. Please, therefore, move as quickly as you can to send my reply directly to *Berliner Tageblatt*. Unfortunately, I don't remember the exact date. Wasn't it the 28th?? I can count on everything being done as requested, can't I? Thanks in advance!

We are leaving Paris on Sunday. We will be in Leipzig for a short time, then will go home via Copenhagen.

Greet Mrs. Grøndahl![4]

Sincerely yours,
EDVARD GRIEG

---

[3] The draft that Grieg sent to Brækstad—in somewhat faulty English, as Grieg himself acknowledges—was as follows:

Dear Sir!
I am obliged to beg you publish in the *Pall Mall Gazette* that, thanks to my bad English, your interviewer has not understood me at all when I was speaking about my relations to the German art. My intention was only to say, that the great traditions of the German music often make the German musicians and critic unjust in their judge of the works of foreign composers. No music and no musicians has gone to my heart like the German and the Norwegian music generally and my own especially has been met with so much sympathy there, that it would be more than unthankful, if I would forget it.

Believe me, dear Sir,

Yours faithfully,
EDVARD GRIEG

[4] Norwegian pianist and composer Agathe Backer Grøndahl (1847–1907).

4

Christiania, October 31, 1889

Dear Brækstad!

Thank you for your letter! No doubt you have read in the newspapers of the remarkable degree to which the scenes from *Olav Trygvason* have won the hearts of everyone here in Norway.[5] I will not depend on the national enthusiasm but will wait until I see the effect on an unbiased audience.

The performance in Copenhagen is the 15th or 16th of November. Hopefully the music will be in print by the beginning of December. Yesterday my publisher sent me an English translation (probably by F. Corder,[6] the Wagner translator) that seems to me to be excellent. I was very happy to see this, because I think this composition will be suitable for performance in England. If I did not find Mr. Berger,[7] the secretary of the Philharmonic Society, (I am sorry to say this) so totally unbearable I would establish a connection with the Society. But never mind, an opportunity will surely present itself. It is unlikely that I will come to England during the current season. If this decision is changed, however, I will let you know.

Enclosed you will find the program for my last concert with the text of *Olav Trygvason.* I am also sending you, in accordance with your wish, the beginning of a "Sword Dance,"[8] which is the tune accompanying the underlined text on the last page of the program.

Believe me, I am rejoicing over my reconciliation with Bjørnson after a hiatus of sixteen years.[9] He was completely overwhelmed by *Olav Trygvason* and is now thinking about resuming work on the libretto. During these days I have experienced moments that I would never have dreamed were possible in Norway. The whole affair was a grand thawing. You should have heard Bjørnson's after-dinner speech at a farewell party last evening in the Grand Hotel! It's too bad there wasn't a stenographer!

We leave tomorrow for Copenhagen, where the rehearsals will begin immediately.

Warm greetings, also from my wife, who, unfortunately, has a sore throat and does not dare to sing.

Sincerely yours,
Edvard Grieg

---

[5] The premiere of the first three scenes of *Olav Trygvason,* text by Bjørnstjerne Bjørnson, took place at a concert of the Music Association in Christiania on October 19, 1889. See Grieg's letters to Bjørnson.

[6] The English composer and author Frederick Corder (1852–1932) translated the texts of several of Grieg's songs into English.

[7] There had been some correspondence between Grieg and Francesco Berger (1834–1933) regarding the honoraria for Grieg's concerts.

[8] Grieg is referring to the so-called "Temple Dance" in *Olav Trygvason.*

[9] Bjørnson and Grieg had had no contact since their falling-out in 1876.

P.S. Would you please write in above the line in the manuscript the English words for "Sverddans af Olav Trygvason" or just "Sverddans". And excuse me for not using proper stationery, but it is late in the evening and all the shops are closed.

5

Christiania, October 27, 1892
Address Hals Brothers Music Store

Dear Mr. Brækstad!
I just read about your marriage in *Dagbladet*,[10] but I didn't know your address, so I was very glad today to find your card. Both my wife and I send heartfelt congratulations and hope that now you will at last find the domestic tranquility that you have sought so long.

For no less than ¾ of a year I have suffered so much that my art has virtually had to take a rest. But now I'm coming back to life again, and in about fourteen days—after I have conducted my music to Bjørnson's *Sigurd Jorsalfar*—we leave for Germany, where we will stay for some time.

Next summer I may go to Chicago, where I have been invited to conduct four concerts of my own works.[11] Just tell me some way to avoid dying of seasickness on the way!

Now I have made a note of your new address, so in the future there will be no way for you to avoid either me or my wife, both of whom send our heartiest greetings.

Edvard Grieg

6

London, December 6, 1897
47 North Side, Clapham Common

Dear Mr. Brækstad!
I'm not crazy about court goings-on, as you well know, but this was in a class by itself. The queen is *sweet*, if one can use this word to describe an old lady.[12] She was delighted. She knew practically the whole program, enjoyed having Nina sing in Norwegian, and asked for more. I then played the "Gavotte" from the *Holberg Suite*.

---

10 *Dagbladet*: a Christiania newspaper.

11 Mr. Harry Randall (1858–1955), a Norwegian-American who was actively involved in planning and promoting a big song festival in Chicago in 1893, had invited Grieg to participate in the festival. See Grieg's letter to Randall.

12 Nina and Edvard Grieg, assisted by Dutch violinist Johannes Wolff (1863–?), gave a concert for Queen Victoria (1819–1901) in Windsor Castle on December 6, 1897. The Norwegian word he used to describe the queen was "søt".

When I was introduced to her she said, "I am a warm admirer of your music." It was all natural and genuine. She talked about *Peer Gynt* and would like to have heard "The Death of Åse" and "Last Spring" for string orchestra. I declined all meals and took the next train home.

See you soon!

Sincerely yours,
EDVARD GRIEG

7

London S. W., December 8, 1897
47 North Side, Clapham Common

Dear Mr. Brækstad!

We were received in the drawing-room and the concert also took place there. Present, in addition to the queen, were only her daughter, Princess Beatrice,[13] and numerous courtiers of both sexes. I see that the *Times* has secured a copy of the program without mentioning that all the music is by me; indeed, it looks almost as if Bjørnson, H. C. Lumbye and Paulsen[14] are composers! Never mind!

It is impossible for me to meet you in the city either Thursday or Friday. This whole week is my worst, with concerts every other day. I hope to see you Monday at the Promenade concert and with your wife after the recital in St. James Hall on Wednesday. Between the concerts all I do is rest. Otherwise I can't survive.

I assume that you received my letter to the editor of the *Century*.[15] How goes it with my answer?

We leave for Cheltenham in a couple of hours. Warm greetings.

Sincerely yours,
EDVARD GRIEG

8

Leipzig, February 6, 1898
Hotel Hauffe

Dear Mr. Brækstad!

First of all I must express my pleasure over the nice article about you in [the Christiania newspaper] *Verdens Gang*. It's a good thing that once in awhile something happens according to one's merits! (. . .)

---

[13] Princess Beatrice (1857–1944), youngest daughter of Queen Victoria.

[14] Norwegian poets Bjørnstjerne Bjørnson (1832–1910) and John Paulsen (1851–1924), Danish conductor Hans Christian Lumbye (1810–74). Why Grieg mentions Lumbye in this context is unknown. Bjørnson and Paulsen were each the authors of several of Grieg's song texts.

[15] *The Century Illustrated Monthly Magazine*, an American publication for which Grieg wrote articles on both Schumann and Mozart. The articles will be printed in new English translations in Benestad & Halverson (eds.), *Edvard Grieg: Diaries, Articles, Speeches* (Columbus, Ohio, 2001).

But now to the music festival, which shall indeed become a reality. Apropos your kind offer, I ask that you—by means of notices to as many English (and American) editors as possible—let it be known that a music festival will be held in Bergen this coming summer between June 27 and July 3 (in conjunction with the international fishing-industry exhibition). The festival will be held under my *auspices* (be sure to use this expression, not "leadership" or "direction") and will be devoted entirely to performances of Norwegian compositions. The famous Concertgebouw Orchestra of Amsterdam, out of interest in the event, has obligingly agreed to participate. A music hall is being built for this purpose in the area where the exposition is to be held. It is designed to accommodate an audience of between 2,000 and 3,000 in addition to providing space for 500 performers.

This is enough for now. The program, which we have not been able to firm up as yet, will come later. The committee chairman now is John Grieg, the book publisher, to whom I ask you kindly to write if there should be any practical questions about which it might be of interest to the English to get information.

In view of some possible expressions of chauvinism in the Christiania newspapers in connection with the involvement of the Amsterdam orchestra, I will ask you—assuming that you share this view—to make propaganda as you are able for the concept that a Norwegian music festival is one in which Norwegian music gets the most ideal performance possible. And here, where it is a matter of an international gathering in which continental Europe is represented, this view of the matter acquires a double significance.

I am up to my ears in letters and telegrams to promote the festival. So excuse this scribbling!

Warm greetings to you and your wife from my wife and from

Yours truly,
EDVARD GRIEG

P.S. Since Mr. N. Vert,[16] because of his interest in the matter, has promised to work at publicizing [the festival], I will ask you to confer with him if you find that he can contribute to the task in some way.

9

Leipzig, February 23, 1898
Hotel Hauffe

Dear Mr. Brækstad!
Thank you for the material you sent! You are right: Now there will be a temporary lull. Later I will send you the program, and then it should also be reported that the famous Concertgebouw Orchestra of Amsterdam will participate.

---

[16] Narcisco Ramon Domingo Vert (1845–1905) was Grieg's concert agent in London.

I can't tell you all the chicaneries to which I have been subjected by people in Christiania because I hold the incomprehensible opinion that a Norwegian music festival is a festival in Norway in which Norwegian compositions get the most ideal performance possible so that, as a result, they are understood by the people—and it matters not, for this purpose, whether the performers are Dutchmen or Japanese! This, it seems to me, is a national view, and if it is also yours then let it be heard. To be a chauvinist is not to be a Norwegian! God deliver me from such people! They do their country irreparable harm! Their "unmasking" is indeed instructive!!!

Warm greetings to you and your wife from

Yours truly,
EDVARD GRIEG

10

Troldhaugen, August 9, 1898

Dear Mr. Brækstad!
Thank you for your English article! It was kind of you to send it to me, for we indeed live in a country where, to be sure, the press reprints interesting foreign articles about our writers' influence on the continent and elsewhere in the world. But we know nothing about our composers, for the relevant [music] journals are not subscribed to and read as are *Deutsche Rundschau, Athenæum, Revue de deux Mondes* etc.. The article you have sent is important, and since you clearly are of the same opinion it would be a just course of action to get it translated for one of our leading Norwegian newspapers. If you will be the agent of justice in this case, you will have the sincere thanks both on my behalf and on behalf of Norwegian music.

I have been working eight hours a day here for several weeks to get my two new compositions—which will be published by Peters this autumn—ready for printing. They are the song cycle based on Garborg's[17] *The Mountain Maid* and *Symphonic Dances* for orchestra. There is not even any interest in our country that such works are being published! And yet—that only makes Norway all the more delightful a place to live! There is here this blessed innocence that is so good for the artistic imagination!

Warm greetings to you and your wife from

Yours truly,
EDVARD GRIEG

---

[17] Norwegian author Arne Garborg (1851–1924).

11

Troldhaugen, September 30, 1898

Dear Mr. Brækstad!

Thank you for the material you sent! And thank you for your interest in the art environment up here. The article in question has appeared in [the Christiania newspaper] *Morgenbladet* and *Bergens Tidende*. In my naiveté, I thought these papers were on top of things to such an extent that they had gotten hold of the article on their own initiative. But no! That would be too much for a Norwegian newspaper. The music festival controversy, which is still provoking articles and brochures criticizing me—all-out, vulgar attacks—has now reached the point where *Morgenbladet* and *Verdens Gang* have decided to give me their full support. And by damn, it was about time. Just think: A protest meeting of musicians was called recently in Tigerville[18] to consider a resolution to the effect that henceforth no one in Christiania would ever again play under my baton! Isn't that the height of foolishness! But almost nobody showed up, so no decision could be taken. There are, then, just a few whiners who can't accomplish anything. But unfortunately—for the moment I had better be careful about appearing in Christiania.

My opinion about the American music journal is that its music supplement is beneath all criticism. I haven't had time to plow through the whole big volume.

My *Symphonic Dances* for orchestra and the songs from Garborg's *The Mountain Maid* have just been published in Leipzig by Peters. The songs with German and English texts. The Nordic edition will be published in a few days by Wilhelm Hansen in Copenhagen.

I will send you pictures of Troldhaugen before I leave from here twelve days from now. We will stay in Copenhagen for the time being. (Address: Wilhelm Hansen's Music Store, Gothersgade 11.) Warm greetings!

Sincerely yours,
EDVARD GRIEG

18 "Tigerstaden": a derisive name for Christiania coined by Bjørnstjerne Bjørnson.

Correspondence with Johannes Brahms

Grieg met Johannes Brahms (1833–97) for the first time during a stay in Leipzig in the winter of 1878–79. Grieg probably was present at the premiere performance of Brahms's *Violin Concerto* on January 1, 1879, with Joseph Joachim as soloist. Two days later he received a special musical greeting from Brahms: the first four measures of the second movement of the *Violin Concerto* in the composer's own hand. Grieg had by then been familiar with Brahms's music for several years, and through his Dutch friend and colleague Julius Röntgen, who was a friend of Brahms, had increasingly become an admirer of the works of the great German master. Röntgen reported in his Grieg biography that Brahms especially appreciated Grieg's *Ballade* for piano.

Brahms and Grieg met again at a New Year's Day party in 1888 at the home of the Russian violinist Adolf Brodsky, who was working in Leipzig at the time and had just premiered Grieg's *Violin Sonata No. 3*. In her book *Recollections of a Russian Home* (Manchester, 1904), pp. 158–59, Mrs. Anna Brodsky reports a delightful incident that occurred at this party: "After the introductions and greetings were over we passed to the dining-room. Nina Grieg was seated between Brahms and Tchaikovsky, but we had only been a few moments at the table when she started from her seat exclaiming, 'I cannot sit between these two. It makes me feel so nervous.' Grieg sprang up saying, 'But I have the courage,' and exchanged places with her. So the three composers sat together, all in good spirits. I can see Brahms now taking hold of strawberry jam, saying that he would have it all for himself and no one else should get any. It was more like a children's party than a gathering of great composers."

Grieg was with Brahms on several occasions in January of 1896. On January 24 he wrote to his Norwegian friend Frants Beyer, "Last week we were frequently with Brahms in Leipzig, where he was visiting for a few days, and we enjoyed his company immensely. I don't understand how a one-sided person like Brahms—one-sided in his greatness, that is—can have such a positive opinion of my music, which, as far as I can see, goes in a very different direction from his. But, taciturn though he is, he nonetheless showed me that he does. His *Symphony No. 4* in E Minor was performed in the Gewandhaus. The first movement of that work, which I had never heard before, is one of his most beautiful creations."

After Grieg's concert in Vienna on March 24 of the same year, Grieg and Brahms and a number of others who had participated in the concert celebrated the event until the early hours of the morning. Röntgen reported in the above-mentioned biography that on this occasion Grieg stood up and addressed a few remarks to Brahms, "speaking so warmly and beautifully that we all were deeply moved. He didn't say anything about his own triumphs, which we all still had fresh in our minds. Brahms listened with bowed head, and when Grieg had finished he slowly rose from his seat, walked over to Grieg and, without saying a word, pressed his hand."

Their last times together were in Vienna in December–January of 1896–97, when Grieg gave one orchestral and two chamber-music concerts. Brahms attended the orchestral concert, which took place on December 19. On January 2, 1897, they both attended a performance of Brahms's *String Quintet* op. 111, which was received with great enthusiasm. That was to be the last time they would see each other.

Three months later—on April 3, 1897—Brahms died. The same day, upon hearing the news, Grieg wrote to Röntgen: "Only now do I fully realize what a man of integrity he was, both as an artist and as a person, as far as I knew him. How glad I am that I was so fortunate as to make his acquaintance!"

The letters from Grieg to Brahms are preserved in Gesellschaft der Musikfreunde, Vienna, the letters from Brahms to Grieg in Bergen Offentlige Bibliotek (Bergen Public Library).

Brahms to Grieg 1

Leipzig, January 3, 1879

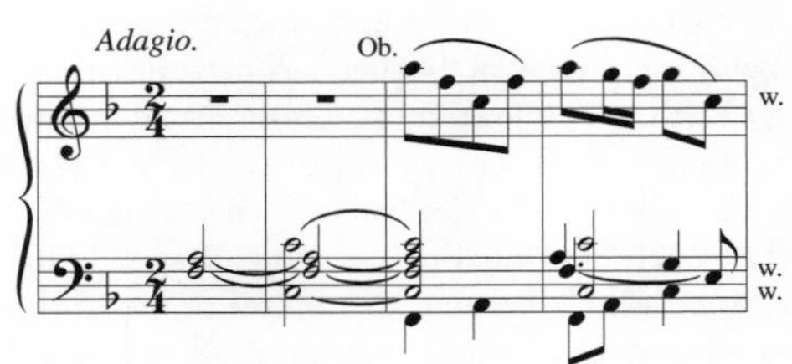

To Mr. Edvard Grieg as a friendly memento,[1]

J. Brahms

Grieg to Brahms 1

Leipzig, April 1, 1896
Hotel Hauffe

Dear Maestro!

The most beautiful and enjoyable hours of my stay in Vienna were those that I was given the opportunity to spend with you, but as a Norwegian I perhaps have not managed to reveal this feeling. Permit me, therefore, to take up my pen to express my most sincere thanks for your friendly courtesy during our last, brief time together.[2]

Just think if you could some day come to Norway! Then, to be sure, I wouldn't be able to show you a "fantastic"[3] night, but I would show you something much better, namely, "a white night!"[4] And quite certainly I would show you something more that, as a matter of fact, I solemnly promised in Leipzig: the secret place where the treasure—your fifth symphony—lies hidden![5] So please, please, do

---

[1] Brahms's handwritten music example shows the opening measures of the second movement of his *Violin Concerto.*

[2] Grieg arrived in Vienna on March 19, 1896, and remained there for one week. He conducted a concert on March 24 with the soprano Ellen Gulbranson (1863–1947) and the pianist Dagmar Walle-Hansen (1871–1954) as soloists.

[3] Grieg here uses the German word *toll* and presumably is referring to Pierre-Augustin Beaumarchais' play *Le mariage de Figaro ou La folle journée* (1781), which as early as 1785 was performed in Vienna in a German translation under the title *Der tolle Tag oder Figaros Hochzeit.* It was this play that provided the initial idea for Mozart's opera *The Marriage of Figaro* (libretto by Lorenzo da Ponte). But Grieg may also be referring to a gathering after the concert of March 24 in Vienna, where Brahms also was present. On April 2, Grieg wrote to Frants Beyer (1851–1918), "Yes, these 8 days I shall never forget. You certainly have gotten word of the artistic success through the newspapers. But to give a full account of those 8 days I would need 8 big sheets of paper. What put everything in the right perspective was the association with Röntgen, Messchaert and Brahms. We had many good times together in the local restaurants, and Brahms was with us to the very end at the party in the hotel the night after the concert."

[4] Grieg is alluding to the fact that at mid-summer at Troldhaugen the sun barely dips over the horizon, with the result that the nights are not only very short but also very light.

[5] As is well known, Brahms composed four symphonies, the last of which was premiered in 1885.

your utmost to come! Norwegian nature, like your most beautiful inspirations, is powerful and serious. It *must* appeal to your inner self!

You absolutely can't imagine how beautiful the day at Semmering was. The blue sky and the white, snow-covered fields were filled with quiet music.[6]

Apropos music: We talked together one day about the critics, toward whom, in fact, I have an insurmountable feeling of shyness. Mr. Ed. H.[7] in *Neue Freie Presse* is now slaying me with silence, certainly as thanks for my not paying him a visit. And he is supposed to be the "foremost" of the lot! To me it fortunately doesn't really matter, but how many younger artists there must be who have to suffer under such uncivil treatment!

Ah well—no more these sounds![8] But once again I send heartfelt thanks and best wishes, also from my wife!

Respectfully yours,
EDVARD GRIEG

Brahms to Grieg 2

[Vienna, April 4 (?), 1896]

Dear Colleague!
When one has been as happy to see someone as we were to see you here, a friendly follow-up greeting such as I received from you is extraordinarily welcome.

For that reason I am very grateful to you for all the friendly and jolly words you wrote regarding Vienna and Semmering. Your tempting description makes me look with genuine longing toward your beautiful homeland.

A little dissonance disturbs me in your letter, but I really have no right to try to resolve it. It has to do with your complaint against Ed. Hanslick, to whom in my opinion you do an injustice. (I suppose we can just as easily wrong critics as

---

6 Semmering is a popular excursion spot in the mountains south of Vienna. In a letter to Frants Beyer on April 2 Grieg wrote, "I got to bed at 2:30, and at 5:30 I got up in all secrecy—to avoid company—in order to join Röntgen for a trip up to Semmering."

7 Grieg is referring here to Eduard Hanslick (1825–1904), who since 1864 had been music critic in *Neue Freie Presse* in Vienna. Through his work as a critic, musicologist and author Hanslick had a significant impact on musicians and on the music-loving public of his day. He was a great admirer of Brahms but a fierce critic of Wagner and the program music of the so-called "new German school". Hanslick's book *Vom Musikalisch-Schönen: ein Beitrag zur Revision der Ästhetik der Tonkunst*—published in 1854 and translated into English as *The Beautiful in Music* in 1891 (and in a revised edition as recently as 1974)—is a penetrating analysis of many important issues in musical aesthetics. Grieg's reference to Hanslick constitutes something of a *faux pas*, for Brahms and Hanslick were close friends—as is clearly evident from Brahms's response to Grieg's letter.

8 Grieg writes, *Doch – nicht diese Töne!*—a reference to Schiller's text used by Beethoven in the fourth movement of his *Ninth Symphony*. The passage from which these words are taken reads thus in translation:

O friends, no more these sounds continue,
Let us raise a song of sympathy.

Johannes Brahms, triptych from 1889. On December 21, 1900, Grieg wrote to his American biographer Henry T. Finck, "For me there is no doubt concerning Brahms. A landscape, torn by mists and clouds, in which I can see ruins of old churches, as well as of Greek temples—that is Brahms." (PD)

they can wrong us?) Perhaps you are unaware that H., because of his age,[9] has practically given up going to concerts? Only his ardent interest in new works allows him to make exceptions. But regarding your works, for example, he has always expressed himself at considerable length—a fact that you can easily verify for yourself, as his works have been collected and published.

You must forgive me for arguing his case in this way, but I consider him to be an unusually good, honest and well-meaning man.

Once again: Please excuse the epistle, and accept sincere thanks and hearty greetings from

Yours truly,
J. Brahms

Grieg to Brahms 2

Leipzig, April 9, 1896
Hotel Hauffe

Dear Maestro!
Influenza and bronchitis! (Aftermaths of the Semmering rashness!) Otherwise these lines would have come earlier.

---

9 Hanslick was born September 11, 1825. Thus he was 70 years old at this time.

Even as I thank you most heartily for your answer, I would now just like to add a final word to "the dissonance question". Ed. H. reviewed all the important concerts during the week in question and was also present at the concert I conducted. Had I been mistakenly informed regarding this latter point, I obviously should not only have withheld criticism of him: I should also have regretted that I did not have the good fortune—*without* having paid a visit to the critic—to meet the brilliant author Ed. H.; for that is how I have long regarded him, although from a purely musical perspective he is too conservative for me.

Even more strongly, however, I regret that at the time I wrote to you, the Billroth letters had completely slipped my mind.[10] From those letters I should have known of your close relationship to Ed. H. Had I remembered them—you can take my word for this—I would certainly have exercised the appropriate restraint. So please forgive me!

From what I have said you can see, in any case, that I for my part have made every effort to resolve the dissonance that I myself had conjured up.

With hearty and respectful greetings,

Yours truly,
EDVARD GRIEG

P.S. Welcome, welcome, welcome to Norway! But write in advance so that we (Röntgen and I) can be completely at your service.

Brahms to Grieg 3

[Vienna, April 17 (?), 1896]

Dear Mr. Grieg:

You have given me inexpressible joy with your exceedingly splendid picture[11]—but even more with your friendly letter. The latter was very nearly a necessity for me, for I feared after I had sent it that my rather hasty and unclear letter could have provided many occasions for misunderstanding! Now I thank you most heartily for having read it in a friendly way and having construed everything in the best light.

Everyone here hopes indeed to see you again next year, not least one who sends hearty greetings,

Yours truly,
J. BRAHMS

---

[10] Brahms carried on an extensive correspondence with the German surgeon, Professor Theodor Billroth (1829–94). Grieg presumably was familiar with *Briefe von Theodor Billroth*, published by G. Fischer, Hannover/Leipzig, in 1894.

[11] On April 14, according to his account book, Grieg had sent a photograph of himself to four friends and acquaintances including Johannes Brahms.

To Georg Brandes

Grieg was an ardent admirer of the Danish scholar and literery critic Georg Brandes (1842–1927), and the admiration was mutual. Brandes's most important work, the 6-volume *Hovedstrømninger i det nittende Aarhundredes Litteratur* (*Main Currents in Nineteenth Century Literature*), originated in a series of lectures at the University of Copenhagen that began in 1871 and continued over a period of several years. Grieg was in complete agreement with Brandes's radical outlook, not least his attack on the church and other authorities.

Grieg's letters to Brandes are preserved in Det kgl. Bibliotek (The Royal Library, Copenhagen).

1

Troldhaugen, Bergen, June 26, 1903

Dear Georg Brandes!
You have heaped coals of fire upon my head![1] I can now tell you that last year I got so far as to make a note in my schedule book: Dr. Georg Brandes, Hotel d'Jena, Avenue de Jena, Paris. You understand. I had intended to send you a telegram on your 60th birthday. But—yes, but. Why didn't it happen? I reproach myself, perhaps *too* strongly. For I have a vague feeling of having been far from the telegraph office that day, high up in the mountains.

But all the same: Thank you for the coals of fire! I still have a brain that can take it! Your greeting has made me very happy!

Your old admirer,
EDVARD GRIEG

P.S. By the way, isn't this a somewhat dubious compliment—to be the best-known Scandinavian in the world? But I gobble that up too, albeit with the suspicion that at root you are a big joker!

2

[Copenhagen], April 2, 1905
Hotel Phoenix

Dear Georg Brandes!
It is not all great men who keep their word. Double thanks because *you* did so. Moreover, I knew about your splendid lecture in Paris from excerpts in Norwegian newspapers.

---

[1] Grieg had received a delayed greeting from Georg Brandes in honor of his 60th birthday, which had been celebrated on June 15, 1903. Brandes's greeting included the following words: "No Scandinavian in the world is known and revered so much as you. (. . .) My tribute to you concerns not only your art, which has more expert judges than me. At the purely human level you moved me by your action during the Dreyfus affair, which was manly and courageous."

There is still one thing I must thank you for: the interesting article on Andersen's *The Improviser* and *Only a Fiddler* in the current issue of *Politiken*.[2] You should have gotten a big honorarium from Hegel,[3] for many will do as I intend to do: We will read these books more than once.

I have many times wished to congratulate the country that brought forth Georg Brandes. But today—the 100th anniversary of the birth of Hans Christian Andersen—as a Norwegian I will congratulate you on being a son of the country that brought forth Hans Christian Andersen. The children's poet? No. And not the adults' either. He wrote for just one child: the child in himself. If I were to make a speech for Andersen today, I would say that when Ibsen wrote in a rhymed letter, "It's for *beauty* that we hunger,"[4] it doesn't apply to our times. What applies to our times is this: "For the times are hungering for *the child*." This longing for the child—the lost child!—in ourselves is the hidden spring in Andersen's works, for the sound of which we and the whole world are constantly listening. Go ahead and smile smugly, Georg Brandes—but I am right.

Warm greetings!

Your old admirer,
EDVARD GRIEG

---

[2] Danish writer of children's stories Hans Christian Andersen (1805–75). His novels *The Improviser* and *Only a Fiddler* were published in 1835 and 1837 respectively. *Politiken* is a Copenhagen newspaper.

[3] Jacob Hegel (1851–1918), owner of Gyldendalske Boghandel in Copenhagen, publisher of the Andersen novels to which Grieg refers.

[4] The quotation is from Ibsen's *Balloon-letter to a Swedish Lady* (written 1870, first published 1871), a long poem in which the author philosophizes about art and form and the alleged lack of soul and individuality in both Egypt, which Ibsen had visited in 1869, and Germany, which was at war with France at the time of his writing of the poem. The line is quoted as translated by John Northam in *Ibsen's Poems* (Oslo 1986).

To Breitkopf & Härtel

The Leipzig firm of Breitkopf & Härtel was founded in 1719 and today is one of the world's leading music publishers. The firm published two of Grieg's compositions—the *Piano Sonata* in E minor, op. 7 (1866) and the *Violin Sonata No. 2* in G major, op. 13 (1871). Grieg was not pleased with the way he was treated by Breitkopf & Härtel, however, and thereafter he declined to send them any new compositions.

Drafts in German of the letters included here are preserved in Bergen Offentlige Bibliotek (Bergen Public Library).

1

Leipzig, December 2, 1865

Dear Mr. City Councilman![1]
I was pleased to receive yesterday the news that you will print my *Sonata* [op. 7]. I return it herewith and cherish the hope that its future may contribute to my securing a place in your esteemed publishing company.

Respectfully,
EDVARD GRIEG

2

Christiania, May 4, 1868

Breitkopf & Härtel, Leipzig.
It seems appropriate to me that you do not offer an honorarium for my *Sonata* [op. 13] since my *Piano Sonata* has thus far enjoyed such limited success in Germany.[2]

Respectfully,
EDVARD GRIEG

3

Christiania, August 31, 1882

Breitkopf & Härtel, Leipzig.
Having received your kind letter of August 23, I take the liberty of replying: The orchestral arrangement of the minuet movement of my *Piano Sonata* that Mr.

---

[1] Dr. of Jurisprudence Hermann Härtel (1803–75), who in addition to his work in the publishing firm was very active in Leipzig's political and cultural life.

[2] On December 23, 1867, Grieg had offered Breitkopf & Härtel his new *Violin Sonata No. 2* in G major. Since the sale of the *Piano Sonata* had not been as great as they had hoped, they were reluctant, but they nonetheless invited the composer to send the work to Leipzig so they could hear it. Grieg sent it on April 9, 1868, and received a reply dated April 27 informing him that the firm would risk publishing the work on the condition that Grieg would not demand an honorarium. However, the sonata was not published until 1871.

Henriques has made is so sonorously and capably done that it is in any case worth publishing. I can, therefore, to the benefit of the work, applaud his effort.[3]

It goes without saying that the reaffirmation of your desire to get some new compositions from me is pleasant to hear. However, inasmuch as I still have not received any honorarium for the two sonatas—opp. 7 and 13—which, according to the statement in your letter, have enjoyed good sales in recent years, I must regretfully say that I am obliged to decline the honor of seeing my new works published by you. I mention this matter with the greatest reluctance, but since I have now been virtually provoked to do so I had in the name of truth no other alternative.

With high regard,
EDVARD GRIEG

4

Bergen, Norway, May 10, 1885

Dear sir!
It was not my intention to make a recommendation regarding an honorarium, and I have absolutely no desire to take an initiative in the matter.[4] I think, therefore, the most appropriate thing to do is to lay the question aside since it is useless to discuss it further. To what extent my irritation is justified or not can remain undecided. But I, too, must be permitted to have my own opinions. I have had the honor of working with several renowned firms, in any case, that do not share your opinion—firms which, without any urging from me, have in due time paid me honoraria for works from my youth.

The French say, and not without reason: "Noblesse oblige!"[5]

With high regard,
EDVARD GRIEG

---

[3] In a letter of August 23, 1882, Breitkopf & Härtel had requested permission to print the third movement of the piano sonata op. 7, *Alla Menuetto*, in an orchestral arrangement by Danish composer Robert Henriques (1858–1914). In the same letter they expressed interest in publishing new works by Grieg. Grieg's reply precipitated a long response from the firm, dated September 9, 1882, in which they courteously apologized for the fact that Grieg had not had a share in the profits from the sale of the sonatas and asked him to make a suggestion regarding a suitable payment. From Grieg's letter of May 10, 1885, it appears that he did not respond to this request.

[4] Grieg's letter is a response to a follow-up letter from Breitkopf & Härtel dated April 16, 1885.

[5] *Noblesse oblige*: the nobly born must nobly act.

To Adolf Brodsky

Russian violinist Adolf Brodsky (1851–1929) and his wife Anna were close friends of Edvard and Nina Grieg. They had met for the first time in Leipzig in 1887, and the Griegs were frequent guests in the Brodsky home. Mrs. Brodsky writes in her book, *Recollections of a Russian Home* (Manchester, 1904), about a party at which Brahms and Tchaikovsky were present: "In came our dear friends, Grieg and his wife, bringing, as they always did, a kind of sunshine with them. They knew Brahms, but had never met Tchaikovsky before. The latter loved Grieg's music, and was instantly attracted by these two charming people, full as they were of liveliness, enthusiasm and unconventionality, and yet with a simplicity about them that made everyone feel at home" (p. 158). Brodsky, who at that time was professor of violin at the Leipzig Conservatory, was to premiere Grieg's *Violin Sonata No. 3*, with the composer at the piano. A New Year's party at Brodsky's home a few weeks later became something of an event in music history, for among those attending the party were Johannes Brahms, Peter Tchaikovsky and Edvard Grieg. Four weeks later Grieg again met Tchaikovsky at Brodsky's home, and this time Grieg's countrymen Christian Sinding (1856–1941) and Johan Halvorsen (1864–1935) were also present. Halvorsen, who would later play an important role in Norwegian music history both as a composer and as conductor of the National Theater Orchestra of Christiania, was then a student of Brodsky. Descriptions of these events appear in several places: in Grieg's letters to Frants Beyer, in Anna Brodsky's book and in Tchaikovsky's *Autobiographical Descriptions of a Journey Abroad in 1888*.

From 1890 to 1894 Brodsky was concertmaster of the New York Symphony Orchestra under Walter Damrosch (1862–1950). In 1895 he moved to Manchester, England, as concertmaster of the Hallé Orchestra and senior violin professor at the newly founded Royal Manchester College of Music, now the Royal Northern College of Music, Manchester, which owns Grieg's letters to Brodsky.

The Griegs visited Brodsky in Manchester in November, 1897, and the Brodskys paid a visit to Troldhaugen in August, 1906. Brodsky came from England to play in the orchestra at Grieg's funeral in Bergen in September, 1907.

1

London S.W., May 10, 1888
5 The Cedars, Clapham Common

Dear Brodsky!
I wanted so much to write you a "proper" letter, and for that reason I have stupidly delayed writing day after day. But London is a true predator. The city devours days and weeks like other cities take up minutes and hours, and I can see already that I must give up my good intention in order to be able at least to send you this greeting from the giant city.

What can I say about those days in Leipzig and the great times we had together there?[1] I don't know how in the world I can tell you how I feel, and I don't

[1] On December 10, 1887, Brodsky and Grieg had premiered Grieg's *Violin Sonata No. 3* in Leipzig. Grieg is also referring to parties that he attended at the Brodsky home.

want to use a lot of words on such intimate matters. Let me just say that the hours spent on Kaiser Wilhelm-Strasse were unforgettable for my wife and me.

I think altogether too often about your wonderful violin. I have had some rehearsals with Neruda.[2] She plays very beautifully, and there are even certain things in which "das ewig weibliche"[3] really fascinates me. There is "schwung" in her playing, but it is female "schwung". The big, masculine type obviously is not there. She has been very amiable, and at my concert in St. James's Hall on May 16 we shall perform my *F-major Sonata* during the first part, and in the second part will follow the *Romanza* and *Finale* from the *Third Sonata* [op. 45].

The concert is being arranged by Chappell.[4] He is to have *half* of the net income. Fine conditions! But of course one must howl with the wolves with whom one is associating.

You can't imagine what a reception and success I enjoyed in The Philharmonic Society. I have never experienced anything like it before and probably will never experience it again. I quite simply don't understand it. Just this much I understand, that the string orchestra made a wonderful contribution. I was not very satisfied with the accompaniment in my *Piano Concerto*, but I was all the more diligent in rehearsing the pieces for string orchestra, and in the end I achieved an effect that surprised me. It appeared that the music critics, too, were really enthused. If I find something in the papers I will send it to you.

I shall never forget your friendly offer to come back!!

Now I wish you well and send the warmest greetings to you and yours from both of us.

Sincerely yours,
EDVARD GRIEG

P. S. Please show Fritzsch the reviews. I know that he has such a great interest in me that they will make him happy. But you must tell him that I don't want them to appear in his paper[5] as if I were blowing my own horn.

---

[2] Czech violinist Wilhelmina (Wilma) Norman-Neruda (1838–1911).

[3] An allusion to Goethe's *Faust*: "Das Ewig-Weibliche zieht uns hinan" ("The eternal feminine draws us on").

[4] The English impresario Thomas Chappell (1819–1902) had responsibility for the arrangements in St. James's Hall.

[5] Ernst Wilhelm Fritzsch (1840–1902) was a music publisher in Leipzig and was editor of the Leipzig periodical *Musikalisches Wochenblatt*, to which Grieg refers.

2

Leipzig, November 16, 1895
C. F. Peters, Thalstrasse 10

Dear Brodsky!
Thanks for your quick reply to my last letter. (. . .) That I am expected in England in February is something I know nothing about.[6] I have plenty of invitations, but I have to turn them down. Naturally it would please and interest me enormously to be able sometime to conduct in Manchester while you are there, but to come to England in order to give just one concert makes no sense.

However, since I am not English it would be of interest to me to learn what kind of terms are offered to "famous" conductors. Do you know? For a lot of things depend on this. I will tell you honestly that public appearances are now so profoundly agonizing for me that in addition to the possible laurel wreath I also require English pounds—indeed, quite a few of them. Unfortunately, my wife no longer sings publicly, and so far as the *Piano Concerto* is concerned I would be extremely satisfied with the conductor—Brodsky—but by no means with the soloist—Grieg. I might recommend Arthur de Greef (Brussels) or Raoul Pugno (Paris).[7] Both play the piece superbly. If anything comes of the idea, I shall hope to hear more from you soon—by return mail if possible.

As far as I am able to understand from *Wochenblatt*, you have succeeded Hallé as director of an academy.[8] Congratulations! That must really be a proof that you are enjoying yourself in Manchester.

Yes, people know how to make the best of things. Here in Leipzig they have gone so far as to maintain that the damned coal dust is actually very healthful! Oh well, when one proclaims such a pessimistic world-view that the healthiest thing of all is to lie hidden in the earth, one can apply Holberg's words: "The patient died, but the fever left him!"[9]

But now I had better end this prattle. Many thanks to the dear Brodsky's from my wife and from

Yours truly,
EDVARD GRIEG

---

[6] Brodsky had written to Grieg on November 10 recommending that he give a concert of his own compositions with the Hallé Orchestra. Brodsky himself hoped to conduct the orchestra in the *Piano Concerto* in A Minor with the composer at the piano.

[7] Belgian pianist Arthur de Greef (1862–1940) and French pianist Raoul Pugno (1852–1914), both of whom performed Grieg's works, were highly regarded by Grieg.

[8] In 1893, Charles Hallé (1819–95) had fulfilled his dream of establishing a music academy in Manchester. He himself was appointed Director and Professor of Piano. Upon Hallé's death in 1895, Brodsky became Director as well as Professor of Violin. Since 1962 the institution has been called the Northern College of Music.

[9] From Norwegian author Ludvig Holberg's humorous heroic poem, *Peder Paars:* "He died, it is true, but the fever left him." Holberg (1684–1754) used the same line in several other plays as well.

3

Leipzig, December 9, 1895
Hotel Hauffe

Dear Brodsky!
My health gives me so much trouble that I still don't know for sure if I can go to England. Please send me a few words as to the latest date by which I must make a firm commitment.[10]

I had to smile when I heard about Hallé's heirs. Just to prevent these poor people from dying of hunger, I would of course accept Forsyth's proposal with pleasure. Otherwise I do not wish to conduct for an honorarium of less than 50 pounds. That *you* should pay something in addition in order that we might have the joy of seeing our dear friends the Brodsky's again—this idea is quite simply out of this world! Your proposal regarding the three sonatas is as original as it is moving. But do you really think people would come to a concert where the program consisted of three sonatas? I don't think so. The idea about Liverpool is fabulous. An orchestral concert of my own works in this city would really be something.

A few days ago I found a third artist who can play my *Piano Concerto*. His name is nothing less than Sapelnikov. To be sure, I have not heard him play the work, but he is in process of learning it and he is a colossal pianist. He was here and played in the Liszt-Verein [Liszt Society]. He will be performing my *Piano Concerto* in England this spring (April). Thus it wouldn't be such a dumb idea to let him come from London.[11]

I also received today a telegram from St. Petersburg—from Sapelnikov and Schroeder (I have no idea who the latter is)—asking if I would be interested in giving two concerts there at the end of January. It is a peculiar question, and I have just answered that I can consider invitations only from concert institutions. Two concerts in St. Petersburg given by me! No thanks.

Dear Brodsky! You invite us in such a friendly way to stay with you that it feels downright homey. Thank you so much! If only I didn't have this wretched health that really compels me always to stay at a hotel. Ah well, everything can remain up in the air for the time being.

Let us hear a few words from you soon. Hopefully I will be feeling better than at present, as I am quite down in the dumps.

Warm greetings from house to house!

Yours truly,
EDVARD GRIEG

---

[10] Brodsky had written to Grieg that the business manager for Charles Hallé's heirs, Mr. James Forsyth (?–1907), would offer Grieg only 35 pounds, but that Brodsky himself would guarantee the balance of Grieg's honorarium. Brodsky would also play Grieg's three violin sonatas with him.

[11] Grieg had met the Russian pianist Vasilij Sapelnikov (1868–1940) in 1888 at the Brodsky's, in Leipzig, where he had played the piano part in the *Piano Quintet* of Christian Sinding (1856–1941).

4

Leipzig, December 25, 1895
Hotel Hauffe

Dear Brodsky!
My most sincere thanks![12] Everything looks fine so far as the pounds sterling are concerned, but my health is now such that without hesitation I must give up the trip to England altogether, especially because it is scheduled for February and not for late April and May. This is sad, especially because you have had so much inconvenience on my account. How wonderful it would have been with two sonatas, and songs sung by Miss Pettersen[13] (who is enormously talented), but it's no use. Since my answer must be given right away, in my present poor condition I absolutely cannot find the courage to say yes.

Your idea about playing violin pieces by me is brilliant, for as a matter of fact I haven't written any. But make me healthy again and I will shake something out of my sleeve. But then you must also go along with the idea that either these as yet unborn pieces or that damned *String Quartet*, that constantly lies there unfinished like a piece of Norwegian "old cheese", be adorned with your name.[14] (. . .)

Yes, the visit *must* some day become a reality, perhaps as early as next year. In this hope, and with the warmest greetings from both of us, we conclude the unsuccessful Manchester event of 1895. Or, as old Hauptmann used to say at the end of his harmony classes, "And thus we close the pigsty!"[15]

Yours truly,
Edvard Grieg

5

Troldhaugen at Bergen, September 3, 1897

Dear Brodsky!
Among the many plans that you have proposed in your life, the last one is not the worst: the idea that my wife would also pay you a visit! It is in any case a proof that you continually hold us in friendly remembrance, and this has moved us so

---

12 On December 20 Brodsky had mentioned to Grieg that the "sonata story" could become a profitable affair. Instead of the 15 pounds that Brodsky himself had guaranteed, he could now offer him 42 pounds, bringing the total for two concerts to 77 pounds.

13 The Norwegian singer Ingeborg Pettersen (1851–1918) had been very successful in Christiania in the 1880's and 1890's with her premieres of Norwegian songs.

14 Grieg is alluding here to the unfinished *String Quartet* in F Major. He wrote the first two movements in Copenhagen in 1891. After Grieg's death, Julius Röntgen (1855–1932) arranged for their publication by C. F. Peters Musikverlag of Leipzig. Grieg's sketches for the two remaining movements have been printed in *Edvard Grieg: Complete Works*, vol. 20. Röntgen completed these movements, but they have never been published. They have, however, been recorded on a CD in Holland.

15 Moritz Hauptmann (1792–1868) was one of Grieg's teachers in music theory at the Leipzig Conservatory. When he placed a thick double line at the end of a harmony exercise, he often said with a pleasant smile, "Und so machen wir denn den Schweinestall zu!"

deeply that we have totally altered our previous plans. Accordingly, both of us will come to England at the end of October. As far as I know, the concert is in Manchester on November 9. I will give you more detailed information about this.

How I am looking forward to seeing you again! Things have changed so much since we were last together! Tchaikovsky and Brahms have begun the long journey[16] and no longer need to be annoyed by each other's compositions! How clearly I remember the dinner with those two masters at your house on Kaiser Wilhelm Strasse! Those were beautiful days! Later (last year) I had a few happy hours with Brahms in Vienna, but I never saw Tchaikovsky again. His compositions have become ever dearer to me. *Symphony Pathétique* is a masterpiece of the highest order.

Lastly, a request: During our stay in Manchester you must give that damned fog a leave of absence! As I understand it, you have a job in which you are accustomed to giving orders! So: if you please!

Hearty greetings to the splendid trio:
Brodsky!
Mrs. Brodsky!
The four children![17]
(Quite especially the G string!)

Yours truly,
EDVARD GRIEG

6

Troldhaugen at Bergen, July 27, 1898

Dear Friends!

The music festival is over and I can breathe again.[18] I have suffered under more than six months of tension and some unbelievably chauvinistic howling in the press. My cause had the truth on its side, however—and I have triumphed, triumphed wonderfully. There were performances such as we have never before experienced in Scandinavia and never will experience again—yes, as good as I have *ever* heard *anywhere*. Svendsen[19] thinks so too. Everyone who is capable of judging agrees. A well-known Norwegian man of letters[20] who lives in London and who was present has written to me that in his opinion the music festival was

---

[16] Peter Tchaikovsky died on November 6, 1893, Johannes Brahms on April 3, 1897.

[17] Grieg is referring to Brodsky's violin with its four strings.

[18] The reference is to the Norwegian music festival in Bergen June 26–July 3, 1898. Grieg encountered opposition, not least in Christiania, because he engaged the Dutch Concertgebouw Orchestra instead of the Christiania Music Association Orchestra.

[19] Norwegian composer and conductor Johan Svendsen (1840–1911), who at this time was musical director of the Royal Theater Orchestra in Copenhagen.

[20] Grieg is referring to the Norwegian author and journalist Hans Lien Brækstad (1845–1915), who since 1877 had lived in London.

"one of the most important events in our cultural life in this century." And he may be right. And the joy and enthusiasm of the audience (ca. 3,000), which in the course of seven days listened continuously to these marvelous performances! You should have seen the farmers who journeyed long distances and who stood there as reverently as in a church during those wonderful *pianissimos* in the string orchestra, all the while trying to conceal the tears trickling slowly down their cheeks! It was moving—and who can measure the cultural significance of these days in view of such a fact! It's such a pity that you couldn't be here, and above all that you, dear Brodsky, couldn't perform the Sinding concerto here. Granted, I'm not familiar with the piece, but what an event that would have been!

As a person, Sinding is unfortunately becoming more and more a mystery to me. There was just one evening when he seemed to melt a *little*; it was after the performance of his *Piano Concerto,* when I led a *hurrah* for him—and the 3,000 listeners joined in with enthusiasm. He had every reason to be satisfied, for the concerto went as splendidly as it possibly could with the wonderfully elastic Concertgebouw Orchestra from Amsterdam under his leadership (which was, unfortunately, very mediocre). His symphony was played brilliantly under Maestro Mengelberg's[21] leadership, and he had a colossal success with his songs, which were sung by our Lammers.[22] And nonetheless! Ah well, each must be allowed to be himself, that's for sure—and in any case not anything more or other than oneself. One can't require of Tolstoy that he be a Turgenev etc.[23] Such is life.

And you are both in Kissingen and are looking out for the welfare of the dear old stove! Good luck! But why the after-treatment in Switzerland? Why not Troldhaugen? Well, well, I suppose that would be impractical. When you come to visit us in Norway it must be at a time of the year when we have white nights. For this year the season for this is almost entirely over—yes, within a few weeks they will be totally gone. But isn't it about time for you to get serious about putting Norway on the program for next year? (Voices from the mountains: Yes! Yes!)

I am now completely exhausted, and in a couple of days I will leave with Nina and her sister to spend a few weeks up in the mountains. For the winter I have no definite plans. Maybe Italy. I would like to work if I could just get peace and quiet without freezing. For that reason I have summoned all my moral resolve and turned down, without exception, all invitations. Italy, America, Germany, Russia—for now, none of these even exist for me.

Apropos Russia: Yesterday I received a visit from a Russian landowner from the region between Moscow and Odessa (really a large area!). He was very amiable and spoke with interest and "not unmusically" about music. Indeed, he seems to be in all respects an extremely well-educated man. His name is

21 Willem Mengelberg (1871–1951) was artistic director of the Concertgebouw Orchestra in Amsterdam.
22 Norwegian baritone Thorvald Lammers (1841–1922), whom Grieg regarded very highly.
23 Russian authors Leo Tolstoy (1828–1910) and Ivan Turgenev (1818–83).

Engelmeyer—quite clearly not a Russian name—but he regarded himself as a true Russian.

César Cui[24] invited me recently to conduct in Russia. Damn it all, just think if *Brodsky came with his quartet and we could also play sonatas together!* (I would then do a better job of turning pages in *Sonata No. 2*!)

Alas! Now I'm getting sentimental and weak! So: I must close!

Heartfelt greetings! I embrace both of you and wish you—to quote the Russian landowner—*a long life!*

Yours truly,
EDVARD GRIEG

7

Copenhagen, April 26, 1905
Hotel Phoenix

Dear Friend!

That you are tied to England until the 14th of August is quite simply "abominable". For the latter half of August, so far as Norway is concerned, is the worst possible time. The long evenings and white nights are over, the rainy season has begun, nature has lost its freshness, the rushing waters in the mountain streams, rivers, and waterfalls are no more—in short, everything has conspired to deprive you of the beauty and originality that are so distinctive and wonderful for Norway. How in the world does it come about that your vacation begins in the middle of August? In Scandinavia vacations are over by that time. Can't you do something about it? Give it some thought. Maybe you can find a solution. We look forward enormously to the possibility of seeing you in Norway, and I must do everything in order to be in some measure in shape for you. I must exercise, walk, do push-ups, get massages, hold to my diet—in short, I must do everything that might transform old age and illness into youth and health.

If we only had three good string players in Bergen I would have tempted you to take your violin with you! Such a quartet evening at Troldhaugen, that is "The Ideal" (NB, not by Liszt, but something even better!).[25] I remember one evening when the Brussels Quartet was at our house. It was absolutely beautiful. And we didn't even know them!

Apropos music: I haven't touched a piano since Christmas and would embarrass myself terribly if I were to play solo for you. As soon as I get home, therefore, I must also prepare myself with finger exercises before you come. But I will gladly do that. Yes, I will try to stand on my head if you will just come for once!

---

24 Russian composer César Cui (1835–1918).

25 Grieg is here making a play on words with a reference to Franz Liszt's symphonic poem *Die Ideale* (1857).

Cheers! We Norwegians never kiss! But I would willingly make an exception for all of the poor, persecuted Russian people. I wish I could place a bomb under the Russian government and administration, starting with the tsar! They are the worst criminals of our time!

Warm greetings to both of you from Nina and from

Yours truly,
Edvard Grieg

8

Christiania, May 29, 1905
Hotel Westend

Dear Friend!
After many mistakes [by the post office] I received your letter yesterday.[26] We have had a bad time. Some weeks ago Nina suddenly became ill and had to be taken to the hospital. It was "erysipelas", an insidious disease that has absolutely laid her low. The doctors now insist that she must go to a sanatorium for a few weeks before she resumes her duties as lady of the house. But the prospect of seeing you dear friends here with us June 11–18 has aroused us to such an extent that Nina will not be dissuaded. So we are leaving for Bergen by steamer in a few days, and I earnestly request that you *cable* us there as soon as possible to let us know on which day and by which steamer we can expect you.

To be sure, you write only about *yourself.* But greet your dear Anna from us, and tell her that she better not dare to let you travel alone. Not only that, but also that without her we neither can nor will have you and enjoy you alone! If this isn't strong enough to make the point, I don't know what is! One must risk a little seasickness for the sake of dear friends. We, too, are exposing ourselves to seasickness in order to get home before your arrival. Otherwise we would travel in all comfort by land. So: an "Our Father" isn't good enough. We expect Brodsky with his wife and children (i.e., violin). The children must, however, play without accompaniment as I have not touched a piano for half a year. Ah well, it will all work out. The main thing is what one says in Norway today: action!

It is a grave time for my beloved homeland. But we stand united as one person, as one will. We have an excellent government that has our full confidence. We are, in fact, prepared for a military assault, so it is unlikely that anything really terrible will occur! Public opinion in both Norway and Sweden is opposed to any such thing. Just think: In reality the king cannot form a new ministry to achieve his purpose, since not much more than a quite small minority support him. He

---

26 Brodsky's letter of May 18, 1905, in which he had written that he could come to Norway for the period June 11–18.

dares to turn against a whole people, and that will soon cost him the throne. The main questions must be answered during the next few days. I spoke last evening with the head of the government, Mr. Michelsen.[27] It was a true pleasure to observe his composure, simplicity and clarity.

Dear friend, forgive me these political digressions. Here, at the moment, the air is completely filled with politics.[28]

With that let me say welcome, welcome, welcome to Bergen and Troldhaugen. *How very much* we intend to enjoy you during the altogether too short time that you will be here.

Faithfully yours,
EDVARD GRIEG

P.S. That's what I call a silver wedding! An ideal complement to the first wedding! It's a pity that I didn't know about the day! I send my warmest good wishes *post festum*![29]

9

[Christiania], January 25, 1906

Dear Friends!
It is altogether too kind of you to invite us! We hope very much that we can come. If only I knew how everything is going to work out! It is *possible* that after the concerts in London I will have to return home *prestissimo* because of the coronation in Trondheim in June. But fortunately that is not *likely*, as I have declined to write a cantata for this occasion, and I assume that people are sufficiently offended to leave me alone. In that case nothing will prevent me from going to Manchester as soon as I am finished in London. That presumably will be at the end of May, i.e., if I am still living by then! For it is no laughing matter to go to Warsaw at the end of March. My friends advised me against undertaking this trip, but my contacts in Warsaw have no misgivings about having me come. And since the people there pay a good price, I am naturally a slave of Mammon.[30]

Each evening Nina reads from Tchaikovsky's life and letters.[31] You can't imagine how vividly I recognize myself in him! It's appalling—this melancholy

---

[27] Prime Minister Christian Michelsen (1857–1925).

[28] Norway had been in a union with Sweden since 1814, but on June 7, 1905, the Norwegian Parliament (Stortinget) declared Norway's independence.

[29] In his letter of May 18 Brodsky had told Grieg that he and his wife had celebrated their silver wedding privately in Southport, a small seaside village near Manchester.

[30] Grieg did not make the trip to Warsaw in 1906. He did, however, give concerts in Prague, Amsterdam and London.

[31] Grieg presumably is referring to a German edition of Tchaikovsky's *Autobiographical Description of a Journey Abroad in 1888.*

temperament, the most intimate and tense states of mind, everything. He was absolutely not a happy man. In that, too, I recognize myself. But being happy does not, in fact, seem to be the meaning of life. "The nightmare," as Tchaikovsky calls this internal monster that threatens to crush us, seems to manifest itself more and more the older we get.

But—in May there must be a beautiful ray of morning sunshine! Thank you for that![32]

Yours truly,
EDVARD GRIEG

10

Troldhaugen, August 20, 1906

My Dear Brodsky!
If only you had had the slightest idea of how you and your wife—with the obligato, charming and original accompaniment[33]—have gladdened me by your visit! And not only gladdened. Your visit was medicine for body and soul, that is something I feel most clearly of all now that it is over. I thank you again and again because you did not shy away from the long voyage that was required for you to come here.[34]

I have just received the pictures that provide a visual account of your visit. But I feel very ashamed. It really is an upside-down world when you send me the pictures that I should have sent you. As a gesture of thanks I should at least have finished the *String Quartet* for you! In that area, in any case, you can't compete with me![35]

Nina and I both think the pictures are wonderful. A lucky star has shone over the picture-taking.

We have been so happy about your meeting with the [Johan] Halvorsens. He is truly a splendid artist and human being. As an artist he has only one vacant spot in his brain. In other words: He doesn't love Schumann. I have tried to find an explanation for this sad fact, but in vain. I just can't understand it. Maybe it has something to do with Schumann's orchestration. For Halvorsen is first and foremost an orchestra man. I very much regret that you have not gotten to know his achievements as a conductor. And there is one more thing that I regret, NB

---

32 Grieg visited the Brodsky's in Manchester in May of 1906 and while there invited them to think seriously about a trip to Troldhaugen.

33 Grieg is alluding here to Toni Maaskoff (1893–?) and Alfred Barker (1895–?), two pupils that Brodsky had brought with him on the visit to Troldhaugen. See Grieg's diary entry for August 6, 1906 in Benestad & Halverson (eds.), *Edvard Grieg: Diaries, Articles, Speeches* (Columbus, Ohio, 2001).

34 The Brodskys' visit to Troldhaugen lasted from August 6 to 10. Grieg gives an account of the visit in his diary.

35 During one of their conversations at Troldhaugen, Brodsky had reminded Grieg of his promise to write a new string quartet.

as an egoist: that you came to Christiania one day too late to see and hear *Peer Gynt*. In view of that, there is only one thing to do: You must come back!

Along with this letter I am sending the song, "With a Water-lily", which Anna wanted to get acquainted with. It has both German and English translations, each of which is as poor as the other. Since I don't have it as a separate item she'll have to take the whole volume in the bargain.

Nina and Tonny[36] are talking right now about how beautifully Anna expressed herself when she served as your "spokesperson" at dinner. I felt exactly the same way. A spokesperson like that can serve you well.

We send our warmest greetings to all of you and wish you the best at Marienbad—also that you will not be treated like "golden geese!"

And so, for now, cheers. Send us a postcard soon about how things are going!

Yours truly,
EDVARD GRIEG

P.S. Nina has just told me that [the song Anna was interested in] wasn't "With a Water-lily" but "Hope". This song is no. 26 in the same volume, and the German translation is pretty good.

11

Christiania, December 14, 1906
Hotel Westminster

My Dear Brodsky!
It's a damn shame that Mr. Urbánek[37] doesn't give me any definite dates. The concert agencies in other cities where I have been invited are impatient and are pressing me to such an extent that I can't wait any longer. I have already had to make commitments up until April 1. After April 15, though, I will be available, NB, if the dates are firmed up by December 24. Is it negotiations with your quartet that are taking so much time? It would be a pity if everything should come to nothing.

I enclose the score of an orchestral piece that has just been published and about which I either spoke or wrote to you several years ago.[38] You thought at that time that I should send it to Hans Richter.[39] For that I am much too modest—and arrogant! But of course I would be very happy if you could find an

[36] Nina's sister Tonny Hagerup (1844–1939).
[37] Mojmir Urbánek (1873–1919) was Grieg's impresario in Prague.
[38] Grieg is referring to *Old Norwegian Melody with Variations*, which was published by C. F. Peters Musikverlag in Leipzig in 1906.
[39] Austro-Hungarian maestro Hans Richter (1843–1916) became conductor of the Hallé Orchestra in Manchester, England, in 1899.

opportunity to show it to Richter—if, after reading through it, the piece interests you. I think it is one of my best works, but unfortunately it is not likely to bring forth X number of curtain calls. I must stress that immediately—and that is very awkward, because orchestral conductors, including the best ones (Nikisch,[40] for example), are very concerned about curtain calls. That is perfectly evident from the composition of Nikisch's programs!

An unusually fascinating book has recently captured my interest: the correspondence between Brahms and Mr. and Mrs. von Herzogenberg![41] I had a long-lasting friendship with the von Herzogenbergs. (By the way, it was at their house that *we* met each other for the first time!) Yes, that book gives one a glimpse into noble souls! What lofty, pure air! Those wonderful people become so alive for me that I absolutely cannot believe that all three of them are dead—and that I am still living! You really must have a look at this book.[42]

We continue to cherish the memory of those beautiful summer days that you gave us! I am so grateful to you. How much I enjoyed you! Hearty greetings to both of you!! You dear, dear friends!

Yours truly,
EDVARD GRIEG

P.S. What are the boys doing? Give them our warmest greetings!

---

[40] Austro-Hungarian maestro Arthur Nikisch (1855–1922) conducted the Boston Symphony Orchestra in 1889–93 and the Budapest Opera 1893–95. In 1895 he became artistic director of both the Berlin Philharmonic and the Leipzig Gewandhaus orchestras.

[41] German composer Heinrich von Herzogenberg (1843–1900) and his wife Elisabeth (1847–92), a pianist.

[42] Max Kalbeck (1850–1921), (ed.), *Briefwechsel von Johannes Brahms mit Heinrich und Elisabeth von Herzogenberg*, Berlin, 1906.

To Alexander Bull

Alexander Bull (1839–1914), the son of virtuoso Norwegian violinist Ole Bull (1810–80) and his first wife, Félicie Villeminot (1818–62), was trained as a violinist but spent most of his time as an impresario, primarily in Paris. With his background in both Norwegian and French culture, Bull served as a bridge-builder between Norway and France around the turn of the century. He assisted Grieg at his concerts in Paris and translated several of Grieg's letters to French recipients. When he was in Norway he lived in the family home built by his father at Valestrand, near Bergen.

Grieg's letters to Bull belong to Bull's great-great-grandson Knut Hendriksen (b. 1944) of Stockholm, who found them in the house at Valestrand. They were published in the book *Arthur de Greef—en venn av Edvard Grieg* [*Arthur de Greef—a Friend of Edvard Grieg*], by Bernard Huys and Eivind A. C. Eikenes, Stavanger 1994. The letters included here in translation are derived from this book and are used with the kind permission of Messrs. Hendriksen and Eikenes.

1

Bergen, January 1, 1889

Dear Bull!

Before I leave Bergen (tomorrow) I feel impelled to ask you to convey to the head of the Pleyel firm my greetings and many thanks for the piano, which now stands properly installed at Troldhaugen. My old instrument will be shipped from here in a few days via Rotterdam. Immediately upon receiving the new piano, I wrote to Mr. Lyon[1] (that is his name, is it not?) and hope that he has received my letter. I have not heard anything from him to date.

I take this opportunity to ask you to greet De Greef[2] when you write and to tell him—no, don't tell him, for one ought never to praise people as kind and brilliant as he is to their face—but rather say *of* him that he is the best interpreter of my piano music that I have ever encountered. It is surprising how he understands my intentions. Whether I refer to the mountain or the valley, whether I am refined or coarse or even rough-hewn in a typically Norwegian fashion, he is with me through a strange instinct that I am at a loss to explain. But this you must tell him, that I feel very happy and honored by his sensitive appreciation

---

[1] Gustave Lyon (1857–1936) became proprietor of the piano firm Pleyel, Lyon & Cie (previously Pleyel & Wolff) in Paris in 1887. The firm also arranged concerts and had its own concert hall. The instrument Grieg is writing about was a gift from the Pleyel firm and Gustave Lyon. Grieg wrote about the gift in a letter to Frederick Delius (1862–1934) dated December 9, 1888: "Think of my surprise: A few days ago the Pleyel firm, about which I know nothing whatsoever, sent me a wonderful grand piano as a gift! The man must be out of his mind!" Grieg already owned an old Pleyel grand that stood in his living room, and it was this instrument that he was sending back to the factory via Rotterdam.

On January 9, 1890—five days after playing a concert in the Pleyel auditorium in Paris—Grieg wrote an effusive letter of thanks to Gustave Lyon, presumably translated into French by Alexander Bull.

[2] Belgian pianist and composer Arthur de Greef (1862–1940).

for my music. He is a true master, that I see more and more clearly—definitely one of those whom one must search high and low in the entire music world to find.

And to yourself I say, lastly, happy new year! We do not want a revolution, but on the contrary a reunion in the elevated peace of Norwegian nature!

Yours truly,
EDVARD GRIEG

2

April 1, 1889
5 The Cedars, Clapham Common, London S.W.

Dear Bull!
I have been pondering, hence my silence. But at this moment I am sending telegrams to you and [Édouard] Colonne,[3] from whom I have seen a letter to Durand & Schönewerk[4] stating that if I come to Paris he will *do the impossible* although his Sundays are not open. My plan, therefore, is: 1) matinee (or soirée) for the press at Pleyel on the eighth (short concert: Nina and I and hopefully Johannes Wolff[5]), 2) concert at Pleyel on the eighteenth. In other words: Lyon's proposal with the modification that I do *not* want an orchestra. If I could then perhaps get my *String Quartet* performed with Wolff playing *primo*, hurrah! That would be to my liking. I must have only modern people, none of the oldsters. You must be sure to say this to Lyon if the concert is to be arranged. If Colonne would give an orchestral concert a couple of days after the eighteenth (or, with Lyon's permission, between the eighth and the eighteenth), then everything would be all right. Please inform Colonne *immediately* of the arrangement with Pleyel so that he can be up to date.

I hope that April first will not make a fool of me with respect to my decision, which is now firm. We arrive Thursday evening the fourth. If it should be Friday, you will hear further. We will stay at the Grand Hotel. You understand that since I will not be having an orchestra at the Pleyel concert, I could perhaps include the *Piano Concerto* with De Greef at the Colonne concert. Tell this to Colonne. I am burdening you—but you yourself have been so kind to reach out both in attack and in assistance! I don't know four words of French. How will it go!!

Be sure to engage Johannes Wolff! I will talk to him today and will tell him what I have cabled to you.

---

3 French conductor Édouard Colonne (1838–1910), founder of the Colonne Orchestra in Paris.
4 A music publishing company in Paris.
5 Dutch violinist Johannes Wolff (1863–?).

Greet Lyon. I would have cabled him directly but didn't know his address.

Do ask Colonne to excuse me for not writing to him today, but it takes me eight days to compose a letter in French and I don't have time for that.

Cordial greetings.

Your devoted
EDVARD GRIEG

3

Copenhagen, January 13, 1891
Hotel King of Denmark

Dear Bull!
I am sitting here reading a book about your father by Oddmund Vik,[6] and each moment I get wet on the cheek. You say that he was a great comedian. I say that he was a wonderful human being who, with the vision of a genius, has shown the right way in many directions. You are often mentioned in the book, so I said to myself: Today he shall have a letter! You can thank your father for that!

But now I want to wish you a good new year and to send you hearty thanks for your company in Paris during the year just past. If I had been healthy at that time, that whole visit would have been different. That episode with Societé Nationale irritated me and irritates me still.[7] But I do indeed have so much to be happy about, for what I did went well.

I will certainly come back again sometime if I still have some music in me a few years hence. This is a damned boring place to be. Devoid of spirit and uninspiring. I am indeed looking forward to seeing old Norway. Yes, patriotism is inalienable!

There is so much in your father's letters and talks that sounds as if it came from my own soul. If I did not love him for anything else, I would have to do so for this constantly recurring longing for home, for the rugged terrain of West Norway. For here we are at the foundation on which your father's whole identity has been built. He felt the same gratitude toward West Norway that I, too, have always felt. Having had a French mother, you don't understand this. Still, even

---

[6] Oddmund Vik (1858–1930): *Ole Bull*, Bergen 1890.

[7] In early December, 1889, Grieg had received an invitation from Vincent d'Indy (1851–1931), secretary of "La Societé Nationale de Musique", to participate in a chamber-music concert to be given in his honor on December 28. Grieg had originally accepted the invitation, but because of illness he had to tell d'Indy that he could not perform but that he would attend the concert. Then, to the great disappointment of the arrangers of the concert and the audience, Grieg sent word that for reasons of health he could not even attend the concert.

It cannot be denied that Grieg's absence from the concert on December 28 looks strange, for the very next day he conducted a program of his own works at a big concert of the Colonne orchestra in the Châtelet Theater. See Grieg's letter to d'Indy of January 15, 1890.

you are not entirely free of a certain longing for Norway. In that you are your father's son! For that reason you will also be heartily welcome at Troldhaugen at any time.

Who is the Norwegian composer "Svendske" whose "Romance" was played?[8] If you are the one who read the proof, you're not going to be my impresario!

We will probably be staying here. Warm greetings also to Paolini[9] from both of us!

Your friend,
EDVARD GRIEG

4

Troldhaugen, January 20, 1892

Dear Bull!
I knew, of course, that you were in America, but I had long ago given up finding you there. Naturally you have gone there only to prepare for my arrival! Yes, I understand that. And for that reason have naturally begun to practice on the piano! The fact is that I have just read Garborg's new book *Trætte Mænd* (*Weary Men*), and I see there that as long as one is in one's thirties one thinks, "Oh, let's take it easy, we still have plenty of time left!" But when one gets up into one's forties one says, "No, damn it all, this won't do. I want to live before it is too late. Take along the whole kit and caboodle!" But—he didn't mention seasickness. And that I don't want to take along! If you can get rid of that for me, all you have to do is assure me one million and I will come at once.

This is all grim humor, you understand. Behind it, no doubt, lies a strong feeling of rural winter loneliness and spiritual emptiness. I won't repeat it in the near future. There aren't any people in this city who want to have anything to do with a non-materialist. Moreover, the sentiment is mutual—unfortunately. I think there is a great deal of spiritual decadence here. These people who boast about their interest in art—there are 55,000 of them, and they are letting their only music society fold up. They turn their dramatic artists into starving artists. All they are interested in is money artists and highball artists. But believe me, it is glorious up here: minus 8 to 10 to 12 degrees Réaumur[10] and a lot of snow with

---

[8] Grieg is making fun of a printing error in a concert program in which the name of Norwegian composer Johan Svendsen was mistakenly spelled "Svendske", which to Scandinavian ears sounds like "Swedish". "Romance" is Svendsen's *Romance for Violin and Orchestra* (1881).

[9] A Monsieur Paolini (first name unknown) was director of the Hotel de Sèze, where Grieg usually stayed when he was in Paris.

[10] "Réaumur" denotes a temperature scale in which 0° represents the freezing point and 80° the boiling point of water. Thus –10° Réaumur equals –13° Celsius and +9° Fahrenheit.

constant frost such as no one can remember. Cold feet are an unpleasant reality out in the country. Otherwise I am fairly comfortable.

Both of us send our warmest greetings! Happy new year!

Your friend,
EDVARD GRIEG

5

Menton, April 4, 1894
Hotel de Russie & Allemagne

Dear Bull!

No, you will have to become a wet nurse after all, for now things are really crazy. Just listen: At the request of Madame Colonne[11] I have orchestrated a song—"Le Cygne" ("A Swan" [EG 177 no. 4] by Henrik Ibsen)—which, together with another song—*Le Solitaire* [*The Mountain Thrall*], also with orchestra—is to be sung on the 22nd by one Mr. Grimaud.[12] Today I have seen the French translation of "A Swan" for the first time, and it is so miserable, so absolutely impossible and destructive for both Ibsen and me, that it must not be tolerated. The poem is made into something totally different, and the notes of the melody are often completely changed. Now that Ibsen is a famous man in Paris, the poem must have a translation that at least makes sense. It must be a rendering of *Ibsen*, and it must be capable of being *properly declaimed* when sung to my melody. Can you manage this? After all, you are familiar with the sources. Couldn't you translate the poem into French prose for the person in question, who must not be unmusical? Dear friend, do the impossible—and do it as soon as possible. On the following pages are Ibsen's poem and my melody.

In great haste,

Yours truly,
EDVARD GRIEG

[Here follows in Grieg's hand the melody line of "A Swan" as well as the complete original text of Ibsen's poem and the "miserable translation" by Alfred Tranchant to which he refers in the letter.]

---

[11] French singer Eugénie Élise Vergin Colonne (1838–1910), wife of Édouard Colonne.

[12] The Belgian singer Grimaud (first name unknown), to whom Grieg also refers in a letter of July 17, 1900, to his American biographer, Henry T. Finck (1854–1926). The concert on April 22 was a huge success, and "A Swan" had to be repeated.

To Schak Bull

Schak Bull (1858–1956), who was Grieg's first cousin, was one of Bergen's most respected architects and was the obvious choice when the Griegs sought help in planning their villa on the outskirts of Bergen. The letters to Schak Bull show the enthusiasm and insight with which Grieg entered into the planning of Troldhaugen.

Grieg's letters to Schak Bull are preserved in Bergen Offentlige Bibliotek (Bergen Public Library).

1

Lofthus, August 5, 1884

Dear Schak!

Since it now appears that we are getting serious about the idea of building a house, I come to you a-courting. The external contours of your earlier drawing have more and more become a part of me. I have become so fond of them that I would be more than glad to retain them, NB, unless your imagination during these two years has raced off toward newer and better ideals.

As for the interior of the house, on the other hand, I have been thinking of something more adapted to my practical use—something along the lines of what is indicated on the enclosed "amateur drawing." I repeat: It is an amateur drawing. Therefore you are not permitted to laugh at my stupidities—no, not even to break into a smile. To the contrary, you ought to praise my efforts. The enclosed measurement shows the same length, width and height as Beyers' house.[1] Length: 17 *alens*, width 13 *alens*.[2] Your plan showed a length of 15 *alens* 18 inches and a width of 13 *alens* 9 inches,[3] and the estimated cost of the lumber at that time was 6,000 Norwegian crowns. My request to you now is this: Will you kindly, one day when you have time (as soon as possible), get together with Beyer—to whom I have written about this—and visit the site, and then tell me what you think of my plan. Thereafter I would ask you as soon as possible to inquire of Gjelvik what the lumber would cost. Salomon,[4] the owner of the farm "Hestetrædet" in Hop, has agreed to lay the foundation, and it is very important to me that he begin as soon as possible so that, if possible, I could get the house under roof before winter sets in, or in any case before Christmas.

I hope that you will please attend to the matter with all the "enthusiasm" that

---

1 Grieg's close friend Frants Beyer (1851–1919) had built a villa called "Næsset" on the lot next to Grieg's property in the spring of 1884. Indeed, it was in order to live near the Beyers that Grieg bought this property.

2 The *alen* was a unit of measurement commonly used in Norway in Grieg's day. 1 *alen* =.6275 meters or 2 feet and ¾ inches. Thus Beyer's house had a length of 10.7 meters (35 feet) and a width of 8.16 meters (26 feet and 10 inches).

3 15 *alens* 18" = 9.9 meters (32 feet and 5 inches), 13 *alens* 9" = 8.4 meters (27 feet and 7 inches).

4 Grieg had bought the property on which "Troldhaugen" was to be built from Salomon Monsen Hop (1846–1927) for five hundred Norwegian crowns. Gjelvik was to be the builder.

your time and your "cousinly" interest can muster. To what extent a completely new drawing is necessary, or whether a less detailed sketch for Gjelvik is sufficient—this I of course leave entirely to you.

I depart tomorrow for the mountain plateau where, according to Ibsen, are found both "freedom and God."[5] Supplied with these two benefits, I will come back down in eight days and will go directly to the city to meet you and clear everything up. So these lines are being sent today just to avoid wasting time.

With warm greetings to your wife, your parents and the whole family from Nina and from

Sincerely yours,
EDVARD GRIEG

P.S. Under separate cover I am also sending you my heart's blood in the form of your own drawing, as I assume you perhaps will need it for comparative calculations.

2

Lofthus, August 29, 1884

Dear Schak!

"Das war eine grausame Salbe!"[6] But in the first place, both Nina and I are very enthused about the drawing, and in the second place, as the years have passed I have grown rash. To be sure, I don't know where the money is going to come from, but hell! It doesn't have to be paid right away, and by spring I can surely work something out. So I accept the proposal in its entirety, thereby giving up the reduction of 493 crowns. But stop! A reduction shall be made, not so much for the sake of the money, for it is only 75 crowns, but because I don't want the windows any larger than Frants [Beyer's]. Since I would like to write down some of the most important features of your drawing before I return it, you won't be getting it until the next mail run. Just these lines today, as the steamboat leaves in a little while.

A couple of small remarks for your consideration:

Should not the flagpole on the balcony (on the tower) be part of the contract? Maybe this and the omission of the larger windows can cancel each other out.

Can't I get along without a window in the northwest wall of the guest room? It seems to me that it would be nicer and plenty light with the one window on the gable side, and it would give more room.

---

5 The reference is to Ibsen's poem "På Vidderne" (translated by John Northam in *Ibsen's Poems* as "On The Moors"), Section IX, stanza 13.

6 "That was a hard blow", a line from *Jacob von Tyboe*, a play by Norwegian author Ludvig Holberg (1684–1754). Grieg's use of the expression was owing to the fact that he had just learned what it was going to cost him to have his house built, and he thought the sum was frightfully high.

Why do you want tar paper on the balcony veranda? It buckles in the heat, that I know from experience. If some other kind of roofing is much more costly, then I would rather give up the flagstone floor. Think about this. As you can see, I have punched out places for two windows in the wood cellar so that at least a *little* light can come in.

One unfortunate thing is that in the dining room there is so little space between the two windows that the only possible place for the sideboard is lost. Can something be done about this? In the wood cellar I have still indicated a place for a coal bin, and between the two storerooms in the attic I have marked a place for a glass window. The tower room will also provide very little space. I think I would prefer that the triple windows be slightly smaller than Frants's—yes, if you don't think it would mar the outward appearance of the house I would like to give up one or both of them and use double ones instead. In any case I will raise the question with you whether it wouldn't give a little more space in the room if the entrance to the balcony on the northwest side were a double door.

As regards the payment to Salomon, Frants has my power of attorney and a bank book.

Of course, you won't be able to consider the things I have been jabbering about here until you get the drawing back, and that will happen soon. Thanks for your work and your interest, and congratulations on making the house so beautiful! Warm greetings!

Yours truly,
EDVARD GRIEG

P.S. NB: 1) The concert room must have a wooden floor. 2) The maid's room must have a stove! Thus a total of six stoves, not five! You must promise me that you will monitor the quality of the stoves and the window glass.

To Michel-Dimitri Calvocoressi

The French musicologist Michel-Dimitri Calvocoressi (1877–1944) was a music critic in Paris and a foreign correspondent for English, Russian, German and American journals. He was also very active as a translator. He wrote several books, many of them dealing with Russian music.

Grieg's letter to Calvocoressi (in German) is preserved in The Pierpont Morgan Library, Mary Flagler Cary Music Collection, New York.

Paris, May 2, 1903

Dear Sir!

I wish very much that you had not called my attention to Mr. Claude Debussy's review of the last Colonne concert.[1] For now that the whole affair is over, I have read it, and I am really surprised about the tone that he as an artist dares to strike regarding a fellow artist. Naturally I also regret the complete lack of understanding of my art that finds expression in the same review. But that is not the main point. The main point is and must be the vitriolic and disrespectful tone he employs. A true artist should always aspire to a high intellectual level and show respect for the standpoints of other serious artists and people.[2]

With respect to politics, I have never said—as he writes—that I would "ne voulai plus mettre les pieds dans un pays etc." ["never set foot in a country etc."]. I have written that *maintenant,* i.e., *at that time,* I didn't feel that I could come to Paris.[3]

It is completely unworthy of a talented artist such as Mr. Debussy knowingly and deliberately to say something that is not true in order to smear a colleague. I strongly emphasize this: "a talented artist such as Mr. Debussy." For it is my good fortune that not only am I independent of his judgment of me, but I can also regard his music with admiration. I have read through his three "Nocturnes" with great enthusiasm. They reveal a significant talent for coloration and an exceptional degree of inventiveness, and I am most grateful to you for having given me the opportunity to get acquainted with this work. I hope that I will be able to perform it in Scandinavia.

---

[1] Grieg gave two concerts in Paris in 1903. On April 19 he conducted the Colonne Orchestra at the Châtelet Theater, and on April 27 he participated in a chamber-music concert in Salle Pleyel. See Grieg's own humorous account of the Châtelet concert in his letter of April 20, 1903, to the publisher John Grieg (1856–1905).

[2] After the Colonne concert, Claude Debussy (1862–1918) wrote a somewhat condescending critique in *Gil Blas* to which Grieg is here reacting. Debussy had a number of positive things to say—regarding *Peer Gynt Suite No. 1,* for example—but the praise was almost drowned in caustic observations. Debussy respected Grieg's use of folk music but, he maintained, "when we look beyond this, Grieg is nothing more than a clever musician who is more concerned about effects than about true art."

[3] For Grieg's involvement with the Dreyfus affair in 1899, see his letters to Édouard Colonne (1838–1910) of September 12 and October 4 and 5, 1899.

Regarding *Pelléas et Mélisande*,[4] I dare not venture an evaluation on the basis of a piano reduction. I hope to hear the opera in Berlin. But it goes without saying that also in this work I observe the high seriousness that has inspired the artist. It is precisely this seriousness, which he so mistakenly fails to see in *my* art, that attracts me to his, and that I myself aspire to achieve.

Since you gave me the impression during our conversation of being a deep-thinking and serious art critic, I am confident that you will accord these remarks your full understanding.

Accept, dear sir, the assurance of my sincere respect.

EDVARD GRIEG

[4] *Pelléas et Mélisande*, opera by Claude Debussy.

To Johan Andreas Budtz Christie

Johan Andreas Budtz Christie (1842–1919) was a clergyman and a competent amateur pianist with whom Grieg often had contact, both during his stays in Ullensvang and through correspondence. Christie was a curate in Ullensvang for several years, then (in 1886) became parish pastor in Kvam, and in 1904 became dean in the sub-diocese of Hardanger and Voss.

Grieg's letters to Christie are preserved in Bergen Offentlige Bibliotek (Bergen Public Library).

1

Copenhagen, December 10, 1879

Dear friend!

An awful-sounding hand organ with drums and trumpets that almost shakes the ocean and threatens to break my eardrums is making it impossible for me to work—and you are the unfortunate fellow who has to suffer the consequences. I had said to myself that the letter was to be posted during these days so as to reach you by Christmas Eve, so there is no time to waste. I have often felt a desire to write to you but have not known where I should send the letter. And that desire is a result of the simple fact that in your company I felt happier than otherwise, so that I like to think back on the time we spent together. It did me so much good amidst all my restless yearning and doubt to associate with you in all your cheerful contentment and tranquility. Yes, I certainly learned more from you than you did from me, so perhaps it was good for you that I didn't go along to lovely Italy. Well, now that you are really there you must tell me about your impressions.

I am living here in the Hotel King of Denmark, so that is where you must address mail to me. Think how much fun it is: We are living in the same two rooms that we had last autumn. We have chosen the larger one as a bedroom and are living in the smaller one, and we have it exceptionally nice. No doubt you think it is luxurious, so I must inform you that because we are staying for an extended period the proprietor has given us a very big discount. I am thinking of staying here until well after Christmas. Thereafter I perhaps will go to London, though nothing is definite as yet. I am studying English until my head swims. I practice two hours a day using Ollendorff's method, and I have already reached lesson No. 42. When I have completed 100 lessons I will be able to handle the language.[1]

---

[1] Heinrich Gottfried Ollendorff (1803–65) was a German linguist and author of textbooks who had developed a special method for the rapid learning of foreign languages. The method was first made public in 1835 in the form of a textbook aimed at teaching German to French and English students. The title of Ollendorff's textbook, in translation, was *A New Method for Learning to Read, Write and Speak a Language in Six Months.* In 1843 he published a course in French, in 1846 one in Italian, and in 1848 one in English—the one used by Grieg. To Grieg's disappointment, he never became very proficient at either speaking or writing English.

I have rented a small room where I work and where I am now writing these lines. I say no to most party invitations, so I can't complain about an irregular life. One doesn't hear much music; the theater is the only thing that now and then offers something ennobling for the soul. This evening I will go to see Holberg's[2] *Pernilles korte Frøkenskap* [*Pernille's Brief Maidenhood*]. Next week Ibsen's new play, *Et Dukkehjem* [*A Doll House*], will be performed—a remarkable work, which you must read. I am very anxious to see how it comes off on stage. He is really a colossal spirit, this Ibsen. He is a man who—in contrast to other people! —[piece torn off] himself in his task!

[piece torn off], I think in this connection [piece torn off] Bjørnson—is staying here in the city these days, but of course I won't see him unless he, contrary to my expectation, should think to ask me.[3] He is on his way home from Germany to attend the wedding of a friend. The bridegroom is Wollert Konow, a man from eastern Norway who is involved in the folk high school movement. The bride is a Miss Bojsen, who is Danish.[4] (. . .)

[Grieg's signature has been clipped off]

P.S. Greet those who may remember me, for example Ravnkilde.[5] Don't forget to send me your address!

2

Copenhagen, January 27, 1880
Address: Hotel King of Denmark

Dear friend!
Where might these lines find you in the world? Someplace, hopefully. I know nothing of the fate of my previous letter. I addressed it to the Scandinavian consul in Rome, or maybe it was the Danish consul, I don't remember exactly. But I want you to know that I have written, and I did so some time before receiving your friendly letter from Florence. I am very curious to hear about your Roman experiences, your impressions, your health, etc. etc. Yes, health: that is indeed the main thing. That is how I have come to feel lately. The rising generation, the youth—or rather, the male of the species—is poor. That part of humankind, at any rate, that has spiritual interests.

After Christmas I had a cold and fever with sore throat that certainly was

2 Norwegian author Ludvig Holberg (1684–1754).

3 The reference is to Norwegian author Bjørnstjerne Bjørnson (1832–1910). Grieg and Bjørnson were not on speaking terms at this time because of a serious disagreement that arose over their attempt to collaborate on a national opera.

4 Wollert Konow (1847–1932) operated a folk high school at Halsnøy Kloster, a tiny village on an island off the west coast of Norway, from 1868 to 1873. In 1879 he was elected to Stortinget (the Norwegian parliament) for the Liberal [Venstre] party and in 1884 became president of Stortinget. He was a friend of Bjørnson.

5 Grieg's Danish friend Niels Ravnkilde (1823–90), who lived in Rome.

unpleasant, but of course that is nothing to complain about. The worst part was that I began to suffer from insomnia, which unfortunately produced some nasty results after the cold went away. I have lost my strength, especially in my arms and legs. I see black spots in front of me all day long, my scalp is numb, I can scarcely stand to play or even to hear music. In short, I have acquired the modern illness: nervousness. The doctor says that my nerves are very weakened. God knows how it happened. I don't understand it, for I have not over-exerted myself in any way. And I, who have always been so proud of my nerves, who have never been really ill but, on the contrary, have braved all the choir rehearsals, private lessons and everything else under the sun. Believe me, this has been a wake-up call for me, and that certainly is a good thing. I have labored under the false belief that I had a strong constitution. Now if only I have not learned my lesson too late!

I am dreading a concert that I am to give here next week before I leave Copenhagen.[6] I had thought of going to London but must now change may plan. I probably will go directly to Christiania in the middle of next month and then travel overland through snow and ice to Lofthus, where I will hopefully get my nerves cured if they are still curable. If I am going to be ripped out of my activity, I will remember with double gratitude the many enjoyable things that it was given to me to experience—beyond what is given to many, many others. Then I will also remember with double joy the faithful friendship that has been shown to me by a few people. You know that you are one of these. I hope—yes, I know—that you will be the same no matter what may happen to me. I feel that, however different we may be, you have responded to the human being, not merely to the artist.

If you write soon after receiving this, just address your letter here, and I will leave word at the hotel to have it forwarded to me. Then let me know about your plans, about when you are coming home, and give me some hope that I may be able to see you this summer in Hardanger. If only we could take a short trip to the mountains together!

Yes, the mountains, the mountains! I feel for them as if they were human beings! Thank God that there is something called love of the homeland; that is indeed something more than a mere phrase.

And with that, farewell for this time. My head is already reminding me of its existence. Greet friends in Rome, and gladden me soon with a few words.

Yours truly,
EDVARD GRIEG

P.S. Nina sends greetings! She is doing a lot of singing down here and having success—which she deserves, too, for she simply sings better here than at home.

---

[6] Grieg gave concerts in Copenhagen on February 4 and 11, 1880.

3

Bergen, December 19, 1881

Dear friend!
No, this is going too far! An envelope with your address has lain ready for such and such a time. *All* that is lacking is the content. To date I have tried to stifle the voice of conscience, but as you know, in the long run it doesn't work. And now, with Christmas just around the corner, one feels, as is well known, an instinctive desire to settle old debts in order that the new year shall not see the old Adam. Well, however that may be: a merry Christmas for both you and me! That I certainly may be permitted to say, for even if I do not believe in the same *literal details* as you, I certainly do believe without reservation in the same great spirit of love. Everything is created for the good, and love has never manifested itself so completely as through him whose birth we now shall celebrate. For that reason I, like you, rejoice in Christmas and wish only for strength to struggle to possess just a little spark of that spirit of love which Christ radiated in his life.

I hear that things are not going well for you. That, in any case, is how it sounded a month ago. Tell me what led you to settle in Christiania. You are certainly amidst family life there as well, aren't you? Is it the climate that has been the decisive factor? I can console you with the fact that the weather cannot be any worse than it has been here lately. Rain and storm week in and week out, month in and month out.

I have worked in the sweat of my brow in the hope of better times. At least my health has improved to the point that I have had enough strength to lead Harmonien. But I wouldn't do it for another winter for all the gold in the world. One really gets infected by all the pettiness and indifference with which one is surrounded. To date we have had four concerts, in the course of which there have been some performances that must be described as fairly good. After Christmas I shall begin rehearsing Mendelssohn's oratorio *Elijah*. It is to be performed at the end of March. It is a marvelous work, and I hope you will be here at that time. The performance presumably will not take place in the church. For of course I won't try for that. There is no point in proposing anything to a clergy about whom it must be said that they systematically suppress everything having to do with cultural life. I can back up this assertion with proofs. I will just remind you of the *Requiem*[7] last year, of the decision not to appoint Cappelen[8] to the position of cathedral organist, and recently, as you may remember, of the appointment of the least well qualified of all the candidates—a certain Mr. Johannesen (who goes around tuning pianos)—to the new organist position in Sandviken.

---

7 Grieg was conductor of the Music Society Harmonien, predecessor of the modern Bergen Philharmonic Orchestra, during the years 1880–82. He conducted a performance of Mozart's *Requiem* on March 31, 1881. To his exasperation, the clergy refused to allow the performance to be given in a church.

8 Christian Cappelen (1845–1919), who, however, became organist at Our Savior's Church in Christiania in 1887.

I have been on the verge of going to Christiania several times in recent weeks, because I had a strong desire to get away to some different surroundings for a short time. But a trip in December is too strenuous. I will remain a Philistine and a provincial until summer, but then, if I'm still living, I will shake the dust off my wings.

When Mrs. Thoresen[9] says that the human being's most beautiful feeling is longing, I say no and again no. *Hope* is the most beautiful sentiment we have. Long live hope! Also, therefore, the hope for a good year in 1882!

Yours truly,
EDVARD GRIEG

4

Amsterdam, December 28, 1883

Dear friend!
Before the old year runs out I still want to tell you that you have so often—so very often—been in my thoughts without my realizing my plan to write to you. Then your dear letter arrived, and with it a renewed incentive. Now at last there is a lull in my busy schedule, and I intend to take advantage of it. To be sure, it is unfortunately not a voluntary lull. I must for now abandon the real goal of my trip, which was Paris, because the long concert tour—especially the last part of it—has so sapped my strength and overtaxed me that I can't continue. Just recently I had to decline appearances in both Paris and London, where I had been invited to perform. Instead, I will try to regain my health with a two-month visit to Italy; Nina will join me in January. I hope to be home again in the spring and am already looking forward to the thought of seeing my dear, dear Norway again, walking in the mountains and hiding myself away in the bosom of nature, which never disappoints.

You think that my stay abroad might demoralize me. Dear friend, do you really think that I am so low a person! I have traveled abroad ever since my early youth, and I have learned what is and is not worth getting involved in. At first one meets a lot of trash, that is true, but now when I travel I meet only the best and the noblest. Only now am I beginning to appreciate the value of culture. In Norway, the new culture is crammed with learning and makes the individual antagonistic toward everyday life and its demands. Not so here.[10] In precisely the people who stand at the pinnacle I have seen how the true culture—that, namely, which includes nourishment for both the spirit and the heart—how it makes

---

[9] The Danish-Norwegian author Magdalene Thoresen (1819–1903), Henrik Ibsen's mother-in-law.

[10] Grieg was staying at this time with his Dutch friend Julius Röntgen (1855–1932) in Amsterdam and was very impressed with the culture and human understanding he encountered here.

people natural, happy, straightforward, humane and nobler in their way of thinking. I am, unfortunately, suspicious by nature, so I have often enough made my quiet observations about the extent to which culture was merely a good polish that in a disappointing manner covered a multitude of sins. But when the thought is expressed in the deed, then I think we have proof of its genuineness. I have indeed had my eye on the danger of a certain kind of demoralization, and that is the danger that arises from too much recognition and admiration. I have encountered this in a richer measure than ever before, and as much good as it does, thrown into one's life like sunbeams in moments when one needs light and warmth, to that same degree it becomes dangerous when it continues without interruption.

I do not know what Paris and London would have brought me. Perhaps there I would have gotten the weight pulled down appropriately on the other side of the scale. But still, I know that for the time being I have gotten exactly enough of the kind of praise that, like caviar, is best enjoyed in small portions, and this knowledge is to me a guarantee that I still have not become demoralized. If one senses the danger one is, in general, more certain to avoid it than if one does not sense it. That certainly is an indisputable truth.

Perhaps you have read in the newspapers about my artistic journey. And if not, I will tell you about it when we meet. It is altogether too long-winded a story to put on paper. But I do wish you had heard the string orchestra in my music for Vinje's poems[11]—had heard it, for example, in Weimar, in Breslau, in Cologne and in The Hague—and had seen the audience's appreciation. The first time I conducted this music for a German audience was in Weimar, and I do not remember many times in my life when I have been so moved. I hardly knew where I was, in the palace theater in Weimar or out in the somber, brooding Norwegian mountains. The truth is that I was in neither of these places but rather on the ethereal wings of harmony in outer space. And what a performance! The eyes of the musicians followed my every movement, and I saw this strangely supportive cast in their expression that let me know what they were thinking and feeling. When the orchestra is enthused and wants to show its enthusiasm, it is the practice in Germany—and also here—to rap on the back of the violins with the wood of the bows. It is not a beautiful sound, but for me it was wonderful, that I admit. It was as if the walls were going to fall over on our heads. In Meiningen, after we had played "Last Spring" [op. 34, no. 2], the duke shouted out in a loud voice, "Da capo". The most beautiful performance, however, was the one by the well-staffed orchestra in the splendid old Gürzenich auditorium in Cologne.

Did you, on your trip, see the Cologne cathedral after it was finished? I went

---

11 Aasmund Olavsson Vinje (1818–70), author of the poems set by Grieg in op. 33. Grieg arranged two of the songs for string orchestra as *Two Elegiac Melodies* op. 34.

into it the same afternoon that I was to perform, and I sat and then walked around for a long time. It's a sanctuary, that's for sure.

Yesterday I walked for a long time down by the harbor here, and in the course of my walk I went past the Norwegian Seamen's Church. I wanted to go in, but it was closed. It's not really a church, however, but a quite ordinary building with, I think, no more than three banks of windows on each floor. A strange city, Amsterdam! And a strange, original country, Holland. One can understand that such a singular power was able to free itself from Spanish domination. I have still not gotten to the museums and art galleries, as we are having uninterrupted fog here. Still, I hope it will let up a little before I leave, for it is my intention to stay here one or two weeks.

Today I received my certificate as a member of "The Association for the Promotion of Music"[12] and an invitation to play my new *Cello Sonata* in one of the Association's concerts at the beginning of January. I would like very much to do that, if only my health were in agreement with me.

If was very kind of your two nieces to visit me—and apparently very unkind of me not to reciprocate their act of friendship. But the time totally got away from me, and I left Leipzig in such a rush that it was impossible for me to visit them. This by way of excusing myself, for I don't want the privilege of exhibiting bad manners and discourtesy.

It's wonderful that you have regained your desire for active work. It is a mystery to me why you did not seek the position at Balestrand. It is important to act before the desire vanishes again. This is true with everything when one is beginning to get old. You *must* have gotten some benefit from the trip. There is no other possibility. But such benefits often do not appear until half a year—yes, a whole year—later. I hope we can meet in the spring on your way home from southern Europe and that you will be healthy and happy by then.

And with that, farewell and warm greetings from

Yours truly,
EDVARD GRIEG

P.S. Your portfolio[13] is my daily companion and friend and reminds me—reminds me!

My address is always: Dr. Max Abraham, Thalstrasse 29B, Leipzig.

---

[12] "Maatschappij tot Befordering der Toonkunst", founded in Amsterdam in 1829. This nationwide association sponsors choirs and music schools throughout Holland.

[13] Grieg appears to be referring to a letter portfolio that he had received as a gift from Rev. Christie.

5

Leipzig, January 30, 1888

Dear friend!
I am about to write a letter to someone or other, and I open your letter portfolio. Then my eye falls on your lovely initials, and immediately the feeling of guilt vanishes so noticeably that Nina looks up from her knitting and says, "Yes, you dear Budtz Christie!" And then I take a new sheet of paper and start this letter. You won't get much from me. But this much you already know, that when you do not hear from me, the reason is not that I am not fond of you! It is strange that no matter how much there is that divides us, still there is so much that unites us! There are so many people whom I meet in life. I recognize them, but they come and go, and before I know what is happening they are out of my thoughts and my memory. But you are like a part of those mountains that I love above everything else in the world. And you are much more—like a part of the truth. For you are what you are. However much you might wish to help people better understand what you are thinking, that which you feel and believe is so genuinely felt and believed that any sincere human being must love you for that. I certainly will never reach the point where you would like to have me, but—I believe in people, and I believe in God, and I still believe that the God who has created human beings has had something good in view for them. Otherwise I would not want to live for another moment. And you are warm-hearted enough to understand such a God, are you not? If you would now like to show me that *you* haven't forgotten me either, a letter will always reach me.

I have promised to go to London in March. I don't have a lot of enthusiasm for this plan, but it must be done nonetheless. Then this summer—I think in June—there is a music festival in Copenhagen where I must, in fact, be present, NB, if homesickness doesn't absolutely consume me before then. Yes, this love of the homeland that grows year by year despite the fact that I see ever more clearly so much that is not good—what in the world is this strange, lovely feeling, and where does it come from? You must answer that for me!

And with that I send the warmest greetings from Nina and from

Your old friend,

[Grieg's signature has been clipped off.]

P.S. Write soon! Address: C. F. Peters, Thalstrasse 10, Leipzig.

6

Troldhaugen, August 14, 1904

Dear friend!

Yes, those were some lovely days! Thank you for them! I found in you some of the peace that life's autumn desires so much but seldom achieves. I know that we are both, each in our own way, seeking the same thing, namely, the truth. Therefore our varying views at the purely confessional level can never come between us. "All roads lead to Rome." Or, as the farmer says, "The roads meet in the distance." It seems to me that I have achieved a wider horizon since we talked together in the old days. And it strikes me that you have done the same thing. Never have I enjoyed your company more than I did this time. Yes, I even have the feeling of being closer to you than before. I hope this feeling is mutual.

You have hidden something from me. Why? It indeed interests me in the highest degree. On the steamship I was told that a powerful Pietistic movement is raging in your parish—a movement that you are firmly opposing, as a result of which you have been subjected to many unpleasantries. Write to me about this. This matter of the *spirit* and the *letter* is the eternal dilemma. If one wishes to awaken people to life—or, more correctly, if one has, like you, received the task of doing so—then I surely know you well enough to know that you will do battle with the letter. I am anxious to hear more about this.

Now you must thank all the good fairies who live around you for all their kindness and hospitality toward us. It is no small matter to be oneself and to feel happy in such supportive surroundings. If I had a pleasant home with an equally pleasant workroom in your vicinity, who knows whether we might not be able to gladden both ourselves and others more than once. It seems to me as if I still have something to say—if the right peace and the right surroundings fall to my lot. And I do not doubt for a moment that your surroundings are precisely what is good for me. But—from thought to deed is a long way at my age! That, unfortunately, is something I feel strongly.

Accept, now, heartiest thanks for everything both from Nina and from

Your old friend,
Edvard Grieg

To Édouard Colonne

The French violinist and conductor Édouard Colonne (1838–1910) was one of his country's leading orchestra conductors. In 1873 he initiated the so-called Colonne Concerts, which continued under his leadership to the end of his life. The first such concert was given in the Odéon Theatre, but the following year the concerts were moved to the Châtelet Théâtre. Colonne was a great admirer of Grieg's compositions and regularly performed them at his concerts. Grieg first made contact with Colonne in 1881 inviting him to consider a performance of *Before a Southern Convent.* Grieg's first personal appearances in the Colonne concerts occurred on December 22 and 29, 1889, when Colonne, for only the second time in his life, departed from his usual practice and turned over the baton to someone else. The previous year he had done the same thing for Tchaikovsky. Grieg's second concert appearance in Paris was on April 22, 1894. Colonne tried several times during the 1890's to get Grieg to come to Paris again, but for various reasons Grieg declined to do so. In 1899 Grieg's very visible involvement in the Dreyfus affair[1] soured his relationship with France and for some years made him *persona non grata* among the French. It was not until 1903 that he accepted a new offer from Colonne.

Grieg's letters to Colonne, which are owned by Bibliothèque Nationale in Paris, are uncatalogued and have not been accessible. The translations that follow, therefore, are based on Grieg's drafts in Norwegian and French which are preserved in the Bergen Public Library. A detailed account of Grieg's contacts with Colonne and France will be found in Harald Herresthal and Ladislav Reznicek, *Rhapsodie norvégienne,* Oslo 1994. This book also contains translations into Norwegian of several letters from Colonne to Grieg.

---

[1] In 1894 Captain Alfred Dreyfus (1859–1935), a French army officer of Jewish descent, had been convicted of high treason and condemned to life imprisonment on Devil's Island. In due course it became clear to many that the conviction had been based on falsified evidence, but a series of scandalous legal proceedings resulted in the acquittal of the person actually guilty of the crime. A number of prominent people became engaged in the controversy at this time, notably French author Émile Zola (1840–1902), who published his famous article "J'accuse" ("I accuse") in the Paris newspaper *L'Aurore* on January 15, 1898.

On June 3, 1899, Dreyfus's conviction was overturned and the case was referred to a new court martial in Rennes. Meanwhile, Dreyfus's supporters in France (the "Dreyfusards") sought to win public sympathy for the unjustly accused army officer by soliciting statements from cultural leaders all over the world. In mid-June, 1899, Grieg received a letter from French musicologist Jules Combarieux (1859–1916) asking him to respond to a series of questions of principle highly relevant to the Dreyfus case. Grieg's reply, dated June 22, 1899, will be printed in translation in Benestad & Halverson (eds.), *Edvard Grieg: Diaries, Articles, Speeches* (Columbus, Ohio, 2001).

At the time of the court martial in Rennes, Edvard and Nina Grieg were guests of Norwegian author Bjørnstjerne Bjørnson (1832–1910) and his wife at their estate "Aulestad" in Gausdal. To their consternation, they learned that the court martial in Rennes, despite overwhelming evidence that Dreyfus was innocent, had reaffirmed the verdict of 1894. The day after hearing the news from Rennes, Grieg received an invitation from French conductor Édouard Colonne to give a concert with the Colonne Orchestra in Paris. Grieg, who was unable to separate the artistic opportunity from the human-rights issue, found himself in a moral dilemma. Emboldened by Bjørnson, on September 12 he wrote to Colonne pointedly declining the invitation. With Grieg's permission, Bjørnson's son-in-law, German writer Albert Langen (1869–1910), had the letter published in *Frankfurter Zeitung,* and it was soon reprinted in newspapers all over Europe.

1

[Aulestad, September 12, 1899]

Dear Maestro!

Although I thank you for your kind invitation, I greatly regret that I must inform you that in view of the outcome of the Dreyfus affair I cannot make the decision to come to Paris at this time. Like all foreigners, I am so indignant about the contempt with which law and justice are treated in your country that I am not inclined to appear before a French audience. Forgive me that I cannot feel otherwise, and try to understand me.

My wife and I send you our warmest greetings.

Respectfully yours,
Edvard Grieg

2

Copenhagen, October 4, 1899
Hotel King of Denmark

Dear Maestro!

Allow me to thank you for the charming and noble manner in which you have characterized my answer to your friendly invitation,[2] and I ask you to kindly take a few moments to hear a bit more about the matter. The French translator of my answer to you asked me for permission to publish it in *Frankfurter Zeitung*. In the indignation of the moment (it was the day after the conclusion of the trial at Rennes) I gave him permission to do so. But in so doing I should have been clearly aware of the possibility that I might hurt you by failing to secure your advance approval to publish the letter. I very much regret this, but I hope you can easily put yourself in my place. When I wrote my answer, I was out in the country at the hospitable home of the poet [Bjørnstjerne] Bjørnson, and he and his whole family as well as my wife and I are sworn advocates of Dreyfus. In this situation, the matter acquired its own momentum. I remember that I asked the German translator who was there with us, "Do you really think that anything good could come out of the publication of the letter?" Both he and the others answered, "Yes, without doubt."

I should have liked to show you all the vile letters that I receive every day from

---

[2] Colonne, after Grieg's very public response to his invitation, felt obliged to clarify his own position regarding Grieg's harsh letter of September 12. On September 30, 1899, therefore, in a letter to *Le Figaro*, he expressed surprise that Grieg's letter was published in the German press at the same time that it was sent to him, but he assumed that the intent of the letter had been misunderstood. He concluded thus: "I am convinced that this misunderstanding is of a temporary nature. For that matter, Edvard Grieg himself says that he cannot make the decision to come to Paris just now. I will add that I shall continue to place Grieg's works on my programs. I admire him as a musician and regard him very highly as a human being."

your country. For me they are only proofs of a bad conscience, new testimony to the innocence of the wretched Dreyfus!

Yesterday I received Mr. Henri Rochefort's[3] "noble" newspaper *L'Intransigeant,* addressed to "the Jewish composer Edvard Grieg!" Finale! I am proud of it. "Long live Mendelssohn!"

One of the letters from Paris threatens that if I dare to go there again I will get "a powerful kick in the least noble part of my body" (!).

I cherish the hope, however, that the easily ignited passion of the great French nation will soon be replaced by a far healthier view, consistent with human rights as proclaimed by the French Republic in 1789.

I hope first and foremost for France—but also for myself—that once again I shall have the opportunity to see your beautiful country.

My warmest greetings to Madame Colonne and to you, Dear Maestro, on behalf of my wife and myself.

Respectfully yours,
EDVARD GRIEG

3

Copenhagen, October 5, 1899

Dear Maestro!
After sending my letter yesterday, I have at this moment received *Le Temps* together with your letter to me.[4] I only repeat that it does not persuade me to change the views that found expression in my letter.

With all good wishes,

Respectfully yours,
EDVARD GRIEG

---

[3] French journalist and politician Henri Rochefort (1830–1913).

[4] Colonne's letter to Grieg (which was in French) reads as follows:

Dear Maestro!
The letter that you sent me in the passion of the moment after the guilty verdict at Rennes is surely one to which you have not given much thought.

My dear maestro, France has by no means ceased to be a country where freedom, justice and law are permitted to reign. Here, as in other places, the passions of politics and religion are intense. Sometimes they poison and disregard all questions regarding the human spirit. But in such cases it is a matter of temporary crises which we will always overcome, so that we can again be the France that the world has become accustomed to seeing—a France of equality and justice, a France of the year 1789. This, dear maestro, is part of what you forgot when you published your letter, and your many friends here hope with me that you have already regretted what you wrote.

It is with this hope, dear maestro, that I send you my warmest greetings.

ÉDOUARD COLONNE

4

Troldhaugen, September 22, 1902

Dear Maestro!

Thank you for your kind invitation.[5] But unfortunately! I have no program to offer. My few orchestral works have already been played in Paris. And if I am not mistaken, you do not perform works for choir and orchestra.

And lastly, the most important question: Mr. Henri Rochefort and several anonymous letter-writers have promised me a caning if I dare to set foot in Paris! Unfortunately I am not strong enough to defend myself!

How do you think these unpleasantries could be avoided? I would like to hear from you regarding this matter.

[Respectfully yours,
Edvard Grieg]

5

[Troldhaugen, October (?) 1902]

Dear Maestro!

Thank you for your friendly letter![6] Please excuse my silence, but as a matter of fact I have not had time to answer you until today. I regret having to say it, but in January, February and March it is impossible for me to come. The best time for me would be toward the end of April. If this time is convenient for you, I shall defy all difficulties and rely on your word that "France is now in the hands of reasonable people"—because the handling of the law regarding the religious schools does not appear to strengthen these schools.

I would like to perform, among other things, *Before a Southern Convent*, a short work for soprano and alto solo, female chorus, orchestra and organ (text by Bjørnson, op. 20). The choral part is very short and easy.

Would you please give me some information regarding your terms?

Farewell for today, dear maestro! All good wishes to you and Madame Colonne from my wife and myself.

Respectfully yours,
EDVARD GRIEG

---

[5] Colonne had written to Grieg on September 10, 1902, once again inviting him to visit Paris.

[6] Colonne had written on September 25, 1902, "There is no reason for your anxiety. . . . You can come back without fear. The storm has passed, and France is now in the hands of reasonable people." On October 20 he wrote, "A reception is now being planned for you in Paris that will cause you to forget all of the old enmity, and I for my part am happy to be an instrument of this reconciliation."

6

[Berlin, March 27(?), 1903]

Dear Maestro!
Hearty thanks to Madame Colonne for the translation.[7] I am anxious to familiarize myself with it. Permit me to advise you that I have written to C. F. Peters in Leipzig regarding the vocal parts for *Before a Southern Convent*, and they have informed me that they will send the parts to Durand & Co. in Paris as soon as possible.[8]

Along with these lines I take the liberty of sending the scores for the *Piano Concerto* and the *Peer Gynt Suite*. In the concerto I have improved the orchestration in a couple of places, and the suite you will find marked with the bowings etc. that I customarily use.

Since it seems likely that I will have just one rehearsal in Paris, I would be very grateful if you would arrange to have my bowings marked in the orchestral parts and used in the preliminary rehearsals.

I am conducting in Warsaw on the fourteenth of April and will leave that same night for Berlin. If I am feeling strong enough, I will leave the following evening for Paris and will then arrive there on the sixteenth of April. Unfortunately, however, it is not likely that I will be able to handle two night journeys on successive nights, so I dare not count on being in Paris before the seventeenth of April. I assume, however, that you will have an orchestra rehearsal on the seventeenth, and I ask you in any case to please write me a few lines at Hotel de Sèze, 16 rue de Sèze, so that I can know *where* and *when* your next-to-last rehearsal will take place. It is also very important to me to have an opportunity to rehearse with the women's chorus and the soloists *before* the dress rehearsal.[9]

May I ask you to give me your home address so that I can inform you of my arrival?

With warm greetings to you and Madame Colonne,

Respectfully yours,
EDVARD GRIEG

P.S. My address until April 8 is: Berlin, Continental Hotel, thereafter Warsaw, Hotel Bristol.

---

7 The French singer Eugénie Colonne (1854–?), wife of Édouard Colonne, had revised the French translation of the text of *Before a Southern Convent* made by Frank van der Stucken (1858–1929).

8 Grieg wrote to the Peters firm from Berlin on March 27, 1903, that Colonne had asked him to send the conductor's score and orchestral parts for *Before a Southern Convent*. He was now passing along this request to the firm.

9 Grieg's concert with the Colonne Orchestra at the Châtelet Theatre on April 19, 1903, proved to be a colorful, dramatic affair. It ended as a great public success, but the critics were by and large negative. See Grieg's lively account of the concert in his letter of April 20, 1903, to the publisher John Grieg (1856–1905). For a more detailed account of the event, see Harald Herresthal and Ladislav Reznicek, *Rhapsodie norvégienne*, pp. 213–24. Grieg also refers to the concert in his letter to Michel-Dimitri Calvocoressi (1877–1944) of May 2, 1903.

To Knut Dahle

Edvard Grieg's *Norwegian Peasant Dances* op. 72 is his most advanced work. Here, in a quite remarkable way, he entered into the world of Hardanger-fiddle music and succeeded in adapting its uniqueness to the piano. He based the seventeen dance tunes of op. 72 on the transcriptions by Johan Halvorsen (1864–1935) of the tunes as played by the outstanding Hardanger-fiddle player Knut Dahle (1834–1921) from Tinn in Telemark. Dahle had learned the tunes from Torgeir Augundson (1801–72, known affectionately in Norway as Myllarguten, "the miller boy"), Håvard Gibøen (1809–73) and other well-known fiddlers.

Dahle had written to Grieg as early as 1888 asking for his help in getting the dance tunes written down, and Grieg had responded positively. Thrond S. Haukenes (1840–1922), in his book *Telemarken* (Bergen 1892, p. 91), tells of visiting Dahle in Vestfjorddalen at the beginning of September, 1889: "Knut took out a letter that he had just received from the musician Edvard Grieg, a letter wherein Grieg told him that sometime during that fall season he intended to pay him a visit in order to hear him play these indigenous tunes. Grieg also writes in the same letter that no one could be a greater lover of authentic Norwegian music than he was." Unfortunately it has not been possible to locate this letter.

Various obstacles prevented Grieg from making the trip in 1888, however, so the visit had to be postponed. Dahle sent a second letter in 1890, but this time it appears that Grieg did not reply. Only in 1901 did Grieg react to yet a third appeal from Dahle. That time he wrote to his friend and colleague, the violinist and conductor Johan Halvorsen (who in 1899 had become musical director at the National Theater in Christiania), asking if he would take on the task of transcribing Dahle's dance tunes. Halvorsen immediately accepted the challenge.

The complete extant correspondence between Dahle, Grieg and Halvorsen concerning this matter was published in an article by Øyvind Anker (1904–89) entitled "Knut Dahle – Edv. Grieg – Johan Halvorsen. En brevveksling" ("Knut Dahle – Edv. Grieg – Johan Halvorsen. Correspondence").[1] Anker borrowed from Knut Dahle's grandson the three Grieg letters from 1901 that are given below. See also Grieg's letters to Halvorsen of October 18, November 4 and 23 and December 6, 1901.

Knut Dahle's letters to Grieg are preserved in Bergen Offentlige Bibliotek (Bergen Public Library).

1

Troldhaugen, Hop Station at Bergen
October 18, 1901

Mr. Knut Dahle.

I have just received your letter. It goes without saying that my interest in the peasant dance tunes and your preservation of them is the same as before, but for the moment I cannot do anything personally as I am sickly and unable to pay you a visit for other reasons as well. But there is one very important consideration: The dance tunes must be transcribed by a *violinist* (I am a pianist) for the sake of the bowing, tuning, fingering and tone color. The Norwegian Parliament [Stortinget] has paid people to collect folk *songs* but has not understood that the collection

[1] *Norsk Musikkgranskning. Årbok 1943–46*, pp. 71–90.

of folk *dance tunes* is a job for a specialist. Thank you for writing, for I feel more strongly than ever that something must, should and will be done.

I am writing to Christiania about the matter today. If a violinist from there who understands how to *transcribe* and who has a feeling for this work can be secured, either he must come to you or, if that is not possible, you must go to him in Christiania if you are still up to such a trip. Your expenses would be covered one way or another. I will request an immediate answer from Christiania, and as soon as I have it you will hear from me again.[2]

Tell me at your convenience how old you are, when you were in America, how long you were there, and where you performed in public.[3]

With friendly greetings,
Edvard Grieg

---

[2] Knut Dahle's letter of October 11, 1901, to which Grieg is here replying, reads as follows:

Mr. E. Grieg
Today I read in [the newspaper] *Varden* about a concert you had given in Bergen, so you must have come home from abroad. By this letter I will let you know that I have also been to America and have come home. Many of my dance tunes have been preserved there, especially the ones I learned from Myllarguten, but I would like it so very much if a composer here would do the same thing and write them down. I am now the only one alive who has learned from Myllarguten himself. I still have the letter that I got from you many years ago, when I am gone the dance tunes will also be gone, those now being played are entirely different.

Please write to me again either telling me that you are interested in the old dance tunes or if you know someone else who is. The enclosure is from Professor Hanssen in Dekora [Decorah, Iowa], a great musician.

Greetings with much regard,

Respectfully,
Knut J. Dahle
Tinn Telemarken

[3] On October 25, 1901, Dahle answered Grieg's letter as follows:

Mr. Edevart Grieg
I have received your letter and thank you so much for it. It makes me happy to hear that you will do so much in order that the old national tunes can be preserved.

What occasioned my going to America was that my youngest son wanted to go and I didn't want to be separated from him, and the place we decided to go to was northwestern Minnesota. As soon as possible my son hired out as a harvest hand and I went out in the countryside and played now and then in the schoolhouses and sometimes in the small towns. The next spring I went to Dakota and did some playing and some working, in the fall I traveled eastward through Minneapolis St. Paul and on to Harmony, where I stopped. Next, during Christmas I went to Decorah and on to Kolmer Konover, Regyvay Leraai, Spring Valley. But everything was on a small scale. In the big cities there was no way for someone who didn't have a lot of money to perform, for a good hall one had to pay 20–25–30 dollars and more, plus many other expenses, and I couldn't afford it. In Morssi I got a letter from Mr. Gaustad, the painter, telling me that Professor H. Hanssen in Decorah wanted desperately to get hold of me, and as soon as I could I went there and was received cordially and Hanssen helped me so that I gave a concert there in Luther College for the students, teachers and professors Hanssen, Rekve and Larson. I got everything free and, in addition, a lot of praise in the newspapers, so that helped a lot.

In order to get in a position to perform in the big cities I again traveled west to meet my son, and we were going to travel together, but some obstacles came in the way. He was attacked by nerve fever and died after three weeks of suffering. All hope of success in America now having disappeared, my next thought was to return to Norway and live with my daughter, she is a teacher in Tinn, but for reasons of health she had to resign her position this fall. She suffers from a breast disease, and my stay in America lasted just four years,

Knut Dahle, the peasant fiddler whose playing of traditional Hardanger-fiddle tunes provided the raw material from which Grieg composed Norwegian Peasant Dances *op. 72. (Nasjonal-biblioteket, Oslo)*

2

Troldhaugen, Hop at Bergen
October 25, 1901

Mr. Knut Dahle.
Johan Halvorsen, musical director at the National Theater in Christiania, has indicated that he is willing to transcribe the dance tunes. He is an excellent violinist and Norwegian from head to toe. But—you will have to go to him in Christiania as his duties at the theater make it impossible for him to come to you. If you can take the trip I will see to it that you are reimbursed for your travel expenses.

Let me hear a word from you as soon as possible as to whether this proposal is acceptable to you. Halvorsen lives on Bygdø Allee, I think it is No. 21, upper floor. But he can also be seen in the forenoon at the National Theater.

---

and some over one year ago I came home again. My age is sixty-seven years, born the 14th of October 1834, hale and hearty, thank God, so I am willing to take a trip to Christiania if it must be. If only I had money.

Please accept my photograph. I now wear a full beard so I look much different than I used to.

I send the most cordial greetings and I hope that my wish will be fulfilled so that the genuine national tunes can be preserved.

Greetings with much regard,

Respectfully,
Knut J. Dahle
Tinn Telemarken

P.S. My dear wife died thirteen years ago as of October 13th of this year.

You must promise me to stay long enough so that he gets *all* of the best dance tunes written down. I shall then arrange them for piano, and they will become known both in Norway and abroad.

If you decide to make the trip, take this letter with you and show it to Halvorsen. You can be assured of a good reception.[4]

With friendly greetings,

Respectfully yours,
EDVARD GRIEG

3

Troldhaugen at Bergen
November 4, 1901

Mr. Knut Dahle
Tinn
Thank you for your letter and photograph. Poor man! You have lived through much in your life. It's good that you are healthy. At the age of 67 you will of course be able to travel to Christiania. You must do this right away, and for that purpose I am sending you 100 crowns.

I have written to Maestro Halvorsen that he can expect you one day soon, and I hope that all will go well.

With friendly greetings,

Respectfully yours,
EDVARD GRIEG

---

4 On October 31 Dahle wrote to Grieg as follows:

Mr. E. Grieg
I have received your very welcome letter of 25 and thank you so much. I have decided that God willing I will leave home on the 12th or 13th of November. The shortest route is via Kongsberg and from here to Christiania is 18 Norwegian miles [=180 kilometers or ca. 112 miles], but at this time of the year most people travel via Skien and take the train from there to Christiania but that is a little more expensive. If you have confidence in me, I wish that you would help me with a few crowns for the travel expenses. I have some money and could have had enough but my daughter has not gotten her unemployment pay yet so I have to provide for her, and as far as the stay in Christiania is concerned I can stay there as long as you wish if my living expenses are paid and I am given money for the trip home and then I will be content to have delivered my best dance tunes. Next time I will be writing from Christiania.

Accept the friendliest greetings from

KNUT J. DAHLE
TINN TELEMARKEN

I hope you have received the letter and photograph.

K. DAHLE

All the dance tunes that have names and legends associated with them I will explain exactly as I have heard them.

To Edward Dannreuther

The English pianist and musicologist Edward Dannreuther (1844–1905) was born in Germany but came to England as a young man and made his home there for the rest of his life. In 1863 he played the London premiere of Chopin's *Piano Concerto No. 2* in F minor and was soon acclaimed as one of England's foremost pianists. He became a strong champion of Wagner's music in his adopted country. His interest in contemporary music also led him to introduce the piano concertos of Grieg, Liszt and Tchaikovsky in the British Isles.

Letters 1–3 are preserved in Bergen Offentlige Bibliotek (Bergen Public Library), letter 4 in Nasjonalbiblioteket, Oslo (National Library of Norway, Oslo Division). All were written in German.

1

Bergen, June 7, 1874

Dear Mr. Dannreuther!

Naturally I was very happy to receive the surprising news that you have played my *Piano Concerto* in London.[1] I won't have to find out from the newspapers that you have done an outstanding job. When the author of the program notes (is it you?) surmises that Liszt and Wagner have not been of importance to me, he is profoundly mistaken. Since my visit to Liszt in 1870[2] I have known and admired many of his works, and so far as Wagner is concerned I don't know how you could find any musician with a modicum of spirit who has not been inspired by his genius. But it is quite true: It is one thing to be inspired, quite another to show it.

This winter in Christiania I conducted a significant portion of *Lohengrin* for choir and orchestra as well as Liszt's *Tasso.*[3]

I have read with pleasure of your beautiful efforts in London. It is truly about time that the newer school in the English capital gets as warm and gifted an advocate as you.

Farewell for now. Warm greetings from

Yours truly,
EDVARD GRIEG

---

1 Dannreuther had played Grieg's *Piano Concerto* at a "Crystal Palace Saturday Concert" in London on April 18, 1874.

2 See Grieg's letter to his parents, Alexander (1806–75) and Gesine Grieg (1814–75), regarding this visit.

3 Richard Wagner's opera *Lohengrin* and Franz Liszt's symphonic poem *Tasso: lamento e trionfo.*

2

Copenhagen, December 2, 1879
Address: Hotel King of Denmark

Dear Mr. Dannreuther!
Since it is my intention to come to England next spring, you probably can easily guess why you are getting a letter from me today. Here is the situation: A word of advice from you would mean very, very much to me as you, based on collegial feelings, would give me the right counsel. I have written to Manns[4] about playing my *Piano Concerto* in the Crystal Palace. I have been told that this is where one must begin. What advice would you give me regarding a longer stay? Next season I would like to play as much as possible in London (England) in order to show my compositions. I would mainly like to perform my chamber works and arrange for my songs to be sung—and, if possible, to conduct my little choral work, *Before a Southern Convent.* But I just don't know whom I should approach. I wouldn't want to fall into the wrong hands and thus waste my opportunity—and it is altogether too easy to do that in London!

I have heard of Chappell![5] Does he engage artists for the whole season? Or does he just arrange for chamber-music concerts? Unfortunately, my financial circumstances do not permit me to come to London on the basis of vague possibilities. I must have definite assurances, preferably an engagement for the complete concert tour. But for one thing I am afraid to approach the first and best "entrepreneur" who comes along, and for another I need a so-called "name".

Which leads me to a question strictly between us: Do you think my art has chances for success in London, both artistically and financially? A naive question! Kindly give me an equally naive answer! Kindly regard me as a little child and write:

1. You must do that and that!
2. You must do thus and so!
3. You must do etc. etc.

When must I be in London in order to accomplish something?[6]
With the warmest greetings to you and your wife, I remain

Sincerely yours,
EDVARD GRIEG

---

[4] Sir August Manns (1825–1907), who was born in Germany, conducted the Crystal Palace concerts from 1855 to 1901.
[5] London impresario Edward Chappell (1819–1902).
[6] Grieg did not realize his plans for a visit to England until 1888.

3

[London, May 1 (?), 1888]
5 The Cedars, Clapham Common

Dear Dannreuther!
That we have been able to reach neither Mr. Manns nor his wife appears to be an extremely common occurrence in London. At the very least, my wife and I have been very unlucky during these few days. Moreover, I live so far away that I think it would be difficult to make another try at a visit.[7] I am, therefore, all the happier that you (and hopefully your esteemed wife) will come to the rehearsal to hear how poor a pianist a composer often is!

Hopefully the enclosed calling cards will not fail to produce the desired result. (I do not know any of the leaders of "The Philharmonic Society", and the secretary is absolutely invisible.) But if my calling card does not have the necessary authority, you must please insist on talking with me personally.

So: I'll see you later!

Yours truly,
EDVARD GRIEG

4

[London], May 5, 1888
5 The Cedars, Clapham Common

Dear Dannreuther!
What a pity! Today I am totally unable because of business and tomorrow, Sunday, I have declined all invitations in order to take a little trip out into the countryside. But perhaps it is just as well that I cannot accept your kind invitation, for after the last concert[8] I was so physically exhausted that I need all the rest I can get. For that reason I absolutely do not dare to go to parties or to participate in a trip through the sights of London.

You appear to be made of iron and perhaps cannot understand such a thing. But we can speak of this and many other things later. I will be here for some time in order to give a concert.[9]

With cordial greetings, I am

Yours truly,
EDVARD GRIEG

---

[7] Grieg was staying with music publisher George Augener (1830–1915), who was also the general agent in England for Grieg's publisher, the C. F. Peters Musikverlag of Leipzig.

[8] Grieg had performed as soloist in his *Piano Concerto* at a concert in St. James's Hall on May 3, 1888, with Frederic Hymen Cowen (1852–1935) conducting.

[9] The last concert during this visit to London took place in St. James's Hall on May 16. Appearing at that concert, in addition to Grieg himself, were his wife Nina and violinist Wilhelmina Neruda (1838–1911).

To Arthur de Greef

Grieg developed a warm friendship with the Belgian pianist and composer Arthur de Greef (1862–1940), one of the foremost pianists of his generation. De Greef was an ardent admirer of Grieg's music, not least the *Piano Concerto*, which he performed publicly for the first time at a Colonne concert in Paris on February 26, 1888. That autumn he was on a concert tour to Norway and took the opportunity to pay Grieg a visit at Troldhaugen. Grieg was enchanted with the integrity of his playing, as is evident from his enthusiastic comments in a letter to Alexander Bull (1839–1914) of January 1, 1889 (see p. 179).

In November and December of 1889 Grieg and de Greef appeared together at three concerts in Brussels, where the latter was a professor at the conservatory. On December 8, de Greef played the *Piano Concerto* with the composer conducting. On December 22 and 29 they repeated the successful performance in Paris. The last time they performed together was during Grieg's farewell concert tour in Germany in the spring of 1907, when they performed the *Piano Concerto* at a concert in Munich on April 6. Five months later Grieg passed away.

Grieg's letters to de Greef were written in German. Letter 1 is preserved in the Bergen Public Library, which also owns all of de Greef's letters to Grieg, which are in French. Most of Grieg's letters to de Greef are preserved in Koninklijke Bibliotheek Albert I, Brussels. They have been printed in the original German in Bernard Huys's article "Onuitgegeven autografische brieven van Edvard Grieg en Nina Grieg en Alexander Bull aan Arthur de Greef, bewaard in de Koninklijke Bibliotheek Albert I te Brussel" in *Academiae Analecta*, Brussels, 1988, and in the book *Arthur de Greef—en venn av Edvard Grieg* by Bernard Huys and Eivind A. C. Eikenes, Stavanger 1994.

1

Copenhagen, December 29, 1890
Hotel King of Denmark

Dear de Greef!
Was my last letter really so gloomy? If so, the reason must have been that I was vexed about the fact that I have still not finished your piano concerto.[1] And that we shall not meet is indeed sad. I had been greatly looking forward to it. But I understand very well your reasons and can only say that you are absolutely right.

Tomorrow we will bury the old master, Gade.[2] He visited us just last Sunday, was jolly and happy, and that very evening he suddenly died. That's the way it always ought to be! Death is natural, but suffering is unnatural, and the "why" of suffering absolutely defies understanding. It's a shame that you never got to know Gade personally. You would immediately have recognized in him a significant artist. He flourished during the 1840's and 1850's, and during those years he was indeed one of the leading composers.

---

[1] Grieg is alluding here to his *Piano Concerto No. 2* (EG 120), which he wanted de Greef to premiere. As early as September 7, 1888, Grieg's editor in Leipzig, Max Abraham (1831–1900) of the C. F. Peters Musikverlag, had urged Grieg to write another piano concerto, and Grieg made several attempts to do so but never managed to complete it. The sketches for the intended concerto are preserved in the Bergen Public Library and have been published in *Edvard Grieg: Complete Works*, vol. 20.

[2] The Danish composer and conductor Niels W. Gade (1817–90) died in Copenhagen on December 21 at the age of 73.

We plan to spend the winter quietly here. As soon as spring is approaching, though, I'm going home to my mountains. I am already longing for them like a child.

And now I wish for you and your wife everything good and beautiful in the new year! Warmest greetings to both of you from my wife and from

Your friend and admirer,
EDVARD GRIEG

2

Troldhaugen at Bergen, July 15, 1907

My dear de Greef!
It pains me that I can't write to you in French. How strongly I feel the things you say in your letter! So much that should have been said [when we were together] remained unsaid. And the reason is that because of the language problem our conversation never gets beyond a purely superficial level.

But through your music I have gotten back the things that I missed! You played *more beautifully than ever!*[3] Since then the thought has not left me that you could once again concertize in Norway. I have spoken with Vogt Fischer,[4] the impresario whom I previously mentioned (Thomas Heftyes gate 14, Christiania). Unfortunately, he has engaged two pianists to appear in Norway this autumn, one of them being Ernst von Dohnányi.[5] I have therefore suggested next spring and have encouraged him to begin negotiations with you as soon as possible since you are much in demand. Mr. Fischer is a very proud person and really doesn't want to be called an "impresario". (I mention this just as a hint.)

What you write about Alexander Bull surprises me greatly. There is, unfortunately, no longer any possibility of his getting well again. If he sees someone he smiles sadly, and if he hears them talk about bygone days, even in French, his face might light up for a moment, and perhaps he would say something, thereafter only to sink ever deeper into his melancholy. Poor man!

I very much enjoyed my concerts in Berlin and Kiel.[6] But afterwards, unfortunately, I fell ill—it was a nerve problem—and I had to spend some time at a Danish sanatorium.[7] It's going better now, but things still are not as they should be. Summer is finally here and with it the hope of improvement.

Let me soon hear from you again! Warm greetings from house to house from

Yours truly,
EDVARD GRIEG

---

[3] De Greef had been the soloist in Grieg's *Piano Concerto* in Munich on April 6, 1907, with Grieg conducting. This proved to be the last time they would meet.

[4] Norwegian impresario Peter Vogt Fischer (1863–1938).

[5] Hungarian pianist, composer and conductor Ernst (Ernö) von Dohnányi (1877–1916).

[6] Grieg's concerts in Berlin were on April 12 and 14, the one in Kiel—the last concert of his life—on April 26.

[7] Skodsborg Sanatorium near Copenhagen.

To Frederick Delius

The English composer Frederick Delius (1862–1934) was an ardent admirer of Grieg's music from childhood onward. The two men met for the first time in Leipzig in December, 1887, when Delius was a conservatory student. They soon developed a warm friendship that continued to the end of Grieg's life. Grieg quickly perceived Delius's talent; indeed, his first letter to him is in reality a strong letter of recommendation that was probably aimed at Delius's father, who was reluctant to let his son devote himself totally to music.

Delius was a fanatical nature-lover. As early as 1881 he made his first visit to the "Hardangervidda", the barren mountain plateau that covers thousands of square miles in West Norway. He visited there again during the summer of 1887, and when he and Grieg were together in December of that year they shared their impressions of the vastness and rugged beauty of the mountains of West Norway. Grieg later enjoyed calling Delius "the Hardangervidda man", and through the years Delius made a number of trips to Norway, especially to the Hardangervidda and the mountains of West Norway.

Grieg and Delius carried on an extensive correspondence in German. The letters from Grieg to Delius are preserved in The Delius Trust in London, those from Delius to Grieg in Bergen Offentlige Bibliotek (Bergen Public Library). The complete extant correspondence has been published in an English translation by Lionel Carley in the book *Grieg and Delius: A Chronicle of Their Friendship in Letters*, London 1993.

1

Leipzig, February 28, 1888

Dear sir!

I am pleasantly surprised by your manuscripts—indeed, I am really excited—for I see in them evidence of a truly exceptional talent for composition in the grand style, a talent that strives toward the highest goal.[1] Whether or not you will reach that goal depends solely on how the circumstances of your life work out. If you will permit me—for the sake of your future—to give you a word of advice (as an older artist I surely may be allowed to do that), it would be this: Now when you are young, instead of taking up an external vocation,[2] just immerse yourself in the study of your art and follow your own true nature and the inner voice in your quest for the ideal. But with this in view it is absolutely essential that you choose the national and artistic environment that your guardian spirit prescribes for you.

It is my most fervent wish that in your homeland you will receive the recognition that you deserve and get the resources that are needed to enable you to

---

1 The works "in the grand style" to which Grieg refers probably are the orchestral suite "Florida" (1887) and the symphonic poem "Hiawatha" (1888).

2 Delius's father, a prosperous manufacturer of woolen products, wanted his son to go into the same line of work. This, presumably, is what Grieg means by the expression "an external vocation" ("eine äussere Stellung"), i.e., a vocation that had nothing to do with music. Grieg's letter, as Lionel Carley points out, is somewhat similar to the recommendation that Franz Liszt wrote for Grieg in 1869. Liszt's recommendation is given in English translation in footnote 3 to Grieg's letter to Niels Ravnkilde (1823–90) of November 2, 1868.

reach your beautiful goal, and I do not doubt for a single moment that you will reach this goal.

With the assurance of my warm understanding and support,

Yours very truly,
EDVARD GRIEG

2

Leipzig, April 16, 1888

Dear Delius!

You say that I should write when I have inclination and time. Well, I have plenty of the former but absolutely none of the latter. But as you know, nothing seems hard to a willing mind. I well understand that you are now breathing in a different atmosphere in more ways than one.[3] But that is also the case with us since *you* left.

I must tell you that *very* seldom have I enjoyed an acquaintanceship so much! Now if only we could meet again! Unfortunately we cannot accept your kind invitation to come to Bradford. And our reunion in London? Well, that probably will not be much more than a handshake. But in Norway! *There it shall happen*—after you have returned from Spain, bringing with you a whole world of new impressions. Then we will sit down together someplace in the Norwegian mountains and hear reports of things seen with Spanish eyes!

We leave Sunday for London, traveling by way of Calais. We will arrive in London on Monday afternoon. That is to say, if I am ready, for I still have altogether too many things to attend to. But I *must* be ready.

Yesterday I was with Sitt,[4] and I visited him again this evening. He was most cordial and manifested an enormous erudition. I think, however, that his style of orchestration is at times somewhat crude. I can't deny that I got that impression, but I will not make a final judgment for now.

Our dinnertime whist games are now continuing with Mr. Brown,[5] who appears to be a very charming and natural person—and, as Sinding says, gifted as well.

My wife asks me to greet you warmly.

Goodbye for now, and don't forget May 3[6] and

Your devoted friend,
EDVARD GRIEG

---

[3] Delius had written to Grieg on April 12 telling him that he was home in Bradford, England, and that he hoped to see Nina and Edvard there.

[4] Bohemian violinist, violist, conductor and composer Hans Sitt (1850–1922) had been commissioned by Max Abraham (1831–1900) of the C. F. Peters Musikverlag to orchestrate Grieg's *Norwegian Dances*, a composition for piano four hands. Sitt's version was published by Peters in 1891.

[5] Grieg had often played whist with Johan Halvorsen (1864–1935), Christian Sinding (1856–1941) and Frederick Delius in Leipzig. "Mr. Brown" was Delius's English fellow student at the conservatory, Charles Brown (1868–?), who also had received instruction in music theory from Sinding. (Grieg spelled his name "Braun".)

[6] Grieg was scheduled to make his first public appearance in London on May 3 as soloist in his *Piano Concerto* with Frederic Cowen as conductor. The concert proved to be an outstanding success.

To Ernst von Dohnányi

The Hungarian pianist, conductor and composer Ernst (Ernö) von Dohnányi (1877–1960) was one of the foremost pianists of his day. Grieg had great confidence in his pedagogical insight and contacted him in the hope of enlisting his help in guiding the young Norwegian pianist Fridtjof Backer-Grøndahl,[1] whose potential Grieg rated very high.

Grieg's letter to Dohnányi is translated from the German original that was published in *Studia Musicologica Academiae Scientorum Hungaricae* 9, 1967.

Christiania, January 8, 1906
Hotel Westminster

Dear Maestro von Dohnányi!
I thank you most heartily for your exceedingly kind reply regarding Mr. Backer-Grøndahl.[2] Needless to say, Mr. Grøndahl accepts your proposal with the greatest pleasure. When *you* have told him what he must learn (above all more moderation, a more beautiful *cantabile* and better use of the pedal), then I am sure that he, gifted as he is, can work on his own until you again have time to work with him.

You write that you will be playing in Copenhagen sometime—and maybe in Christiania? I hereby request that you change this "maybe" to "quite certainly!"[3]

I will be here until the middle of March and would be very happy to be able to greet you in our new Norway.[4]

With warm greetings, also from my wife.

Respectfully yours,
Edvard Grieg

---

[1] Fridtjof Backer-Grøndahl (1885–1959) was the son of Olaus Andreas Grøndahl (1847–1923) and Agathe Backer Grøndahl (1847–1907), both of whom were professional musicians. Agathe Backer Grøndahl is regarded to this day as Norway's foremost female composer.

[2] Dohnányi had responded to Grieg's request in a letter dated January 4, 1906. He advised Grieg that he did not take private pupils but that he would make an exception in this case since "Mr. Grøndahl is recommended by you." He warned that the lessons would have to be at somewhat irregular intervals because he so often was away on concert tours. He also informed Grieg that he would not accept pay for such lessons.

[3] Dohnányi did in fact give a number of concerts in Norway later that year. See Grieg's diary entries for October 8 and 18, 1906, in Benestad & Halverson (eds.), *Edvard Grieg: Diaries, Articles, Speeches* (Columbus, Ohio, 2001).

[4] Grieg is alluding to the fact that Norway had only recently (in 1905) won its independence from Sweden.

To Bella Edwards

During a visit to Copenhagen in October, 1895, Grieg met two Danish artists—Margrethe Petersen, a singer, and Bella Edwards, a pianist. Grieg was much taken with the latter, as is evident from the six letters he sent her. The letters were first published in the *Bergen Arbeiderblad* on March 16, 1985—two days after they had been released for publication by the governing board of Bergen Offentlige Bibliotek (Bergen Public Library), where the letters are preserved. None of the letters are signed. Grieg undoubtedly destroyed his letters from Bella Edwards.

1

Leipzig, November 6, 1895

[Dear!]
Finally! If only you knew how I have been longing! And how happy you have made me in this present moment. It is as if I can feel your breath in every puff of wind. The few lines—far, far too few and too cautious, why?—shall we be ashamed of the most noble and most beautiful feelings? Yes, altogether too few—and yet, they reveal a whole world. But I must be permitted to write without suppressing my passion. You must not say "thank you" for the loveliest hours of your life—and yet, these words resound like no music on earth! For what shall I say, then? Well, they were not just hours. They were mere seconds, yet they held a reflection of eternity. Since we met each other I have begun to believe in hypnotism! Do you know that you have become a part of my consciousness, that it has become cold and empty around me when you are not there? Promise me that I can see you and talk with you when we are both in Denmark. Promise me that!

How sweet you are when you write, *We* sang "A Swan"! *Yes*, you dare to say that, for the tones vibrate in the depths of your soul, that is true. I only wished that your piano technique could have been further improved, and I feel confident that you will succeed in doing that. Can I not have the pleasure of working a bit with you in Copenhagen when you come home in January–February? For in that case I will do everything I can to be there. I think I should be able to teach you something regarding the interpretation of my own compositions. I could also teach you a few things with respect to piano technique if you are really interested.

And now may these lines find their way to you. I could not formulate them in any other way. May a lucky star hover over you—the same star that caused us to meet in order that we might become friends! Yes, write to me now as a friend—as *soon* as you get this. I am counting on it. Write about your life, about your plans, about how "we" sing together! About everything! Farewell, my dear!

Warm greetings to Margrethe Petersen if she knows of our correspondence. I dared to take her into my confidence that memorable day at the hotel. An instinct told me that it was safe to confide in her. She will certainly have understood that something quite different lay beneath my jocular tone. And then she would treat it as something sacred, wouldn't she?

Promise me: Burn this letter!

2

[Leipzig], November 15, [1895]

Dear!
If I really am your friend, don't call me master, for that is something I neither am nor wish to be. Furthermore, the masters are dead—and I am living, living in order to search for something that I never find. That is my unhappiness and my happiness as an artist and as a man. In your eyes I beheld the profoundest beauty that I have seen in my life, but your letters, dear though they are to me, are stubbornly silent about all that is wonderful that I read in your eyes. Why? Are you afraid? Or have you no confidence in me? Of course that is the problem. How could you have it when you don't know me? And yet, I trust you *without* knowing you. Do not deprive me of this trust! Or have I made a mistake? Was it really just the harmonies? No, no! Those sweet eyes conveyed so infinitely much more! That strange, stunning moment when I said, "Is it possible?" And you did not reply. But you gazed—gazed at me for a long, long time with an expression that was a singular, blessed *Yes.* That moment was surely no figment of the imagination. It really happened! Tell me, then, in a single word that this expression was not a lie, that I may read between the lines in your letters, may believe in that which I wanted so much to find there—but which isn't there. Tell me this with nothing more than a little *"Yes"* in the corner of the letter. For things cannot go on like this. I can't stand it. Each letter will torture me, and that cannot be your intention. But—if you don't say it, I will understand—and then it's all over. Then I will try to forget, and in my art I will try to rise above what you call "all sorrows and gloomy thoughts." And then you must forgive me for momentarily misunderstanding an altogether too affectionate expression in the eyes of a woman.

As you see, a storm is raging within me. But let it rage! Since I risked the previous letter, I can risk this one. I am a lonely man, and you had become my better world. That is the complete explanation.

So, then, farewell, my dear! I, too, send many greetings—not, however, "surrounded by lovely harmonies" but by an even lovelier hope for the whole "Yes"!

Promise me as before: Burn this letter! And one thing more: *No third party* must see these lines—not even M[argrethe] P[etersen], even though I like her very much. Promise me that! But greet her and thank her for "A Swan", which I think she will be able to sing so beautifully that I will get the urge to take up the baton. What a shame that I will not be there! Well, who knows. Maybe some other time. Tell her that the words "to trumpet your sound, then" must be *fortissimo* all the way to the end, not *diminuendo* as incorrectly indicated in the piano edition. "Ne'er a sound to foretoken your bright voice, my mute one"[1] must be one long *pp* with no hint of a *crescendo.*

---

1 From the translation by Rolf Kr. Stang in *Edvard Grieg: Complete Works*, vol. 14.

3

Leipzig, December 5, 1895

[Dear!]

If only you knew how many times I have read and reread your lovely letter! You wonder if the "yes's" gladden my heart? No, "gladden" is not the right word. But they carry me away into a fairytale world. I forget that I am standing at the noontime of my life and feel like a love-struck schoolboy who is giddy over the girl who is the object of his affection! (Tell me: Is that really what one calls "friendship"!?)

So: My "storm" letter was what it took to get you to talk. Therefore I do not regret it. Yes, our "beautiful, wonderful three-day relationship without regret!" Where have you found these wonderful words? I could never have hit upon such expressions!

But let us tell it like it is. There is no use denying it: There may be no *regret*, but our happiness is mingled with *sadness*. Tell me: Is it happenstance that shall bring us together again? Is that really your opinion? And can you accept this? Impossible! Now you must be nice and give me hope! How long will you be in England? Tell me about your plans for late winter.

There is a Danish man here, Folmer Hansen,[2] who (just between us) definitely wants me to conduct in several German cities. He knows you and has traveled with you. Allow me, therefore, to ask a question: What do you know about him? Is he clever and dependable?

And then tell me about both "swans"—about both the one whose eyes were secret lies and still more the one whose eyes were *not* that.[3] Greet M[argrethe] P[etersen]. She is the only one of the younger generation of singers who has had the courage to be not just a singer but herself. There are certain Nordic songs, especially mine, that absolutely require that kind of personality. I admit, I had already given up—but I had forgotten nature's beautiful secret: that life renews itself. Yes, we three must meet somewhere in the world! Whether I shall dare to believe that it is possible—that *you* must tell me. And then I will try to be happy—and will write about the "jubilant unattainable happiness." How remarkable that you should mention this particular goal, which is precisely what I long for in the depths of my soul. That must be a good omen!

Farewell, my dear! Write soon (and include the date)! Give me your exact new address, and—burn [my letters]! Tell me plainly whether you have done this?????

---

[2] Folmer Hansen (?–1918) was the director of a company that published materials for the theater and who also worked as an impresario.

[3] Grieg is alluding to the text of "A Swan".

4

Leipzig, December 24, 1895

Dear!
Forgive my silence! I have been much too agitated to write. That is to say, I have written at least four letters but have torn them up. But today I must get everything off my chest. And it will be from the bottom of my heart. For I can't keep up this correspondence any longer! It shakes the foundations both of me personally and of my art! For I feel it: Our letters are not speaking the same language. Each word from you increases my growing longing for you and tells me that while you have taken my whole heart, what you give me in your letters is only a tiny fragment of yours. When we were together up there it was different. But now I no longer know what I should believe. Your letters confuse me because they reveal no ardor, no longing! For my sake, and for your own, tell me fully and from your heart what you think about what I am now asking you. I *think* that you warmly desire to see me again, even if you do not write that you do. But I must know. And above all, I must see you and talk with you again. Can we not, during the two months you will be home, meet regularly at the piano and revive those blessed moments that we shared the last time we were together? Trust me, no one will suspect anything. Wherever I am, I have a workroom that not a soul knows about. Shall we dream the beautiful dream? If so, I will come to Copenhagen the latter part of January at the latest and will abandon all my other plans!

If you do not have enough longing—or enough courage—tell me candidly. As you see, I am completely candid. For in that case I *will* attempt the impossible: to forget you! There is no middle way for me. Either/or! If this should be my last letter, I thank you again and again for all the loveliness that I read in your eyes. It is not your fault if Eros is unable to affect you as deeply as he does me. If this is not my last letter, I will nonetheless no longer risk writing to your address in Copenhagen. I will address any future letters to E. G. B. E. c/o *poste restante* and will inform you when a letter is waiting for you.

But now: You must answer right away—and fully. Speak directly to me, as your eyes did! Caution, now that you see how things stand with me, would be a sin and—a game. And surely you don't want to play with my affections! I am a lonely person. That is the source of my infinite longing for understanding. In Woman I have found it; in Life, never!

I had to talk candidly with you! Warm Christmas greetings!

5

[Leipzig], December 30, 1895

[Dear!]
Thank you for the quick response! I awaited your reply with indescribable anguish! So this is how it stands: You lack the courage! Ah, but then you also lack

that which gives courage! But—to act contrary to your wishes is the last thing I wanted you to do. Therefore, I have cast the die: I will *not* come to Copenhagen until the middle of March, when you will have left for Norway, and by the time you get back I will be gone!

Now it has been said—it cost every ounce of my strength to say it. Feeling as I now do, I could not bear to be for a single day, a single hour, where you are without seeing and talking with you privately. I would die from the agony of privation.

You must not talk about never separating—you who do not want *us* to meet. It is nothing but empty sound!

As far as Copenhagen is concerned, I think you would have had nothing to worry about. For a long time I have had my various workrooms so well hidden that nobody—neither my best friends nor my wife—have known where they are. I have required this in order to be able to work in peace, and people have understood that. I say this just to help you understand. But be assured that I shall not try to change your mind, for your lack of courage has been like a cold shower on the heat of my passion. And this shower shall give me strength to preserve for myself and my art all of my pride and sincerity as an artist and a man. How, then, could I be angry! It is wistfulness, not anger, that completely fills my soul! You would certainly not cause sorrow for anyone else—but me!

Still, thank you for everything! Thank you for the Christmas card and thank you for the inexpressibly lovely—and bitter—year!

Dear, thoughtless creature, from the enclosed piece of envelope you will see how you have closed your latest letter!! It was unsealed!! And still I am supposed to rely *confidently* on you!

6

[Leipzig], January 27, 1896

[Dear!]
I cannot reply to your letter without reopening all the wounds! Therefore just this: Do not write any more! Still—since you wish it so, we shall not absolutely sever our relationship! Let us then meet again as friends!![4]

---

[4] In one of the letters Grieg enclosed the following musical passage, which constitutes the principal motive in Hector Berlioz's "Dance of the Sylphs" from the second part of *The Damnation of Faust* op. 24 (1845–46). According to popular legend a sylph is an imaginary being, usually thought of as female, who inhabits the air. The term is also applied figuratively to a slender, graceful girl or woman.

To Emil Erslev

Emil Erslev (1817–82) was a music publisher in Copenhagen, having founded the firm Horneman & Erslev in collaboration with Johan Ole Emil Horneman (1809–70) in 1846. He became sole owner in 1859 and a decade later sold the firm to Sophus A. E. Hagen (1842–1929). Many of Grieg's earliest compositions were published by Horneman & Erslev including *Humoresques* op. 6 and *Songs and Ballads* op. 9.

Grieg's letters to Erslev are preserved in Nasjonalbiblioteket, Oslo (National Library of Norway, Oslo Division).

1

Christiania, November 5, 1866

Dear Music Publisher Emil Erslev:
Just a short time ago I received word from Miss Hagerup[1] that my songs have already been sent to the engraver. Without delay, therefore, I am sending the enclosed song in case it might still be included in the set—and I surely hope that may still be possible.

The fact is that I would have much preferred that the two songs to texts by Hans Christian Andersen be omitted and the enclosed song, "Outward Bound", be included instead—partly because all the texts would then be by Munch,[2] partly because the published set would otherwise be too complex.

The new song, as you will see, is fairly long and has the character of a ballad from beginning to end. My wish, therefore, is that it should be the last piece in the set. And since one of the earlier songs—"The Harp"—is also somewhat balladic, in order to maximize the unity of the entire set I would like the sequence to be as follows:

1. The Harp
2. Sunset
3. Cradle Song
4. Outward Bound

The set should have the following title:

Songs and Ballads to Poems by A. Munch
composed by Edvard Grieg
op. 9[3]

---

1 Nina Hagerup, who at this time was engaged to Grieg.
2 Norwegian poet Andreas Munch (1811–84).
3 "The Harp" and "Outward Bound" constituted the first and last songs, respectively, of op. 9 as Grieg

Hopefully you will do everything in your power to see to it that the change can be made, for I am convinced that by so doing the set will be much improved. I think "Outward Bound" fits exceptionally well into the overall structure of the set. I now look forward with great anticipation to receiving a proof of the whole set, both to see how the new song looks and also because I want to add a few pedal indications etc. to the earlier ones.

I heard from Warmuth[4] recently that *Humoresques* is sold out. If there is going to be a new edition I definitely want to make a few small changes.

And now you must excuse me for troubling you at such great length. It's not easy to deal with matters like these when we are limited to correspondence.

With warm greetings, also to Professor Gade,[5]

Respectfully yours,
EDVARD GRIEG

2

Christiania, December 29, 1867

Mr. Emil Erslev, Copenhagen

Thanks so much for what you sent me. I would be glad to send you another little song when I have time—but you must not *press* it out of me, for then I foresee that it would be colorless. But I do make it a practice to keep my word. (. . .)

Could you give me some information about Miss Stenhammar?[6] Is she coming up here—and when? Do you think I could engage her to sing the part of Armida in "The Crusaders"?[7] It's scheduled for performance in April or possibly earlier. Please be so kind as to give me your advice in this matter.

Is Gade not writing anything new?

As you can see, I have questions by the dozen, but how could it be otherwise? I'm sitting up here at the edge of the world and feeling a need to live and make a contribution to art. If you have an organist position for me, I'll come straight to Denmark and will gladly write you a song each week. When I would leave Norway on such conditions you can draw your own conclusions about the state of affairs up here. If I don't get away from here soon I will have to say like Bjørnson in *The Newlyweds*,[8] "There is something in here that is dying."

Yes, next summer I shall hope to greet you in beautiful Denmark. Then I will

---

requested. The order of the other two songs, however, was reversed. The songs to texts by Hans Christian Andersen (1805–75)—"Love" and "Folk Song from Langeland"—were included in *Four Songs* op. 15, which was published in 1868.

4 Carl Warmuth Sr. (1811–92), a music publisher in Christiania.

5 Danish composer Niels W. Gade (1817–90).

6 Swedish singer Fredrika Stenhammar (1836–80).

7 *Korsfarerne (The Crusaders)*, a cantata by Danish composer Niels W. Gade.

8 *De Nygifte (The Newlyweds)*, a play written in 1865 by Norwegian author Bjørnstjerne Bjørnson (1832–1910).

compose and forget all this inertia and pettiness. That Norway has no prominent composers is not due to the fact that none are born. It is because they are stifled in their home country before they have developed fully— and because as a rule material need makes it impossible for them to liberate themselves. A sad truth.

But as clearly as I see this, it is equally certain that I will not succumb to it. If I get a stipend I will go to Leipzig, where I hope to be able to live.

But enough for now. Please give my warm greetings to Winding and his wife[9] when you see them. Also Professor Gade.

With wishes for a good new year, please accept sincerest greetings from me and my wife.

Yours truly,
EDVARD GRIEG

P.S. Do you want more "Humoresques"? But you must remember: One has a duty not to commit suicide! Do you understand me?

I venture to send you the enclosed picture as a Christmas greeting.

---

[9] Danish composer and pianist August Winding (1835–99) and his wife Clara (1839–1925), who was a daughter of Danish composer J. P. E. Hartmann (1805–1900).

To Henry Theophilus Finck

The American music historian Henry Theophilus Finck (1854–1926) was an enthusiastic admirer of Grieg's music. On February 2, 1900, he wrote to Grieg requesting some first-hand information that he might use in a book that he was writing (*Songs and Songwriters*, New York, 1900). He was interested in Grieg's views concerning poetry, the folk song, local color, accompaniment questions, and other matters. This request was the beginning of an active correspondence between the two men that continued until December 30, 1905.

On July 17, 1900, Grieg sent Finck a letter in German together with a long enclosure that has become an important source for our understanding of Grieg's art. Unfortunately, as Finck mentions in his reply to Grieg of September 7, 1900, the book was already in galley proofs by the time he received this information. Thus he was able to make use of the new material in *Songs and Songwriters* only in the form of footnotes. He made extensive use of it, however, in two later books: *Edvard Grieg* (London, 1906) and *Grieg and His Music* (New York and London, 1909).

Though neither Grieg nor Finck was aware of it at the time, they were both in Bayreuth in the summer of 1876 to cover the Wagner performances in the new opera hall, Grieg for the Norwegian newspaper *Bergensposten*, Finck for the New York magazines *World* and *The Atlantic Monthly*. The two men met for the first time in 1901 (see footnote 3).

All the extant letters from Finck to Grieg are preserved in Bergen Offentlige Bibliotek (Bergen Public Library), which also owns Letter 3 from Grieg to Finck as well as two versions (both in German) of the enclosure to Letter 3. The longer of the two, which presumably was the one used by Finck and returned to Grieg at his request (see Letter 3), is given here in translation. This letter and enclosure have been published in the original German in Øystein Gaukstad (ed.), *Edvard Grieg: Artikler og taler* (Oslo, 1957) and in English translation in Bjarne Kortsen (ed.), *Grieg the Writer I* (Bergen, 1975). Letter 6 is a translation of a facsimile of the German original reproduced in Finck's book, *Grieg and His Music* (New York and London, 1909). The remaining letters, the originals of which have not been located, are given in Finck's translations as included in the same book. Finck rarely indicates whether he is quoting a letter in whole or in part, but presumably in most cases it is the latter.

1

Copenhagen, February 23, 1900

Dear Sir!
Accept my best thanks for the kind gift of your book on Wagner. As a matter of course, your name as that of an excellent writer on music had been familiar to me for many years. In addition to this, I had, before my article on Mozart was printed, a very special reason to be grateful to you, because you prevented the appearance in it of an erroneous assertion on my part regarding Wagner.[1]

Some time ago a new method of carrying out contracts was introduced in

[1] In his first letter to Grieg, dated February 2, 1900, Finck informed Grieg that he had translated his article on Mozart (written in German) for publication in *The Century Illustrated Monthly Magazine* (Vol. 55, No. 1, November 1897). Finck informs the readers of *Grieg and His Music* that in the course of making this translation he had "suggested the omission of the error referred to by Grieg."

America, in consequence of which my works are reprinted there in a way which affects me grievously. The thought of becoming popular in America, therefore, has for me, as you see, exclusively an ideal charm. But in order to give expression to the feeling of gratitude that, as just stated, I entertain toward you, I take great pleasure in meeting your wishes to the best of my powers. Now, however, comes a "but". I read very little about music—my poor health makes the greatest possible concentration imperative—and of the things written about me, most of those I have seen were quite too stupid and ignorant to be of any use. Consequently, I regret that there is nothing of this nature that I could recommend to you. . . . I am very glad, indeed, to have my faults and weaknesses censured if I can only detect at the same time some comprehension of my intentions. Wagner says somewhere that one must feel sympathy with him in order to understand him. I have often thought this over and asked myself if Wagner does not here invert cause and effect. Well, however that may be, I shall be glad to make some jottings for you regarding my songs. The matter seems, however, *intime* and I feel sure I may take it for granted that what I have to say will be used with the greatest circumspection and friendly tact [*Pietät*]. I regret to say that at present I am too busy to be able to promise that my notes will reach you as early as the end of April. I shall do the utmost—that I can promise you. It will be a pleasure for me to do anything that will contribute to your work.

America I shall probably never visit. I cannot endure the sea voyage, nor perhaps the climate. The many invitations to give concerts in America, some of which are very tempting, I am therefore obliged to decline without hesitation.[2]

Should you actually come to Norway this summer, I would be very happy to meet you and your wife.[3]

Sincerely yours,
EDVARD GRIEG

2

Copenhagen, April 13, 1900

Dear Sir!
I wanted to write to you, but fell seriously ill with influenza and am far from well now, which, I regret very much to say, has prevented me to this day from writing anything about my songs, and very probably will continue to prevent me. For some

2 In his letter of February 2, 1900, Finck had strongly urged Grieg to visit America: "You could give concerts [in the big cities on the East Coast] in October and November and then go to southern California for the winter."

3 The Fincks did in fact visit Grieg at Troldhaugen in July, 1901. Mrs. Finck reported her impression of Grieg in a letter to her family from which Finck quotes in *Grieg and His Music*: "His face is as individual, as unique, as attractive, as his music; it is the face of a thinker, a genius. His eyes are keen and blue; his hair is long, straight, and almost white, and brushed over backwards, like Liszt's."

weeks I am not permitted to do any mental work, and late in April I have some concerts to conduct in Christiania. Not until the middle of May shall I be back in my home near Bergen. But that would leave me only eight days for the work, if it is to be in your hands by the middle of June. It is too bad. Now comes another thing, I have read Waldmann's *Conversations with Franz*[4] and have become quite perplexed. For, that sort of thing I cannot do. I am simply sorry that I read the book. Even a master of song like Franz ought not to talk about Schubert, Schumann, and Mendelssohn as he has done, and especially about his own points of superiority to these masters. If he was not privileged to see that Schubert and Schumann possessed much greater powers of imagination than he did, then he will appear in my eyes—I regret to say this—somewhat less great than heretofore. His horizon must have been limited. How great were Liszt and Schumann for the very reason that, beside their other *geniale* [brilliant] qualities, they also possessed a wide horizon, purified chemically, as it were, from all one-sidedness and overestimation of self. All that is great is great! That is and remains my motto! However, I am going astray—it is due to the influenza-affected head! I am very sorry you are not coming to Europe this summer. You might then have played the role of Waldmann so nicely—better, in any case, than he did!

To sum up: I cannot at this moment make you a promise. But should circumstance permit my doing something to meet your wishes, I shall certainly do it.

Sincerely yours,
EDVARD GRIEG

3

Troldhaugen, July 17, 1900

Dear Sir!
The enclosure is a jumbled confusion. It is formless from beginning to end. But I have a purpose in this: that through this private soliloquy you might get to know as much of my personality as I think is necessary in order for you to evaluate my songs. Much more could, of course, be said, but—I don't feel inclined to do that.

As I now send you these remarks for your use as source material, I do so under the following explicit assumptions:

1. that you will return them as soon as you are finished with them,
2. that you will extract from them *only* what is necessary for your work —in other words, that so far as possible you will avoid using my own words. As a matter of fact, you must in any case not quote me directly,

[4] German song composer, conductor and organist Robert Franz (1815–92). The book to which Grieg refers is W. Waldmann (ed.), *Robert Franz. Gespräche aus zehn Jahren*, Leipzig 1895.

3. that you—as I would expect from a writer such as yourself—will regard my communications as totally confidential, and
4. that you, consistent with your promise, will send me a copy of the relevant pages of your manuscript or galley proof for me to read and approve.

Forgive me if now and then I have been too long-winded. Also, you must kindly forgive my poor German. When it comes to the use of *der, die, das* I have always been a poor wretch.

I am very anxious to see your work on the modern art song. That is a subject that has not been adequately dealt with heretofore. To one who has written on Wagner with such deep insight as you have done, I dare to say something that Liszt once said to me in Rome: "You have the talent for it!"[5]

When you look at the pictures of me and my wife, please imagine that your planned trip[6] has already occurred and that you have taken the pictures with you as souvenirs from Troldhaugen (my villa), where I am writing these lines!

Sincerely yours,
EDVARD GRIEG

[Enclosure]:

1. The relationship of my songs to the Norwegian folk song
Norwegian folk life, Norwegian sagas, Norwegian history, and above all Norwegian nature have had a profound influence on my creative work ever since my youth. It was only later, however, that I had an opportunity to immerse myself in the Norwegian folk song. When I wrote the piano pieces in op. 3 and especially op. 6,[7] in which a national element often appears, I knew, so to speak, virtually nothing about our folk songs. This is an important fact in view of certain German assertions to the effect that I am nothing more than a copy-machine of Norwegian folk music.

Regarding my songs, I do not think that on the whole they have been greatly influenced by the folk song. In cases in which local color *had to play* an essential role, the influence probably is evident—for example, in "Solveig's Song" from *Peer Gynt.* But this is perhaps the only one of my songs where an imitation of a folk song can be traced.[8]

---

[5] See Grieg's letter to his parents of April 9, 1870, in which he tells of his associations with Liszt in Rome in 1870.

[6] In his letter of February 2, 1900, Finck had written, "Perhaps my wife and I will visit Norway next July. Could you give us an hour or so at that time when we might have a brief chat together?"

[7] *Poetic Tone Pictures* op. 3 (1863) and *Humoresques* op. 6 (1865).

[8] The Norwegian folk tune that comes closest is "Jeg lagde mig så silde" ("I lay down so late"), which Grieg arranged for male chorus in *Album for Male voices* op. 30 (1877–78). But "Solveig's Song" also has a certain similarity to the Swedish folk song, "Ack Värmeland du sköna."

Edvard and Nina often performed Grieg's songs together. " I loved a girl with a wonderful voice and an equally wonderful gift as an interpreter. My songs . . . were written for her." (Det kgl. Bibliotek, Copenhagen)

There is, however, one peculiarity of our folk music that has always had a strong appeal to me: the treatment of the leading tone, in particular when the progression is from the leading tone down to the dominant. But the same melodic pattern occurs also in the works of other composers.[9] In opp. 17 and 66 I have arranged folk tunes for piano,[10] in op. 30 I have freely arranged them for men's chorus.[11] In three or four of my other works I have tried to make *motivic* use of folk tunes.[12] But inasmuch as I have now published 70 opuses, I dare say that the assertion by certain German music critics that my so-called originality is limited to the use of folk tunes (!) is grossly unfair. That the spirit of the homeland, which from time immemorial has been expressed in the folk tunes, hovers over my compositions is another matter. But I am not aware of any deliberate imitation.

---

[9] The pattern wherein the melodic line descends from the tonic to the leading tone to the fifth has received various designations in the Grieg literature: "the Griegian *leit motiv*", "the Grieg motive", "the Grieg formula", "the Grieg hall-mark". The most striking example is its use as the opening motive in Grieg's *Piano Concerto* in A minor: *a – g♯– e.*

[10] *Twenty-five Norwegian Folk Songs and Dances* op. 17 (1869) and *Nineteen Norwegian Folk Songs* op. 66 (1896).

[11] *Album for Male Voices* op. 30.

[12] Grieg very frequently made use of motives from folk music, not least the "Grieg motive"—for example, in the first two *Violin Sonatas*, opp. 8 and 13, and in the *String Quartet*, op. 27.

When the late talented French composer Edouard Lalo made use in his *Norwegian Rhapsody* for orchestra of the first movement of my op. 19 in the belief that it was a folk tune, I take the liberty of construing this thievery as a compliment.[13]

When I speak my own musical language, which has nothing whatever to do with the folk tune, the conservative German music critics have found an insulting term for that, too. They call it "Norwegerei".[14]

This much is certain: I have only followed my own natural bent. That is the very thing that most people do not do, because they lack the courage to do it. (Georg Brandes,[15] one of the greatest intellects in the world, says: To have talent requires courage.) If my nature—insofar as I try to express it through music—strikes certain people as strange, I cannot with the best will in the world do anything about that. But to construe my natural mode of expressing myself as "Norwegerei" proves that these gentlemen have only a very superficial knowledge of what they are talking about. Regarding their malice I shall remain silent.

My great-grandfather was Scottish, and today, when my works have achieved a worldwide distribution that I myself do not understand at all, it certainly is not due exclusively to the national element in it but perhaps much more to the fusion of cosmopolitan and national factors. Cultural history shows us that all lasting art forms have been national. Like every modern artist who wants to achieve something with his art, I stand, consciously or unconsciously, on national ground, and it goes without saying that I also feel national, especially when I have occasion to deal with national literature. But my songs often have a less national tinge than the rest of my compositions for the simple reason that I have been inspired to a great extent by Danish and German poets. In such songs, *I* at least cannot discern any direct relationship to the Norwegian folk song.

I will go a step further and make the following statement: When the *Norwegian* poets are not depicting nature or folk life and legends but purely and simply universal human-spiritual phenomena, it has never occurred to me to seek a national coloring. By and large I have never explicitly tried to achieve such coloring. It came about of its own accord. I think it is utterly impossible to successfully create a national coloring with the help of thought. Where the national element has not entered into one's *blood*, it has no legitimacy in "creative" art. It has legitimacy only in "photographic" art.

---

[13] Edouard Lalo (1823–92): *Rhapsodie norvégienne* from 1879 is an arrangement of his *Fantaisie norvégienne* for violin and orchestra from 1878. The "thievery" to which Grieg refers has to do with the fact that Lalo made use of Grieg's "In the Mountains", the first piece in *Pictures from Folk Life* op. 19 (1869–71). "In the Mountains" has an unmistakable similarity to a *springar*, a distinctively Norwegian type of dance tune in 3/4 time.

[14] "Norwegerei", a pejorative German word for "Norwegianness", i.e., an exaggerated and conscious use of Norwegian characteristics.

[15] Danish aesthete and man of letters Georg Brandes (1842–1927).

2. The use of church modes and other harmonic innovations

In my songs I have only in a few exceptional cases preferred the old church modes, and I dare say that it has happened almost unconsciously—and in any case not to the same extent that Brahms, for example, uses them. But that many of our oldest folk tunes are based on old hymns seems to me to be beyond doubt, and it would be very interesting to be able to show this. Unfortunately there is a lack of sources in this area, and our scholarship with respect to art is so primitive that thus far no one in our country has tried to write a work dealing with the Norwegian folk tune and its history. With each day that passes this task becomes more difficult, and when it finally is too late—then, perhaps, it will be done!

I find it difficult to talk about harmonic innovations. The realm of harmony has always been my dream-world, and the relation between my sense of harmony and Norwegian folk music has always been an enigma to me. I have found that the obscure depth in our folk melodies has its foundation in their undreamt-of harmonic possibilities. In my arrangements in op. 66 and elsewhere I have tried to give expression to my sense of the hidden harmonies in our folk tunes. In so doing I have been rather especially fascinated by the chromatic lines in the harmonic texture. A friend once told me that I was "born chromatic". And I still remember quite precisely something that Dr. Papperitz,[16] my first teacher in harmony at the Conservatory in Leipzig, said upon perusing my assignments (I was 15–16 years old): "But all this chromaticism! Why, you'll be a Spohr no. 2!"[17] This was not at all what I had intended. For even at that time, Spohr and all his chromatic saccharinity struck me as extremely distasteful. In the use of the chromatic scale, my ideal teachers were names such as Bach, Mozart, and Wagner. I have observed that when these immortal masters gave expression to their deepest and most fervent thoughts they had a marked fondness for chromatic lines, each in his own original way. On this basis I quietly evolved little by little my own sense of the importance of the chromatic element. Several of my songs show how I have proceeded, for example Album III[18] no. 30: "A Swan" [op. 25, no. 2], and especially no. 33, "Departed" [op. 25, no. 5]. See also *Ballade* op. 24.[19]

3. Choice of poets

My choice of poets is closely related to what I have experienced. At the Conservatory in Leipzig (1858–62), where I concerned myself only with German music and literature, it was also natural to compose in the German manner. I had not

[16] German music teacher Robert Papperitz (1826–1903), instructor in harmony and counterpoint at the Leipzig Conservatory.

[17] German composer and violinist Louis Spohr (1784–1859).

[18] Grieg is referring here to Albums I–V which were published by C. F. Peters Musikverlag 1875–85. Each album contains 12 songs. The albums were later published in revised editions.

[19] *Ballade in G Minor* (*Ballade in the Form of Variations on a Norwegian Melody*) for piano op. 24 (1875–76).

yet fully emerged from the egg. When I went to Copenhagen in 1863, I began to breathe Nordic air and got in contact with Danish poets, both personally and musically. This group also included Hans Christian Andersen, the writer of fairy-tales.

After moving back to my homeland (at the end of 1866 I settled down in Christiania) I became mightily captivated by our modern national poets. Even while I was in Copenhagen I had become acquainted with the old Norwegian lyricist Andreas Munch, and for songs such as "Outward Bound" [op. 9, no. 4] and "Cradle Song" [op. 9, no. 2] I am indebted to his beautiful poems. But in Norway I turned to the two dioskurs,[20] Bjørnstjerne Bjørnson and Henrik Ibsen, who were still bursting with youthful vigor. A little later I became acquainted with the works of the important poet of the people, Aasmund Olavsson Vinje. I also set poems by the Norwegians Vilhelm Krag, Nordahl Rolfsen, John Paulsen and others. In 1884 in Rome I learned to know the brilliant Danish lyric poet Holger Drachmann, whose poems have often inspired me to compose songs.[21]

For my most recent published songs I am indebted to Norwegian poet Arne Garborg,[22] who writes in a rural dialect. The fragments that have been translated into German give absolutely no idea of the beauty and originality in his book *Haugtussa* [*The Mountain Maid*]. They who lack the happy ability to intuit things will for that reason also not really be comfortable with the music. A few years ago a critic in *Signale*[23] used six columns to show that he understood these songs as little as a bull understood a red flag!

My new songs [opp. 69 and 70], which will come out this fall and which are settings of texts by the Danish poet Otto Benzon,[24] are thoroughly cosmopolitan in character. The lyricism of, respectively, German, Danish and Norwegian poets is for the attentive observer so totally different that the music, too, must be equally varied in order that the contrasts among the several nationalities can be perceived, yet not in such a way that the differences can be precisely described verbally. Whatever might be said about my songs in this regard I must leave to the insightful critic who is familiar with my way of composing.

4. The relationship between German and Norwegian songs

Anyone who reads the *Elder Edda* soon becomes aware of its wonderful power and pithiness of expression, its remarkable ability to say much in a few words. Such a reader will admire the simple, plastic formulation of the sentences. The same is true of the sagas about the Norwegian kings, especially those written by

---

20 The term comes from Greek mythology and is an allusion to Zeus's twin sons, Castor and Pollux.

21 The poets to whom Grieg refers are: Norwegian authors Andreas Munch (1811–84), Bjørnstjerne Bjørnson (1832–1910), Henrik Ibsen (1828–1906), Aasmund Olavsson Vinje (1818–70), Vilhelm Krag (1871–1933), Nordahl Rolfsen (1848–1918), John Paulsen (1851–1924), and Danish lyric poet Holger Drachman (1846–1908).

22 Arne Garborg (1851–1924).

23 The German music periodical *Signale für die musikalische Welt.*

24 Otto Benzon (1856–1927).

Snorre Sturlason.[25] The more deeply the heart is moved, the more condensed and enigmatic is the mode of expression. The language is constantly bold, serious and dignified. One senses more than one sees the stormy ocean of the passions. To display one's innermost feelings was considered brutal. For the feelings, too, the mode of expression is as brief as it is chaste. This saga literature is the foundation on which Bjørnson and Ibsen built.

One can say that in a similar way the folk song is a musical reflection of the innermost soul of the people. What the poets have achieved in this respect is what I have striven for in music, perhaps above all in setting to music the profound poems of the national poets Vinje and Garborg. The exaggerated external trappings so typical for the Germans is foreign to Scandinavians. To be sure, history provides exceptions—for example, in the story of Sigurd Jorsalfar,[26] a king who brought back to Norway a feeling for South European—even Oriental—splendor. From his time, in any case, come a number of chivalric songs that little by little acquired the character of folk songs. These songs are for the most part balladic in character and are solemn and dignified. The basic feature of the Norwegian folk song, however—in comparison with the German—is a deep sense of melancholy that can suddenly change into wild, unbridled humor. Mysterious gloom and unrestrained wildness—these are the contrasting elements in the Norwegian folk song.

5. Biographical events that give a Romantic tinge to various of my songs
There are many things that I would like to have said on this topic, but I must decline to give you a complete account. For many of my songs—especially the best ones—are closely related to experiences of an intimate personal nature. I, too, have received my share of the above-mentioned shyness about revealing my innermost self, which is a fundamental trait of the Norwegian national character. No doubt you think that that sort of biographical material will be of interest to the reader and will inspire him to acquaint himself with the songs. That may be, but as the English say "My house is my castle," I say, "My inner life is my mighty fortress!" Thus I must ask to be excused if with respect to this question I reply only briefly. If I should live a long life, perhaps in an autobiography I would include the missing information.[27] I can, however, make space for a few explanations.

---

[25] Icelandic historian and poet Snorre Sturlason (1179–1241).

[26] Sigurd Jorsalfar (1090–1130), who after his father's death shared the throne with two brothers, became absolute monarch in 1123. In 1107 he led a fleet of Norwegian crusaders (the Saga states that there were 60 ships, which implies ca. 5,000 men). Sigurd fought against the Moors on the Iberian peninsula, participated in the conquest of Sidon, then returned home via Constantinople. The Saga tells the story of his journey with glowing enthusiasm. Bjørnson wrote the play *Sigurd Jorsalfar*, for which Grieg wrote incidental music.

[27] Grieg never wrote an autobiography. He did, however, produce a diary as well as a number of articles, letters and speeches that are autobiographical in nature. All these materials will be published in English translation in Benestad & Halverson (eds.), *Edvard Grieg: Diaries, Articles, Speeches* (Columbus, Ohio, 2001).

I found the song "Autumn storm"—written in the summer of 1865 [op. 18, no. 4]—well suited for a broader symphonic and orchestral treatment, so I made use of it in the concert overture *In Autumn* (op. 11), which was composed the following winter in Rome. Ibsen's poem "Fiddlers"—Album III, no. 34 [op. 25, no. 1]—captured my imagination so vividly and lastingly that I used the beginning of the song as the core motive in the string quartet that was composed a short time later (op. 27, G minor).

The winds of my homeland are blowing in Album IV. In these songs, which are different from all the preceding ones, I introduced a mode akin to the Norwegian folk tradition—one that at that time was new. I got very excited in the spring of 1880 when I became acquainted with Vinje's poetry, filled as it was with the profoundest wisdom, and in the space of 8–10 days I composed not only the songs of Album IV but also others to texts by this poet. These latter have still not been published.[28] Vinje's background was that of a farmer. In his prose writings he tried to enlighten the Norwegian people, and through these as well as through his poetry he gained great national significance. Of the songs I have mentioned, no. 38, "Spring" [op. 33, no. 2] and no. 39, "The Wounded One" [op. 33, no. 3] have also been published in a version for string orchestra under the title *Two Elegiac Melodies* (op. 34). In this form they have achieved wide popularity outside my homeland. The profound wistfulness in these poems is the background for the solemn character of the music, and this led me in the arrangements for string orchestra, where the poems are not readily at hand, to clarify their content by giving them more expressive titles: "Last Spring" and "The Wounded Heart". Unfortunately "The Goal"—no. 48 [op. 33, no. 12], the last of these songs—will probably be totally incomprehensible to foreigners. Vinje was the publisher of *Dølen*,[29] a newspaper that was written in a Norwegian dialect, and because of its efforts to make propaganda for the language of the farmers, as well as its folkish character, he had many enemies among the spokesmen for the bourgeoisie in Christiania. One New Year's Day toward the end of the 1850's Vinje published "The Goal" as an appeal to his subscribers. I was totally unaware of this when I composed the song. I thought that this energetic poem was addressed either to a friend or even to the poet's wife! The following translation is absolutely incorrect, and ridiculous as well: "Komm denn, Klugheit, wir gehen Beide" (!) ["Come then, wisdom, we shall both go"]. The literal translation would be, "Komm denn, Liebe, wir wollen die Last zusammen tragen!" ["Come then, dear, we will bear the burden together!"]. Vinje employed alliteration, which misled

---

[28] The first edition of op. 33 was published in 1881 as *12 Melodier til Digte af A. O. Vinje (Twelve Songs to Poems by A. O. Vinje)*. The Vinje songs not included in op. 33 were printed in vol. 15 of *Edvard Grieg: Complete Works* (1991).

[29] *Dølen*, literally "The Man from the Valley", was published weekly, with several interruptions, from 1858 to 1870. This publication was Vinje's *alter ego*, giving a true picture of his complex, irregular, brilliantly eccentric personality.

the translator to write the unfortunate and incomprehensible line, "Komm denn, Klugheit!"[30] Perhaps with a better translation the song could make some headway.

This brings me to a point on which I am obligated to dwell a little longer. I refer to the matter of translations. That my songs—compared with my other compositions—have thus far gained so little ground abroad, while they have won wide acceptance throughout Scandinavia, is undoubtedly due in part to difficulties with the translations. When I compose songs, my principal goal is not to write *music* but first of all to do justice to the *poet's* most secret intentions. To let the poem come to the fore as strongly as possible—that is my task. If this task is performed well, then the music is successful too. Otherwise it is not, even if in and of itself it is ethereally beautiful. But when Scandinavian poets, whose language foreigners neither understand nor sing, are maimed by the translations, both the poet and the composer suffer.

Unfortunately I have often had very bad luck in my efforts to find good translations. True enough, the task of translation presupposes a versatility that is very rare, for the translator must simultaneously have insight into poetry, language, and music. In addition to that there is the sad fact that most publishers don't know better than to value a *good* translation no higher than a *cheap* one. To be sure, C. F. Peters, my Leipzig publisher, has tried very hard to get hold of good things. But the result, even when the translations have been pretty successful, is that when they are incorporated into the *music*, they usually sound forced and unnatural. I am a friend of good declamation. I have always taken great pains regarding declamation in my mother tongue. That is perhaps the main reason that my songs are sung throughout Scandinavia. But when a rhythmically poor translation is unpoetic and banal as well—yes, when it almost distorts the poet's meaning, as is altogether too often the case with German, English and French translations of my songs—then, to tell the truth, it is no wonder that nobody enjoys having anything to do with the songs. I cannot see that my songs are any more unusual than the rest of my works. On the contrary, the words should help to make the spirit of the song more evident, which, of course, is what happens with songs in the original language. But when one hears a declamation like that in "The Princess" [EG 133]: "Du fesselst mir, *ach!* all *meine* Gedanken!" etc., it is only too easy to understand that one closes the songbook never to open it again. A sad fate for Bjørnson's wonderful poem!

I have indeed said that my songs are *frequently* sung in Scandinavia, but in so saying I have not meant to suggest that they are also sung *well*. To the contrary, I have had the sad experience that there is no one in the present generation of Norwegian singers who interprets my songs in a manner consistent with my intentions. There is a lack of musical training and, therefore, of understanding.

---

30 Vinje's original line here is "Kom då, Snille, vi slita saman". A later translation by Hans Schmidt, which may have been approved by Grieg, rendered the line "Also laß uns, Geliebte, wandern".

One should at least be able to expect understanding in the composer's homeland. But no. That one publicly performs songs that easily bring success is no heroic deed. But our singers have neither the artistic conviction nor the requisite courage to perform an unfamiliar work that lies beyond the grasp of the wider public. There is absolutely no understanding here of how to appreciate that which is *intimate*. No one dares to sing a so-called "ineffective" song in public. That requires a divinely gifted artist, one who really knows how to "score a success" also with such a work. Then the whole flock of sheep would immediately fall in line!

As you can see, I have had the same thoughts as those for which you have found such an extremely apt expression in the chapter on singers in your excellent book on Wagner.[31] One incident taught me something that I previously regarded as impossible, namely that everything—even that which is most intensely personal—can be used in the concert hall *if only the right interpreter is available*. A few years ago I was horrified to note that my "Cradle Song"—Album I, no. 7, G-sharp minor [op. 9, no. 2]—was on a program at the Gewandhaus in Leipzig. I considered this song totally unsuited to the concert hall. The singer, however, was Johannes Messchaert[32] and the pianist Arthur Nikisch.[33] After the first few measures I was struck by a great hush that pervaded the auditorium. I began to hope, for the interpretation was incomparably beautiful. And my hope was realized! After the last measure there was a long, continuing storm of applause. Everyone had been carried away. I am sure that the audience had rarely heard such a deep intensity in *piano* and *pianissimo*, or such ideal declamation. Fortunately, the poem had also been well translated into German.

One major obstacle to the wider dissemination of my songs is the faulty choice of tempi made by the singers. I have been told this many times and have often experienced it first-hand myself. One would think, for example, that a song such as "Good Morning!"—Album I, no. 8 [op. 21, no. 2]—would be interpreted in a light and lively manner. The female singers in Germany think otherwise, however, and the conductors accompany according to the divas' prescription. Wherever I have had to listen I have always heard an *Allegretto quasi Andantino* instead of the *Molto Vivace* that is indicated. It's dreadful to listen to that sort of thing.

And then we have these examples of prima-donna impudence in the endings:

Instead of  always this: 

---

31 *Wagner and His Works*, New York 1893.

32 Dutch baritone Johannes Messchaert (1857–1927) was one of Grieg's favorite singers.

33 The Hungarian-born German conductor Arthur Nikisch (1855–1922), who became musical director of the Gewandhaus Orchestra in Leipzig in 1895, was also an outstanding pianist.

When will it be legal to punish someone for such things?! Not more than four weeks ago at a concert in Bergen I heard "A Mother's Grief"—Album II, no. 23 [op. 15, no. 4]—performed exactly *twice as slowly* as is indicated! One should have a feeling of the correct tempo in one's blood. If this is not the case, you can swear to it that the rest of the composer's intentions will be mutilated as well. I have often had to ask myself: Why has Mother Nature so consistently bestowed a singing voice only on those who have neither the intelligence nor the depth of feeling to make their voices serve a higher end?

The Mountain Thrall [op. 32], a song for baritone, string orchestra and horns, has had a special significance in my creative work. I have sought here to emulate the compact terseness of style that is expressed with such awesome power in the Old Norse poetry, and I think perhaps that in this little piece I have best succeeded in doing this.

One song that in recent years has often been sung abroad is "A Swan"—Album III, no. 30 [op. 25, no. 2]. The translation does not preserve the verbal enchantment of Ibsen's dark, weighty original poem. In Paris (Colonne concert) the Belgian singer Grimaud sang it with orchestra under my leadership, and he sang with astonishing beauty and great dramatic force. No Norwegian would dare to give this kind of intense expression to the musical interpretation of a poem having such a tragic content. Our nature would have had to struggle with our characteristic national diffidence.

In the area of theater, above all in Bjørnson's and Ibsen's national dramas, we already have some important representatives who can give expression to the poets' ideal intentions. With respect to our *music* literature, however, it appears, as I have said, that our present generation is not yet mature. Language education is universal in our country, but music education is not. That is why the poets are better understood. Let me also call your attention to the fact that the words "Ja da, – da sangst du!" ["to trumpet your song, then!"[34]] in the aforementioned "A Swan" should be sung *sempre ff,* if possible even with a *crescendo,* not with *diminuendo* and *piano.*

The songs *Reminiscences from Mountain and Fjord* (op. 44) call for a special explanation. Everything here was experienced by me personally. In the summer of 1886 I took a trip to the mountains with the poet Holger Drachmann, who was visiting me in Norway. During the trip we met some charming young women who inspired both of us to write songs. I regard "Prologue" [op. 44, no. 1] as one of my best inspirations. But the daring poem must, if possible, be declaimed in its original language if it is to be fully realized. "Epilogue" [op. 44, no. 6] fails because of the banal phrase "Auf der Alm, da giebt's ka' Sünd".[35] Drachmann sang

---

[34] From the translation by Rolf Kr. Stang in *Edvard Grieg: Complete Works,* vol. 14. Ibsen's original Norwegian text is "Ja da – da lød det" ["Yes, then – then it sounded"].

[35] "In the mountain pasture there is no sin."

this phrase to me as he had heard it sung in the Tyrol, and in a way he obligated me to use it. Perhaps in a future edition I will *eliminate* this phrase.

I don't think I have any greater talent for writing songs than for writing any other kind of music. Why, then, have songs played such a prominent role in my ouevre? Quite simply because I, like other mortals, once in my life (to quote Goethe) had my moment of genius. And it was love that gave me this glory. I loved a girl with a wonderful voice and an equally wonderful gift as an interpreter. This woman became my wife and has been my companion through life down to the present day. I dare say that for me she has remained the only true interpreter of my songs. During the time when I was music director in Christiania 1866–74 (that is the time when her voice was at its peak) she performed frequently. But the level of the concert-going public in Christiania at that time was very primitive, and most importantly, the understanding of the art of interpretation was altogether too undeveloped for them to properly assess performances that gave the greatest emphasis to the inner life of the spirit. In the end we just made our music for ourselves, in our home or among a circle of friends. But in Copenhagen, where I gave concerts almost every year, my wife became a favorite among the artists and the musically literate public. My songs from this period came to life as if they were the products of a natural law, and all of them were written for her. From this time onward, embodying my feelings in song became as much a necessity of life as breathing.

In the songs from my second period (beginning approximately with Album III), a keen observer can sense a greater tendency toward deeper contemplation. In accordance therewith, my wife's interpretations gradually became more and more profound.

The third period—the present one—seems to me to be almost a combination of the two preceding ones. "On revient toujours"[36]—NB! with the addition of life's experiences!

I am well aware that when I emphasize so strongly my wife's influence on my songs, and when I so deliberately call attention to her achievements, I run the risk that you may get the impression that I, as a devoted husband, am doing advertising for my wife! Well, that is a risk that one must take. To you, and in view of the task you have given me, I consider it my duty to speak with ruthless honesty and without petty sentimentality. I must assume that nothing regarding my wife's achievements has ever reached you. She has never done anything to acquire fame in Europe. It is perfectly clear to me, however, that this is primarily my fault. I did not understand at the time how important her interpretations really were. For me it was only natural that she should sing so beautifully, so tellingly—from a full heart and from the innermost depths of the soul. How could it have

[36] "One always returns."

been otherwise? Now that she no longer sings, I realize that I have wasted the very best opportunities for the wider dissemination of my songs. But this has also contributed to the fact that we have both been spared the demoralizing effect that concert touring has on one's personality.

In the winter of 1874 we went together to Leipzig. There we heard many famous *Lied* singers, both male and female—and it was there that I realized for the first time how much attention my wife's singing was capable of arousing also among artists outside Scandinavia. Then it dawned on me: The ability to sing beautifully wasn't something to take for granted. Old Mrs. von Holstein[37] (the late widow of the composer Franz von Holstein), who had been a friend of Mendelssohn and Schumann, once said to me that my wife's way of interpreting songs reminded her of Jenny Lind.[38] I have never heard the famous Swedish singer. According to Mrs. Holstein, her strong points were a charming "schwung", a dramatic vivacity, a brilliant handling of language, and an utterly unsophisticated, non-primadonna-like manner. These are the very qualities that are also descriptive of my wife. In her singing she did exactly what I have striven for in my creative work: above all to interpret the *poem*.

It is possible that I should have regarded it as a duty to make my wife's achievements as a performer known abroad, but my health has prevented me from doing so much traveling. Once in Paris (at Salle Pleyel) and a few times in London she sang my songs and earned enthusiastic ovations. But by that time her voice was already past its prime. Her last public performance occurred almost two years ago in London and at Windsor Castle in response to an invitation from old Queen Victoria. Since then she has never sung in public. She has won—and that is the most important thing—the acclaim of some of the leading personalities of our time. I will mention just one episode. In the late 1880's she sang at some private parties in Leipzig at which the only people present were artists, one of whom was Tchaikovsky. The parties were given by the violinist Brodsky and the pianist Siloti.[39] At the last of these parties she sang, among other things, "Last Spring" (Album III, no. 38) in such a way that Tchaikovsky got tears in his eyes.

Since I have dared to describe her vocal art so panegyrically, it is comforting to know that other artists have done the same. Edmund Neupert,[40] the pianist who died in America, wrote on a copy of his wonderfully poetic *Etude*: "To Mrs. Nina Grieg, who sings more beautifully and warmly than all others." Ibsen, after she had sung one of my songs to a poem written by him, whispered just a single

---

[37] German composer and author Franz von Holstein (1826–78) and his wife Hedwig (1819–97).

[38] Jenny Lind (1820–87), "The Swedish Nightingale".

[39] Russian artists Adolf Brodsky (1851–1929) and Alexander Siloti (1865–1945), who were living in Leipzig at the time.

[40] Norwegian pianist Edmund Neupert (1842–88), soloist at the first performance of Grieg's *Piano Concerto* in Copenhagen on April 3, 1869. Neupert, who had gone to America in 1882 as a professor at the new conservatory in New York City, had died suddenly on June 22, 1888.

word: "understanding". Tchaikovsky sent her his songs with warm acknowledgments. Why, then, should I hold back—and especially here, when the purpose of what I write is to show you the secret wellspring of my songs. But even though that is the case, I would never have risked telling you had not your own book on Wagner given me unconditional artistic confidence!

• • •

You ask me to give you the names of the best contemporary young Nordic composers of songs. Those most deserving of this appellation are the Norwegian Christian Sinding, the Dane Peter Lange-Müller, and the Swede Emil Sjögren.[41] Sinding's songs, in particular, include works of great significance. He is criticized for being too Wagnerian, but in my opinion this is only superficially the case. It is precisely in his songs that he is above all—Sinding himself. I find his settings of Drachmann's poems especially brilliant. Lange-Müller and Sjögren are also extremely poetic and sensitive lyricists, the former with a somewhat Danish coloring, the latter with a more cosmopolitan tinge. Lange-Müller's incidental music for Drachmann's fairy tale *Der var engang* [*Once upon a time*]—the same material that was recently employed in an opera by Zemlinsky in Vienna[42]—has had eminent success in Denmark, with more than 100 performances at The Royal Theater. Messchaert has songs by both Sinding and Lange-Müller in his repertoire.

The mention of the name Wagner reminds me that I should add a few words about his influence on my songs. It would be difficult to demonstrate such influence, however; in any case it would certainly be only indirect. It goes without saying that I am an enthusiastic admirer of the great master. On the other hand, I hate the Wagnerites—these pompous, self-important, brutal clique-mongers who aren't worth a tinker's damn. And I hate no less the composers who think that the more Wagnerian they compose the better it is. If one has nothing more to say than that which Wagner has said better thousands of times, one should rather remain silent. It is, however, quite a different thing to make use of what Wagner has achieved in the realms of musical declamation and technique. These achievements can also easily be combined with ideas native to one's own imagination. In the songs that date from my second period, and even more from my third, I have aimed at perfecting declamation in the Wagnerian sense. Occasionally I have written almost recitatively—for example, in "Prologue" from op. 44. By and large, however, it is contrary to my nature to go as far as the modern German composers of songs. I do not want to see the melodic element

---

[41] Christian Sinding (1856–1941), Peter Lange-Müller (1850–1926), and Emil Sjögren (1853–1918).

[42] Austrian composer Alexander Zemlinsky (1872–1942) wrote the opera *Es war einmal* in 1897–99. It premiered at the Vienna Hofoper January 22, 1900.

primarily concentrated in the piano part, and I am not supportive of the efforts to transfer the Wagnerian opera style to the art song. The lyric dramaticism of a song must, in my opinion, always be totally different from that of the music-drama. These views throw an important sidelight on my song production.

4

[Troldhaugen], September 24, 1900

Dear Sir!
I have just received the proof-sheets and hasten to return them. I need not tell you how I rejoice at your approval and your comprehension of my art. Hitherto I have always been, as regards critics, a great pessimist. Always these gentlemen have pointed out my least important things as my best, and unfortunately also *vice versa*. How happy I am that this is not the case with you. You have in the main dwelt on the very songs that I myself consider the best.

Now, however, comes a big 'But.' You have, after all, cited my own words and very often, in fact, where it was not necessary. That must be avoided, and I have, as you see, indicated the way of doing so. I beg you urgently to carry out the changes I have marked with ordinary lead pencil (not blue pencil). Only in a few places have I left myself as the speaker. . . .

Sincerely yours,
Edvard Grieg

5

Christiania, December 21, 1900

Dear Sir!
If I had a catalogue of my books, your volume on song writers would be marked with two stars. Higher praise I could not utter. And yet: Everything in this world has its faults. I confess that your judgment of Brahms was a great disappointment to me. That you, with your great, wide horizon, have failed to discover the real Brahms, is really quite extraordinary and shows how the most many-sided men have their limitations. For me there is no doubt concerning Brahms. A landscape, torn by mists and clouds, in which I can see ruins of old churches, as well as of Greek temples—that is Brahms. The necessity of placing him by the side of Bach and Beethoven is as incomprehensible to me as the attempt to reduce him *ad absurdum*. The great must be great, and a comparison with other great ones must always be unsatisfactory.

That you have not only appreciation for my art, but a deep comprehension of it, is a real boon for my heart. Believe me, I have hitherto nearly always fared badly with the so-called critics. Where there was sensitive appreciation there was no comprehension, and for so-called comprehension without such appreciation I do not give a penny. As for America, I doubt if I shall ever see it. But I hope you will soon come to Norway so we can shake hands.

For reviews of your book in the local papers I regret that no copies can be obtained here. Allow me to suggest that a copy be sent to our leading liberal paper, *Verdens Gang*, of which the editor is Mr. Olav Anton Thommessen.[43]

Sincerely yours,
EDVARD GRIEG

6

Troldhaugen, June 14, 1901

Dear Sir!
If nothing unexpected occurs, I will in any case be at home during the first week of July, and it will be a pleasure for me to have the opportunity to welcome you and your honored wife.

Sincerely yours,
EDVARD GRIEG

7

[Troldhaugen], September 30, 1902

Dear Sir!
I was glad to see your handwriting again. And I was egotistic enough to hope that you were going to write me this time about Seidl's[44] orchestration of "Bell Ringing". Instead of that, it was something quite unexpected. It is indeed most kind of you to take my part in America, and that, too, in a purely business matter. I am, as you quite correctly say, not a millionaire. But I am not in such dire straits as to be willing to take money from American publishers who are inclined to reprint my works. Moreover, my relations to the Peters firm are such that for this reason alone I cannot entertain the offer made by Mr. Ditson.[45] It will be different if Mr. Ditson makes an arrangement with Peters. Then it would perhaps be possible to have my works appear legitimately in America too. But if he is not

---

[43] Olav Anton Thommessen (1851–1942) was editor of the liberal Christiania newspaper *Verdens Gang*.

[44] Austro-Hungarian conductor Anton Seidl (1850–98). Seidl became conductor of the New York Metropolitan Opera in 1885 and of the New York Philharmonic Society in 1891.

[45] American music publisher Oliver Ditson (1811–88). In 1902 Finck had been approached by the Oliver Ditson Company of Boston to make a selection of Grieg's fifty best songs for publication in their Musicians' Library. Although it was at that time legal for an American publishing company to print the works of European composers without their permission (and without paying them a royalty), Finck had responded that he would accede to this request only on condition that the composer be paid a royalty on every copy sold. The Ditson Company accepted this condition and also authorized Finck to offer Grieg in their name $1,000 for a dozen new songs and piano pieces. Grieg was unable to accept this offer because of an exclusive agreement with the C. F. Peters Musikverlag of Leipzig to publish all of his new compositions.

willing to do this, things will have to remain as they are: The smart Messrs. Pirates reprint and enrich themselves without considering the composer. Well, I am glad at any rate that an American edition, if it cannot be avoided, is to be placed in your hands.

It is possible that, as an American, you will not find my standpoint "smart" enough. As a German, however (and especially as a German *idealist*) you will, I feel sure, agree with me.

If I really told you that I was not composing any more, this must not be taken literally. Last Christmas there appeared the tenth volume of *Lyric Pieces*. Soon all the ten parts will be published in a sumptuous volume by Peters.

Accept once more my best thanks for your kind intentions. With hearty greeting from house to house,

Sincerely yours,
EDVARD GRIEG

8

[Christiania], January 16, 1903

Dear Sir!
I told you [at Troldhaugen] what is a well-known fact, that C. F. Peters at one time reprinted pieces not protected by copyright, among them my own. But very many years ago Peters made an arrangement with the original publisher of these works by which he acquired all rights, except for Scandinavia. I should like to see the royalties offered me by an American publisher! Should such a thing come to pass, I shall promptly inform C. F. Peters. The only correct thing would be a direct arrangement with Peters, without whose agreement I would in no case accept a royalty. You may think this is foolish. But I happen to be so foolish.

Sincerely yours,
EDVARD GRIEG

9

Copenhagen, May 2, 1905

Dear Sir!
I would have written you long ago to thank you for the excellent photographs of yourself and your wife. (What a pity I cannot show yours to anyone because of the extravagant words on my art which you wrote on it.) What prevented me from writing was—illness and always illness. Hardly had I arrived here toward the end of December when I was confined to my bed (influenza, bronchitis, asthma), and I have not recovered. More recently a complicated stomach problem was superadded which brought on such complete prostration that I am

good for nothing, unable either to write or to make music. Even the writing of this letter is a colossal effort for me. I am much grieved to be obliged to tell you that for this reason with the best intentions I cannot comply with your wishes.[46] In connection with this I must tell you that a German publisher has offered me a brilliant honorarium for an autobiography—a work that, for the reasons just given, I have not begun, nor am likely to begin for some time and probably never will begin.

But now arises the question: In what way can I be of use to you in your task? How gladly I would help! Unfortunately, since the days of my youth I have saved hardly any of the articles written about my works, my concerts, etc. I cannot, therefore, refer you to the periodicals containing them. The article on me in the so-called "Scandinavian" number of *Die Musik* is by reason of its lack of understanding and its superficiality sheer nonsense. Its author contents himself with designating me a "Kleinkünstler" (miniature artist) and acts as if I had written only short things, although he ought to know that as a matter of fact I owe my name to my larger works. It is unheard of that a serious periodical not only is so unjust but in addition indulges in cheap witticisms such as that I "never reached the ocean but got stuck in the fjord."

I shall inform Peters that you intend to apply to him and shall ask him to send you the necessary material. The few things that I possess are at Troldhaugen, my villa near Bergen, which I shall probably not reach until the beginning of June. A few years ago there appeared here in Copenhagen a book on me in the Norwegian language written by the Norwegian composer Gerhard Schjelderup.[47] He asked me for contributions to his book but I had to refuse them firmly. The book consequently contains many erroneous details. The author was also obliged to prepare it for the publisher in a short time. Yet it is written by a sympathetic and genuine artist hand, and while I do not agree with all of the author's views, his book contains much that must be of interest for your purposes. Perhaps you can also use the illustrations. The letter to my parents relating to Liszt (of the year 1870 from Rome), which was printed in 1892 at Bergen in a festival book issued on the occasion of my silver wedding, will also interest you. I shall do my best tomorrow to get a copy and will send it to you at once.[48] Whatever I can find at Troldhaugen I will send you from there as soon as possible. Pardon me, however, if I unfortunately cannot comply with your request that I should send my photographs directly to Mr. Lane.[49] Such things I avoid as a matter of principle. In

[46] Finck had been asked by John Lane (1854–1925) of London to write a book of 20,000 words on Grieg's life and works for the series *Living Masters of Music*, and in this connection had asked Grieg to provide him with any information that might help him in this project.

[47] *Edvard Grieg og hans Verker (Edvard Grieg and His Works)*, Copenhagen 1903, was written by Gerhard Schjelderup (1859–1933) in connection with Grieg's sixtieth birthday.

[48] Finck adds in a footnote, "He did so, after writing in it a number of marginal comments and further details which were of much use to me."

[49] John Lane, publisher of Finck's book, *Grieg and His Music.*

fact I have for many years refused without exception all requests for biographic material and photographs from persons unknown to me and especially from publishers. I simply have neither time nor desire for this. And in the latest years the wan thing, illness, has been added. I shall, however, make an exception from this philistine "without exception" in favor of the esteemed and excellent author of the book on Wagner and "Songs and Song-Writers", out of gratitude for his sensitive appreciation of my art, and shall gladly send you what I have when I get home.

But now I am done! Completely exhausted by this exertion. The parole now is: Go to sleep. I hope soon to write you more, from Troldhaugen.

Sincerely yours,
EDVARD GRIEG

10

Troldhaugen, June 22, 1905

Dear Sir!
Hardly had I got home when I fell seriously ill and not until today have I been able to delve among my papers. Without result, I regret to say. Newspaper clippings of value there are none. Those of my early days are too stupid, and the later ones I did not save. . . . My wife has found some interesting pictures.[50]

Sincerely yours,
EDVARD GRIEG

11

[Troldhaugen], July 30, 1905

Dear Sir!
You want to know something about the origin of the *Peer Gynt* music. How gladly I would meet your wishes. But my memory says no. However, I will see if anything is left in my brain. I believe it was in the winter or spring of 1873 that Ibsen asked me to write the music to *Peer Gynt.*[51] I began it in the summer of 1873 [1874] in Sandviken near Bergen, continued it the following winter in Copenhagen, and orchestrated the whole thing at Fredensborg in Denmark during the summer of 1875. Unfortunately I was not able to decide myself at what points the music was to be introduced and how long each number should be. All that was determined by the Swedish theatrical director [Ludvig] Josephson, at that time

---

[50] Finck adds, "The rest of this four-page letter is devoted chiefly to remarks about the pictures he is about to send me and to references to a few reliable sources of information, notably Aimar Grønvold's book [*Norske musikere*, i.e., *Norwegian Musicians*, Christiania, 1883] and Holter's article in Salmonsen's Konversations-lexicon, which, he says 'is written in many respects with intelligence'."

[51] Grieg is mistaken about the year. Henrik Ibsen's letter asking Grieg to compose music for a stage version of *Peer Gynt* is dated January 23, 1874. It is printed on pp. 441–442.

chef [director] of the Christiania Theatre. I was thus compelled to do real patchwork. In no case did I have an opportunity to say all I wanted to say. Hence the brevity of these pieces. The performance of the music by the very inadequate (*bescheidene)* forces of that time was anything but good. I did not hear the first performance as I was living at that time in Bergen. But I was told that the orchestral effects were not well brought out (*dass die Klangwirkung sehr mittelmässig war*). It was really not until the last years in the eighties, after the numbers printed as suites by C. F. Peters had appeared, that the music won its chief success.[52] In the new National Theater in Christiania Ibsen's inspired work was taken into the repertoire again a few years ago [1902], and it always draws a full house. The music, which is played by the new orchestra under the direction of our excellent conductor, Johan Halvorsen, now goes well, and as executed at present contributes materially to the success. If you had an opportunity to attend one of these representations you would discover that it requires the stage performance to clearly bring out the musical intentions. It is greatly to be regretted that the local coloring and the philosophical tone of much of the dialogue present a great obstacle to the success of Ibsen's work outside of Scandinavia. In Paris, where it was staged a few years ago [1896], the music (played by the Lamoureux orchestra) had a colossal success, but Ibsen was not understood. In Berlin, last year, the work was simply a failure. And yet I hold it to be Ibsen's greatest creation. In the Fatherland it will always be considered a monument to him and keep its place on the stage even as a folk-play (*Volksstück*). . . .

Sincerely yours,
EDVARD GRIEG

12

[Troldhaugen], September 4, 1905

Dear Sir!
I greatly regret that I do not possess my complete family crest, yet I am really glad, because I do not like the idea of using that. The flag would be a thing that has special interest at this moment, and, like my music, it points directly at my nationality. Why not simply use a portrait? . . . The interview you referred to is, like all interviews, incorrect. . . .

I hope Mr. Lane will send me a few copies of your book, and I regret that it does not appear simultaneously in a Norwegian version.

Sincerely yours,
EDVARD GRIEG

---

[52] Grieg's *Peer Gynt Suite No. 1* was published in 1888, *Peer Gynt Suite No. 2* in 1893, both by C. F. Peters Musikverlag.

13

Christiania, September 29, 1905

Dear Sir!

I feel very guilty! But it was quite impossible for me to answer your two letters immediately. Then came another journey, followed by the political excitement, which still continues. In short, I must beg your pardon. . . . Your idea about the Norwegian flag is, I think, a very good one. But I hope the right one has been chosen and not the old one with the Swedish colors in the corner. That would never do (*das fehlte noch*)![53]

Yes, I did write articles on the Bayreuth performances in August, 1876; they appeared in *Bergensposten*, a newspaper which does not exist any more. Today I can only say this, that I was at the same time wildly enthusiastic and strongly inclined to criticize. The undue lengthening of some of the scenes affected me very unpleasantly; so did the dialogue, which is often fashioned too much after a theory. In other words, without being a Wagnerite, I was at that time already what I am still: an adherent, nay a worshipper, of that mighty genius.[54]

Apart from articles on Mozart, Schumann, and Verdi[55] I have not written anything worth mentioning, only here and there a short paper in the journals, which I have never gathered together. You express surprise that I endured all the stupidities of the critics so patiently instead of laying about with a club long ago. Well, had I done that, I would, in my opinion, have lost all that remained of my artistic pride. If there is in my music anything of lasting value it will live; if not, it will perish. That is my belief, for I am convinced that truth will prevail *ultimately*.

It is not probable that you will hear from Bjørnson.[56] He seems to be in a bad humor, and apart from that I cannot, for obvious reasons, appeal to him personally. . . .

Fortunately I am now getting along somewhat better here in Christiania. But creative work is still out of the question.

If you have really succeeded in correcting the many erroneous current notions regarding my works, you will have done me and my country a great service and I shall take pleasure in thanking you therefor cordially. Unfortunately I am somewhat pessimistic; yet I am none the less cordially obliged to you for your good and artistically correct intentions.

Sincerely yours,
EDVARD GRIEG

---

[53] Finck had written to Grieg informing him that he had suggested to London publisher John Lane that the medallion to be stamped on the cover of Finck's book should represent the Norwegian flag.

[54] See Grieg's articles on the Bayreuth performances in Benestad & Halverson (eds.), *Edvard Grieg: Diaries, Articles, Speeches* (Columbus, Ohio, 2001).

[55] All three articles will be printed in English translation in *Edvard Grieg: Diaries, Articles, Speeches.*

[56] Finck had written to Bjørnstjerne Bjørnson asking if he could write a few introductory words for Finck's book on Grieg.

14

Christiania, October 8, 1905

Dear Sir!

Yesterday I received from Mr. Lane the proof-sheets of your book, which have occupied me uninterruptedly (excepting a few intervals for my meals and sleep). In consequence of my imperfect command of the English language it was a great exertion, and I have just finished the task. I admire the keen scent with which you track facts—like an expert hunter pursuing his quarry. But so far as your estimate of my works is concerned I must echo the words of our poet A. O. Vinje in his "Last Spring": "More I got than I deserved—and everything must end." There are certainly passages in which you have done yourself and me a questionable service by an excess of superlatives!? But the many truths that you did not hesitate to express bluntly have gladdened my heart.

Somewhere in your book you express the indubitable truth that in art quality is more important than quantity. From this point of view I am much surprised that you make no mention at all of a short composition that to me is of the greatest importance: I mean *Der Bergentrückte* [*The Mountain Thrall*] for baritone solo, string orchestra, and two horns. The text follows some very old specimens of folklore which greatly absorbed me during my stay at Lofthus. This piece contains drops of my heart blood. Schjelderup speaks of it in his book. Apart from this I have nothing to add. The political situation takes up much of my attention.

The compositions of mine that are about to appear in print are: op. 73, *Moods*, piano pieces; op. 51, *Old Norwegian Melody with Variations* for orchestra; and op. 54, *Lyric Suite* (from the *Lyric Pieces*, op. 54). . . .

I am of course delighted that you, who have so much sympathy with my art, were asked to write a book about me, and I am under great obligations to you because you are endeavoring to carry out your task with so much interest and carefulness. At the same time I wish, and cannot refrain from saying so, that you might have had four times as much time at your disposal, so that you might have written a complete and definitive record of my career. This wish you will easily understand.

Those musk melons I envy you! They are my favorite food! We have them here, too, in great abundance, moreover, and very cheap. You are wise in devoting as much time as possible to your garden. That keeps the mind fresh and preserves the love of nature!

P. S. Have you seen in the *North American Review*, edited by George Harvey, September, 1902, an article by A. M. Wergeland: "Grieg as a National Composer"? It was written by a woman who was born in Norway, and contains much that is good and true.

Sincerely yours,
EDVARD GRIEG

15

[Catholic Hospital, Christiania], December 30, 1905

Dear Sir!

As you see, I am in a hospital because of my sins. I have had a bad time with my disordered organs of digestion and my whole nervous system. But for this, I would have written to you long ago, to express my most cordial thanks to you for your book on me. I have now read it again in as sober a mood as possible. I still must reproach you with having placed me too high. But the whole book breathes sympathy and love for my art, and you have made excellent use of the material. Of most particular importance is the chapter on the relation of Norwegian folk songs to my originality. For this I must express to you my gratitude in the highest degree. You have succeeded brilliantly in rehabilitating me in face of the many unjust and ignorant foreign criticisms.

I was deeply grieved to read about the illness of MacDowell and have written to his wife, in your care.[57] He may improve, of course, but whether permanently, that is the question. He is indeed the most ideal of the American composers I know of.

Should you soon come to Norway again, as I hope you will, you will find a free, independent people. What has happened in our country this year seems like a fairy tale. The hopes and longings of my youth have been fulfilled. I am deeply grateful that I was privileged to live to see this.[58]

And herewith the best New Year's wishes to you and your dear wife from my wife and from

Sincerely yours,
EDVARD GRIEG

---

[57] American pianist and composer Edward MacDowell (1860–1908). The letter to Mrs. Marian MacDowell (1857–1956) begins on p. 487.

[58] Norway had been subject to the Danish crown for over 400 years. In 1814, at the conclusion of the Napoleonic wars, Norway's bid for complete independence was frustrated when Norwegians were compelled to accept a union with Sweden in which Norway was subordinate to the Swedish crown. The yearning for independence remained alive, however, and was a burning issue throughout Grieg's lifetime. Grieg was deeply involved in the struggle for political freedom. The union with Sweden was dissolved on June 7, 1905, when the Norwegian Parliament (Stortinget) declared Norway's independence. See also Grieg's diary entries for November and December, 1905, in Benestad & Halverson (eds.), *Edvard Grieg: Diaries, Articles, Speeches* (Columbus, Ohio, 2001).

To Peter Vogt Fischer

The Norwegian impresario Peter Vogt Fischer (1863–1938) had close contact with Grieg during the last year of the composer's life. Grieg was especially concerned that Fischer should do everything possible to advance the career of his young protégé Fridtjof Backer-Grøndahl (1885–1959).

Grieg's letters to Fischer are preserved in Nasjonalbiblioteket, Oslo (the National Library of Norway, Oslo Division).

1

Skodsborg Sanatorium,[1] June 7, 1907

Dear Fischer!
First and foremost, hurrah for the great day today[2] and then on to life's gravity. You surely understand how deeply I wanted to be present for Agathe G.'s[3] funeral, but unfortunately it is not possible. And in not coming for it, I am following both the doctors' and my friends' insistent advice not to travel until I am feeling better. Today, therefore, we have had to make the decision to stay here for eight more days, so we will not be getting to Christiania until about the sixteenth. Details later by telegram.

Be sure to tell me about Agathe Grøndahl's last days, about her death and whatever else there is to say about her and Fridtjof and all the Grøndahls. I had a telegram from O. A. Grøndahl[4] shortly after Agathe's passing. But I was feeling so miserable that I couldn't comply with a request from the editor of [the Christiania newspaper] *Morgenbladet* to write an obituary. I can't tolerate either reading or writing, so you understand that it is my brain that is afflicted. This and the bowels as well. I hope you got the letter in which I asked you to please secure a beautiful wreath with a ribbon bearing the colors of the Norwegian flag and the inscription "From Nina and Edvard Grieg." Thank you for your trouble!

Hearty greetings to all!

Your devoted
EDVARD GRIEG

---

[1] Skodsborg Sanatorium near Copenhagen.

[2] On the morning of June 7, 1905, the Norwegian Parliament (the Storting) had unanimously passed a resolution declaring that the union with Sweden had ceased to exist.

[3] Norwegian composer Agathe Backer Grøndahl (1847–1907), mother of Fridtjof Backer-Grøndahl. See Grieg's letters to her.

[4] Norwegian choral conductor and composer Olaus Andreas Grøndahl (1847–1923), husband of Agathe Backer Grøndahl.

To Ernst Wilhelm Fritzsch

The Leipzig music publisher Ernst Wilhelm Fritzsch (1840–1902) was the first one who, in 1872, risked publishing Grieg's *Piano Concerto*—three years after its highly successful premiere performance in Copenhagen. Seven years later he took another chance when he published Grieg's *String Quartet* in G minor. Fritzsch also published many of the works of Grieg's friend and fellow composer, Johan Svendsen.

All of Grieg's letters to Fritzsch were written in German. Letter 1 belongs to Nasjonalbiblioteket, Oslo (National Library of Norway, Oslo Division), Letter 2 to Bergen Offentlige Bibliotek (Bergen Public Library), Letter 3 to The Pierpont Morgan Library, Mary Flagler Cary Music Collection, New York, and Letter 4 to Stiftelsen Musikkulturens Främjande (the Society for the Promotion of Musical Culture), Stockholm.

1

Rome, February 22, 1884

Dear Fritzsch!

I regret infinitely much that you have lost my arrangement of the second piano part,[1] for I put a lot of work into it and I no longer remember a thing about it. Since I have neither a score nor orchestral parts here, you will have to be content with the changes I have been able to undertake from memory. For safety's sake, please send me a proof.

You would have enjoyed the performance of my *String Quartet* in Sgambati's matinee.[2] It was *outstanding* and the reception was better than ever before. How they are able to appreciate this music in Italy is a mystery to me. With cordial greetings,

Sincerely yours,
EDVARD GRIEG

2

Copenhagen, March 15, 1891
Hotel King of Denmark

Dear Fritzsch!

I don't know if you have a correspondent in Copenhagen, but this much I know —that it is of significance for your paper[3] that you hear about the musical event that is taking place here these days. On March 7 there was a performance of Wagner's *Die Walküre* [*The Valkyrie*] in the Royal Theater—the first performance

---

[1] Grieg is referring to an arrangement of his *Piano Concerto* for two pianos instead of piano and orchestra.

[2] Italian pianist and composer Giovanni Sgambati (1843–1914) gave a concert in Rome in Grieg's honor on February 15, 1884.

[3] Grieg is referring to *Musikalisches Wochenblatt*, a weekly newspaper edited and published by Fritzsch.

not only in Copenhagen but, as a matter of fact, in all of Scandinavia. The performance must be described as outstanding. The text has been excellently translated into Danish by the poet Karl Gjellerup,[4] and the singers have done a praiseworthy job. The orchestra, meanwhile, under the brilliant leadership of Johan Svendsen, deserves nothing but praise. The passion and richness of color that were created here was truly enchanting. The splendid work is now playing to a full house every other day.

These comments must of course be used without any mention of my name.

Friendly greetings,
EDVARD GRIEG

3

Vienna, December 23, 1896
Address Gutmann, Opera House

Dear Fritzsch!
You will note in the enclosed copy of *Neue Freie Presse* the peculiar fact that Hanslick[5] has actually spoken approvingly of me. Of course, that doesn't mean much. But he discusses my article on Schumann in *The Century Magazine*[6] in such a way that one must conclude that I am not an admirer of Wagner. Anyone who reads my article will see that this is absolutely not the case. Unfortunately, however, my article is unknown in Germany. Earlier this would have been utterly immaterial to me. For that reason I have not made any effort to get it published in German. But now when the "Wagnerites", citing Hanslick's article, use the opportunity to smear me, the time has come when my article *must* be published in Germany. As soon as I can get hold of a copy of *The Century Magazine* I will send it to you with a request that you get the article translated for use in your own magazine. Obviously I do not want any honorarium.

The three concerts that I planned to give here had to be postponed because of my illness (influenza), but now I have taken care of a chamber-music concert and an orchestral concert and they went very well.[7] But the famous Böhmer quartet didn't play my *String Quartet* op. 27 nearly as well as the Hilf quartet played its pieces.

During the Christmas holidays we are going to Semmering,[8] and on the evening of January 6 I am collaborating with Sistermans[9] in a song recital. Thereafter, hopefully, we will head for Leipzig.

---

[4] Karl Adolf Gjellerup (1857–1919) won the Nobel prize in literature in 1917.

[5] Austrian musicologist Eduard Hanslick (1825–1904), music critic for the *Neue Freie Presse* of Vienna, was known as a warm advocate of Brahms and an equally harsh opponent of Wagner.

[6] See Benestad & Halverson (eds.), *Edvard Grieg: Diaries, Articles, Speeches* (Columbus, Ohio, 2001).

[7] Grieg's concerts in Vienna took place on December 16 and 19, 1896, and January 6, 1897.

[8] Semmering is a well-known resort area in the mountains south of Vienna.

[9] Dutch baritone Anton Sistermans (1865–1920).

So: Merry Christmas to you and yours, and we hope to see you soon!

Your old friend,
EDVARD GRIEG

P.S. Brahms is unusually amiable, but he looks *sad.* His illness is definitely serious.[10] We will be spending New Year's Eve with him and Joachim.[11] He tries to give the impression that he is healthy, but the intention is all too obvious—unfortunately.

Your old friend,
EDVARD GRIEG

4

Amsterdam, February 27, 1897
13, van Baerlestraat

Dear Fritzsch!
It is incorrect to say—as you write in *Musikalisches Wochenblatt*—that I have "arranged for" a choral and orchestral concert of my own works here. I was invited by "The Association for the Promotion of Music"[12] to give a concert of choral and orchestral music as well as a chamber-music concert. Both have now been successfully carried out.[13] Oh well, the error is a very trivial one, but the phrase "arranged for" gave me a pain in the pit of my stomach.

However—to speak of something more pleasant than my stomach pains—I can tell you that I am completely overwhelmed at the quality of the choral and orchestral ensembles here. The orchestra is *absolutely first class.* Some of my works were performed more beautifully than I have ever heard before—and after all, I have had to do with the most famous orchestras in Europe. And then this seriousness and this enthusiasm that the people demonstrate for art. It is really a very high level.

On March 3 I have been invited by "Diligentia"[14] to conduct a similar choral and orchestral concert. On March 8 I will play chamber music in Arnheim, and then I will either go north or—to Leipzig, I don't know yet.

I have had two chamber-music concerts here in which my wife had to fill in

---

[10] Johannes Brahms died April 3, 1897.

[11] Austro-Hungarian violinist Joseph Joachim (1831–1907).

[12] "Maatschappij tot Befordering der Toonkunst", founded in Amsterdam in 1829. This nationwide association sponsors choirs and music schools throughout Holland.

[13] Grieg conducted the Concertgebouw Orchestra in Amsterdam on February 13. Three days later he gave a chamber-music concert.

[14] The "Diligentia" concerts were a concert series in The Hague sponsored by "Maatschappij voor Natuur en Letterkunde", which was founded in 1793 and is still in existence. "Diligentia" is also the name of a concert hall in The Hague.

for Messchaert,[15] who was suddenly taken ill, and with what remains of her voice she achieved a major success. You cannot imagine how happy she was after previously having lost all her courage.

Kindly let me hear a few words about what is happening with the Schumann article. Do you dare to print it [without having secured permission from the American journal] and—do you dare to print it after you have read what it says? Those are the two questions I ask you. I certainly don't want you to print it just to do me a favor—I say this quite explicitly—and we will be the same good friends if you do not venture to print it because Wagner (as a human being) doesn't come out of it unscathed.

So, please, some *unambiguous* (!) lines!

Warm greetings to you and yours, also from my wife.

Yours truly,
EDVARD GRIEG

15 Dutch baritone Johannes Messchaert (1857–1927).

To Lyman Judson Gage

Lyman Judson Gage (1836–1927) was an influential American banker and politician. In 1897 he was Secretary of the Treasury in Washington, D.C., and in 1902–06 was President of the United States Trust Company in New York City.

Grieg's letter to Gage is presented here without alteration from an English draft preserved in Bergen Offentlige Bibliotek (Bergen Public Library). Around the turn of the century, when this letter was written, Grieg was very concerned about his rights as a composer. See also his letters to Henrik Ibsen (1828–1906) of December 25, 1898, and January 13 and 16, 1899.

Dear Sir! *Bergen, Norway, September 1900*

It is animated by Mr. O. W. Meysenburg of Chicago, whom I had the pleasure to meet during his stay last summer in my native country Norway, that I take the liberty to write to you. He communicated me your position to the American Copyright bill. He told me also, that you take great interest in music and therefore I am bold enough to direct your peculiar attention to the present arrangement between America and Norway, according to which Norwegian literary and musical works printed outside Norway may be pirated and have been printed in America on a large scale in spite of Norway having joined the *Convention of Bern.*[1]

As to me it is *only* the American printers who reap the material advantage of the popularity that my name has the honor of enjoying in America. This seems to me a barbarity. I therefore profit by the occasion respectfully to refer to your interest of the art and your sense of justice to try to obtain an alteration in these unfortunate circumstances. If you will do my country and myself the favor to throw your personality into the affair, I have no doubt that better conditions will be the result.

I beg you kindly to forgive me my straightforward application and send you beforehand my warmest thanks for what you will do to forward the matter.

Believe me, dear Sir,

Yours truly,
EDVARD GRIEG

P.S. I have seen the Norwegian Culturminister, Mr. Wexelsen,[2] who takes great interest in the matter. Denmark has—without joining the Convention of Bern—conducted the particular agreement, which is required for having the benefit of the Copyright protection, while the countries which—as Norway—only have joined the Convention of Bern without also joining the particular agreement, have been excluded.

---

[1] The Bern Convention is an international agreement regarding the copyright protection of literary and artistic works. Its central provision is the requirement that each country signing the Convention shall provide protection for works first published in other countries signing the Convention. The original agreement was adopted in Bern, Switzerland, on September 9, 1886, and has been modified several times since. Norway signed the convention in 1896. The United States did not sign it until 1988.

[2] Vilhelm Andreas Wexelsen (1849–1909), Norwegian bishop and politician. He had the honor of crowning King Haakon VII and Queen Maud in the Trondheim cathedral in 1906.

To Arne Garborg

Arne Garborg (1851–1924) published *Haugtussa* (*The Mountain Maid*) in 1895, and Grieg, who read the book immediately, was thoroughly enchanted. This poetry impressed him as "a sea of unborn music," and that same summer he wrote most of the songs of op. 67. These songs and the Vinje songs of op. 33 are generally considered Grieg's most important contributions to song literature. Garborg's mature works were all written in "New Norwegian", an indigenous form of the Norwegian language that explicitly sought to avoid Danish influences. Through his novels and plays, and also as an active participant in the public discussion of the language question—which was a hotly debated issue at this time (see letter 2)—Garborg became a leading spokesman for "New Norwegian" and Grieg became one of his standard-bearers in the realm of music.

Grieg's letters to Garborg are preserved in Nasjonalbiblioteket, Oslo (National Library of Norway, Oslo Division).

1

Leipzig, January 13, 1898
C. f. Peters, Thalstrasse 10

Mr. Arne Garborg.
I wrote several songs based on your beautiful *Mountain Maid* immediately after the book came out. These are now going to be published. But where will I find the German translation? Do you know of one? NB, one that is not only literarily and linguistically mature but also musically so to the extent that the declamation is not faulty.

Dare I ask you for a few words as soon as possible.

Your admirer,
EDVARD GRIEG

P.S. The songs are: 1) "The Enticement", 2) "Veslemøy. The Young Maiden", 3) "Blueberry Slope", 4) "The Tryst", 5) "Love", 6) "Kidlings' Dance", 7) "Hurtful Day", 8) "At the Brook".[1]

2

Stockholm, November 9, 1899

Dear Arne Garborg!
I am glad that you like my *Mountain Maid* songs. And I am doubly glad because

1 It was these eight songs—in precisely this order—that were published in the 1898 edition of *The Mountain Maid*. Grieg wrote six additional songs based on this cycle of poems, however, and these, together with Grieg's sketches for still other songs that were never completed, have been printed in *Edvard Grieg: Complete Works* vol. 15 (1991).

then Mrs. Nansen must have performed them well. And I am sure that Mrs. Grøndahl was the best accompanist in Norway.[2]

It was not many weeks ago that I had an argument with B. B.[3] regarding the language issue. Unfortunately, he and I are in complete disagreement. It is nothing but a damn shame that we don't have B. B. with his dazzling abilities on our side. And yet, I think his opposition is a good thing insofar as it give the *fanatics* something to think about.[4] What shall we poor folks do who were born to a Danish-speaking mother and father and have only received the gift of *loving* the language, but without being able to write or speak it? Shall we, for that reason, be regarded as enemies by the fanatical advocates of New Norwegian? That would be unfair and unwise. I do not regard either the city man or the farmer as holding a patent on the refinement of spirit and heart, and I don't think the language makes any difference for those who possess that for which language is only an expression—whether it be Dano-Norwegian (a condemned word) or a rural dialect. But there are two things that B. B. and those who share his opinion have not mentioned that I think are of the greatest importance:

1) Our Danish language has been *forced upon* us through school and church. Justice requires, then, that what is currently only the language of farmers shall get the same right. For a few generations (or for just one) it must be compulsory. I'm not worried about the rural culture. It gives us an abundance of substantial materials and will merge with city culture in a higher unity. From that will come the language of the future in which I believe.

2) B. B. does not mention that *four fifths* of the nation speak a rural dialect. That, for me, settles the issue.

I had to take the opportunity to say this since you mentioned the matter in your letter.

Hurrah for the future! Warm greetings and thanks to you and your wife!

Sincerely yours,
EDVARD GRIEG

---

[2] Garborg had written Grieg on November 7, 1899, that he had heard Eva Nansen (1858–1907), accompanied by Agathe Backer Grøndahl (1847–1907), in a performance of the *Mountain Maid* songs (November 2). He wrote, "I have come to love them more than I can tell you. It is precisely this deep, soft, subdued character—the music of the underworld—that I in my way have tried to express in words, but that you have really captured. And then suddenly once again blazing sun and the joy of summer, as in the marvelous "Kidlings' Dance". But one of the most enchantingly moving songs of the lot is "At the Brook". Yes, now I am happy and proud—absolutely disgracefully proud—that you were able to use these verses. Thank you!" Grieg was in Stockholm at this time, where on November 7 he had presented four of the *Mountain Maid* songs in collaboration with the Norwegian-born Swedish singer Dagmar Möller (1866–1956).

[3] Norwegian author Bjørnstjerne Bjørnson (1832–1910).

[4] In his letter of November 7 Garborg had written, "B. B. is outspoken now. But I don't think it will have much of an effect. Maybe it will do some good instead, liven things up."

To Hulda Garborg

Hulda Garborg (1862–1934), wife of Arne Garborg (1851–1924), was a writer in her own right who played an important role in Norwegian cultural life. In addition to her work as a writer, she was an early promoter of the Norwegian folk-dance movement, a collector and publisher of indigenous folk songs and a driving force behind the successful effort to get people to wear the colorful national costumes (called *bunader*) on festive occasions. In 1910 she established a drama society that later evolved into Det Norske Teatret (The Norwegian Theater), a theater devoted to the performance of dramatic works written in New Norwegian—an indigenous form of the Norwegian language that explicitly sought to avoid Danish influences.

Grieg's letters to Hulda Garborg, one of which is included here, are preserved in Nasjonalbiblioteket, Oslo (National Library of Norway, Oslo Division).

Troldhaugen at Bergen, August 18, 1898

Mrs. Hulda Garborg.

How gladly I would have accommodated your wish, both for your sake and for the sake of the matter itself! Especially since I had hoped that Mrs. Nansen[1] might be the first interpreter [of the songs]. But unfortunately it is impossible. To be sure, the *Mountain Maid* songs will come out at the end of September, but simultaneously in Denmark and Germany—and my German publisher guards his treasure like a brooding hen sitting on her eggs to make sure that not a single note reaches people's ears prior to publication.

Moreover, how curious it is that your letter came today of all times. For just last evening I asked my wife if she thought it would be a good idea if I sent my manuscript of the piano reduction of *Olav Trygvason* to *Den norske Marknad*,[2] which I of course regard with great interest. I think I may take a chance on it. To be sure, both the *Marknad* and I will be running the risk that here in our beloved Norway my gift will be sold as wastepaper, for despite all our boasting we have not advanced beyond that point. But good God! We must not hold that against our beloved Norway. Lack of good manners is a fault that I for my part, in any case, will gladly overlook.

Greet your husband and tell him that he is not permitted to be sick. We can't afford that. In the past I have never been able to imagine Norway without people like Bjørnson and Mrs. Sars.[3] But when I hear that Garborg is sick, it immediately strikes me that Garborg is an extremely big part of the Norway that I am happy to call my own. How much I owe to him on the purely personal

---

1 Norwegian singer Eva Nansen (1858–1907), wife of polar explorer Fridtjof Nansen (1861–1930).

2 *Den Norske Marknad*: "The Norwegian Market", an agency that sought to raise money to support "New Norwegian" literature.

3 Maren Sars (1811–98), a sister of Norwegian poet J. S. Welhaven (1807–73), was married to Michael Sars (1805–69), a zoologist.

level! If I did not feel so strongly how wonderful it is to belong to this bounteous, half-wild country precisely now, when it is in process of forming itself anew—I could wish to live a few generations later, simply to be along in speaking the Norwegian language that I love with the power of instinct.[4] And especially in reading its poetry as it has found expression in such works as *The Mountain Maid.* What a plumbing of the depths of the soul of the language—and what a world of unborn music! In truth, reason enough for me to be crazy about the language even if I were not enthused out of national sentiment.

Excuse the prolixity—the very opposite of my customary practice. But I had to avail myself of the opportunity! With respectful greetings,

Yours truly,
EDVARD GRIEG

---

[4] I.e., "New Norwegian."

To Børre Giertsen

Børre R. Giertsen (1851–1905) was a shipowner who was a member of Grieg's circle of friends in Bergen. His wife Nancy (1859–1911) was a sister of Marie Beyer (1852–1929), wife of Grieg's close friend and confidante, Frants Beyer (1851–1915). Giertsen made an important contribution to the cultural life of Bergen and had an impact throughout Norway as a strong advocate of forest preservation.

Grieg's letters to Børre Giertsen are preserved in Nasjonalbiblioteket, Oslo (National Library of Norway, Oslo Division).

1

Voksenkollen Sanatorium,[1] *January 2, 1901*

Dear Giertsen.

Thank you for the telegram—just received, as it was delayed—and the warmest wishes to all of you for a happy new year at Solbakken![2]

And now regarding Harmonien.[3] You show me the honor of allowing *me* to make the decision regarding the name of the new music society. But I cannot accept that honor. I will have nothing to do with it. I once stated my view publicly and was met with such withering scorn and contempt—culminating in the city's giving support to the so-called Music Society—that I have had enough. Either people do not understand or else they refuse to understand. Both possibilities demonstrate that I should have nothing further to do with this matter. If I am asked publicly, then of course I must say what I think. But I hope this does not happen. With respect to you personally, dear friend, it is a different matter. You have been so kind as to share with me all of this information that you know is of deep interest to me, so I will try as briefly and concisely as possible to tell you how I view the matter. But, it is only to a friend—or more correctly, to friends, to you and Frants—that I am speaking.

There is one thing that exasperates me over and over again in this country,

---

[1] Voksenkollen Sanatorium was located on the outskirts of Christiania, near Holmenkollen.

[2] "Solbakken" was the name of Giertsen's villa on the outskirts of Bergen.

[3] The Music Society Harmonien (Musikselskabet Harmonien), an orchestra of professional and advanced amateur musicians that Grieg conducted during the years 1880–82. In 1894, however, an organization calling itself the "Music Society" (Musikforeningen) was established exclusively for amateur musicians, and it soon found itself in competition with Harmonien. In March, 1899, the "Music Society" applied to the city for operating support and another group called the Bergen Orchestra Association (Bergen Orkesterforening) sought support for a permanent city orchestra. The "Music Society" received a grant of 2,000 crowns whereas a minority of the councilmen were willing, on certain conditions, to commit funds to the "Bergen Orchestra Association". Grieg had been furious over what he perceived as a decision to support dilettantism in preference to professionalism. On June 7, 1899, he had published an article in *Bergens Tidende* in which he heatedly argued that the organizations had to cooperate but that dilettantism had no place in true art. See "Our Musical Conditions" in Benestad & Halverson (eds.), *Edvard Grieg: Diaries, Articles, Speeches* (Columbus, Ohio, 2001). In 1901 the various organizations involved all came to the realization that Grieg was right and joined together as "The Music Society Harmonien" (Musikforeningen Harmonien).

and that is the boundless lack of reverence. Good God! We can't be such total barbarians that we do not understand the importance of a tradition! Harmonien was established in the last—no, I think it was in the next-last—century by *cultured* businessmen as a *protest* against a one-sided preoccupation with business. Now a group of businessmen who are anything but cultured have established a society whose goal it is to kill Harmonien—namely, a society that not only does not manage to set loftier ideals than the older organization, but that sails under a false flag and fights with the dirtiest of weapons. *That Harmonien should pay the Music Society's debt in order to put an end to strife and division is both practical and noble.* I can also understand that if this is all that is involved you could go along with calling the new organization "Filharmonien" ["The Philharmonic"] NB *when it obviously is Harmonien that is continuing under the statutes of the new organization. But to go along with allowing Harmonien to be disbanded would in my opinion be disgraceful.*

Do you know that the famous Gewandhaus concerts in Leipzig were established more than 1½ centuries ago by cultured amateurs and that this Society, which has since become world-famous, clings to tradition to the extent that it retains the old name even after having moved into its splendid new concert hall. And yet, this word "Gewandhaus" doesn't even have anything to do with art.[4]

If one has no feeling for the value of tradition it is of little use to preach about it. But to *you* I say: Try to understand me, and if it finally dawns on you that perhaps I am right, then convey this understanding to others. A good word always finds a good place, as the saying goes. There was a time back in the 1850's and 60's when Harmonien was given the name "Filharmonien". That was when Otto Lübbert was conductor. It is indeed possible that Harmonien was inactive at this time and that the philharmonic concerts were substitutes.

But whatever you do, *don't let Harmonien be inactive now!* For if that happens it will never come to life again. Mr. Bugge[5] and his cohorts will see to that. It is contemptible to use art in the service of a "caste". That is what is now being done at home. But do the members of Harmonien go along with the idea of the Society committing suicide? You say nothing about that. It is, in the final analysis, the decisive question. How deeply will Harmonien prostrate itself in the dust for those narrow-minded city officials—or, more accurately, those misguided party toadies? And that for the sake of a paltry 7–8,000 crowns? To hell with it! Here, with Henrik Ibsen, I don the kid gloves—which, God knows, I otherwise do not love. No, and again I say no! Harmonien has the qualifications to exist and should continue to do so. But: *There must not be two music societies!* Absolutely

[4] *Gewandhaus* means, literally, "woollen merchants' exchange".

[5] Cornelius B. Bugge (1865–1934), businessman and local politician in Bergen, chairman of the board of Harmonien.

not! And to achieve this I go along with the idea of the name "Filharmonien". That's as far as I can go.

I see that the Englishmen are now engaging a corps of Boers to fight against —the Boers![6] That's sheer madness. I find myself thinking of this in the present connection. No, let us begin the century with our self-respect intact—also on this point. I see that you indicate that the Music Society has not declared itself unwilling to retain the name Harmonien. And after what you have said about the financial arrangements appurtenant thereto, it is easy to see why. Now I do not doubt for a moment that a man as resourceful and enterprising as Mr. Bugge could just as well be used for a good purpose as for a poor one. And it is to be hoped that he would certainly find greater satisfaction in so doing. I have previously supported the idea that the Music Society and Harmonien should join together into one orchestra with two conductors. But as matters now stand, you should go all the way. The goal must be *one* music society, for Bergen cannot support more than one. If it were true—as you say and as the newspapers here assert—that Bergen is tired of music, then there would be only one thing to recommend: to free Bergen from all music societies. But the expression used is highly misleading.

I page through your letter and stop by the statement that it would be *financially* indefensible to throw away a society with "Harmonien's" traditions. This strikes me as inessential. *No, it is precisely the ideal side of Harmonien's activity that I want preserved*—in contrast to that of the Music Society. I am so totally confident that *if only* Harmonien does not surrender, it will triumph. The city will see in the end that Harmonien *will* not be killed. *Cannot* be killed. Let it get such a feeling *as soon as possible.*

Answer: You have wanted what is best. But you have gone too far. Without wanting to do so, you are working to assassinate the institution whose champion you are called to be. Here I am coming very close to Frants's views. And here I think Frants's concept of justice is the right one. Yes, I agree with Joachim's[7] statement: One must believe in oneself, otherwise no one else will do so.

You must excuse the fact that my answer was not brief and concise as I promised. It isn't clear either. But I was not in a mood for conciseness. Many greetings from

Yours truly,
EDVARD GRIEG

---

[6] Grieg is referring to the so-called Boer War between Great Britain and the two Boer (Afrikaner) republics—the South African Republic and the Orange Free State. The war lasted from Oct. 11, 1899 to May 31, 1902 and so was much in the news at the time of this letter.

[7] Grieg's second cousin, Joachim Grieg, who was a driving force in Bergen's cultural life.

2

Berlin, April 1, 1903
Continental Hotel

Dear Børre Giertsen!
Thank you for the letter from the heights![8] And thank you because you always think of me from the heights! That is Norway and friendship all wrapped up in one, the best thing I can get here in my exile. When I read about your heights with storm and snow and rain and slush, my thoughts glide over to my own heights of quite a different sort—but heights, after all, are heights. And I know for sure that a few words from these heights will interest you. I am speaking of my reception in Prague a few days ago. Just as you did at Fossli, I took delight in letting the storms down there blow over my head.

Just as you were received by Ole Garen,[9] I was received like an old friend by all the people in Prague. I don't know of anything else in life that so moves me to gratitude as the awareness of having won unknown friends through the power of music. There is something so unmerited in that. For indeed, I do not compose in order to please others but only because I feel a need to use the language in which I am best able to express my innermost thoughts. You should have seen the kind of reception I got when I walked in. And when the "Homage March" from *Sigurd Jorsalfar* had sounded through the auditorium, the path from the podium was blocked by people who came with laurel and palm wreaths as big as millwheels—and under a glass, on a silk cushion, a silver wreath. The applause grew steadily throughout the concert. And when I drove home, crowds of people ran along beside the coach, and like a king I had to stand part way up and bow to right and left. Yes, this of course has nothing directly to do with art. But I know that as a friend you will rejoice to hear about the sincere appreciation that was shown to me.

Now I am sitting here waiting for Mrs. Ekman[10] in order to rehearse with her. Then we will travel together to Warsaw, where a concert is scheduled for the fourteenth. That same night I leave for Paris, where I must conduct on the nineteenth. If this goes well, everything will be fine. Unfortunately, it couldn't be arranged any other way, and I do indeed feel that I am taking a terrible chance. Oh! If only I get to see my beloved West Norway again!

What I know about Harmonien is principally what I have heard from you. Frants has only touched lightly on the subject. I understand so well what you have had to deal with. And in addition to that, people like the undersigned have irritated you—inadvertently, to be sure. But of course I knew absolutely nothing

---

[8] Giertsen had written the letter from his stone hut on the Hardanger Plateau.
[9] Ole Garen (d. 1915) was the owner of the Fossli Hotel and a well-known guide in the Jotunheimen mountains.
[10] Finnish soprano Ida Ekman (1875–1942).

about the sale of the library, and that made me rather "dumbfounded" in the beginning. You deserve a lot of gratitude because you bought back "Harmonien's" library. But it should never have been done in the way you indicate. I had thought that all of us (a few private individuals) should have provided money rather quietly to get it done. It is more than unjust that this should land entirely on your shoulders. But the worst thing would be if your interest in our music life should have been lost. A contrary wind certainly cannot alter our perceptions and our sympathies. That would be illogical. Now if only you may have reaped some good from your stay in the mountains! Unfortunately I do not know the day of Gina's[11] wedding. I am sorry about that. I would have liked so much to send a greeting!

Farewell for now, dear friend, and thank you again for your letter from the heights. You can't imagine how much good it does me. Sincerest greetings to all!

Your devoted
EDVARD GRIEG

---

[11] Gina Giertsen, Børre Giertsen's daughter.

To Percy Grainger

The Australian-born composer, pianist and conductor Percy Grainger (1882–1959) spent most of his adult life in the United States, becoming a naturalized citizen in 1918. Prior to moving to America, however, he lived in London (1901–14), where he established a reputation as a gifted performer of contemporary music. It is not known exactly when he became acquainted with Grieg's *Norwegian Peasant Dances*, op. 72, but presumably it occurred before 1905. He met the Norwegian composer for the first time in May of 1906 when Grieg went to London to give several concerts. They became friends immediately and were together on several occasions. Grainger, among other things, played some of the op. 72 dances for Grieg, who was thoroughly pleased with his interpretations.

In the summer of 1907, Grainger visited Grieg at Troldhaugen from July 25 to August 5. On July 27 and August 5 Grieg made long entries in his diary about his new, young Australian friend. See Grieg's diary entries for these dates in Benestad & Halverson (eds.), *Edvard Grieg: Diaries, Articles, Speeches* (Columbus, Ohio, 2001).

Grainger had a reading knowledge of Norwegian, so Grieg was able to write to him in his native language. The letters to Grainger are preserved in The Grainger Museum, University of Melbourne, Australia.

1

Troldhaugen, Bergen, June 30, [1906]

Dear Percy Grainger!

Thank you for your letter! Let me say it right away: I like you! I like your healthy, wholesome view of art, your unspoiled nature—which even "high life" has not been able to destroy—and also your deep feeling for the folk song and all the possibilities it carries within its bosom. Your understanding of the English folk song is brilliant and has within it the germ of a new English style. And your feeling also for the Norwegian folk song and Nordic language and literature demonstrate that you are not a slave of partiality. And in addition to all that there is your marvelous piano playing and—your appreciation of the *Norwegian Peasant Dances!*

I will tell you one thing: I have met plenty of appreciation in my life, more than I have deserved. But it has rarely been of the right kind. I have often been the victim of appreciation *without understanding*. It is your understanding of what I have aimed at, even if I have not achieved it—that is what makes me so happy.

Greet Sandby[1] and tell him that I must be permitted also to count him among my few understanding friends. And in so saying I will gratefully include both of you in this understanding.

---

[1] The Danish cellist Herman Sandby (1881–1965), whom Grieg was with on several occasions during his visit to London in 1906. We know from Grieg's diary that Sandby and Grainger played Grieg's *Cello Sonata* for him in order to get his opinion of their interpretation. See his diary entry for May 30, 1906 in Benestad & Halverson (eds.), *Edvard Grieg: Diaries, Articles, Speeches* (Columbus, Ohio, 2001).

I wish you luck apropos the invitation to play under Svendsen's leadership.[2] That is art of the highest rank.

But—when shall we meet again? My sun is already low in the western sky, so it better happen soon. Both my wife and I would like so very much to see both of you here at Troldhaugen. How unfortunate that you are tied up in the middle of the season!

We hope to see Brodsky[3] and his wife in August. Do you know them? They are wonderful people. And he is a great artist.

I'm sure the scenery of West Norway would thrill you. It is full of musical motives that each person can make use of in his own way. It is lying here in its majestic tranquility and waiting for you. But you must come while you are young and receptive. Later it will be too late. I am still living on the powerful impressions of my youth.

My wife and I send our warmest greetings to you and also to your mother! Write again soon!

Sincerely yours,
EDVARD GRIEG

2

Christiania, November 27, 1906
Hotel Westminster

Dear Percy Grainger!
If you were to get a letter from me each time we talk about you, it would soon be too much for you. But my failing is at the opposite extreme, and that is the result of old age. Letter-writing is hard work when one is 63 years old. But I must thank you for your letter today, and I'm going to do it this evening without delay—because tomorrow something might get in the way.

It's great that you are coming to Leeds next autumn. Might it not be possible, if I were to include my *Piano Concerto* among the works that I shall conduct, that I could have the great joy of seeing Percy Grainger as soloist? I have no idea whether concertos are performed at such a festival—or whether one must limit oneself to symphonies, overtures and choral works. Please look into this for me and tell me what you find out.

This festival has one big problem, namely that it won't take place until next year! At present I am still capable of participating, but it's more than doubtful

---

[2] Johan Svendsen (1840–1911), music director at the Royal Theater in Copenhagen, each year gave a series of philharmonic concerts with members of the Royal Theater Orchestra. Grainger played Grieg's *Piano Concerto* under Svendsen's baton at a large memorial concert for Grieg on October 19, 1907. Grieg had passed away on September 4 of that year.

[3] The Russian violinist Adolf Brodsky (1851–1929) visited Grieg August 6–10, 1906. See Grieg's diary entries for that period.

whether I will be able to do so a year from now.[4] Can you tell me the dates of the festival? I have forgotten them, and my letters are in Bergen. I think it is in the beginning of October, but I'm not sure.

I hope to hear from you again soon, and then you must tell me a little more about yourself and your plans. A young fellow like you is absolutely forbidden to be sick! You, who have so much to achieve—you must take good care of yourself!

Next year you *must* come to Norway! The air here is wonderful and healthful. We will be staying here all winter—until March, when I will be conducting at several places in Germany and farther south.

My wife asks me to greet you "again and again". I, too, add my own most heartfelt greetings—and equally warm greetings to your mother from both of us!

Your old friend and admirer,
EDVARD GRIEG

3

Christiania, January 17, 1907
Hotel Westminster

Dear Percy Grainger!
Let me first and foremost take the opportunity to wish you everything good in the new year: No illness, imagination and fingers in perfect working order, and—we shall meet again! Both at Troldhaugen—where you can only expect to share the simple manner of our life here[5]—and in Leeds. Let us hope that this can come about. But I have learned from bitter experience that I cannot make a firm commitment. My health is much too fragile for that. But what a joy it would be for me and my wife to see you—and even to *hear* you—at Troldhaugen! There we could go through the *Piano Concerto* together. I have written about this matter to Leeds, but I have no idea as to the probability of a favorable reply.

I often receive highly informative brochures from "The Folksong Society". I admire the way in which the enterprise is organized and regret that something similar cannot be organized in my homeland. But here we lack a feeling for *anything* except politics and—sports!

I know that in England there are still many forms of coarseness to contend with. But in Norway, unfortunately, we have much, much more of that sort of thing. But there is a future in our people, and I am happy to have had the opportunity to live in the dawning day.

---

[4] Grieg's fears were well founded. He died on September 4, 1907, while making final preparations for the trip to Leeds.

[5] See also Letter 6. Grieg evidently feared that Grainger might expect to be grandly entertained during his visit to Troldhaugen.

My youth and manhood occurred in the beautiful sunrise of Romanticism. But that is now fading and is being supplanted by a flat, material Realism that is increasingly dominant in all spheres. I then flee back to nature, to mountain and forest and fjord, and from afar look with wondering eyes at the growing youth. But do not think that I am forgetting that which is most important! That in the last analysis youth is always right! But *they* ought not to forget that they have grown out of us, that they stand on our shoulders!

No, enough of these ruminations. Warm greetings from my wife and from

Yours truly,
EDVARD GRIEG

4

Christiania, February 26, 1907
Hotel Westminster

Dear [Percy Grainger]!
It's damnably unfortunate! We come to Copenhagen the 8th or 9th of March, and you are leaving on the fifth! But I *can't* be there until the 9th or maybe the 10th.

And then the fact that I shall not hear you play! Therefore, there is only one thing to do: I will look forward to seeing you again this summer—at Troldhaugen. If I survive my concerts in Germany in April. For I am sicker than anyone thinks.

But: Cheer up! I just say: See you soon!

Warm greetings also from my wife.

Sincerely yours,
EDVARD GRIEG

5

Christiania, March 10, 1907
Hotel Westminster

Dear Percy Grainger!
These few lines before my departure from Christiania to thank you for your letter and because you have been such an outstanding interpreter of the *Norwegian Peasant Dances* in Copenhagen! You have thereby made me happy and have done a favor to Norwegian folk music.

I have received an answer to my letter to Leeds, the one in which I recommended your participation—but there is no mention of this matter! I don't understand it. But I will try once more. Still, it will have to wait until I am finished with all the rehearsals and concerts that await me and require all my time, thought and strength in the immediate future.

The Griegs with two distinguished guests at Troldhaugen on July 26, 1907, just a few weeks before the composer's death on September 4. L to r.: Dutch composer and pianist Julius Röntgen, Nina, Grainger, Edvard. Röntgen wrote to Nina on September 13: "Do you know what Edvard said to me when we went to the station? He said, 'We won't see each other again; the end is near for me now!' It made me feel so indescribably sad. It was good that I didn't have any idea of how soon his words would be fulfilled. But we had some wonderful days together this summer." (Nasjonalbiblioteket, Oslo)

If I get back to Norway alive, there at home I will look forward to your coming—and then we will get the Leeds affair straightened out! It *must* succeed!

Warm greetings also to your mother from my wife and from

Sincerely yours,
EDVARD GRIEG

6

Skodsborg Sanatorium, May 28, 1907

Dear Percy Grainger!
It is unfortunately a sick man who is writing to you. I am in a lot of pain. I was feeling relatively good when I came to Copenhagen after my concerts.[6] In order to fully restore my health, I made use there of the famous Finsen electric light-baths. But I was not able to tolerate these. My nervous system got totally shattered, and

[6] Grieg's farewell concert tour in Germany in 1907 had included concerts in Munich on April 6, in Berlin on April 12 and 14, and in Kiel on April 26. The concert in Kiel proved to be his last public performance.

now I am as low as I have been in a long time. Insomnia, breathing difficulty (asthma) and hallucinations make my life a continuous torment.

This sanatorium is near Copenhagen. It is situated on the magnificent Øresund (the sound between Denmark and Sweden) and is surrounded by the no less magnificent beech forest. But after being here for only two days I have gotten even sicker, so I think that today or tomorrow I will go to Copenhagen and from there go home to Norway as soon as possible.

I had to tell you all this so that you can understand that I am in no condition to make the beautiful summer plans that I had hoped to make. Still, I am counting on the peace and quiet of home so that in July I might have the joy of seeing you with us at Troldhaugen. It is likely that my friend Julius Röntgen from Amsterdam will be coming between the 15th and the 25th of July, and I would be happy if you two could get to know each other. I will therefore recommend that you plan to come on July 15. But I must warn you that at our house everything is simple and modest.

If my illness continues and forces me to be alone, you will of course hear from me. But still, I have some hope that the change of climate will help me.

I am very glad that you are playing the *Norwegian Peasant Dances* at your concert in London. At Troldhaugen we will have a piano rehearsal in preparation for Leeds! They have written me from there as if your participation were definite.

My address until June 15 is Brødrene Hals Musikhandel, Christiania; after June 15 it is Hop Station at Bergen.

Please give my warmest thanks to your mother for her kind letter. The reason I have not answered is that I don't want to make a fool of myself with my wretched English.

Warmest greetings to both of you from my wife and from

Sincerely yours,
EDVARD GRIEG

7

Troldhaugen at Bergen, June 30, 1907

Dear Percy Grainger!
Thank you for your friendly birthday greeting! I have been so poorly that I really have not wished for "many happy returns of the day!" Until a few days ago I was quite sure that I would have to give up the pleasure of seeing you here. But during the few days I have spent here in peace and quiet, I have begun to sleep again—and with sleep has also come a strengthening of the nerves.

It does not surprise me in the least that you have so much to do. Just be careful to choose what is essential, and don't load yourself down with little things like I, unfortunately, have so often done.

That you can arrive here around the twenty-first of July suits me perfectly. I hope that by then my health will have improved even more. I will write to Julius Röntgen immediately urging him to try to be here at the same time as you. If only the weather could be better. It is constantly cold, rainy and windy. For that reason I have a man from the city come here each day to give me a massage.

As you can see, I am doing everything possible to avoid being a "graybeard" when you arrive. Now let me have a word from you with definite information as to when—which day—we can expect you in Bergen. Both my wife and I send greetings and assure you of our warmest welcome!

Sincerely yours,
EDVARD GRIEG

P.S. We ask that you convey our friendliest greetings to your mother.

8

Troldhaugen, August 11, 1907

Dear Percy Grainger!
Thank you for your postcard! But above all, thank you for the days you gave us! I wanted so much to get to know you better, both as an artist and as a person, for I had the feeling that we would understand each other. And that is what happened. You have become a dear young friend to me, one who has enriched my life's evening.

I have always found that those people who make a distinction between the artist and the human being are wrong. On the contrary: The two are inextricably interconnected. Every characteristic of the artist—yes, even the very tiniest—has its parallel in the human being. Even your indefatigable "unnecessary" fifths (!) I could trace in the person of my dear Percy G.! Moreover, I have no doubt that they will sound good in your choral arrangements. But I *hear* them, and precisely as fifths, and it annoys me to hear them in a manner different from that in which I hear, for example, fourths and sevenths, which float past my ear without my even noticing them. And in so saying, I am at the heart of your music.

//I have once again immersed myself in your folk-song arrangements, and it is becoming clearer and clearer to me how brilliant they are. You have given here a very important indication of the way in which the English folk song (which in my opinion is very different from both Scotch and Irish folk songs) has the requisite qualities to be elevated to the level of art, thereby creating an autonomous English music. It could without doubt constitute the material foundation of a national style, as it has done in other countries—including the culturally most developed countries. It has impressed me to observe the seriousness and the energy with which the English "Folksong Society" is pursuing its work. May it receive ever new infusions of strength and zeal to continue its work! And may you, too, in the midst of your diverse—and for you and your art most important—activities, spare time and strength to give this cause the benefit of your personal efforts!//

Since you mentioned to me that "The Folksong Society" would appreciate a statement from me, you are welcome to make use of what I have written here if you find it usable. If not, just let me know how it ought to be. I have placed what I think you might be able to use in the paragraph marked //–//.

With that I send a warm greeting, also to your mother. Write soon!

Sincerely yours,
EDVARD GRIEG

P.S. Please, don't write to Mr. Plumkit Green. Mr. Sistermans *will sing.* In his last letter he says that the songs suit him very well! Oh, these singers![7]

7 Oddly enough, Grieg wrote this postscript in English. Anton Sistermans (1865–1920) was an outstanding Dutch baritone. Mr. Plumkit Green presumably was someone involved in arranging the concerts in Leeds.

To Alexander and Gesine Grieg

There are 57 extant letters from Grieg's father, Alexander Grieg (1806–75), and six from his mother, Gesine Grieg (1814–75) to Edvard, but nearly all the letters from Edvard to his parents are lost. The two letters that we do have from Grieg's four-month stay in Italy in 1869–70 are, therefore, especially valuable. In 1892 these two letters were printed in the Norwegian journal *Samtiden* (pp. 219–24). Grieg himself made copies of the letters for this purpose, but in so doing he abbreviated them somewhat and changed the wording in several places. He also wrote the following brief introduction: "Excerpts from two youthful letters from Rome, graciously placed at our disposal with Edvard Grieg's permission by the composer's brother, Mr. Consul John Grieg." The first two and a half pages of the letter of February 17 and the last four pages of the letter of April 9, 1870, were omitted from the *Samtiden* version. On the other hand, in the last letter Grieg added a paragraph that is not in the original one. It is given below in footnote 29.

Grieg's letters to his parents are preserved in Bergen Offentlige Bibliotek (Bergen Public Library).

1

Rome, February 17, 1870

Dear Parents!

The last letter really gave me a surprise, and it was my intention to reciprocate the same day by sitting down at my desk immediately, but then something got in the way. Still, not so much time has passed but that these lines will certainly arrive before they are expected. It could have happened that there would have been no writing today either, for just now I was busily at work—that is to say, I pounded on the piano like a madman in order to forget everything around me, for that is the only way I can get in the mood—but then fate decreed that I should hear the residents of the room next door come home. These people are Scandinavians, and that's all it took; the mere thought of being criticized in my workroom destroys my concentration, and I can just as well quit at once. I commend and envy painters, sculptors and poets, who don't have to struggle with that sort of thing. It is also a completely unanticipated bit of bad luck that these Scandinavians should move in right beside me. It happened about eight days ago, and only the gods know when they are leaving—certainly not soon, for Carnival begins the day after tomorrow, and then everyone is glad to have a roof over his head.

But what I was going to say is that nothing is so bad that it isn't good for something. It gives me an opportunity to converse a little with you, my dear ones at home.

How much things can change in a short time! Who would have thought that Dr. Heyerdahl's time had come.[1] No, that is just the point. One thinks too

[1] Dr. Valentin Christian W. S. Heyerdahl (1821–1970), who had been chief of staff at the newly established maternity hospital in Bergen, died of pneumonia on January 26, 1870.

little, but an event like that sets one thinking. In Christiania, too, things will seem different for us. The brilliant Schweigaard[2] is dead. I heard his lectures at the university and was enthused. He just seemed to be a natural part of the Christiania milieu. We cling to any touch of genius, even if it be far removed from our own fields.

A close acquaintance of ours has also died recently: Mrs. Cappelen, the wife of the book dealer.[3] She was so friendly toward us, and we have spent many pleasant evenings in her home. It will be empty in our home, too—yes, dear me, I often think forward to that time. Perhaps that is when the loss will really hit home. I ask only for the strength to work; then everything else will fall in place.[4]

Dad, I have now read through your dear letter, and I am again surprised at how much of your valuable free time you have devoted to me. You fish up all the news for me so faithfully that I, who have much more newsworthy material at my disposal, can only be ashamed that I still can't produce as meaty a letter as that. But I will tell you a few things that will be of interest to you anyway.

Tomorrow we and several other Scandinavians (Windings, former minister in Slesvig Wolfhagen and his wife, landscape painter Aagaard and the sculptor Hasselriis[5]) were going to take a trip to Tivoli for two days. But what happens? Last evening, as I was sitting in the Scandinavian Society playing a game of whist, Sgambati[6] (an outstanding pianist, I certainly have written about him before) came up with a message from Liszt[7] that he wanted to see me at his place tomorrow morning at 11 A.M. As much as I had been looking forward to the trip to Tivoli, this naturally takes priority, so the plan has been changed.

This, however, will not be my first meeting with Liszt, and wait till you hear this. Ever since the beginning of the council[8] (he can't stand either it or its principles) he withdrew to Tivoli, where he inhabits Villa d' Este. (See Tasso's[9] biography for further information about that.) He comes here only rarely, and on one of those occasions I learned that he was coming and went to see him the following forenoon. I did not meet him then, but left my card.

A couple days later he left again, but soon thereafter I met Ravnkilde,[10] the Danish musician, who lives down here. He told me that he had just gotten a note from a lady, a German painter, whom Liszt had asked to get in touch with me

---

[2] Norwegian economist, politician and professor of law Anton Martin Schweigaard (1808–70).

[3] Frederike Helene Cappelen (1819–70), wife of Jørgen Wright Cappelen in Christiania (1805–78).

[4] The Griegs' only child, Alexandra, had died of meningitis on May 21, 1869, at the age of one.

[5] Danish pianist and composer August Winding (1835–99) and his wife Clara (1839–1925), possibly the Danish politician Fredrik Herman Wolfhagen (1818–94), Danish landscape painter Carl Frederik Aagaard (1833–95) and Danish sculptor Louis Hasselriis (1844–1912).

[6] Italian pianist and composer Giovanni Sgambati (1843–1914).

[7] Hungarian pianist and composer Franz Liszt (1811–86).

[8] A meeting of leaders of the Catholic church in Rome.

[9] Grieg is referring to the Italian renaissance poet Torquato Tasso (1544–95), court poet of the Este family, which had erected Villa d' Este.

[10] Danish composer Niels Ravnkilde (1823–90), with whom Grieg had developed a friendship in Rome in 1865.

through Ravnkilde. I was to be informed that he was so sorry that he had not had time to pay me a visit but requested that I come to see him the next day at 10 A.M. So he was in the city and was expecting me. Thus I went out to see him. He lives in a monastery near the Arch of Titus and the old Forum Romanum.

But Ravnkilde had told me that Liszt liked very much to have people bring some gifts to him, and unfortunately all of my best compositions were at the moment either at home or in Germany. So I had to go up to Winding, to whom I had earlier given a copy of my latest *Violin Sonata*,[11] and become an Indian giver. Winding kept the cover, I took the insides, wrote upon it "To Dr. F. Liszt with admiration", took in addition my *Funeral March for Nordraak*[12] and a volume of songs (the one that includes "Outward Bound")[13] under my arm and trudged down the Via del Corso—with a bit of a knot in my stomach, I don't deny it. But I needn't have worried, for you would have a hard time finding a person with greater amiability than that exhibited by Liszt. He came toward me with a smile and said in the most pleasant way, "We have exchanged a few letters, haven't we?"[14] I told him that it was thanks to his letter that I was now here,[15] a remark which elicited a truly Ole Bullian[16] laugh from him.

All the while he eyed with a sort of voracious expression the parcel I was carrying under my arm. "Ha, ha," I thought, "Ravnkilde was right." And his spidery fingers hovered so menacingly that I decided the most prudent course would be to make a move to open the parcel without delay. He then started to leaf through it, i.e., he read quickly through the first part of the *Sonata*, and that this was no mere bluff was immediately obvious when he indicated the best passages with a significant nod of his head, a "bravo," or a "very beautiful".[17]

My spirits rose, but when he then asked me to play the *Sonata* my mood immediately dropped to below zero. It had never occurred to me to play the *Violin Sonata*—both the violin and the piano part—on the piano, and on the other hand I was anxious to avoid having to sit there and mess things up. But there was no way out, so I sat down at his lovely American piano and began to play. At the very start, where the violin breaks in alone with a somewhat baroque but national passage, he exclaimed, "Ah, how daring! Listen, I like this. Let me hear it again, please."[18] And when the violin comes in again, this time *adagio*, he

---

[11] *Violin Sonata No. 2* in G major, composed in 1867.

[12] *Funeral March in Memory of Rikard Nordraak* (EG 107), composed in 1866.

[13] Grieg is referring to *Songs and Ballads* op. 9, texts by Andreas Munch (1811–84). "Outward Bound" is the fourth song of the set.

[14] "Nicht wahr, wir haben ein Bischen correspondirt?" Liszt and Grieg conversed in German. In the letters to his parents Grieg reports Liszt's remarks in German as he remembered them.

[15] In November, 1868, Niels Ravnkilde had relayed a written request from Grieg to Liszt for a letter of recommendation. On December 29, Liszt had responded with a strong recommendation which Grieg attached to his application for a travel grant. The application was successful. Liszt's letter is given in translation in a footnote to Grieg's letter to Ravnkilde of November 2, 1868.

[16] An allusion to the renowned Norwegian violinist Ole Bull (1810–80).

[17] "sehr schön."

[18] "Ei, wie keck! Nun hören Sie mal, das gefällt mir! Noch einmal, bitte."

played the violin part an octave higher on the piano, and he played with an expression so beautiful—so absolutely, amazingly authentic and *cantabile*—that I smiled to myself. These were the first tones I heard from Liszt.

And now we came straight into the *Allegro*, he playing the violin part, I the piano. My courage steadily increased, because I was so pleased with his approval, which in truth flowed so abundantly that I felt the most wonderful gratitude. When we had finished the first movement, I asked if I might play something for piano alone, choosing the Minuet from the *Humoresques*,[19] which you of course remember. When I had played the first eight measures, and repeated them, he sang the melody with a certain heroic expression of power in his gesture, which I very readily understood. I noted, of course, that it was the national peculiarities that appealed to him. I had suspected this earlier, and for that reason had brought along a number of pieces in which I had tried to touch some national strings.

When the Minuet had been played, I felt strongly that if there was to be any possibility of getting Liszt to play, it had to be now, when he was visibly elated. I asked him, and he gave me a little shrug of the shoulders. But when I said that it couldn't be his intention that I should leave southern Europe without having heard a single note from him, he made a little flourish and mumbled, "All right, I'll play whatever you wish, I'm not so [expensive]!"[20] and in a flash he brought out a score that he had recently finished—a kind of sacred procession to Tasso's grave, a supplement to his famous symphonic poem for orchestra entitled *Tasso: lamento e trionfo*.[21] And then he sat down and set the keys in motion. Yes, I assure you, he belched forth—if I may use so ugly a word—one cluster after another of glowing embers and fire and thoughts clothed in sound. It was as if he were conjuring up Tasso's own spirit. His way of playing is garish, and such a subject is just the thing for him. To depict tragic greatness is precisely his strength. I hardly knew which I should prefer here, the composer or the pianist, for he played mightily. No, one can't really call it playing. One forgets that he is a musician. He sets the spirits in motion, he roots around in your innermost self with uncanny power.

When this was finished Liszt said quite offhandedly, "Now we must go further with the *Sonata*!"[22] And of course I said, "No, thank you, after this I would rather not." But now comes the best part. Liszt said, "Well, why not give me the music and I will do it."[23] Now first you must remember that he was not familiar

---

[19] *Humoresques* op. 6, composed 1865. "Tempo di Menuetto ed energico" is no. 2.

[20] "Nun, ich spiele was Sie wollen, ich bin nicht so!"

[21] *Tasso: lamento e trionfo*, symphonic poem from 1848, inspired by the work of English poet Lord Byron (1788–1824).

[22] "Jetzt wollen wir mal weiter gehen in der Sonate!"

[23] "Nun warum nicht, geben Sie mal her, dann werde ich es thun."

with the sonata, had never heard or seen it before, and second, it must be remembered that it was a violin sonata with a violin part that develops autonomously—now it goes up, now down, independent of the piano. So what does Liszt do? He plays the whole thing lock, stock and barrel—violin part, piano part, and even more than that. Yes, he played fuller, more broadly, in such a way that the violin part came into its own right in the middle of the piano part. He was literally all over the keyboard at the same time, without missing a note. And how did he play? With the ultimate greatness, beauty, and brilliance in his understanding of the piece. I think I laughed—laughed like an idiot. And when I stammered a few words of admiration he mumbled, "Well, you must at least trust me to be able to sight-read a bit. I am, after all, an old, experienced musician."[24]

Isn't that kindness from beginning to end? None of the other great men I have met are like that.

Then, at the end, I played the *Funeral March*, which was also to his liking. I then talked with him a little. I told him that my father had heard him in London in 1824, which amused him ("I have played much in various parts of the world—too much!"[25] he said). Then I took my leave and walked homeward, strangely warm in my head but with the consciousness of having spent two of the most interesting hours of my life. I have now been invited for tomorrow and naturally look forward to it very much.

The day after this visit, the Italian artists Sgambati and Pinelli[26] played my first *Violin Sonata* at a matinee that was attended by all of the cultured people in the area. Liszt came in the middle of the concert, just before my sonata, and this was good. Because I can't take credit for the applause my sonata received. The thing is, when Liszt claps, everyone claps, each one louder than the other.

I'm sure Nina will tell a little about the concert in the Scandinavian Society that same evening. It was a strenuous but enjoyable day.

Now I have made myself important enough, but I hope that my ten pages will be read with the same pleasure with which I have sent them to you.

Our current plan is to leave for Naples on April 1. Until then, therefore, I must have some money, not because what I have will be all used up by that time but because I need it to get back to Denmark.

Farewell for now. I shall hope for another surprise as splendid as the last one.

Warm greetings!

Affectionately,
EDVARD GRIEG

---

[24] "Nun, das werden Sie mir doch zutrauen, etwas vom Blatt zu spielen, ich bin ja ein alter, gewandter Musiker."

[25] "Ich habe in der Welt viel herumgespielt, zu viel!"

[26] Italian violinist Ettore Pinelli (1843–1915).

2

Rome, April 9, 1870

Dear Parents!
This time I can say in all seriousness: Where shall I begin and where end! All the impressions, everything I have experienced crowds together in my brain in a mighty chaos. The best thing I can do, then, is just to give a biographical sketch of the last few weeks. So: First I must report on a visit to Liszt that took place shortly after the dispatch of my last letter and that was no less interesting than the first one. Fortunately I had just received from Leipzig the manuscript of my piano concerto, so I took it along. Present in addition to me were Winding, Sgambati, and a German Liszt enthusiast who mimics his hero to such an extent that he wears the Abbé garb, also a Chevalier de Concilium, and lastly some young women whose admiration for Liszt was comical. They competed with each other to get close to him, touch the edge of his long Abbé robe, and finally to take his hand—yes, later, when he played, the women stood around the piano with their eyes stiffly glued to his fingers as if the fingers were destined in the next moment to become a sacrifice to those greedy admirers.

Winding and I were very eager to see if he really would sight-read my *Concerto*—something that I, for my part, considered an impossibility. Liszt, however, was of an entirely different opinion. He said, "Will you play?"[27] I quickly said, "No, I can't!" Then Liszt took the manuscript, went to the piano and said with a characteristic smile to all those present, "Well, then I will show you that I can't either."[28] And then he began. And in view of what he now achieved, I must say that it would be impossible to imagine anything of the kind that would be more sublime. Oh yes, he played the first movement somewhat rapidly, and the result was that the opening passage sounded rather slapdash; but later on, when I had an opportunity to indicate the tempo, he played as he alone and no one else can. It is typical that he played the cadenza, which is among the technically most difficult parts of the concerto, perfectly. His gestures are priceless. You see, he doesn't just play; no, he converses and criticizes at the same time. He carries on a brilliant conversation, not with one person but with the entire audience, distributing significant nods to right and left, mainly when he is particularly pleased with something. In the *Adagio*, and to an even greater extent in the *Finale*, he reached a peak both in execution and in the praise he gave.[29] Finally, as he handed

---

27 "Wollen Sie spielen?"

28 "Nun, dann werde ich Ihnen zeigen, dass ich auch nicht kann."

29 In the version of the two letters to his parents that Grieg prepared for publication in *Samtiden* in 1892 he added at this point the following passage:

> "There is one perfectly divine episode that I should not forget. Towards the end of the *Finale*, as you will remember, the second theme is repeated in a great *fortissimo*. In the very last measures, where the first note of the first triplet of the theme—G sharp—is changed to G in the orchestra, while the piano in a tremendous scale passage traverses the entire keyboard, he suddenly stopped, rose to his full height, left the piano,

me the score, he said: "Hold to your course. Let me tell you, you have the talent for it, and—don't get scared off!"[30] This last is of infinite importance to me. It is almost like what I will call a sacred mandate. Time and again when disappointments and bitterness come I shall think of his words, and the memory of this hour will have a singular power to sustain me in days of adversity; that is my confident hope.

Since you enjoyed my first report I have also added this one, but I hope that it will reach only a small audience. Something that is to be read by many would have to be assessed differently.

But on with the story. On March 31 a large group of us left Rome, the group consisting of the Windings; the painter Aagaard; the Swedish estheticist, Professor Ljunggreen;[31] the merchant, Mr. Tvermoes;[32] Mr. Kleisdorff (Danish); and Miss Hilsinger from Finland. Believe me, we had an enjoyable trip to Naples. A whole throng of Scandinavians gave us a jovial send-off at the train station, and then we chugged off in a cheerful mood. The first two days in Naples were devoted to visiting museums—the great collections from antiquity, about which I have already reported sometime or other. Then one beautiful Sunday morning we took the train out to Pompeii, where we spent some exceedingly interesting hours. That evening we arrived in Castellamare, a true paradise. The next day to Salerno, then a carriage tour to Amalfi—yes, what shall I say when I have called Castellamare a paradise, and yet Amalfi is much more beautiful. The road from Salerno to Amalfi goes by way of some breath-taking structures that remind one of our big road construction projects at home—up on the mountain, in daring curves, it follows the picturesque, winding course of the coastline with the great, wide sea stretching to infinity along one side. Above and below, like birds' nests here and there in the mountains, are many small villages. On the cliffs down near the sea stand the ruins of Norman towers, and right beside the road grew trees, with oranges and lemons hanging directly above our heads in such profusion that it seems to me a pity that a couple dozen of them didn't fall into my mouth, which was half open in delight. Add to that the warm sun, the fresh sea wind, the blue sky and the clear horizon as far as the eye could see—what more could one ask for! The memory of *such* a day enriches one for a lifetime.

---

and with mighty theatrical steps and raised arms strode through the great monastery hall, literally roaring out the theme. When he got to the above-mentioned G, he gestured imperiously with his arm and cried: 'G, G, not G sharp! Fantastic! That's really a genuine Swedish Banco!' ['g, g, nicht giss! Famos! Das ist so echter schwedischer Banco!'] And then, as if in parentheses, quite *pianissimo*: 'Smetana (gifted Bohemian composer) has recently sent me some of it.' ['Der Smetana hat mir neulich Etwas davon geschickt']. He then went back to the piano, repeated the whole phrase, and concluded." [Liszt's cryptic remark about "Swedish Banco" may have been a reference to Swedish banknotes or, perhaps more likely, to a Swedish alcoholic beverage that was exported all over Europe under the French trademark "Caloric Banco Suédois".]

[30] "Fahren Sie fort, ich sage Ihnen, Sie haben ganz das Zeug dazu und—lassen Sie sich nicht abschrecken!"

[31] Professor of esthetics and art history Gustaf Ljunggreen (1823–1905).

[32] Danish merchant and legator Emil Tvermoes (1831–93)

The following day we let the women stay in Salerno and drove out to the temple ruins at Pestum. The fact is that the road is insecure, and none of us felt much inclined to watch the bandits sail off with our wives, so we acted like cautious generals. Except for a temple at the Acropolis in Athens, Neptune's temple at Pestum is the most beautiful example of Greek art that has come down to us. You can understand to what extent this is true when I say that everything in Rome is a mere plaything compared with this temple.

When we came home we found our ladies in seventh heaven, but we were so tired that it is no exaggeration to say that we were asleep before our heads hit the pillows. The next day we went by train to Naples, then to Capri, where we parted company with our travel companions. I suppose you are expecting to hear about the blue grotto, but that's a story that is better told orally in a jocular setting. Last evening we returned here full of impressions—yes, surfeited with pleasures.

Today I received Kirchner's[33] letter with the draft for 250 *spesidalers*. Well, there's nothing to do about it now. Dad, you received my last letter after you had sent your letter to Kirchner, but it doesn't make any difference. Now I need just 50 more *spesidalers*, which can be sent to Copenhagen next time.

Thank you for your last letters—the last ones, in fact, to Rome, for we will be leaving one day soon, Wednesday the 13th at the latest. So, God willing, we will receive your next letter in Copenhagen.

Farewell, then, and many loving greetings.

Your devoted
EDVARD GRIEG

---

[33] On January 10, 1869, Grieg had applied to the Ministry of Church and Education for a travel grant of 500 *spesidalers* "in order, by means of an extended stay abroad, to continue his studies as a composer." He received the grant, and in December, 1869, he and Nina went to Italy. It was stipulated that Grieg was expected to stay abroad for at least ten months. The grant was paid out in two installments at five-month intervals. His father handled the transmission of the grant funds through Hermann Theodor Kirchner, a book dealer in Leipzig who from time to time helped Grieg with currency exchanges. Grieg's grant applications as well as his report to the Ministry dated September, 1870, will be printed in English translation in Benestad & Halverson (eds.), *Edvard Grieg: Diaries, Articles, Speeches* (Columbus, Ohio, 2001).

To Joachim Grieg

Edvard Grieg's second cousin Joachim Grieg (1849–1932), a ship broker and politician in Bergen, had strong cultural interests. He was a member of Stortinget (the Norwegian parliament) representing the Liberal Left ("Frisinnede Venstre") party in 1906–09 and held a number of other responsible positions both public and private. During the controversies surrounding the music festival in Bergen in 1898, Joachim Grieg was one of his cousin's strong supporters. In 1919, when Troldhaugen was sold at auction, he purchased the property and in 1923 gave it to Fana, the suburb of Bergen in which Troldhaugen is located. (Fana was incorporated into the city of Bergen in 1972, thereby conveying ownership of Troldhaugen to the city of Bergen.)

Letters 1 and 2 are preserved in Bergen Offentlige Bibliotek (Bergen Public Library), letter 3 in Universitetsbiblioteket i Bergen (University of Bergen library).

1

London, November 8, 1897
47 North Side, Clapham Common S. W.

Dear Mr. Consul!
My sincerest thanks for your kind letter. It did me considerably more good than the dreadful medicines I have to swallow. Yesterday I crawled out of bed, but it's going very slowly. I hope to be all right to perform at St. James's Hall on the 22nd. But I feel that it is extremely doubtful that I will be able to recover my strength by that time. A radical bronchitis attack has practically wiped out the small reserve of strength I had stored up during the summer. In four days, in accordance with the doctor's advice, I will go down to Hastings, and since this is a very well regarded health resort I expect everything from the change of atmosphere.

And now to the main subject. The circular to the exposition committee[1] strikes me as on the whole excellent. I regret the expression "big Norwegian Music Festival" and would recommend that in the future we be content with "Norwegian Music Festival". Then there is an expression about me that I cannot approve. Least of all now. It reads, "as well as to undertake the organization of the musical part." This "undertake the organization" goes too far. No, I can't handle that. Rather use the expression "assist with" the organization, which is all the more correct in that Holter[2] has promised to assume the chief responsibility and Halvorsen[3] some of it as well.

Holter, to whom I have sent two letters—important letters regarding the

---

[1] The committee coordinating plans for an international exposition to be held in Bergen in the summer of 1898. Grieg had proposed that a festival of Norwegian music be held in connection with this exposition.

[2] Norwegian composer Iver Holter (1850–1941), who was also conductor of the Music Association in Christiania. See Grieg's letters to him during the period October 10, 1897–June 2, 1898 regarding the music festival.

[3] Norwegian composer and conductor Johan Halvorsen (1864–1935), who was working in Bergen at this time.

orchestra question, with a request for a swift reply—has not written a word, however, which surprises me. Yesterday I sent a postcard requesting an immediate answer. The fact is that if the Christiania orchestra question encounters the slightest difficulty, that would in fact (just between us) be the very best thing that could happen, because then we can immediately take the outstanding Dutch orchestra, which according to a letter received recently (from Julius Röntgen[4] in Amsterdam) is deeply interested and very receptive to the plan and presumably will require only: free travel, free board and room, and a couple *gulden* a day for each member of the orchestra for incidental expenses. You will understand that this indicates the highest interest, but of course it adds up nonetheless. If we say a minimum of sixteen days, and an orchestra of eighty members, allowing, let us say, 3 *gulden* (= 4½ Norwegian crowns) per day, it comes to 3,840 *gulden* or 5,760 crowns. As you can see, this does not even exceed what the Norwegian orchestra would cost. In other words: If we were not obligated to Christiania, we would be just as well off financially and 100 percent better off with respect to both performance quality and freedom to operate. If you note the slightest little problem regarding the Norwegian orchestra question (for example, that a couple—or even just one—of our better artists cannot participate) send me a telegram and I will engage the Amsterdam orchestra by telegram.

I am Norwegian, not hyper-Norwegian. Therefore I cannot see anything other than that a Norwegian music festival is one consisting of Norwegian music. In a Norwegian orchestra, however, there are many Germans. If there is any sign of chauvinism, therefore, unjustified as it is, it must be nipped in the bud. These are the thoughts I have communicated to Holter with a request for a swift reply. One thing: If the Amsterdamians would be content with 2 Fl.[5] (3 crowns) per day, it would be cheaper than the Norwegian orchestra and this, in my opinion, would be reason enough to engage them immediately apart from other motives. So: all of this between us, and it would please me greatly to hear your opinion as soon as possible.

With hearty greetings and thanks for your work in the interest of the music festival,

Your devoted
EDVARD GRIEG

P.S. That the exposition committee should give all the concert-goers free admission to the exposition seems to me to be asking a lot, but if they are willing to do so it is very good indeed.

---

[4] Dutch pianist, composer and conductor Julius Röntgen (1855–1932).
[5] Fl. is an abbreviation for *florin*, which was the original name of the Dutch *gulden*.

2

London, December 16, 1897
47, North Side, Clapham Common, S. W.

Dear Mr. Joachim Grieg!

First and foremost, I send my condolences on your election as chairman [of the music committee], (which makes me very happy)! Secondly, I congratulate you on having such a sweet daughter in Frida. She completely captivated us! It's too bad that we didn't see more of her![6]

And now I will turn to your letter (thank you for both letters!) and answer it point by point.

1) The festival *appears* to be in good shape *financially*, but this cannot be regarded as a certainty until the orchestra question is decided. On this matter you must confer immediately by telegram with Holter. I understand that it has not been possible to carry out my wish, which I think I have confided to you—*immediately* to engage the Amsterdamians, who have been unbelievably cooperative. And now it is probably too late. In a letter received today from Amsterdam I see that the orchestra has just received a very lucrative offer for the very same days during which the music festival is to be held—an offer which it most likely is considering. And it is right for them not to wait any longer for such ungrateful people as we have shown ourselves to be in this matter. You certainly should recommend to Holter *the last days of June* and *the first days of July*. Perhaps in this way we can best take account of all the concerns.

2) The exposition committee's position *now* in contrast to its *earlier* one (according to Johan Bøgh's[7] statements) is incomprehensible to me. Indeed, it makes no sense that we should pay 14,000 for 8–12 days and the exposition 9,000 for the whole summer. Wouldn't it be better to have nothing to do with the exposition and build *outside* its domain? Maybe in the face of such an eventuality the exposition committee would take a more accommodating stance. Still, strictly speaking this is no concern of mine since, in your opinion, the festival is financially secure.

3) I think that, like me, Holter would find it impractical to approach privately the conductors involved before we send a formal invitation. We will put certain compositions on the program and then will invite the respective composers to conduct them. If they decline, Holter will do the conducting. We must remember that the main thing is the compositions, not the conductors.

4) I think that *all* the reputable composers in the country should be invited and request that you ask Holter to give you a list of these, which I shall then be permitted to see.

---

[6] Joachim's daughter Frida (1880–1955) had attended a concert given by Grieg in Brighton, England.

[7] Johan Bøgh (1848–1933), Bergen art historian and museum curator.

5) I think the hall can be started independently of everything else. It doesn't matter whether or not one has received an affirmative reply from all the guests before one begins to build. Was not the estimate 2,500 attendees, 500 performers? I hope that is the case.

6) You say it is important to schedule works that will fill the auditorium. So be it, but—things that at the same time, and above all, represent the best music in the country.

7) There should of course be an art committee consisting of Halvorsen, Schjøtt, Frants, John[8] (and others?). Likewise a building committee, and to your idea of a publicity committee headed by your brother John[9] I say *bravissimo*!

8) A notice from the committee regarding the holding of the music festival could be published in England without significant expense. I have talked about this with my agent (England's foremost), Mr. Vert,[10] and he has promised to get such a notice published in the newspapers—so far as possible without costs worth mentioning. I understood him to say that it could be done as a news item, not a paid advertisement. We will also have a warm friend of our cause in the local Norwegian journalist, Mr. Brækstad,[11] with whom I shall speak. He will be *able to accomplish much* and is a Norwegian to his fingertips and at the same time an influential man in the press through his acquaintances. In Germany the situation is worse. I don't think we dare to expect much from that quarter. I will inquire in Leipzig, where I am going right after Christmas, and will tell you what I find out.

9) Three concerts with three repetitions. All right. I would ask you to inform Holter of your suggestion—a good one, to be sure—that each concert, by means of a suitable mixture, should indeed contain something new.

One important matter that you do not mention is the form for the invitation of the orchestra. I would request that you ask Holter to draft it and inform you of the content before it is sent. Above all: If Holter handles the matter, as he has promised to do, it is in good hands, for he is as thoughtful as he is conscientious.

At this moment my eyes are focused on your words, "Half moons with plum filling," so not one more word regarding the music festival must be required of me today. Is it old Mrs. Sars[12] in Christiania who has told your wife that, like her, I am crazy about these childhood memories? Do you know Mrs. Sars? The loveliest Norwegian woman! Eighty-five years old, I think. When she is gone, Norway will no longer be what it was. That is true in a completely selfish sense, I must

---

8 Bergen singer and choral conductor Ingolf Schjøtt (1851–1922), Grieg's close friend Frants Beyer (1851–1918)and Grieg's brother John Grieg (1840–1901).

9 Book dealer John Grieg (1856–1905).

10 Narcisco Ramon Domingo Vert (1845–1905) was Grieg's impresario in London.

11 Norwegian journalist Hans Lien Brækstad (1845–1915) was living in London at this time.

12 Maren Sars (1811–98), sister of Norwegian poet J. S. Welhaven (1807–73) and wife of Michael Sars (1805–69), a zoologist.

admit, for she has sent me "Half moons" and knitted stockings for me in our national colors!

I do not use any trumpeters in the press. For that reason you presumably will see no visible evidence of what I have here described. But I not only am not ashamed, I am proud to be able to say that London has been a little Norwegian-crazy of late. The only thing that pains me a little is that the sold-out concerts consist of too many "schoolgirls". But—after all, they are the mothers of tomorrow! So: respect.

Now I ask you to accept hearty greetings from my wife (who yesterday sang —to the delight of the audience and the press—with what remains of her voice but with her never-failing interpretation) and from

Your devoted
EDVARD GRIEG

P.S. How goes it with Johan Bøgh? That I would like to know.

My address between the 23rd and the 31st is Amsterdam, 13, Sarphatikade, c/o Mr. Julius Röntgen. Thereafter: C. F. Peters, Thalstrasse 10, Leipzig.

3

Copenhagen, April 4, 1905
Hotel Phoenix

Dear Joachim Grieg!
Thank you for your statements regarding the consular question.[13] You do not cut me to the heart in the slightest, and you have absolutely no need to cut your own for my sake! We are not in as much disagreement as you think. For you *must* agree with me that until we can get the union *improved* or *changed* or *dissolved* there is no use thinking about achieving peace with the Swedes. From an ideal point of view, the union is indeed the sick point. But this sickness has manifested itself practically in the consular question. Whether to "follow the law" or to pursue the matter as we do now—that is a matter about which there certainly can be different opinions. But be assured that I loyally accept the decision that is taken, in order to join in the unanimous demand that Norway's rights be respected.

Your characterization of the Swedes is certainly correct. But I want to distinguish between the people and politics. Viewed strictly from a human perspective, one people is more like another than one might think. No people is completely dishonorable. But a political stance, like that of the Swedes—that can be so. It is the politicians who must be eliminated when they have as narrow-minded a

[13] The so-called "consular question" was a major issue between Norway and Sweden during the years 1892–1905. See Grieg's letter to Bjørnstjerne Bjørnson (1832–1910) of December 7, 1904.

view as Boström[14] and his cohorts. But it can never be narrow-minded of Bjørnson and Hagerup[15] to look beyond the consular quarrel, to look way out to the horizon that is blocked by the damn union.

I must take the liberty of telling you that at the beginning of January, in a letter to the Danish newspaper *Nationaltidende* written in response to an inquiry, I expressed my opinion regarding the union and set forth the very view that some days later I discovered was the view espoused by Bjørnson. Otherwise you might be tempted to think that I agree with Bjørnson through thick and thin. The question is simply: What is No. 1, the union or the consular matter? I think it is the union.

When I wrote to your brother that your statements would be of interest to me, I assumed that you must have means of judging the difficulties that inevitably will arise in relation to the Swedes when our own consuls begin to exercise their duties. May it not be the case that the intimate relationship between the consulate and the office of foreign affairs will then make it impossible to avoid a new collision—and NB: a continually recurring collision—with the Swedes? Well, we will see. One thing I do feel: This crown prince regent will become our worst enemy. Indeed, he is that already. And this brings me to the point where we really are in serious disagreement. It is true that *we* are the ones who should act, but if the consequences of the action that is now taken constitute what is called "war", then I break all the old concepts of honor to bits and shout: not one drop of blood for the sake of the consular affair! Militarism must not be allowed to celebrate that triumph. And not inhumanity either!

You are right: There is an eastern European spirit at the other side of the border—NB, among the politicians and press people, not to forget the nobility. But it remains for our culture to show how high we are elevated above this spirit. It must not happen through gunpowder and bullets. You say yourself that the consular affair is a *small issue* on which to launch the struggle. It is indeed. To redden Norwegian soil with our blood for the sake of a financial question would be sheer madness, even if someone would call me a traitor [for saying it]. The few young people who do not go to America—they would be the ones to be maimed and killed for the sake of mercantile interests and chauvinism.

People speak about the idea of peace. About the idea of arbitration. Why not combine these ideas until we find the right solution instead of beating the drum for war, as Mr. Stang[16] did recently. It's a cheap course he has chosen. It's easy

---

14 Erik Gustaf Bernhard Boström (1842–1907) was the Swedish prime minister in 1902–05 and was a leading figure in the union negotiations between Norway and Sweden.

15 Francis Hagerup (1853–1921), a Norwegian lawyer and politician who was involved in the negotiations that led to the dissolution of the union between Norway and Sweden in 1905.

16 Grieg presumably is referring to the Norwegian military officer and politician Georg Stang (1858–1907), who was a saber-rattler during the union negotiations.

enough to act the rabble-rouser in that way. It is more difficult and more thankless to stand in the breach against chauvinism and against the old-fashioned saber-rattling. This war talk becomes doubly remarkable when one considers that it is a monarch who is to declare war on his own people. I hope that Norway's good genius will prevent it, that's all I can say. When the leaders seem to be blind, luck must do the leading.

Believe me, the whole thing looks peculiar from abroad. Often I wish that I were home. But the distance certainly gives one clarity.

And with that, farewell. I will only say in addition that it really is true that a masseur here has completely cured Frits Thaulow[17] of diabetes—but of course the doctors in Bergen smile in supercilious greatness, just like the ones in Copenhagen.

Warm greetings to you and your wife, also from Nina.

Your devoted
EDVARD GRIEG

---

[17] Norwegian painter Frits Thaulow (1847–1906).

To John and Marie Grieg

Edvard's brother, John Grieg (1840–1901), was married to Marie Ehrhardt (1845–1931) of Dresden. John and Edvard were students together at the music conservatory in Leipzig, but John never became a professional musician although he participated actively in the music life of Bergen as a cellist. His principal occupation, however, was in the family seafood exporting business, which he took over upon his father's death in 1875. He also succeeded his father as British vice-consul in Bergen. John and Marie had a very large family—a fact to which Grieg alludes in his letter of November 26, 1885.

The letters included here are preserved in Bergen Offentlige Bibliotek (Bergen Public Library).

1

Copenhagen, November 26, 1885

Dear John and Marie!
Thank you for the telegram! So that will be the last one! Well, I can only congratulate you. It is impossible for me to view the matter in any other way. And presumably you see it the same way. But the joy certainly is purchased at a high price. For poor Marie, you clearly have suffered a lot of pain—but can you now not be content with what you have and trust that the world will be sufficiently populated without your further contribution? I have a feeling that this view would not be too bad.

And with that I take my leave of the subject of productivity and switch to the delivery of a biographical sketch of the undersigned and his wife since the moment of our departure from the Norwegian capital. You heard about the theater affair, so I leave Norway as a morally compromised person and come here, where instead of recovering the high ground I sink steadily downward: the morass of well-being and pampering.

The Concert Association concert was a huge success, with orchestral flourishes at the beginning and the end.[1] You should have heard Simonsen[2] in *Landsighting.* He absolutely made the eardrums tremble. Svendsen,[3] who sat in the dress circle, said the piece sounded powerfully imposing from beginning to end.

The first concert without orchestra also was exceptionally successful. Nina sang more beautifully than ever, and the cellist Robert Hansen[4] played the *Cello Sonata* very well. He is a skillful cellist with a faultless technique. He is also a talented musician, but he lacks a full tone and a dramatic flair—two characteristics which, unfortunately, happen to play important roles in this case.

---

[1] Grieg took part in four concerts in Copenhagen in November and December 1885: at the Concert Association on December 14, evening concerts of his own on November 23 and 27, and the first Music Association concert of the season on December 10. He also appeared at a concert of the Student Glee Club on December 18.

[2] Danish baritone Niels Juel Simonsen (1846–1906).

[3] Johan Svendsen (1840–1911), who in 1883 had assumed the post of musical director at the Royal Theater in Copenhagen.

[4] Danish cellist Robert Emil Hansen (1860–1926).

Tomorrow we have the last concert. I will conduct *The Mountain Thrall* in the Music Association, and then I will get to work on the re-orchestration of *Peer Gynt*, which is going to be performed at the Dagmar Theater here on December 26.[5] Thus it seems likely that we will spend Christmas here. It is incomprehensible that people come to our concerts, for the mood of the city is extremely depressed, both politically and most of all with regard to commerce.

Well, that's enough for now. It was just a thought. Loving greetings to all of you, big and small!

Warm regards,
EDVARD

P.S. What in the world is it that Tonny[6] writes about that you, John, have played "Last Spring" and "Outward Bound"? The latter you perhaps have adapted from Sauret,[7] but "Last Spring?" That I don't understand.

We have just received Agnes's[8] letter, from which we see that you have double reason to be congratulated, but that this time the solemn occasion has unfortunately been fraught with danger. Give Marie our warm greetings and tell her that our loving thoughts are with her. May we all be together next summer! There are illnesses in the world other than childbed fever that can kill a person; that is something I often think of, especially in these days. Yes, well, who knows!

Agnes, you are clever and kind to write! Let us hear from you again soon, even if it be only a few words!

Yours truly,
EDVARD

2

Odnes,[9] October 28, 1898

Dear John and Marie!
These are my first scribblings since illness got the best of me. Therefore I am counting on you to lay aside all demands. I have been sicker than you at home know, for what I have left in the way of lungs was so chock full of phlegm that I could hardly breathe. I caught a cold as we were leaving Bergen, and the three days of traveling have naturally made the illness worse. It turned out to be bronchitis, not pneumonia. But I am still very weak. Today I have been outside a bit, and

[5] The Danish premiere of *Peer Gynt* took place at the Dagmar Theater on January 17, 1886.
[6] Tonny Hagerup (1834–1939), Nina Grieg's sister.
[7] The French violinist and composer Émile Sauret (1852–1920) had arranged several of Grieg's works for violin and piano.
[8] Agnes Grieg (1869–?), daughter of John and Marie Grieg.
[9] Odnes is a village on Randsfjorden, an inland lake north of Oslo.

if I continue to make progress we will leave here on Monday or Tuesday.[10] It was a stroke of good luck that I ended up here, among nice people who have provided good service and excellent provisions in the way of food and drink. And it is so beautiful here, a great place for convalescents. A fine new physician, Dr. Einar Hoff, has come once or twice each day the whole time. What makes me happier than I can tell you is that, through his kindness, I have read a lot of things that I would not willingly have missed. *Robert Elsmere* by Humphrey Ward was interesting. But still, this was nothing compared with *Darwin's Life and Letters with Autobiography*, which I think has made me a better person—as long as it lasts! You absolutely must read this work, which has been published in the "Library for the Thousands" series.

And now to the main point of this letter: Good luck on your birthday, dear Marie. Nina reminded me of it, and although I am not one to write birthday letters, the principle applies also here: Every rule has its exceptions.

We are getting old. Yes, it is true. But lately it has seemed to me that we have no right to feel that we are old as long as our health doesn't go completely to pot. For to the end, life has so much that is beautiful and interesting to sustain us—if only we are in a position to see it. Still, you don't have to be told that, for you are lucky enough to possess a full measure of optimism. But we who have Hagerup blood in our veins always have to think about it in order to see the brighter side of life. It's a pity that our ancestors have not left us a bit of autobiography. It would be interesting, indeed, to see if our pessimism comes from the Hagerup or the Janson side of the family.[11] I rather suspect it is the latter.

Excuse me, but the effort of writing these few pages is making me sweat. So let me conclude this letter—which unfortunately is not exactly "unmarenic"[12]—with thanks for your friendly letter and because you so kindly accepted what I sent. I know well enough that it is easier to give than to receive, especially when the giver has been in the chips as much as I have the last couple of years. Thus it has not been a burden for me in any way. Be assured of that. If this should occur, I would just let you know. But as long as I am able to work, everything is all right.

Unfortunately, we will certainly have to travel right through Christiania, as I absolutely cannot tolerate the exertion that would be required to stop and say hello to friends and family. But be assured, John, that if possible I will contact Bjørn.[13]

Farewell, then! Warmest greetings to all of you.

EDVARD

---

[10] Grieg was en route for a five-month stay in Denmark. Thereafter he went to Italy, where he remained for the following two months.

[11] Grieg's grandparents on his mother's side were Edvard Hagerup (1781–1853) and Ingeborg Benedicte Janson (1768–1849).

[12] Maren Grieg (1837–1905) was Edvard's eldest sister.

[13] Probably Bjørn Bjørnson (1859–1942).

To John Grieg (book publisher)

Edvard Grieg's second cousin, John Grieg (1856–1905), was a book publisher and book dealer in Bergen. In 1882 he took over the Dahl book printing company and greatly enlarged the business. At the same time he launched his own publishing company as well as a book bindery and lithography business. His firm's publications included *Samtiden* (*The Present Time*, published in Bergen until 1899) and *Kunst og kultur* (*Art and Culture*, published in Bergen until 1913.) Both journals are still in existence but are now published in Oslo. Edvard Grieg often used his second cousin as a press contact in Bergen to relay information about concert successes at home and abroad.

Grieg's letters to John Grieg, one of which is included here, are preserved in Nasjonalbiblioteket, Oslo (National Library of Norway, Oslo Division).

Paris, April 20, 1903
Hotel de Sèze, 16, rue de Sèze

Dear Mr. book printer!
One more glass of Canarisec! If the Bergensians want to read about how it went in Warsaw, let them have the enclosure, which has been translated from Polish.

Regarding the concert yesterday, perhaps you will get information from another quarter. Yes, it was fun. I have never been involved in anything like this, and I honestly admit that if I had gotten the invitation from Colonne[1] *after* Jaurés had revived the passions regarding the Dreyfus affair,[2] I would not have accepted it. But now I couldn't back out without looking like a coward. The press had already urged people to demonstrate—indeed, in a meaner way than I had anticipated. At the beginning of the concert a small group among the 3,500 people present greeted me with boos and catcalls, so I quite calmly put the baton down, left the podium and just stood and waited. When it sounded like it was about over I mounted the podium again, but then it started anew. This time, however, it was I who made music. I didn't hesitate a second, but made an energetic signal to the orchestra to begin—*fortissimo*, fortunately! And once I managed to begin, I had the upper hand. Moreover, everybody else in the audience was on my side, and the police—*three times* the usual number for a concert—threw these *paid* troublemakers out of the hall.

The concert itself was one great crescendo, and it ended with the most tremendous ovations. It was a triumph in every way. The orchestra played magnificently!

---

[1] Grieg had been invited by the French conductor Édouard Colonne (1838–1910) to give a concert with his Paris orchestra.

[2] In 1894 Captain Alfred Dreyfus (1859–1935), a French Jew, had been falsely convicted of high treason and condemned to life imprisonment on Devil's Island. Grieg followed the case with great interest and in 1899 published an "open letter" that aroused international attention. He pointedly declined an invitation to conduct in Paris at that time, and his public defense of Dreyfus made him a target of many angry statements in the French press. French politician Jean Jaurés (1859–1914) was a socialist leader who had whipped up public sentiment against Grieg when it became known that he was returning to France for a concert in April, 1903. See Grieg's letters to Colonne.

When Nina and I got into the carriage that was to take us to our hotel, it was surrounded by a cordon of police. I felt like a Cromwell or Emperor so-and-so. The newspapers today are furious about my triumph and are as mean as possible. There is only one person—the composer Gabriel Fauré[3] in *Le Figaro*—who has shown a noble heart.

Yes, what strange people! Just think that the very same critic in *Le Temps* who a few years ago praised me to the skies now chides me for the same things he previously commended![4] Another critic insinuates that I was well paid for risking a visit to Paris. He concludes like this: "A few omnibuses with gallery[5] awaited Grieg at the end of the concert to escort him to Gare du Nord with his waistcoat *better lined* than by all that fur that he needs up in the fjords." If only it were true! But unfortunately the hotel and the trip gobble it all up. That and more.[6]

How I long for home! Warm greetings to all!

Sincerely yours,
EDVARD GRIEG

---

[3] French composer Gabriel Fauré (1845–1924).

[4] The conservative critic Pierre Lalo (1866–1943), son of composer Edouard Lalo (1823–92).

[5] An "omnibus with gallery" (French *galerie*) was a kind of primitive double-decker that provided space for luggage and second-class passengers on top of the cab.

[6] See also Grieg's description of this concert in his letter to Frants Beyer (1851–1918) of April 21, 1903.

To Modesta Grieg

Modesta Grieg (1809–79)—"Aunt Mone"—was a sister of Edvard's father, Alexander Grieg (1806–75). She was his favorite aunt, as is evident from his letter to her. The letter, which was written on the occasion of her 70th birthday on August 11, 1879, reached her just about two weeks before her death on August 29 of the same year.

Grieg's letter to his aunt is preserved in Bergen Offentlige Bibliotek (Bergen Public Library).

Lofthus, August 9, 1879

My Dear Aunt Mone!

With your fine Griegian nose you will no doubt detect that this letter smells of fish. For I have just come home from a fishing outing and am sitting down, cold and numb, at my desk. But my feelings for you, dear Aunt Mone, fortunately are not cold and numb, and as a weak proof thereof I am sending you these poor lines on the occasion of your big day of celebration.

Yes, it is great to be seventy years old and to feel happy, as I know you do, even if one's body feels the age. Here there certainly is more reason to send congratulations than on most other occasions. And you will be receiving hundreds of congratulations from both near and far. How I would have liked to be with you and to have seen your joy on this day. But since that cannot be, accept my sincere thanks for always having been a loving and good aunt to me. I know that you have always followed me with great interest, and you know that I have always had a weakness for my dear, old Mone.

Thank you for each time you have elicited everything in me that is good and noble—and that you have done every time I have set foot inside your doorstep. When I went in to see you, for me it was always as if I lived the happiest moments of childhood all over again—yes, it has been that way right up to these last days. For me your home has always been like a refuge, a place where conflict and controversy could not gain access. An illusion, perhaps, but in any case a beautiful one, and I thank you again and again for managing to call it forth.

If I have not learned anything else in life, I have at least learned this, that the most beautiful thing of all is to preserve the child in oneself. And this most beautiful thing you have had in such rich measure that you have been able to share it with others—and the more you have given, the more you have received in return.

Yes, dear auntie—you epitome of a world that for me has vanished, but which I nonetheless grope for day in and day out—if only I could tell you how much I love you and the extent to which my love is concentrated on you on this particular day! It's a good thing I'm not in Bergen! I would *crush* you to death—both in love and—in drunkenness! Yes, of course I know about your Malaga and other sweet things with which you lead people astray up there in your innocent-looking little flat!

And with that, goodbye. See you soon!

Yours truly,
EDVARD GRIEG

To Agathe Backer Grøndahl

Agathe Backer Grøndahl (1847–1907) was Norway's first important female composer. Her strength was in the small forms—piano pieces and songs. She was also a world-class pianist who gave concerts in several European countries. She often performed Grieg's works, including his *Piano Concerto* in A minor, in which she appeared three times as soloist with Grieg on the podium. Born Agathe Backer, in 1875 she married Olaus Andreas Grøndahl (1847–1923), one of the leading Norwegian choral conductors of his day. The pianist Fridtjof Backer-Grøndahl (1885–1959) was their son.

Letters 1 and 3 are taken from O. M. Sandvik, *Agathe og O. A. Grøndahl 1847–1947. Et Minneskrift* (*Agathe and O. A. Grøndahl 1847–1947: A Memoir*), Oslo 1948. Letter 2 is a translation of an original letter owned by the Grøndahl family. The remaining letters are taken from Gunnar Hauch (ed.), *Breve fra Grieg* (*Letters from Grieg*), Copenhagen 1922.

1

Lofthus, September 28, 1884

Dear Mrs. Grøndahl!

. . . It is indeed possible that I have told you how highly I regard your talent. But since this was a long time ago, and the ability to judge a talent grows in concert with a person's development generally, I want now to tell you my current opinion. And that is that in this moment I consider your gift greater than I did before. The very fact that you, though limited by unrelated duties and in precarious health, continue to sing is of the greatest significance, it seems to me, when one would estimate the true creative urge. You can therefore understand how happy you made me with your friendly communication.[1] . . .

I hope it does not go for me with your songs as it did with Godard's trio. I still have not seen it. How is it? It would indeed interest me to know. I am asking you because I seem to remember having read in some newspaper or other that you have played it.[2]

Sincerely yours,
Edvard Grieg

---

[1] In 1881 Grieg had dedicated his *Twelve Songs to Poems by A. O. Vinje* op. 33 to Agathe Backer Grøndahl, and on December 3 of that year she had written him a letter thanking him for the honor. She had added, "Would that some day I could produce something that was approximately good enough to bear your name! So far I have never dared to [dedicate anything to you]." Less than three years later, however—on September 22, 1884—she wrote to Grieg: "Will you allow me, in all modesty, to dedicate to you some *Sange ved Havet* [*Songs by the Sea*] which I composed this summer and hope to have published by Wilhelm Hansens Publishing Company for Christmas? (. . .) That you have earlier voiced a positive judgment about some of the little things I have written has always been one of my greatest encouragements. I think, therefore, that even if much of this is more or less unsuccessful, you will feel what *is* in them, be patient with the rest, and in any case accept it—as it is intended—as an expression of my deepest admiration and gratitude for all the pleasures I have enjoyed because of you." *Songs by the Sea* op. 17 consists of settings of texts by the Danish poet Holger Drachmann (1846–1908).

[2] In January, 1884, Mrs. Grøndahl had joined with violinist Gudbrand Bøhn (1839–1906) and cellist Johan Hennum (1836–94) in a performance of *Piano Trio* op. 72 by French composer Benjamin Godard (1849–95), a

2

Troldhaugen, May 28, 1897

Dear Mrs. Grøndahl!

Thank you for the heroic ballads![3] I think the idea is excellent, and although your piano arrangements of folk dances seem to me to be superior you have, nonetheless, produced so much that is noble and genuinely felt in the heroic ballads that you need have no misgivings about making your work available to the public. I was especially struck by "Haugebonden" ("The Hill Farmer") and "Store bror og lille bror" ("Big Brother and Little Brother"). In the latter, the harmonic treatment near the end is surpassingly beautiful. These heroic ballads are indeed wonderful! It is as if the deepest harmonies lie hidden in them, longing to be finally brought into the light of day! My collection of folk songs published recently also contains a few that must be classified as heroic ballads. What should be of special interest to Norwegians about this collection is that none of these melodies have been published heretofore. They have been written down as sung by milkmaids and cowherds in the Jotunheim mountains during the past two years. The main feature in them is the deepest melancholy, interrupted only here and there by a momentary ray of light.[4]

That the music people in Christiania can nonchalantly look on as the young Mr. Lindeman hovers like a Fafner[5] over all the treasures of folk songs that were left in manuscript form by his father, without allowing our generation—which feels explicitly called to elevate this treasure by means of an artistic treatment—to get acquainted with them is one of the dark points (of which, unfortunately, there are quite a few) in the music life of our capital city. Believe me, if I were younger, and if I had a scrap of legal knowledge, this scandal would not be allowed to continue much longer. Our folk songs can never in a thousand years belong to just one man, especially in this case, where it was with public support that they were collected.[6]

---

composition dedicated to Grieg. By September of that year Grieg had still not received a copy of the composition. Strangely enough, a long time was also to pass also before he would see a printed copy of *Songs by the Sea*. It was not until January 12, 1887, that Mrs. Grøndahl was able to send him the first copy: "Finally they come—in the most unpretentious garb, to be sure; but still I am glad that they have finally seen the light of day."

3 On May 17, 1897, Mrs. Grøndahl had sent Grieg a manuscript containing piano arrangements of Norwegian heroic ballads and had requested his advice. They were published later that year as *Åtte Kjæmpeviser* [*Eight Heroic Ballads*] op. 43, I. "The Hill Farmer" and "Big Brother and Little Brother" are nos. 4 and 5 of the collection. Op. 43, II, *Tyve Folke- og Skjæmteviser* [*Twenty Folk and Humorous Songs*] was also published in 1897.

4 Grieg is referring here to *Nineteen Norwegian Folk Songs* op. 66. Except for "Gjendine's Lullaby" (no. 19), these arrangements were made from tunes transcribed by Grieg's close friend from Bergen, Frants Beyer (1851–1919).

5 The giant Fafner, one of the leading characters in *The Ring of the Nibelung*, who steals the Rhine gold and guards it so that no one else can get his hands on it.

6 In 1848 the Norwegian organist and composer Ludvig Mathias Lindeman (1812–1887) had received a public grant to enable him to collect Norwegian folk tunes. His work resulted in the multi-volume collection *Ældre og nyere norske Fjeldmelodier* [*Older and Newer Norwegian Mountain Melodies*], which was published one volume at a time during the years 1853–67 and comprised a total of 636 melodies in simple arrangements

Well, I'm off the subject. But once again: thank you!
With warm greetings, also from Nina,

Your old admirer,
EDVARD GRIEG

P.S. The heroic ballads are enclosed herewith.

3

Leipzig, February 18, 1898

Dear Mrs. Grøndahl!
I have just received your friendly letter,[7] from which the nature of your illness is clearly evident. It is called: lack of self-confidence. But watch out: The days are growing lighter, spring will soon be here, everything in nature wakens anew—and so will your belief in yourself.

I have to smile when you thank me. You should know what I am in the middle of at the moment in connection with the music festival and you would understand how happy *you* have made *me* and how grateful I am to both you and Dr. Westerlund.[8]

But listen: Let me now at this early date ask Knutzen[9] if he is willing to fill in for you if necessary. This is more courteous to Knutzen and more reassuring for the rest of us. And with respect to the public announcement, it would be very difficult for the committee to wait until after Easter to announce the soloists. I do not doubt for a moment that, so far as your condition is concerned, it is also best for you to proceed on the assumption that you will play. Last fall, after having been seriously ill in London, if I had not had the pressure of having made a commitment that *required* me to play, I quite certainly would not have been

---

for piano. The final volume in the series was published in 1907 by L. M. Lindeman's son Peter Brynie Lindeman (1858–1930), whom Grieg is here reproaching for withholding the unpublished melodies from scrutiny by others. L. M. Lindeman is known to have collected over 3,000 melodies, but it is only in recent years that plans have been made for publication of the full collection. A large volume (840 pages) containing the texts of the collected songs was published in Oslo in 1997: *Ludvig Mathias Lindemans samling av norske folkeviser og religiøse folketoner. 1. Tekster* (*Ludvig Mathias Lindeman's Collection of Norwegian Folk Songs and Religious Folk Tunes. 1. Texts*).

7 In February, 1898, Grieg had sent a telegram to Mrs. Grøndahl asking if she would be the soloist in his *Piano Concerto* at the Norwegian music festival in Bergen in the summer of 1898. After discussing the matter with her physician she had responded affirmatively, but on February 15 she wrote that she was "absolutely beside herself" when she thought about what she had promised. "If it works out, I cannot thank you enough! In any case you have performed a great act of friendship by remembering me and wanting to help me recover, for I think I was half dead. But you must also remember that there has been about a five-year lull in my playing—which is to say, a five-year regression. There is no other possibility." Nonetheless, she played Grieg's *Piano Concerto* in Bergen with great success and also accompanied performances of some of her own songs.

8 Mrs. Grøndahl, who was often plagued by illness, was at this time a patient of the Swedish neurologist Ernst Otto Theodor Westerlund (1839–1924) in Enköping, Sweden.

9 Norwegian pianist Martin Knutzen (1863–1909).

able to do it.[10] And in the present case we are not even talking about a commitment, for Knutzen can step in if necessary. I mean: You don't *have* to play, but you should just say to yourself, "I *want* to play *because that is the best medicine for me.*"

Don't give another thought to the wretched newspaper announcement. That is merely a formality. The main point is that you will play if you are healthy enough to do so, and it cannot be avoided that this good news will spread from mouth to mouth among your many friends and admirers. What difference does a little news item make? I think Dr. Westerlund will agree with me. I will do nothing, however, until I hear from you. I only ask that this be soon.

Nina has been going around for months with a stubborn case of influenza. As you know, she has gone through a lot of sickness in recent years. But that didn't stop her, notwithstanding her 52 years, from singing in London to the great enjoyment of many. Art is just the wonderful opposite of suffering. Therefore it must be supported by every means possible.

If it can be of help, let me conclude by saying: *I* believe in you! It is precisely the ability of the *great* talent, the *true-born, genuine* talent, to be able to shake off both mental and physical suffering in a way that is not possible for the *small* ones. So: It *must* work out and it will!

Best wishes for improvement, and warmest greetings from Nina and from

Yours truly,
EDVARD GRIEG

4

Christiania, November 12, 1905
Hotel Westminster

Dear Mrs. Grøndahl!
While others today are voting at the ballot box, I will also celebrate the day in my own way as I let "the mood" prevail.[11]

Poor you, who are not well! It is only for that reason that I have not given in to my desire to visit you, above all to congratulate you on your [son] Fridtjof. But I'm not the kind of person who likes to give up, so now I will resort to the pen.

It is astonishing how much Fridtjof's talent has developed since I last heard

---

[10] In November and December of 1897 Grieg gave ten concerts in England, of which four were given in London.

[11] Norway had just succeeded in dissolving the union with Sweden without bloodshed and had invited Prince Carl of Denmark (1872–1957) to become king of the newly free and independent country. Prince Carl had declared that he would accept the throne only if it was clearly the will of the Norwegian people that he do so. A plebiscite was held on November 12 and 13, 1905, with the result that 259,563 voted for a monarchy, 69,264 for a republic. Prince Carl then accepted the invitation and took the name Haakon VII. Grieg himself was a republican, but in the situation in which the country found itself in 1905 he accepted the conclusion that a monarchy was the best alternative.

him. His concert was for me the happiest musical event among us in a long time. I cannot but remember what Liszt wrote to me in my youth: that I would achieve such and such if my talent was permitted to "follow its natural bent."[12] Liszt touched on the great secret of every talent. I understand "following its natural bent" to mean following *that which is best* in its natural bent. But one does not do that unless one is born under a lucky star—unless, like "Parsifal". one is "der *reine* Thor."[13] That is what I think Fridtjof possesses in such rich measure, and for that reason I believe in his future. What a reserve of vital strength, what invincibility! That is the hallmark of a brilliant young person. Like the river that forces its way onward through all obstacles, like the waterfall that casts itself carelessly over the precipice. It is this surplus of strength that really constitutes the creative element, and that one encounters so very, very seldom.

The artistry of most performers seems to me to be built out of surrogates for this gift—nature's own overabundance—which Fridtjof possesses, and which needs to be managed well. I have recommended that he study with Dohnányi, one of the few truly great pianists.[14] I know him slightly from Copenhagen, so if Fridtjof wants me to I can write a few words of introduction.

I would be extremely happy if fate would allow me to arrange something for Fridtjof abroad. To be sure, your own significant name would enable you yourself to do most anything that needs to be done. But there is something so strange about it. There is something in me that wants to show you what an infinite debt of gratitude I feel that I owe you for all the beauty that you have brought to my life in the course of the years. Back when we were quite lonely here at home—*I* was so, in any case—you were the quiet, richly compassionate and co-creative musical soul-mate. I say *quiet*, for you did not say much. But your gentle support was evident nonetheless and reached me indirectly. I can never forget this. As for myself, I not only had the greatest admiration for your beautiful work—I think especially of the time when you wrote *Songs by the Sea*—but in fact, you had more significance for me and my art than I myself realized.

Fortunately we are influenced by that which we love, and what we care about

---

[12] In 1868 Grieg had asked Franz Liszt for a recommendation in support of his application for a travel grant. On December 29 of that year Liszt had responded with a strong letter in which he stated, among other things, that Grieg had "a talent that needs only to follow its natural bent in order to attain to a high level." Grieg got the grant and visited Liszt in Rome in 1870. For details see Grieg's two letters to his parents, also his letter to Niels Ravnkilde of November 2, 1868.

[13] In a diary entry dated August 5, 1907, Grieg used the same expression to describe the Australian-born American pianist Percy Grainger (1882–1961). The quotation is from Wagner's opera *Parsifal*: "Durch Mitleid wissend, der reine Thor." Literal translation: "Knowledge through compassion, the guileless fool." Grieg perceived Fridtjof Backer-Grøndahl as an innocent young man—"der reine Thor"—and thought this quality also found expression in his piano playing. One might also conjecture that just as Parsifal was led by good powers, so also Grieg desired to lead his young Norwegian friend on toward high artistic goals.

[14] Hungarian pianist Ernst von Dohnányi (1877–1960), who became Fridtjof Backer-Grøndahl's teacher. See Grieg's letter to Dohnányi of January 8, 1906, and to Backer-Grøndahl of June 1, 1907.

is precisely the means to understanding. Wagner hit the nail on the head when he said, "Only he who loves me understands me." How much good your understanding did in those days! Thank you for it! Why in the world have I never said this to you before—this and more? Is it I and my increasing inflexibility that are responsible or is it your mimosa-like—if I may call it that—unapproachability?

But—now the mimosa is opening up in the form of Fridtjof! It must be a great consolation to you, and a great joy in the midst of your illness and loss, that he is continuing your life work in such a genuinely artistic fashion.

Nina and I speak so often about this, and we share your joy, even though conditions at the moment make it difficult for us to share our thoughts with you as we would like. Meanwhile, I am still not giving up hope. I think your ear trumpet serves you well in conversation, and if it tires you out as time goes by—well, then we of course have paper and pencil. If people have something to say to each other, they can always find a way to say it.

Congratulations, then, to both you and Grøndahl on your Fridtjof! I repeat the *leitmotiv*: "His talent needs only"—I forgot this *only*—"to follow its natural bent." One should think that would not be terribly difficult!!

Greetings to both of you from Nina and from

Your old friend and admirer,
EDVARD GRIEG

5

[Christiania], November 17, 1905
Hotel Westminster

Dear Mrs. Grøndahl!
Thank you, thank you!

Believe me, I shall also preserve *your* letter, with all the beautiful and true words that it contains. But I will again answer you immediately so that you do not misunderstand me. I am so *fully* and *completely* in agreement with you in your assessment of Fridtjof. Like you, I see that some things are still lacking, and I am amazed that you as his mother see it just as clearly as I do. But I have not wanted to mention it, because I am convinced that life's own process of maturation will supply what is lacking—the soft element, let us call it. This about the pianist and the composer pressing down, each on its own side of the balance, one temporarily more, the other less—this is not a bad thing in a person in whom a dual talent is present. I do not doubt that Fridtjof possesses a strong but quite undeveloped talent for composition. But we need time, we Norwegians. And we shouldn't be concerned if it appears at some time that the one talent is thriving at the expense of the other. But I would like it if he as a pianist would *soon* begin to work on *cantabile* piano-playing. To such a talented young person one needs only to say, "Forward with the right hand, back with the left in *cantabile* passages!" This applies to a great extent to, for example, the *cantabile* themes in my *Piano Concerto*, which I still hope to talk with him about when we meet again at the piano—and I hope it will be soon.

The altogether too severe self-criticism of which you speak is touching and is indicative of the depth of your artistic temperament. It is said that art requires talent. True, but to the same extent it also requires character. And what is indeed remarkable is that the best features of our character have a double effect. Consider your "mimosa-likeness". It is possible—yes, it is certain—that it has harmed you externally. But without it, your most beautiful songs would not have been sufficiently pure and delicate to continue to live long after you are gone. To have the ability to withdraw into yourself and forget *everything* around you when you are creating—that, I think, is the sole condition for being able to bring forth something beautiful. The entire process of creation is—mystery. And the older I get the more I feel like Hamlet: "There are more things in heaven and earth" etc.[15] This duality in everything, such that evil is changed to good when we view it from a distance—this is so incomprehensible in itself, but so beautiful, that you certainly have a right to say in the midst of the mystery that "the backward glance reconciles."

Warm greetings to both of you, also from Nina!

Yours truly,
EDVARD GRIEG

6

46, Grosvenor Street, London W., May 26, 1906

Dear Mrs. Grøndahl!
Finally, finally! For several weeks I have written to you each day in my thoughts but have not found time and quiet. And here in London life has been absolutely crazy. Hundreds of letters are still lying here waiting for an answer. But now that I am finished with the concerts and all the anxiety and nervousness they entail, I must push all of that aside to tell you how very honorably Fridtjof acquitted himself during his appearance in Amsterdam.[16]

I do not doubt that the two-week stay there has been of the greatest significance for him. I know it from my own experience. The same circle of genuine musical families that Röntgen,[17] to my benefit, introduced me to many years ago now became Fridtjof's circle. And the enthusiasm over his artistic talents and

---

[15] The allusion is to *Hamlet*, Act 1, scene 5: "There are more things in heaven and earth, Horatio, than are dreamt of in your philosophy."

[16] On April 26, 1906, Fridtjof Backer-Grøndahl scored a great success in Amsterdam as soloist in Grieg's *Piano Concerto* with Grieg conducting.

[17] Dutch pianist and composer Julius Röntgen (1855–1932).

lovable, noble personality quickly won him the hearts of all. I believe, in fact, that he developed during these weeks. We in Norway have little concept of what it means to have a high level of musical understanding among lay people. The banker Tiefenthal[18] and his wife—my best friends [in The Netherlands] next to the Röntgens—are thoroughly imbued with this understanding. I think Fridtjof, who stayed with them, has realized that he was regarded as a friend and almost as a son, and that the house was filled with music in the best sense of the word. But Röntgen is the soul of the whole group, and he is faithful to that which he has learned to cherish. Therefore Fridtjof should go to Amsterdam again as soon as there is an opportunity.

And in this connection I must emphasize what great help he has received from Fischer,[19] whom I have come to regard more and more highly. At first I, like so many others, was a bit put off by his somewhat feminine demeanor. But that is just on the surface. Even in Christiania I began to realize—and now I have seen it first-hand—that he is at root as genuine and good as he is capable. He is no ordinary impresario when it comes to the artists whose careers he cares about. He is interested as a friend. (. . .)

Like you, I do not doubt that a creative spirit slumbers within Fridtjof. But let him now in his early youth devote himself to being the pianist he is. The ability to compose develops more slowly and in concert with character. For now Fridtjof is indeed the pure child, which makes him doubly dear to me. I must tell you about our departure. We were at the Röntgens in the evening. We took each other's hands—and suddenly he pressed his cheek to mine and whispered, "Thank you!" How un-Norwegian! And yet: how infinitely moving because it was so genuinely felt. I was quite captivated by it—but you must not tell him I said so. May he just keep this childlikeness for a long time and may he, in addition, keep this "traveling father and traveling mother" that he has in Fischer.

Believe me, it was a great pleasure for me to introduce him to Julius Röntgen. I was afraid of exaggerating, so I said as little as possible beforehand. I merely mentioned the word "talented". Then—I think it was the next day—there was a lot of music-making at the Röntgens, and after awhile I said to Fridtjof, "Play the Toccata" (Schumann). I knew what I had chosen. And you should have seen Röntgen, who is an excellent pianist and who has the Toccata in his repertoire—you should have seen how flabbergasted he was. And then he has the ability—as so few artists in Norway have—of being able to recognize the truly great talent. From that moment on those two were friends. Then he played your beautiful "Sommervise" ["Summer Song"][20]—but in this case the admiration undeniably had to be shared with the composer.

---

[18] Dutch banker Benno [Benjamin] Tiefenthal (1851–1906).

[19] Norwegian impresario Peter Vogt Fischer (1863–1938).

[20] "Sommervise" is no. 3 in a collection entitled *Fantasistykker* (*Fantasy Pieces*) op. 45, which dates from 1897.

I am so glad that Fridtjof learned that it is important for a significant artist also to be a significant human being—and that the one underscores the other, as it does with Röntgen. I am glad for those few days! If only, for Fridtjof's sake, they could have lasted another three weeks! I noted how, like a bee, he sucked in all the genuine music that was being made around him. And often it was compositions one doesn't hear in Berlin. There are Dutch musicians of great significance and originality—people like von Brucken-Fock[21] (painter, composer and pianist), who played his remarkable *Preludes* at Röntgens.

But why am I writing all this! You surely will hear it from Fridtjof himself. Yes, dear friend, I am so happy to have gained a young friend in Fridtjof. I find him so engaging that it was the greatest joy for me to collaborate with him. May the collaboration continue when the opportunity presents itself!

I heard from Fridtjof while we were together that you are not well. And this spring has indeed not been suited to eliciting improvement either. But believe me, summer will bring it. That's how it usually goes with me, and I think that our ailments are to some extent similar.

Warmest greetings to you and Grøndahl both from Nina and from

Your devoted old admirer and friend,
EDVARD GRIEG

7

Christiania, February 27, 1907
Hotel Westminster

Dear Mrs. Grøndahl!
That in me Fridtjof has a warm friend—*that is something you can be sure of!* But I think life will slip away from me before it does the same for you, for I am sicker than many believe. One thing, however, is certain: Fridtjof's talent and unspoiled nature are his best friends and support and will continue to be so throughout his life. If he can avoid the two rat-traps—controversy and Bohemianism—he will have triumphed.

We have just returned home from a seven-day stay at Slemdal. But so far as improvement is concerned I can say in the words of Lassen's song, "Es war ein Traum!"[22] We now understand, both you and I, what I in any case did not understand the significance of when we were young: the statement in the preacher's book about when those days come about which we must say, "I have no pleasure

[21] Gerard von Brucken Fock (1859–1935), who was called "the Dutch Chopin" by his contemporaries.

[22] "Es war ein Traum" ("It was a Dream") is a setting of a poem of Heinrich Heine (1797–1856) by German composer and conductor Eduard Lassen (1813–1904).

in them."[23] The meaning seems clear enough, but one must have one's life behind one in order to understand it in all its seriousness.

Dear Mrs. Grøndahl, let me yet once again thank you for all the poetry you have laid around my existence as well! I think it results from the fact that our talents have been so similar.

Warm greetings to all of you and the best wishes from

Your old friend and admirer,
EDVARD GRIEG

8

Copenhagen, May 15, 1907
Hotel Bristol

Dear Agathe Grøndahl!
Each day I have wanted to tell you what a great joy it was to be with Fridtjof recently, but as soon as I got here I had to begin a kind of therapy (electric light-baths) that until now has rendered me incapable of doing anything at all.

Yes, dear friend, now the days have come for both of us of which we must say, as it is written: "I have no pleasure in them!" But—we have the great, great joy of recollection. And when I am with Fridtjof and rejoice over him as an artist and as a person, my thoughts are led to you and to all that I owe to your beautiful art and your noble personality. Yes, we lived the best days of our life in a society that was not in the habit of expressing its likes and dislikes. Maybe such confinement within the self was one of the last vestiges of the saga period. I don't think I see many of those vestiges any more. But perhaps *we* have both exhibited that kind of behavior. And I do not regret it. Who knows? We have, as it were, appropriated more completely and more inwardly all of that which we have admired in each other's art. Frequent personal association often brings unclarity and disappointments. Kindred spirits have ways of relating to each other apart from purely personal association, and I value these infinitely highly—yes, highest of all! Thank you for everything that your music has meant to me! It has been the medium of our most beautiful conversations! Yes, ten times more beautiful than those—albeit far too few—conversations in days gone by, without paper or ear trumpet!

Goodness, how much Fridtjof has developed since last year in Amsterdam! It was a pleasure to hear how his feeling for contrasts and coloration has grown. I only wish for him the same thing that I wish for myself: that the concert devil will not succeed in corrupting us! That fellow should be in *our* pocket, not we

---

[23] Grieg is alluding to Ecclesiastes 12:1, "Remember also your Creator in the days of your youth, before the evil days come, and the years draw nigh, when you will say, 'I have no pleasure in them'." (RSV)

in his! One should think it would be so easy to say "No thanks" to all the invitations, but it isn't! There is something demonically tempting about the concert hall for one who hears shouts of understanding and appreciation. The concert hall can affect one in either of two ways, depending on one's character. I think that Fridtjof and I are made the same way. Young or old—that is not what determines it. But we both trust *our artistic instinct.* That, in my opinion, is the central point. I hope to have further opportunities to spend some time with Fridtjof in the days that remain to me, but if that is not granted to me I nonetheless feel sure of him precisely with respect to artistic instinct. And if I should outlive you, be assured that as long as I live he will have in me a friend in the best sense of the word![24]

And with that, thank you again and again for everything. The very warmest greetings to both you and Grøndahl from Nina and from

Yours truly,
EDVARD GRIEG

---

[24] Agathe Backer Grøndahl died on June 4, 1907, three weeks after Grieg's last letter to her. Just three months later—on September 4, 1907—Grieg passed away.

To Olaus Andreas Grøndahl

Olaus Andreas Grøndahl (1847–1923) was one of the leading Norwegian choral conductors of his day. He first studied theology but terminated these studies in 1870 when he decided to devote himself entirely to music. After studying in Germany during the years 1870–74 he became a voice teacher at several schools in Christiania. In 1878 he established "Grøndahl's Choir", which he led in performances of great sacred choral works. He also served as conductor of several other choirs in Christiania including the Craftsmen's Chorus (1884–90), the Businessmen's Chorus (1888–1912) and the Students' Male Chorus (1889–1913). As a composer he is known primarily for his works for male chorus. In 1875 he married Agathe Backer (1847–1907). The distinguished pianist Fridtjof Backer-Grøndahl (1885–1959) was their son.

Grieg's letters to Grøndahl, one of which is included here, are owned by the Grøndahl family.

Copenhagen, January 16, 1900
Hotel King of Denmark

Dear Grøndahl!

First of all a happy new year to you and yours! I was just about to write to you regarding the Nordraak matter[1] when your letter arrived. I went immediately to Svendsen,[2] who gave me "full authority" to tell you that he would like very much to participate if he can be assured a first-rate, big French orchestra and a substantial honorarium. For me, however, it is out of the question. You evidently have forgotten my letter to Colonne in connection with the Dreyfus affair[3]—in response to which I received at least forty threatening letters. According to all the rules of the game, I'm sure I could expect such a colossal cacophony of whistles and catcalls that not a note of my music would be heard. Therefore Svendsen has promised to conduct the orchestral music with which I may be represented. I would, with good reason, also feel personally insecure down there, as I have been promised a physical beating if I set foot in Paris. Such is the current crop of Frenchmen.[4] Moreover, I would rather not subject myself to all that turmoil,

---

1 Grieg had taken the lead in raising money for a monument honoring his late friend, Norwegian composer Rikard Nordraak (1842–66), and he wanted to give a benefit concert in Christiania for this purpose. The concert took place on April 28, 1900, with Grieg conducting.

2 Norwegian composer and conductor Johan Svendsen (1840–1911), who was musical director at the Royal Theater in Copenhagen.

3 See Grieg's letters of September 12, 1899, to Édouard Colonne (1838–1910) and September 14, 1899, to Bjørnstjerne Bjørnson (1832–1910).

4 A Norwegian music festival was being planned for August 4–7, 1900, in connection with the Paris World Fair. Norwegian music was to be sung and played at three concerts in the Trocadero Palace. O. A. Grøndahl, who was a member of the program committee, had been given responsibility for a 100-voice men's chorus whose members were drawn from four Christiania choirs. Grieg's music was included at all three concerts, with *Land-sighting* as the concluding number at the last concert. All of the other living Norwegian composers of consequence were also represented. The programs included three works by Johan Svendsen: *Norwegian Rhapsody No. 3*, *Zorahayda*, and *Symphony No. 1*.

Grieg, who had conducted concerts in Paris with great success in 1889 and 1894, declined to appear there in 1900 because he realized that there would be problems with the French public. He was extremely unpopular in France at this time because of his very public involvement in the so-called Dreyfus affair.

so it is no sacrifice for me to decline. Nonetheless, I send my warmest thanks for the invitation to you and all the others who wanted to have me along!

And now to Nordraak.[5] The songs for male chorus that you mention are the very ones I had thought of doing. In addition, of course, "Yes, we love this land"—and, if possible, the "March" with chorus and the "Jagtsang" ("Hunting Song") from *Maria Stuart i Skotland.* Will you kindly ask Sigurd Hals[6] to talk with Bjørn[7] about which day in the latter half of April I am to conduct at the National Theater, and then reserve the Masonic Lodge Hall for 4–5 days thereafter. I have conceived of a concert *without* orchestra, partly because Nordraak himself did not orchestrate anything and partly in order to achieve a result consistent with our goal. I would much have preferred to begin the concert with my *Funeral March in Memory of Rikard Nordraak*[8] for winds, but of course I must give up on that for the same reason, unless the musicians could be persuaded to contribute their services. Tell me your opinion about this as well as the choice of the Masonic Lodge Hall. For it is of course conceivable that the National Theater would be made available to us for this purpose.

Thank you for your interest and your work! And a warm greeting, also to Agathe, from Nina and from

Sincerely,
EDVARD GRIEG

5 Norwegian composer Rikard Nordraak (1842–66), whose setting of a text by Bjørnstjerne Bjørnson became the Norwegian national anthem, "Ja, vi elsker dette landet" ("Yes, we love this land, our country".)

6 Sigurd Hals (1859–1931), proprietor of a piano manufacturing company, music publishing company and concert bureau in Christiania.

7 Bjørn Bjørnson (1859–1942), director of the National Theater in Christiania.

8 *Funeral March in Memory of Rikard Nordraak*, written for piano in 1866, was published in an arrangement for wind ensemble and percussion in 1899.

To Aimar Grønvold

Aimar Grønvold (1846–1926) was an attorney. From 1884 onward he held a series of important government positions and in 1906 was appointed the king's cabinet secretary. He also had a life-long interest in music and music history. He was a competent amateur pianist and once studied composition with Norwegian composer Johan Svendsen (1840–1911). He served as music critic for the Christiania newspapers *Aftenbladet* (1867–81) and *Aftenposten* (1881–86). In 1883 he published a book entitled *Norske Musikere* (*Norwegian Musicians*), in which one chapter was devoted to Grieg. Much of the information in this chapter came directly from Grieg, as is evident from his letter to Grønvold of April 25, 1881. The letter of February 3, 1899, shows Grieg's efforts behind the scenes to get Johan Svendsen appointed as musical director at the newly constructed National Theater in Christiania.

Grieg's letters to Grønvold are preserved in Nasjonalbiblioteket, Oslo (National Library of Norway, Oslo Division).

1

Bergen, April 25, 1881

Mr. A. Grønvold, Christiania

I have finally reached the point that I have time to send you a few lines. But I will tell you honestly that the kind of work you are asking me to do is the worst thing I know of. No matter what I may end up jotting down, I make one urgent request: Do not quote a single word from me directly. Just recently I have learned the hard way that this directive is necessary. (Don't misunderstand me. I can't imagine that it would ever occur to you to be so tactless.)

Some time ago I received a request from a man in Holland whom I do not know—a man who writes about music—to send him some clippings containing material for use in a review of my works for a Dutch readership. A few days ago I received a copy of his article and discovered to my horror one direct quote after another.[1] I am sending you this article in the hope that you can use some of it, for in this way I avoid having to rehash the details of my youth. But return it to me when you are finished with it.

It is strange how different various people are from one another. I must say, in contrast to Svendsen, that I left the Conservatory in Leipzig as stupid as I was when I arrived there. I had learned something, of course, but my individuality was still a closed book for me.

Then came the Copenhagen period, when I— in association with Nordic art and Nordic artists, in the process of studying Nordic sagas and Nordic folk life—began to understand and to find myself. During the tremendous ripening process

[1] Grieg is referring to an article by J. de Jong, "Een Norweegsch componist: Edvard Grieg", which appeared in the Dutch journal *De Tijdspiegel*, The Hague, 1881. The article was printed in four installments in the Bergen newspaper *Bergensposten* on May 29 and June 2, 3 and 5 of the same year.

that I experienced at this time, one fine day I stumbled upon a Norwegian fellow whom I did not know: Rikard Nordraak,[2] who went home with me and sat down at the piano, where he sang and played his songs to texts from Bjørnson's[3] peasant stories, his incidental music to *Sigurd Slembe*, his "Purpose" from *Maria Stuart i Skotland*[4] and more. I will never forget the impression. Suddenly it was as if the scales fell from my eyes and I knew what I wanted to do. It was not precisely what Nordraak wanted, but I think that the way to me went through him.

Now came a happy time of excitement and productivity. This was in 1864–65. There in Copenhagen, in daily association with Nordraak and other young people who were enthusiastic about everything Scandinavian, in a short time I wrote many songs, *Humoresques* op. 5, *Sonata* op. 7, and *Sonata* op. 8. It was touching how fond Nordraak and I were of each other. How he adored my *Humoresques*! "Yes," he shouted in triumphant self-confidence upon hearing the "Menuetto", "it is as if I had written it myself!"

And I! How I adored his songs every bit as much! We indiscriminately hated everything that belonged to the establishment and dreamt of a new super-super-Norwegian future. But this dream didn't last long—fortunately for both of us, perhaps.

As for Nordraak, it is now clear to me that he was a brilliant prophet, but he would never have become a mature artist in the fullest sense of the word. Thus it is good for him that he passed away before reality surprised him. As for me, it was at the end of his life that I achieved clarity about myself. His contempt for the technical side of art, which I did not share, became for me a spur to serious work.

When you ask about Nordraak's influence on me, it is as you assume: His view of our folk music has strengthened my own. But my national enthusiasm had already been awakened by the time I became acquainted with him, albeit without having yet borne artistic fruit. It was the encounter that called forth the productive manifestation of enthusiasm. Besides, who knows the hidden laws of influence? I know only that he came as a good spirit upon my pathway, and that I am infinitely indebted to him, and that without him I would perhaps have had to struggle for who knows how long without finding myself. We were so extremely unlike each other, in spite of our intimate mutual understanding. Perhaps it was precisely for that reason that his influence could be effective.

I remember distinctly that one summer day in 1865 on a street in Copenhagen I bumped into Halfdan Kjerulf,[5] to whom I spoke enthusiastically about

---

[2] Norwegian composer Rikard Nordraak (1842–66).

[3] Norwegian author Bjørnstjerne Bjørnson (1832–1910).

[4] *Sigurd Slembe* and *Maria Stuart i Skotland*: plays by Bjørnson.

[5] Norwegian composer Halfdan Kjerulf (1815–68).

Nordraak. He clapped his hands together and shouted, "Now, isn't that something! Les extrêmes ses touchent!"[6] At the time I thought Kjerulf was mistaken, but since then I have come to realize the truth of what he said.

The winter of 1864–65 was notable for the artistic life of Copenhagen in a number of ways. Several young composers—C. F. E. Horneman, G. Matthison-Hansen,[7] Rikard Nordraak and I—established a society whose aim it was to present performances by young Nordic composers. It was called "Euterpe"[8] and it flourished marvelously. This is where Nordraak conducted "Kaare's Song" from *Sigurd Slembe* for the first time and where I presented some movements of a symphony which I later published for piano four hands under the title *Pièces symphoniques.*[9] But in May, 1865, Nordraak went to Berlin, where he found an early grave the following spring.

I also left Denmark, and after some time "Euterpe" was dissolved. What strongly influenced me at that time and inspired many of my songs—for example, *Melodies of the Heart*[10]—was my acquaintance with and engagement to the woman who is now my wife, Miss Nina Hagerup, whose lovely singing voice and singular gift of interpretation at that time conquered people's hearts wherever she went. She sang my songs and has certainly contributed to the fact that all of my songs are known in Denmark in quite a different way than they are at home.

I spent the winter of 1865–66 in Rome, where in March, upon hearing of Nordraak's death, I wrote my *Funeral March* in memory of him. During this stay in Rome I also wrote *In Autumn*, a concert overture for orchestra, which has been published for piano four hands as op. 11.[11]

In the fall of 1866 I came to Christiania, where a variety of activities were to occupy me for an extended period of time. Upon my arrival in the city I gave a concert at the Hotel du Nord in collaboration with Mrs. Norman-Neruda,[12] with whom I performed my *Sonata* op. 8, and with Miss Nina Hagerup, who sang songs by Nordraak, Kjerulf and myself. It was the first time an all-Norwegian music program had been presented in Norway's capital, and I still think back with deep gratitude on the warm reception that was accorded me at that time.

---

[6] "Opposites attract one another!"

[7] Danish composers Christian Frederick Emil Horneman 1840–1906) and Gottfred Matthison-Hansen (1832–1909).

[8] "Euterpe" was also the name of a similar organization in Leipzig.

[9] Grieg's *Symphony* in C minor was first published in *Edvard Grieg: Complete Works*, vol. 11 (1984). The two inner movements were published as *Two Symphonic Pieces* for piano four hands in 1869.

[10] *Melodies of the Heart*, settings of four poems by Hans Christian Andersen (1805–75).

[11] Grieg revised and orchestrated this composition in 1887, and the following year it was published by C. F. Peters Musikverlag in Leipzig as *In Autumn. Concert Overture.*

[12] In 1864 the Czech violinist Wilhelmina (Wilma) Neruda (1838–1911) married the Swedish composer Ludvig Norman (1831–85) and thereafter went by the name Norman-Neruda. In 1888, after Norman's death, she married Sir Charles Hallé (1819–95) of Manchester and became Lady Hallé. She and Grieg performed together a number of times through the years. See Grieg's letter to her (under the name Neruda).

I would prefer to skip over my long Christiania period. To write my biography covering these years would be to write about artistic life in general in Christiania, and God knows it was thin. I stood all alone. Kjerulf, who warmly supported me at first, fell away in 1868, and regarding the years that followed, until Svendsen came home again and won people's hearts, I can only recall with bitterness the indifference—yes, the contempt and scorn—that was displayed toward Norwegian music. I could tell things regarding this period that sound unbelievable. There was in fact a total lack of that which is called artistic morale. Kjerulf, who represented a striving for high ideals, had in his later years withdrawn into himself, and the prevailing public opinion was totally degenerate. Dilettantism ruled the roost. I remember, for example, an evening program that my wife and I gave in the Student Association in 1872, in collaboration with Bjørnson, to raise money for Danish people who had lost their homes as a result of a flood. About fifty people showed up, while about 1,000 attended an amateur concert given for the same purpose in the auditorium of the Masonic Lodge that evening. That was the extent of interest in Norwegian art.

A brighter day dawned in 1873 [1872]. Svendsen came home, and he and I now shared the Music Association conducting duties that I had previously handled alone.

In the spring of 1874 I left Christiania, and since then I have lived there for just one winter, that of 1876–77.

There is nothing to report about my personal relationship with Kjerulf beyond what I have already said. I am not aware of any deeper influence by Kjerulf despite my warm admiration for many of his songs.

I have been all the more attracted by Svendsen's music, although nothing could be more different than our respective artistic inclinations. He has taught me to believe in myself and in the power and legitimacy of individuality. There was a time in Christiania, you know, when to be an individual was identical to being a criminal. But then Svendsen came and he, too, was an individual, and then the miracle occurred: From then on I was also tolerated. There are, therefore, few artists to whom I owe as much as I owe to Svendsen. In 1872, when he came home, there were a few people who really wanted to sow enmity between us. Thanks to our mutual appreciation of each other's music, however, the plan failed completely.

I have read in a few biographical sketches of Svendsen the statement that for me the national element was the end whereas for Svendsen it was the means. On this point I would only ask you in the name of truth to protest. I will say nothing about the super-super-Norwegian ferocity of my youth. My goal as a modern artist is that which is universal—or more correctly, that which is individual. If it turns out to be national, well, that is because the individual is national, and that is not something deserving of blame.

I must not forget to mention a man who, in the musically empty Christiania during the years 1868–72, filled me with his powerful personality. That was Bjørnson. He was a true friend to me in those years and deserves much of the credit for my survival. Although he did not understand music, he believed in what I wanted to accomplish—and that gave me courage.

I prefer not to speak about my own art and the deep struggle and longing related thereto. It can speak for itself. And if it does not do so sooner or later, it is because it is worthless. But—history is fair; that is my firm conviction.

And now I have spoken as if to a friend who understands me. If I had not valued this "understanding" on your part so highly I would certainly not have been able to avoid empty phrases. So: Regard everything I have said as a mere glimpse, and use what you will and can—but use no direct quotations.

Let me hear from you soon.

Yours truly,
EDVARD GRIEG

NB: If you are in need of a stack of reviews from various times and countries, I will send them to you immediately. But take good care of them and return them to me as soon as you are finished with them. Do not forget to send me your exact address.

Although recognition from the so-called higher places does not always rest on the best motives, for the sake of completeness I will tell you, in case you wish to include it: that in 1872 I became a member of the Royal Swedish Academy, and that in 1875 I was invited to play for the Queen of Denmark (that was during the summer, in Fredensborg).

There was, indeed, an honor of greater significance for me one day in December, 1868—just as the gloom surrounding me in Christiania seemed the darkest—when I received a letter from Liszt that brought some sunshine into my life. There was at that time no one in my homeland who paid any attention to me as a creative artist. I expressed my feelings of discouragement in a letter to a friend in Rome. My friend passed it on to Liszt, who he knew was warmly interested in me. It shows a very noble trait in Liszt that he immediately sat down at his desk [and wrote to me] in the awareness of the good that he might thereby bring about.[13] I was thinking just then about applying for a stipend, but I didn't have much hope of getting it since I was not well regarded by our conservative older musicians and other leading musical dilettantes. But Liszt's letter worked wonders. I included it in my application to the Ministry of Church and Education,

---

[13] Grieg's memory is a little faulty at this point. He wrote a letter to Liszt requesting a recommendation. This letter was delivered to Liszt by one of Grieg's friends in Rome, Danish composer Niels Ravnkilde (1823–90). See Grieg's letter to Ravnkilde of November 2, 1868.

from where without my knowledge it was shortly stolen by *Aftenposten* (a newspaper which I, for certain financial reasons familiar to most artists, subscribed to at that time) and now, to my great consternation, I read Liszt's letter in its entirety in this newspaper.[14]

This was in the spring of 1869. And what happened now was incredible: Upon my departure I became the object of a whole shower of undeserved recognition from all sides, totally inappropriate—in other words, nothing but a consequence of the recognition imported from Rome.

When I visited Liszt on my trip to Rome, I wasn't disappointed either. I count the time spent with him that winter among the most beautiful and instructive hours of my life.[15] I enclose Liszt's letter with the request that if you are going to use it, copy it immediately and return the original to me.

In later years as well, I have not had a warmer friend of my art than Liszt with his remarkable understanding of and warm appreciation for precisely the uniquely national elements in my music. Thus, for example, the violinist Robert Heckmann[16] (concertmaster in Cologne) tells me in a letter of October, 1879, that after a performance of my *String Quartet* at a gathering of musicians in Wiesbaden, Liszt came up to him "and spoke at length and in detail about the deep impression the quartet had made and the significance it had. He said, 'Not for a long time has a new work—especially a string quartet—interested me so deeply as precisely this singular, excellent work by Grieg. Greet him from me in any case, and tell him that I greatly enjoyed his composition'."[17]

I tell you this, just as the reviews from Cologne and St. Petersburg will perhaps be of significance to counterbalance the harsh treatment that same composition has received from other quarters, especially conservative ones. For I feel that in this work are hidden specimens of the heart-blood of which the future hopefully will see more than just a few drops.

No, now I must quit!

So, then: take of this what you will, but—only as information, not direct quotation!

---

14 Liszt's recommendation is reproduced in a footnote to Grieg's letter to Ravnkilde of November 2, 1868.

15 For an account of Grieg's meetings with Liszt in Rome, see his two letters to his parents, Alexander (1806–75) and Gesine Grieg (1814–75).

16 Grieg's *String Quartet* in G minor is dedicated to Robert Heckmann (1848–91), who also played an important role in the final shaping of numerous details relating to string technique. A detailed discussion of Heckmann's involvement with the quartet will be found in Bjarne Kortsen: *Zur Genesis von Edvard Griegs g-Moll Streichquartett*, West-Berlin 1967. See also Grieg's letters to Heckmann.

17 Grieg quotes Heckmann's letter in German: "und sprach lange und eingehend über den tiefen Eindruck und die Bedeutung des Quartetts. Er meinte: 'Es ist mir lange kein neueres Werk spec. Streichquartett begegnet, das mir so sehr interessiert hätte, wie gerade dieses eigenartige, vortreffliche Werk von Grieg. Jedenfalls grüssen Sie ihn von mir und sagen Sie ihm, dass ich grosse Freude von seinem Werk gehabt'."

2

Bergen, March 18, 1883

Dear Mr. Grønvold!

I say with the man from Sogn: "We could promise it all right, but we couldn't keep the promise!" I have been promising myself for a long time to write to you and thank you for the biography.[18] But since I had to cease all letter-writing for awhile, the number of letters I owed grew so great that it scared me just to think about it. But now I have a free Sunday and I am going to start with you.

I once sent you a greeting through Svendsen, so you already know that I was pleased with your work. And now I want to tell you personally that I was surprised and moved by the sensitive understanding of my art that sounds forth through every line of what you wrote. That is the main point. Of secondary importance is the fact that you have been fortunate with respect to form as well. And of still less importance is the fact that now and then you "cast aside fetters, bonds and constraints"[19] and act like a real story-teller. I refer especially to your account of my meeting Nordraak. You have painted this so vividly that I couldn't help but say to myself, "Se non è vero, è ben trovato."[20]

But my first meeting with Nordraak as it really happened was so characteristic of Nordraak that I can recall it at this moment as if it were just yesterday. What happened was this. One evening at Tivoli in Copenhagen I was presented by Mrs. Thoresen[21] to a young man by the name of Nordraak who introduced himself thus: "Well, shall we two great men really meet one another at last!" His bearing, his gestures, his voice—everything about him indicated that I was in the presence of a man who considered himself to be both the Bjørnson and the Ole Bull[22] of the future. And yet there was such a touching naiveté and charm about him that he took me by storm. Until that moment I had never considered the possibility of being or even having the ability to become a great man. I was a student, no more. Moreover I was timid, shy, and sickly. But this cocksureness was just the medicine I needed. From that moment on it was as if we had always been friends.

You could certainly have learned of this in time to include it in your book, but I didn't think you were going to include so many details. But nonetheless: It is fine as it is so far I am concerned. It would have been different if your aim was to portray Nordraak. I have always thought it might be interesting for me to write down my recollections of him from those days. I probably will never do so,

---

[18] Grønvold's book *Norske Musikere*, 1. Række (*Norwegian Musicians*, vol. I) published in 1883.

[19] Grieg is quoting a line from Johan Nordahl Brun's song "Norges Skaal" ("Norway's Skoal").

[20] "If it isn't true it certainly is well fabricated."

[21] Danish-Norwegian writer Magdalene Thoresen (1819–1903), who was Rikard Nordraak's cousin and Henrik Ibsen's mother-in-law.

[22] Norwegian virtuoso violinist Ole Bull (1810–80).

however, for time races by without my completing the tasks that are more important than that.

Are you soon leaving on a trip? I am just beginning to think about doing some stupid thing or other in order to get to Paris next winter. See to it that you do the same! One must not be in Norway too long at one time. Now when Svendsen leaves, the capital city will become a musical wasteland as well.[23]

Warm greetings from

Yours truly,
EDVARD GRIEG

3

Copenhagen, February 3, 1899
Hotel King of Denmark

Dear Grønvold!
I will forgive your faithlessness on one condition: that you do something about the Svendsen question. Naturally you have seen the interview in *Dansk Nationaltidende*,[24] from which it is clear 1) that Svendsen is not unwilling, 2) that no one has approached him.[25] So: the position is to be filled by the end of February (this is evidently the smart procedure). Is the real intention here a trick maneuver in the press—apparently designed to win Svendsen, but undertaken with the help of uninformed people and, above all, people who have nothing to do with the matter—*so that no direct approach will be made in the short time that remains*? And then one fine day we will read in the newspapers that the post has been filled by a surrogate—someone who perhaps has never conducted an opera in his whole life. Shall this ploy really succeed while *you* sit there looking on and doing nothing to prevent it and when you know that Svendsen was not unwilling?

To me the matter looks like this: If people *don't* want Svendsen, then Halvorsen should be the obvious first choice and Holter should retain the leadership of the Music Association.[26] If they *do* want Svendsen, then the solution is simple. You would avoid putting Winge[27] out of a job but could retain him to work with Svendsen. He also has the important advantage of being a pianist. So: Winge would keep his position and Holter his. This strikes me as something that should

[23] Grieg's friend and colleague Johan Svendsen had just accepted the position of musical director at The Royal Theater in Copenhagen.

[24] *Dansk Nationaltidende*: a Danish newspaper.

[25] Grieg is referring to the question of who should become musical director at the new National Theater in Christiania.

[26] Norwegian conductors Johan Halvorsen (1864–1935) and Iver Holter (1850–1941).

[27] Per Winge (1858–1935) had been conductor of the Bergen Music Society Harmonien 1886–88, the Music Association in Christiania 1893–94 (substituting for Iver Holter) and at the Christiania Theater 1894–99.

be given a lot of weight, as I do not understand how one is justified in throwing people out of their jobs when it can be avoided.

Now the financial side of it: Winge's salary as assistant would indeed be somewhat less. Was not the salary for the new musical director set at 4,000 crowns? This, then, could, for example, be shared equally. And now I contend that when Svendsen, each week or each fortnight, conducted big popular concerts on Sunday afternoon or noon in the theater, the theater could easily assure him 6,000 crowns for these concerts—for it would be a new era with a full house. Add to that the state grant of 1,600 crowns. There we have a total sum of 9,600 crowns.

All of this is obviously just my own imagination. Svendsen knows nothing about this proposal. *I* cannot come out into the open here, for all the people in Christiania whose surnames begin with H would then raise a hue and cry about camaraderie and mutual life assurance.[28] Yes, isn't it a scandal that one cannot set forth a purely objective opinion without being accused of having base motives! Svendsen himself is the noblest person you can imagine. It would never occur to him to say a single word to get one of his friends—me, for example—to plead his case, and we must honestly admit that it would have been very easy for him to do so. But I would be ashamed of myself if I didn't make an effort to get you to do something in this matter. For me it is both a national and an artistic duty. But I assume that you will not show this letter to anyone but simply use the ideas that it contains as if they were your own—if you agree with them. I mean: Facilitate a direct approach from the *right* people as soon as possible. Let an exchange of views take place before we are suddenly surprised by the news that the position has been filled by the person whose friends have chosen it for him—despite the fact that they let it be announced that it was vacant in order to mislead the public. You *must* do this. If I were up there, by damn it would happen—or else I would publicly declare the press to be a humbug machine.

I have learned via a private letter that Bjørn[29] really has also said that he, too, was in favor of Svendsen. Well, you'll have to take that for what it's worth—but something must be done. It is an altogether too great scandal that an opportunity that in fact will *never* come again should not be seized. The big words about national pride in the newspapers are enough to make one vomit. Here we have the Norwegian big words, the famous Norwegian big words. People have a right to scorn us, because we deserve it. Yes, even if Svendsen had been a *foreigner*, the step should have been taken—that's how national I am. But since he is even

---

[28] Grieg uses the English expression "mutual life assurance" here. Among the "H" people to whom he refers with obvious irony are certainly Norwegian composers Johannes Haarklou (1847–1925), Otto Winter-Hjelm (1837–1931) and Iver Holter.

[29] Bjørn Bjørnson (1859–1942), son of Bjørnstjerne Bjørnson and director of the new National Theater in Christiania.

Norwegian, I don't know of a word in the language that adequately describes those who would pass over him or those who look on in silence as it is happening.

Now, look at this: Fortunately my fingers can be used despite disturbing bronchial tendencies.

Svendsen has been right down in bed with bronchitis for several days. Yesterday his temperature was between 39 and 40![30] Today it has slowly gone down somewhat. But it is something that has gone on for 2–3 weeks—to the greatest detriment of concerts and opera.

We probably will be leaving here sometime between the 20th and the 24th.

Warm greetings from

Yours truly,
EDVARD GRIEG

[30] Celcius; the Fahrenheit equivalent is approximately 103 or 104.

To Ellen Gulbranson

Ellen Nordgren Gulbranson (1863–1947) was born in Sweden but was married to Norwegian Lieutenant Colonel H. P. J. F. Gulbranson (1860–1946). She scored many great triumphs as a dramatic soprano in Wagner operas. Her first great international success occurred at Bayreuth in 1896, and she continued to perform at the music festivals there until 1914. Grieg often used her as a soloist at his concerts.

Grieg's letters to Ellen Gulbranson are preserved in Bergen Offentlige Bibliotek (Bergen Public Library).

1

Troldhaugen, Hop Station at Bergen, July 28, 1894

Dear Madam!

How very kind of you that you will come here and take part in *Scenes from "Olav Trygvason"*. Accept my preliminary thanks! I have the confident hope that the concerts can take place in the middle of October. For you cannot have any idea of how many difficulties must be removed to make possible such an undertaking. In this connection I will ask you to make mention only of your participation in the second concert, for which I will be releasing subscription lists next month. I have been advised to exercise this caution. We can then decide on the basis of the subscription response how far we dare to go with preparations for the *four* planned concerts. I hope we can do all four, for otherwise the whole project could easily run aground.[1]

This, then, in confidence.

But who wants to think about concerts during this marvelous summer that we are having in West Norway! It's an absolute paradise here at the moment, and I am completely caught up in pure nature worship! Hopefully we will get a few beautiful autumn days when you are here, for such days in this region have their own special poetry.

I look forward to hearing your beautiful voice again! You will see that the "vølve" will be even better than before, if that is possible, for she obviously has matured along with you!

So: My sincerest thanks! When things have progressed sufficiently I will take the liberty of sending you some further details.

With warm greetings, also to your husband!

Most sincerely yours,
EDVARD GRIEG

---

[1] Grieg gave four identical concerts in Bergen on November 16, 18, 20 and 21, 1894. The program consisted of *Bergliot* and *Scenes from Olav Trygvason*. Ellen Gulbranson appeared as the "vølve" in the latter work. (In Old Norse mythology the "vølve" was a woman who practiced witchcraft and had the ability to foresee the future.)

2

Troldhaugen at Bergen, September 11, 1895

Dear Mrs. Gulbranson!
As you will already have learned from Mr. Holter,[2] I am coming to Christiania at the beginning of October and will conduct a piece for string orchestra at the first concert of the Music Association. At the same time I will then have the pleasure of hearing you sing the three songs with orchestra [EG 177].[3] I don't have the score or the vocal parts at the moment as everything is in Leipzig, where it is being printed. But I have written to Leipzig, and it will be sent to Christiania in time for the concert.

I have heard through the newspapers about your grandiose preparations for Bayreuth. Yes, those Germans! There is one thing that they appreciate, and that is hard labor. In that respect it is healthy to learn from them. The big lie that we Norwegians have lived by—among other lies!—is the belief that artistic results come flying in the window like roasted pigeons. I have struggled against this lie for a generation. It's about time we got our eyes opened.

Shall I really succeed in seeing your home at Haug? It would be a great pleasure for both me and my wife, who joins me in sending the warmest greetings to you and your husband.

Sincerely yours,
EDVARD GRIEG

3

Christiania, October 17, 1896

Dear Mrs. Gulbranson!
I just received your postcard. So everything is arranged. Bravo! But listen! You *will* have time to at least *think* a little about the songs before November 17, even if you won't have time to practice them. Don't *just* be a prima donna now!! Mozart sat and wrote out a fugue while he *thought about* a prelude that he was conceiving at the same time—and in the same way you must sing *Walküre*[4] and *think* about the songs. NB: Not *while* you are singing *Walküre*—my expectations are not that inhuman—but in betweentimes.

So: The printed music will be waiting for you at Gutmann's[5] when you get to Vienna—since you don't have "time to think about them before"—but please take care of the collection of songs that I sent you in my last letter, for I have no copy myself. I will later send both Danish and German editions.

---

[2] Iver Holter (1850–1941), conductor of the Music Association in Christiania at this time.
[3] The concert took place on October 12, 1895.
[4] Wagner's music-drama *Die Walküre.*
[5] Albert Gutmann (1862–1915), a music publisher and concert agent in Vienna.

From the bottom of my heart I congratulate you on your great success in Germany. We will certainly enjoy some of the benefits of that success in Vienna.[6] And you must not give up on Amsterdam. If you have not already heard from there directly you certainly will do so one of these days.

I will be getting to Vienna on November 18 in the hope that you will be there at that time. If not you must please let me know, for in that case I will look for you in Dresden en route to Vienna.

The best option, though, is to meet in Vienna on the 18th.

Warmest greetings to you and your husband, also from Nina.

Your devoted
EDVARD GRIEG

P.S. Tomorrow I go to visit your compatriots! While there I will miss hearing your beautiful voice![7]

---

[6] Ellen Gulbranson performed at a concert in Vienna on November 23, 1896. Some of Grieg's songs were on the program, but Grieg was unable to attend due to illness.

[7] Grieg gave concerts in Stockholm on October 24, 29 and 31 and November 1, 1896.

To Albert Gutmann

Albert Gutmann (1852–1915), a music publisher and concert agent in Vienna, had responsibility for Grieg's concerts in that city in 1896 and 1897 as well as one in Munich in 1907.[1] Grieg's letters give a clear picture of his careful attention to details in planning his concerts—details regarding program, soloists, and financial arrangements.

Grieg's letters to Albert Gutmann were written in German. Letters 1–7 are preserved in Nasjonalbiblioteket, Oslo (National Library of Norway, Oslo Division), letters 8–9 in the Lincoln Center Library, New York City.

1

Bergen, May 5, 1892

Dear Sir!

Unfortunately I must now completely rule out any hope of coming to Vienna this summer.[2] Since my last letter I have been chained to the sick bed for more than three weeks and am still so poorly that for now all I can think of is getting well again. For this reason it would also be very difficult for me to send anything worth mentioning for your album—since you are wanting it so soon. I very much regret this. But if you will be satisfied with the enclosed "Volkston",[3] you are welcome to use it. My only condition is that I retain all rights *except* for your album.

Respectfully,
EDVARD GRIEG

2

Copenhagen, November 28, 1894
Hotel King of Denmark

Dear Mr. Gutmann!

Forgive me that until now I have left your last so exceptionally kind letter unanswered. I will not dissemble but quite simply, in accordance with the truth, admit that I couldn't make up my mind sufficiently to give a definitive answer. My health has been too poorly. Now that it is improving I am getting more courageous. I have, therefore, made a preliminary decision to accept your invitation, which is so flattering to me, to come to Vienna in the spring—for example, at the end of March or the beginning of April.

---

[1] The concerts in Vienna were given on March 24 and December 16 and 19, 1896, and January 6, 1897. The Munich concert was given on April 6, 1907.

[2] Grieg had been invited by Gutmann to give a concert during an "Internationale Ausstellung für Musik und Theaterwesen" in Vienna. In the same letter Gutmann had asked Grieg to send a small composition for an album that he was planning to publish.

[3] See p. 319. "Volkston" was an early version of "Gjendine's Lullaby" op. 66, no. 19. It is somewhat different from the piece published in 1897 in both harmony and notation: The latter is written in 2/4 time and has halved note values.

Because of the great exertions that would be required I must, however, decline to present choral works this time. I only hope that an evening orchestral concert, a chamber-music concert and an evening program of songs will not be altogether too much for me. Moreover, at the orchestral concert I would only conduct, so I would need a suitable soloist for my *Piano Concerto*. For this role I take the liberty of suggesting Professor Raoul Pugno of Paris, Professor Arthur de Greef of Brussels, or Mad. D'Albert-Carreño.[4] At the chamber-music concert and the program of songs I will, of course, be at the piano myself. In the *Violin Sonata* and the *String Quartet* no one captures the style of my works better than Mr. Johannes Wolff[5] of London (N. Vert, 6 Cork Street, London W.), and I would

---

[4] Raoul Pugno (1852–1914), Arthur de Greef (1862–1940), and Venezuelan pianist Teresa Carreño (1853–1917), who during the years 1892–95 was married to German pianist Eugène d'Albert (1864–1932).

[5] Dutch violinist Johannes Wolff (1863–?).

be most pleased if he could be engaged for this occasion. To interpret my songs is a truly difficult task. Kindly tell me if you have had someone specifically in mind. For a complete concert program, in any case, it would be desirable to divide the program between a female and a male singer. But I leave this matter completely to your discretion.

As for the financial side of the matter, I have been thinking of 1500 fl.[6] for all three concerts, i.e., 500 fl. for each concert.

Anticipating your esteemed reply, I am,

With profound respect,
EDVARD GRIEG

3

Copenhagen, February 22, 1895
Hotel King of Denmark

Dear Mr. Gutmann!
Is it really the case, as is written in the newspapers, that it is the Berlin Philharmonic that I shall be conducting in Vienna? That was really a great disappointment. Don't misunderstand me: I am familiar with the Berlin Philharmonic Orchestra and have high regard for it, but when I am going to visit Vienna I had been looking forward to getting acquainted with Vienna's best orchestral resources. Oh well, everything will work out. But I do want to ask you the following question: How many orchestra rehearsals can I have? And with regard to the Berlin orchestra: Would it not be practical if, en route to Vienna, I stayed in Berlin for a few days to conduct a rehearsal with the orchestra? I would like to have this question answered immediately as I am soon leaving Copenhagen.

Lastly a request, esteemed Mr. Gutmann: Can you arrange things so that I will have uninterrupted peace and quiet at the hotel? As a matter of fact, I cannot accept invitations and visits since my health is not up to such things—and of the former I have already received so many that it makes me quite concerned!

I need a *clever* porter who understands what he has to do!

And one thing more: a good little piano that is placed in such a way that people in the stairwell cannot hear when I am playing.

You understand that I am a little "difficile". Unfortunately! But starting the day after tomorrow, when the philharmonic concert here will be behind me, I will live healthily so that in some measure I can be at my best when I come to Vienna.

In cheerful hope of hearing from you again soon, I am,

Sincerely yours,
EDVARD GRIEG

---

[6] Fl. = florins. The florin was a unit of currency in Austria at that time.

P.S. My friend and countryman Johan Svendsen[7] has recommended Hotel Metropole. Is that in your vicinity?

4

Copenhagen, March 2, 1895
Hotel King of Denmark

Dear Mr. Gutmann!
Thank you so much for your last letter! Your explanations show that you are a man with great energy, and on that account you immediately have my envious good will! Naturally I am greatly looking forward to making music together with the Berlin orchestra. The rehearsal days also suit me fine, but I want very much to know whom I shall contact in Berlin. The thing is, I have to go there a few days ahead of time because of some revision of the orchestral parts. It is very important, therefore, that you arrange to *place the orchestral parts at my disposal ca. eight days before the rehearsal.* I do not yet know what my address will be in Berlin, but you can be quite sure that a letter addressed to me c/o C. F. Peters, Thalstrasse 10 in Leipzig will reach me.

Your recommendation regarding *Peer Gynt Suite No. 2* would have been great if I were not going to conduct the first suite. Playing two suites—from the same play, even—does not strike me as a good idea. The program would shape up much better if instead of the second suite we chose the concert overture *In Autumn.* I hope that you, too, will share this view.

Now to some questions that it is very important for me to get answered in your next letter. With whom shall I play the *Violin Sonata*? Who is the female singer and who the male? Which songs have been chosen? I need not tell you that if one fills an entire evening *exclusively* with songs, the voices must be *absolutely first class.* Mere renown, in my opinion, is not enough. It is more important that the artists in question have lived themselves into my way of thinking and are, as a result, sympathetically disposed.

I express my heartfelt thanks for your information regarding the hotel.

I venture to ask you to remind the violinist that the first priority is the *Sonata in C Minor.* If there is to be a second sonata, I recommend *No. 2 in G Major.*[8]

I see in the newspapers that I have been made an honorary member of the "Gesellschaft der Musikfreunde" in Vienna. Is that correct? Thus far I have not received any direct notice of this, and for that reason I cannot thank for the honor either.[9]

---

[7] Norwegian composer and conductor Johan Svendsen (1840–1911).

[8] The sonatas are *Violin Sonata No. 3* in C minor and *Violin Sonata No. 2* in G major.

[9] On February 12, 1895, Grieg was named an honorary member of the "Gesellschaft der Musikfreunde" in Vienna. The famous Czech composer Anton Dvořák (1841–1904) was awarded the same honor at the February 12 meeting. Grieg eventually received official notification of the honor and responded with a brief letter of thanks on February 15, 1896.

It is my intention to go to Berlin in the middle of this month. That is to say: I am thinking of first spending a week in Leipzig and then going on to Berlin. My wife is traveling with me; in Vienna, therefore, I need a double bedroom and a sitting room.

With that I hope that I have mentioned everything of prime importance. Looking forward to receiving further details, I am,

Sincerely yours,
EDVARD GRIEG

P.S. I would request that you also send the parts for the *Piano Concerto* to Berlin as they need revision.

5

Copenhagen, March 23, 1895
Hotel King of Denmark

Dear Mr. Gutmann!
I have finally crawled out of bed, and my first lines go to you. I am very disheartened about the disastrous confusion I have created in your papers. But what could I do? I can't do a thing about it. I have had an incredibly unpleasant bit of bad luck. The illness has taken such a hold on me that I know only too well how impossible it would have been to perform in public now. If I could only have hoped for a fourteen-day postponement, or maybe even just eight days, I would have come. But of course, with a foreign orchestra one is obviously bound to the day and time. And besides, Easter comes right afterward and then the Viennese have other things to do than go to concerts.

I need not tell you that I now feel obligated to accommodate your wishes regarding any date in the 1895–96 concert season. It would be especially nice if I could come right at the beginning of the season—ca. October. By then I will have recovered my strength in the Norwegian mountain air.

Let me above all learn via a few lines that you are not angry with me! I feel, to tell the truth, almost like a criminal; indeed, if you wish it I will make a pilgrimage to Rome in the hope that it will go better for me than it did for Tannhäuser![10]

So: with wistful regret, I am,

Sincerely yours,
EDVARD GRIEG

---

[10] Tannhäuser, in Wagner's opera by the same name, had to make a pilgrimage to Rome to beg for the pope's forgiveness for having sung a hymn in praise of Venus, goddess of carnal love. The pope refused to give him absolution.

6

Aulestad,[11] *Gausdal near Christiania, January 2, 1904*

Dear Mr. Gutmann!
Once again I have been sick abed. To regain my strength I have spent the Christmas holidays with my friend Bjørnson at his estate. But unfortunately the illness has taken such hold of me that I must simplify my spring tour. And so, regretfully, I must first cancel the long trip and the three concerts in Vienna. It is extremely painful to me to do this, but it has to be. I note in a letter from Johannes Wolff that he still has not heard from you. It would have been difficult, therefore, to count on his participation. It's a good thing for me, however, as this was very important to me. Oh well, who knows whether in a year I will be mobile enough to go to Vienna. I hope so.

And in this hope I wish you, your dear wife and your daughter—also on behalf of my wife—a happy new year!

Sincerely yours,
Edvard Grieg

Address: Hotel Westminster, Christiania.

7

Christiania, December 6, 1906
Hotel Westminster

Dear Mr. Gutmann!
I greatly regret that d'Albert cannot participate, not least because of the piano ballad.[12] It is most likely that you will be turned down by all the virtuosos who do not have my *Piano Concerto* in their repertoires, for it is almost unthinkable that they will learn a large work while they are on the road in the middle of the concert season. I take the liberty, therefore, of mentioning the following first-class artists who might be considered: 1) Carreño, 2) Pugno, 3) Arthur de Greef (Brussels), 4. L. Borwick (London), 5) Busoni.[13]

Please use this order when you send your inquiry. I think very well of Dohnányi, but he does not play my concerto. Mr. Lamond,[14] whose name I of course know, would not be acceptable since I have never heard him play and do not know how his art corresponds to mine. The first condition when it comes to choosing a performing artist is that the person in question have an understanding

---

[11] Aulestad was the estate—in Gausdal, near Lillehammer—of Grieg's friend Bjørnstjerne Bjørnson. Most non-Scandinavians would have been unfamiliar with either Gausdal or Lillehammer at that time, and this is presumably why Grieg wrote "near Christiania"—even though Christiania was more than a hundred miles south of Gausdal.

[12] Grieg's *Ballade in G Minor.*

[13] Teresa Carreño, Raoul Pugno, Arthur de Greef, Leonard Borwick (1868–1925) and Ferruccio Busoni (1866–1924).

[14] Scotch pianist Frederic Archibald Lamond (1868–1948).

of my music. With respect to the artists listed above, with whom I am personally acquainted, I know that this is the case.

I hope the arrangements with Mrs. Gulbranson[15] are proceeding favorably. With respectful greetings,

Sincerely yours,
EDVARD GRIEG

8

Christiania, December 23, 1906
Hotel Westminster

Dear Mr. Gutmann!
I am pleased to learn from your last letter that Mrs. Gulbranson has responded affirmatively to your inquiry. Hopefully Madame Carreño will also be able to make a commitment. If not, you will in any case find the needed replacement among the artists I have suggested. It should perhaps be emphasized that the artist in question must also play some of my solo pieces in addition to the *Piano Concerto.* Madame Carreño has a number of them in her repertoire, as do also De Greef and Borwick.

With regard to Bucharest, I cannot under any circumstances make that long trip for just one concert. If the planned second concert were to be a repetition of the first one, I am prepared to come for 3,000 francs—if the round trip travel expenses Berlin–Bucharest for my wife and me will be covered in addition to a room at a first-class hotel for two persons. If what is intended is two concerts with different programs, I would have to ask for 4,000 francs in addition to the above-mentioned travel and hotel expenses. I would be able to start from Berlin on April 14. But since for reasons of health I cannot travel at night, I probably could not get to Bucharest until the evening of April 16. The first concert could then take place after two or three orchestra rehearsals (depending on how much is needed). The last rehearsal must not, however, be held on the same day as the concert.

If my health should be so bad that my doctor cannot allow me to travel, I must be free of all obligations. Though I hope that this will not happen, I mention it nonetheless in order to avoid any misunderstanding. The selection of the program and choice of soloists must be left to me. These are my conditions, and I would be grateful to you for a clarification of these matters. At present I am free at the times indicated above, but nonetheless I should like just as soon as possible to have free hands.[16]

With warm wishes for a merry Christmas, I am,

Sincerely yours,
EDVARD GRIEG

---

[15] Swedish-Norwegian singer Ellen Nordgren Gulbranson (1863–1947).
[16] Nothing came of the plans for a concert in Bucharest.

To Nina Hagerup and her Sisters

Nina Hagerup (1845–1935) and Edvard Grieg were first cousins inasmuch as Nina's father, Herman Hagerup (1819–1900), was a brother of Gesine Grieg (1814–75), Edvard's mother. After Edvard had completed his studies in Leipzig in 1862, he spent a year in Bergen. Here, from "Aunt Mone's front room"—Aunt Mone was Modesta Grieg (1809–79), his father's sister—he wrote his first letter to Nina of which we have knowledge. It is evident from this letter that he wanted above all else to get to Copenhagen. In the second letter he goes so far as to describe Bergen as "the city of horrors".

In spring of 1863 Edvard got a loan from his father that enabled him to live in Denmark for a few months. The "dear cousins" to whom the letter is addressed were Nina, Tonny and Yelva, all of whom were living at that time with their parents in Aldersfred, Helsingør (Elsinore).

After Grieg's death, most of his letters to Nina were destroyed because of their intensely personal nature. The two that remain are preserved in Bergen Offentlige Bibliotek (Bergen Public Library).

1

[Bergen], February 23, 1863
Aunt Mone's front room, 5 P.M.

Dear cousins!

Auntie wants me to write you a few words on this note. Well, I'll obey, but I take no responsibility for any of the rubbish that will result. Although this note paper is very small I don't think I'm capable of filling it with any decent substance, for each day here passes like every other—no, that was a stupid way to say it. I mean that each day is as monotonous as every other, and whatever is monotonous is poison to me—so you can understand that it will be a great joy for me if I can go to Copenhagen in April as father has promised. Notwithstanding this promise, the old man is inwardly vexed any time I so much as hint at leaving. Yes, just a few days ago when father noted that we had April weather, and in connection therewith I expressed the wish that it really were April, he got unbelievably exasperated and gave me a sermon about what the youth of today are coming to. I've never heard the likes of it from his lips before. Well, that's how it is when things get to him, but thank God it doesn't happen often.

Well, look at this, the little thing is filled with writing. Adieu!

Sincere greetings from

Your devoted cousin,
EDVARD GRIEG

This famous portrait of Nina Grieg was made by German painter Franz von Lenbach in Rome in 1894. The original now hangs at Troldhaugen.

2

Copenhagen, July 14, 1863

Dear cousins!

Thanks for your letter. As usual, it naturally made me indescribably happy. Yes, I admit that even though I can't stand "Zukunftsmusik"[1] this nonetheless sounded sweet to my ears. I seemed to hear transfigured (improved by Nina) Schumannesque melodies sounding clear down here to me, etc. etc. But dear little Nina, I can hear you saying "no crudities"—so on to something else.

As for news that might be of interest to you, I know of none. *I*, on the other hand, am very much occupied with something that is anything but pleasant. About half an hour ago I slashed my left index finger. The instrument was a most ordinary bread knife about the usefulness (with respect to sharpness) of which I have been in serious doubt until today. But what a job it did! It slipped down from a poor four-skilling sandwich and gave me a deep slash all the way to the bone. For a quarter of an hour the blood gushed out in torrents. Well, there's nothing to do about it. I can say good-bye to the piano for several weeks.

But back once again to crudities! Nina, you did not succeed in writing me a letter without crudities. To the contrary, your whole letter is a crudity from beginning to end.[2]

---

[1] "Zukunftsmusik": music of the future.

[2] None of Nina's letters to Edvard are extant.

Surely you know, to begin with, that it is a crudity when you write that you are going to find out *if it is possible for you* to write without crudities, that the lofty expressions are crudities, that everything you write about Andersen[3] is a crudity, that your treatment of the civilized human being is a crudity, that the cute little parenthesis (her own words) is a crudity of the highest order—in a word, that the whole letter is a veritable "Satyre"[4] from the very first word. Still, as you very correctly observe, within the family all is forgiven; it's so good to have it on one's side.

For quite the same reasons I ask you to excuse this paper and this handwriting, neither of which could be described as being of prime quality—*but of course, within the family. . . !!*

The same day I got your letter I also received one from home. From it I learned that fat Bull (whom Uncle certainly knew) is dead and buried, further that Ole Bull[5] has given three concerts in the city of horrors—concerts in which mother has accompanied him as he played original compositions as well as works by Paganini.[6]

So long for this time. Warm greetings, write again soon. You can thank my finger for this terribly long pile of nonsense.

Most cordially,
EDVARD GRIEG

---

[3] Danish author of children's stories Hans Christian Andersen (1805–75).

[4] Grieg presumably means *satire.*

[5] Norwegian virtuoso violinist Ole Bull (1810–80).

[6] Grieg's mother, who received professional training as both a singer and a pianist, played an important role in Bergen's music life. She was considered the city's best piano teacher, and it was she who gave Edvard his first piano lessons. Violin virtuoso Ole Bull, regarded by many as the equal of the Italian virtuoso Nicolò Paganini (1782–1840), had an enormously important influence on Edvard Grieg. He was a kind of "shirt-tail relative" of both Edvard and Nina: His brother Jens Munthe Bull (1815–1905) was married to Edvard and Nina's aunt, Johanne Margrethe Hagerup (1817–88), who was a sister of Edvard's mother and Nina's father. The identity of the "fat Bull" to whom Grieg refers is unknown.

To Charles Hallé

The English pianist and conductor Charles Hallé (1819–95) was born in Germany and received his musical training there as well. In 1836 he went to Paris, where he became acquainted with Chopin, Liszt, Berlioz and Wagner, and he became the first pianist to perform all of Beethoven's piano sonatas in the French capital. Later he performed the same feat in London. In 1848 he left Paris and settled down in London, which he had visited for the first time in 1843. He did not find London to his liking, however, and upon receiving an invitation from Manchester he moved there and immediately initiated a revitalization of the city's music life. In 1858 he launched the Hallé concert series, which in time became very famous, and he continued to conduct and perform as a pianist at these concerts until 1895. In 1893 he also became Director and Professor of Piano at a new music conservatory in Manchester.

Charles Hallé was knighted in 1888. That same year he married the Czech violinist Wilhelmina Neruda (1838–1911), and thereafter they concertized together in England, Australia and South Africa.

Grieg conducted the Hallé orchestra at a concert in Manchester on February 28, 1889.

The first and third of Grieg's extant letters to Charles Hallé are preserved in Bergen Offentlige Bibliotek (Bergen Public Library), the second is owned by Tore Severeide Johansen of Moss, Norway. All were written in German.

1

Leipzig, February 13, 1889

Dear Maestro Hallé!

Since writing to you about four weeks ago[1]—in a very somber mood, as a matter of fact—my health has taken such a fortunate turn that I feel that I have gotten a new enthusiasm for life. Therefore I cannot refuse the pleasure of doing something extravagant, so I will make an attempt with respect to the 28th of February,[2] even though I fear that my offer comes too late.

So: It would be an honor for me—since I will be free at that precise time—to play my *Piano Concerto* with you on the day specified and also to conduct an orchestral piece (perhaps my *Two Elegiac Melodies* for string orchestra, assuming that you have enough strings). I do not wish for an honorarium, only reimbursement for travel expenses and hotel for me and my wife.

I repeat: I would consider it an honor to collaborate with you in your concert, and in order that you in any case can see my sincere desire to accommodate your wishes, all that remains is to send these lines and at the last minute hope for a happy result.

---

[1] The letter to which Grieg refers is not extant.

[2] Grieg mistakenly wrote the 29th. At the concert in Manchester Grieg conducted *Two Elegiac Melodies* and the *Piano Concerto* in A minor, the latter with Charles Hallé as soloist. He also performed his *Violin Sonata No. 1* with Mrs. Hallé (Wilhelmine Neruda) and accompanied Nina in some of his songs.

We are coming to London on February 17. I must participate in "Popular Concerts" on the 23rd and 25th, but I could be in Manchester as early as the 25th if necessary.

Please address your reply to London, 5 The Cedars, Clapham Common (Mr. Augener).

With most cordial greetings,

Sincerely yours,
EDVARD GRIEG

2

[London], February 20, 1889

Dear Maestro Hallé!
Since no one understands Norwegian, perhaps it would be a good idea if I could see a proof of the texts (NB, if time permits).

E. G.

P.S. I hope that you are using the printed (not the autograph) score, for otherwise there will be a lot of trouble and disagreements.

3

Leipzig, February 2, 1893
Thalstrasse 10 (Edition Peters)

Dear Maestro Hallé!
I have only one excuse for my long silence, but it—unfortunately—is a very good one. I have been sick. The truth is that I am still sick, but nonetheless I do not want to delay my answer any longer. Accept, therefore, my warmest thanks for your good advice regarding the matter mentioned in my last letter. Richter,[3] with the greatest cordiality and interest in the matter, has been obliging, so I hope that the end of the story will be that one fine day I will have the pleasure of welcoming you and your wife as our guests.

In this hope, and with the best wishes, also from my wife, I remain,

Sincerely yours,
EDVARD GRIEG

---

[3] The Austro-Hungarian conductor Hans Richter (1843–1916). See Grieg's letter to Richter of January, 1893, regarding a possible performance of the opera fragment *Scenes from "Olav Trygvason"* in summer 1893. The plans did not work out, and the performance did not occur. The "last letter" mentioned in the previous sentence is not extant.

To Sigurd Hals

Sigurd Hals (1859–1931) was the son of Karl Hals (1822–98), who, together with his brother Peter Hals (1823–71), had founded the firm Brødrene Hals (The Hals Brothers) in Christiania in 1847. In 1883 Sigurd Hals joined the firm, and two years later his brother, Thor Hals (1852–1924), did the same. At first the firm built only studio pianos, but in 1852 it began to build grand pianos and in 1886, harmoniums. The instruments made by the Hals Brothers were highly regarded at the time. In 1880 the firm opened its own concert hall and at the same time launched a concert bureau. In 1887 they also established a music publishing division and a music store.

Grieg's extensive correspondence with Sigurd Hals is preserved in Bergen Offentlige Bibliotek (Bergen Public Library).

1

Copenhagen, November 14, 1885
Hotel King of Denmark

Dear Sigurd!
Thank you for the famous telegram. I just about died laughing when I saw "Melodrama by Berlioz" in the newspaper. And so did many others around me who heard about it.[1]

I will remain in your debt for the time being, but I promise not to run off to America.

This evening I am conducting a concert here with *Land-sighting* (solo by Simonsen[2]), *Before a Southern Convent* (solo by Nina) and *Holberg Suite.* Yesterday's rehearsal went very well. The only things the lovable Danish nation is missing in life are rhythms. It's enough to make you fly off the handle when you stand there with a baton in your hand.

Ask Ole[3] to send me a postcard telling me how *Bergliot* went at the later performance—or somebody else if Ole wasn't there. And lastly, ask your father to let me see more of him next time. Tell him it was the biggest disappointment during my stay in Christiania that I did not get to see him oftener.

Svendsen[4] lives just a few rooms away from us. He is as spry as a twenty-year-old.

---

[1] Grieg's melodrama *Bergliot* op. 42, a setting of a text by Norwegian author Bjørnstjerne Bjørnson (1832–1910), was premiered in Christiania on November 3, 1885, by Norwegian actress Laura Gundersen (1832–98) with Grieg conducting. Grieg's allusion to a "Melodrama by Berlioz in the newspaper" evidently is an amusing typographic error whereby "the melodrama *Bergliot*" was referred to as "the melodrama by Berlioz."

[2] Danish baritone Niels Juel Simonsen (1846–1906).

[3] Norwegian composer and conductor Ole Olsen (1850–1927), brother-in-law of Sigurd Hals.

[4] Norwegian composer and conductor Johan Svendsen (1840–1911), who in 1883 had become musical director at the Royal Theater in Copenhagen.

Greetings to you, my dear Sigurd, to Thor and his wife, to your fiancee, to the old man and Ole and family from

Yours truly,
EDVARD GRIEG

2

Brussels, December 6, 1889

Dear Sigurd!
Under separate cover I am sending you various reviews to be translated and hopefully reproduced in all the Christiania newspapers. After the main event—the concert tomorrow—I will send you some more. There is tremendous appreciation of my music here. I had never imagined the possibility of such a thing. Monday we leave for Paris.

Warm greetings.

Sincerely yours,
EDVARD GRIEG

P.S. You write nothing about my *Funeral March* at Neupert's funeral. How did it sound? Thank you for arranging for a wreath! Nordgren[5] left from here for Stockholm on the 3rd and will be staying in Copenhagen for two days en route.

Address in Paris: 16, rue de Sèze, Hotel de Sèze.

3

[Brussels, December 9, 1889]

Dear Sigurd!
In all haste: I received the enclosed item from Elliot & Fry[6] recently, but the bill has been paid, hasn't it? If not you must by all means pay it immediately on my behalf. As you will recall, I paid you my half when I was in Christiania.

The concert yesterday was splendid in every way.[7] But to send a telegram about my own you-know-what—that's something I won't do. This evening, unfortunately, I am sick and have to stay in because of a fever. Tomorrow we leave for Paris. Unfortunately it didn't help that you did not send me a report of Neupert's funeral. I got it from Mrs. Neupert[8]—and it was like a stab in my heart

[5] Ellen Nordgren Gulbranson (1863–1947).
[6] Elliot & Fry, photographers in London.
[7] Grieg gave three concerts in Brussels: November 30 and December 2 and 8, 1889. The pianist Arthus de Greef participated in all three concerts.
[8] Hilda Elisabeth Neupert (1848–1934).

when I read about Rossini's funeral march.[9] Yes, yes, silence is golden—but this is a sacrilege for which there is *no* excuse. God help me, how petty we are there in Norway!

Cordial greetings.

Sincerely yours,
EDVARD GRIEG

4

Paris, December 17, 1889
Hotel de Sèze, 16, rue de Sèze

Dear Sigurd!

How can you say that I have *upbraided* you. Something in connection with my *Funeral March*? I have not done so. Not a single word. I expressed to you my indignation about what had happened, and I thought you and I knew each other well enough that I could do that. I am not quick to express myself—quite the opposite—but I have learned to like you and have come to have confidence in you, so it seemed very natural to me to let my feelings come out. How you can take offense at this is incomprehensible to me. I don't want to be so hogtied that I can't speak to my best friends about things that trouble me. That is why I also wrote to you, and I believed it was *intentionally* that you had not sent me the newspaper accounts of Neupert's funeral. I credited you with—for the sake of friendship—not wanting to contribute to creating unnecessary annoyance for me. That would in any case be a beautiful characteristic that could be hereditary, for I still remember as if it were yesterday a lovely evening many years ago when your father deliberately refrained from telling me that I had been vilified in *Signale*[10]—and I have many times been grateful to him for this. You, to be sure, are much younger, but still, you must understand this way of thinking. In your last letter you sound almost as if you are stepping aside, and you're not permitted to do so with me, dear Sigurd—me, who wish you only what is good. Unfortunately, whether you find the right target for my reproaches or not makes no difference. I only know that what was done was done out of either ill will or ineptness—or both—and besides, I really don't want to have anything to do with that kind of stuff. Perhaps you don't understand how deeply I have been offended. It was a sacred promise to a deceased friend. However: I will say no more about it.

---

[9] Norwegian pianist Edmund Neupert (b. 1842), who died in New York City on June 22, 1888, was buried in Christiania on November 26, 1889. It is evident from Grieg's letter to Hals of December 17, 1889, that Grieg had given Neupert his word of honor that his (Grieg's) *Funeral March in Memory of Rikard Nordraak* (EG 107) would be played at Neupert's funeral. Grieg thought this understanding between Neupert and himself was well known in Christiania, and he reacted angrily when he learned that a funeral march by Italian composer Gioacchino Rossini (1792–1862) had been played instead.

[10] The German music journal *Signale für die musikalische Welt*, Leipzig.

Thank you for the newspapers and sheet music. I will have my first orchestra rehearsal with Colonne's orchestra[11] the day after tomorrow. However: I have been sick with influenza ever since I came here. I am inordinately weak and decrepit, so I will more than likely have to bow out altogether. It's a nice kettle of fish, but it must be handled without regard to personal safety.

Greet your poor wife. Good God! Five weeks is a long time. She must drink quinine water. That's what I do. She can be glad she isn't here. If I get home alive I will send the gods a hymn of thanksgiving!

Warm greetings and merry Christmas to all of you!

Sincerely yours,
EDVARD GRIEG

5

Copenhagen, December 26, 1890
Hotel King of Denmark

Dear Sigurd!
I am still sufficiently alive that I will not let the old year pass without thanking you for it—and also for your Christmas greeting with the "Pilots".[12] Down here Christmas has been largely overshadowed by Gade's death.[13] Just think: Sunday morning he was with us in the café, where he sat for a long time and chatted with us. He was in high spirits and seemed more animated than ever. That evening he died suddenly; the next morning I saw him cold and pale—but smiling in death! If one could pass away like that there would be nothing to it. He will be buried on Monday. Naturally memorial wreaths are streaming in from all over Europe.

I just finished reading *Aftenposten*, and I see that Winter-Hjelm is not pleased with Beyer's songs[14]—nor with anything, I think, except Olsen's *Intrepid*.[15] Lawdamighty!

Moreover, it makes a strange impression on me to see all—yes, all—the new works discussed except mine. Am I living or dead? If I am dead, fortunately it is

---

[11] On December 22, 1889, Grieg conducted his *Piano Concerto* with the Colonne orchestra, whose regular conductor was the Frenchman Édouard Colonne (1838–1910). The soloist on this occasion was Belgian pianist Arthur de Greef (1862–1940).

[12] Grieg is referring to a book—*Lodser* (*Pilots*)—that had just been published by Norwegian author Christian Krohg (1852–1925). The book was illustrated by Krohg himself, a leading figure in Norwegian cultural life around the turn of the century who made his mark both as a painter and as a writer. The "pilots" are, of course, boat pilots.

[13] Danish composer Niels Wilhelm Gade (b. 1817) died on December 21, 1890.

[14] Grieg's close friend in Bergen, Frants Beyer (1851–1918), an attorney who was also a capable amateur pianist, had at Grieg's suggestion published some songs that he (Beyer) had composed. Otto Winter-Hjelm (1837–1931) was music critic for *Aftenposten*, a newspaper published in Christiania.

[15] Grieg is referring here to Ole Olsen's incidental music to *Svein Uræd* (*Svein the Intrepid*), a fairy-tale comedy by Norwegian author Nordahl Rolfsen (1848–1928). The play was premiered at the Central Theater in Christiania on March 4, 1890.

only in Norway—and maybe Denmark. Of course I understand very well how it all hangs together—and I hold my tongue.

Thanks, too, for the newspapers and clippings. Yes, that was one sorry mess! It would have been tempting to speak my mind. But damned if I am going to get my hands any dirtier than I have to!

Happy New Year, dear Sigurd, to you and yours, and greetings to all of you!

Sincerely yours,
EDVARD GRIEG

P.S. Thank Ole Olsen for his letter. I will write soon.

6

Copenhagen, January 18, 1891
Hotel King of Denmark

Dear Sigurd!
(. . .) Recently I had two great pleasures. One was a telegram from St. Petersburg signed by a whole bunch of Russian musicians reporting that my *String Quartet* had scored a great success there. The other was an elegant certificate from Geneva making me an honorary member of "Deutsche Liedertafel" ("German Glee Club") in that city. When someone is stagnating as I am doing these days, this sort of thing affects me like a *Lebenswecker.*[16]

I wish I had stayed in Christiania this winter, for the situation here is worse than deadly. And then there is all the artistic pettiness now after Gade's death. Lucky are those who are not a part of it. I have also been mentioned as Gade's successor in the Music Association, but I respectfully decline—and if it keeps on, I am going to state publicly that I do not aspire to this honor. People go around here looking askance at me as if I wanted to take the bread out of the mouths of the honorable Danish gentlemen. We Norwegians are less popular than ever—and it's a good thing, too, for it demonstrates once and for all that we are two different nations, with totally different ideals.

Greet your sweet wife and the whole family from both of us.

Sincerely yours,
EDVARD GRIEG

---

[16] *Lebenswecker*: something that awakens to life.

7

Leipzig, January 14, 1897
Address C. F. Peters, Thalstrasse 10

Dear Sigurd!
Don't tell anyone yet, but it is possible that I will be taking a trip to Finland and Russia in March. In this connection, will you do me the great favor of getting me a diplomatic passport? Presumably you will have to apply directly to Hagerup.[17] However, you yourself know best how to go about it. Send it to me at the above address as soon as possible.

We have just returned here from Vienna, where I was forced to stay for almost two months because of illness. But fortunately my three concerts there went splendidly. We won't be going to Amsterdam until February. I will be conducting there and in The Hague.

I was surprised to learn via a letter from Amsterdam that Mrs. Gulbranson, who was engaged a long time ago to sing in *Olav Trygvason*, [op. 50] *Before a Southern Convent* [op. 20] and *Six Songs with Orchestra* [EG 177], has sent word that she cannot come *for reasons of health*. She hasn't communicated a word of this to me personally, but nonetheless I don't doubt that the report is true. Well, I'll have to get along as best I can. Fortunately Europe has other talented singers, but I feel bad for Mrs. Gulbranson, whose singing of Wagner is beginning to take its toll. Is she very sick, and what is wrong with her? Both Nina and I are very sorry to hear of her illness.

And now, farewell for today. Warm greetings from both of us, also to Antonie!

Sincerely yours,
EDVARD GRIEG

P.S. Please ask the people preparing the diplomatic passport to exercise discretion until it is decided whether or not the trip is going to occur. It is strictly a matter of health, and I don't want people talking about it until it is firmed up.

8

[Copenhagen],[18] April 30, 1902

Dear Sigurd!
I have just received your letter en route northward from Warsaw. Since I do not know Bjørnson's address in Stockholm, I am requesting that you kindly send him these lines.

---

[17] Norwegian attorney and politician Francis Hagerup (1853–1921), who headed a coalition government during the years 1895–98.

[18] The stationery on which this letter was written is from "Der Kaiserhof" in Berlin, but the letter is dated April 30, 1902, and Grieg was in Copenhagen at that time.

I, too, find Vigeland's[19] model very moving as an expression of pent-up power. But Nordraak's power was not pent-up. Quite the opposite. He died quite simply from an altogether too great consumption of power. So the symbolism is all wrong.

And then: On the 17th of May,[20] shall the Norwegian people use their tribute for this product of imagination that has no more to do with Nordraak than the cat? Even if a thousand authorities support it, they do not outweigh my own common sense that says: No. I have told Werenskiold[21] the same thing.

If we get enough money I would like to go along with acquiring Vigeland's model (NB when the symbolism is changed) as a relief on the pedestal. But then the bust must be at the top. We certainly are not committed to Vigeland to do the bust, since he has not expressed interest in this task.

This, then, is my standpoint today. And I hope in the course of further conversation with Werenskiold to come to a concept that is acceptable to both of us. When I was in a meeting with Werenskiold and he urged so strongly that we give the artist a free hand, I jokingly asked, "Is it not even permissible to tell the artist that what we want is a bust of Rikard Nordraak?" Well, it is now clear that this question was right on target.

One thing is certain: I will not be a party to using the money I have worked so hard to gather for this purpose in a manner that is contrary to my conviction.[22] And this conviction is so strong that I— despite the fact that I am an amateur in this area—cannot submit to Werenskiold's considerable professional authority. And I have also told this to Werenskiold.[23]

Warsaw was unique in my experience.[24] Never before have I enjoyed such enthusiasm. The concert that was supposed to last from 8 to 10 was still not over at 11 o'clock, and it wasn't encores that were responsible, because I rarely

---

[19] Norwegian sculptor Gustav Vigeland (1869–1943) had been commissioned to create a monument honoring Rikard Nordraak (1842–66), the creator of the melody of the Norwegian national anthem.

[20] May 17 is Norway's Constitution Day.

[21] Norwegian painter Erik Werenskiold (1855–1938).

[22] As early as April 28, 1900, Grieg had given a concert in Christiania to raise money for a Nordraak monument in that city. He had also participated in a benefit concert in Bergen on October 5, 1901, for the same purpose. See Grieg's letter to Bjørnstjerne Bjørnson of January 16, 1900.

[23] Erik Werenskiold was artistic advisor to the committee making plans for the Nordraak monument in Christiania. Gustav Vigeland was given the commission to design the monument and in 1902 presented a model in which a nude, heroic Nordraak figure sits facing the mountains, playing the piano. Grieg rejected this design. Vigeland, in accordance with Grieg's wish, then tried to work the performing figure into a relief at the bottom of a high plinth on which rested a realistic bust of Nordraak. Grieg didn't like this either, but he finally agreed to allow Vigeland to sculpt a whole figure for the same honorarium as he was to have received for just the bust. Grieg did not live to see the statue erected, however. It was indeed finished by 1905, but it could not be unveiled at Nordraak Square on Wergeland Street in Christiania until 1911—four years after Grieg's death. In the meantime Vigeland had received permission to construct a cast-iron fence around the monument as well as two chained dragons sitting in the front, probably because he thought the statue was a bit tame. The portion of Grieg's letter to Hals in which he discusses the Nordraak monument was sent by Hals to Bjørnson as Grieg requested.

[24] Grieg's concert in Warsaw took place April 22, 1902.

responded to such requests out of concern for the exhausted orchestra. No, it was just ovations. Finally I took a curtain call with my overcoat on, and then they followed me along the aisles, down the steps, out into the vestibule and finally out on the street, where crowds of people stood shouting.

So much for that. But the orchestra! Never have I heard the *Peer Gynt Suite* and the "Homage March" from *Sigurd Jorsalfar* performed so brilliantly. As a matter of fact, I have had to promise to come back again next year. People tell me that nobody—absolutely nobody—has been received like that before, not even the Poles' own Paderewski.[25] I don't understand it. But I sense a deep sympathy for Norway's aspirations in the air. That explains a lot.

And farewell for now! See you soon. Warmest greetings to all!

Sincerely yours,
EDVARD GRIEG

9

Troldhaugen at Hop, August 4, 1905

Dear friend!

I heard one day recently that you were making progress, albeit slowly. I hope that is the case. But the fact that you have not yet gone to the spa is evidence that you are not strong enough to go. Yes, it is a son-of-a-gun of an illness. And precisely of the kind that demands a radical cure. But you will have to put up with that. It simply won't do to say "to hell with it" about such things. Knowing you, I'm sure that's what you would sort of like to do. As young as you are, it should be possible to accomplish great things if the problem is attacked head-on. It's worse for an old graybeard like me, who just has to give up. Now you must see to it that you get so much out of your summer up there that we can get together over some delicious oysters in the fall.

We are thinking of spending the winter in Christiania. We have not secured lodging yet. We probably will come in the first half of September, and there should still be hope of securing something then.

I was supposed to be going to Finland in September to conduct two concerts with the Philharmonic Orchestra from Warsaw. But I have recently sent word that I won't be coming. I can't travel through Sweden in view of the way people are acting in that country.[26] And say, hasn't everything been turned upside down?

---

25 Polish pianist and composer Ignaz Paderewski (1860–1941).

26 Norway had been an unwilling partner in a political union with Sweden since 1814, but on June 7, 1905, the Norwegian Parliament (Stortinget) had declared Norway's independence. Thus relations between Norway and Sweden were very tense at the time this letter was written. See also Grieg's diary entries for November and December, 1905, in Benestad & Halverson (eds.), *Edvard Grieg: Diaries, Articles, Speeches* (Columbus, Ohio, 2001).

We are supposed to be the barbarians and the Swedes the old, chivalrous, noble people of culture—and now we see that the very opposite is the case. All that culture appears to be merely on the surface. There is indeed a crudeness in the leaders' way of thinking in that country that fortunately is foreign to us: It does not look good. The desire for war that in fact is present is part and parcel of this crudeness—despite all the speeches about a peaceful resolution. I will not be surprised the day the dreaded event occurs, i.e., that we are attacked. I will be much more surprised if the storm passes over.

Yesterday Michelsen[27] came home to Bergen—in poorer condition healthwise, unfortunately. If only he could soon get this matter settled and then step down. That is what he most desires. And then he will have earned the gratitude of his countrymen as no one else since 1814. Then it was Christie[28] who negotiated with the Swedes' delegates. It's actually kind of interesting how much these two are alike. Both with a cold head and a warm heart—precisely what is needed.

Yes, it is a proud time in which to be living. I get scads of congratulatory letters from abroad. People envy us our government. And with good reason, as a matter of fact. What impresses me more than almost anything else is the fact that the government has managed to keep the press in check. But that cannot last long. For that reason we must hope for a *quick* solution, otherwise the whole process will collapse.

Everyone here sends you the warmest greetings. So also, with wishes for steady improvement, does

Sincerely yours,
EDVARD GRIEG

P.S. If you yourself are not able to write, then Antonie must please send a few words on a postcard. Just so that we know how you are getting along.

---

[27] Prime Minister Christian Michelsen (1857–1925).

[28] Wilhelm Frimann Koren Christie (1778–1849), one of the framers of the Norwegian constitution, who in his capacity as president of the Norwegian Parliament (Stortinget) participated in the negotiations with King Carl Johan (1764–1844) regarding the terms of the obligatory union with Sweden. Christie's success in negotiating terms more favorable to Norway than had been anticipated won the praise and gratitude of his countrymen. Christie was a first cousin of Grieg's maternal grandfather, Edvard Hagerup (1781–1853). A statue of Christie was unveiled in Bergen on May 17, 1868, and Grieg wrote a cantata for the occasion (EG 158) that has been printed in facsimile in *Edvard Grieg: Complete Works*, vol. 16. The text is by Norwegian author Andreas Munch (1811–84).

10

London, May 23, 1906
46 Grosvenor Street, W.

Dear Sigurd!
I have just received word of Henrik Ibsen's death.[29] Please arrange for a beautiful wreath with a silk ribbon and the words "From Nina and Edvard Grieg." I have just sent a telegram to Mrs. Ibsen, but I assume that this letter will reach you in time. Ibsen's death was, of course, expected, but even so it casts an exceedingly somber mood over my concert preparations. I wish I were home.

Things have gone well for me beyond all expectation, so to date I have fulfilled my commitments with flying colors. Tomorrow is the last concert, and there is no way that I can be persuaded to give more.[30] For pre-concert stage fright is just like seasickness: It gets worse and worse as the years go by.

London is a terrible city for a person with a well-known name. Several hundred letters are lying on my desk that I have not even had time to open. There are obligations all over the place. And then these female singers! To hell with the lot of them! They are as stupid as they are conceited. And these journalists! Interviewers by the dozens—but I won't talk to a single one of them, as a result of which I have to put up with a few churlish newspapers. But you should have been at the first concert and seen the audience.

The 17th of May[31] was fun. And then the party that evening: Nansen[32] is marvelous. He spoke in such a way that tears came to my eyes.

I hope that we will see each other in the middle of June. Warm greetings to all!

Sincerely yours,
EDVARD GRIEG

---

[29] Upon hearing of Henrik Ibsen's death on May 23, Grieg made the following entry in his diary: "How much I owe him! Poor, great Ibsen! He was not a happy man, for it is as if he carried within him a chunk of ice that would not melt. But beneath this chunk of ice lay a fervent love of humankind."

[30] Grieg was in England May 10–31, 1906, during which period he gave three concerts. In the first two he conducted. In the last—in Queen's Hall on May 24—he performed as a pianist.

[31] May 17 is Constitution Day in Norway.

[32] The famous explorer Fridtjof Nansen (1861–1930)was Norway's first ambassador to England.

To Johan Halvorsen

Johan Halvorsen (1864–1935) was a native of Drammen, a port city about twenty miles southwest of Christiania. He made his public debut as a violinist at the age of eighteen and soon began an active career as a soloist both in Norway and abroad. In 1893 he became conductor of Harmonien, predecessor of the modern Bergen Philharmonic Orchestra, and also musical director of The National Stage in Bergen. In 1899 he became the first musical director of the newly established National Theater in Christiania. Halvorsen was also an excellent composer. In 1894 he married Annie Grieg (1873–1957), daughter of Edvard Grieg's brother John (1840–1901). Grieg and Halvorsen first became acquainted in 1887, when they both spent several months in Leipzig.

Most of Grieg's letters to Halvorsen are preserved in Bergen Offentlige Bibliotek (Bergen Public Library). The rest are in Nasjonalbiblioteket, Oslo (National Library of Norway, Oslo Division).

1

Copenhagen, February 12, 1895
Hotel King of Denmark

Dear Halvorsen!
So: Your superbly orchestrated *Boyars*[1] resounded throughout the grand auditorium of the Concert Palace at 4:30 in the afternoon on Sunday. It sounded great and, as I said in my telegram, the conductor took several curtain calls. His name is Joachim Andersen.[2] He started out as an outstanding flutist playing for operas and concerts in Berlin and later alternated with Kogel[3] as conductor of the popular philharmonic concerts in Berlin and at the Scheveningen spa.[4] He is an excellent conductor—not brilliant, but intelligent and experienced. The concert will be repeated next Sunday afternoon at the same time. Andersen is engaged for the summer for a big undertaking in Lübeck—a north-European exposition. Each day he will conduct a concert consisting primarily of Nordic music, and yesterday he asked if he might use your piece there. I thought I could speak on your behalf and I said yes.

But now, with respect to the matter of getting it published I have been so bold as to tell Hansen[5] that I represent you and that he must, therefore, deal with me. If he had approached you directly he would certainly have tried to avoid paying an honorarium. But remembering how I was treated in my youth, I want to make damn sure the same thing doesn't happen to you. So: Let me handle the matter. I will do the best I can.

---

[1] *Bojarernes Indtogsmarsch* (*Entrance of the Boyars*), Halvorsen's best-known composition. It was composed in 1893 for the small theater orchestra at The National Stage in Bergen and was re-orchestrated for full orchestra in 1894.
[2] Danish flutist, conductor and composer Joachim Andersen (1847–1909).
[3] German conductor Gustav Friedrich Kogel (1849–1921), who in 1887–91 was musical director of the Berlin Philharmonic orchestra.
[4] At that time an ocean spa on the outskirts of The Hague.
[5] Copenhagen music publisher Wilhelm Hansen (1854–1923).

But there is one thing you must do *immediately*: Prepare a piano reduction that is well adapted to the piano and that sounds good on the instrument—even if you have to leave out some of the witticisms. And one more thing! I am displeased in that after the trio you do not repeat the G-major section. That is unfortunate and must still be subject to change. So: Get going on the piano reduction today!

The reviewers' comments on your piece are so brief that they do not lend themselves to reprinting in the papers at home. It's better if you just announce that the piece has been performed [in Copenhagen] and that it was well received.

We speak often of you and look forward to seeing you this summer!

Warm greetings to both of you from Nina and from

Yours truly,
EDVARD GRIEG

P.S. Send the piano reduction *to me*: Hotel King of Denmark!

2

Copenhagen, March 25, 1895
Hotel King of Denmark

Dear Halvorsen!

I hope you have heard of my illness, for otherwise you must have thought me to be remarkably disinterested—and that I am not. So: Back to the "Boyars"! I have carefully studied your two piano reductions and, like you, I have found the second one better than the first. But not nearly good enough—that I had to say to myself at once. Either no piano reduction or else one that "fits the fingers". Much of your later version could be used, of course, but the whole thing has to be totally redone. Well, before I knew what I was doing I had produced something else myself. I then wrote this down and—in the hope that I was acting in your best interests—gave it to Wilhelm Hansen. He thought it was just fine and wanted—on the condition that I would attach my name as the arranger of the piano reduction—to change the financial arrangements such that you will receive 400 crowns in cash and, if it becomes a success, a share in the profits at a later time. Since I have nothing at all against having arranged the "Boyar" march, of which I am so fond, I agreed on your behalf. If you have any objection, just say so. You will not see any expression of chagrin on my part as a result. But as I have said, I think you will benefit by welcoming Wilhelm Hansen's proposal with open arms, for it is quite *unusually* favorable.[6]

---

[6] With Halvorsen's approval, the piano reduction of *Entrance of the Boyars* (EG 187) was published with Grieg's name as arranger on the title page. When Halvorsen visited Copenhagen in the summer of 1896, Chr. F. E. Horneman (1840–1906) told him that the publisher had earned a great deal of money from the piece. Halvorsen never received a share in these profits, but the foundation was laid for a life-long business relationship between composer and publisher.

I am still confined to my room, but as soon as I can go out I will get the papers in order for you and send you the result. Regarding my arrangement there isn't a lot to say. It is easy to play, and often with only a slight change is made to "fit the fingers" better and to sound better as well. For it is your intention that Misses Pedersen, Olsen, Larsen etc. will want to sit and give it a try, is it not?

Couldn't you send me a nickel's worth of enthusiasm for life! For the influenza has taken away every shred of that which I had. A wretched illness! But—I am counting on Norway! It has helped me many times before when I was at my wit's end. I had to cable Vienna that I was not coming. There was nothing else to do.

I hope we will see each other in May. Fortunately I have enough feeling that I can still look forward to something with childlike excitement!

Warmest greetings to the *trio*!

Yours truly,
EDVARD GRIEG

P.S. If you see the Beyers,[7] greet them warmly.

3

Leipzig, April 2, 1896
Hotel Hauffe

Dear Friend and Kinsman!
I beg your pardon? Do you want to supplant my *Peer Gynt Suite*? If so, then it's high time I learn to handle a revolver. Moreover, you must not suppose that you were telling me anything new. No, of course you forget that there is something called reporters and something else called the telegraph. Two days after the performance of *Vasantasena*[8] I read in *Verdens Gang*[9] here in Leipzig about the success your music had achieved. From this I can well understand that here you have found your way to the very center of your talent. I will only hope that this center is so large and so flexible that you will be able to pluck one *Vasantasena* out of another, like Chinese boxes.[10] Thank you for offering to dedicate this to

---

[7] Frants Beyer (1851–1918) and his wife Marie (1852–1929).

[8] Halvorsen had composed incidental music for the staging of the Indian play *Vasantasena* at The National Stage in Bergen in 1896. The premiere performance had occurred on March 24. Somewhat later he arranged this music in a suite for full orchestra. Grieg is suggesting good-naturedly that this music was good enough to eclipse his *Peer Gynt* suites. *Vasantasena* was attributed to the Indian King Çudraka, who lived ca. 400 A.D. During the nineteenth century the play was produced in various languages in theaters throughout Europe.

[9] *Verdens Gang* was a newspaper published in Christiania.

[10] Grieg's characterization of Halvorsen's special talent as a composer of stage music proved to be prophetic. During his tenure as musical director at the National Theater in Christiania, Halvorsen wrote incidental music for about thirty plays.

me. I accept it with pleasure—even if my *Peer Gynt Suite* goes down the drain as a result! I admire you for finding time to write such a large work in the midst of all your activity. And still, when I think back, it is just when one is your age that one can do everything at once without blinking an eye.

We have had a very difficult time. Perhaps you know that Nina had to undergo a breast operation which, it seems to me, has greatly exhausted her. (But don't report this to the old folks and Tonny!)[11] You can understand what it was like, under such circumstances, to go on alone to Vienna. Something always goes wrong. Were it not for this, these days would have been among the most beautiful days of my life. You should have heard the strings!! And such people, such a city! Joy, a capacity for enthusiasm, kindness, spontaneity. Yes, I don't know of any other group of people like them![12]

We hope to be home early in May! Guess if I am looking forward to it and longing! Warm greetings to all three of you!

Greet Müllers[13] and congratulate them most warmly!

Yours truly,
EDVARD GRIEG

4

Leipzig, January 26, 1897
C. F. Peters, Thalstrasse 10

Dear Halvorsen!
Before I leave "das grosse Vaterland"—in order to clear my conscience in relation to you—I want to send you a few words with thanks for your letters. Not merely to clear my conscience, however, but because yesterday Dr. Abraham[14] asked me to tell you that he would like to have both your score to *Vasantasena* and your honorarium requirements as soon as possible—both because he wants to get the matter taken care of and because he wants to get the work engraved in time to avoid a mad rush with proofreading and such. So: Dr. Abraham is aware that *I* have suggested 800–1,000 German marks. (Parenthetically, I told him that the piece was well worth 1,000. Hm!) I remember that I recommended to you that you ask for 800, but if you have not already done so, just say 1,000. Strike while the iron is hot. Who the hell knows when the opportunity will come again.

---

[11] Grieg is referring to Nina's parents, Herman Hagerup (1816–1900) and his wife Adeline (1813–1907) and to her sister, Tonny Hagerup (1844–1939).

[12] On March 24, 1896, Grieg had conducted a concert in Vienna with soprano Ellen Nordgren Gulbranson (1863–1947) and pianist Dagmar Walle-Hansen (1871–1954) as soloists.

[13] The actor Ludvig Müller (1868–1922) and his wife, the actress Signe Grieg (1868–1960), who was a daughter of John Grieg and a sister of Annie Grieg Halvorsen.

[14] Dr. Max Abraham (1831–1900), proprietor of the distinguished C. F. Peters music publishing house in Leipzig, was Grieg's good friend as well as the publisher of most of his compositions.

Unfortunately, Abraham—so it seems to me—does not have much time left to live. And his successor is of a completely different caliber.[15] So: Go to it.

Believe me, having had both a personal friendship and a business relationship with Dr. Abraham for so many years, I have all kinds of feelings at the thought of his passing. He has contributed so mightily to creating a name for me—a bigger name than I deserve, that I know in my heart of hearts. But he is such a complete gentleman that for many reasons I wish that both you and he would derive so much pleasure from your suite that it would, as an obvious consequence, bring the two of you into a closer relationship.

And you are hard at work and perhaps many a time longing to get out into a broader art environment. I am hard at work in my own way, and I am longing for home—I almost said: to get away *from* an art environment. The thing is, down here art is so exceedingly much just art—and not nature. That is why I long for the great natural scenery at home, which more than anything else is akin to great art. German art today—especially the performing arts, perhaps—are either *school* art or *intestinal* art! Both are lacking the high, pure standard and as a result smell like it does in a schoolroom or anatomy laboratory. My kingdom for a good, stiff drink![16]

Next week I'm off to Holland. The atmosphere there is healthier, I hope. And there one also finds the wonderful, old paintings that sparkle with humor to such an extent that one could wish to live life all over again.

Warm greetings to the whole trio, also from Nina.

Yours truly,
EDVARD GRIEG

5

Rome, March 31, 1899

Dear Halvorsen!
Dear Annie!
Dear Åse![17]
Hurrah, hurrah, hurrah! I just came home and found the enclosed item from Bjørnstjerne Bjørnson,[18] and it will amuse you. So I ran to the telegraph office, and here I am, full of jubilation over the outcome.[19] Yes, I am as happy as if it had

15 Max Abraham's successor as director of C. F. Peters was his nephew, Henri Hinrichsen (1868–1942), who had already been working with him in the firm for several years at the time this letter was written.
16 An allusion to the famous line in Shakespeare's *Richard III*: "A horse, a horse, my kingdom for a horse."
17 Åse Halvorsen (1895–1978), daughter of Johan and Annie Halvorsen.
18 Bjørnstjerne Bjørnson (1832–1910), like Grieg, was in Rome at this time.
19 Grieg is referring to Halvorsen's appointment as musical director of the newly established National Theater in Christiania. Halvorsen was one of three candidates for the position, the other two being Iver Holter

to do with myself. That justice finally triumphs makes one feel so good that one can't help but think that life is worth something after all. No doubt there were some interesting attempts to undermine your candidacy there in Tigerville,[20] and the *bagler* bishop[21] will see to it that you will not get roses without thorns. But you have a good fist and a good temperament, and with them you will triumph. My task has been to achieve via letters the following: If not Svendsen[22] plus Halvorsen, then Halvorsen. But I must confess that I didn't have a lot of hope, for I know the people up there. But then came your big—absolutely convincing—success, and it determined the outcome by disarming the rumor-mongers and the cliques.[23] How happy your brother[24] must be, for he actually played the decisive role! Greet him warmly from me, and give him my best wishes!

Fortunately we will be coming home soon enough for us to lift a glass together to celebrate this event that is so decisive for your entire life and for much else!

I have had three orchestra rehearsals. Tomorrow I will have the last one and on Monday April 3 a concert for the whole kit and caboodle, with the queen leading the pack. Here is the program:

1. The *Sigurd Jorsalfar* pieces
2. Songs (Mrs. Bergliot Ibsen[25])
3. Piano concerto (Gulli[26])
4. *Elegiac Melodies* for strings
5. Songs (Mrs. Bergliot Ibsen)
6. *Peer Gynt Suite No. 1.*

The orchestra is a bit of a disappointment in that it is not of the highest quality. The discipline is poor, and I have done an incredible amount of bullying. But

---

(1850–1941) and Per Winge (1858–1935). The decision by the governing board on March 28, 1899, to offer the position to Halvorsen was a major triumph for the brilliant young man, placing at his disposal a permanent 46-piece orchestra (reduced to 43 the following year). The telegram that Grieg sent to Halvorsen upon hearing the news was as follows: *Eviva il nuovo maestro di capella. Bravo! Griegs.* ("Long live the new musical director. Bravo!")

20 "Tigerstaden": a derisive name for Christiania coined by Bjørnstjerne Bjørnson.

21 The "baglers" were a 13th-century political party founded by the bishops in opposition to King Sverre Sigurdson (1150–1202), who had reaffirmed the supremacy of the king over the church. Grieg is referring derisively to the organist, composer and music critic Johannes Haarklou (1847–1925), who was a strong opponent of Grieg.

22 Norwegian composer and conductor Johan Svendsen (1840–1911).

23 On March 18, shortly before the decision regarding the National Theater musical directorship was made, Halvorsen had given a big concert of his own works in Christiania in which he appeared as both soloist (violin and viola) and accompanist (piano) as well as conductor.

24 Rolf Hakon Halvorsen (1862–1926), proprietor of "The Silk Store" ("Silkehuset") in Christiania. It was he who had assisted in making arrangements for the concert on March 18.

25 Soprano Bergliot Ibsen (1869–1953), daughter of Bjørnstjerne Bjørnson and wife of Sigurd Ibsen (1859–1930).

26 Italian pianist Luigi Gulli (1859–1918).

the musicians are pleasant and willing and want to do the best they can, so I hope the result will at least be something worth listening to. Tonny and Nina send greetings and congratulations. And I for my part embrace all three of you as

Your old friend,
EDVARD GRIEG

6

Troldhaugen, October 18, 1901

Dear Halvorsen!
It is not about the sad family matter[27] that I want to write today but about something that in its own way is as sad as anything, namely the fact that our fiddle dance tunes are dying out. I recently received the enclosed letter from the fiddler Knut Dahle in Tinn (Telemarken), and I feel more strongly than ever that now something clearly must be done. *You absolutely must return Dahle's letter to me.*[28] There was a time when Frants and I set out to visit him, but unforeseen circumstances forced us to give up the trip. But it is clearer to me now than it was then that *only a violinist with a Norwegian emotional makeup who knows how to transcribe music* can do the job that needs to be done. It is in fact crazy that the Norwegian Parliament pays people who are not violinists to collect folk songs, when these people are incapable of recording the other half of our folk music, which is at least equally important: the folk dances.

What is now to be done? To get Myllarguten's dance tunes written down in their original form—that is the task that cannot be delayed a single day, for Knut Dahle is an old man. I would prefer that *you* would undertake the task. But I suppose you are too busy, even if I could get Dahle to go to Christiania in a few weeks and call on you some morning. If no wealthy man will pay his travel expenses and board and lodging, I will do it myself. So the financial side of the matter is not an issue. But just think if you did this, and if I then arranged the dance tunes for piano, and then we made them world-famous through C. F. Peters right under the noses of that very *un*-Norwegian Parliament of ours! If it is *absolutely impossible* for you to take the time we could, of course, turn to Gustav Lange,[29] who no doubt has as little time to spare as you do. Still, I think

---

[27] Grieg's brother John, who was Halvorsen's father-in-law, had taken his own life on October 10, 1901.

[28] Knut Dahle's first letter to Grieg is dated April 8, 1888. In that letter Dahle (1834–1921) gave an account of his relationship to Torgeir Augundson ("Myllarguten'—1801–72) and other well-known fiddlers in Norway. The letter had captured Grieg's interest and, as we learn from the present letter, Grieg and his friend Frants Beyer had set out to visit Dahle, but something had happened to prevent them from completing the trip. Encouraged by Grieg's reply, Dahle wrote to Grieg again on August 8 and November 9 and 16, 1890, pleading for Grieg's interest and help. Grieg did not respond, however, until he received a letter from Dahle dated October 11, 1901. See Grieg's letters to Knut Dahle.

[29] Norwegian violinist and composer Gustav Fredrik Lange (1861–1939).

the possible loss of private-lesson fees and additional loss of time could be made up in another way—for example, through the publication.

The question that you must kindly answer immediately, then, is this: Can you either receive Dahle yourself, or can you identify some other *suitably qualified* man in Christiania—or, let me say, in Norway?

We will stay at home through Christmas and will hope for a pleasant visit with you in the new year!

Warm greetings to all of you from Nina and from

Yours truly,
EDVARD GRIEG

P.S. Greet Schjelderup, and tell him that he will hear from me soon. Tell him why I am not in the mood for writing letters at the moment.[30]

7

Troldhaugen, November 4, 1901

Dear Halvorsen!
Hopefully you will see Knut Dahle one of these days. I got a letter from him yesterday telling me that he doesn't have any money, so today I am sending him 100 crowns. Please let me know your impression of him as soon as possible so that I can get to work to raise what he will need for a longer stay in Christiania if necessary.

Now if only he proves to be the right man. In any case it is, of course, a matter of rescuing the fragments that remain.

Yesterday we, together with Frants and Marie, visited your mother-in-law. It was hard for her to get past the birthday this time, but she is *worthy of admiration.* In her sorrow she is so outgoing, so wise, so free of all sentimentality.

Warmest greetings to all!

Yours truly,
EDVARD GRIEG

---

[30] Norwegian composer Gerhard Schjelderup (1859–1933) was in process of writing a biography of Grieg and his music in connection with Grieg's forthcoming sixtieth birthday. The book, *Edvard Grieg og hans Værker* (*Edvard Grieg and His Works*) was published in Copenhagen in 1903. On October 27, 1901, Halvorsen conducted an all-Schjelderup program of symphonic music at the National Theater with the composer in the audience.

8

Troldhaugen, November 23, 1901

Dear friend!

Thank you for the report![31] I was so happy that I felt like dancing. If Knut is just intelligent and solid we can manage all right, even if he isn't brilliant. Besides, he is, of course, an old man. The main thing is *the stamp of authenticity*. Squeeze out of him everything you can. As far as the money is concerned, it's a clever peasant's strategy that the man, after having asked and begged for the opportunity and having gotten travel money, still wants more. But unfortunately he's not likely to get it. I can't spare any more now. And if *you* don't know some well-heeled person in Christiania who, if necessary, will come up with the rest, then I will write to somebody or other over there. But I hope you can take care of it with a patron of the arts in your area. Thanks for keeping an eye on Knut's secret dealings with Bacchus. It's damn important. But—of course he wouldn't be a real fiddler if he didn't like his liquor.

Naturally you will transcribe using the original tuning. I hope my brain is still capable of figuring it out.[32]

Warm greetings tutti!

Yours truly,
EDVARD GRIEG

P.S. Your mother-in-law is doing fine. We see her often. She is incomparably brave. Eager to work and absolutely free of sentimentality and prejudice. Tomorrow we are all getting together up here in winter weather like that in eastern Norway. (12 degrees Réaumur[33] last night!)

Nina asks me to greet you so warmly!

Poor Bjørnson! We are so sorry for him. Well, you can get him to believe anything. For me L. Holst is just "schmutzige Wäsche".[34]

---

[31] Knut Dahle reached Christiania on November 16, and Halvorsen began transcribing the dance tunes the following day. Everything took place at Halvorsen's office at the National Theater during the forenoons of November 17–26, 1901. Grieg subsequently arranged Halvorsen's transcriptions as *Norwegian Peasant Dances*.

[32] The Hardanger fiddle—the instrument on which Norwegian fiddlers typically played their dance tunes—is tuned in several different ways depending on the tune that is to be played. These tunings are often very different from the standard $g - d^1 - a^1 - e^2$ of the modern violin.

[33] "Réaumur" denotes a temperature scale in which 0° represents the freezing point and 80° the boiling point of water. Thus 12° Réaumur is equivalent to 15° Celsius and 57° Fahrenheit.

[34] Lars Holst (1848–1915) was a newspaper editor in Christiania who in 1898 became clerk of the local municipal court. "Schmutzige Wäsche" means "dirty laundry".

9

Troldhaugen, December 6, 1901

That's what I call a real Saturday evening, dear Halvorsen. Outside a storm is raging, with a fierce south wind that shakes the house, and on top of that a veritable deluge is pouring down from the heavens. But here in the living room it is cozy. I recently received your peasant dances and have just finished reading through them—all the while absolutely trembling with delight. But at the same time I have fretted and fumed about not being a fiddle player. How I hate that conservatory in Leipzig!

But to the matter at hand: This "peculiarity" you speak of—this use of G♯ in the key of D—was the thing that drove me wild in 1871. Naturally I stole it immediately and used it in my *Pictures from Folk Life.*[35] This phenomenon is something that should be researched. The augmented fourth also occurs in peasant folk songs. It is a holdover from one or another of the old scales. But which one? It defies comprehension that no one among us engages in musicological study of our national music, when we have such rich sources in our folk music for anyone who has ears with which to hear, a heart with which to feel, and the intelligence to write things down.

At the moment it feels to me as if it would be a sin to arrange these dance tunes for piano. But sooner or later I no doubt will commit that sin. It is too tempting. I thank you heartily for your work, which has made me very happy. And as time goes on it will become clear that you have done more than that.

I probably won't be able to get to work on them until next summer. When the time comes, do you want me to try to get both your work and mine published by Peters?

Thank you also for playing patron of the arts![36] I will reimburse you as soon as I can. It's not worth bothering a wealthy person for such a small amount. But just between us, I have had a lot of expenses recently, so it has not been easy to take care of every little thing that has come along.

I have enjoyed your letters, both the one with "the trout" and the one with the "rosemaling".[37] It surely was a good thing that it was done, that I see from a cursory reading. And you were just the man for the job. If only we could sit and play them and talk about them at your apartment. But we have to stay at home.

It was good that you sent Knut Dahle home again before he committed any

---

35 *Pictures from Folk Life*, composed 1869–71.

36 When Dahle was ready to leave Christiania he had a bill at the hotel that he claimed he was unable to pay because he apparently had "lost" some of his money. So Halvorsen paid it for him. The amount was 58 crowns and 10 øre (= ca. $8).

37 In a letter dated November 17, 1901, Halvorsen had written that Knut Dahle's dance tunes were difficult to transcribe: "Small leaps and trills that are like a little trout in a swift-flowing stream. When you are ready to take them they are gone." On November 28 he characterized the ornamentation as "rosemaling", a type of decorative floral painting widely used in rural Norway.

more blunders. This evening I got a divine letter from him. He says he was totally baffled in Christiania because he couldn't "remember" where he had hidden forty crowns. "When I travel I never have my money in one place but hide a little here and a little there, and sure enough, when I got home I looked carefully through my hiding places and found [the forty crowns] in my innermost jacket pocket, so I did not lose anything during the trip." As you can see, he has imagination. Well, one must excuse the old fellow and just be happy for the result. I'm surprised that he wasn't dead drunk the whole time he was there.

I see that you and I have similar tastes in various areas, for I, too, am fond of Alfvén's symphony.[38] It is grand and straightforward. But you absolutely must learn to love Schumann, even if he is not a charming colorist.

If it is true that your salary has been increased from 4,000 to 6,000 crowns, congratulations! Now you will be a big shot, and when you swear that this will be your last child,[39] then . . .

Well, farewell for this evening. Warm greetings to large and small from Nina and from

Yours truly,
EDVARD GRIEG

I am searching for a brilliant female singer for my songs. Can you think of anyone who has had a great success this year?

10

Berlin N. W., April 16, 1903

Dear Halvorsen!
In great haste en route from Warsaw to Paris. Thanks for your letter. I will send the *Peer Gynt Suite* at the earliest possible time, as soon as I have used it in Paris. Your program is excellent. I only think that "The First Meeting" should not *precede* "Last Spring". Rather the other way around. But perhaps I am wrong. (The Warsaw orchestra played "The First Meeting" *wonderfully.*)

So: Now you have become a hero in the muckraking paper *Aftenposten,*[40] just as I did at an earlier time. I am just amazed. Amazed that he can keep dishing out that bullshit for such a long, long time without being hoisted on his own petard. You are right: Keep looking up! And in that we shall stand together.[41]

---

[38] Halvorsen had performed Swedish composer Hugo Alfvén's *Symphony No. 2*, composed 1899, at concerts on November 24 and December 1, 1901.

[39] Grieg is alluding to the fact that Annie Halvorsen was expecting their third child, who turned out to be a girl and was named Nina (1901–58). But she was not their last child. A boy was born to the Halvorsens in 1909 and was named Stein Grieg Halvorsen.

[40] *Aftenposten*: one of Christiania's oldest and most distinguished newspapers.

[41] In a letter dated April 8, 1903, Halvorsen had informed Grieg that he (Halvorsen) had been attacked in

The Warsaw concert the day before yesterday was so successful that it had to be repeated last evening. The newspapers are singing hymns. You should have heard those fellows play the overture *In Autumn.* I have never heard it played so well. Last evening I went directly from the concert hall (after a hot shower there) to the night train, and I will do the same thing—take the night train—at 11 P.M. tonight. I didn't think I could demand this much of myself, but so far it's going all right.

It's a damn shame that the Dreyfus passions have once again been aroused.[42] I have been warned on good authority that I can expect whistles and catcalls when I come on stage at the Colonne concert. Well, cheer up, Antonius! You haven't done anything wrong.[43]

Warm greetings to all five of you! Congratulations on little Nina! That was great news.[44]

Greetings also to the sisters and nieces.

Yours truly,
EDVARD GRIEG

11

Paris, April 23, 1903
Hotel de Sèze, 16, Rue de Sèze

Dear friend!
Today I sent the score of *Peer Gynt Suite No. 1.* Address: 11 Arbiens Street. You mentioned "Bridal Procession"[45] in your last letter. That is certainly an excellent idea and it will be fun to hear.

Now I have had the experience of being hissed off stage. What strange

---

Aftenposten by Johannes Haarklou: "Things are not exactly pleasant for me these days. *Aftenposten* has opened its pages to the vilest attack on my person and my work. It is, of course, Haarklou, who in several columns rants and raves about the fact that his opera *Væringerne i Miklagard* (*The Viking Mercenaries in Constantinople*) has not been performed at the National Theater. He contends that I am not competent and that I am acting out of impure motives, also that he himself is a conductor and composer without peer in Norway. His performance of Beethoven's symphonies has never been excelled either before or since etc. He has a couple of anonymous supporters, one of whom (between us, it sounds to me like Ole Olsen) brings up the music festival, the Dutch orchestra, that I am bound by Uncle Grieg's wishes, etc. Fortunately the whole thing is so vile that all perceptive people just get a kick out of it. My position for the time being is to work and keep looking up!"

42 For a summary of Grieg's involvement in the so-called "Dreyfus affair" see his letter to Bjørnstjerne Bjørnson of September 14, 1899.

43 This is a quotation from the comedy *Den politiske Kandestøber* (*The Political Tinker*) by Ludvig Holberg (1684–1754).

44 Nina Halvorsen had been seriously ill with pneumonia but had now recovered.

45 Halvorsen wanted to bring the National Theater orchestra to Bergen to give two concerts in connection with Grieg's sixtieth birthday and had proposed that the orchestra play his arrangement of Grieg's "Bridal Procession", which he—with Grieg in the audience—had performed for the first time in the National Theater on February 22, 1903, at a concert given to raise money for unemployed workers. The piece was published by C. F. Peters later that year.

people, these Parisians. I was ready for just about anything, as the press had encouraged demonstrations. But that morning I had taken five drops of opium (following the advice of Danish Professor Rovsing[46]), and it worked so well that I was totally calm. As I came on stage the applause was so great, notwithstanding the hissing, that I had to bow again and again. But when I turned toward the orchestra in order to begin, the whistling and shouting ("A la porte", "des excuses"—and the funniest thing, a chorus of voices from the balcony shouting:

à la the rhythm in "Dance of the Mountain King's Daughter") became so loud that I had to put down the baton, leave the podium, and wait quietly for whatever was going to happen. It was a wild contest, but all the noise got drowned in the most powerful applause, and in the meantime the worst instigators of the commotion were thrown out by the *tripled* staff of gendarmes.

When it looked for a moment as if calm had returned, I again mounted the podium—but so help me, they started in anew. But now I had had enough of it. I wasn't going to let them get going again. I gave an energetic sign to the orchestra, and since the overture *In Autumn* fortunately begins *fortissimo*, the situation was saved. During the whole overture they didn't make a sound. But between numbers there was some shrill shouting of opinions. Some yelled, "Down with the Jews!" Others: "We have come to hear the musician, not the politician!" And so on.

The whole concert was one great crescendo. Despite the fact that Colonne[47] chose to run off to Spain instead of rehearsing the music, and despite the further fact that I had just *one* rehearsal, the orchestra played so marvelously that the newspapers had to admit that they had never heard the *Peer Gynt Suite* played like that.

It was poor Mrs. Gulbranson[48] who suffered by Colonne's absence. For the assistant conductor[49] led the conclusion of *Götterdämmerung*[50] so mechanically that her voice couldn't be heard above the sound of the orchestra.

The proudest moment occurred when Nina and I were about to climb into the carriage that was to take us to our hotel. It was surrounded by a triple cordon of gendarmes! It was a real comedy!

---

[46] Danish physician and professor of medicine Niels Thorkild Rovsing (1862–1927).

[47] Édouard Colonne (1838–1910), founder and conductor of the famous Colonne Orchestra which Grieg conducted on April 19, 1903.

[48] Swedish-born Norwegian soprano Ellen Nordgren Gulbranson (1863–1947).

[49] French conductor Louis Laporte.

[50] Richard Wagner's *Twilight of the Gods*, the fourth opera in the famous *Ring* cycle.

But the press reports the next day! This furious anger over the great success! I have never seen anything more vile. There were indeed some noble critics, including Gabriel Fauré in *Le Figaro*, but on the whole it was filth and not music review at all.

You should have been with us that evening when Johannes Wolff joined Nina and me at an oyster bar! Wolff asks me to greet you. He had played the composition you dedicated to him at a concert in London the previous day.[51]

Monday the 27th I will give a program of chamber music in Salle Pleyel,[52] and then I will head for home via Leipzig. How I look forward to the mountains and the fjords and everything!

Many greetings to all!

Yours truly,
EDVARD GRIEG

12

Bergen, May 30, 1903

Dear Halvorsen!
It was great to see you again! You mentioned "Fløjen"[53] in connection with the orchestra. This gives me an idea. I want so much to do something nice for the orchestra. Couldn't I invite all of you to be my guests for breakfast at Fløjen? Answer: Yes, thank you. Hopefully this will work out. But in that connection a very important question which you must answer *immediately*: Dare I (out of concern for the concert) offer the orchestra *wine* at this breakfast, or must we be content with beer and a shot of liquor, or must it be a non-alcoholic breakfast? The last option would be downright dull. *But*, we don't for anything want inebriated people at the concert. So: Answer without delay. Naturally I can invite them only on the condition of good weather. If the weather is bad it won't work at all. So for now, don't say anything to anyone about it.[54]

Warm greetings. In haste,

Yours truly,
EDVARD GRIEG

---

[51] Dutch musician Johannes Wolff (1863–?) was one of Grieg's favorite violinists. The piece Halvorsen had dedicated to him was *Air norvégien* for violin and piano, comp. 1896.

[52] One of the pieces performed at this concert was Grieg's *Violin Sonata No. 3* in C minor. The violinist was Johannes Wolff, who was living in Paris at this time.

[53] "Fløjen" is the name of one of the mountains overlooking the city of Bergen. Atop the mountain is a restaurant, also called "Fløjen", which has long been used as a venue for festive occasions.

[54] Johan Halvorsen brought the National Theater orchestra to Bergen to assist in the celebration of Grieg's sixtieth birthday on June 15, 1903. The weather cooperated, the breakfast atop Fløjen took place as planned, and the beverages were "beer, a shot of hard liquor and red wine." See Grieg's letter of June 26, 1903, to Johan Svendsen.

13

Copenhagen, February 28, 1905
Hotel Phoenix

Dear Halvorsen!
It is not I who am sending you these lines. It is only a shadow of my former self. So totally has this illness finished me off. I am absolutely no good for letter-writing, but I want you to know that I have followed your activities and rejoiced over the fact that you have gotten the recognition that you deserve. Yes, I have rejoiced as intensely as if it were I who had been so honored. Or, more correctly, even more than that. For the feeling of joy over one's own good fortune is always mingled with the feeling of something undeserved.[55]

For the past week I have wanted each day to write to you and thank you for your letters, but I never got to it. Today, however, the egotist is on the loose, so it's happening. I have a favor to ask of you.

The thing is, in last evening's issue of a local newspaper called *Ekstrabladet*, a contemptible interviewer put some statements in my mouth that I never could have uttered.[56] It has to do with our political situation, and I am terribly agitated about it. My hope is that a worthless newspaper like that won't be quoted in Norway. But please be on the lookout, and if you should see anything about it in Christiania, insist that the newspaper in question—preferably at my request—print the correction that *Ekstrabladet* is running this evening. It reads as follows:

> Edvard Grieg
> We should report that in the interesting interview with *Edvard Grieg* that we carried yesterday, a number of statements were included that Mr. Grieg cannot acknowledge and that he had corrected in a proof

---

[55] Grieg is referring here to the enormous success of Halvorsen's incidental music to *Fossegrimen*, a play by Sigurd Eldegard (1866–1950). (A "foss" is a waterfall, a "fossegrim" a fiddle-playing supernatural being said to live beneath the waterfall.) The premiere performance occurred at the National Theater on January 29, 1905, and a total of 45 performances were given during the winter and spring of that year. *Fossegrimen* is the first composition ever written in which the Hardanger fiddle, Norway's national instrument, is used as a solo instrument with orchestra. Halvorsen's interest in the Hardanger fiddle was a direct result of his experience in transcribing the peasant dances as played by Knut Dahle in 1901.

[56] The interview in *Ekstrabladet* on February 27, 1905, was titled "Edvard Grieg on the Norwegian Consular Controversy. An Interview". The statement attributed to him to which Grieg objected presumably was this: "In my opinion, therefore, there is nothing to do but raise the question of the dissolution of the union, i.e.: Norway's relationship with Sweden must be based on a defense alliance. It is a necessity. Our future is at stake. We cannot expect anything from the Swedish side as long as we proceed on the present assumptions—especially since [Swedish] foreign minister Boström so shamefully altered the communiqué." He is quoted as saying in conclusion, "One thing more: Not a single drop of blood must be shed over the consular issue!" Grieg always supported a peaceful solution to the issues that had brought Norway and Sweden to the brink of war and no doubt was concerned lest people in Norway should perceive him to be vacillating with respect to the consular question. See also Grieg's letters to Bjørnstjerne Bjørnson of December 7, 1904, and to Henry T. Finck (1854–1926) of December 30, 1905.

> copy which, as agreed, he had submitted, but which mistakenly did not reach the composing room before the paper went to press.[57]

When the paper is obligated to report this, you can understand that the people into whose hands I have fallen are nothing but scoundrels. I even told the guy that I *didn't want* any interviews, but he dragged the words out of my mouth, and then he wrote down words that I never said—and after he had *promised* me that the completely rewritten proof would be used, he had the impudence to use his own manuscript, which had already been delivered to the printer. So here I stand—completely disgraced, in my opinion. I am singularly unlucky when it comes to these damned reporters. Early this morning a reporter from another newspaper showed up, but believe me he got a quick answer and left in a hurry.

Dear friend, do what you can *if necessary*, but only if necessary.

The only music I have heard is *Twilight of the Gods.* How it *is* filled with brilliance, notwithstanding the length. And this orchestral sonority! The performance is irreproachable.

Now I must conclude before I get totally crazy in the head.

Warm greetings to all of you from both of us!

Yours truly,
EDVARD GRIEG

P.S. As far as Olaf[58] is concerned, the only person who should be thanked is Sigurd Ibsen. He has been a gentleman and has kept his promise.

14

[Christiania, December 10, 1906]
Monday

Dear Mr. Musical Director!
It was good seeing you! Thank you again! Both because you performed Debussy and because you did so in such a way that I wish I could have embraced you for it! But I was ill that evening.[59]

Please give me an answer regarding the enclosure. She (Boje-Jensen) *used* to be excellent. I don't know how she is now. I was going to answer her that I am

---

[57] Grieg's "disclaimer" was printed word for word in *Ekstrabladet* on Tuesday, February 28.

[58] Halvorsen had been made a knight of the Order of St. Olav.

[59] On December 9, 1906, Halvorsen had conducted the National Theater Orchestra in a concert of French music in which *Prelude to the Afternoon of a Faun* by Claude Debussy (1862–1918) was performed for the first time in Norway. Grieg had attended the dress rehearsal on December 8. See his diary entry for that date in Benestad & Halverson (eds.), *Edvard Grieg: Diaries, Articles, Speeches* (Columbus, Ohio, 2001).

lucky enough not to have any influence on either the musical director or the theater director—but then my better feelings got the best of me, so I am sending this to you.

Yours truly,
EDVARD GRIEG

P.S. What a music lover that theater director must be to opt for a good dinner rather than attending yesterday's concert!!!

To Angul Hammerich

The Danish music historian Angul Hammerich (1848–1931) was for many years the music critic in *Nationaltidende* in Copenhagen and often had occasion to write about Grieg and his music. In 1896 he became a lecturer in musicology at the University of Copenhagen. The following year he established in the Danish capital an institution that is known today as the Musikhistorisk Museum Carl Claudius Samling, which is famous for its large collection of old musical instruments.

The Hammerich letters given below are preserved in Det kgl. Bibliotek (The Royal Library), Copenhagen.

1

Bergen, December 8, 1881

Dear Hammerich!
I don't know if you are the person I should thank for a copy of *Nationaltidende* in which you have reviewed my "Melodies for String Orchestra." [1] Be that as it may, however, I want to tell you how happy I am that you have been sufficiently discerning to conceive of the possibility of another understanding of "Last Spring" than the prevailing one. I admit that it is a mistake that the main outline of the content of the poem is not provided, and you would be doing me a big favor if you would make up for this lack—if your position gives you an opportunity to review them as new works in some newspaper or other. I have asked Hansen[2] to send you a copy of my new songs to poems by Vinje.[3] Among them you will find the two songs that I arranged for string orchestra [in op. 34]. Both of the poems, in my opinion, are so wonderful—each in its own way—that they certainly deserve publication. In one newspaper up here I see an excerpt from *Berlingske Tidende*[4] in which it is stated that "Last Spring" is a disappointment after one has heard Gade's[5] *Foraarsfantasi* [*Spring Fantasy*]. When you have read the poem you will have the means at hand to tell the writer of that article that this is pure nonsense. In any case, thank you for what you are doing with respect to this matter.

With sincere greetings to you and your wife from Nina and from

Yours truly,
EDVARD GRIEG

NB: Danish and Norwegian publishers do not see the advantage of arranging for reviews abroad of newly published Nordic works. To the contrary, they suppress them if possible. You will, therefore, serve the cause of justice by spreading the word so that my three compositions that have just been published by Peters—

---

1 *Two Elegiac Melodies.*

2 Music publisher Alfred Wilhelm Hansen (1854–1923), Copenhagen.

3 *Twelve Songs to Poems by A. O. Vinje.* Aasmund Olavson Vinje (1818–70) was a Norwegian poet and journalist who championed the use of *landsmål* (later called *nynorsk*), an indigenous form of the Norwegian language that explicitly avoided Danish influences.

4 The Copenhagen newspaper *Berlingske Tidende,* which is still in operation.

5 Danish composer Niels W. Gade (1817–90).

opp. 31 (*Land-sighting*), 34 (*Two Elegiac Melodies*) and 35 (*Norwegian Dances* for piano four hands)—will not be killed by silence in Scandinavia.

2

Copenhagen, November 21, 1889

Dear Mr. Hammerich!

I don't want to leave Denmark without thanking you for your review of the performance of *Scenes from Olav Trygvason.*[6] It made me feel so good because it was the only review of my work that seemed to me to be written out of understanding and appreciation. To this expression of thanks I must, however, add a correction—and it is a vitally important one. You, like several other reviewers, think that my op. 50 is an expression of the "cosmopolitan" credo that I recently felt compelled to publish in Wilhelm Hansen's music journal.[7] The fact is, though, that *Olav Trygvason* was drafted in its entirety in 1873, i.e., sixteen years ago. Only the orchestration is of recent date. You can see, therefore, that a certain "cosmopolitan" strain was in my blood even in the fiercely nationalistic days of my youth—NB, if this work contains anything especially cosmopolitan, which I cannot concede. The subject *requires* that the music be Nordic (albeit not just Nordic à la J. P. E. Hartmann[8]), but as *dramatic* music it must *at the same time* have *something* of a cosmopolitan touch. For the life of me I can't understand how anyone can think that I would choose such a subject to confirm a cosmopolitan credo.

It is true that the designation of this work as op. 50 is misleading, but this misleading is good. It is my opinion that just as the human being is both *individual* and *social*, so the artist is both national and cosmopolitan—but he does not always have occasion to reveal both sides of his personality in the same degree.

I would ask you kindly to do what you can to prevent the word "cosmopolitan" from being applied to me as a catchword that is alleged to signal a fundamental change in my music. That was never my intention. In the above-mentioned article I myself explicitly asserted the presence of *both* elements, the national and the cosmopolitan.

Your appreciation of my art has led me to write this because I didn't want you to have a mistaken view of the matter. Ordinarily, as a matter of principle, I refrain from such tirades.

Friendly greetings also to your wife, and thank you for your visit!

Sincerely yours,
EDVARD GRIEG

---

[6] Grieg's opera torso *Scenes from Olav Trygvason*, which premiered in Christiania on October 19, 1889, was performed in Copenhagen on November 16 of the same year.

[7] Grieg's so-called "cosmopolitan credo" will be printed in translation in Benestad & Halverson (eds.), *Edvard Grieg: Diaries, Articles, Speeches* (Columbus, Ohio, 2001).

[8] Johan Peter Emilius Hartmann (1805–1900), who was an organist and conservatory professor as well as a prolific composer, was a dominant figure in Danish music life during the latter half of the 19th century. See Grieg's letters to him.

To Gerhard Armauer Hansen

In 1874 Gerhard Armauer Hansen (1841–1912), a physician and scholar from Bergen, published an epoch-making article on leprosy in which he demonstrated that the dreaded disease was not hereditary but bacterial in origin. Soon thereafter he waged a successful campaign for new laws to prevent the further spread of the disease in Norway. His contribution to the eradication of the disease in Norway made him world-famous ("Hansen's disease" is an alternative name for leprosy in medical circles), and the laws developed at his urging have served as a model for other countries desiring to institute preventive measures to control the disease.

A photocopy of Grieg's letter to Armauer Hansen is preserved in Nasjonalbiblioteket, Oslo (National Library of Norway, Oslo Division).

Leipzig, January 19, 1896
Hotel Hauffe

Dear Armauer Hansen!
I'm beginning to get genteel in my old age. I have just written a letter to our ambassador in Paris, and now it is your turn. For that you are also one of the genteel I infer from the fact that you wrote to me in connection with the honor [that I recently received].[1] Shame on you! But you will be forgiven for it because it is you.

Moreover, I can assure you that as soon as I get my hands on the bauble in question it will be consigned as quickly as possible to some drawer or other at Troldhaugen, where in company with other colleagues it will have plenty of time to meditate on the world's lack of good judgment.

That the first congratulations from Norway in this connection should come from you—that is absolutely unbelievable! It's different here in Germany, where —ever since the newspapers reported this "honor" that I share with "legions"— people bow and scrape and stand in silent awe on the streets as I pass by.

By the way, you must not think that I am as stupid as I let on, for I suppose an official French recognition is of some significance. Moreover, like you, I have an appreciation for England that leads me to value more highly the fact that my work is regarded with interest there.

I read *Verdens Gang*[2] regularly and am pleased with the freshness and good sense with which it looks at our circumstances. On the other hand, I am not pleased about the speech from the throne[3] in Stockholm that tries to give people the impression that everything is fine just the way it is and that the purpose of the rearmament is to protect our neutrality. There should be some kind of

---

[1] In January, 1896, Grieg had been awarded the French "Legion of Merit". Through the years he received many honors, none of which he took very seriously. On March 14, 1897, after having been awarded the Order of Orange-Nassau in Holland, he wrote jokingly to Max Abraham (1831–1900) in Leipzig: "If you know me you will understand that I was overjoyed! Such medals serve a good purpose in my suitcase, for the customs officials at the border are always extra pleasant when they see them."

[2] *Verdens Gang*: a Christiania newspaper.

[3] "Speech from the throne" (*trontale*): a formal speech by the king setting forth the government's official position on one or more current issues of importance.

punishment for a king who, contrary to better judgment, dupes his people. But of course it is only the small fry who are punished for their crimes; the big shots are allowed to go free.[4]

In the blessed assurance of belonging to the latter category, I hope to be able for some time yet to move about in freedom with the right to speak my opinion as a good Norwegian.

It was kind of you to write! Warm greetings to you and your family, not forgetting your brother Klaus[5] and his wife, from

Sincerely yours,
EDVARD GRIEG

[4] Grieg is alluding here to the growing tension between Sweden and Norway as Norway struggled to free itself from the union with Sweden that had been forced upon it in 1814. See Grieg's letter to Henry T. Finck (1854–1926) of December 30, 1905, footnote 58.

[5] Dr. Klaus Hanssen (1844–1914), who was Grieg's personal physician in Bergen.

To Charles Harding

In August, 1888, Grieg participated in a music festival in Birmingham, England, where he conducted the concert overture *In Autumn* op. 11 on the 29th and the *Holberg Suite* op. 40 the following day. It was at this time that he became acquainted with English attorney Charles Harding, who was vice president of the Birmingham Festival. The stay in Birmingham also proved to be significant for Grieg in another way: Through Harding he came in contact for the first time with the Unitarian movement, the dogma-free religious outlook of which greatly attracted him and which he soon adopted as his own.

Letters 1–5 are preserved in the Charles Alvar Harding Collection of The Pierpont Morgan Library in New York City. Letter 6 is in Stiftelsen Musikkulturens Främjande (Society for the Promotion of Musical Culture), Stockholm, and a fair copy of letter 8 in Bergen Offentlige Bibliotek (Bergen Public Library). Letter 7 is privately owned. All are in English except letter 2, which is in German. The letters written in English are given in Grieg's original versions.

1

Lofthus via Bergen, August 26, 1884

My dear Sir,
Through my brother I received the other day your offer, so flattering for me, to go to Birmingham next summer to introduce some of my works. Excuse my first mentioning the pecuniary side of the affair. Is it an engagement or a matter of honor? I am obliged to know this.

If my delicate health will not prevent me, I hope to be able to receive[1] an invitation if such a one should officially be presented to me. Having, during my last journey in Germany and Holland, overworked myself by piano playing, I should prefer, if my concerto in a-moll for piano should be in question, to direct this work myself with a good pianist, for instance d'Albert.[2] If works with chorus should be chosen, I shall propose the two shorter pieces: 1) "At the cloister gate" for female chorus, two solo voices and orchestra [and] 2) "Sight of land" for chorus of male voices, baritone solo and orchestra.[3]

Being for the time occupied with other compositions, probably I shall not next year have finished some new greater work with chorus.

Letters must for the time be directed: Lofthus pr. Bergen, Norway.
Believe me, dear Sir,

Your faithful servant,
EDVARD GRIEG

---

[1] Grieg presumably means "accept".
[2] German pianist and composer Eugène d'Albert (1864–1932).
[3] *Before a Southern Convent* op. 20 and *Land-sighting* op. 31.

2

Leipzig, December 21, 1887

Dear Sir!
Hopefully you will forgive me for writing in German. My English is so poor that misunderstandings could easily arise.

I am pleased that the committee accepts both of the works I have proposed, for all the time until next summer I am unfortunately so fully occupied that I really could not find time and the requisite leisure to write a large composition. The score of the orchestral fantasy "Autumn Songs"[4] is now finished in manuscript form. The "Suite in Olden Style"[5] is for string orchestra. With respect to the orchestral fantasy I promise you that it will not be performed anywhere else before the performance in Birmingham. Naturally I cannot make the same promise regarding the suite inasmuch as the score has already been printed. But I promise nonetheless not to perform the work at my appearance in London next spring (March 1888). The music publishing company that is publishing "Autumn Songs" (C. F. Peters, Leipzig) has already commenced the process of writing out the orchestral parts, so the committee will not incur any expense in this connection. The publisher has nonetheless guaranteed not to publish the work until *after* the Birmingham festival.

My proposal regarding an honorarium, as you will see from my previous letter, was not definitive. I only desire assurance that my travel expenses and my time will be reimbursed at a level such that I can come out of the whole process without a pecuniary loss. If you think that this can happen with 50 Guineas,[6] I not only am content but I naturally regard it as a great honor to be invited to take part in the famous festival.

In the program that was kindly sent to me I am enormously impressed with the magnificent size of both the chorus and the orchestra. But in general, of course, I have long been acquainted with the significant traditions of the Birmingham Music Festival.

With high regard, dear sir, I remain,

Yours truly,
EDVARD GRIEG

---

[4] *In Autumn. Concert Overture* op. 11.

[5] *Holberg Suite* op. 40.

[6] A Guinea was equal to 21 shillings or approximately $3.

3

Bergen, July 7, 1888

Dear Sir!
I am very sorry not having been able to write to you before, but my time has been so very occupied of the musical festival at Copenhagen and later I was obliged to make a long journey. I therefore hope you will kindly excuse my silence.

I was told in a letter from Leipzig that the string orchestra band-parts to *In Autumn* now are finished and to be had by the edition C. F. Peters. The wind instruments I have got copied and shall take them with me when I am going to Birmingham. The band-parts and the score to the suite in old style "from the time of Holberg" are also to be had by the edition in Leipzig, before mentioned.

Will you do me the favor to send me the program of the festival as soon as it may be decided and let me know on what day the rehearsals in London will take place. Will you also be kind enough to let the notices of both my works in the program be printed as follows:

1. *In Autumn.* Concert Overture for orchestra, op. 11. (The themes of this work are taken from a song by the author, entitled "Autumn-song" and a Norwegian harvest-men song.)[7]
2. *From Holberg's Time.* Suite in old style for string orchestra, op. 40. (Ludvig Holberg—1684–1754—the Molière of the north, is the creator of the newer Danish-Norwegian literature.)

As a musical friend of mine intends to accompany me to Birmingham, I should be very happy if you could be able to procure him a room, near your house, for the festival days. With kind regards,

Yours truly,
EDVARD GRIEG

P.S. I hope you will find my music better than my English!

4

Hop Station pr. Bergen, July 28, 1888

Dear Sir!
To my letter of the 7th of July I have not yet had the honor of your answer. However I hope you have got it and now I take the liberty of asking you to tell me

---

[7] The "Autumn-song" to which Grieg refers is "Autumn storm" op. 18, no. 4. The "Norwegian harvest-men song" is a folk-dance tune that Grieg knew from the collection *VIII Norske Slåtter for Hardangerfele* (VIII Norwegian Folk Dances for Hardanger Fiddle) published in Bergen in 1865.

whether by coming to London for the rehearsal on the 22nd in the morning I may reckon on an equal number of rehearsals as will be granted to the other works. I must necessarily know about this to be able to decide my route and therefore I should be very much obliged to you for some lines in reply to this.

Yours truly,
Edvard Grieg

5

Bergen, August 5, 1888

My dear Sir!
From the programs you kindly sent me I am sorry to see that to my astonishment incorrect titles are given to my works, which is completely misinstructing to the public as to my intentions and which therefore I cannot possibly allow to pass. I feel obliged to entreat you in the programs exactly to give the titles which you have got from me and which to be quite safe I repeat once more:

3. *In Autumn*, Concert Overture for orchestra (op. 11).
4. *From Holberg's Time*, Suite in Old Style for string orchestra (op. 40).

I am very sorry to make you so much trouble but you will see how important the thing is to me. With kind regards,

Yours truly,
Edvard Grieg

6

Bergen, October 23, 1888

My dear Mr. Harding!
I am very glad to hear that you have received my first letter because you will have found there something of the heart, of which I have left so much in your home. Knowing that my native home too has got a part of your heart, you will permit me to send Mrs. Harding and your daughters a bit of Norway in shape of the enclosed national "Søljer."[8] How happy I would be if they would wear them when we shall meet again.

Let me not forget to add that I sent my last letter the 13th of October after receiving the photographs. In the same letter I also sent my answer to the vote of thanks.

---

[8] *Søljer*: distinctively Norwegian silver brooches.

Many kind regards to you and your whole family from my wife and from your faithfully,

EDVARD GRIEG

P.S. Please tell Mrs. Harding that I used three of the powders from Mad. Albani and was not seasick at all!

7

Leipzig, January 18, 1893

Dear Mr. Harding!
How kind you are as to remember such a bad fellow in letter-writing, as I am. But you should know how much trouble I had the whole last year and you would certainly forgive me. It is just now a year since the beginning of my sufferings—Rheumatismus in the feet and a very earnest stomach-catarrh. You will understand, it has not been easy to exist under such circumstances. And still I am not at all restituted. But I hope, the spring shall bring me all sound again and in this hope I bring you my and my wife's best thanks for your kind invitation to come and see you and your dear family in Birmingham. It should be for us such a great pleasure, and if my health shall permit me to visit Cambridge in the beginning of June, it should be very delightful to spend a few days in Birmingham afterwards.[9] If possible, I should wish to have Frants Beyer in my pick-pocket. Then he is, what the Germans say: "Mein guter Geist"—my good spirit. Please, do invite him to come with us! How he should enjoy it![10]

But my dear Mr. Harding! I am afraid, you would not recognize me, because I am grown old. You must take on your spectacles to find me, so thin I am! But I remember, you have a pair [of] very good ones and this consolates me.

Now I will spare you for your hearing more of my bad English! My love to all and many good wishes for a happy year!

Faithfully yours,
EDVARD GRIEG

P.S. My address: C. F. Peters, Editor of music, Thalstrasse 10, Leipzig.

---

[9] Grieg was to have received an honorary doctorate from Cambridge University in 1893 but because of poor health had to postpone the trip to 1894.

[10] Grieg's Bergen friend Frants Beyer (1851-1918) had accompanied Grieg to Birmingham in 1888.

8

Troldhaugen via Bergen August 28, 1903

Dear Mr. Harding!

Since I got your telegram, I have been very, very ill. (Bronchitis and Asthma.) Still I am not permitted to write letters. But I *must* send you some lines, that you and your dear family may feel how grateful I am that you remembered my 60th birthday. I beg you to be assured, that if writing or not, I will ever keep the same friendly feelings for you all. I never forget the happy days in the autumn 1888, and I shall always feel thankful for your kindness and hospitality.

We have a very bad summer and then we are without our dearest friends Beyers, who are obliged to stay at Christiania from July to October. We intend to leave Bergen in the middle of September and hope to meet with Beyers in Christiania.

I am so sorry, that it is for me out of question to visit England. My health should not at all permit it. If it was possible to cross the sea by railway, then I would surely come, but to travel through six kingdoms before reaching England, that is too much for me.

And now, dear Mr. Harding, my best love to you all and the kindest greetings from my wife!

Thankfully Yours,
EDVARD GRIEG

P.S. I beg you kindly excuse my very bad English!!

To Johan Peter Emilius Hartmann

In his youth, Grieg regarded Danish composer Johan Peter Emilius Hartmann (1805–1900) as one of Scandinavia's greatest composers. Although he eventually rejected pan-Scandinavianism in favor of the nationalistic style for which he is known, Grieg acknowledged his debt to Hartmann and admired him greatly. Grieg's tribute to Hartmann on the occasion of the latter's 80th birthday will be found in Benestad & Halverson (eds.), *Edvard Grieg: Diaries, Articles, Speeches* (Columbus, Ohio, 2001).

Grieg's letters to Hartmann are preserved in Det kgl. Bibliotek (The Royal Library), Copenhagen.

1

[Christiania], October 12, 1871

Dear Professor!

While I thank you very much for your letter and your kindness in sending me the two compositions of yours, I write to inform you that in order to avoid misunderstandings I of course withdraw the request for the honor of associating your name with my *Before a Southern Convent.*[1] I will ask you to accept instead something that cannot have the same interest for you personally, but that I nonetheless do not want to be overlooked simply because of the broadly national coloring that characterizes it. I refer to a volume of piano pieces that will be published before Christmas entitled *Pictures from Folk Life.*

It was an odd coincidence that rendered impossible the first dedication, and I don't have to tell you that for reasons other than the usual ones I am anxious to get acquainted with your composition. I told Bjørnson what had happened, and he had a good laugh over it.

I conclude these lines with a request that you give my sincerest greetings to the Windings[2] and beg you once again to be assured of my deepest appreciation for your compliance with my wish. Both works will in all probability be performed during the current season.[3]

Most respectfully yours,
EDVARD GRIEG

---

1 Grieg had planned to dedicate his new choral work *Before a Southern Convent* to Hartmann. Then he heard that Hartmann had also set this text from Norwegian author Bjørnstjerne Bjørnson's poem *Arnljot Gelline*, so he dedicated the composition to Franz Liszt and instead dedicated *Pictures from Folk Life* to Hartmann.

2 The Danish pianist and composer August Winding (1835–99) was one of Grieg's friends in Copenhagen. His wife Clara (1839–1925) was the daughter of Hartmann.

3 The two Hartmann compositions to which Grieg refers—the introduction to the ballet *Valkyrien* [*The Valkyries*] and "Zigeunersang" ["Gypsy Song"] from the incidental music to Goethe's *Götz von Berlichingen*—were both performed at the Music Association in Christiania under Grieg's leadership on December 16, 1871.

2

Leipzig, February 8, 1893

Dear Professor!

A telegram is not enough.[4] I feel an uncontrollable urge to say a few words of a more personal nature. First and foremost, then, let me thank you once again for your splendid composition, *Vølvens Spaadom.* You had to wait a long time for it to be performed in Germany, but I daresay on the other hand that the first performance as a whole was a credit to the composition. The chorus of the Teachers' Singing Association is Leipzig's finest, and the orchestra, though not made up of Gewandhaus players, fortunately also did not display this corporation's indifference in its interpretation. The effect of the winds was at times—especially in the most important places—so wild and demonic in character that in Copenhagen people might have thought it went beyond what was proper, but I'm sure it would have gladdened your heart. The first movement, unfortunately, was taken too fast, as a result of which the somber character was lost. The rest of the tempos were correct, and the conducting of the whole was broad and to the point. The effect of the last movement was considerably greater than what I heard in Copenhagen. The concert was given in Albert-Halle, a splendid auditorium with seats surrounding the stage on three sides, and it was filled to the rafters with what I would judge to have been over 2,500 people. These surroundings were absolutely perfect for *Vølvens Spaadom,* which really was presented in all its awesome majesty. The silence during the performance, and the intensity of the applause, also showed how greatly the listeners were enthralled.

As you see, dear Herr Professor, I am actually playing the role of a concert reviewer, but my excuse is that I wanted you to get at least one correct account in addition to the unavoidable newspaper scribblings. Yes, these reviews! I have just read a review by one wise man who has no better ears with which to hear than that he finds—Wagnerian influences! Now may your brilliant composition just find its way around Germany. I not only hope that: I firmly believe it. And this summer, may I once again shake your hand!

With this wish and with the warmest greetings, also from my wife, I am, as always,

Your grateful and warmly devoted admirer,
EDVARD GRIEG

---

[4] On February 7, 1893, Grieg had sent the following telegram to Hartmann: "Last evening *Vølvens Spaadom* in a brilliant performance by [Hans] Sitt. Effect impressive. Applause warm. Greetings and admiration. Edvard Grieg." *Vølvens Spaadom* [*The Vølve's Prophecy*] is a cantata in which Hartmann tried to create an "Old Norse" style. In Old Norse mythology the "vølve" was a woman who practiced witchcraft and had the ability to foresee the future.

To Robert Heckmann

Robert Heckmann (1849–91) was one of the foremost German violinists of his day. He received his training at the Leipzig conservatory in the mid-1860's—at the same time that Grieg's friend Johan Svendsen (1840–1911) was a student there. Grieg approached Heckmann in the spring of 1878 after he had composed his *String Quartet* in G minor, op. 27. He wanted to hear Heckmann's opinion of the work and to get advice and suggestions regarding questions of string technique. This approach marked the beginning of an extensive exchange of letters, all in German, that provide convincing evidence of a very close collaboration between the two artists.

All of Heckmann's letters to Grieg are preserved in Bergen Offentlige Bibliotek (Bergen Public Library). Grieg's letters to Heckmann have been difficult to locate, however, and his earliest letters to Heckmann evidently are not extant. The Bergen Public Library owns the letters from July 4 and December 16, 1878, while the Pierpont Morgan Library, Mary Flagler Cary Music Collection, New York, has the letter of July 22, 1878.

Grieg dedicated op. 27 to Heckmann, whose string quartet premiered the work in Cologne on October 29, 1878.

1

Lofthus, July 4, 1878

My dear Heckmann!

I can just see your face when you receive the second page filled with notes! But to begin with: The first page comprises the whole *Andante* movement and—well, other than that I have nothing to say in my defense. It was something I have been very displeased with all along, and now that I have seen your interest the desire has reawakened in me to make the things as good as possible. The irksome figure in the development of the *first* movement has been shortened to a minimum. The newly inserted slow passage will better emphasize the slow theme *agitato pp* that follows. I for my part am very happy today over the change. It goes without saying that I am not requesting any further testing of the material, both because of the bother and because of the delay this would entail. A quick glance will show you that the things are now better, and hopefully you will tell me in a couple of words the same day you get this letter that you agree so that I can soon send the manuscript to Peters.

Just a few comments regarding your last changes.

First movement: 14 measures after letter C, that poor E-flat can be removed. Four measures before letter Q is fine, of course. *The beginning is outstanding, but not the end.* The melody

must be maintained in the three octaves throughout. In order that the notes

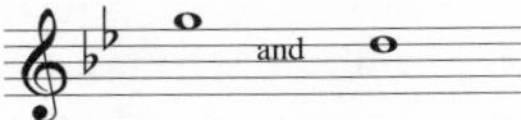

at NB shall not get lost, the passage should rather be played like this:

The cello part shall be as before.

You are certainly right about the *Intermezzo* at letter *B.* It irritates me that the chords in the whole pizzicato passage have to be played arpeggio. If I had been writing the piece for string orchestra I would have *divided* the parts (divisi). I am in agreement regarding the concluding chord in the first part of the *Intermezzo.*

In the trio at letter H I am *very reluctant* to have the cross relation.

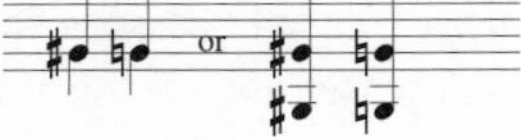

Surely there is some other way to achieve a doubling of the parts. Either in both of the upper voices

Thus either

To be sure, the *b* is missing in the last case, but that doesn't matter. The chromatic voice leading becomes clearer. Choose whichever you think is best.

Your idea of beginning with the repeated

at letter *H* in the Finale would probably sound fine. I have nothing against it. As you can see, I have included your modification at letter *W*. As for the passage 9–12 measures after letter *V*, I have never said that it sounds and looks strained. It is something completely new, though, and it looks marvelous and will certainly sound good as well. I only fail to understand why you write as follows:

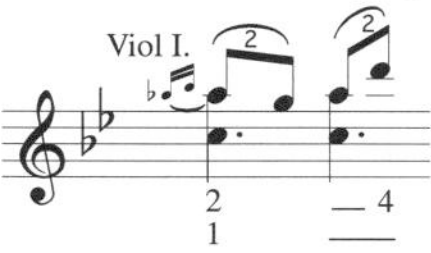

Surely it should be like this:

In the *Andantino* section I would prefer not to have any pizzicato chord in the cello 9 measures *after letter G* (NB in the *enclosed new version*). If it remains as it now stands it corresponds to the parallel place at letter *C*.

In the *Andantino* section you will also find that the viola in the first *Allegro agitato* plays almost *staccato*. It is better if, so far as possible, the figure is like this:

Where the two last notes are not tied together it is important that the following measure can begin *fz* with a *down-bow*. Hopefully the *pizzicato* in the second violin four measures before letter *G* (in the new version) is playable.

In the *Intemezzo*, in any case, you are right about the following passage:

So: the *f-sharp* at NB is fine, but at "?" I do not want to have it held over.

Thanks so much for the cue notes. And don't be angry with me because I have caused you so much bother. This much is certain: The most recent changes have pleased me.

Just think if I had been able to play the violin a *little*!!! Damn that Leipzig conservatory! What I am able to do I *did not learn there*—that is a fact.

Greet your colleagues from me! I look forward to getting acquainted with them.

And with that, warm greetings to you and your wife from

Your grateful friend,
EDVARD GRIEG

P.S. I am happy about the place in the *Andantino* section and hope it will sound great!? I am waiting with great anticipation for the score!!!!

2

Lofthus, July 22, 1878

Dear Heckmann!
Along with this letter I am sending you the new score.[1] That's the best thing to do. Read through it, and immediately thereafter do me the favor of sending the manuscripts (including the enclosed piano pieces[2]) to Leipzig (Address *Dr. M. Abraham*, C. F. Peters, Thalstrasse). You must not be cross with me for loading you down with another communication. I wrote Dr. Abraham[3] today that you are to receive the manuscript later, so all you have to say is that you want to have *two* proof copies. (I assume that you will not say no to my proposal in the previous letter.)

The reason that I am sending you the score is this: It would be going altogether too far afield if I were to write out all of the *innumerable little* changes. I hope you agree with me that much has been improved. I am dubious about some of the changes so far the performance is concerned. Therefore the following:[4]

In the first movement, four measures after letter F in the new score, the violins have:

Later they have the same pattern twice, each time a minor second higher. If this is too difficult (difficult, I mean, to get the fifths *perfect*), please kindly change those places, either like this:

---

1 Grieg had earlier sent Heckmann the first manuscript of his *String Quartet*. On the basis of suggestions made by Heckmann he had now revised it, but instead of sending a manuscript containing numerous changes he chose to make a fair copy of the revised score.

2 Grieg probably is referring to *Album Leaves*, which was published simultaneously by Carl Warmuth in Christiania and C. F. Peters in Leipzig.

3 Max Abraham (1831–1900), proprietor of C. F. Peters Musikverlag, Leipzig.

4 Readers who wish to follow the details of Grieg's music examples are referred to Bjarne Kortsen's book *Zur Genesis von Edvard Griegs g-Moll Streichquartett. Op. 27* and to the score and comments regarding the work in *Edvard Grieg: Complete Works*, vol. 9.

or this: 

or in whatever way you yourself think results in the fullest sound. It must sound *furioso*. Still, I would prefer that if possible that passage could stay as it is now.

The G-major conclusion with the leap

comically enough, is *exactly* as I have conceived it. I was just afraid that I had written something that was questionable.

So that you will not have too much trouble finding the changes, I will direct you to the most important ones.

First movement: In the opening chord you have let the cello stay on *d*, which I also think is best. 17 measures before letter *A* (second violin); 12 and 8 measures before letter *A* (cello); 10 measures before measure *A* (all voices); *A* (second violin and cello). In the cello figures, I was in doubt as to whether it should be

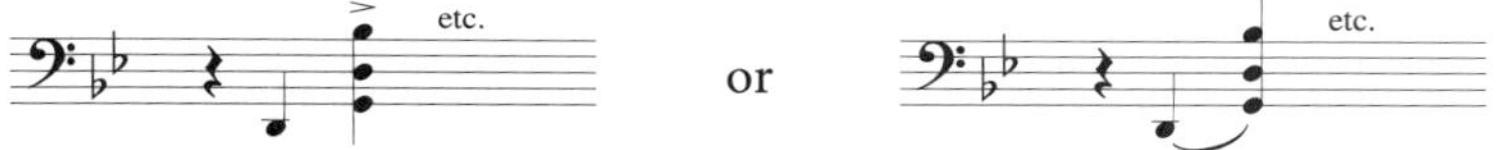

Nonetheless it was important to me to get

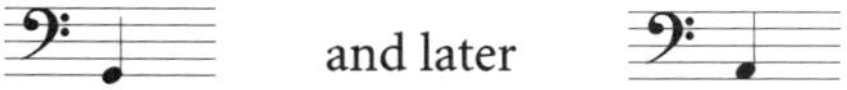

to sound forth clearly. That is why I did not write *legato*, even if this would be easier to play. If *legato* would absolutely sound better, please change it. 23 measures after letter *A* (cello); 33–34 after letter *A* (second violin and viola); 18 after letter *C* (all voices); at letter *D* (bowing); 19 after letter *D* (second violin); 17 before letter *E* to 5 after letter *G*; 23 after letter *G* (abbreviation, delete imitation); 9 after letter *H* (viola); 24–36 after letter *H* (second violin); 11 after letter *K* (second violin); 3–14 after letter *L* (first violin and cello); 7 before letter *M* (not *ritardando*, just *diminuendo*, and thereafter no *stretto*, and *molto ritardando* does not begin until just before letter *N*); at letter *N* (cello) and viola (bowing); 4 before letter *O* (second violin and viola); 3 after letter *O* (second violin); at letter *R* (tremolo); 41 after letter *R* (Presto) the first four measures in all voices.

Second movement: the beginning (cello and viola); second repeat (cello and viola); in the fifth measure, the second violin also; *Allegro agitato* (cello); 8 after letter *A* (first and second violin); 10 after letter *A* (first violin); 7 after letter *C* (first and second violin); 1 before letter *F* (first violin); at letter *F* (bowing in first violin and viola); 2 before letter *G* (first violin and viola); 2 before letter *G* (first violin and viola shall have the note *f-sharp* instead of *f*); 1–4 after letter *G* (all voices); 10 before letter *H* (bowing); 1 after letter *H* (bowing); 12–14 after letter *H* (bowing, first violin).

Third movement: 8 measures after the opening I have indicated *legato* for the first two notes in the viola in order to facilitate an *up-bow* in the next measure. I assume that the rhythm will then be perceived like this:

NB

If you see it differently, omit the *legato*. Just now it occurs to me that perhaps you take both notes with a *down-bow*, in which case the *legato* obviously is unnecessary.

Nine measures after letter *A*, both violins shall have *legato* in one measure and *staccato* in one measure. It certainly must sound better that way, and only now do I realize that this is how I have sung this passage in my mind; 14 after letter *A*; at letter *B* (viola and cello); 8 before letter *C* (first violin and viola); 14 after letter *F* (viola, *legato*??); 7–9 after letter *F* (cello); 15 (17) after letter *F* (cello); at letter *G legato*; 4 before letter *H* (cello and viola); 1 and 3 after letter *H* (cello); 8 after letter *H* (first violin).

Fourth movement: 1–26 after letter *A*; 4 before letter *D* (I will discuss this passage later); 5 before letter *D* (viola); 1, 3, 5 after letter *D* (viola); 16–18 after letter *D* (cello); 19 after letter *D*; 11 after letter *E* (second violin and viola, later cello); 5 after letter *K*; 8–12 after letter *K*; 11 before letter *L*; 8 before letter *L*; 4 before letter *M* (viola); *O* (?); 16 before letter *P* to 8 before letter *Q*; 4 before letter *S*: here I would prefer that the chord

not be played arpeggio, and for that reason I have deleted the lower B-flat which you had added in the first violin; I have done the same at a corresponding place (4 before letter *D*); 3 before letter *S* (viola); 1, 3, 5 after letter *S* (viola); 8 before letter *T*. At 4 after letter *T* I have rewritten the whole passage in order to avoid the high position in the *ff* that follows. I think it will sound better this way. My last mailing contained a notation error in the cello part 4 measures after letter *W*; it obviously should be as I have now written it. Also the first violin shall be as before (the so-called presentiment was a bit of nonsense); at letter *X* (cello); 4 before letter *Z* (viola, remains as before); 13 after letter *Z* the first violin has

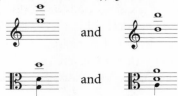

and

and the viola has and

That's it! In view of the indescribable inconvenience that I have caused you —and will continue to cause you—it is now my greatest desire that in the future you will come to experience a little joy from the composition. For in this case I know you well enough to understand that you will not regret—or be annoyed by—your work with it.

And now enough. Since my last mailing (*Andante* and changes) I have still heard nothing from you. Hopefully there won't have to be a lot of changes.

Goodbye for now, dear friend, and warm greetings to you and your wife from

Yours truly,
EDVARD GRIEG

P.S. Yesterday I received the news that I have been awarded the royal stipend; thus it is quite certain that I will be coming in the fall.[5]

I also request that you kindly leave the small notes (cues) enclosed in the quartet manuscript in the score (for the engraver).

3

Leipzig, December 16, 1878

Dear Heckmann!
Welcome back from Scandinavia! And thanks for your letter! I was so glad to hear that everything went so well.

I have never experienced anything like what I went through here after your departure. I thought the concert in Gewandhaus had been a decisive success—yes, some said that it had been a rare success—and in my naiveté I had already sent a telegram to my wife. But then all hell broke loose! Oh well, it's all over now and the newspapers are in the trash.[6]

The person who has annoyed me the most, however, is Dr. Abraham.[7] Well, I am his guest, so no more about that. But you will be surprised when you hear that the *Quartet* is going to be published by Fritzsch. More about this some other time.

---

[5] Grieg had applied for a travel grant of five hundred *spesidalers* in April of 1877. That application was not approved despite a unanimous recommendation by the appropriate committee in support of Grieg's request. When the application was resubmitted in 1878, the decision was positive. Soon thereafter Grieg began a "living-out-of-a-suitcase" life that was to continue for nearly two years.

[6] Grieg's *String Quartet* in G minor was premiered by the Heckmann quartet in the great hall of the Cologne Conservatory on October 29, 1878. The concert was a great public success. On November 30 the work was played in the Gewandhaus in Leipzig. The reaction of the audience was again very positive, but Leipzig music critic Eduard Bernsdorf (1825–1901) wrote a scathing review of Grieg's composition in *Signale für die musikalische Welt.*

[7] Grieg was hurt that Max Abraham of the C. F. Peters firm was not very enthusiastic about the *Quartet.* He said that he would print it, but Grieg understood that he was reluctant to do so and submitted it instead to E. W. Fritzsch (1840–1902), who published the first edition. The work was later reissued by Peters.

December 18

Since being interrupted the day before yesterday, it has been impossible for me to get a quiet moment until now. You ask me about the change at the conclusion of the third movement. That's how I have conceived it. After the ending, therefore:

This has the great advantage, seen in connection with the last movement, that it ends in G major and in so doing gives the beginning of the following movement an improved effect.

One could also very simply do it like this:

I think, however, that the first solution is best. Try both solutions and tell me your opinion, also if you find both unsatisfactory.

In the same movement there are two things that I have always regarded as poor, and that I have now altered. At the beginning of the second section it must be like this (NB: the first section *without* repetition!):

or—if you think the effect is more powerful—if *first violin and viola exchange parts*. The same holds true for the parallel passages that follow.

And now comes the place after letter *E* where I have twice eliminated four measures. Thus 6 measures after letter *E*:

In the first section the beginning of the passage was poor. The three long chords in B-flat minor must be omitted, and immediately afterward it begins like this (NB: the last B-flat major chord with a *fermata*).

And five measures after letter *E*:

Hopefully you agree! You would make me very happy with a quick reply, for Fritzsch is anxious to get the manuscript.

And with that, farewell for today! Greet your wife and the little singer, and don't forget

Your grateful friend,
EDVARD GRIEG

To Johan Hennum

Johan Hennum (1836–94) was musical director at the Christiania Theater from 1866 until his death. During his tenure in this position he made an important contribution to the cultural life of the city. Among his many achievements, he was responsible for the premiere performance of *Peer Gynt* in 1876 and for the new production of the play in 1892. Grieg's letters to Hennum are important to the understanding of Grieg's work with the incidental music to Ibsen's dramatic poem. Hennum was also an excellent cellist and often participated in chamber-music programs in the Norwegian capital.

Grieg's letters to Hennum are preserved Nasjonalbiblioteket, Oslo (National Library of Norway, Oslo Division).

1

Bergen, December 14, 1875

Dear Hennum!

Here I am sending you a letter for which I cannot think of a better name than a "Peer-Gynt" letter. The fact is that there are several things in the score that naturally are not stated as clearly as one might wish, and I have recently observed a few places in which the orchestration could have been improved. I will not ask you to take care that it comes off as well as possible, for I know that you will do that on your own initiative. I just want to thank you in advance for all your trouble, which, as I can foresee, is likely to be considerable. The fact is that there are only a very few places where the music is just music; it moves out on thin ice to caricature, and it often characterizes so crassly that it is important to perform it in such a way that the audience will understand the intention. There is so much that I wish we could talk about that does not lend itself to a simple summary. I will, therefore, set the score in front of me and go through it, and I ask you to now do the same.

First we have the metronome indications.

No. 1. *Allegro con brio* ♩ = 168. *Poco Andante* ♩ = 76. *Un poco Allegro* (*halling*[1]) ♩ = 112. *Poco Andante* as before. *Vivace* ♩ = 192. *Poco Andante* as before. *Largamente poco agitato* not slower but broader. *Allegro con brio* as before with *stretto* approaching the *halling.*

No. 2. Halling. *Allegro* ♩ = 112.

No. 3. Springar.[2] *Allegro vivace* ♩ = 192.

No. 4. *Allegro furioso* ♩ = 176. *Andante* ♩ = 56.

---

[1] A *halling* is a type of Norwegian folk-dance tune in 2/4 time.

[2] A *springar* is a type of Norwegian folk-dance tune in 3/4 time.

No. 5. *Allegro marcato* ♩ = 112. *Un poco più Allegro* ♩ = 116. *Allegro vivace* ♩. = 112, *Quasi Presto* 𝅗𝅥 = 120.

No. 6. *Andante* ♪ = 100. *Allegretto pastoral* ♩. = 69. *Allegro capriccioso* ♩ = 168 etc. as before.

No. 7. *Presto* ♩. = 192.

No. 8. *Alla Marcia e molto marcato* ♩ = 138.

No. 9. *Allegretto* ♩ = 104.

No. 10. *Presto* ♩. = 120.

No. 11. *Andante* ♩ = 56. *Allegro* ♩. = 88. *Andante* ♩ = 80.

No. 12. *Adagio* ♩ = 52.

No. 13. *Allegretto pastorale* ♩. = 48.

No. 14. *Presto* ♩. = 144.

No. 15. *Allegretto vivace* ♩ = 126.

No. 16. *Tempo di Mazurka* ♩ = 152.

No. 17. *Andante* ♪ = 120. *Allegretto* ♪ = 176. *Allegro* ♩. = 88. *Allegretto* as before. *Poco più lento* ♪ = 168. *Allegro molto* ♩. = 96.

No. 18. *Allegro vivace* 𝅗𝅥 = 152. *Prestissimo* 𝅗𝅥 = 200. *Molto più lento, quasi Moderato* 𝅗𝅥 = 104.

No. 19. *Un poco Andante* = 72. *Allegretto* ♩ = 132.

No. 20. *Largo* ♩ = 50.

No. 21. *Allegro molto* ♩. = 120.

No. 22. *Allegro molto* ♩. = 144. *Allegro marcato e sempre stretto* ♩ = 176.

No. 23. *Poco Andante* tempo as in No. 19, perhaps a bit calmer or, better, more somber.

No. 24. *Andante mystico* ♩ = 84. *Poco Allegro* ♩ = 100. *Poco Andante* ♩ = 72. *Andante* ♩ = 60. *Meno Andante* ♩ = 72 etc. as before until *Quasi Allegro agitato* ♩ = 96. *Andante* ♩ = 69. *Andante molto* ♩ = 56. *Allegro mystico* ♩ = 126.

No. 25. *Lento* ♩ = 72.

Well, that was that! Please add these tempo indications to the score. It is unfortunate that the score contains only handwritten notes, including many that have not even been written by me personally, so I must ask you to keep your eyes open for any possible copyist errors—and kindly inform me if you should find any such cases about which there might be some doubt.

Now I really come to the main business at hand, namely the understanding of the most dangerous passages and small changes in orchestration (of which, however, there are not so many). Let us, therefore, go through the work together once more. I think this is the most straightforward way to get the job done. Complexity is unavoidable, so you must excuse that. Thus:

No. 1. [Prelude. At the Wedding]

The two fragments of "Halling" and "Springar" I have thought of as being played by a *solo viola.* They must sound as if from afar, but sharply accentuated and authentic. In the "Halling" fragment, two measures have been mistakenly omitted. After the 12th measure following the 2/4 the following should appear once more:

and thereupon the next three measures. The conclusion of the *Allegro* from the point just before the curtain rises must be played *stretto.*

Nos. 2 and 3. ["Halling" and "Springar"]

On page 27 of Ibsen's book the beginning of the "Halling" must be heard as coming from *very far away.* On page 28, on the other hand, the ensuing "Halling" is heard in its entirety, and I have visualized the fiddler being seen in the distance on the meadow. It would be best if the fiddler [in the play] really were the one playing. If this is not possible, the one playing must stand right behind him, unseen by the audience, and in such a way that the illusion is preserved. I have supplied the bowings in the "Halling" and the "Springar" as well as I can. But since I have only a theoretical knowledge of the instrument, I am amenable to changes in bowing details that would improve the effect. But I do ask you for one thing: the fiddler must *know* both dances, not as an *orchestral* part, but almost by heart, and both dances must be played in perfect accord with folk-dance traditions, with sharp jerks against the beats and powerful strokes, so as to make the picture credible and authentic.

No. 4. [Prelude. The Abduction of the Bride. Ingrid's Lament]

Here I have had to make a change in the orchestration that must be inserted in the relevant parts and the score. It affects the winds and extends for eight measures beginning with measure 51 *[see page 382].*

The notes in the strings marked "–" preceding the quarter rest must absolutely not be short but must be sustained the full quarter note. Trumpets and timpani must come in strongly in *f* and execute a pronounced *dim.*, becoming steadily weaker and more muffled. Thereupon the timpani must again produce a mighty *crescendo.* Above all, much weight must be given here to the contrasts, since different characters are portrayed—the *Andante* Ingrid who toward the end

complains beseechingly, even threateningly, and in the *Allegro furioso* Peer Gynt, who tells her to go to hell. The horn motive in the Andante

signifies the demonic, which is later echoed by the Herd Girls:

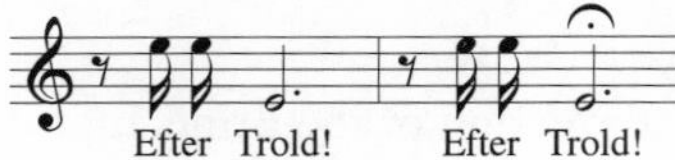

No.5. [Peer Gynt and the Herd Girls]

This is a risky piece that will either produce a downright bad effect or an altogether splendid, wild, devilish, and sensual one—all depending on how the performers *sing* and *play*. This is just one of the places where I think the music ceases to be music. The herd girls must first scream the words: "Trond of the Valfjeld!" etc., as if they were shouting all at once. They must not address themselves to the audience but only to the mountain scenery around them. Later they must just speak the lines clearly, that's the main thing, and then they must not stand still for a second, but must circle around Peer Gynt in wild desire, first a little, then more and more. Naturally, when the actors and actresses are so preoccupied with what is happening on the stage, it will be difficult to get them to pay attention to the baton, but *the situation must not be allowed to suffer as a result of that.* Before Peer Gynt's line, "And where are your boys then?" the preceding "When there aren't any boys, we'll settle for trolls" must be worked out with attention to *ritardando*, diction, precision, and the last word, especially—*trolls*—must be worked out with respect to both the bowing in the strings and the vocal sound in such a way that the *fz* that follows becomes both wild and coarse. Then comes the ensuing laughter, which must sound altogether witchlike and be accompanied by mimicry and gesture—still more the second time, and most of all the third time. Following that I suggest that Peer Gynt come forward right up to the footlights, with the herd girls following, so that everything they say to him can be picked up by the audience. However, Peer Gynt must first leap into their midst at *Allegro vivace* 3/8. In the concluding *Quasi Presto* the orchestra has a demanding task, and if they get it right I think it should sound absolutely devilish. With respect to this scene as a whole I would ask you to request of Josephson[3] that he, in consultation with you, do what can be done. Naturally you are having trouble with the singers, for the female singers, *ex professio,* consider it beneath their dignity to sing that sort of thing—because they don't win laurels in that way—and the actresses may not have enough vocal resources. If only it can be lively! That is the main thing.

No. 6. [Peer Gynt and the Woman in Green]

Here the curtain does not rise until the *Allegretto pastorale.* The double-basses must produce a big *crescendo* in the next-to-last measure of *Allegro capriccioso.* The oboe solo portrays the Woman in Green; the double-basses, on the other hand, depict Peer Gynt. The "amorous gestures" mentioned by Ibsen must, therefore, be adapted to the music.

No. 7. [Peer Gynt: "You can tell great men by the style of their mounts!"]

In this piece there is nothing to do but to go strongly ahead and then make a clear *diminuendo* to indicate that the actors are leaving the stage.

No. 8. [In the Hall of The Mountain King]

This piece must begin calmly and little by little become more agitated in a steady *crescendo* and *stretto* so that the theme will be a lot faster as the curtain rises. Then there must really be a whole crowd of people on the stage. The lines of the Troll Children—"May I slash his finger?" etc.—must be spoken in rapid succession with the rest; my concept is that the Troll Children come running across the stage

---

[3] Ludvig Josephson (1832–99), a Swede, Director of the Christiania Theater. See Grieg's letters to him.

toward the Mountain King one by one, each speaking his line when he reaches front stage. This will enhance the effect. Thus the speakers gather expectantly in front of the Mountain King until he shouts with a thundering voice: "Cool your blood!" etc. This, strictly speaking, is a matter for neither you nor me, but suggest it to Josephson. The change in the piccolo is to be used only if there is not time enough for the piccolo player to complete the figure:

The change will then be partly to 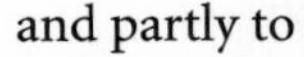 and partly to

depending on whether the figures begin with F ♯ or with A. The bass drum and cymbals must thunder and crash for all they're worth.

No. 9. [Dance of the Mountain King's Daughter]

Here the music must be an absolute parody, and in such a way that the audience understands that it is a parody. Only then will the effect be comical. The cowbell, obviously, can be replaced by a triangle. I would prefer to have an oboe solo because I think it provides a greater opportunity for comedy, but of course it depends mainly on the player. The piece must begin *piano* and steadily grow in intensity. The conclusion in the oboe part is changed as follows from two measures before *fermata* No. 1:

The reason is to make it more convenient for the player to take a breath after the long C ♯ than before it. Otherwise the notes are the same as before.

On the other hand, I would like to have the last two measures of the piece deleted and replaced instead by the following *one* measure *[see facing page, top]*.

It must be played with a tremendous jerk that brings the dance to an abrupt end. This is followed immediately by the Courtier Troll's line: "How do you like it?" etc. During the dancing and playing, Peer Gynt must make it clear (to the audience) that he can't stand either of them—and yet, he must do this while trying very hard to conceal his displeasure from the Mountain King and his cohorts.

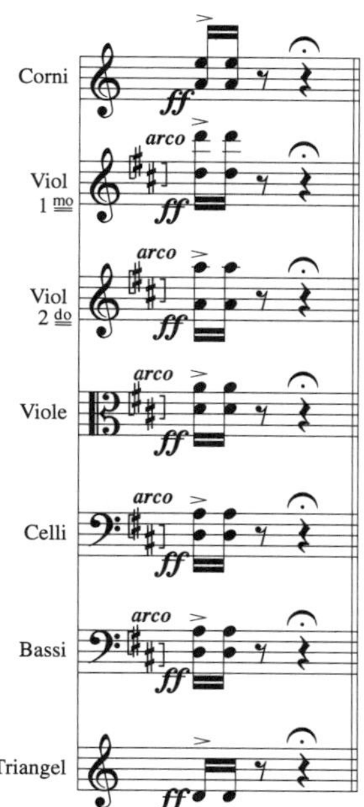

No. 10. [Peer Gynt Hunted by the Trolls]

This is yet another piece where it is essential that everything be strictly coordinated and that what occurs on stage be exactly what is prescribed and that there be no hiatuses. You must make very sure that Peer Gynt's lines can be heard by the audience. There is a small error in declamation that I would ask you to correct. In the line, "Goblins, block all the exits!" it should not be

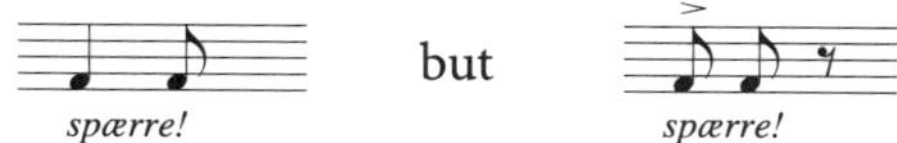

at all three occurrences.

After Peer Gynt's line, "Oh, were I a louse!" where the whole orchestra comes in *ff*, the trombones have been inadvertently omitted. Their parts must be added as follows:

The low-pitched *bell* in the distance I would like to have tuned to D in order to form a diminished fifth with the double-bass *tremolo* on G-sharp: that should give quite a frightening effect. If you can't find a bell, I suppose you could trim down a huge piece of iron or copper until it has this tone. And then it is important that the Troll Child does not scream until *you give him the sign at the sixth iteration of the bell sound*, for the racket in the orchestra and on stage must come immediately after the Troll Child's line. I hope the theater has a tom-tom (gong) that is more complete and more resonant than the cracked piece of junk that was there in my day, for the one time it is struck it must resound as if heaven and earth were coming to an end.

No. 11. [Peer Gynt and the Boyg]

Naturally, this is not a matter of making music but simply of trying to make the chord sound as hollow and muffled as possible. I suppose that this is achieved not only by having the winds stand backstage but also by having them turn their backs to the stage. If this is not enough, then try having them stand with their bells facing each other so that the sound from one player's instrument more or less goes into that of the other. From the measure before the chorus comes in backstage, the horns must sound more distinctly—because the chorus imitates the horns and gets its pitch from them. Toward the end, where I have tried an experiment with *the bells of the instruments pointed upwards* I have had in mind an extremely garish and sharp sound. The organ must have 8- and 16-foot stops and must be distant.

No. 12. [The Death of Åse]

This piece is played twice, first from the orchestra pit as a Prelude to Act 3, and again as Åse dies—this time off stage, and infinitely softly.

No. 13. [Prelude. Morning Mood]

This piece has merely to be treated as music, so everything depends on the musical interpretation. It is a morning scene where I think of the sun breaking through the clouds at the first *forte*. Two measures preceding this *forte*, i.e., measures 19 and 20 of the piece, there is a small change in the orchestration for the bassoons, horns, second violins and cellos, namely:

The other instrumental parts remain unchanged. The horns have rests in order to be more effective in the next measure. Despite the relatively few instruments, I would like to have a marked *crescendo* in the two measures preceding the *forte*. In the 70th measure the flutes and clarinets must be added. Like this:

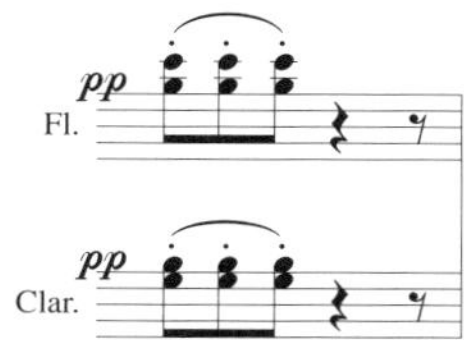

The other woodwinds have rests. Six measures later the flute has a figure that is mistakenly notated thus:

It must be like this:

In other words, the trill must be shorter. This change applies for each iteration of the figure. The three last chords in the piece should be very calm. This leads immediately, without a pause (only the horn and the clarinet must have time to change [instruments or crooks]), to No. 14.

No. 14. [The Thief and the Receiver]

A very fast tempo, and the whole thing must sound conspiratorial. It is important that the words of both the Thief and the Receiver be clearly heard. That is why I have kept their music so simple, so that anybody can sing it—but that does not mean that just anyone can act in these roles. Only when the piece is completely finished does Peer Gynt enter the stage.

No. 15. [Arabian Dance]

This is a piece which I think will be effective. I think it might be difficult to ensure that the chorus doesn't run away from the orchestra, but otherwise I have kept it as easy as possible. I hope that each of the dancing girls will have a tambourine, for that is the only way to get the sound I have in mind. I heard something similar last winter, and it sounded splendid. You must make very sure that everything occurs precisely on the beat. If Mrs. Juell[4] sings Anitra, I would be very pleased. Greet her warmly from me and tell her what I have said. The orchestra must sparkle and the *pizzicatos* must be kept together. Where the chorus sings:

---

[4] Johanne Juell (1847–82), an actress at the Christiania Theater.

I would like to have the piccolo play an octave higher, so with the two preceding measures it would be like this:

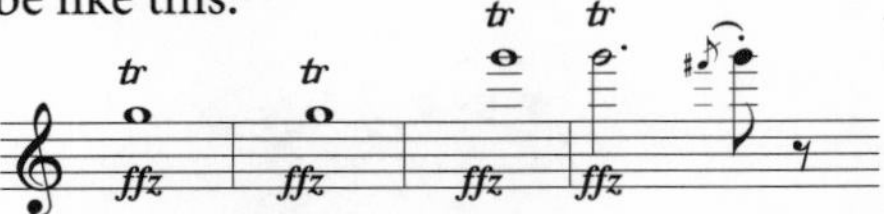

I have placed Peer Gynt's line at the end of the piece a little too early. He should not begin until the flutes have played their last notes as Peer Gynt follows the departing dancers with his eyes. The bassoons and bass drum *pp* must sound really Turkish.

No. 16. [Anitra's Dance]

This is an elegant little dance which I hope will sound really delicate and beautiful. It is essential that there be only a few dancers. It is orchestrated in such a way that, if necessary, it can be played *ppp* so that Peer Gynt's lines during the dance can be heard by the audience. I would be grateful if you would treat this piece with special affection. After the repetition sign, the double bass part at the beginning of the second section should be changed thus:

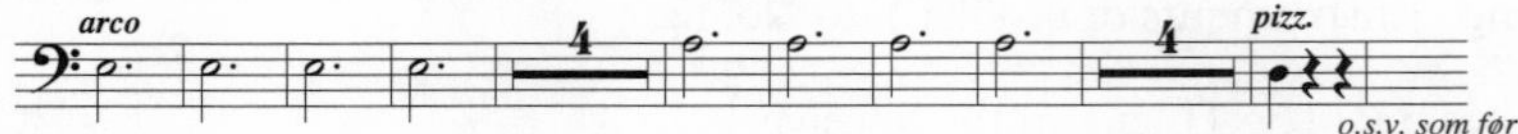

If we count 22 measures from here, we come to a place where the second violin *divisi* and second viola should be changed thus:

As you see, the strings are divided, and I am assuming that at that point—as I have marked No. 1—there will be four instruments on each part among the strings and two cellos—and this as a minimum.

No. 17. [Peer Gynt's Serenade]

Here I have added in the score that Peer Gynt should preferably sit far back on the stage, and in this case the accompaniment must be offstage and the first five measures omitted. Peer Gynt can then sit and mouth the words while he accompanies on his lute, and a singer offstage can sing the song in a vocally correct manner. It must sound partly amorous, partly ironic. In the measures where the text has the words "Fair maidens mourned the sacrifice," the cello part mistakenly has

instead of

Later in the song, where the words are "Like bird on highest branch's tip," the cello part must be changed in the same way. During the interlude and the instrumental conclusion Peer Gynt must handle his instrument with a certain affected passion. My concept is that the violin's *pizzicato* and the clarinet's *staccato* should produce a unique sound when both instruments are played precisely and simultaneously. If it proves to be too difficult for the clarinet I would recommend that it be played like this:

In other words, omit the middle note in [each group of three]. In any case, the [figure containing the] third grace note should *always* be played like this:

and not like this:

as it is in the score. That would be too heavy.

No. 18. [Peer Gynt and Anitra]

Here the strings must play with sharp accents.

No. 19. [Solveig's Song]

The actress who sings this song must make the most of it, for it reveals Solveig's character. Once in a moment of weakness I noted in the score that if the actress couldn't manage the humming part it could be played instead by a solo clarinet, and Solveig could sit spinning until it was finished. But I have totally abandoned this idea—first and foremost because it doesn't make sense to have her spinning in 3/4 time, secondly because it is inconsistent with the character of the song, and finally because the unique character of the piece is ruined. So you absolutely must rehearse the humming with the actress. It certainly is not difficult technically and can be sung quietly. Moreover, I have made the following change in the *Allegretto* that will make the last stanza easier to sing. Measures 13–17 of the *Allegretto* mistakenly have this:

instead of this:

Please change this in all the parts, also in the last stanza. The result is three measures instead of five, which makes it easier for a less experienced singer to hold the high A to the end without taking a breath. A folk-song style must be maintained throughout.

No. 20. [Peer Gynt at the Statue of Memnon]

The four horns must be played very muffled and softly, and the whole piece must have a foreign flavor.

No. 21. [Prelude. Peer Gynt's Homecoming. (Stormy Evening on the Sea)]

The aim of this piece is to characterize a stormy evening on the sea. Every *crescendo* and *diminuendo* must, therefore, be strongly emphasized and the tempo must be very agitated.

No. 22. [The Shipwreck]

The foundering of the ship is depicted. The actual grounding is indicated by the bass drum, timpani, and the *tremolo* in the double-basses, which should accordingly make a murderous noise. The groaning sounds in the woodwinds beginning at measure 27 must at each iteration begin very softly and make a pronounced *crescendo.* Thereafter the tempo is a bit calmer until the next 2/4, *Allegro marcato.* Here a change has to be made in the horn parts. The first and second horns beginning at *Allegro marcato* must be changed as follows:

The *presto* and the outcry must sound absolutely frightening, and the ensuing timpani solo depicts the expectant calm.

No. 23. [Solveig Sings in the Hut]

Offstage. Subdued and solemn.

No. 24. [Night Scene]

This piece, in which the music depicts Peer Gynt's pangs of conscience and the deeds that accuse him with increasing intensity until the final "Till you cry, *Enough*!" depends heavily on the interpretation. Where the woodwinds begin offstage, they must make the strongest possible *crescendo.* Likewise the strings in the pit, which shortly thereafter come in *tremolo,* begin *pp* and each time make a big *crescendo* and *diminuendo.* I have anticipated a bit of an effect from the experiment at this point of placing the winds offstage and the strings in the pit. But there are two things which you must be sure to tell the winds and the chorus backstage. First, it mustn't drag. And secondly, this is how it should sound: first soft, distant, and then a continually increasing intensity. The unison chorus must sound more and more ominous, and there must be a bit of *stretto* character as the piece progresses. Where the chorus sings "Doubt that strangles" etc. the first bassoon has sixteenth-note triplets, both here and later, until the next *Andante.* If he can't manage this, he can just play in unison with the second bassoon like this:

and later in the same way—only, of course, in the measures containing chromatic sixteenth notes. The hymn that is on page 254 of Ibsen's book must only be hummed offstage, not sung aloud.[5]

[5] This hymn, "Whitsun Hymn" ("O Blessed Morning") is in reality piece no. 25. Originally Grieg wrote just the melody, but he later made a four-part arrangement which is printed in *Edvard Grieg: Complete Works,* vol. 18.

No. 25. [Solveig's Cradle Song]

Here I am hoping for a poetic effect using all of the available musical resources. My concept is that during the prelude Peer Gynt lies as though hidden in Solveig's arms while the horizon heralds the imminent sunrise—which, however, must not occur until the place that I have indicated it, i.e. such that Ibsen's stage directions "her voice rising in the early light" have their intended effect. I hope the strings at this point will play in a balanced, quiet and graceful manner, and I hope that the actress will sing quietly and sincerely, then louder and fuller toward the end. In order that the song not feel excessively long, I recommend that where the three horns come in—at the words "Calmly he lay upon his mother's breast"—Solveig should sing *un poco animato*. At "all the whole livelong day," however, she should again sing *tranquillo*. Where it goes into *d minor* it must be sung and played fervently, and each iteration of the word "rest" must be given its own character. Steadily softer and softer, and always in such a way that the sounds of the horn and Solveig's "rest" are heard in contrast to one another. Therefore the strings must always accentuate the beginning of the measure and then immediately change to *pp*, so that the whole song becomes almost dream-like when the off-stage organ and voices join in, *distinctly and softly*. If the grace notes in the choral parts sound garishly out of tune or jerky, they can be omitted. The organ must have 8- and 16-foot stops. If it is an instrument with *Gr. Jeu*, use it. From the place where I have wished the sun to break through, the orchestra must little by little broaden and the performance indications must be carefully observed. Likewise Solveig's last stanza must be *very broad and fervent*. The curtain must fall *very* slowly as Solveig remains sitting, bowed over Peer Gynt. In the last measure the timpani's *tremolo* should be on

and not, as in the score, on

I know that you will regard what I have written with interest, and I request that you make all the necessary changes in the score and parts.

Thank you for your efforts for the benefit of the work. It will a big job for you, as it is for many others.

If you have anything to tell me, my address is just Bergen. How gladly I would have come to Christiania if I had not lived through such sad events[6] that quietude is the only way in which I think I might find myself again.

---

[6] Grieg's father died on September 13 and his mother on October 23, 1875.

Merry Christmas, and warm greetings from

Yours truly,
EDVARD GRIEG

P.S. Greet Josephson warmly from me!

2

Bergen, November 12, 1882

Dear Mr. Hennum!
In recent years I have received requests from several foreign concert organizations for the score and instrumental parts for the *Peer Gynt* music, but I have always responded negatively as I do not want it disseminated in that way in its present form. As you will recall, it was orchestrated strictly for the resources available in the Christiania Theater, and if the orchestration was not pleasing to me at that time, it is much less so now. On the title page of the score I have also made sure that there will be no concert performances by explicitly noting that the music is intended for "dramatic performance".

I am sending you this information so that, if you should receive the same request, you would not have to refer the inquiry to me but can simply say no.

Warm greetings.

Sincerely yours,
EDVARD GRIEG

3

Troldhaugen, February 16, 1892

Dear Hennum!
Herewith the music to "The Boyg" as requested by [Bjørn] Bjørnson.[7] From a strictly musical point of view it is very easy, but the trick is to integrate it well with the action on stage. The horn players must blow as if they had twenty lungs!

In addition to the Boyg music, I enclose a couple of small changes that I would ask you to kindly observe. How I wish I could be there. Then I could help you with this and that.

Warm greetings.

Sincerely yours,
EDVARD GRIEG

---

[7] The music to which Grieg refers was an expanded version of the music for the "Boyg" scene in *Peer Gynt*, which was to be staged at the Christiania Theater under Bjørn Bjørnson (1859–1942). Bjørnson himself played the title role and Johanne Dybwad (1867–1950) scored her first major stage triumph as Solveig.

Good luck!

While I think of it: I have not had time to send Bjørnson a piano reduction for use in rehearsing the melodrama. But I hope that neither you nor he will rest until everything is being done correctly and going like clockwork.

If the violas should be too thin in the *tremolo* of the first *Andante*, the second violins can just as well play along with them throughout that section. But I have written it that way to make it as soft as possible while lines are being spoken on the stage.

4

Leipzig, February 8, 1893

Dear Hennum!

I am sending herewith the score of *Peer Gynt Suite No. 2*, which has just been published. I ask you to accept it as a small token of my gratitude. In it you will see that "Dance of the Mountain King's Daughter", the orchestration of which I was not pleased with in Christiania, now is the way I think it ought to be. The piano can, of course, be omitted, as can the harp—NB in the theater—but I would much prefer that the xylophone (Holter[8] has an instrument that one or another of the percussionists should be able to play) be retained.[9]

You will also note that the "Arabian Dance" has undergone some small changes which I ask you to kindly enter into the score and parts. Last evening I conducted the new suite in an "Akademisches Koncert" in Albert-Halle (there were between two and three thousand people) and it went very well. Moreover, the Russian pianist Siloti[10] played my *Piano Concerto*.

My health situation, unfortunately, is not good. We are thinking of going to Italy at the beginning of March to see if I might be able to improve a little in a more southerly climate. Hopefully we will see you next summer. With warm greetings,

Sincerely yours,
EDVARD GRIEG

---

[8] Iver Holter (1850–1941), conductor of the Music Association orchestra in Christiania.

[9] The first printing of *Peer Gynt Suite No. 2* included "Dance of the Mountain King's Daughter" as the fifth movement. However, after Grieg had conducted the suite in Leipzig on February 7, 1893, he had second thoughts about the inclusion of the piece in the suite, and he insisted that it be withdrawn from the work. C. F. Peters complied with his wish, omitting the piece from all subsequent printings of the suite.

[10] Alexander Siloti (1865–1945).

To Robert Henriques

The Danish cellist, composer and music critic Robert Henriques (1858–1914) played an important role in Copenhagen's music life during the latter half of the nineteenth century, not least as music critic and associate editor of the newspaper *Vort Land*. Grieg was a frequent guest in the family home at Tordenskjoldsgade 1.

Grieg's letters to Robert Henriques are preserved in Det kgl. Bibliotek (The Royal Library), Copenhagen.

1

[Copenhagen,] December 21, 1885

Dear Mr. Henriques!

I would request that you send me an immediate reply to the question I asked you concerning a possible performance in Berlin.[1] And I have one more thing to ask of you: Will you please lend me your orchestration of my Dances for four hands[2] as I plan to use some of them in *Peer Gynt*.[3] Don't misunderstand me! This will be a loan to me personally, not something for which I can get you an honorarium or any kind of compensation from the theater. The theater is planning a more elaborate dance scene than was used in the Christiania production—and I, unlucky fellow that I am, must practice the piano, because I have promised Svendsen[4] that I will participate in his next philharmonic concert and don't have time to orchestrate the dances myself. I could, of course, get somebody here to do it, but that would look as if I didn't approve of your work, and my clear recollection is that I did. If you have the score with you, please send it to me. If not, tell me where in your house I can find it.[5] But above all: *without delay.*

Written in haste. With friendly greetings,

Sincerely yours,
EDVARD GRIEG

---

1 Grieg had asked in a postscript to a letter sent to Henriques on December 13, 1885, "Who conducts the philharmonic concerts [in Berlin], and with whom shall I communicate in order to play my *Piano Concerto* and conduct a few short pieces in February?"

2 Grieg is referring to *Norwegian Dances* for piano four hands. On December 2, 1882, Henriques had sent Grieg an orchestral arrangement of the dances which he asked Grieg to look over. Grieg himself never orchestrated these dances, but when C. F. Peters Musikverlag later published an orchestral version of them they did not use Henriques's orchestration but rather that of Bohemian violinist, violist, conductor and composer Hans Sitt (1850–1922).

3 The Danish premiere of *Peer Gynt* at the Dagmar Theater in Copenhagen on January 15, 1886, was a great success. A total of 42 performances of this production were given during the period January–August, 1886.

4 Johan Svendsen (1840–1911), musical director of the Royal Theater Orchestra in Copenhagen and conductor of annual series of philharmonic concerts in the Danish capital.

5 Grieg was using Henriques's workroom in Copenhagen while Henriques was in Berlin.

2

Copenhagen, January 16, 1886

Dear Henriques!
Will you please convey the enclosure to Prof. Mannstaedt[6] as soon as possible? It occurred to me that a direct approach would be the most courteous way to handle this.

I can greet you from your Dances,[7] which at yesterday's performance of *Peer Gynt* accompanied the dance scene in the hall of the mountain king and at some places really sounded quite good. In general for this purpose I would have liked a more rhythmic emphasis in the orchestration, but who could have guessed that these dances would be used in *Peer Gynt*?

I am writing these lines in your room, and that leads me to ask: How long may I continue here? In other words: When are you going to chase me out? Because I'm not going until then. I would very much like a word from you on this soon.

The other day I got a telegram from Hamburg inviting me to appear at the philharmonic concert there on the 21st, but unfortunately I had to decline because I don't want to make such a trip unless it can also include Berlin. So you can see that the Mannstaedt issue is an urgent one for me. The Klindworth[8] option must, therefore, according to your letter, be regarded as futile.

I nodded to your father at *Peer Gynt* last evening, but I haven't talked with him since, so I don't know if he was completely bewitched by the trolls!

With fond greetings from

Yours truly,
EDVARD GRIEG

3

Troldhaugen at Bergen, April 24, 1887

Dear Henriques!
Recently I happened to come across the volume of piano pieces that you have been so kind as to dedicate to me. Why have you not sent them to me, so that I could have thanked you earlier? I will tell you that you have made me very happy, for the things you have written are very nice. To be sure, the physiognomies that one encounters here are familiar ones. But good Lord, why be a novelty-chaser! Beauty is first and foremost beauty. And your pieces are so deeply felt, so fine in form, so noble in sound, that with respect to beauty they must be ranked very

---

6 Fritz Mannstaedt (1852–1932) was conductor of the Berlin Philharmonic concerts from 1893 to 1897.

7 Henriques's orchestral version of Grieg's *Norwegian Dances.*

8 The German pianist, conductor and composer Karl Klindworth (1830–1919) was conductor of the Berlin Philharmonic concerts for several years beginning in 1882.

high. The little "Tin Soldiers March" is just right. I would have guessed that it was written by Saint-Saëns or some other sophisticated Frenchman. But when I single out this one piece it is not my intention to denigrate the others, for all of them deserve full attention, and I will not fail to mention and disseminate them as I have opportunity.

Since I am now writing to you, however, I will not shrink from telling you how much it hurt me that you, in an article about Ole Olsen, wrote as you did about Johan Svendsen.[9] For let us be honest with each other. It is a simple fact that Svendsen does not care for Olsen's music. That being the case, it is only honorable of him to withdraw and not pretend; to do otherwise would be a lie. I have often talked with Svendsen about Olsen, whose fresh and vital talent—despite the rough-and-ready crassness that permeates it—I value highly. But unfortunately I have not been able to get Svendsen to share my opinion. You must remember that integrity is more important than compatriotism. If I had Svendsen's brilliant technique, perhaps I would reason as he does. But since technique does not play so large a role for me, I find it easier to enjoy the other outstanding aspects of Olsen's talent. And you with your artistic outlook should draw the same conclusion.

This, then, was about last year's snow;[10] but you will not misunderstand me. From where I sit, in any case, I could not pass by in silence a matter that lay so near at hand when I was writing to you.

Now you must bring the warmest greetings to everyone in your home. Tell your brother Edmond[11] that I miss him greatly these days: I have written a new *Violin Sonata*[12] that in this desert I have not been able to hear. Since my autumn travel plans hopefully will take me through Copenhagen, I look forward to revisiting Tordenskjoldsgade No. 1 and its amiable inhabitants.

Sincerely yours,
EDVARD GRIEG

P.S. Nina asks me to greet you!

4

Troldhaugen, July 26, 1898

Dear Robert Henriques!
I just come in from the breakfast table, my eye falls on the music shelf, and—at

---

[9] Ole Olsen (1850–1927) was a Norwegian composer, conductor and teacher. It was common knowledge in Copenhagen that there was no love lost between Henriques and Svendsen. The reason for this was that Svendsen was firmly opposed to Henriques's appointment as a cellist in the Royal Theater Orchestra.

[10] An allusion to François Villon's *Ballade des Dames du Temps*: "But where are the snows of yesteryear?"

[11] Robert Henriques's brother Edmond (1860–1910) was a Copenhagen banker.

[12] *Violin Sonata No. 3* in C Minor.

the bottom of it—on your name. I fetch the magnifying glass: It is your miniatures. And with the cover of the grand piano raised—play through them all! From there *presto* to the writing desk—two steps—to send you a declaration of love. What beautiful little things you have given us here! Genuine poetry, fine piano sound, excellent form, and often perfect characterization. I will just mention as pearls "Traveling Musicians" and "Tin Soldiers March"—but I should mention them all together. Apropos "should"! You "*should*" after this have achieved ——. Yes, isn't it a damn shame that no joy can be complete! Forgive me, that just came out of its own accord.

Yet another "should": You *should* have been at the music festival.[13] It was simply incomparable. To be sure, I had a hand in it, but a well-known Norwegian writer who lives abroad[14] recently wrote to me as follows: "The music festival, in my opinion, was one of the most important events of this century in our cultural life."

And now I'm off to spend a whole day in proof-reading![15] Damn, damn, damn!

Warm greetings to all of you from Nina and from

Yours truly,
EDVARD GRIEG

5

[Copenhagen], March 26, 1901

Dear Robert!
Of course I would rather be a "brilliant" composer than an "old" one.[16] But the word "brilliant" absolutely doesn't fit in this case, for the unanimous judgment of the reviewers is that my new songs are insignificant. I, for my part, even thought they provided evidence of a kind of evolution! And I also believed that I had a fairly advanced sense of self-criticism! When I saw all these scornful dismissals of my songs I felt the same as I once did in Leipzig when, after the premiere of my *String Quartet* in G minor, all the critics trashed it. I had given my

---

[13] The Norwegian music festival held in Bergen, Norway from June 26 to July 3, 1898.

[14] Grieg is referring to Hans Lien Brækstad (1845–1915), who worked in London as a correspondent for Norwegian newspapers. See Grieg's letters to Brækstad of February 6 and 23, 1898..

[15] Probably the proofs of the song cycle *The Mountain Maid,* which was in process of publication at this time.

[16] Grieg's *Five Songs* op. 69 and *Five Songs* op. 70, both to texts by Otto Benzon (1856–1927), had been performed at a concert in Copenhagen on March 21, 1901. Henriques had written in *Vort Land* that Benzon's texts were nothing but versified journalism but that "the lovely music will certainly survive when a real poet writes other texts to fit it or the composer arranges them as 'Songs Without Words' for string orchestra." What hurt Grieg the most, however, was that Henriques had referred to him as an "old" composer. "Old", in this context, could almost be regarded as a term of derision. Henriques must have quickly contacted Grieg and told him that there had been a typographical error: The word he had written was *genial* (brilliant), not *gammel* (old)!

best, my very soul, and I received nothing but scorn. I was so sad that I wanted to burn my piece. But time has proven that the critics were wrong. I hope the same thing will happen with these songs.

Thank you for your understanding! Warm greetings from

Sincerely yours,
EDVARD GRIEG

6

Christiania, October 20, 1906
Hotel Westminster

Dear Robert Henriques:
Let me through these lines solicit your interest and good will for my young countryman Fridtjof Backer-Grøndahl,[17] who in a few days will appear for the first time on a concert stage in Copenhagen. You know and prize as highly as I do our superb young pianist Karl Nissen,[18] who has just recently given a concert in your city. The still younger Grøndahl is no less talented than he.

What is interesting about the personalities of these two artists is not least the fact that they complement each other in the most remarkable way. Karl Nissen is serious, tranquil, reflective, pliable. Fridtjof Grøndahl is bursting with vital energy. He is a new lion—or, in view of his nationality, a new colt—romping about with *joie de vivre* and a sense of well-being. Both are amiable and modest people whom I like very much. It has been a pleasure for me, as I have had opportunity, to introduce them in various European concert halls. Last spring, for example, Karl Nissen played my *A-minor Concerto* in Prague under my direction, and he not only did an outstanding job but he also had a significant success. A few weeks later Fridtjof Grøndahl performed the same composition in Amsterdam, again under my leadership, and he played equally well and scored a similar triumph.

I hope very much that people in Copenhagen will not be so petty as to think of these two as competitors—though unfortunately it would be easy to do just that. But both of them are too good for that, and it would be a tragedy for our little Norwegian arts community if they themselves should begin to feel like competitors. Moreover, it would demoralize them as artists and as human beings. Both as a musician and as a patriot I am grateful to you for the warm reception you have accorded Karl Nissen in your paper. Now when you have heard Fridtjof Grøndahl and gotten an impression of his great skill, please use your influence to ensure that Fridtjof's talents will be recognized for what they are.

---

[17] Norwegian pianist Fridtjof Backer-Grøndahl (1885–1959).
[18] Norwegian pianist Karl Nissen (1879–1920).

How deeply I desire that these two young eagles, who are leaving the nest at the same time and spreading their wings in order to ascend to the heights, should be granted the opportunity to soar up there unhindered by all the pettiness and foolishness that could impede their flight.

Believe me, I speak on the basis of my own costly experience! How much both Svendsen and I have suffered from time to time from the words of "well-intentioned" friends who, in their lamentable need to draw comparisons, have practically depicted us as enemies! Help me, then, to save these two young men from such friends! Remember what Goethe said when somebody wanted to denigrate Schiller: "You should be happy that you have two such fellows!"[19]

Accept, then, my sincere thanks for what you have done and are doing both for the one and for the other! I need not add that Grøndahl is unaware that I am writing to you.

I often long for Denmark more than I should. Old age and youth reach out toward each other in such a way that the longing grows. But unfortunately: It *cannot* be. Winter in Denmark belongs to the past.

If you have a moment to spare, give me the pleasure of a few lines. Warm greetings to everyone in Tordenskjoldsgade!

Sincerely yours,
EDVARD GRIEG

---

[19] Grieg quotes the response of Johann Wolfgang von Goethe (1749–1832) to someone who sought to curry favor with him by speaking negatively of his presumed rival, Friedrich von Schiller (1750–1805): "Sie sollten froh sein, dass sie zwei solche Kerls haben!"

To Henri Hinrichsen

Henri Hinrichsen (1868–1942), nephew of Max Abraham (1831–1900), became an apprentice at age nineteen in his uncle's firm, C. F. Peters Music Publishing Company in Leipzig. In 1891, after further education in Basel, Brussels and London, he became confidential clerk of the firm. Three years later he became co-owner, and in 1900, when Max Abraham died, sole proprietor. He was eminently successful in leading the firm farther along the path laid out by his uncle and, like him, provided solid support for Grieg and his work. Grieg showed his gratitude by taking the initiative that resulted in Hinrichsen's becoming a Knight of the Order of St. Olav in 1904. Hinrichsen's high regard for Grieg is evident from a letter written to the composer on December 21, 1904, which states in part: "I really do not need to assure you that a new opus from your pen is among my *very greatest* joys. If the joy is not exactly the same as that when my wife is about to give me our fourth child, it is at least of almost the same type, and these are the only occasions when the flagpole at Talstraße 10 is adorned with a flag."

The complete correspondence between Grieg and the owners of C. F. Peters—a total of 635 letters, which are preserved in Bergen Offentlige Bibliotek (Bergen Public Library)—has been published by Finn Benestad and Hella Brock in the original German in the book *Edvard Grieg. Briefwechsel mit dem Musikverlag C. F. Peters 1863–1907*, Frankfurt 1997. Many of these letters deal with business minutiae, others give information of great interest with respect to Grieg's biography, and not a few provide a glimpse of the friendship that existed between Grieg and his publisher.

Included here are two letters in translation from Grieg to Hinrichsen.

1

Voksenkollen, December 9, 1900

Dear Mr. Hinrichsen!

That was a hard blow![1] If only I had been in Leipzig so that I could have pressed his hand one last time in a final farewell! From my own state of mind I can imagine how you are feeling the loss. For me he was, in the best sense of the word, a fatherly friend; he has affected my life in an energetic and productive way as have few others. When we first became acquainted with each other forty years ago, our collaboration during the first years was of a purely business nature. But I soon observed, behind the businessman, the philanthropist and the personal good will, qualities that aroused in me an appreciation that has never ceased—no, to the contrary, it was destined to grow more and more. I am deeply aware of the gratitude that I owe to him and his memory. And I regret all the more that I did not have an opportunity to give expression to this at the jubilee. For my letter, which you are requested to open, unfortunately arrived too late.[2]

---

[1] Hinrichsen's uncle, Max Abraham, who was director of C. F. Peters Musikverlag in Leipzig, died on December 8, 1900.

[2] See Grieg's letter to Abraham of December 5, 1900, which he wrote primarily on the occasion of the centennial jubilee of the C. F. Peters Music Publishing Company.

How empty everything around me became when I received the news last evening. And then this morning, like a final greeting from the departed, I received his dear, last letter, in which he expresses his gratitude to *me*![3] This final greeting is a great, great consolation to me! I would not for anything in the world have failed to receive it. Judging from this letter, which was written December 5, it appears to me as if the death must have occurred quite unexpectedly. Please be so kind as to tell me something about his final days and hours!

Today I cannot write anything else! I will add just this much, that I cherish the firm hope that in the future the good spirit of the departed will also reign over your life and work!

With warm greetings to you and your family, also from my wife, I am,

Sincerely,
EDVARD GRIEG

2

Christiania, December 11, 1905
Hotel Westminster

Dear Mr. Hinrichsen!
Well, you certainly are the living, resurrected Dr. Abraham! With what sensitivity you have thought the matter through! And then, in addition, the more than modest request to be kept anonymous in the whole matter! I don't need to tell you that both my wife and I feel a great joy over this new proof of your kindness. So: On behalf of Norway accept my sincerest thanks for your beautiful intention.[4]

But hear now what an old expert regarding his people says: "Among us the word 'reverence' hardly exists except in name." It may be unfortunate for us, but it is a fact that lies deeply buried in our history, and one must take this into account. Up here we don't erect either memorial plaques or museums in honor of the country's outstanding men. We simply have no interest in such things. So: If, after my death, you wanted to bequeath Troldhaugen to the Norwegian state,

---

[3] See the excerpt from this letter in footnote 8 to Grieg's letter to Abraham of December 5, 1900.

[4] Grieg had long considered moving to Christiania because he was no longer able to tolerate the climate of West Norway. But in order to buy a house in Christiania he would have had to sell Troldhaugen, his villa on the outskirts of Bergen. In a letter dated November 28, 1905, Hinrichsen sent Grieg a check for 25,000 Norwegian crowns with the request that he keep the matter secret but merely (for business reasons) confirm that he had received it. Hinrichsen's intention in giving this unusually generous gift from the Peters firm was to enable Grieg to retain ownership of Troldhaugen as long as he lived and that the villa should then be conveyed to the Norwegian state as a Grieg museum or a retirement home for Norwegian composers. The letter came to Grieg like a bolt out of the blue. Hinrichsen wrote later that Grieg himself would have to decide how the money should be used—for which Grieg thanked him in a letter dated December 27, 1905. At that time Grieg expressed the wish that the proceeds from the sale of Troldhaugen after his death should go to the Grieg fund, which had been established in 1903 with gifts received in honor of the composer's sixtieth birthday. Grieg never did buy a house in Christiania. Except for numerous concert tours abroad, he continued to live at Troldhaugen until his death in 1907.

the state would indeed accept the gift with thanks but perhaps would—probably *almost too* strongly—feel the same as Dr. Abraham said to Anton Rubinstein[5] when he, after having made a number of changes in scores that had already been printed, requested that they be engraved anew: "You understand, Mr. Rubinstein, this is for me more an honor than a pleasure!" (A brilliant reply!) In other words: The state would have to accept the villa and then pay the expenses on it.

In other respects too, however, the villa would be as unsuitable as anything imaginable for the purpose you have suggested, and if you had visited Troldhaugen just once you would never have come up with this idea. The villa is in an *out-of-the-way* location and is very exposed to rough weather and storms. During the winter no one would visit a Grieg museum there. Nonetheless, one would have to employ a watchman to prevent the theft of things of value. As a home for composers the situation would be equally unfavorable. The villa—and this is especially true for older people—can, in general, *only* be used as a summer residence. Don't you think it would be more to the purpose—if I were to leave Troldhaugen—to sell the villa and then, in accordance with your magnanimous idea, let the proceeds together with my other effects go either to the Music Society Harmonien[6] in Bergen or to "the Grieg fund"? This fund will in any case go to a home for composers.[7]

Please forgive me for expressing my views in accordance with my deepest convictions, and give me soon the pleasure of a reply.

With friendly greetings,
EDVARD GRIEG

P.S. With respect to the consul matter,[8] I have conferred with a cabinet minister whom I know well. As soon as possible he will speak with the minister of foreign affairs, in whose hands this matter falls. I have been advised that the idea of decreasing the number of consulates is currently on the agenda but that the question is still undecided.

---

5 Russian pianist and composer Anton Rubinstein (1829–94).

6 Grieg was conductor of the Music Society Harmonien, predecessor of the modern Bergen Philharmonic Orchestra, during the years 1880–82.

7 After Grieg's death in 1907, Mrs. Grieg retained possession of Troldhaugen for more than a decade. In 1919, however, the villa was sold at auction. The buyer was Joachim Grieg (1849–1932), Edvard's second cousin, who four years later gave the property to the municipality of Fana, within whose borders it is situated, on the condition that the municipality would "take care that the place be used for purposes that could be assumed to be consistent with the spirit and interests of Edvard Grieg and worthy of Troldhaugen's tradition." Grieg's former home was opened as a museum in 1928.

8 Hinrichsen had asked Grieg about the possibility of becoming Norwegian vice-consul in Leipzig. Grieg carried the matter all the way to Prime Minister Christian Michelsen (1857–1925), but it became evident that the government had someone else in mind for the job. Hinrichsen did not, therefore, submit a formal request for consideration.

To Hedwig von Holstein

Hedwig von Holstein (1819–97) was married to German composer and author Franz von Holstein (1826–78), who made German translations of a number of Norwegian and Danish texts used by Grieg in his songs.

Letter 1 to Hedwig von Holstein is preserved in Nasjonalbiblioteket, Oslo (National Library of Norway, Oslo Division), Letter 2 in The Pierpont Morgan Library, Mary Flagler Cary Music Collection, New York. Both are in German.

1

Copenhagen, December 29, 1890
Hotel King of Denmark

Dear Mrs. von Holstein!
Today we saw Gade[1] to his grave! He had requested that there be no music or speeches, just a short prayer. And that is how it was. The only unbelievable person was, naturally, the minister, who didn't miss the opportunity to utter a bunch of nonsense. Were it not for this, the solemn occasion in all its simplicity would have had something uplifting about it. The king and queen, the princes and princesses all participated in the ceremony. First there was a prelude, then a hymn, then the sermon, then another hymn (melody by Gade), and then the church choir—with organ accompaniment—sang the old crusader song:[2]

(Perhaps you are familiar with the melody.) And then the solemn occasion was over. Gade will not be buried; he will be entombed in the church chapel among the country's great men.

I have admired Gade as I have admired few others, especially in my youth, and I know that you have done the same. That is why I am sending you this farewell impression from him. Just think: Last Sunday he visited us in the hotel, joked and was happy and healthy. That same evening he suddenly died. A beautiful, enviable death! The following day I saw him pale and cold, but smiling in death.

In Germany he is already by and large forgotten. How unfair! For he has written great and singular works that contain much more than mere echoes of Mendelssohn. And moreover: what a noble spirit! A tolerant nature, without the slightest tinge of narrow-mindedness!

---

[1] Danish composer Niels Wilhelm Gade (1817–1890) died on December 21.

[2] Grieg is referring to the Silesian folk tune known in English as "Beautiful Savior", in German as "Schönster Herr Jesu", and in Scandinavia as the Christmas hymn, "Deilig er jorden".

I cannot speak of anything else today. Goodbye for now, dear Mrs. von Holstein! A happy new year, hopefully also one in which we shall meet again, is wished to you by my wife and by

Yours truly,
EDVARD GRIEG

P.S. Warm greetings to Miss von Holstein and Miss Hauptmann.

2

Troldhaugen, Hop Station at Bergen, February 26, 1892

Dear Mrs. von Holstein!
Accept my sincerest thanks for your swift reply! I had, after all, no hope of hearing anything quickly from poor Herzogenberg, and I was terribly worried! I *had* to inconvenience somebody or other—and the choice fell on you. Forgive me![3]

Now he himself has written, and I can only say that I admire in the highest degree the manner in which he is taking his bitter loss. Even—how shall I say this?—his Olympian optimism is intact. For example, he writes thus: "In spite of everything, the dear Lord is fond of me, for he has immediately given me something to work with!" It's really unbelievable! But from the top of his spiritual vantage point perhaps one may have a right to an Olympian joviality such as that.

The commemorative ceremony in your home must have been very moving. Dr. Wach[4] has sent me a copy of his beautiful talk. It would make me very happy if, when you have the opportunity, you would convey to him my sincerest thanks for his kindness in thinking of me.

An awful lot has now changed in Leipzig! I think your home on Salomonstrasse is the only true music home that remains from the old, wonderful time. May it long remain so!

With the sincerest greetings, also from my wife, I am

Yours truly
EDVARD GRIEG

---

[3] On January 7, 1892, the Austrian composer Heinrich von Herzogenberg (1843–1900)—one of Brahms's close friends and a friend of Grieg as well—had lost his wife, pianist Elisabeth von Herzogenberg (b. 1847). In 1872, Herzogenberg had moved from Graz to Leipzig, which is where Grieg had become acquainted with him. In 1885 he had moved to Berlin as professor of composition at the Hochschule für Musik. After an extended sick leave that lasted from 1889 to 1892, he was finally about to resume his position at the Hochschule.

[4] Leipzig attorney Adolf Wach (1843–1926).

To Iver Holter

Norwegian composer and conductor Iver Holter (1850–1941) was in many ways a kingpin in the cultural life of Norway for two generations. As a young violinist and student of medicine, he played under Grieg in Christiania in the late 1860's. Later he also played viola under Grieg and Johan Svendsen (1840–1911) in the Music Association orchestra. After studying composition in Leipzig in 1876–78 and in Berlin in 1879–81, on Svendsen's recommendation he was chosen to succeed Grieg as conductor of the Music Society Harmonien in Bergen. After another period of study in Leipzig in 1884–45 he returned to Christiania, where in 1886 he replaced Johan Selmer (1844–1910) as conductor of the Music Association orchestra. He remained in this important position for 25 years, in the course of which he had a profound impact on the cultural life of the Norwegian capital. He kept abreast of new currents in European music and gave first performances in Norway of a long list of works by such composers as Richard Wagner, Johannes Brahms, Camille Saint-Saëns, Jean Sibelius and Carl Nielsen. He was also a highly regarded choral conductor. In 1897 he founded "Holter's Choral Society", which he conducted until 1920 and with which he performed many choral masterworks.

Holter's opus list is not long, and his compositions are not especially forward-looking, but they do show a secure sense of form. His best-known work is his orchestral suite from the incidental music for Goethe's *Götz von Berlichingen.*

Grieg had a close working relationship with Holter for many years. Their friendship was severely tested when they found themselves on opposite sides of a major controversy that developed in connection with the Norwegian music festival held in Bergen in 1898 (see Grieg's letters to him in 1897 and 1898), but they became reconciled before the festival took place.

Grieg's letters to Holter are preserved in Nasjonalbiblioteket, Oslo (National Library of Norway, Oslo Division).

1

Bergen, September 24, 1889

Dear Holter!

Herewith the piano reduction.[1] Excuse the delay, but the copyist did such an outrageously incomplete job that both my wife and I myself had to supply what was lacking. That is why there are three different handwritings. The baritone solo, the mezzo soprano solo and the quartets can be sung from the choral parts. I won't send the viola part until I know for sure whether or not Miss Nordgren[2] will sing. I spoke briefly with her last evening but was not able to pin her down. She talked about having to consult Mr. Knutzen[3] (is she engaged to him?). You will hear something definite in a few days. Presumably she doesn't want to buy a pig in a poke, but will first familiarize herself with the part, and one can't object to that. However that may be, it seems to me that it is the Music Association that is being

[1] The piano reduction of *Olav Trygvason*. Regarding the premiere performance of Grieg's opera fragment, see his letters to Bjørnstjerne Bjørnson (1832–1910) of October 6 and 15, 1889.

[2] Swedish soprano Ellen Nordgren (1863–1947), who later married Norwegian Lieutenant Colonel Hans P. J. F. Gulbranson (1860–1946).

[3] Norwegian pianist Martin Knutzen (1863–1909).

hurt by the fact that Miss Nordgren is performing a few days before its concert, not the reverse.

By way of introduction to the piece itself I will just tell you that the sketches are from 1873! I have undergone an enormous development since that time, so I cannot honestly say that it is flesh of my flesh and bone of my bone such as I am today. On the other hand, I felt that it contains things that were worth rescuing from the oblivion of the wastebasket. I think it will come off well on the stage. As for the concert hall I have my doubts, but I have hope. That the piece was not continued back then was owing to the fact that Bjørnson didn't want to write any more text.[4] It is representative of him and his stage of development at that time. Naturally there will never be any more, nor should there. A continuation now would be at the expense of stylistic unity both for him and for me. I say this to you quite privately as a friend and an artist.

We leave from here Monday the 30th and arrive by train in Christiania Friday evening. I am thinking of giving a concert in the Hals auditorium on Wednesday the 9th, but I haven't decided for sure. My wife is so miserable that I don't dare to proceed as I would otherwise.

Warm greetings! Thank you for your interest! Remember to correct the mistakes in the choral parts! You presumably will hear from me by telegraph before you receive this letter.

Sincerely yours,
EDVARD GRIEG

2

Troldhaugen, June 17, 1891

Dear Holter!
Thank you for the telegram! My friend Frants Beyer and I took a wonderful trip to Odland in Samnanger on my birthday. It's a spot that is so bountiful and beautiful that it can compete with the best of Hardanger. It is also a place where the grass will be trampled bare when the vacation period arrives. There is going to be an extraordinary "brood" at Troldhaugen: Brodsky with his wife and his sister-in-law Mrs. Piccard, Dr. Abraham, Delius, Holter, and hopefully Sinding.[5] There will be room for all of you, NB if you aren't too choosy. As far as I know, Brodsky's and Abraham are coming around the 20th of July. So you must not come later than that. I don't know anything definite about Delius, but he will

---

[4] See Grieg's letters to Bjørnson from 1874 and 1875.

[5] Russian violinist Adolf Brodsky (1851–1929); Olga Piccard, his sister-in-law; Max Abraham (1831–1900), owner of the C. F. Peters Musikverlag in Leipzig; and English composer Frederick Delius (1862–1934). Grieg had a trip to the mountains with Delius and Holter in July and with his Bergen friend Frants Beyer (1851–1918) and Dutch friend Julius Röntgen (1855–1932) in August. Max Abraham, Christian Sinding (1856–1941) and the Brodskys were not able to come.

come. I must choose the date for the trip to Jotunheimen to accommodate Abraham, whose time is limited, but we can work that out. I think it will be enjoyable. I suppose you have heard that Brodsky is going to New York. Unfortunately! This get-together will be a kind of farewell celebration. As for yourself, you are warmly welcome! The bath house and fishing tackle are ready! Frants has a sailboat. You yourself must bring good weather and good humor—that's an order! Write and tell me when you are coming!

Sincerely yours,
EDVARD GRIEG

P.S. Nina hopes you will be content with what we have to offer even if it isn't the "fleshpots of Egypt".

3

Troldhaugen, September 5, 1891

Dear Holter!
Your description of the trip wasn't bad. Both Nina and I got a good laugh. Otherwise I for my part wasn't inclined to laugh, for in recent days—for the third time since our departure from Haukeliseter—I have had stomach problems, and they have finally started to rob me of my strength. In Odda I was in bed for four days. It was a fairly serious attack. Thereafter Röntgen and I went from Lofthus to Turtegrø, where we met Beyer, with whom we had an exceptionally wonderful and felicitous ten-day trip to the mountains. Right when I came home I had the second stomach attack, and a few days later the third, both times after a rather cold swim in the sea—so now I will have to be careful about that.

I have not been in shape to date to make plans for the winter. What I would like most of all is to stay home and work in peace and quiet. But perhaps this would prove to be altogether too lonely, as spoiled as I have now become. Apropos your renewed friendly invitation, I spent some time yesterday pondering what could be done there.[6] If I go first to Christiania and subject myself to all the agonies that for me are connected with public performance, then I might as well go all the way: first a little concert in the Hals auditorium, then the Music Association, and then my own big concert—as before. And then it makes little sense to perform only *Olav Trygvason,* which was done recently. You ask if I have something more, and I have been thinking about what I would dare to serve in Tigerville,[7] where I have indeed performed a lot of my compositions in recent years. One piece that I have not conducted there for many, many years is *Before*

---

[6] Holter had invited Grieg to Christiania to give a concert to mark the 25th anniversary of his (Grieg's) first concert there on October 15, 1866. Grieg went to Christiania and participated in concerts there on November 1, 14 and 21, 1891.

[7] "Tigerville": a somewhat pejorative name for Christiania coined by Norwegian author Bjørnstjerne Bjørnson.

a Southern Convent, and something else that has never been performed there is a part of the *Album for Male Voices.* If I could add to that a new *Peer Gynt Suite No. 2,* I would then have the following program:

1. New *Peer Gynt Suite* (or, failing that, *Holberg Suite*)
2. Songs?
3. *Before a Southern Convent*
4. Songs for male voices—baritone solo and male chorus
5. *Olav Trygvason*

I could bring the score and orchestral parts for *Olav Trygvason* with me, but the Music Association would have to purchase the choral parts. (The old offprints can no longer be used because of changes.) I have all the music for *Before a Southern Convent.* As for the songs for male voices, however, you will have to gladden Warmuth's[8] heart by purchasing the music. I might make arrangements myself to have the parts for the *Peer Gynt Suite* written out in Christiania, and I have all the *Holberg* music. The soloists would of course be Lammers and Mrs. Gulbranson or Oselio[9]—though it would make more sense to choose Gulbranson, who has sung in *Olav Trygvason* before, if she is available. The question of an honorarium is immaterial to me. But if I do this program I naturally would repeat it at my own concert, and for that reason I am afraid that I wouldn't want to risk a public dress rehearsal in the Music Association.

Well, what do you think of this? If you say yes, then we'll plan on the 9th of November, and I would ask you to immediately let Sigurd Hals[10] know so that he can reserve the auditorium for my own concert. If you say no, I will regard it as the hand of fate and will stay home on my cozy little hillock. So: My winter is completely in your hands. I would not come home afterward, that's for sure, for all the fears of seasickness prevent me from doing so. Consult the Norns[11] immediately. You must chant over what they have woven so that it doesn't happen here as it did in *Twilight of the Gods*: "Es riss, es riss, es riss!"[12]

Be sure to let me know the date of the first concert so that if possible I can be present to hear Delius's piece.

Do you know if *Peer Gynt* is going to be performed at the theater?[13] That would undeniably give wings to my wanderlust. Especially if my wayward health

---

[8] Christiania music dealer Carl Warmuth Jr. (1844–95).

[9] Norwegian baritone Thorvald Lammers (1841–1922), Swedish-born soprano Ellen Nordgren Gulbranson and Norwegian soprano Gina Oselio (1858–1937).

[10] Christiania piano manufacturer Sigurd Hals (1859–1931).

[11] Norns: In Nordic mythology, the goddesses of fate, usually represented as three maidens (Urd, Verdandi and Skuld) who spun or wove the fate of men.

[12] Rikard Wagner's music drama *Twilight of the Gods.* "Es riss!": "It tore!"

[13] The first three acts of *Peer Gynt* were staged at the Christiania Theater on March 9, 1892. Bjørn Bjørnson (1859–1942) directed the play and also played the title role. Grieg wrote some new music for the Boyg scene but could not attend the performance. See his letter to Bjørn Bjørnson of February 7, 1892.

would behave itself. But you can understand that there is no surplus of energy when one feels as dejected as I do now. Still—today I again feel that things are improving.

Warm greetings from both of us!

Sincerely yours,
EDVARD GRIEG

P.S. Let me know if you are thinking of having Lammers's choir participate, especially in the songs for male voices, so that I can talk with Lammers personally when he comes here soon.

To spare you the unpleasant visit with Sigurd H[als], I will rather write him a few words and ask him to get further details from you a couple days after receiving my letter. I am telling him that for now the matter is just between us.

4

Geneva, March 16, 1894
Hotel Beau-Rivage

Dear Holter!
I promised you a letter from Munich, but everything got so topsy-turvy with our hurried departure that I had to postpone it. The concert was a triumph for me and a victory for Norway such as I have not experienced since the one in London. The orchestra played marvelously. I had to take 12–14 curtain calls, and at the end, when people left, the young folks stayed behind and called me out 5–6 times with loud shouts of "Hurrah" and "Wiederkommen! Wiederkommen!" It wouldn't have taken much more, God help me, to get me to commit the blunder of talking to the people à la Ole Bull[14] and inviting the whole lot of them up to Norway. But reason prevailed.

Afterwards we ate oysters with Levi,[15] and the next day we came here. In the evening there were several people who wanted to send a telegram to Norway, so it was no wonder that today I eagerly looked through *Verdens Gang*[16] for Monday the 12th. But not a word. Does this perhaps have something to do with the parole? Who knows. For I *can* read between the lines. I pity you, who have a permanent position there under the conditions at home—now more than ever lacking in music reviewers. It's bad enough when the reviews are handled by untalented so-called artists. But there is something that is even worse, that I see now. But take heart. I was trampled on in Christiania for seven years in a row—so badly trampled that one would think I could not survive. The fact is that

---

[14] Norwegian virtuoso violinist Ole Bull (1810–80), who often made impromptu speeches to his audiences after taking several curtain calls.

[15] German conductor Hermann Levi (1839–1900).

[16] *Verdens Gang*: a Christiania newspaper.

when the pear is ripe it falls off. And the strangest turns occur when one least expects them.

Tomorrow I will conduct here. From a musical standpoint Geneva is a small city, but I have had four rehearsals and have made good use of them, so I hope it will go okay. The day after tomorrow we may go to Menton, for we can't stand it here. It's full winter here, with slush and rain, wind and cold. And no hope of being able to get anything done, for people bother the life out of me.

Let me hear from you soon. The address is always: C. F. Peters, Thalstrasse 10, Leipzig.

Nina asks me to greet you warmly. So also does

Yours truly,
EDVARD GRIEG

5

Leipzig, January 12, 1896
Hotel Hauffe

Dear Holter!
I really should address you as Mr. Cantata-composer, for what you are producing along that line is indeed colossal.[17] For me, the very mention of the word "song festival" (in the Behrensian[18] sense of the word) makes me nauseous, and when I am so unfortunate as to have write something for such a festival I write music that makes one vomit. Therefore, in setting a poem by Jonas Lie[19] (which may be okay as poetry but is rhythmically impossible), I have now inked over a piece of staff paper so painstakingly that it has become a solid waste receptacle for the gentlemen songsters in case they should get upset to their stomachs during the festival. To whom shall the song be sent? You must tell me that, and then you must tell Lammers that he is involved in it.

Recently I got a telegram from Trondheim with a request to set a poem by Skavlan[20] entitled *Griffenfeldt at Munkholmen.* Obviously I had to decline, as I don't intend to have any more to do with song festivals than is absolutely necessary and since, above all, I think that other Norwegian composers should also be involved.

Now I see from the newspapers that Mr. Haarklou[21] is reminding people of

---

[17] Holter was in process of completing a cantata (text by Nordahl Rolfsen, 1848–1928) to be sung at a big song festival on May 25, 1896. The previous year he had composed a cantata entitled *Til Fædrelandet* (*To the Fatherland*) to a text by Theodor Caspari (1853–1948).

[18] Johan Didrik Behrens (1820–90) was the foremost choral director in Christiania during the second half of the nineteenth century.

[19] The composition to which Grieg is referring so disparagingly is "Greetings from Christiania Singers", a setting for baritone solo and male chorus a cappella of a text by Norwegian author Jonas Lie (1833–1908). It was performed at a song festival in Christiania in May, 1896.

[20] Norwegian clergyman and author Sigvald Skavlan (1839–1912).

[21] Norwegian composer and organist Johannes Haarklou (1847–1925).

his existence with the greatest work for men's voices ever published in Norway. Yes, if it were a matter of length he would be a tough opponent with whom to compete. What a disgusting advertisement, that one in *Verdens Gang*. When all is said and done you are going to have to conduct Norway's "biggest/greatest" work.[22]

But now: Thank you for our altogether too short meeting last year, and best wishes to you for the new year. May it lead us together in one way or another. That I am staying in Leipzig is not good for me. If I were healthier I would be conducting here and there, but now I am feeling so miserable that I have to turn down every opportunity. Unfortunately, the idea of getting together during the song festival is out of the question, for I absolutely cannot tolerate that sort of thing. No, either you must come to West Norway during your vacation or I must get to East Norway in the fall. But that's a long time to wait.

Delius was here recently. His new opera contains some excellent things, indeed brilliant and unique, but without a superb performance the whole thing will come to nothing.[23]

Now you must not return evil for evil, but write soon. We will remain here for the time being.

Warm greetings from both of us, and—good Lord!—thank you for the songs,[24] *the most beautiful ones you have written.*

Sincerely yours,
EDVARD GRIEG

6

Leipzig, March 28, 1896
Hotel Hauffe

Dear Holter!

Thank you for your friendly letter to Nina. She greets you most warmly and asks me to tell you that if she had been able to write she would have done so immediately. It is a difficult time that we have gone through and, I may say, are still going through, for her health is improving ever so slowly. You can understand that this robbed me of the full enjoyment during the otherwise so successful visit to Vienna. My, what a wonderful city it is! What light-hearted, lively, warm people! That must be a good place to live. And then you should have heard the orchestral sound—or perhaps more to the point, the sound of the strings! And then this fire and rhythm, this *schwung*! This *ff* and this *pp*! Yes, that's the way it ought to be.[25]

---

[22] Grieg presumably is referring to Haarklou's *Varde*, a setting for male chorus of a text by Norwegian poet Per Sivle (1857–1904). The Norwegian word for "greatest"—*største*—also means "biggest". Grieg is playing on this double meaning in using it to describe Haarklou's composition.

[23] Frederick Delius's opera *The Magic Fountain*, for which the composer also wrote the libretto.

[24] Iver Holter's *Fem Sange* (*Five Songs*, 1895).

[25] Grieg had conducted an orchestral concert in Vienna on March 24, 1896.

The day after the concert, Julius Röntgen and I went up to the Semmering mountains[26] in the most glorious summer weather and became absolutely newborn after all the exertion and partying.

I was with Brahms a lot. He was cheerful and gracious. I cannot say the same of Dvořák, with whom, however, I developed only a superficial acquaintance. Then I visited old Bruckner—a trembling old graybeard, but touchingly childlike.[27]

There is one item in your letter to Nina that requires an answer. You say that the chairman of the committee informed you that it was with Grieg's consent that Grøndahl[28] had assumed responsibility for it (conducting *Land-sighting*). I will just say that this is plucked out of the air and that I know absolutely nothing about this arrangement. I think it is totally inappropriate to use my name in this way—not to mention the fact that deceptions of that sort are not very high-minded.

Your view of "the mountain king"[29] is much the same as mine. I like him in his grotesque greatness, comical though it is, because at root he is a good, honorable fellow. His idea with the folk songs is good; I only wish they could earn him a decent living in his old age.

You will soon be finished with a season on which, according to the newspapers, there is every reason to congratulate you. You have worked like a trooper with inadequate musicians, and you thoroughly deserve the rest that you will be able to get after the song festival. Hopefully we will see each other before then. I hope we will get to Christiania around the 1st of May.

Warm greetings!

Sincerely yours,
Edvard Grieg

7

Vienna, January 8, 1897

Dear Holter!

The press of concert duties during the past few days has unfortunately made it absolutely impossible for me to answer you before today. And the worst thing is that I neither have [with me] here nor can I remember any biographical sources of any kind worth mentioning. Everything that has been written strikes me as having missed the target, and I myself have never produced anything other than a few scattered items when requested to do so. But even this was a long time ago. More recently, when inquiries regarding biographical information naturally have

---

26 Semmering is a well-known resort area in the mountains south of Vienna.

27 Grieg is referring to his well-known contemporaries: German composer Johannes Brahms (1833–97), Czech composer Antonín Dvořák (1841–1904) and Austrian composer Anton Bruckner (1824–96)

28 Norwegian composer and conductor Olaus Grøndahl (1847–1923).

29 Grieg is alluding to baritone singer Thorvald Lammers, who on March 7, 1896, initiated a popular series of folk-song concerts.

increased, I have agreed with Dr. Abraham to refer them to C. F. Peters, where the requisite facts are on file and will be provided upon request. Taught by bitter experience, I personally will no longer write anything about myself—even if I had the time. So much for that.

But listen: You, who have followed me through many years, can certainly construct a meaningful whole out of all the independent bits and pieces, and all you need is the skeleton that can be found in any encyclopedia. Moreover, there is so much in the way of lies and slander that is known to me and that you yourself can easily correct. How lucky is Jonas Lie, who has gotten an Arne Garborg as his biographer![30] I will tell you honestly that basically I know nothing about your feelings toward me as an artist. I cannot say in advance, therefore, whether I would be happy to have you as my biographer—despite the fortunate happenstance that you are who you are and not just any old pen-pusher who writes only to make a little money. But the deep, sympathetic understanding that a great personality like Garborg has for one who is as different from him as Lie has made a powerful impression on me and has led me to say in my heart: Think, what a happy coincidence!

However that may be, if I were to give you any advice it would be this: Write without regard to me or anyone else. Just let the completely independent "I" speak.

The most essential data in the encyclopedia generally conclude during the 1880's. So: 1880–82, conductor in Bergen. 1883–84, Rome. Then we got to work on Troldhaugen, whence we moved in April, 1885. In 1888 I went to London, participated in the music festival in Birmingham that summer, also in Copenhagen. Autumn 1889 to Paris, in recent years repeatedly to London, Paris, Leipzig. March 1896, Vienna.

The period that began after my parents' deaths in 1875[31] was of prime importance to me. I stayed home during the winter of 1876, and in addition to many songs wrote the *Ballade* op. 24. In autumn 1876 I went to Christiania for the winter, but I left Tigerville for good in the spring of 1877. I spent the summer at Børve in Hardanger (where I started on my *String Quartet,* which I finished during the winter at Lofthus). I remained at Lofthus continuously until autumn 1878 (where I wrote, among other things, *Album for Male Voices* and the piano pieces of opp. 28 and 29). Then I went to Cologne, where I presented a concert in collaboration with Heckmann's quartet.[32] From there I went to Leipzig, where, as you remember, we were together when the *Quartet* was viciously attacked in the press. That

---

[30] Norwegian author Arne Garborg (1851–1924) published a biography of his fellow author Jonas Lie in 1893.

[31] Grieg's father died on September 13 and his mother on October 23, 1875.

[32] The quartet of German violinist Robert Heckmann (1848–91), to whom Grieg dedicated op. 27, premiered the work at this concert. Grieg himself performed the *Violin Sonata* in G major with Heckmann as well as a number of his newer compositions for solo piano.

summer was again spent at Lofthus, the next winter (as far as I remember) in Leipzig. In the spring of 1880 I came home to Bergen in March, and at my brother's home on Strand Street (in a little attic room) I wrote all the Vinje songs [op. 33]. Then I went back to Lofthus.

I don't know if you have taken notice of a song by Ibsen: "My dreams were of my beloved, through the warm summer night, but by the river I wandered, in an eerie and pale moonlight. Heigh, do you know song and terror? Can you dazzle the heart of the fair, that in mighty halls and cathedrals she'll covet to follow you there?" etc.[33] It was the motive from this song (from 1876) that I used in 1877 in the string quartet. And in this, as *you* will understand, there lies a piece of personal history. I know that I had a big spiritual battle to fight, and I used a great deal of energy creating the first movement of the quartet there among the dark mountains of the Sørfjord in that sad summer and autumn.

But what's going on here? Now I have written something after all! Yes, dear Holter, you can see that what you are so friendly as to hope for is coming to pass: I have confidence in you!

Moreover, that was not the only time that I used song motives in orchestral pieces. I made use of the song "Autumn storm" (text by Richardt),[34] which I wrote at Rungsted in 1865, in the overture *In Autumn,* written in Rome the following winter. When I brought this to Copenhagen and showed it to Gade,[35] he said, "That's a goddam piece of junk, Grieg; go home and write something better." So I went home—and with all due respect: wept. The overture was not well orchestrated, that I remember. So out of pure dejection I let it lie, arranged a version for piano four hands, and played this with Nina at home. Then I sent it to Stockholm as an entry in a contest sponsored by the Swedish Academy. The judges were Rietz[36] in Dresden, Söderman[37] in Stockholm—and Gade in Copenhagen. The overture won the prize, was printed and came out in a version for piano four hands in Stockholm. (Gade presumably had forgotten the whole affair.) Well, such is "the way of the world". In 1887 I re-orchestrated the piece and had the score published by Peters. There you have the whole story, which, moreover, is fairly typical. If you can use it, welcome to it. For me, to tell the truth, it has not been without significance.

But do not conclude from this that I think I am not deeply indebted to Gade. I admire as highly today as I always have the composer of *Elverskud* [*Elf-king's Daughter*], of the *Symphony in G Minor* [no. 6] and of the *Efterklange af Ossian* [*Echoes from Ossian*] overture. I also admire much in the *Symphony in A Minor*

---

[33] "Fiddlers" to a text by Henrik Ibsen (1828–1906).

[34] "Autumn storm" to a text by the Danish poet Christian Richardt (1831–92).

[35] Danish composer Niels W. Gade (1817–90).

[36] German composer, cellist, conductor and music publisher Julius Rietz (1812–77).

[37] Swedish composer August Söderman (1832–76).

[no. 3]. But Gade was one-sided; that, at least, is how we Norwegians felt. When I as a young man (1865) showed him my *Humoresques,* he sat paging through the manuscript, initially without saying a word. Then he began to grunt a little, then a little more, and finally he blurted out: "Tell me, Grieg, is this stuff supposed to be Norwegian?" And I, somewhat hurt, replied: "Yes, Herr Professor, it is." Still, I was a young beginner and he the famous master. That must always be remembered in connection with these anecdotes. He harbored a friendly appreciation for me—often very visible, but equally often more concealed—right up to his death.

As for a few facts about Nina—well, she was born in 1845 at Haukeland, near Bergen. When she was eight she moved to Denmark, where she lived throughout her youth and where she took singing lessons from Carl Helsted.[38] I became acquainted with her there in 1863. We got engaged in 1865 and married in 1867. Our wedding was in St. John's Church in Copenhagen, and immediately thereafter we went to Christiania (No. 2 Øvre Vold Street), where my hard spiritual struggle began. Up there—no, nothing about that. If there is any justice left, some day something will be written about this period that is true.

Look at this! I intended to write a short letter, but the memories took over and ran away with me!

You, too, must let subjectivity rule! It alone is right! I mean, of course, the genuine, unalloyed subjectivity!

Happy new year, and warm greetings from both of us!

Sincerely yours,
EDVARD GRIEG

P.S. When is the Stockholm event?[39] Aulin[40] wrote that it would come off as planned.

Julius Steenberg, the singer from Copenhagen, once wrote some biographical notes about Nina that I sent to a German fellow—who proved to be a dirty dog because he never returned them. It would be good if Steenberg still has these notes and would allow you to make use of them. His address is: c/o Wilhelm Hansen. He could also tell you about my youthful years in Copenhagen. Prof. G. Matthison-Hansen[41] could also tell you a lot about those years.

---

38 Danish flutist and singing teacher Carl Helsted (1818–1904).

39 Grieg had made an effort to secure an engagement for Holter to conduct a symphony concert in the opera house in Stockholm in the latter half of the 1897–98 season.

40 Swedish violinist and composer Tor Aulin (1866–1914).

41 Danish singer Julius Steenberg (1830–1911) and Danish organist and composer Gottfred Matthison-Hansen (1832–1909) were among Grieg's closest friends during his early years in Denmark.

8

Amsterdam, February 9, 1897
Van Baerlestraat 13 (Julius Röntgen)

Dear Holter!

I'm up to my ears in rehearsals and concerts. Accept, therefore, the good will contained in these few lines. I will try to hit the main points.

Nordraak's[42] importance for me is *not* exaggerated. It really is so: Through him and only through him was I truly awakened. The history of Danish literature provides a completely parallel case: If Oehlenschläger had not met Steffens[43] it is unlikely that he would have found himself. It is as Kierkegaard[44] says: The occasion is nothing and the occasion is—everything. What we all know from [Bjørnstjerne] Bjørnson's life was true to a large extent of Nordraak, too: His personality was captivating. He was a dreamer, a visionary, but he lacked the inborn ability to bring his art to the same level as his vision. That is to say, he could do so in short songs, but he would hardly have been able to live up to his promises if he had lived longer. For me, he was exactly what I needed. I came to see what Bjørnson in *Arnljot*[45] calls "Norway in the rising sun".

I was destroyed after my stay in Leipzig. I didn't know which way to turn when a vague longing drove me toward Copenhagen. Gade, despite all the admiration I felt for his brilliant early works, understandably could not still this longing. But that I at that time had his clear artistic mastery in addition to Nordraak's youthful enthusiasm (which I fully shared)—that was my good fortune. I didn't exactly want to be Norwegian, much less super-Norwegian. I just wanted to be—myself. I wanted to find expression for something of the best that was in me, something that lay thousands of miles away from Leipzig and its atmosphere. But that this "best" lay in love for the homeland and a feeling for the great, melancholy, natural scenery of West Norway—that I did not know and would perhaps never have learned if I had not, through Nordraak, been led to self-contemplation. This found its first expression in the *Humoresques* op. 6 (dedicated to Nordraak), in which the direction of my development is clearly evident. I willingly admit that the influence of Nordraak was not exclusively musical. But that is precisely the thing for which I am most grateful to him: that he opened my eyes to the importance of that in music which is *not* music.

You ask about [*Olav*] *Trygvason.* The first act was sent to me in Bergen in the

---

42 Norwegian composer Rikard Nordraak (1842–66).

43 In 1802 the Norwegian-German philosopher and physicist Henrich Steffens (1773–1845) gave a famous series of lectures at the University of Copenhagen that played a role in paving the way for Danish Romanticism. He had a profound influence on the young Danish poet and dramatist Adam Oehlenschläger (1779–1850), whose *Guldhornene* of 1802 (published in English translation as *The Golden Horns* in 1913) is regarded as the first important example of Romanticism in Danish literature.

44 Danish philosopher Søren Kierkegaard (1813–55).

45 Bjørnstjerne Bjørnson's poem *Arnljot Gelline.*

summer of 1873 and I conceptualized it immediately out in Rolfsen's[46] gazebo in Sandviken, where my parents lived at that time. Unfortunately for me, just at that time Bjørnson went through the inner upheaval that suddenly brought his historical period to an end and led him to write *En Fallit* [*The Bankrupt*].[47] The text for the remaining acts was not sent to me and when, not long thereafter, we were estranged from each other for no less than 16–17 years as a result of pure trifles—after having been friends from youth (I certainly can say that even though Bjørnson is eleven years older than me)—there was no possibility of resuming work on it. Finally—I think it was in 1889—as I was digging around in my sketches, I one day reached the conclusion that my draft of the first act of *Olav Trygvason* could be orchestrated and played as a concert piece. I went to work on it immediately, and I think it was in the fall of 1889 that I first conducted the piece in Christiania. Then I also had the great joy of renewing my friendship with Bjørnson—this time, I think, for good—as some of Bjørnson's friends (Sars[48] and others) had prevailed upon him to come to Christiania to hear it. There was some talk of Bjørnson continuing work on *Olav Trygvason*—but that was only a momentary fantasy. He had more important tasks in mind and could no longer get excited about the standpoints he had previously occupied, which is understandable. So *Trygvason* will always remain a fragment.

You will have to be satisfied with these bits and pieces. If there is something special that you want to know, just ask and I will give you an answer.

It will surprise you to hear that the choir and orchestra resources here are *absolutely* first rate. The choir rehearsal on *Olav Trygvason* one evening recently was brilliant. There are *340* people—who really can sing. And the orchestra rehearsal today! Yes, you probably won't believe me when I tell you that I have never heard anything like it—not in Paris, not in London, not (yes, least of all!) in Germany. What happens on the 13th (Saturday) is going to be something quite exceptional. The "vølve"[49] is being sung by Miss Marie Brema[50] (her performance is supposed to be absolutely outstanding) and the bass solo by Messchaert.[51] So everything is in the best hands. Perhaps you know that Mrs. Gulbranson suddenly withdrew on grounds of overexertion—but still, during these very days, she is appearing in Copenhagen both in concerts and on the stage. And I can only say that I am happy to be free of the obligation to deal with people like that. At the same time, however, I regret that she has disappointed me so grievously both as an artist and as a person.

---

[46] Rasmus Rolfsen (1812–1903), owner of a factory in Bergen, lived in a villa called "Elsero" in Sandviken, a community on the western edge of the city. Grieg also wrote much of the *Peer Gynt* music there.

[47] Bjørnson's play *The Bankrupt* (1875).

[48] Grieg may be referring to the historian Ernst Sars (1835–1917).

[49] In Old Norse mythology a "vølve" was a woman who practiced witchcraft and had the ability to foresee the future.

[50] The English mezzo-soprano Marie Brema, whose real name was Minny Fehrmann (1856–1925).

[51] Dutch baritone Johannes Messchaert (1857–1927), whom Grieg regarded very highly.

What's the deal with Stockholm? The secret must lie in the fact that Aulin has been sick and that his relationship to the chamberlain[52] perhaps is—partly for that reason—not the closest. Still, I advise you to correspond with Aulin and him alone, for whatever is going to be achieved will certainly be through him. I do not know Nordquist[53] as a person. These are, as you know, his concerts. I think that Nordquist and Aulin together must formulate a firm statement to the chamberlain. Then it will work out. I wrote to the chamberlain after returning home from Stockholm, but he has not answered me. For that reason it would be difficult for me to approach him again. Who knows? If it doesn't work out this winter perhaps the music festival[54] will provide an opportunity for an approach.

Well, enough for today. Excuse the lack of form, but I am exhausted, tired and very chilled.

Hearty greetings!

Sincerely yours,
EDVARD GRIEG

P.S. It is a sacred duty for me to call attention to the great influence that my association with [Bjørnstjerne] Bjørnson from the autumn of 1866 to the spring of 1873 had on my art. He formed my personality in countless ways—that is to say, he contributed mightily to that process. He made me a democrat, both artistically and politically. He gave me the courage to follow my own natural bent. This time (the 1870's) was a wonderful time, with its surplus of courage and faith! That was followed by the reaction—the one that still holds sway, in spite of everything!

9

Copenhagen, April 4, 1897

Dear Holter!

I do not know any "vølve" in Stockholm. (In Amsterdam I had an absolutely superb one: Brema.) Also in Norway we have one person who *earlier*, in any case, could have been good: Oselio. But how she is now I don't know. She *is* middle-aged. However that may be, I still say what I said in my telegram: A good "vølve" is essential. Don't force the issue. If a good "vølve" cannot be found, omit *Olav Trygvason*. I have no other wish—except I would like to have the *String Quartet* performed *well*.

Brahms is dead! I understand his greatness all the more clearly now after having observed the meanness of the honorable Danish music critics upon his

---

52 Chamberlain Axel Burén (1842–1923), head of the Stockholm Opera.

53 Conrad Nordquist (1840–1920), court musical director of the Stockholm Opera.

54 Grieg is referring to the Scandinavian music festival to be held in Stockholm in June, 1897. Holter was chairman of the Norwegian committee preparing for the festival. Grieg did not participate in the festival, but Johan Svendsen did.

passing. Fortunately Brahms did not suffer any further pains. It was liver cancer that let him slowly slip away.

I am sitting and reading in *Also sprach Zarathustra.*[55] The mountains tremble, a mouse is born! No, *that* is not the future!

Warm greetings.

Sincerely yours,
EDVARD GRIEG

P.S. How will Norway be represented at the music festival in other ways?

10

Copenhagen, Sunday Morning [October 10, 1897]
Hotel King of Denmark

Dear Holter!
I spoke with Svendsen last evening. He is enthusiastic about the idea and is with us. He read the program and was also in agreement there.[56] Also, in our draft at the Grand Hotel we forgot Neupert[57] and Agathe Grøndahl,[58] both of whom can be represented with solo piano pieces or songs. But the reason I am dropping you these lines is to tell you that if you encounter the *very slightest* difficulty regarding the orchestra question—be it enterprising people outside the theater who make demands or anything like that—don't agree to *anything* for now but just let the matter rest. For (just between us):

1. According to a letter from Röntgen received yesterday, the Amsterdamians are answering in a very accommodating manner, and
2. Svendsen (big secret!) probably will be touring in Swedish, Norwegian and Danish cities with the Royal Opera Orchestra in June and proposed that it could take over the music festival in Bergen! I looked very surprised, confided in him about Amsterdam, but above all we were in

---

[55] Richard Strauss's tone poem, composed 1895–96.

[56] Grieg and Holter had had a discussion in the Grand Hotel in Christiania about the possibility of holding a Norwegian music festival in Bergen in the summer of 1898. This is the first time the subject of this music festival was brought up, but in the ensuing weeks it was to create a great deal of controversy among Norwegian musicians. It is clear that from the very beginning Grieg wanted to bring the Concertgebouw Orchestra of Amsterdam to the festival, no matter what it might cost. As the plans developed, Grieg incurred the anger of several important figures in Norwegian music life, but he got his way. The music festival was a huge artistic success, and the concerts were received with enthusiasm by the public. Grieg's sharp criticism of Holter during the months preceding the festival seems unreasonable, so it is not surprising that for a time their friendship was broken off. It was Holter's magnanimity in response to an overture from Grieg's second cousin, John Grieg, that eventually led to a reconciliation. See Grieg's letter to Holter of June 2, 1898.

[57] Norwegian pianist and composer Edmund Neupert (1842–88), who spent the last six years of his life as professor of piano at the then new music conservatory in New York City.

[58] Agathe Backer Grøndahl (1847–1907), Norway's first important female composer.

> agreement that if a *complete* Norwegian orchestra is placed at our disposal *without difficulties*, we cannot for a moment be in doubt about choosing this. But also only then. Here artistic and national interests collide—unfortunately. But of course you understand that this is what we must publicly be in agreement about, that we would have preferred to have a Norwegian orchestra. If we encounter difficulties we break off negotiations and without hesitation take a foreign one—and then, in any case, we will triumph *artistically*.

Let me know your opinion on this as soon as possible. Address: G. Augener, 47 *North Side, Clapham Common, London S. W.*

In great haste with warmest greetings,

Sincerely yours,
EDVARD GRIEG

P.S. The music festival should preferably be held the *first week of July*. Otherwise the schedule gets tight for Svendsen! And we don't want to do it without him.

11

Amsterdam, December 25, 1897
13 Sarphatikade

Dear Holter!
Thanks for your letter, which I received upon my arrival here on the 23rd. I won't waste a word on the exposition committee nonsense. The committee can untangle that itself. But this I know, that if you were here you and I would be in agreement with respect to the artistic dimension. For the Dutch orchestra's offer is so uniquely noble that such an opportunity obviously should be accepted without a thought. The Dutch orchestra will be much cheaper than the Norwegian one, for *in reality* its participation is *gratis!* Consider: In addition to travel, food and lodging they are asking for two Fl.[59] (= three crowns) per day for private expenses. The orchestra has about 70 members—(and what a 70!!). This comes to 210 crowns per day. Now I estimate on the high side and allow for *19 days*. 19 x 210 totals 3,990 crowns. Just think: one of Europe's *finest orchestras* for *19 days* for 3,990 crowns!!! And after all, we are first and foremost artists who want to have Norwegian compositions performed in the best possible way.

Obviously: If there were no reason *except* the artistic one to choose the Dutch orchestra, *then the Norwegian one should be preferred.* But since the financial reason is a principal consideration, I think we are completely free as far as the

---

[59] Fl. is an abbreviation for *florin*, which was the original name of the Dutch *gulden*.

chauvinists are concerned. *Of course* all of the decent Norwegian musicians will be invited *in any case.* These *must* understand that when we chose the Dutch orchestra it was both for financial reasons and because the Norwegian Parliament does not provide money to enable Norway to field a *first-rate* orchestra. If they cannot understand it, their lack of understanding in any case cannot prevent me from stating my conviction and acting accordingly. With respect to Halvorsen,[60] I think you are totally mistaken—fortunately. But he, in my opinion, is completely impractical and disorganized by nature. That, after all, is why you have to answer all kinds of questions from the committee.

Your idea regarding Copenhagen is wonderful.[61] It was damnably attractive to me. But to no avail. It won't work. I am spending Christmas here. I go from here to Leipzig. It's a damn shame that we can't discuss the matter together *now.* It always looks different in writing. You could easily regard me as partial, but I am not. Moreover, I understand so very well the joy that *you* must have at the thought of presenting the Norwegian orchestra on the development of which you have expended so much energy and love. But remember that you have no responsibility in the matter if the Dutch orchestra should be chosen. That responsibility falls back on the committee in Bergen and on me. I hope you will try to stand as free and high as possible despite the bonds that *seemingly* would restrict you.

Well, enough for today. I have to stay in to avoid catching cold. I have to be *extremely* careful.

Christmas is not being celebrated here at all. Röntgen, as you undoubtedly have heard, recently lost his father, so the mood in his family is somber.

Farewell, then! Thank you for the old year—though it didn't give us much time together—and may we meet (to speak with J. S.[62]) in "collegial" joy in West Norway!

Warm greetings! Also from Nina!

Sincerely yours,
EDVARD GRIEG

P.S. We probably will be leaving Amsterdam the 1st or 2nd of January.

---

[60] Johan Halvorsen (1864–1935), who was a member of the committee planning the Bergen music festival, had mentioned to Holter that he thought his rough estimate of the Christiania musicians' honorariums was too low as the musicians would be unlikely to "give up their more remunerative summer engagements for the sake of the music festival. It makes me all the happier that such is not the case." On the basis of this statement, Holter wrote to Grieg in a letter dated December 18, 1897, that "Halvorsen is trying to throw suspicion not only on me but on the performing musicians here." Holter was really mistaken about this, however, for it was precisely in response to Halvorsen's advice that the committee chairman, Joachim Grieg (1849–1932), shortly thereafter engaged the Christiania musicians.

[61] Holter had indicated that he could meet Grieg in Copenhagen during the Christmas holidays to discuss the matter.

[62] Presumably Johan Svendsen.

Negotiations are under way these days for a very advantageous engagement for the Dutch orchestra. But I am not in a position to put off a decision longer than until the end of the year. That I am here just now is incredibly fortunate if the goal is to get them under contract. Today I sent a telegram to the committee (Joachim Grieg) that I am expecting an answer before the end of the year.

12

Amsterdam, January 1, 1898

Dear Holter!
First of all, happy new year! And then directly to the matter. To my surprise, I have learned via a telegram from the committee in Bergen that you have made a binding commitment to the Christiania orchestra. This is undeniably beyond all calculation. As you know, in accordance with our agreement you should merely have inquired in Christiania about the possibility of and the conditions for the participation of the Christiania orchestra. I was to do the same in Amsterdam. It obviously is impossible for me to negotiate with the Dutch orchestra when you are at the same time making definitive arrangements in Christiania. It strikes me as indubitable that you have gone too far here and that you must have misunderstood me. Of course you were supposed to negotiate, but not definitively, as if the question of the Dutch orchestra did not exist.

My beautiful dream is now shattered, and in addition to that I have been placed in such an awkward situation that my only choice is to withdraw from the whole affair. The total of 3,900 crowns that I calculated for orchestra expenses will be significantly increased when the Bergen string players and the foreign cellists are added in. Thus the Norwegian orchestra will be more expensive despite the enormous reduction you have achieved in comparison with your first budget.

That the great artistic success should founder on the tiny difference in travel expenses is too incredible. And I, who have told the Dutch musicians that the question has to do with orchestra expenses—I must now stand by what I have said. I honestly admit that once you have acted definitively you, too, are in a sorry situation. But when it becomes apparent that the Norwegian orchestra will be more costly, then it really is altogether too annoying that such a unique opportunity to get a first-rate performance should slip between our fingers.

There are other considerations in support of the Dutch orchestra as well—the time question, for example. If the musicians in Christiania are not available until July 2, then the festival can hardly begin before the 7th or 8th. And this creates the very conflict with vacations that one would like to avoid.

But as I said, the issue of orchestra expenses is the main point, and since I do not want to be in disagreement with you or with the committee I would rather resign now than to be forced to do so later. For on the principal issues we should be in agreement, which we apparently are not at present.

I deeply regret this development, which for me completely bars the way to further progress on the matter.

If you can still make the case that your approach to the orchestra should be construed as provisional, it would be wonderful. But unfortunately, I don't have much hope for this.

Warm greetings!

Sincerely yours,
EDVARD GRIEG

13

Leipzig, January 25, 1898
Hotel Hauffe

Dear Holter!
As you have of course already heard, the situation became unsustainable for the committee. I reaffirmed my resignation, and the same evening I had communicated this I received word that what you indicated in your letter should occur, did occur—namely, that the committee should disband. The telegram was categorical: The music festival is abandoned, the committee dissolved. After its last telegram from you it didn't have any other choice, either. Thus ended the first Punic War! And I cannot deny that I was quite simply relieved.

But what happens? The very next morning a telegram from Johan Bøgh[63] informs me that a new committee has been formed and that this committee has given me the task of engaging the Dutch orchestra. I thought it over for quite awhile, because I knew very well what I was letting myself in for, but in the end I accepted. I did so partly on the basis of artistic considerations but equally because of the resolution adopted at the meeting of orchestra musicians in Christiania—a resolution with which I am in such complete disagreement that I consider it an absolute duty to take a stand against it. If the resolution had expressed regret and disapproval that the committee did not feel itself bound by its word—well, that I could understand. But if the wording of the resolution is as it has been reported to me—that "All the musicians here assembled express their regret and disapproval of the use of a foreign orchestra at a Norwegian music festival when a Norwegian one is available"—then I must say that I distance myself as far as possible from such a view. Yes, if the resolution had stated "when an equally good [Norwegian one]," or even just "when a good Norwegian orchestra is available." But just this: "when a Norwegian one is available." No, this is too much for

---

[63] Art historian Johan Bøgh (1848–1933), Director of the West Norway Museum of Decorative Art in Bergen. When the committee was dissolved, Joachim Grieg (Edvard's second cousin) stepped down as chairman. The chairman of the new committee was Joachim's brother, book publisher John Grieg (1856–1905).

me, and I greatly regret that *you* have allowed the resolution to come out in this crass form.

I would have been rather surprised at your behavior on this occasion if I did not understand so well that, for the sake of your musicians, you had to stretch as far as possible, and that you have gone farther than you as an artist can, strictly speaking, defend. For both verbally and in writing you have been involved with the idea of engaging the Dutch orchestra. If you had held the views expressed in the resolution when we first discussed the matter, then of course the whole confounded mess would have been avoided and I would have known where I stood. But I am not forgetting that the situation during the meeting was difficult for you and that you had to act under enormous pressure. This certainly explains the resolution that diverges from your real view.

As things look to me, I think you will understand that, with the prospect of getting one of Europe's finest orchestras on such uniquely favorable terms, I am not of a mind to let myself be bullied by the chauvinism—or perhaps more accurately, the restricted field of vision—of the Christiania orchestra musicians. Their limited horizon is easily explained and therefore very excusable.

I don't have to tell you that the slap in the face that has been given to me personally via the resolution has hurt me. I have a strong feeling that I have not deserved it. But it is true: The musicians' lot in life is not always the easiest, and with the memory of so many beautiful occasions when we have worked together through the years it is easy for me to get over it. Nor is it to be expected that the average Norwegian orchestra musician should be able to see that some of the most indispensable musicians in Christiania—and most of those in Bergen—are of such a caliber that one would not let them represent Norway at a music festival where Europe is in attendance unless one absolutely had to.

Moreover, this business of representing Norway through the orchestra: Tell me now—hand on your heart!—doesn't it contain just a little humbug? Have you yourself not engaged German woodwinds without anyone objecting? Isn't the nationality of an orchestra of a dubious sort? Aren't there German musicians all over the place?

I have not yet received a final answer from the Dutchmen, but since they reported a short time ago that they were available for the festival from June 26 to July 3 I have reason to believe that this offer is still in force. This much is now clear: Either we have the Dutch orchestra or there will be no festival.

Please tell me without delay:

1. Whether you still have the draft program that we together wrote down in the Grand Hotel last fall. If so, please send it to me. I have unfortunately lost my copy.
2. Whether there is a possibility that your choir will participate in the festival.

It is true: I have heard such tepid comments about Elling's oratorio[64] (albeit not from competent sources) that I am afraid to put it on the program until I have heard how it came off at your performance and until I have gotten acquainted with it myself.

And with that, farewell for today! Write soon!

Sincerely yours,
EDVARD GRIEG

14

[Troldhaugen, June 2, 1898]
Thursday Morning

Dear Holter!
I am so happy today! You and I cannot be enemies! Away with all expressions of opinion. Blot it all out! Here is my hand. Let us meet as in the old days![65]

Sincerely yours,
EDVARD GRIEG

15

Troldhaugen, September 15, 1902

Dear Holter!
Thank you for urging me to conduct the Music Association orchestra on October 4. But I will not be coming to Christiania until the latter part of the month, so it can't be done. Moreover, I couldn't very well conduct in Christiania at just that time inasmuch as I, for reasons of health, have had to decline an invitation to conduct on October 7 and 8 at a music festival in Bristol. It is quite true that it is primarily the long trip (through six kingdoms!) that has scared me, but perhaps it would not be well received over there if they heard that on approximately the days in question I conducted in Christiania. However that may be, I certainly hope that we will see each other next month.

I would have set out earlier if I were not in the middle of a job that vitally interests me. It is a set of piano arrangements of a whole bunch of still unknown

---

64 The oratorio *The Prodigal Son*, by Norwegian composer Catharinus Elling (1858–1942), composed 1895–96, was first performed in Christiania in 1914 at a music festival initiated by Holter.

65 Book publisher John Grieg, chairman of the festival committee, had taken the initiative in bringing about a reconciliation between Grieg and Holter. Prior to the festival—on June 1, 1898—he had sent a letter to Holter, to which Holter reacted positively. The letter stated in part:

"You, like me, are in good health and have a good stomach, and in such circumstances one certainly can delay a resolution. But since it is now evident from your letter to Hammer that you are coming, don't you think it would be best for both parties if you wrote a few lines, expressed regret that you did not meet [Grieg] in Christiania, and told him that you would come earlier in order to effect a reconciliation? Whenever there is a controversy, of course, each party feels wronged; but since you now intend to come with a friendly mien, why not let Grieg know that? Hammer let me read your letter to him. I have not told anyone that I have written to you about the matter and am reluctant to have it be official."

Norwegian dance tunes from Telemark [op. 72]. They are so genuine and wild and bursting with creative vitality—with a moving undercurrent from time to time—that I am happy that they were rescued in time. What happened was that I sent the fiddler to Halvorsen, who transcribed them in their original form. That is somewhat different from starting with Lindeman's collection,[66] where one doesn't know what is original and what has been added by Lindeman. I will now see to it that the original is printed along with my free arrangement so that one can see which is which. All in all it is a pity that we don't have an authentic primary source [of Norwegian folk music].

Well—where in the world am I wandering? Once again: Thanks for the invitation. I hope to see you soon.

Sincerely yours,
Edvard Grieg

16

Christiania, December 7, 1905
Hotel Westminster

Dear Holter!
Thank you for yesterday! Thank you because the Music Association once again gave me an opportunity to make music with Norwegian musicians![67] And promise me one thing more: When you meet with the Businessmen's Chorus again, convey to them my warmest thanks for the outstanding way in which they performed their task yesterday. Each of them did his duty, and for me the whole piece—especially near the end—sounded so impressive that I myself was profoundly moved. But I saw the genuine glow of enthusiasm in the singers' eyes as well. *You* have played a role in creating this, and I could wish that you *yourself*—remembering Goethe's famous words, "Nur die Lumpen sind bescheiden!"[68]—would make the singers aware of the fact that the *good* conductor is the source of his singing group's capacity for enthusiasm. Then you would immediately receive the ninefold "Hurrah" that you so honestly have deserved!

Warm greetings to all of you!

Sincerely yours,
Edvard Grieg

---

[66] Ludvig Mathias Lindeman (1812–87) published his collection of *Ældre og nyere norske Fjeldmelodier* (*Older and Newer Norwegian Mountain Melodies*) in simple piano arrangements *seriatim* during the years 1853–67.

[67] Grieg conducted the Music Association orchestra on December 6, 1905. The program included the premiere of *Lyric Suite, Land-sighting,* and three of the *Six Songs with Orchestra* EG 177 with Ellen Gulbranson as the soloist. Iver Holter conducted Johan Svendsen's *Symphony No. 2.*

[68] Grieg often used this passage from Goethe's poem *Rechenschaft*, published in 1810. His quotation in this case is not quite accurate, however: He substitutes "Lumpen" ("rags") for "Lumpe" ("rogues"). The first two lines of the poem are "Nur die Lumpe sind bescheiden,/Brave freuen sich der Tat" ("Only rogues are unassuming/Good men celebrate their deeds").

To Louis Hornbeck

The Danish composer, violinist and organist Louis Hornbeck (1840–1906), was one of the youthful friends who joined Grieg and others in founding the music association "Euterpe" in Copenhagen in 1865. Grieg was very fond of this noble, modest friend. Upon Hornbeck's death in 1906, he wrote an obituary that appeared in the September 28 issue of the Copenhagen newspaper *Politiken* in which he said, among other things, "He was in fact nothing less than a highly gifted lyrical composer who wrote songs that are among the best in Danish song literature."

The first letter to Hornbeck is taken from *Norsk Musikkgranskning. Årbok 1937*, pp. 49–50. Copies of the other two are preserved in Nasjonalbiblioteket, Oslo (The National Library of Norway, Oslo Division).

1

Berlin, October 22, 1865

My dear friend Hornbeck!

In order to avoid being counted among those people who do not keep their word I will today try to get off a letter to you, though God knows I am anything but in condition for writing. To begin with, I feel physically unwell after a big night on the town yesterday—with plenty of oysters and Rhine wine. Secondly, at the moment I am depressed about my bad luck. For it surely must be called bad luck when I come to Berlin to fetch Nordraak[1] for the trip to Italy and then the man lies down and is deathly sick! He has now been in bed for fourteen days with the most severe pneumonia, and he would certainly have died if his fabulously strong constitution had not kept him going. When his illness was at its worst I cabled his father (in accordance with Rikard's wish and the doctors' advice), but he replied that circumstances prevented him from coming.

Now the greatest danger is past, but Rikard is still suffering terribly. He sweats so profusely that it just runs off him, and he doesn't dare, or more correctly is unable, to speak a word. He only whispers softly when he is unable to make himself understood with gestures.

I have no idea what is going to happen to our planned trip; I will probably leave the first of December. That's hard to take, because the trip to Italy at Christmastime is no joyride. There is even a question as to whether we can tolerate the exertions of a winter journey.[2]

---

[1] Norwegian composer Rikard Nordraak (1842–66).

[2] Grieg went to Berlin at the beginning of October, 1865, and remained there for several weeks to see if Nordraak would improve sufficiently to accompany him on a planned trip to Italy. On November 2, when Nordraak's condition had not improved, Grieg went to Leipzig to give some concerts. He had promised Nordraak that he would return to Berlin, but he did not do so. On November 30 he wrote to Nordraak telling him that he would go directly from Leipzig to Italy. Nordraak reacted angrily to this news, giving vent to his rage in an eight-page letter. Grieg received in Rome a letter dated December 15 from Rikard's father, who at the doctors' persistent urging had gone to Berlin to be with his son. Nordraak died on March 20, 1866. Grieg received word of his death on April 6, and that same day he composed his *Funeral March for Rikard Nordraak*. Grieg's letters to Nordraak from this period are not extant. See, however, his letter of May 7, 1866, to Nordraak's father, Georg Marcus Nordraach (1811–90), in which he expresses in gripping terms his sorrow over the passing of his dear friend.

Since I am not a fatalist, I dare say with confidence that everything would have gone better for Rikard if he had taken my advice. To begin with, he should have just stayed in Copenhagen for the summer and worked, for here he has accomplished next to nothing—"Mary Anne", a song to a text from *Maria Stuart*, and the beginning of an overture to the same play, that's all.[3] Secondly, he should have left the minute I came here to fetch him instead of telling me that he had had second thoughts and that he intended to stay here all winter, as he first said. Still, the man is fairly pliable, and it wasn't hard for me to get him to abandon that crazy idea. So we agreed to leave on November 1, but excuse me, by then he was ill.

Berlin is an abominable hole. Would that I were with you in Copenhagen, which is a different story. Everything there is inspiring: poetry in the air, poetry in people. Ah, Denmark! The memory of the days spent there is my life's highest joy. Write to me soon in such a lively and friendly manner that I can again feel that I am with you for awhile. Perhaps in that case I could get in shape to accomplish something worthwhile, for I'm doing a miserable job of it here.

Good-bye for now, and greet everyone whom we care about from

Yours truly,
EDVARD GRIEG

2

Lofthus, Hardanger, August 23, 1884

Dear Hornbeck!

First of all, thank you for your letter and best wishes on the occasion of your engagement. I will carefully refrain from philosophical observations regarding my personal opinion on the subject. May you have acted from a lucky instinct, and may your fiancee understand what it means to have an artist as a husband. If the famous words of Kierkegaard[4]—"Marry or remain single, you will regret both"—apply to anyone, they certainly apply to the artist. For if it is true that by his art he is able to make others happy, it is even truer that he himself never will be so. He can therefore marry or not marry: He will be equally far from that for which he yearns.

As you see, on this subject I am a complete pessimist, and the reason is that I don't think there is a woman who can make an artist happy. Maybe I am wrong, and if so—if there are women created for the artist—then I have no doubt that you, with your finely tuned observer's eye, have found the right one. Give your sweetheart a misanthrope's respectful greetings and good wishes.

As for the second point in your letter, circumstances were such that I have

---

[3] *Maria Stuart i Skotland* was a play published in 1864 by Norwegian author Bjørnstjerne Bjørnson (1832–1910). Nordraak wrote several pieces of incidental music for this play. The piece that Grieg refers to as the overture probably is "Purpose", which is played at the beginning of Act 1. "Mary Anne" is a setting of a text from Act 4, Scene 9. It is sung by William Taylor and is often referred to as "Taylor's Song". The last part of each of the two stanzas begins with the words "Mary Anne".

[4] Danish philosopher Søren Kierkegaard (1813–55).

not been able to answer it until today. I have been up in the mountains, and your letter has been waiting for me here for at least eight days. Unfortunately, it is more than likely that my letter to Svendsen[5] will have no effect, as it will certainly reach him too late. I have written it nonetheless and am posting it at the same time as this one to you. May luck be with it.

You don't write anything about how things are going for you in other respects. I know almost nothing about my old Danish friends any more.

Oh, the air in Tivoli Park is light! Since we last spoke I have been on a long journey. I have concertized in Germany, Holland and Italy and have enjoyed a lot of artistic success. But my health is downright bad, and without good health nothing else counts.

Let this now be the beginning of a continuing correspondence. Warm greetings to you and your sweetheart both from Nina and from

Your devoted
EDVARD GRIEG

3

Troldhaugen at Bergen, September 9, 1895

Dear Hornbeck!
You gave me a wistfully happy surprise by sending me the old group[6] from bygone happy days. Hearty thanks both for thinking of it and for doing it. Obviously I still treasure the original as a holy relic, but for one thing this copy is from you and for another thing it is enlarged, so it has for me considerable value in its own right. I have a similar picture—a copy based on a calling card from Nordraak—and I will now have them both framed and hung side by side.

Yes, dear friend, although our paths do not often cross, you may be sure that I am not one of those who forget memories of the kind that you and I share. I don't own a safe—I'll leave such things to the merchants. But I have an invisible *mental* safe that is fastened more securely than that in which any banker keeps his dough. Memories are—with all due respect—like flounder: They live on the bottom and stay there until someone brings them up to the surface. But they ought not to come up, because then their eyes explode and it's all over for them. So let us hide our treasures like misers and count them every day. That is what I do, anyway, and I am often inspired by this exercise.

Greet your family, which unfortunately I do not know. I have yet to get acquainted with my godson. But the day will surely come, for Copenhagen is my old love—so we certainly will meet again some day.

Thank you for thinking of me. Accept fond greetings from

Your incorrigible old friend,
EDVARD GRIEG

---

[5] The Norwegian composer and conductor Johan Svendsen (1840–1911), who in 1883 had assumed the position of musical director at The Royal Theater in Copenhagen.

[6] Grieg is referring to a group picture of himself, Chr. F. E. Horneman (1840–1906), and Louis Hornbeck.

To Christian Frederik Emil Horneman

The Danish composer Christian Frederik Emil Horneman (1840–1906) was Grieg's best friend during his student days in Leipzig and a close ally in the mid-1860's in Copenhagen. Grieg was deeply devoted to his friend and wrote of him in glowing terms on a number of occasions. His characterization in a letter to August Winding (1835–99) dated September 3, 1886, is typical: "Horneman, whose noble heart and deep musical feeling I have to thank for several of the most significant influences of my youth."

After Horneman's death Grieg wrote a letter to the Danish Minister of Culture that included the following words: "Your Excellency has requested a statement from me regarding the late Prof. C. F. E. Horneman. I hereby comply with great pleasure because I have followed both Horneman and his art from his earliest days, and in him I have seen one of Denmark's most gifted artists. In the course of a long career, Horneman has created many great works. Among them are the opera *Aladdin* and most recently the cantata written on the occasion of the death of King Christian IX (1818–1906)—works that have assured him national significance. His widow, according to what I have heard, is virtually penniless. Therefore, in my opinion, there is no place where a public subsidy would be more appropriate than here. Your Excellency will honor Danish music by making possible such a subsidy."

There was a voluminous correspondence between Grieg and Horneman. A number of Horneman's letters to Grieg are preserved in Bergen Offentlige Bibliotek (Bergen Public Library). Most of Grieg's letters to Horneman are lost. The six included here are preserved in Nasjonalbiblioteket, Oslo (The National Library of Norway, Oslo Division).

1

Christiania, November 21, 1866

Dear friend!

My reason for writing to you just now is partly that I want very much to know how you are getting along, partly because I am desperately in need of some music that I once loaned to "Euterpe" and that is still in "Euterpe's" files.[1] It is a rather thick book with compositions by Mozart. Don't you remember the sonata for two pianos that you and I once talked about playing? In the same book there is a quintet for piano, oboe, clarinet, bassoon and horn—this is the piece I will be using very soon. The book is bound in brown cardboard, oblong shape. Ask your father to please send it to Warmuth[2]—and the sooner the better.

By all means write and tell me about "Euterpe". If I manage to finish something this winter I hope you will perform it. I know perfectly well that they won't perform my *Violin Sonata* [op. 13] in The Music Society, so you must make sure

---

[1] In 1865 Grieg, Horneman, Louis Hornbeck (1840–1906), Gottfred Matthison-Hanson (1832–1909) and Rikard Nordraak (1842–66) had established in Copenhagen a music association to which they gave the name "Euterpe." The name was borrowed from a similar older music association in Leipzig. "Euterpe" was conceived as an alliance that would challenge the established dominant cliques in Danish music life—cliques represented in the first instance by the conservative "Musikforeningen" ("The Music Association") in Copenhagen. "Euterpe" gave several concerts during the two years that it survived. The first of these was given on March 18, 1865. Nordraak conducted a 37-piece orchestra and a chorus "scraped together in a mad rush" in a performance of "Kaares Sang" ("Kaare's Song") from Nordraak's incidental music to *Sigurd Slembe*, a play by Norwegian author Bjørnstjerne Bjørnson (1832–1910). The last "Euterpe" concert was given on April 23, 1867. By then Nordraak was no longer living and Grieg had settled in Christiania.

[2] Carl Warmuth Jr. (1844–95), music publisher and owner of a music store in Christiania.

that "Euterpe" gets it—if for no other reason than to restore my honor, but it must have been a scandal to hear Jähnigen[3] and his sister play in the Casino small auditorium.

These days I'm digging into the proceeds from a concert we gave here some time ago that earned me 150 *spesidalers.* I think it's going to go well for me up here. I have assumed the leadership for concerts of the Philharmonic Society, which will start after Christmas. At the first concert I will do the C-minor Symphony [by Beethoven], the overture to *The Magic Flute* and, if possible, Nordraak's *Sigurd Slembe* or *Maria Stuart* music.[4]

I am also strongly considering establishing a conservatory. If anything comes of the idea you will soon read of it in the Norwegian newspapers.[5]

If everything goes well, as I have reason to believe it will, we will see each other next summer as I, God willing, plan to get married in beautiful Denmark.[6] What a time that will be! It almost seems to me like something I should only dream of and never expect to experience in reality.

Warm greetings to your wife. I will not soon forget those splendid days down in Fredensborg last summer. Hopefully that was not the last time.

So long for now. If you don't write to me again and send me Mozart, you will have forever

Your devoted friend
EDVARD GRIEG'S
enmity

P.S. Greet your father. He will soon get a letter, also Gottfred Hansen.[7]
My address is: *Urmager Smiths Gaard*, Kirkegaden 13, 2nd Floor.

2

Christiania, May 5, 1867

Dear friend!
It is true that I wrote that you would be my enemy forever if you didn't answer me, but it's easier said than done. Yes, you're the same splendid fellow whether you answer or not, and I will always be very fond of you. May I congratulate you

---

[3] The German-born conductor and violinist Christian Jähnigen (1830–1910), who came to Norway with the Schwarzenbacher orchestra in 1850 and settled in Christiania, where he played in several theater orchestras during the 1860's. Jähnigen had given a public performance of Grieg's *Violin Sonata* op. 8 in Copenhagen.

[4] Rikard Nordraak had written incidental music for Bjørnstjerne Bjørnson's plays *Sigurd Slembe* and *Maria Stuart i Skotland.*

[5] On December 12, 1866, Grieg and his colleague Otto Winter-Hjelm (1837–1931) published an article in *Morgenbladet* outlining their plans for a Norwegian music academy. The article will be printed in translation in Benestad & Halverson (eds.), *Edvard Grieg: Diaries, Articles, Speeches* (Columbus, Ohio, 2001). The academy began operations on January 14, 1867. It limped along for a couple of years, but when Grieg went abroad in the autumn of 1869 it faded into oblivion.

[6] Edvard and Nina were married on June 11, 1867, in Johanneskirken (St. John Church) in Copenhagen.

[7] Danish organist and composer Gottfred Matthison-Hansen (1832–1909), a close friend of Grieg.

on your new title? True enough, it doesn't bring in much—it even costs a little—but so what? Honor is costly. When we see each other you must explain more fully to me the feeling of being a father. It must make you very proud to have composed a little baby girl such as that. Too bad I can't become your son-in-law as we talked about one time.

Do you remember the last time we talked? At the train station in Fredensborg. Yes, how vividly I see the whole scene, and how different everything has become since that time.

Only now for the first time do I see that lovely period that we spent together in the proper light. Now I look upon it as something in the past, for it will never return! Euterpe, Fredensborg, Rungsted, love affairs, engagements, enthusiasm and friendship—all these things from a vanished time are for me like the elements of a composite picture.

Next month I am coming to Denmark, but only for a short time—three or four days. I'm getting married. But we absolutely must get together.

While I think of it: From now on I regard myself as no longer a member of the board of Euterpe. My position up here is now so secure that I certainly will not be coming to Denmark any more, so it's nothing but a meaningless formality to continue using my name. Gottfred Hansen resigned a long time ago, so now you are completely in charge, and that certainly is best. Both of us can now work for the same cause better than ever.

I absolutely must get the overture to *Aladdin* [8] performed next year. You can count on getting the music that you want from here.

Sigurd Slembe has created an enormous furor up here. I have re-orchestrated it to make it more powerful. You should have heard the chorus of our students. It sounded very different than it did in Denmark. I myself was so deeply moved as I was conducting that something like a shudder went through my body.

No doubt you have worked like a horse with Euterpe this winter. Still, not more than I have worked with the Philharmonic here. And then in addition I have the Music Academy and private lessons. What has become of the composer you can easily imagine. But just wait: It will certainly come. Now you absolutely must not leave the city in June—so that I can talk with you about many, many things.

Your devoted friend,
EDVARD GRIEG

P.S Greet your wife and your little—yes, what is her name?

---

[8] Horneman's *Aladdin* is a fairytale opera in four acts (eight scenes). The libretto, which was based on a play by Adam Oehlenschläger (1779–1850), was written by Grieg's and Horneman's mutual friend, Benjamin Feddersen (1823–1902), and later revised by Julius Lehmann (1861–1931). The overture had been performed at a concert as early as 1865. The whole opera was premiered at the Royal Theater in Copenhagen in 1888 as part of the jubilee celebrating the 25th anniversary of King Christian IX's ascension to the Danish throne. Horneman had then been working on the opera for more than twenty years. The premiere under Johan Svendsen (1842–1911) in 1888 aroused little interest, but when the work was staged again in 1902 it became a huge public success.

3

Christiania, April 24, 1869

Dear friend!

(. . .) Now you must do me a favor: Get Neupert[9] to go to Leipzig this fall and play my *Concerto*. If it really is true that it shows him at his best, I won't deny it. For one thing, it is his duty as an artist, and it is also the only way to get it printed by Senff[10] (whom I would like to have publish it), for it would be impossible for me to promote it in any way myself even if I were in Leipzig. If you think the concerto deserves it, do it. That would be fun: a Norwegian pianist playing a Norwegian composition.

You expect me in Denmark this summer. No, unfortunately, that cannot be. I will get a stipend all right, but I will have my wife with me, so it's not worth digging into those funds for now. This summer I will live at my parents' country house in Bergen because, you see, that won't cost me a penny. If I can then earn something from concerts in my home town I will come to Copenhagen in the fall and will stay for a month en route [to Leipzig]. I would like, if possible, to give a concert in Copenhagen at that time.

This summer I hope to write something for chorus and orchestra. I have the feeling that I might be able to accomplish something in that area, but I haven't been able to find a text.[11] Since we last parted I haven't composed a single note. I've just given lessons and concerts. I have become so unmusical that the idea of getting my imagination going again looks impossible to me. But I have had the same experience in the past, and that is my consolation.

Can you believe that I recently got a letter from Liszt![12] It made me dizzy. I sent it in support of my application for a stipend, and yesterday it appeared in one of the newspapers without my knowing anything about it in advance. God knows how it came about. Just think, he invites me to visit him in Weimar. But I'm stuck up here with a wife and maybe children![13]

I agree with you: There is so much about which to speak and write. Do you know what? You could devote a few lines to me again some time. The address is *Bergen*. Greet your wife and the little Kierkegaardian.[14]

Your devoted
EDVARD GRIEG

---

[9] Norwegian pianist Edmund Neupert (1842–88), who played the world premiere of Grieg's *Piano Concerto in A Minor* in Copenhagen on April 3, 1869.

[10] The German music publisher Bartolf Wilhelm Senff (1815–1900).

[11] Grieg did not find a text to his liking until 1871, when he wrote *Before a Southern Convent*, a setting of two pieces from Bjørnstjerne Bjørnson's poem *Arnljot Gelline*. A piano reduction was published in Copenhagen in 1871 by Horneman & Erslev, an orchestral score in 1876 by E. W. Fritzsch in Leipzig.

[12] The letter from Liszt, which is dated December 29, 1868, is reproduced in a footnote to Grieg's letter to Niels Ravnkilde (1823–90) of November 2, 1868.

[13] Grieg's only child, Alexandra, was born on April 10, 1868, but died of meningitis on May 21, 1869. See Grieg's letter to Ravnkilde of June 29, 1869. Grieg's use of the phrase "maybe children" may indicate that another child was on the way, but if so the pregnancy did not reach full term.

[14] Grieg is alluding to Danish philosopher Søren Kierkegaard (1813–55). The remark is somewhat cryptic, however.

4

Troldhaugen, June 25, 1892

Dear friend!

Believe you me, that "Album"[15] shook me up something fierce! I really thought I could keep my emotions under control. For with age, according to Ibsen, there comes "all sorts of evidence of petrification". But no, the urge became too strong and I became, so to speak, as soft as cheese—a cheese drenched in tears. In other words, it touched me in the depths of my soul. Thank you, thank you, all three of you. I think I understand you when, instead of calling me friend, you call me comrade, and I would be the last person to chastise you because you hold your ideals so high. But you see, my feelings for you—them you do not know, and it may be the most Norwegian thing about me that I keep them to myself. And I know this, that if for me anyone is a friend, you are. I, too, have my ideals. I have not yet written anything that was good enough for you—good enough, I mean, to bear your name. This has now been vexing me for twenty years. But either you shall have the best, something that I myself am pleased with, or else I will declare bankruptcy. What I owe you for the thoughts and hopes that we shared in our youth is the very best music that I can write, and to date that work remains unborn! But I still believe that I am not finished. If only this damned health of mine would behave better. Since February, when I got rheumatism in my legs, I haven't been able to write a note! I lack inclination, will, everything. Now I'm talking to Nina about Fredensborg, Søllerød, or some other quiet place like that with a piano, but of course nothing will come of it. Here at home I won't get well. The climate is too bad.

What are you doing this summer? I know absolutely nothing about you. What became of all that beautiful material in *Kalanus*? And how is it going with *Tamyrus*[16] or whatever it was called? Write a few lines. Let's forget about the long letters, but let's send a postcard now and then!

Warmest greetings to all three of you from both Nina and

Yours truly,
EDVARD GRIEG

5

Troldhaugen at Bergen, June 3, 1895

Dear friend!

Please know that we have indeed thought about you and talked about you these days! But now it's all over, that happy-wistful time, and you and yours are alone again! I understand, of course, that such an experience stirs up many thoughts,

---

15 The album for which Grieg is expressing thanks was a gift from Horneman, Gottfred Matthison-Hansen and August Winding on the occasion of Edvard and Nina's silver wedding anniversary on June 11, 1892.

16 In 1880 Horneman had written incidental music to *Kalanus* (1854), a play by Frederik Paludan-Müller (1809–76). The premiere occurred in 1906 at the Dagmar Theater in Copenhagen. What Grieg is referring to as *Tamyrus* is unclear.

and I only wish that it were this very day that you were coming up here—both because just now you need new impressions of a bright and happy nature and because summer is so inordinately beautiful that I am afraid it won't continue like this. I have just written to Winding and given him some practical travel advice that he must pass on to you. The main point, however, which remains unchanged—that you will be our guests from Christiania [to Troldhaugen] and back to Christiania again—is something that you must not tell anyone. The reason is that if it becomes known, my taxes will be raised so much here at home that I'll have to pay the whole bill for the war against the Swedes. But damn it all, I won't contribute a thing to that war. It's nothing but old-fashioned barbarism.

Despite all your admonitions to the contrary, I must be permitted to be as happy as a child as I look forward to your forthcoming visit. It's so damn nice of you to give up your peaceful summer in Denmark to come and visit us that I have decided to let Edition Peters bleed profusely so that we can show you how beautiful Norway is![17]

Yesterday I was on an eight-hour hike in the mountains. We descended 2,000 feet from a pass of singular wildness. And I am healthier today than I have been for a long time. There must be some life-enhancing stuff up there in the lofty heights. But you have to go up and get it yourself, for only then do you feel the pleasure and the effect on your mind that are as indescribable as they are incomprehensible. So: July 10, departure from Copenhagen. I will be in Christiania the same day. Hurrah! Hearty greetings to both of you!

Yours truly,
EDVARD GRIEG

6

Troldhaugen, September 15, 1896

Dear friend!

Now the summer is over. No letters and no getting together. Well, so it goes. What is really annoying about getting old is that one turns into a grumbler and withdraws into one's lair. I tell myself ten times that I won't do that because it is stupid and fruitless, but—Frants[18] just walked in, so: see you later!

(Frants has left, so on with the letter.) About your summer all I know is that you first went to Stettin (?) and then to Espegjærde, where you composed as if your life depended on it. Therefore your silence will be most graciously forgiven.

---

[17] Horneman, Matthison-Hansen and Winding and their wives all came to Troldhaugen as guests of the Griegs. Unfortunately, for reasons that Grieg was never able to understand, a feeling of ill will developed between him and Horneman in the course of the visit that permanently poisoned their friendship. See Grieg's letter to August Winding of August 16, 1895.

[18] Grieg's close friend and neighbor, Frants Beyer (1851–1919).

My silence is unforgivable, for I have, so to speak, done nothing except for the so-called *Lyric Pieces* [op. 65] that swarm around me like lice and fleas out in the country. And I've been working on some folk songs [op. 66]. But I have also spent a few days in the mountains and have had a wonderful time up there. It was in a stone hut up in the middle of the Hardanger Plateau, where I slept in a reindeer-skin sleeping bag.[19] Some days it was very cold, and then I crawled into the sleeping bag and wrote a long article that I had promised to prepare for an American periodical. Can you guess what it was about? Mozart![20] No doubt I have not expressed my admiration for him to your satisfaction, but it is as a not altogether untalented man once said: "My thoughts are not your thoughts".[21] In the end one must be content with one's own. And I was.

What is unique about being up on the mountain plateau is that you do exactly what you please, and you forget that there is such a thing as people who have theories, opinions—yes, even philosophies of life. Up there, this last-mentioned strikes me as pure idiocy! But then I came down again and, unfortunately, recovered my lost memory!

I regret to say that we will not be coming to Copenhagen this winter. I gave the devil a finger and he took the whole hand. Next month I go to Stockholm. Then to Vienna. Then to Amsterdam. In general: I do that which I do not want to do, and that which I want to do I do not do.[22] *Facit*: bad person!

Warmest greetings to both of you!

Yours truly,
EDVARD GRIEG

---

[19] Grieg spent several days during this summer with his friends Frants Beyer, Julius Röntgen (1855–1932) and Børre Giertsen (1851–1905) in "Trondsbu", Giertsen's new hunting cabin near Lake Tinnhølen.

[20] The article on Mozart was commissioned by *The Century Illustrated Monthly Magazine*, New York and London, and published in November, 1897. It appeared in Norwegian in a slightly extended form in *Samtiden*, Bergen, in 1898 and in an abbreviated version in German in the Austrian weekly *Die Zeit*, Vienna, on December 10, 1898. It will be included in a new translation from the original Norwegian in Benestad and Halverson (eds.), *Edvard Grieg: Diaries, Articles, Speeches* (Columbus, Ohio, 2001).

[21] Grieg is quoting from *Isaiah* 55:8, "For my thoughts are not your thoughts, neither are your ways my ways, says the Lord" (RSV).

[22] Grieg is paraphrasing Romans 7:19: "For I do not do the good I want, but the evil I do not want is what I do." (RSV)

Correspondence with Henrik Ibsen

Grieg met Henrik Ibsen (1828–1906) for the first time at the Scandinavian Society in Rome in 1865. His diary for 1865–66 contains several references to Ibsen, some of which are quite amusing. Although Grieg set one poem by Ibsen as early as 1868 (op. 15 no. 1), the two artists did not actively collaborate on anything until 1874, when Ibsen approached Grieg about the possibility of writing incidental music for a staging of his dramatic poem *Peer Gynt.* As is well known, Grieg responded positively to Ibsen's inquiry. Shortly after completing the *Peer Gynt* music (op. 23) Grieg also composed the *Six Songs* of op. 25 to texts by Ibsen. The two men never became close personal friends—indeed, Ibsen, so far as we know, had no close friends —but they met on several occasions through the years. At one time they toyed with the idea of collaborating on an opera based on Ibsen's early plays *Olaf Liljekrans* and *The Vikings at Helgeland,* but nothing came of it.

Grieg's letter of December 25, 1898, is in Riksarkivet (The National Archive of Norway), the others in Nasjonalbiblioteket, Oslo (National Library of Norway, Oslo Division). Ibsen's letters to Grieg are preserved in Bergen Offentlige Bibliotek (Bergen Public Library).

From Grieg to Ibsen 1

Copenhagen, June 10, 1866

Mr. Henrik Ibsen, Rome

Excuse me for taking up your time for a moment. It can't be helped: There are things I have to know about and concerning which, therefore, I must ask your advice.

In accordance with your friendly counsel in Rome I wrote to Bjørnson[1] already during my stay in Leipzig—about six weeks ago. I told him exactly what I was thinking, how much I would love working with him, how I thought that the influence from him would help me survive amidst the chaos of pettiness and misunderstanding that I am fully prepared to wade through daily up there, told him what hopes I had for the future of our Nordic music if it should fall to my lot to work on its behalf—in short, I thoroughly described my views to him, and lastly I applied for the position of musical director at the theater, assuming that the present incumbent, Hennum,[2] has only a provisional appointment. I let him know how important *his* opinion would be to me and urged him to answer me as soon as possible. But to date the man has not let me hear a single syllable from him, which strikes me as almost worse than inconsiderate. I know very well what Bjørnson has had to contend with up there recently, and I can well understand that he must have plenty of things to think about besides letter-writing. But that does not in the least excuse his silence in this case, which has to do with such important business matters.

---

1 Norwegian author Bjørnstjerne Bjørnson (1832–1910), who at that time was director of the Christiania Theater.

2 Unknown to Grieg, the cellist Johan Hennum (1836–94) had been appointed musical director at the Christiania Theater in March, 1866. Hennum went on to present a number of important operas and operettas and in 1876 conducted the premiere of *Peer Gynt.*

Henrik Ibsen, for whose play Grieg wrote his famous "Peer Gynt" music. Upon hearing of Ibsen's death in 1906, Grieg wrote in his diary: "How much I owe him! Poor, great Ibsen! He was not a happy man, for it is as if he carried within him a chunk of ice that would not melt. But beneath this chunk of ice lay a fervent love of humanity." (Norsk Folkemuseum, Oslo)

You can undoubtedly imagine what a state of mind I am in at this time. My whole future is at stake. When I wrote to Bjørnson I was enthused about the idea. I lived in it and longed to hear that my plan would also please him. Now, when his lack of interest in the matter seems clear to me, I have become rather listless. I am constituted in such a way that I cannot divide up my hope and my longing. I stake everything on one throw, and if that fails I fall apart.

But I suppose it is still too early to abandon the beautiful idea. Therefore I am asking that you write to Bjørnson and ask him at least to answer me so that I can make a decision and put an end to this numbing uncertainty. I know that he has received my first letter, and I am too proud to write him a second one—that you can understand. Therefore, if you have some interest in me, help me now and give Bjørnson a tongue-lashing that he won't forget. It seems to me that he must not like me, I must have taken the matter in a wrong way, or some such thing. Now, hopefully, you can make it right again. I hope very much to hear that some lines from you to me are awaiting me at Hegel's.[3]

[3] Danish book publisher Jacob Hegel (1851–1918), owner of the Gyldendal Publishing Company in Copenhagen.

I have now also read your magnificent *Brand*. There is something remarkable about the truth. People can tolerate it when it is expressed in poetry; it doesn't touch one's life so closely but that one can enjoy it. When it is expressed in pure prose, however, it is, as Kierkegaard[4] has said, too sharp, too impertinent. In no other way can I make the slightest sense out of the enormous furor that *Brand* has created, the huge circle of readers that daily devour it.

Farewell for now. Warm greetings from

Very sincerely yours,
EDVARD GRIEG

P.S. Greetings to Ravnkilde,[5] who will hear from me soon.

From Ibsen to Grieg 1

Frascati, August 24, 1866

Dear Grieg!
Hopefully you have long since received an answer from Bjørnson. Your letter was fairly old by the time I received it down here, but I wrote to Bjørnson immediately, and although I am afraid that my letter didn't reach him until he was in Stockholm, he surely has now had enough time to think it over. Uncertainty about his own future position at the theater has certainly been the reason for his silence.[6]

But no matter how this turns out, you have no right to say that your whole future is at stake. No, dear Grieg, your future is certainly something more and better than the position of musical director. It would be ungrateful of you to measure the talents you have received by so small a measuring stick. But of course I understand what you actually mean.

Be assured that I have plainly stated your case and told Bjørnson what kind of a man you are.

Now I assume that the theater controversy will soon be settled, and then I hope I will also learn of your appointment. Don't hold a grudge against Bjørnson; I'm sure he is not against you. Write to him one more time if necessary. Tell him that he *shall* let you have the position. Tell him you have a right to it. Make him answerable if he refuses, and if all of this is of no avail, then your musical accomplishments will demonstrate how badly people have behaved—and the whole affair will have to do only with a postponement of the time [of your

[4] Danish philosopher Søren Kierkegaard (1813–55).

[5] Danish composer Niels Ravnkilde (1823–90) was one of Grieg's close friends during his stay in Rome in 1865–66. See Grieg's letters to him.

[6] After disagreements with the governing board of the Christiania Theater, Bjørnson resigned in 1867 after only two years in the position.

triumph], nothing more. Just don't become dispirited; that you have neither a reason nor a right to do.

Farewell. My wife asks me to greet you, and receive also warm greetings from

Yours truly,
HENRIK IBSEN

From Ibsen to Grieg 2

Dresden, January 23, 1874

Dear Mr. Grieg:
I am writing to you in connection with a plan that I propose to implement, and in which I wish to invite your participation.

The plan is this: I intend to adapt *Peer Gynt*, which will soon go into its third printing, for a stage performance. Will you compose the music that will be required? I will indicate briefly how I am thinking of arranging the play.

The first act is to be retained in its entirety, with only a few cuts in the dialogue. I would like to have Peer Gynt's monologue on pages 23, 24 and 25 treated either as melodrama or in part as a recitative. With the help of ballet, much more must be made of the wedding scene on page 28 than is suggested in the book. For this scene a special dance tune must be composed, which then continues to be played softly until the end of the act.

In the second act, the scene with the three herd girls, pages 57–60, should be handled musically in whatever way the composer thinks best, but there must be deviltry in it! I would prefer that the monologue on pages 60–62 be accompanied by chords, i.e., handled as a melodrama. The same goes for the scene with Peer and The Woman in Green, pages 63–66. Some kind of musical accompaniment must also be provided for the episodes in the hall of the Mountain King, although the speeches in this section are to be considerably shortened. The scene with the Great Bøyg, which is to be given in full, must also have a musical accompaniment; bird calls must be sung, and church bells and hymns must be heard in the distance.

In the third act I need chords—but only a few—for the scene with Peer, the Woman [in Green] and the Troll Child, pages 96–100. I have also thought that there should be a slow accompaniment from the top of page 109 up to and including the bottom of page 112 [the scene depicting the death of Åse].

Nearly the whole of the fourth act is to be omitted in performance. In its place I have imagined a large-scale tone picture suggesting Peer Gynt's wandering throughout the world; American, English, and French melodies might be interwoven, growing and fading one by one. The chorus consisting of Anitra and the other girls, pages 144–45, is to be heard singing behind the curtain at the same time that the orchestra is playing. While this is occurring the curtain will rise and the audience will see, as in a distant dream picture, the tableau described on page 164 where Solveig, now a middle-aged woman, sits singing in the sunshine outside her hut. After her song the curtain will be slowly lowered. The orchestra will continue to play, but the music will move toward a description of the storm at sea with which the fifth act begins.

The fifth act, which in performance will be called either the fourth act or an epilogue, must be shortened considerably. A musical accompaniment is needed for pages 195–99 [for the scene with the Stranger]. The scenes on the overturned boat and in the graveyard are to be omitted. Solveig will sing, page 221 [Scene 5], and the postlude will accompany Peer Gynt's spoken lines. After that the choral scenes will take over, pages 222–225 [Scene 6]. The scenes with the Button-molder and with the Mountain King will be shortened. The churchgoers sing on the forest path, page 254 [Scene 10]; the ringing of bells and the distant singing of hymns are suggested in the music that follows, and this continues until Solveig's song brings the play to an end. As the curtain falls, the hymn-singing again sounds nearer and louder.

That is more or less how I have conceived the whole project. Please let me know if you are willing to undertake this task. If you agree to do so, I will immediately contact the board of the Christiania Theater, deliver a corrected script and get advance assurance that the piece will be performed.

As an honorarium I intend to request 400 *spesidalers*, which shall be shared equally between us. I think there is no doubt that we can also count on the piece being performed in Copenhagen and Stockholm. But I ask you to keep the matter a secret for now and to answer me as soon as possible.

Cordially,
HENRIK IBSEN

P.S. My address here in Dresden is: Wettiner-Strasse, No. 22, Second Floor.

From Ibsen to Grieg 3

Dresden, February 8, 1874

Dear Mr. Grieg!
From your friendly letter[7] I note with pleasure that you agree with my proposal. How much music and for which scenes you will compose it I naturally leave entirely to you; in this a composer obviously must have a completely free hand.

Nor is there any problem with your delaying the project until summer, for in any case the play cannot be produced until the next season.

[7] This letter and the one referred to in Ibsen's letter of March 3, 1875, unfortunately are not extant.

At the same time that I send you these lines I am writing to Mr. Josephson.[8] Will you perhaps be so kind as to talk with him and tell him everything I told you in my previous letter regarding my plan for shortening the play etc. When he, as I hope, gives his consent or preliminary assurance that he will accept the piece for performance, I will send him a corrected copy of the book which you will be able to get from him for your own work.

We should set forth our conditions regarding honoraria and related matters only when the completed score is delivered. The score should be accompanied by an official letter to the whole board of directors of the theater, which letter I will compose and transmit to you—for it should be signed by both of us.

I regard this matter with great interest, and it is my hope that you will do the same. I will probably visit Norway this summer, and then I could perhaps have the pleasure of discussing this project with you—and also of reviving old memories of Rome.

Cordially,
HENRIK IBSEN

From Ibsen to Grieg 4

Dresden, March 3, 1875

Dear Mr. Grieg!
In answer to your friendly letter I can today give you some news that, judging from what you tell me about the Christiania Theater orchestra, will not be unwelcome to you.

The fact is that *Peer Gynt* is not scheduled for performance during the current season. Thus you will have the whole spring and most of the summer at your disposal. I earnestly beg you not to make any concessions to poor orchestral resources. Orchestrate your music according to an ideal standard and let the people up there see to it that it is properly performed. Anything less than that would be unworthy of a man such as you and moreover would harm us both.

In the middle of April I am changing my place of residence to Munich. Before then I probably will come to Leipzig for a couple of days on literary business. It would be a pleasure for us if we, here in Dresden, could have the pleasure of seeing you and your esteemed wife before our departure.

With warm greetings,

Cordially,
HENRIK IBSEN

---

[8] Ludvig Oscar Josephson (1832–99), a Swede, was Director of the Christiania Theater 1873–77.

From Grieg to Ibsen 2

Fredensborg, July 25, 1875

The Playwright Henrik Ibsen, Munich

I send you these lines to inform you that the music for *Peer Gynt* is now ready for mailing. Do you want it sent or—if, like me, you find this a little risky—shall I send the play and the music after having received your official letter to the board of directors of the theater? This I must know as soon as possible.

When you have assigned the staging responsibility to Josephson I suppose it is appropriate that I inform him of what I thought should be done to strengthen the impact at certain points. If you are amenable to this idea, fine; if not, either I would have to send you my score so that you could read through all the comments pertaining to the musical-dramatic handling or I would have to write you a mile-long letter in which I explain in detail what I have done and not done. Therefore it is doubly important for me to hear your opinion soon.

If you have no specific wish with respect to the time for the performance of the play in Christiania, I would strongly advise that it not be scheduled for the beginning of the season. I certainly will not be coming home until the end of September, and I think that if I could be present at the rehearsals I might be able to contribute in some degree to eliminating misunderstandings and thereby achieving the best possible result from the musical production of the play.

While I have pen in hand I want also to thank you for your kind invitation to come to Dresden. Unfortunately, it did not fit in with my travel plans.

I am addressing these lines to Mr. Grønvold,[9] the painter, as your present address is unknown to me.

Warm greetings, also to your wife!

Sincerely yours,
EDVARD GRIEG

P.S. My address for the time being is Fredensborg at Copenhagen.

From Ibsen to Grieg 5

Kitzbühel, Tyrol, August 20, 1875

Dear Mr. Grieg!

From your kind letter I note with pleasure that you have now finished the music for *Peer Gynt*. It is my confident hope that we will experience satisfaction from this collaborative effort.

If it has not happened already, I request that you send the music directly to Mr. Josephson in Christiania. The play itself I sent to him already last year. By the

---

[9] Norwegian painter Marcus Grønvold (1845–1929).

same token I request that you communicate all the comments you have to make to Mr. Josephson.[10] But I must firmly counsel you against any effort to get the performance of the play delayed any farther into the season; for in any case it will not be ready until near Christmas, and for that reason the rehearsals should get under way as quickly as possible. That you yourself will be present for the music rehearsals is, of course, a foregone conclusion; but these are unlikely to begin until sometime in October.

I will stay up here in the mountains until the beginning of September. If you should have anything further to communicate to me about these matters, your letter will reach me safely here with no further address required. From October 1 onward I will again live in Munich, No. 17 Schönfeld-Strasse, where I would also be pleased to hear from you at any time.

With the warmest greetings I remain,

Cordially,
Henrik Ibsen

From Grieg to Ibsen 3

Bergen, March 15, 1876

The Playwright Henrik Ibsen, Munich
Yesterday I received a letter from the board of the Christiania Theater which includes the following:

> "Now that *Peer Gynt* is being performed at the Christiania Theater, the board takes the liberty of requesting a statement from you regarding the honorarium for the music that you have composed for this piece."

Obviously, in view of the earlier letter from you, I cannot answer this letter without having heard your view of the matter. You will recall that at that time I declared myself in full agreement with your proposal, which was that you would demand 400 *spesidalers* from the Christiania Theater, which sum would be equally shared by us. Now after the performance I had expected to hear from you, not from the board of directors of the theater, with which I have had no business dealings. But perhaps the matter has entered another phase, and that is why I must know your opinion—as soon as possible.

I will tell you straightforwardly that it is distressing to me to deal with you on a financial matter. Naturally it is a very naive position to take in relation to a poet whom one admires, but as things stand now I can't help it.

---

[10] See Grieg's letters to Josephson. Far more important than these, however, are his letters to musical director Johan Hennum. See, for example, the long letter of December 14, 1876, in which Grieg discusses each number in detail.

It is, therefore, a double joy for me to congratulate you on the marvelous result produced by the stage version of *Peer Gynt.* If I have contributed even a little to that result, I have repaid only a portion of the debt that I feel I owe you.

I was unfortunately unable to be there myself (shattering events in my home[11] have made all public activity loathsome to me for the time being, so this winter I have just withdrawn into my lodgings and into my thoughts), but I nonetheless think I could pronounce a kind of judgment on the impression of the performance as a whole. What I very much regret is that the ending—where I think I have written some of my best music—has, because of a thoroughly mangled musical performance, made a weak impression. But I suppose this can be changed when Solveig is played by someone else.

Where are you spending the summer? I will be in Bayreuth in July and August, and in that connection I cherish the hope of being able to meet you for a few days somewhere in the world.[12]

Warm greetings and sincere thanks!

Yours truly,
EDVARD GRIEG

P.S. Greet your wife!

From Ibsen to Grieg 6

Munich, March 30, 1876

Dear Mr. Grieg!
I see from your friendly letter received last evening that there must be some misunderstanding on both sides regarding the music to *Peer Gynt,* but I hope this matter can be easily resolved to everyone's satisfaction.

As you will recall, our agreement that I would deliver to the theater in my own name both the text and the music could not be fulfilled inasmuch as the latter was not ready at the anticipated time. Therefore, I delivered only the text and have since that time constantly assumed that the terms of payment for the music would have to be a private matter between you and the board of directors of the theater. This has also been the understanding of the board of directors; for in my correspondence with the board concerning the author's honorarium it is

---

[11] Grieg's father died on September 13, 1875, his mother on October 23.

[12] Grieg had received tickets from Max Abraham (1831–1900), his publisher in Leipzig, to the performance of Richard Wagner's tetralogy *The Ring of the Nibelung* in Bayreuth, and the Bergen newspaper *Bergensposten* had commissioned him to cover this international event for a Norwegian readership. He did so in a series of eight perceptive articles that appeared in the newspaper during the period August 20–September 3, 1876. See Benestad & Halverson (eds.), *Edvard Grieg: Diaries, Articles, Speeches* (Columbus, Ohio, 2001). In Bayreuth Grieg was with the Bergen poet John Paulsen (1851–1924), and after the Wagner festivities were over they went together to Tyrol, where they visited Ibsen in Gossensass.

explicitly stated that they were unable to pay me more than such and such an amount "since, of course, the music must be paid for separately." On the basis of this statement I could only assume that at the same time you delivered the score you had reached some agreement regarding the remuneration. That this is not the case, however, is not a serious matter; for I cannot doubt for a moment that the theater, in dealing with a composer of your stature, will show itself to be every bit as liberal as it would have been had the negotiations been handled through me. I think, therefore, that you should answer the board's letter and state the demands that you think appropriate.[13]

I take it for granted that you are not selling the music but only the right to its use at the Christiania Theater; for according to what I have heard, plans are under way to perform the play in Stockholm, and a few days ago I received a communication from a German man of letters who requests permission to translate and arrange it for use in German theaters.

Thus the most important point is for you not to relinquish your right of ownership. You yourself, who are so nearby,[14] can bring all of the negotiations relating to this matter to a satisfactory conclusion much more easily and quickly than I, and I hope soon to hear that such negotiations have been successful.

Permit me, however, to express to you my most cordial and friendly thanks for all you have contributed to the success of my play on the stage in Norway!

We have heard with sincere sympathy of the grievous loss that has recently struck your closest family circle. I assume that this is what you allude to in your letter.

I am pleased for your sake to hear that you will be taking a trip abroad again next summer. It will provide diversion for you and lead you to new works.

It would be especially pleasing to me if we could meet. We are staying here in Munich until the end of July. My address here is: No. 17 Schönfeld-Strasse. In August and September we probably will go to Tyrol, then will return to Munich. So: Plan your trip to include Munich! You have many friends and admirers in the musical world around here.

---

[13] Grieg took Ibsen's advice and on April 8, 1876, sent the following letter to the board of directors of the Christiania Theater:

"That I am only now able to reply to the letter of March 11 of the esteemed board of directors is due to the fact that I have had to await an answer to a letter to Ibsen, from whom I at one time received a proposal regarding an honorarium which I accepted. According to this proposal, he intended to secure from the Christiania Theater a sum that was to be equally divided between the two of us. On the basis of this agreement I concluded that I should deal with the author, not the theater board. Since, however, I see in a letter received from Ibsen today that the situation is otherwise inasmuch as he has already received his honorarium, I take the liberty of recommending 200 *spesidalers* (the sum Ibsen proposed to me) as an honorarium for the use of the music at the Christiania Theater. In so doing I explicitly note that at the time I accepted his proposal I had no idea how much music there would be. Thus the sum I have mentioned is a minimum. Beyond this, in view of the circumstances, I leave the matter to the liberal decision of the esteemed board of directors."

[14] Grieg was in Bergen at this time.

In the hope of hearing soon that the matter with the theater is resolved, and with a warm greeting to you and your wife, I remain

Very cordially yours,
HENRIK IBSEN

From Grieg to Ibsen 4

"Fuglsang",[15] *Nykjøbing at Falster*
December 25, 1898

Dear Henrik Ibsen!
Merry Christmas! And right to the matter which to a large extent has to do with the wish for a "happy new year!"

I recently received from C. F. Peters, my German publisher in Leipzig, a recommendation that I, in collaboration with you, try to get enacted in Norway a system that would make it impossible for the works of Norwegian authors and composers to be abandoned in America to whoever produces the first and best reprinting in that country, such as is currently the case according to the very latest American decisions. I immediately referred the assignment I had received to my Danish publisher, Wilhelm Hansen,[16] who was just in the process of taking an initiative in the same matter. Since I happen to be staying in Denmark just now, he—in collaboration with Hegel, in order to expedite the matter—sent me the enclosure[17] with a request that I pass it along to you.

As you will see, the issue in question is of the greatest significance for the existence of Norwegian writers and composers. A request from *you* to our national

---

[15] "Fuglsang" ("Birdsong") was the estate of Grieg's friends Rolf Viggo de Neergaard (1837–1916) and his wife Bodil (1867–1959) on the Danish island of Lolland.

[16] Alfred Wilhelm Hansen (1854–1923).

[17] The "enclosure" to which Grieg refers was the following letter addressed to Ibsen and Grieg:

Copenhagen, December 22, 1898

To Messrs. Dr. Henrik Ibsen and Dr. Edvard Grieg.

Earlier the United States in North America—for their territory—granted copyright protection for new literary and musical works when the country in which the work in question was published was a signatory to the Bern Convention.

Recently, however, a report was received from the copyright office in Washington that this decision has been modified in such a way that henceforth the right to registration for copyright protection will depend on whether the country of which the author or composer of the work in question is a citizen has concluded a special agreement on copyright protection, whereas the countries that—like Norway, for example—have only signed the Bern Convention without also having concluded the special agreement will be excluded.

Since the undersigned publishers have the honor of having published Norway's most significant literary and musical works, and since Norwegian works will, because of the lacking special agreement, be cut off from the market in America, which in many ways is significant, we request that you gentlemen appeal to the Norwegian government to enter into a special copyright agreement with the United States as soon as possible, for the effects of a failure to do so will be just as serious for the Norwegian authors and composers as for their Scandinavian and foreign publishers.

JACOB HEGEL
Gyldendal Publishing Company

WILHELM HANSEN
Wilhelm Hansen Publishing Company

Parliament or our government to bring the matter up as quickly as possible on the basis of the enclosed document is, of course, the only way to move quickly toward the goal. The form that your request will take naturally is left with thanks to your discretion. But you will surely agree with me and the publishers that something should be done here without delay.

I would indeed be grateful to you for a few lines setting forth your view of the matter.

With warm greetings, I am,

Sincerely yours,
EDVARD GRIEG

P.S. Address: Copenhagen, Hotel King of Denmark.

From Grieg to Ibsen 5

Copenhagen, January 10, 1899
[Hotel King of Denmark]

Dear Henrik Ibsen!
Since I have reason to believe that an important letter, which I sent to you on December 25 during my stay at "Fuglsang" (Nykjøbing at Falster), has not been satisfactorily dealt with [by the postal service], I ask you kindly to send me a few words informing me whether you have received it.

With warm greetings,

Sincerely yours,
EDVARD GRIEG

From Ibsen to Grieg 7

Christiania, January 13, 1899

Dear Edvard Grieg!
Yes, I received your letter, but the reason I have not answered is that I first wanted to await a communication on the same subject from the Norwegian Authors' Association, where I knew it was under consideration.

This communication, which I have now received, assumes that the Association will name a committee which, in collaboration with its legal advisor—Mr. Hoel, a graduate in law and legal assistant in the Ministry of Church and Education—will take the necessary steps to get the matter settled. I am therefore very much in doubt as to how desirable any interference from me would be for the time being. I am no expert in this international domain, so to that extent I have nothing to contribute to the best resolution of the matter.

However, if you want me to do so nonetheless, I will be glad to send Messrs.

Hegel and Hansen's letter to the Ministry of Church and Education accompanied by an earnest recommendation.

With the warmest greetings to you and Mrs. Grieg, I remain

Cordially,
HENRIK IBSEN

From Grieg to Ibsen 6

Copenhagen, January 16, 1899
Hotel King of Denmark

Dear Henrik Ibsen!
I am of course grateful for your kind offer to send Messrs. Hegel and W. Hansen's letter to the Ministry of Church and Education accompanied by your earnest recommendation. As a matter of fact, however, the letter, even if it had been cast in the form of a petition, would not have carried much weight as a communication from foreigners. As such it would only have significance as an enclosed document. I, therefore, am not in doubt for a moment that a weighty word from you—in which you, with reference to the Danish letter, ask the government or Parliament for the necessary protection of our literary rights—is not only the main point, but in support of the petition of the Norwegian Authors' Association will be the best contribution to the most favorable and—what is of the greatest importance—the *fastest* solution of the problem.[18]

Urgently requesting, for the sake of the matter at hand, that you not let a day be wasted, I am, with warm greetings to you and your wife,

Sincerely,
EDVARD GRIEG

---

[18] On January 22, 1899, Ibsen forwarded the letter from Jacob Hegel and Wilhelm Hansen to the Ministry of Church and Education along with the following cover letter, which is preserved in Riksarkivet (The National Archive of Norway):

To the Department of Church and Education:
At the request of the composer, Dr. Edvard Grieg, I take the liberty of sending to the Royal Ministry of Church and Education the enclosed letter, to which I hereby add my warmest and most urgent recommendation that the unacceptable circumstances for Norwegian authors and composers described therein be changed as soon as possible.

Respectfully,
HENRIK IBSEN

To Vincent d'Indy

The French composer Vincent d'Indy (1851–1931) was, at the time of Grieg's visit to Paris in 1889, director of the choir associated with the Lamoureux Orchestra and secretary of the French *Société Nationale de Musique.* The latter regularly gave concerts in Paris, and quite often their programs included Norwegian music. D'Indy admired the music of Johan Svendsen (1840–1911) and in the 1880's arranged two of his songs for piano four hands. Grieg was also very highly regarded in Paris at this time. The Parisians were especially interested in his chamber music.

Grieg's letter to Vincent d'Indy is preserved in the Library of Congress, Washington, D.C. Bergen Offentlige Bibliotek (Bergen Public Library) also has a draft of the letter (in Norwegian) in Grieg's own hand as well as a French version, also in Grieg's hand, which follows a translation by Alexander Bull (1839–1914), son of Norwegian violinist Ole Bull (1810–80).

Paris, January 15, 1890
Hotel de Sèze

Dear Sir!

To my surprise and regret I have just learned that a critic in *Le Ménéstrel* has described my connection to the concert of December 28 in *La Société Nationale de Musique* in a manner that I cannot accept.[1] I have suffered such an irreplaceable loss in not being able to take part in this concert, which you have shown me the honor of devoting in large part to my compositions, that it seems to me more than unfair that some people add to my misery by questioning my motives for not attending. It definitely is not the case, as *Le Ménéstrel* maintains, that I stayed away out of concern for my forthcoming engagement [with the Colonne Orchestra]. Such concern did not exist. I stayed away purely because of my health. I thought I had said this to you and your colleagues so clearly that there could be no misunderstanding.

It is not my custom to respond to criticism that appears in newspapers. Thus I will only request that you, *cher Maître,* do me the favor, wherever you may have opportunity, of protesting in the name of truth against the statement in *Le Ménéstrel.*

Permit me, while I have your attention, to thank you for your *Trio,* which I have found extremely interesting. *Chant élégiaque* is a remarkable piece of music.

Accept, dear sir, my sincerest greetings.

EDVARD GRIEG

---

[1] Early in December, 1889, Grieg had received an invitation from *La Société Nationale de Musique* to participate in a chamber-music concert that was to be given on December 28 in his honor. Grieg had originally accepted the invitation. Because of illness, however, he had to inform d'Indy that he would not be able to perform, but only to be present for the concert. To the great disappointment of the arrangers of the event and of the audience, he then sent word that for reasons of health it would not even be possible for him to attend the concert.

It cannot be denied that Grieg's absence was a bit strange, for the very next day he conducted his own works at a big concert by the Colonne Orchestra in the Châtelet Theater. That he did not forget the episode, which for him was a very painful one, is evident from a letter to Alexander Bull in 1891 in which he mentioned that the experience with *La Société Nationale de Musique* was still an unpleasant memory for him.

To Joseph Joachim

The Austro-Hungarian violinist Joseph Joachim (1831–1907) was a child prodigy who made his public debut with his teacher at the age of eight. He appeared in a Gewandhaus concert in Leipzig at the age of twelve in 1843—the year Grieg was born—and came at this time under the strong influence of both Mendelssohn and Schumann. His reputation grew rapidly and he soon came to be regarded as one of the foremost violin virtuosos of his day. He became a close friend of Johannes Brahms, who sought his advice while writing his violin concerto. In 1868 he moved to Berlin, where he became leader of the newly established Hochschule für Ausübende Tonkunst (College of Music). He was also an outstanding chamber musician; the Joachim Quartet achieved international fame, not least as a result of its interpretations of Beethoven's and Brahms's chamber music. Joachim also composed a number of works, his three violin concertos being the most important.

Joachim played Grieg's violin sonatas from time to time, only rarely with Grieg himself at the piano.

Grieg's letter to Joachim is in German and is preserved in the Staatsbibliothek zu Berlin, Preussischer Kulturbesitz, Musikabteilung.

Copenhagen, December 2, 1879
Hotel King of Denmark

Dear Maestro!

Encouraged by my friend Heinrich von Herzogenberg,[1] I take the liberty of respectfully sending you an urgent request. I am planning to go to London in the spring. Would you show me the extraordinary kindness of providing me with some recommendations? Perhaps you will say that someone who is going to give concerts must either do it without recommendations or simply forget about it. And you are right about that. It is also my view. But there is only one city like London, and there is only one Joachim!

It is my intention to play my own compositions (*Piano Concerto*, violin sonatas, *Piano Sonata*, solo pieces)—and, if possible, to perform other compositions of mine as well.

Completely unknown as I am in London, a few lines from your hand would prepare the way for me in thousands of ways. You yourself know best which recommendations I need; as stated, I do not know anyone there. I have written only to Manns[2] regarding the *Piano Concerto*.

In the hope that you will not take my burdensome request[3] amiss, I am, with great esteem and respect,

Sincerely yours,
EDVARD GRIEG
Norwegian Musician

---

[1] German composer Heinrich von Herzogenberg (1843–1900).

[2] German-born violinist and conductor August Manns (1825–1907) had conducted the popular Crystal Palace concerts in London since 1855.

[3] Joachim sent Grieg a recommendation via Clara Schumann (1818–96), and Grieg enclosed it in his letter of January 4 to the administration of The Philharmonic Society in London. See Grieg's letters to Clara Schumann and Francesco Berger (1834–1933). Grieg's plans for concerts in London in 1880 did not work out, however, and he did not give concerts in England until 1888.

To Robert Underwood Johnson

Robert Underwood Johnson (1853–1937) was associate editor of the American journal *The Century Illustrated Monthly Magazine* 1881–1909 and editor 1909–13. Grieg wrote two articles for the journal, one on Schumann and one on Mozart. Both articles are very long and bear witness not only to Grieg's deep insight into the music of the two masters but also to his love for their works. They will be printed in new translations in Benestad & Halverson (eds.), *Edvard Grieg: Diaries, Articles, Speeches* (Columbus, Ohio, 2001).

The Schumann article, which Grieg wrote at Grefsen Baths in June, 1893, was printed in the journal in January, 1894. A Norwegian version was published in *Nyt tidsskrift* [*New Journal*] the same year. The article on Mozart was written during a trip to the Hardanger Plateau in July, 1896,[1] and was published in November, 1897. In December, 1897, Grieg sent out a correction regarding the introduction that the editor of the journal had commissioned for the Mozart article. This correction appeared in several English, American and Norwegian newspapers.

The six letters that follow are reprinted in the English form in which they were sent. Drafts of letters 1 and 2 are preserved in Bergen Offentlige Bibliotek (Bergen Public Library), letter 3 in the Library of Congress, Washington, D.C., and letters 4 and 6 in the Mary Flagler Cary Music Collection of The Pierpont Morgan Library, New York City. Letter 5 is in Nasjonalbiblioteket, Oslo (National Library of Norway, Oslo Division).

1

Menton, April 4,1893

Dear Sir!

After a long journey your letter at last has reached me here.[2] I am sorry to say I never was happy enough to[3] know Schumann, as he died in 1856 and I came as a child to Leipzig in 1858. But from early youth he is my favorite and therefore I will take pleasure in trying to accomplish your wish. Still you will permit me to take the reservation that I only send you the article when I am anyhow satisfied with it myself. As I am not able to write in English, will you kindly let me know if you can get it translated from Norwegian or from German. I fully agree with your terms: 1,000 francs and remain, dear Sir,

Yours faithfully,
EDVARD GRIEG
Address: C. F. Peters, Thalstrasse 10, Leipzig

---

[1] See Grieg's letter to C. F. E. Horneman (1840–1906) of September 15, 1896.

[2] Johnson had written to Grieg on February 28, 1893, inviting him to write "an article of reminiscence and appreciation of Schumann, with whom, if we mistake not, you associated during the last years of that master's life in Leipzig." Grieg first drafted a letter declining the invitation, but he evidently changed his mind and drafted—on the same page—the reply given here. The draft is undated, but Grieg's account book makes it clear that he sent the letter from Menton, a small French city on the Riviera. Nina and Edvard Grieg and Christian Sinding (1856–1941) had been invited by Max Abraham (1831–1900), owner of the C. F. Peters Musikverlag in Leipzig, to accompany him on a trip to the famous health spa. It is possible that Max Abraham persuaded Grieg to write the Schumann article.

[3] Grieg means "so fortunate as to."

2

Grefsen Baths, June 7, 1893[4]

Dear Sir!
I sent you a letter communicating you my readiness to write the article on Schumann and asking you in what language I was to concept it—German or Norwegian—as I am not able to write it in English. Kindly inform me which you can get translated into English. I have not yet heard from you and therefore I am afraid you have not received my letter. I shall be obliged to you for an early answer.

I remain, dear Sir,

Yours faithfully,
Edvard Grieg

3

Bergen, Norway, July 18, 1893

Dear Sir!
Enclosed I send you my essay on Schumann.[5] You will understand that I better write my own language than a foreign [one], and as I had already finished the article in Norwegian as your last letter arrived, you will kindly excuse me that I am troubling you with a translation from the latter. I don't mind if the German citations are to be translated into English and shall be obliged to you if you will be kind enough not to let the paper appear before I have sanctioned the English version.

Believe me, dear Sir

Yours very respectfully,
Edvard Grieg

P.S. I have made efforts to get a very interesting portrait of Schumann (photo after a painting in watercolors), and if able to procure it I shall send it as soon as possible. A photo of mine you will find enclosed.

---

[4] The draft of this letter appears on the same page as the two letters mentioned in footnote 2. Grieg states in his account book that the letter was sent from Grefsen Baths, Christiania, on June 7. Johnson replied on June 19, 1893: "Kindly write the article in German, if it is as convenient as Norwegian." But the reply arrived too late to affect the outcome: Grieg had already written the article in Norwegian (see letter 3).

[5] Grieg stated in a letter to his Dutch friend Julius Röntgen (1855–1932) dated June 24, 1893, that he had written the Schumann article during a stay at Grefsen Baths in Christiania.

4

Christiania, October 4, 1893

Dear Sir!
Enclosed I return the Schumann article yesterday received. It seems to be *very well* translated.[6] On the pages 1, 2, 11, 13, 18, 23, 24, 25, 26 however I have taken the liberty of choosing some other expressions after my opinion better answering my thoughts. I beg you to ascertain that they are written in correct English.

The German citations are to be carefully corrected.

I thank you and shall feel most honored by appearing in *The Century*. But a proof of the portrait of myself I have not yet received.

Hoping that you will be kind enough to send me the paper, when my article is printed, I remain, Dear Sir,

Yours faithfully,
EDVARD GRIEG

5

Fossli at Eidfjord, Norway, August 8, 1896

Dear Sir!
I take the liberty to tell you, that I have just finished an article on Mozart for the *Century Magazine* and if you should wish it, I shall get it translated into German as soon as possible and send it to you. Will you kindly let me know, at what time you intend to publish my work.

Believe me, dear Sir,

Yours respectfully,
EDVARD GRIEG

6

Vienna, November 18, 1896

Dear Sir!
Thanking you for your sending of 1,000 fr. for my article on Mozart. I beg you, as soon as possible, to let the translator correct two faults in my essay.[7]

1. I mention in the beginning of my article something like the following: "It is good that in his writings Wagner has also inscribed the

[6] The translator was the Norwegian-American author Hjalmar Hjorth Boyesen (1848–95), professor of Germanic languages and literature at Columbia College in New York City.

[7] The translator was the American writer Henry T. Finck (1854–1926). See also Grieg's letter to Finck of February 23, 1900, in which he states, "I had, before my article on Mozart was printed, a very special reason to be grateful to you, because you prevented the appearance in it of an erroneous assertion on my part regarding Wagner." Grieg's remark obviously refers to the suggested correction concerning this paragraph, and it was not included in the article as printed in *The Century*.

name of Mozart on his shield. His belief in Mozart is unambiguous, and thereby he has in the most explicit way disassociated himself from those contemporary musicians who are so modern that they no longer know how to enjoy Mozart."

Instead of these lines I wish to have the following: "It is too bad that in his writings Wagner has not proclaimed the same unambiguous admiration for Mozart that he has expressed for such other great masters as Bach, Beethoven, Gluck and Weber. By this omission he has contributed in no small degree to the emergence in our day of a group of musicians for whom the most important thing is to appear modern, i.e., to adopt Wagner's views on everything. There is a possibility that Wagner has not exactly idolized Mozart. Consequently, there is no need for us to do it, either! Had the Bayreuth master been able to foresee the consequences of his silence regarding Mozart he would certainly have disassociated himself most emphatically from these hyper-modern musicians who fancy themselves so modern that they can no longer stand Mozart's music."[8]

2. Later I have mentioned a picture by a German master entitled *Ein Supplicant.* The motto of the picture is: "I can wait". The name of the master is not, as I have said, Vautier, but Knaus.[9] I beg you also kindly to let this fault be corrected.

Hoping that these lines may reach you in time, I remain, dear Sir,

Yours faithfully,
EDVARD GRIEG

My address: C. F. Peters Musikverlag, Thalstrasse 10, Leipzig, Germany.

---

[8] This passage and the one it was intended to replace are both written in German in this letter. Grieg's article was originally written in Norwegian but translated into German by Grieg himself.

[9] The artists mentioned by Grieg are the Swiss-German painter Marc Louis Benjamin Vautier (1829–98) and the German painter Ludwig Knaus (1829–1910).

To Ludvig Oskar Josephson

The Swedish actor and stage director Ludvig Oskar Josephson (1832–99) was head of the Christiania Theater from 1873 to 1877. His career prior to assuming this position included a number of outstanding productions of plays and operas in Stockholm. He began presenting operas at the Christiania Theater in 1874, and when Ibsen suggested staging his dramatic poem *Peer Gynt*, Josephson enthusiastically endorsed the idea and accepted responsibility for the production.

Grieg's letters to Josephson, which are preserved in Kungliga Biblioteket (The Royal Library), Stockholm, should be read in conjunction with the correspondence between Grieg and Ibsen.

1

Bergen, August 28, 1874

[Dear Mr. Josephson]:

I am pleased to learn from your letter[1] that *Peer Gynt* is not scheduled to be produced until 1875, as it would be impossible for me to finish the music any sooner. The job is proving to be much larger than I had thought, and in some places I am encountering difficulties that have me absolutely stymied. Nonetheless, I hope to be finished by the end of the year. Please tell this to Ibsen.[2]

I will not be coming to Christiania, so I would be most appreciative if you would send me a corrected copy of the book. I am going directly from here to Copenhagen around the 8th of September.

I see to my sorrow how slowly I work these days, so I am extremely doubtful about being able to do anything with *Neckens Polska*. I tell you this in case you might have better use for your beautiful text than to let me keep it with such uncertainty. I hope you understand that I am writing this in a somewhat dispirited mood. Perhaps by tomorrow I will bitterly regret what I have written, but that's the way I am.

It grieves me that you didn't come to see me in Bergen. My residence is not ten minutes away from my parents' home. Naturally I would have gone to see you if you had not left word that you were unavailable the whole day. My address in Copenhagen is: Music Dealer Wagner, Østergade 4.

Warm greetings from

Yours truly,
EDVARD GRIEG

---

[1] In a letter to Grieg dated August 23, 1874, Josephson had mentioned that the presentation of *Peer Gynt* could not take place until some time after January 1, 1875. He also wanted to discuss with Grieg his opera libretto, *Neckens Polska [The Dance of the River Sprite]*.

[2] Ibsen was in Christiania at this time working with Josephson on revisions of the text required in order to stage the play.

2

Bergen, September 2, 1875

Dear Mr. Josephson!
I recently received a communication from Ibsen in accordance with which I take the liberty of dispatching to you the *Peer Gynt* score. A letter from H. Lassen[3] which I received recently gave me a rather unpleasant surprise: He recommended that the fourth act be omitted, but it immediately occurred to me that a disagreement between you and Lassen on this point must rest on a misunderstanding on his part. After all, last winter you yourself sent me a complete list of what I had to compose.[4]

That there are so innumerably many details about which, for the sake of the dramatic effect, I wish that we could talk together, you will readily understand. In many places the text is such that one must simply abandon any thought of real music for the sake of the outward effect. How close this will come to approximating what I have had in mind depends largely on the performance. It is good, therefore, that I can be present and—especially with respect to the singers—give the needed hints. The writing out of the parts should of course get under way immediately and will probably take at least a few weeks.

So that you will not search in vain, I must not forget to tell you that I have not written a hymn for the graveyard scene—partly because I think this scene will be omitted and partly because Hennum[5] can simply make use of one of the traditional hymns.

I will be in Christiania at the end of this month and will then get in touch with you as soon as possible.

With warm greetings, I am,

Yours truly,
EDVARD GRIEG

3

Bergen, September 28, 1875

Dear Mr. Josephson!
I send you these lines in a depressed state of mind. A few days ago I saw my father to his grave, and my mother is so seriously ill that we anticipate her death soon.[6] As you can well imagine, I cannot leave Bergen until mother has closed her eyes. On the other hand, you can also understand that I am extremely reluctant to let

---

[3] Hartvig Lassen (1824–97), consultant to the Christiania Theater.

[4] In a letter dated October 1, 1875, Josephson again assured Grieg that everything was to be as they had previously agreed.

[5] Norwegian conductor Johan Hennum (1836–94), musical director at the Christiania Theater.

[6] Grieg's father died on September 13, his mother on October 23, 1875.

the music to *Peer Gynt* be performed without my being present at least for a few rehearsals in order to make sure that my intentions are realized. It is not necessary for me to see the performance; please tell me, then, when the orchestra rehearsals are to begin. The fact is that I would try to get away from here for 8–14 days. For *me* it would be best if it could be as soon as possible; for the *music*, on the other hand, it would be better if I were to come so late that I would be present for *the last two rehearsals.* I leave this matter to your best judgment; imagine yourself in my situation and you will feel with me. Please, then, inform me as soon as possible:

1. When is it intended to perform *Peer Gynt*?
2. When do the orchestra rehearsals begin?
3. When do you assume the preparations will have advanced to such a point that it would make sense for me to spend a few days in Christiania?

I ask that you let all of this be a private matter between us and I remain, with warm greetings,

Yours truly,
EDVARD GRIEG

One more question: Can the performance of the piece be postponed until after Christmas, or is performance before Christmas a *firm commitment*?[7]

[7] The premiere performance of *Peer Gynt* took place at the Christiania Theater on February 24, 1876.

To Paul Klengel

The German musician Paul Klengel (1854–1934) was an unusually versatile artist who exhibited great skill as both a violinist and a pianist. He was also a highly regarded conductor, composer and musicologist. He served for many years as a choral conductor in Leipzig and later held appointments in Stuttgart and New York. He finished his career as a member of the faculty at the Leipzig Conservatory.

Several of the letters to Klengel (not included here) demonstrate Grieg's deep insight into the German language and the literary judgment he brought to bear in evaluating German translations of Norwegian poetry.

Grieg's letters to Klengel, all in German, are preserved in Universitätsbibliothek Leipzig (University of Leipzig Library).

1

Bergen, Norway, September 14, 1889

Dear Mr. Klengel!

Thank you so much for your friendly lines. I will be in Paris in January, so perhaps it would be possible for me to come in February. However, I no longer perform my *Piano Concerto*. It is altogether too agonizing for me. It requires a first-class talent for it to be effective. Several important pianists now have the concerto in their repertoires. (The Brussels pianist, Professor De Greef,[1] will play it in Paris.) If you could consider finding a suitable pianist, I would be pleased to conduct both this and other works.

My chamber music, on the other hand, I could play. I have had little to do with the piano of late, however, because I have been totally occupied with a large choral work [op. 50] that I shall be conducting in October and November in Christiania and Copenhagen. But I will get back to playing again soon, and it would please me enormously if we could come to some definite agreement regarding a visit to your city.

With friendly greetings, I am

Yours truly,
Edvard Grieg

P.S. What were the financial arrangements? I have forgotten them.[2]

---

[1] Arthur de Greef (1862–1940).

[2] Grieg had been invited by Klengel to give a concert in Stuttgart for an honorarium of 400 marks. The concert took place February 4, 1890. The German pianist Johanna Klinkerfuss (1855–1924) was soloist in the *A-minor Concerto* with Grieg conducting.

2

Troldhaugen at Bergen, August 25, 1903

Dear Dr. Paul Klengel!

Accept my seriously delayed but heartfelt thanks for your kind letter in honor of my birthday. Among the many greetings I received on this day, yours was one of those that I cherished the most.[3] My delay in responding is due to long-lasting, serious illness.

Yes, the years pass, and I had already given up hope of seeing you again. I thought you were lost in the American maelstrom. But thank God! Your "better self" has triumphed. For you are precisely the kind of person who doesn't fit in this maelstrom. And I think the same thing is happening to you that has happened to me: The older I get the less tolerance I have for that commercial art humbug. As a matter of fact, this flourishes also in Europe, just in another form. And in that respect I find the European art-lies much more disgusting and reprehensible than the American ones. For in art, false, affected idealism is the greatest—the unforgivable—sin.

I won't make any promises, but perhaps we will see each other this winter. At least it is my intention to spend some time in Leipzig. If only I could tolerate the climate there I should have liked to spend the whole season in that city. But unfortunately: Bronchitis and Leipzig do not get along—or, more correctly, they get along altogether too well. Nonetheless, I will conclude with a "see you soon".

The most heartfelt greetings from house to house!

Cordially yours,
EDVARD GRIEG

---

[3] Grieg had celebrated his 60th birthday on June 15, 1903.

To Thorvald Lammers

The Norwegian baritone and choral conductor Thorvald Lammers (1841–1922) was trained as a lawyer, but from 1870 on he devoted himself entirely to music. He sang his debut concert in Christiania in 1873 and quickly earned a reputation as one of Norway's most eminent singers. In 1879 he founded the "Choral Society", which in 1902 was reorganized and given the name "Cecilia Society". The latter group, under Lammers's leadership, performed many choral masterworks. He was also well known for his contribution to the dissemination of Norwegian folk tunes and wrote a number of songs in folk-tune style. Lammers was awarded an annual artist's grant in 1899.

Grieg's letters to Lammers are preserved in Nasjonalbiblioteket, Oslo (National Library of Norway, Oslo Division).

1

Leipzig, February 25, 1898
Hotel Hauffe

Dear Lammers!
I have now been waiting for more than fourteen days for an available moment to write to you. I can't say what I want to say in a telegram, which is what I usually do these days regarding matters having to do with the music festival.[1] Yes, if you saw the pile of telegrams that are stacked up on my desk—almost all of which contain material requiring strenuous work and aggravations—you would say: Much good may it do you! And I hope you would add: Poor you!

Well now, old fellow! Permit me, on behalf of the committee and myself, most heartily to invite you and your wife to attend the music festival, and you especially to sing both "You Tyr!"[2] and other Norwegian works that I cannot yet specify. I think I can promise you that the festival will be grand. Naturally I cannot demand that your national-artistic point of view shall be the same as mine—all the more since you there at home in Tigerville[3] obviously are getting an earful from my enemies. So I can only hope that you agree with me that when a music festival in a Norwegian city sets itself the task of performing Norwegian compositions in the *most ideal possible* way, in order thereby to bring Norwegian music closer to the hearts of the people, this is in truth a national duty even if one, in order to perform it, requires Norwegians and Dutchmen and, for that matter, Japanese!!

---

[1] Grieg is referring to the Norwegian music festival held in Bergen, Norway from June 26 to July 3, 1898.

[2] "You Tyr!" is a play on words regarding the baritone part in Johan Selmer's *The Turks Approach Athens*, a setting for baritone soloist, male chorus and orchestra of a text by the French poet Victor Hugo (1802–85). "Tyr", the Norwegian word for "bull", is similar to "Tyrker", which is the word for "Turk". "You Tyr" means, literally, "You bull!"

[3] "Tigerville" ("Tigerstaden"): a derisive name for Christiania coined by Bjørnstjerne Bjørnson (1832–1910).

That this understanding is the right one, and that one who maintains that "cows give cake and bulls give mead"[4] belongs in the hall of the mountain king and not up in the bright summer day—that I do not doubt for a moment.

It would become a long letter if I were to tell you the early history of the music festival up to today as well as all the chicaneries I have had to put up with from Christiania in connection with this matter. You simply would not believe me if the telegrams, which I can show you, did not compel you to do so.

But: "O friends, no more these sounds continue!"[5] Let me, therefore, conclude. *You* know that although I hate chauvinism like the plague, in my heart of hearts I am as good a Norwegian as you could ever find. And one must be permitted to call oneself a Norwegian even if one does not always follow the crowd.

Yes, yes, my dear Lammers, that's the way it is—and the future will confirm that.

Please answer as soon as possible! Warm greetings to you and your Mally both from Nina and from

Your old friend,
EDVARD GRIEG

P.S. Mr. P. Vogt Fischer[6] mentioned something about that you would like to have your choir participate in the festival. I have not taken this seriously, however, because I assumed that if you desired this you would have written. Moreover, when I was with Holter[7] last fall there was some talk about his choir participating. However, since it has not been possible for me to get a definite answer from him in time, despite requests by letter and in telegrams, I have had to give up on his choir. And when it finally became apparent that Bergen could put together a choir of 400, the committee preferred for financial reasons not to make any further efforts to secure a choir from another city.

As a matter of form I will add that the committee pays festival soloists travel and board and room plus 100 crowns per performance.

---

4 The quotation is from a line in Ibsen's *Peer Gynt*, Act II: "Our cows give cake and our bulls give mead, don't ask if the flavor is sour or sweet."

5 The quotation is from Schiller's "Ode to Joy", which Beethoven employed in the last movement of his *Ninth Symphony*: "O Freunde! Nicht diese Töne!"

6 Norwegian impresario Peter Vogt Fischer (1863–1938).

7 In 1897 Iver Holter (1850–1941), conductor of the Music Association orchestra in Christiania, had founded "Holter's Choral Society".

2

Leipzig, March 10, 1898
Hotel Hauffe

Dear Lammers!
Thanks for the letter! And thanks for your assurance that you are coming to the festival! For it goes without saying that I do not expect something so inhuman of you as that you shall only be a "Tyr". But you see, it is as you say: There are so many things to consider that it still is not possible for me to nail down what and how much will be needed in addition. This much, however, is certain: It will not be by me. But I hope it will be something by Sinding.[8] If it is to be art songs, then we must have "Ad kendte Vejer" and "O Mor, vor gamle Mor".[9] We can assume one thing, in any case: It will be pieces that you already have in your repertoire. And that is the most important point, is it not?

The music festival will consist of six big concerts. But NB: The 2nd, 4th and 6th concerts will have the same choir, orchestra and ensemble program as the 1st, 3rd and 5th concerts respectively. Only with respect to the songs with piano accompaniment will each concert present something new. Thus you must appear twice as a devilish "Tyr", but on the other hand just one time as a human being (hopefully without horns!).

Believe me, what you are so kind as to call the high point—that was tempting for me, too. But hopefully it can be done some other time. But: You are coming! Or better yet: Both of you are coming! So everything is fine! Thus there is no doubt about that. One fine day you will see it in the newspaper—and then, of course, it *must* be true! Ow! No, I don't want to conclude with a bad joke but rather with a hearty thank-you for your choice of songs at your concert. It is good! Remember: "Fisherman's Song" *fast* and fresh and rhythmically accentuated![10]

The best songs I have written will be published this fall. They are from Garborg's[11] *Mountain Maid*. I have recently been working very hard to get a German translation into shape. Would that some of the songs were suitable for your splendid voice!

Yes, now I must say farewell for today then, dear Lammers! Duty calls.

Warm greetings to you, your wife and the dear Sars[12] family.

Yours truly,
EDVARD GRIEG

---

[8] Norwegian composer Christian Sinding (1856–1941).

[9] Songs by Christian Sinding: "On Familiar Paths" and "O Mother, Our Old Mother!", both to texts by Danish poet Holger Drachmann (1846–1908).

[10] "Fisherman's Song" is no. 4 of Grieg's *Seven Children's Songs*. The text is by the Norwegian clergyman and poet Petter Dass (1646–1707).

[11] Norwegian writer Arne Garborg (1851–1924), author of *Haugtussa* (*The Mountain Maid*).

[12] The Norwegian zoologist Michael Sars (1805–69) and his wife Maren (1811–98). Lammers's wife Mally (1860–1929) was their daughter.

3

Copenhagen, March 2, 1901
Hotel Phoenix

Dear Lammers!
Thanks for the letter! It was nice to hear from you again. You can see that I'm not at a loss for an answer but cling tightly to old friends. For it is characteristic of me that I am so afraid of being obtrusive, especially in relation to those whom I care about the most. But when I just note the slightest indication that such a friend is taking the bait—the bait that is always out there for old friends—I jerk on the line in a split second. And now in this moment I am as happy as a child to once again have caught the old mountain trout that goes by the name of Lammers. Actually, you are always hanging on the hook, I know that, but you are staying so absolutely still that I don't feel it. It was good that you gave a little tug. I needed that.

Physically I am at a low point. For the past 6–8 days I have had to stay in because of bronchitis, and in addition I have had to don elastic stockings for varicose veins. All of this together has more or less demoralized me. As a result, I have had to postpone my concert. I hope I will come to life again, although many a time I think: Will I ever go back to old Norway again?

About the songs I sent you. There are some that absolutely *must* suit you. I know that despite your gray hair you are still crazy about the god Eros and you can sing "A Life of Longing" with all its wild, concealed passion and pathos. But above all it is "A Poet's Song" that must suit your voice. Sitting up on Olympus and mocking the philistines down below—that is just the thing for you. If I am healthy enough for a concert in Tigerville this spring, it would be just great if you would do me the honor of *creating* them. If only you will now immerse yourself in them and NB like them, the rest will come of itself.[13]

If only I were up where you are! Then the bronchitis would get a move on! Warm greetings to both of you, also from Nina.

Yours truly,
EDVARD GRIEG

---

[13] The songs Grieg mentions are nos. 1, 2 and 5 of *Five Songs* op. 70. The texts are by Danish poet Otto Benzon (1856–1927).

To Albert Langen

The German book dealer and author Albert Langen (1869–1910), who in 1896 had been one of the founders of the German-language humorous-satirical weekly *Simplicissimus* in Munich, was married for several years to Dagny Bjørnson (1876–1974), daughter of the Norwegian author (and Grieg's close friend) Bjørnstjerne Bjørnson (1832–1910). Grieg had frequent contact with him, including an especially memorable occasion in 1899 at Aulestad, Bjørnson's villa in the Gausdal valley near Lillehammer. That was when, at Langen's initiative, Grieg's famous letter to Édouard Colonne regarding the so-called Dreyfus affair became an item of international news. Langen had a hand in arranging for the presentation in Germany of Bjørnson's play *Sigurd Jorsalfar* with incidental music by Grieg, and it was also at his urging that Grieg wrote his autobiographical article, "My First Success".

Grieg's letters to Langen, written in German, are preserved in Nasjonalbiblioteket, Oslo (The National Library of Norway, Oslo Division).

1

Troldhaugen, Hop at Bergen, August 28, 1902

Dear Mr. Langen!

Now I certainly have to laugh. For as far as I know, it is only for unborn children that one makes preparations for their coming—NB! after having determined that the child really is present in the mother's womb. But in this case there is not the slightest hint of an embryo! Therefore, let us for the time being have no talk about either diapers or living expenses for the wet nurse. All of that will come only when the child arrives.[1]

Unfortunately, there will be so many demands on me during the coming year that it will be very difficult for me to begin working on the project at this time. You understand, therefore, that your "sample page" regarding the format of the book came a little too soon. And still, I have enjoyed the content of this sample page so much—yes, it has interested me to such a degree—that I would be happy if I could get acquainted with the whole book (Emil Aarestrup's letters about the first Danish war, 1848).[2] I had not known that Aarestrup was not only a talented writer of lyrical verse but also an incisive political observer. As such, his biting, demonic wit makes him the new Heine.[3] Perhaps you have no idea what you sent me. I shall hope to get more sample pages like that!

It is still very doubtful as to whether I will go to England. My health says no,

---

[1] As early as 1901 Langen had asked Grieg if he would write his memoirs. In a letter dated August 22, 1902, he again raised the question and offered Grieg 10,000 German marks for a manuscript of ca. 240 pages. He even went so far as to suggest some possible titles: *Gedanken und Erinnerungen* (*Thoughts and Recollections*) or *Eindrücke und Erinnerungen* (*Impressions and Recollections*). Grieg was amused by the fact that Langen was already thinking about titles when he—Grieg—had not yet started writing.

[2] Danish physician Emil Aarestrup (1800–56) wrote for publication as a hobby.

[3] German poet Heinrich Heine (1797–1856).

and it must, after all, have the first consideration. This will determine whether or not we shall see each other on December 8.[4]

Carl Nærup has tried to get me to contribute as a writer to a book about Bjørnson that is coming out today. In truth, for me it has been a difficult task which, nonetheless, because of my friendship with Bjørnson, I did not want to avoid.[5]

As you can see, there is always something to keep one busy. And all this mail! Now it is worse than ever! Every day so and so many letters, packages, photographs, books, music and all sorts of things. God knows if I won't soon have to announce in German and English newspapers that I am not in a position to deal with everything. Goethe says, "Only rogues are unassuming".[6] I say, "Only rogues are polite". I don't want to be a rogue. Therefore I must start being impolite.

So long for now to you and your wife. Warm greetings to both of you!

Sincerely yours,
Edvard Grieg

2

Bergen, September 16, 1903

Dear Mr. Langen!

If the Stuttgart Hofbühne[7] pays a total of 6% it really looks unpromising for the author, the composer and you yourself. From where I sit I can only say that I leave the matter totally in your hands, but I insist that my rights as the composer be taken account of.

In 1899, at the National Theater in Christiania they said, "You cannot get any royalty as the play is very expensive to produce and the author must have 5%." In the end I had to be content with 400 crowns, NB! a single payment. That, in my view, is an absolutely disgraceful honorarium for a popular play such as *Sigurd Jorsalfar*, which has become a part of the standard repertoire. The very same thing happened to me at the National Theater with *Peer Gynt*, the music for which had in the meantime achieved international fame.[8] I could not receive a

---

[4] Bjørnstjerne Bjørnson's 70th birthday.

[5] Carl Nærup (1864–1931) was a Norwegian literary critic who in 1902 published a book in Copenhagen under the title, *Festskrift i anledning Bjørnstjerne Bjørnson's 70-aarige fødselsdag* [*Festschrift in Honor of Bjørnstjerne Bjørnson's 70th Birthday*]. Grieg's four-page article, entitled "With Bjørnson in Days Gone By", will be printed in translation in Benestad & Halverson (eds.), *Edvard Grieg: Diaries, Articles, Speeches* (Columbus, Ohio, 2001).

[6] Grieg often quoted these words in German from Goethe's poem *Rechenschaft*, published in 1810. The first two lines of the poem are "Nur die Lumpe sind bescheiden,/Brave freuen sich der Tat" ("Only rogues are unassuming/Good men celebrate their deeds").

[7] The Stuttgart Court Theater had plans to produce Bjørnson's play *Sigurd Jorsalfar* using Grieg's incidental music.

[8] ". . . in the meantime", i.e., since the premiere in 1876. The second production of *Peer Gynt* in Christiania was in 1892, the third—to which Grieg refers here—in 1902.

royalty, as Ibsen had demanded 10%. (It is not true that there were disagreements between Ibsen and me regarding this matter at the opening of the National Theater.) On this occasion, after they first offered me 800 crowns, I finally was given 1,000 crowns.[9] I find this, quite simply, absolutely scandalous.

But now I have gotten smart. A royalty is the only arrangement that is both appropriate and natural. For if the piece does not succeed, why should the composer be able to pocket a large sum as an advance? That is unfair. An advance agreement between author and composer is the only reasonable solution.

It is good that the title "My First Success"[10] is not to be construed literally.

Warm greetings to you, Dagny and the children!

Sincerely yours,
EDVARD GRIEG

3

Troldhaugen at Bergen, August 16, 1904

Dear Mr. Langen!
That was truly a "clarification" of a doubtful sort.[11] They order a long article from me, they decide both the subject and the honorarium, but after receiving my manuscript they refuse to accept my work for reasons that make no sense. I won't stand for it. It is not just an insult, it is also absolutely impermissible legally. I hope that you will tell Mr. McClure the truth in an effective way. To press my rights legally against smart "Yankees" of that sort would presumably be quite futile. I ask you, therefore, as earnestly as I can, not to rest until you have retrieved my manuscript—and that must happen immediately. You know that it was only on your recommendation that I decided to use a month of my valuable time to write the article. I hope, therefore, that in the first place you will give that shameless man a hell of a tongue-lashing, and then do your best to get my article published in America. For the article was written for this country; otherwise I would never have chosen such a form. Therefore it really makes no sense to publish it *only* in other countries.

As I may have told you, a few years ago—at the request of the New York/London journal *The Century Illustrated Monthly Magazine*—I wrote two articles, one on Mozart and one on Schumann, for honoraria of 1,000 francs for each.[12] My

---

[9] At one of the events marking the opening of the National Theater in 1899, Grieg himself conducted his incidental music to Bjørnson's play *Sigurd Jorsalfar*.

[10] As a literery agent, Langen had conveyed to Grieg an inquiry from *McClure's Magazine*, an American publication, regarding the possibility of Grieg's writing an autobiographical article of approximately 8,000 words. Grieg wrote the article in November–December 1903 and sent it to Langen. (See also footnote 1 regarding an earlier proposal from Langen.)

[11] When Langen submitted Grieg's "My First Success" to *McClure's Magazine* the editor declined to use it.

[12] Both were published in *The Century Illustrated Monthly Magazine*, the Schumann article in January, 1894, the Mozart one in November, 1897. They will be printed in new translations in Benestad & Halverson (eds.), *Edvard Grieg: Diaries, Articles, Speeches* (Columbus, Ohio, 2001).

recommendation is that you offer this magazine the new article on similar terms, but retain all other rights—and NB! that you explain the course of events with McClure as it really was. Only in this way can the offer to the noble *Century Illustrated Monthly Magazine* become understandable.

For Germany or Austria 1,000 marks strikes me as too high a figure. How about Scandinavia? It appears, as a matter of fact, that a possible honorarium has been decided on for my "widow"!! The sad thing is—just between us—that I have already used the money, the first half for a sick Danish friend, the rest as a contribution to the education of a young nephew. With this as background I really have become more annoyed over your "clarification" than is good for me. But now I'm going to dinner and will drown the whole rotten mess in a glass of red wine.

I am terribly sorry that this affair makes such great demands on you. "What a lot of fuss for the sake of an omelet."[13] (. . .)

Warm greetings from house to house!

Sincerely yours,
EDVARD GRIEG

4

Copenhagen, March 9, 1905
Hotel Phoenix

Dear Mr. Langen!
It is almost fifteen months since you received the article "My First Success", which I wrote at your request. From this fact I can probably conclude that you—after the shameful behavior by the American [journal editor]—have not succeeded in getting the article placed anywhere else. But you can also easily understand that there comes a time when my patience is exhausted. This time has now been reached. I do not wish to prolong the matter any further and decline, therefore, your continued obliging collaboration. I will, for good or for ill, take the matter into my own hands, and with this in mind I urgently request that you see to it that my manuscript is returned to me as quickly as possible so that I myself can decide what to do with it. I hope that you do not misunderstand me, and I repeat my sincerest thanks for your friendly intention to do everything for my best.

Until I receive your prompt reply, and with warm greetings to yourself and Dagny, I remain

Sincerely yours,
EDVARD GRIEG

---

[13] Grieg uses the French: "Quel bruit pour une omelette!"

5

Troldhaugen, Hop at Bergen, August 7, 1905

Dear Mr. Langen!
To my surprise and annoyance I see that fragments of my article "My First Success" figure in several Norwegian newspapers in a poor—at times meaningless—translation. In response to my wired inquiry, Mr. Hegel[14] in Copenhagen informs me that *you have never offered him the article.* If, as I must assume, this is the case—even though it sounds incredible—the article is thereby rendered unusable in the Scandinavian market. But nonetheless, based on the instinct of self-preservation, I consider it my duty to ask Mr. Hegel today if he will rescue the original manuscript from destruction.[15]

To you I can only say that you have placed me in a most embarrassing situation and that I would not have expected such treatment from you. It was, after all, you yourself who in a most gracious way came with the proposal that you assume responsibility for the sale of the article, and I accepted this proposal without hesitation in full confidence that your intentions were honorable. Thus I regret all the more that I was wrong. Indeed, I am at this moment so furiously angry with you that I am not in a position to find the good, old tone that I have always tried to strike in my dealings with you.

And yet—the new Norway has reconciliation![16] Nonetheless, I am the oldster with life experience, and you are—the youngster. So now the sun breaks through the clouds: "Shame on you, young man!"

Sincerely yours,
EDVARD GRIEG

---

[14] Publisher Jacob Hegel (1851–1918) of Gyldendalske Boghandel in Copenhagen.

[15] "My First Success" was published in *Contemporary Review* in July, 1905. Later it came out in several European journals, and to Grieg's annoyance excerpts were published in unauthorized translations in Norwegian and Danish newspapers. The article was first published in its original Norwegian form in Øystein Gaukstad (ed.), *Edvard Grieg. Artikler og taler* [*Edvard Grieg: Articles and Speeches*], Oslo 1957, pp. 7–30. It will appear in a new translation from the original Norwegian in Benestad & Halverson (eds.), *Edvard Grieg: Diaries, Articles, Speeches* (Columbus, Ohio, 2001).

[16] On June 7, 1905, the Norwegian Parliament (Stortinget) had declared Norway's independence from Sweden.

To Jonas Lie

Jonas Lie (1833–1908) was another of the great writers of his generation with whom Grieg had close contact. With Bjørnstjerne Bjørnson (1832–1910) and Henrik Ibsen (1828–1906), Grieg created both lyrical and grandly conceived dramatic works. With Lie, on the other hand, he wrote only one song for solo voice and piano and one piece for male chorus. He was, however, an enthusiastic reader of Lie's works, not least his many novels.

Grieg's letters to Jonas Lie are preserved in Nasjonalbiblioteket, Oslo (The National Library of Norway, Oslo Division).

1

Troldhaugen at Bergen, August 28, 1887

Dear Jonas Lie!

Since receiving your friendly letter I have been constantly expecting the compositions in question from Mr. Molard.[1] Since to date I have received nothing, I do not want to delay answering you any longer.

First of all, thank you so much for all the beautiful things that have flowed from your pen! If you have something to thank me for in my art, I pay you back in your own coin.

Yes, dear Jonas Lie! We have become famous men. But I for my part find this to be a dubious fortune, for fame exacts a price. Good Lord, how dearly bought it is! If only fame could be paid for with that which one can dispense. But it wears and tears at the tiniest threads, and it doesn't rest until it has unraveled so much that the entire fabric swings and sways in every wind. One must be as wise as the spider: Protect the main point and save as much of the rest as one can. You must have this ability in rich measure, for I do not get the impression from your books that life has gotten the best of you. You see more deeply, more surely, more self-confidently, and you obviously must have managed the point that many of us creatures of both sexes have had such a hard time getting past during the years of our Lord 1860–80.

In about eight days I will go from here to Karlsbad.[2] (Both Nina and I are patients.) From there to Leipzig. And then—yes, I only know that we will stay abroad the whole winter. If I should come to Paris you will of course see me at the earliest opportunity. But—you will not enjoy my company very much, for I have become more despondent and withdrawn than before. Still, you are not one of those who judges by externals, so for you I ought not to be apprehensive.

---

[1] Grieg probably came in contact with the French man of letters William Molard (1862–1937) as early as the beginning of the 1880's. Molard was asked to give advice at that time concerning the translation of the text of "Before a Southern Convent", a section of Norwegian author Bjørnstjerne Bjørnson's epic poem *Arnljot Gelline.* Later Molard himself created French translations of the texts of several of Grieg's songs. In 1894 Grieg was a guest in Molard's home, where he met French composer Maurice Ravel (1875–1937).

[2] Karlsbad was a health spa in Germany. The town of Karlsbad now lies in the Czech Republic and has been renamed Karlovy Vary.

And with that, farewell! Warm greetings to you, your wife,[3] and your whole family, and thank you for letting me hear from you! With fondness and admiration,

Yours truly,
EDVARD GRIEG

2

Leipzig, February 20, 1888

Dear Jonas Lie!
Finally I have reached the point where I have time to thank you for your last friendly letter and for the words of advice you give me therein. That you, an experienced and worldly wise man and author, can be so touchingly naive—yes, this is such a genuine mark of the true artist that I could embrace you for it. So you really think that it is in France that I shall enjoy material success. Then I will just tell you that the little experience I have from correspondence with Frenchmen indicates that down there people make shameless demands on foreign artists without wanting to pay them an honorarium. Several times I have been asked to contribute to this or that journal, but of course: It is supposed to be an *honor for me* to be invited, etc. No, then I commend Germany, where the laborer is indeed worthy of his hire.[4] And the French publishers are misinformed if they think that German publishers are not able to pay just as good honorariums as they. The fact is that they not only are able to, but they really do so. *I*, in any case, have nothing to complain about in that respect. My publisher, the famous firm C. F. Peters in Leipzig, is nobility personified.

But—what a shame that there are no agreements between the various countries! Yes, if creative artists were treated according to the principles of constitutional and international law—principles that apply to all other members of society—I could by now have been a rich man. But without law and justice one can only quietly observe how one is robbed and exploited.

Still, why dig around in this mud pile? My consolation is that the time will come when people will be astonished at the crudity with which creative minds were treated in the nineteenth century.

Unfortunately—Paris comes to nothing for this time. At the end of April we will go to London, where we probably will spend the whole of May. In June there is a music festival in Copenhagen, and then—there is a country by the name of Norway that beckons; and it does not beckon in vain, for even now I am often longing for it so deeply.

---

[3] Thomasine Lie (1833–1907).
[4] An allusion to Luke 10:7, "The laborer is worthy of his hire." (KJV)

I must thank you on behalf of both my wife and myself for your splendid book.[5] It gripped me deeply, for it really is a slice of life.

If you writers weren't so damned uninterested in music, I would like to propose bartering in order to get hold of your collected works! By the way, I think that Ibsen is in a class by himself in this respect; and he obviously regards it as a matter of honor. It is unbelievable.

But now stop! With the warmest greetings.

Yours truly,
EDVARD GRIEG

3

Troldhaugen, Hop Station at Bergen, October 18, 1888

Dear Jonas Lie!

Yesterday I received, in addition to your kind postcard, nothing less than your complete works together with the beautiful dedication. Thank you so much! But please do not think that I am so immodest that *this* was my intention. My idea was that we should send each other our new works as they are published. Now, however, *you* have been the radical one, so you will have to take the consequences—namely, that you will get your house flooded with my dots and dashes. I am not sending you everything I have written, however, since unlike you I did not begin with "The Visionary".[6] I had to fumble my way forward. You will get the most important works—those that I more or less acknowledge as my legitimate offspring—and the ones that belong in the trash can will stay at home. But where shall I send them? Certainly not to Berchtesgaden. Send me a postcard right away telling me your address.

I suppose you are going back to Paris? Yes, this Paris! No doubt it will remain for me the promised land on which I shall never set foot. It won't happen *this* winter, in any case, that much is certain. I have invitations from Berlin, London, Prague, Moscow and St. Petersburg that I cannot refuse. I will stay home in my lodgings until after Christmas, and then I will journey out into the world.

You, who have managed to burn all your bridges, are actually very fortunate. But I can never do that. The mountain regions of West Norway constantly draw me back with irresistible power. It is as if they still have so very much to tell me [some lines of text have been clipped out at this point] and only with a mighty tug can I tear myself away from my distant corner of the world.

Still—it cannot now be otherwise, or in any case it ought not to be. For an

---

[5] Probably Jonas Lie's 1887 novel, *Et Samliv* (*A Married Life*).

[6] *Den Fremsynte,* written in 1870, also published in English under the title *The Visionary* in 1894, was Jonas Lie's first major novel.

artist must live by his best feelings, even if they turn his whole life upside down. But let me not touch on the curse that really hovers like a deep, dark secret over the Norwegian artist! Let me rather conclude by saying: He has a glorious calling, and I would not change places with anyone in the whole world! Warm greetings,

[The name has been clipped off]

P.S. What is your new book about?

4

Troldhaugen at Bergen, August 3, 1892

Dear Jonas Lie!
Finally, finally! The time ever since June 11 has been a desperate period for me. I couldn't tolerate all that partying,[7] got a serious gastric inflammation which has kept me alternately in bed and in the sickroom until just the last few days. I must still exercise the uttermost caution. However, I think I am beginning to come back to life, so I don't want to delay for a moment thanking you in all seriousness. For in the telegram (hopefully you received it, addressed to the consulate in Rome) I was not able to say what I felt. Yes, you cannot know what great joy you gave my wife and me with your poem, your splendid poem! Moreover, it is absolutely one of the most beautiful poems you have written. It is so true—and of course you knew this—that it is the mystery of nature that has captivated me in my best moments. You have hit the nail on the head so precisely—more precisely than I thought it possible to do in words.

Sinding's beautiful music suited the poem brilliantly. The performance (by baritone Ingolf Schjøtt) was commendable, and the effect was thrilling. I will always be indebted to you for this.[8]

And now you must tell me one thing: What are you two doing this winter? We are going south—how far I don't know yet—but if I knew you would be in Rome, that would be a powerful drawing card. There is something called cholera, however, so I suppose it isn't worth it to make one's plans too cock-surely. If you are going to Paris, it would also be tempting to go there for awhile except that I am so afraid of the cold. For all winter I have been an invalid owing to rheumatism in my feet. Life is strange: That from which one expects the most gives the least. I built a little sod-roof hut down in the valley at Troldhaugen, a place where I could find peace and quiet and for which I had the strongest hope. But no: It apparently lay too close to the draft from the sea, and the floor was less than

---

[7] Edvard and Nina Grieg's silver wedding anniversary was celebrated at Troldhaugen with pomp and circumstance on June 11, 1892.

[8] Lie wrote a poem of five stanzas for the Griegs' silver wedding. The setting of the poem by Norwegian composer Christian Sinding (1856–1941) was not included in his opus list but was printed by the Hals Brothers Publishing Company in 1892. Ingolf Schjøtt (1851–1922) was a singer and choral conductor in Bergen.

two feet from the damp earth. The fact is that during Christmas I got something in my feet that began as a cramp and, as I said, turned out to be rheumatism. And with that my hut was doomed. I have not dared to set foot in it since.

The secret, I suppose, is not hard to understand. One begins to get old and dilapidated—at precisely the time in one's life when one thinks one should be doing one's best work. But we are poorly taught, that's the problem. People have led us to believe that the downward course begins at age 60 at the earliest. But that is a contemptible lie and an illusion. For if one is past 40, the decaying process is already under way. For people in the arts in any case. After this time it is no longer possible to completely forget oneself and enter fully into that which one is creating. The body constantly reminds you of its presence. Am I right? I know, unfortunately, that you must grant my point.

But then I think that the south is the only part of Europe where the vital spirits can still be kept alive. That is why I want to go down where there is sunshine and warmth. Though God knows that every Norwegian who feels the significance of the words, "this homeland is ours",[9] should now stay home and speak Norwegian in Norway!

I am now beginning to understand that we have but *one* enemy, but it is one with whom we cannot be reconciled and against whom, when worse comes to worst, it unfortunately is our unavoidable duty to arm ourselves. It is sad that all that money cannot rather be employed, via enlightenment in the country, to air out that damned Pietism that deadens the common sense of our people. Pietism and the Swedes—to arms! Otherwise I am still ready to embrace the whole human race—thank goodness!

No doubt things are just great for the two of you down there in Berchtesgaden! Yes, I must see that paradise some day. For now, greetings to you and your wife, and thank you again for the unforgettable poem—both from Nina and from

Yours truly,
EDVARD GRIEG

5

Mentone, March 21, 1894
Hotel de Russie et Allemagne

Dear Jonas Lie!
Thanks for your letter! And thanks for *Niobe*,[10] which I naturally finished reading long ago. It gripped me deeply, not only by virtue of the masterful writing but because it leads me straight into my own family's secrets. We will talk about this when we are together, and hopefully that will be soon. Naturally it will not

[9] Grieg is alluding to Bjørnstjerne Bjørnson's poem *Jeg vil verge mit land* (*I will defend my country*).
[10] Jonas Lie's contemporary novel *Niobe* was published in 1893.

surprise you that you have seen rightly, but it will surprise you to learn that there are defective people like that in a family in which both beauty and the quest for truth have been present. Still, what nonsense! That can't surprise you either, for both Dr. and Mrs. Bente[11] are "good people", not humbugs by any means. But still, you will listen to some strange reports, that I know. It really is not "very good"[12] of nature to be so wasteful as to throw away whole families. For that, of course, is what it does in Norway just to move forward a step. It strikes down without mercy, worse than any military commander. And that it strikes down so maliciously precisely on us is perhaps due to the fact that we have not lived in close contact with other nations in time—in other words, to the fact that we have had no railroads. Or not *enough* of them.

I warmly agree with your beautiful words about what we can lose in mood and ingenuity as a result of improved communications. That is something that applies especially to me, with my pent-up longings—so characteristic of West Norway—that try to find expression in music. But that doesn't help: All barriers must fall. And the genius that cannot survive without barriers must fall with them. For it does not have the capacity for a long life. Someplace in *Brand*[13] are these words: "Stab, crush, scratch and tear!" That is what dear Mother Nature does—and we are the ones whom she stabs, crushes, scratches and tears. I often think about this, and I love her just as much nonetheless. I think she also dealt roughly with you before you reached the high place where you now stand. Well, I think that the last year has probably been no less strenuous, for there is something about being the recipient of all the outward honor that has rained down on your guilty head these days! But your welcome letter fully reassures me that you are the same as before. There is "good stuff" in you, as Ole Bull[14] said.

Farewell, then, to you and your wife until we meet again, hopefully next month. Warm greetings to both of you from Nina and from

Yours truly,
EDVARD GRIEG

6

Copenhagen, February 13, 1901
Hotel Phoenix

Dear Jonas Lie!
It was so wonderful and so undeserved to hear from you once again. No, there is no reason for you to thank me for those songs, which—just between us—aren't

[11] Dr. Baarvig and his wife Bente are the main characters in Lie's novel *Niobe*.
[12] An allusion to Genesis 1:31: "And God saw everything that he had made, and behold, it was very good."
[13] Henrik Ibsen's dramatic poem *Brand*, published in 1866.
[14] Norwegian virtuoso violinist Ole Bull (1810–80).

so bad after all.[15] What shall I say, then, about the rich outpouring that I receive each year from you? You put me to shame. I am an unproductive ass who is paying the price because in my younger years I did not use as my only motto that which you write about and express in the following well-chosen words: "There is joy so long as one is permitted to work." By "work" I of course mean just *creative* work. In my youth, to *create* and to *starve* were one and the same. That is no longer the case. But now I am beset with a multitude of temptations to which you are not subject: all the tempting offers to perform my compositions here and there. My health is not good enough for that any more. Nonetheless, I cannot resist the temptation. So who knows if some fine day you won't see me again on the banks of the Seine. Good Lord, if I were down there now, you and Bjørnson would not be allowed to hole up in your respective quarters. I would take your hand and his, join them—and bless you both! Old misunderstanding and anger, perhaps. But neither Norway nor we, who love you both, can afford to see this happening. Moreover, I know very well that both of you suffer because of it, much more than you yourselves will admit. I have lost one of the very best friends of my youth and adulthood,[16] a man for whom I have become like a red flag to a bull. I have to stick to trivialities when I meet him—a man who once knew the deepest secrets of my soul—so I know how something like that hurts. It is nothing less than a nail in one's coffin.

I had to take the liberty of making this unprovoked intrusion into your private domain, dear Jonas Lie, but behind the apparent lack of provocation lies a deeper motivation that goes far beyond convenience—and that is that which is genuine! And one thing more: I myself, in a similar case, took the *first* step toward a reconciliation, and even in this very moment, when I think about it, I feel as if I can breathe better.[17]

Yes, indeed, life is short. And it is important to have the beneficent feeling of being able to breath deeply during the few years one has left!

I know that Bjørn[18] *obviously* will perform your new play, and I also know

---

[15] Grieg is referring to his two last collections of songs, *Five songs* op. 69 and *Five Songs* op. 70. Both collections were settings of texts by Danish poet Otto Benzon (1856–1927) and were composed and published in 1900.

[16] Grieg is referring to Danish composer C. F. E. Horneman (1840–1906).

[17] Grieg is alluding to the breach with Bjørnson that occurred in 1876 as a result of their disagreement concerning the *Olav Trygvason* opera project. In 1889 Grieg proposed to Bjørnson that they "blot out" their old misunderstandings and resume their friendship—and they did. See Grieg's letter to Bjørnson of October 6, 1889, and Bjørnson's reply of October 13, which is given as a footnote to Grieg's letter to Bjørnson of October 15.

The background of Lie's breach with Bjørnson is as follows: In 1887, Lie had formed a friendship with the Bohemian circle in Christiania. Bjørnson viewed this as treachery and criticized Lie in the harshest possible terms. Lie, for his part, viewed Bjørnson as a power-hungry man who didn't want him to succeed and made references in several of his writings to Bjørnson and his influence. Grieg's effort to bring the two men together was not successful, but a reconciliation occurred in 1906, when Bjørnson took the initiative and visited Lie in his home.

[18] Bjørn Bjørnson (1859–1942), theater director at the National Theater in Christiania.

that it *will* come off well. That the materials should prevent its being performed —no, we're not that crazy up there any more.[19]

This morning Nina and I had breakfast with Stephan Sinding, whose statue of Ole Bull goes to casting tomorrow.[20] Thank God: It is *brilliant* and visionary. It raises Bull up, high up, for the consciousness of the Norwegian people of the future. People in Bergen will perhaps grumble and complain about the absence of a likeness. That may be. But it didn't take more than two seconds before I began to rejoice within: This is the young, triumphant Bull, with the fairytale power of nature in him, as he listens to the playing of the water sprite! I am as happy today about this vision as if I myself had created something that is really good.

How splendid that you have gotten your dear [wife] Thommasine healed! Wasn't it rheumatism? And where and by what means did she get well? I think it had something to do with San Remo!?

I am in agony these days with rheumatism in my hips, knees, legs and feet. I exercise and get massage, but so far to no avail. I really should get away from snow and winter.

We have spent three glorious months at the new Voksenkollen, a dream come true that the future will give the appreciation it deserves. This Dr. Holm is a good Norwegian in the *best* sense of the word.[21]

Yes, dear Lie, as I said, it was more than nice of you to write. Thank you for doing it! I will gladly let the coals of fire scorch my head a little.[22]

Warmest greetings to all three of you, also from Nina.

Your old admirer and friend,
EDVARD GRIEG

[19] Lie's play *Wulffie & Co.* from 1900. It deals, among other things, with avarice and unethical financial dealings.

[20] Norwegian sculptor Stephan Abel Sinding (1846–1922), brother of the composer Christian Sinding. The Ole Bull statue referred to here now stands in Ole Bull Square not far from The National Stage in Bergen—a theater that owes its existence to Bull's initiative.

[21] Voksenkollen Sanatorium was located on the outskirts of Christiania, near Holmenkollen. It was opened in 1900 under the leadership of the Norwegian physician Ingebrigt Christian Lund Holm (1844–1919). In 1901 Grieg wrote an effusively positive article about the sanatorium entitled "The Soria-Moria Castle". It will be printed in translation in Benestad & Halverson (eds.), *Edvard Grieg: Diaries, Articles, Speeches* (Columbus, Ohio, 2001).

[22] An allusion to Proverbs 25:21–22: "If your enemy is hungry, give him bread to eat; and if he is thirsty, give him water to drink; for you will heap coals of fire upon his head."

To John Theodor Lund

The Bergen politician John Theodor Lund (1842–1913) started his political career in his native city, where he was a member of the city council for thirty years after first being elected to the post in 1879. In 1888–90 he was Lord Mayor of Bergen and he also served intermittently as a member of the Norwegian Parliament (Stortinget) during the period 1882–1900. A prominent representative of the Liberal party, he was one of the pioneers in the struggle for Norwegian independence from Sweden.

Lund was a wealthy man, having earned his fortune as a shipowner and importer of coal. As co-owner of *Bergens Tidende*, the city's principal newspaper, he participated actively in the discussion of the issues of the day.

Around the turn of the century he was chairman of a committee whose task it was to make arrangements for a suitable monument in memory of the great virtuoso violinist Ole Bull (1810–80), a native of Bergen, where the monument was to be erected. The commission was given to the sculptor Stephan Sinding (1846–1922) and the monument was unveiled on May 17—Norway's Constitution Day—1901. Grieg was asked to write a piece for male chorus to be sung at the unveiling. The result was "To Ole Bull" (EG 176), a setting of a text by Norwegian poet J. S. Welhaven (1807–73). He himself conducted the premiere performance.

Grieg and Lund exchanged many letters concerning plans for the construction and unveiling of the Ole Bull monument. The three included here are preserved in Universitetsbiblioteket i Bergen (University of Bergen library). Letters 2 and 3 were published in Norwegian and in English translation in Bjarne Kortsen, *Norwegian Music and Musicians*, Bergen 1975. The present translation was made from the original letters.

1

Copenhagen, March 21, 1897, Hotel King of Denmark

Dear Lund!

Thanks for the letter! In accordance with my agreement with you of last fall, I spoke with Sinding[1] already at that time and he promised me in the most obliging way to do what he has now done: to submit a rough cast to the committee—apart from the formal competition, if it did not produce a winning design. He would do this out of interest in the subject; thus the committee should not feel obligated to accept his design. I was just about to write and tell you this, as I see from the newspapers that the competition was a fiasco—and then I got your letter. You will recall that in the committee meeting last fall I supported an *open* competition or else a direct approach to Sinding. But the compact majority opposed me in this. You understand, therefore, that I have now been proven right.

I have just come from Sinding's, and I am totally enchanted with the beautiful idea that is the inspiration for his design. It seems to me that there can be no question of doing anything except immediately to accept his offer. And even more: to give him a completely free hand to make changes in details that may seem desirable to him during the execution. I mention this because, for example, Sinding has the upper body leaning forward, which, to be sure, harmonizes with

---

[1] Norwegian sculptor Stephan Abel Sinding, brother of the composer Christian Sinding (1856–1941). The Ole Bull statue referred to here now stands in Ole Bull Square not far from The National Stage in Bergen—a theater that owes its existence to Bull's initiative.

the idea of the work but is not fully characteristic of Ole Bull. So I recommended that he straighten the upper body and have it leaning back a little more. Then the fiddler becomes the Ole Bull we all know and love as he strikes up "O the fox he was red" on the G string. And that's something he had just learned from the water sprite! Sinding was a bit taken aback by my suggestion. He adopted the pose of a statue, and after attempting a couple of positions he shouted, "Yes, I've got it! I think it can be done in harmony with my idea! I'll give it a try."

I think, then, that in dealing with an artist such as Sinding the committee can proceed in full confidence. From this point on, however, he won't touch the design until he has the committee's firm decision. I hasten to tell you this, because the matter should be decided without delay so that Sinding can devote himself fully to the task. If the committee is not willing to seize the moment, Sinding will turn to other projects, and perhaps the whole process will be messed up.

It is a splendid idea to raise the monument on August 17, 1898.[2] Let us not talk about the unveiling until the commission has been offered and accepted. Anything in the newspaper now would certainly be negative.

Today at Sinding's I have seen photos of the designs submitted in the competition. All "real men", some well done (I think Utne's[3] is the best), in contrast to Sinding's "mood". And what mood? Precisely the one that slumbers subconsciously in every Norwegian's breast whenever we mention Ole Bull's name. It was the power of nature that was Ole Bull's master and that taught him to play. And to depict this power as the water sprite is simultaneously Norwegian, poetic and musical. In short: right on target!

Today I feel as light-hearted and happy about this conquest as if I had done a good deed and wish you could convey my enthusiasm to the other members of the committee. And now Sinding's artistic brilliance, which is such that one feels secure in advance! So I urgently recommend: Do not require that the rough cast be sent to Norway, for Sinding would prefer to avoid this waste of time. Be content with the photograph and let him, in accordance with his wish, get to work as soon as possible, confident of his own genius. Then there is *every* reason to expect a happy result. Sinding is a proud fellow! That is evident from his letters to you.

Warm greetings!

Sincerely yours,
EDVARD GRIEG

2

Copenhagen, March 11, 1901, Hotel Phoenix

Dear Mr. John Lund!
Thank you for your letter! My situation has changed, but unfortunately not for the better. I have been sick and am so still. And not little things: bronchitis,

---

[2] The original plan was to unveil the statue on the 18th anniversary of Bull's death on August 17, 1880.
[3] Norwegian sculptor Lars Utne (1862–1922).

rheumatism and varicose veins! That's a lot at one time. I have now stayed indoors for a fortnight, have had to further postpone my concert[4] and give up altogether the trip to Holland and England.

To my great sorrow it is very unlikely that I could take part in the festivities on the 17th of May, even if I get home by that time. Yes, I will state plainly that when I can't be along to honor him whom I have admired and loved I don't even want to be home on that day.

What a pity that I don't have a poem that could awaken my slumbering vital spirits. If I had had a copy of Welhaven's poems I would have thrown myself into his beautiful poem to Bull. Is it so difficult, then, to get Garborg or Nordahl Rolfsen (or John Paulsen, if he could be inspired) to write four stanzas, two before the unveiling and two (with a new rhythm) after the unveiling? Of course we have others—Vilhelm Krag, Collett Vogt[5]—but they didn't know Bull!!! I am willing to extend the deadline until the end of this month. It can't be extended beyond that because of the need for rehearsal time. But I must be permitted to set just one condition: that the poem be tolerably acceptable to me, that it fit my style.

Sinding's work is remarkable. I understand now that there is something that is greater than rigid photographic similarity, although I would have preferred to see that too. One thing is certain: Sinding has succeeded in raising Bull up, high up, for the consciousness of the Norwegian people of the future! And that, after all, is what is most important.

And with that, farewell for today. Warm greetings!

Sincerely yours,
EDVARD GRIEG

3

Copenhagen, April 1, 1901, Hotel Phoenix

Dear John Lund!
Since my concert I have unfortunately been suffering. Otherwise you would have heard from me. From my telegram today you will see how matters stand. I can hardly manage Garborg's[6] beautiful poem. The first stanza, as you say, must be omitted, and the whole poem is intended by the poet as a *dråpa*,[7] an elegy. But that sort of song is not suitable for the occasion, and in my opinion the poem does not embody the tone that the occasion demands. Welhaven's lovely poem, on the other hand, fits in so beautifully with the scenery of West Norway.[8]

I will send the song (for male chorus a cappella) one of these first days. I will

---

[4] The concert in Copenhagen took place on March 23, 1901.

[5] Grieg, at various times during his career, set texts by all of these Norwegian poets except Nils Collett Vogt (1864–1937).

[6] Norwegian poet Arne Garborg (1851–1924).

[7] A "dråpa" is an Old Norse lay with refrain composed in honor of a king or chieftain.

[8] Grieg finally chose to set Welhaven's poem, "To Ole Bull".

send it directly to Ingolf Schjøtt[9] along with a few hints regarding my intentions. It can be sung before or after the unveiling ceremony. If it is sung before, then "The Shepherd Girl's Sunday"[10] can follow after—and vice-versa. But one thing I will insist on: that *all* of Welhaven's five stanzas be sung. Partly because they are so wonderful, and partly because each stanza illumines the music in a new way. If I had had more time I would certainly have found the secret of Garborg's poem. But I won't do a routine job. I love Garborg too much for that.

I see that they want to have Admiral Børresen speak at the Tordenskiold unveiling ceremony.[11] That is an excellent idea! If only we had a music admiral of that sort who could give Bull his due both as a musician and as a friend of the homeland! But that we do not have. If *you* speak, then I know it will be *warm*. And warmth *is* appropriate on this occasion. It would be good for the younger generation to know how much we, the older one, loved Bull. And how, in general, we *can* love. For it seems to me as if the younger generation does not have the same capacity for love and admiration. Would that I were wrong!

I see that *Bergens Tidende* has carried a quotation from a private letter written by me (whether the letter was to you or to Jonas Lie I do not remember). I have nothing against my statement about Sinding's work being quoted, but it should have been quoted in its entirety. For I am sure that in the place where the three dashes now stand I said something like "that I am now beginning to understand that there is something that is more important than rigid photographic similarity." No doubt these words were omitted with the best of intentions, but whether it is right to do so is another matter. I think it is good for people to prepare themselves for the fact that such a view exists—and among artists it is even accepted to a degree that is almost unbelievable. For otherwise we might be in danger of experiencing a disappointment. People will, of course—this is how they are—cry out first and foremost for perfect likeness and condemn the work if the likeness isn't there. One good thing: It is the *young* Bull who is represented. And nobody living today knew him, I think.

No, now my letter is beginning to achieve a length à la John Lund! So: Goodbye for now!

Warm greetings!

Sincerely yours,
Edvard Grieg

---

[9] Bergen singer and choral director Ingolf Schjøtt (1851–1922).

[10] Ole Bull had written the melody to "Sæterjentens Søndag" ("The Shepherd Girl's Sunday") in 1849 as part of a larger instrumental work entitled *Et Sæterbesøk* (A *Visit to the Sæter*). Shortly after the premiere of the latter work in Christiania on March 10, 1849, Norwegian poet Jørgen Moe (1813–82) wrote a text to fit the melody.

[11] Peter Wessel Tordenskiold (1690–1720) was a Norwegian naval hero. In 1901, Rear Admiral Urban Jacob Rasmus Børresen (1857–1943), a Norwegian naval officer, published a book entitled *Tordenskiold; en karakterstudie* (*Tordenskiold; a Character Study*). A statue of Tordenskiold by the Norwegian painter and sculptor Axel Hjalmar Ender (1853–1920) was also unveiled in Christiania in 1901.

To Edward MacDowell

Edward MacDowell (1860–1908) was considered the foremost American composer of his generation. His long list of compositions reflects the influence of several of the great Romantic composers, not least Grieg, whom he especially admired and to whom he dedicated two of his four piano sonatas. MacDowell was also an outstanding pianist and teacher.

After spending several years in Europe, first as a student and then as a teacher, MacDowell returned to the United States in 1888. In 1896 he was invited to establish a department of music at Columbia University, where he remained as a professor of music until 1904. Shortly thereafter he was seriously injured in a traffic accident that precipitated a mental illness from which he never recovered.

Grieg's first letter to MacDowell was written in English. The other three were written in German and printed in facsimile in Laurence Gilman's biography *Edward MacDowell*, London 1906. Letters 2 and 4 were made available by the MacDowell Club of Music and Allied Arts, Los Angeles. Letter 3 is preserved in the New York Public Library.

1

Copenhagen, October 26, 1899
Hotel King of Denmark

My dear Sir!
Will you permit me in bad English to express my best thanks for your kind letter and for the appreciation you feel for my music.[1] Of course it will be a great honor and pleasure for me to accept your dedication.

Some years ago I thought it possible to shake hands with you in your own country. But unfortunately my delicate health does not seem to agree. At all events, if we are not to meet, I am glad to read in the papers of your artistic success in America.

With my best wishes, I am, dear sir,

Yours very truly,
EDVARD GRIEG

[1] On October 10, 1899, MacDowell had sent Grieg a letter in English in which he wrote, "A number of years ago a critic in the *Musikalisches Wochenblatt* said that my music itself was a dedication to you. . . . I will confess that the critic was right to some extent, for your music lies closer to my heart than I can well say. I have dedicated much to you in my thoughts, and this will be my excuse for sending you some of my music. If I do not receive your permission for the dedication, I will at least have told you of my love for and loyalty to Edvard Grieg." The reason for the letter was a request by MacDowell that he be permitted to dedicate his *Piano Sonata No. 3* in D Minor, op. 57 (the "Norse" sonata) to Grieg. In a letter of December 13, 1899, MacDowell thanked Grieg for his positive reply and expressed his regret that the publication of the sonata was taking so long. He then ventured to ask of Grieg yet another favor: "Will you, when you receive the music, tell me squarely what you disagree with the most in it. I mean only in very general terms, of course, as I do not wish to bother you nor to take your time." He concluded with the words, "The name of Grieg is adored from one end of this country to the other."

2

Troldhaugen at Bergen, Norway
June 30, 1900

Dear Sir!
Accept my heartfelt thanks for having done me the honor of dedicating to me your splendid piano sonata! I find the work as powerful as it is substantial. I have played it repeatedly and always found new beauties. You are a Wagner enthusiast. It goes without saying that I am one as well—yes, even in an exceptionally high degree. But fortunately one quickly notes that you are not a so-called "Wagnerite". For those Wagnerites are copy-cats, and stupid and arrogant ones at that. In the handling of your Nordic material you are only partly under Wagner's influence. And that is good. For the Edda material[2] that was employed by Wagner is not only Germanic: It is above all Nordic (Norwegian-Icelandic), whereas Wagner was exclusively German and not a Scandinavian at all. Not infrequently in the sonata, your imagination was in the far north. Higher praise I could not give. For the motto you have chosen is not just an external adornment. Far more, it obligated the musician to visit in his imagination the very places where the poet had dwelt. And this you have succeeded in doing—if not always, at any rate many times.[3]

I hope that in America people have reached the point where they will give a man with such a serious will and masterful ability as yours the recognition you deserve. Your songs and piano pieces, which contain so much poetry and beauty, should be the bridge that the American public must cross in order to reach an understanding of a work such as your sonata.

Allow me, dear sir, to assure you of my respect and high regard.

Yours very truly,
EDVARD GRIEG

---

[2] The Eddas comprise two 13th-century Icelandic literary works known as the Prose Edda and the Poetic Edda. They contain a wealth of Scandinavian myths and legends as well as a summary of the rules of Skaldic poetry and remain to this day an important source for our knowledge of Germanic mythology.

[3] MacDowell often wrote short poems in connection with his compositions to indicate in words the "mood" he had in mind while writing the music. The poem ("motto") he wrote for *Sonata No. 3* reads as follows:

Night had fallen on a day of deeds.
The great rafters in the red-ribbed hall
Flashed crimson in the fitful flame
Of smouldering logs;
And from the stealthy shadows
That crept 'round Harald's throne
Rang out a Skald's strong voice
With tales of battles won:
Of Gudrun's love
And Sigurd, Siegmund's son.

3

Copenhagen, April 8, 1901
Hotel Phoenix

Dear Sir!
Need I tell you that I am pleased with your *Norse Sonata* and that I am grateful to you for the dedication? The invisible scarlet thread that unites artists who do not even know each other personally is truly beautiful—indeed, it is one of the most beautiful things in art.

I would indeed have enjoyed seeing you in London this spring. But alas! My health does not allow me to undertake such a voyage.

At the beginning of May I am going home to Bergen, Norway, where I intend to stay during the summer. I hope to get acquainted with your new sonata there, provided it will have been printed by that time.

Yours very truly,
EDVARD GRIEG

4

Bergen, Norway, January 11, 1902

Dear Sir!
I should have sent you long ago my thanks for your last [fourth] sonata.[4] But the seriousness of life prevented it. It is also difficult for me to express my opinion of your beautiful work in the form of a letter. Most of all I would have liked to have you interpret the sonata for me on the piano, and thereafter I could have formed my impressions in words. I don't hesitate for a moment, however, to tell you that I find your composition significant. It is very powerful, often daring—yes, thank goodness, even reckless. But it should have been scored for orchestra, for an orchestral spirit lurks within it. However, with respect to piano technique you have done many interesting things to make the piece exciting for the performing artist.

Perhaps you are familiar with a remark by the late Hauptmann[5] regarding Gade's[6] first orchestral works: "Sea gulls hover over his scores." That was very beautifully said, and I would like to say something equally beautiful to you—for example: "The harp-strings of the skald resound in your sonata!" Hauptmann's picture is as superior, however, as is an original to a copy.

---

[4] In a letter dated February 25, 1901—written in German—MacDowell informed Grieg that he had taken the liberty of "embellishing" his fourth piano sonata with Grieg's name as well. He wrote: "This fourth sonata is to me of Nordic character, and you were so often in my mind that I could not forego attaching your name to it as a kind of motto." MacDowell's *Sonata No. 4* in E Minor, op. 59, composed in 1900, is known as his "Keltic" sonata.

[5] Moritz Hauptmann (1792–1868), one of Grieg's theory teachers at the Leipzig Conservatory.

[6] The Danish composer and conductor Niels Wilhelm Gade (1817–1890).

What I find so appealing in your composition is the noble seriousness and high purpose that you have had in mind. Accept my heartfelt thanks for the dedication!

Last summer I had a visit from Mr. Finck,[7] the music critic for *The Evening Post* [in New York], who told me about you. He has rare qualities as a critic. First by virtue of his objectivity—his antipathy for Brahms is undeniably a regrettable exception—and second by virtue of his imagination. For *imagination* is the very thing that nearly all critics lack. You are lucky to have such an understanding interpreter in your homeland. His biography of Wagner is excellent.

Would you please do me the great favor of relaying to Seidl's[8] widow my desire that Seidl's orchestration of some of my *Lyric Pieces*—especially "Bell Ringing"—be sent to me for my perusal? I would be very grateful to you for that. I talked to Mr. Finck about it, and he told me of the work the brilliant conductor had undertaken, but perhaps he has totally forgotten about the matter.

If you should ever return to Europe, you must not forget that there is a beautiful country called Norway where each summer you will find

Yours truly,
EDVARD GRIEG

My address during the winter months: Wilhelm Hansen Musikforlag, Gothersgade 11, Copenhagen.

---

[7] American music critic and writer Henry T. Finck (1854–1926), who authored two books on Grieg and his music: *Edvard Grieg* (London, 1906) and *Grieg and His Music* (New York and London, 1909).

[8] In 1895 the Austro-Hungarian conductor Anton Seidl (1815–98), who was known especially for his performances of Wagner, had orchestrated four numbers from Grieg's *Lyric Pieces* op. 54 and had performed them in New York City under the title *Norwegische Suite*. Grieg received the Seidl arrangements as requested in 1903 and re-orchestrated them in the summer of 1904. Grieg's arrangement was published by C. F. Peters Musikverlag as *Lyric Suite*. "Bell Ringing", however—the piece that Grieg had especially asked to see—was not included in the suite but was replaced by "Shepherd's Boy". Grieg considered the harmony in "Bell Ringing" to be very modernistic; in a letter of December 8, 1891, to Dutch composer Julius Röntgen (1855–1932) he described it as "crazy" ("verrückt"). Grieg's orchestral arrangement of this piece was published for the first time in *Edvard Grieg: Complete Works*, vol. 13.

To Marian MacDowell

Marian Nevins MacDowell (1857–1956), the wife of American composer Edward MacDowell (1860–1908), was a professional pianist and often gave public performances of her husband's works. In 1907—after the death of her husband—she initiated the process of transforming their farm home in Peterborough, New Hampshire, into a summer school for composers and writers. Since then the MacDowell Colony has served as a sanctuary and source of inspiration for hundreds of composers, writers and painters who use the colony as a working retreat.

Mrs. MacDowell actively managed the colony until her death at the age of 99, and in her old age she also authored a small book entitled *Random Notes on Edward MacDowell and his Music* (Boston 1950).

Grieg's letter to Marian MacDowell, written in German, is preserved in the New York Public Library.

Christiania, December 14, 1905
Hotel Westminster

Dear Madam!

The news of MacDowell's serious illness has affected me deeply. Permit me, therefore, through these lines to express my own and my wife's most heartfelt compassion to him and to you.

I am a great admirer of MacDowell's muse, and I would regard it as a severe blow if his best creative period should have to be terminated so abruptly. But from everything I have heard about your husband as a human being—and to me, this only adds to his significance as a composer—he is also a kind of person who has my full and warm sympathy. He really is a man of integrity, with an unusually sensitive and compassionate nervous system. However, for a personality such as his the possession of such a nervous system is a mixed blessing. For every time that it exalts him to the highest transports of joy, there might be ten times when it is the source of his deepest, most inexpressible suffering. Herein lies the unfathomable riddle. An artist with ideals as high as MacDowell's must ask himself: "For what purpose have I received from nature this delicately strung lyre, when I would have been better off without it?" Life is so unmerciful that every true artist must ask himself this question. The only consolation, then, is work—yes, even the most extreme exertion. That is something MacDowell must have felt intensely, and then being run over was the straw that broke the camel's back.[1]

But: The artist is an optimist. Otherwise he would not be an artist. He hopes and believes in the triumph of the good and the beautiful. He trusts in his lucky star until he draws his last breath. And you—I know that you are the highly

---

[1] MacDowell began to show symptoms of mental illness in December, 1904, and his situation worsened in the winter of 1904–05 when he was run over by a hansom cab in New York City. He eventually withdrew into an infantile state that continued to the end of his life.

gifted wife of an artist—you will not and must not lose hope! In similar cases, fortunately, a seemingly inexplicable recovery has occurred.

If it can give MacDowell a moment's cheer, tell him that in far-off Norway he has a warm and understanding friend who is concerned about him and who wishes from his heart that better times will soon come again both for him and for you!

With warm greetings to you both,

Respectfully,
EDVARD GRIEG

P.S. May I ask you to convey my greetings to our mutual friend, Mr. H. T. Finck![2]

[2] American music critic and writer Henry T. Finck (1854–1926), who authored two books on Grieg and his music: *Edvard Grieg* (London, 1906) and *Grieg and His Music* (New York and London, 1909).

To Gottfred Matthison-Hansen

The Danish composer and organist Gottfred Matthison-Hansen (1832–1909) was one of Grieg's closest Danish friends. He was a brilliant organist, first at Frederik's Church (1859 to 1881) and then at Trinitatis Church (1881 to ca. 1900) in Copenhagen, where he regularly presented the great masterworks of organ music to music lovers in the Danish capital. In 1868 he became a teacher at the Royal Danish Music Conservatory and in 1900 became its Director. Grieg took organ lessons from him in 1866 with the intention of seeking a position as an organist in Christiania.

Grieg's correspondence with Matthison-Hansen is very extensive and provides many insights into the music life of Christiania and Copenhagen in the latter half of the nineteenth century.

All of Grieg's letters to Matthison-Hansen included here are preserved in Det kgl. Bibliotek (The Royal Library), Copenhagen

1

Christiania, December 12, 1866

Dear Hansen!
I am finally getting around to answering your friendly letter. It was nice of you to write, which is exactly what I had planned to do, but I seldom ride the same day I saddle up, so it would have taken a long time for our correspondence to get under way if you hadn't taken the first step.

Before I begin to dwell on the past, present and future, I first have an important matter to deal with. It has to do with a favor that you must do for me as soon as possible. I recently wrote to Horneman asking him to send me a book of mine (containing various things by Mozart including a quintet for piano and winds in E-flat) that I loaned to Euterpe—i.e., to Horneman—last year.[1] It must be in his living quarters or—though this is unlikely—in Euterpe's files. I absolutely must have it, as I am planning to use the quintet. I have told Horneman this, but if I know him right it wouldn't occur to him to do anything but stick my letter in his pocket and at the first opportunity use it as scratch paper or something like that. If you would now be so kind as to look into the matter I would be very grateful. You can send it (C.O.D. of course) as printed matter to Musikhandler Warmuth[2] in Christiania.

So much for the business, and now to friendship. Yes, it is clear to me that in you I have found a friend! What made it hard for me to believe that at first was the fact that we both have the same peculiarity, namely, we are hard to get close to—I mean, when it has to do with a deep, sincere relationship. For that reason it took a long time before I could say that I understand you, and I think the reverse is equally true. You have this wonderful, genuinely Nordic integrity about you,

---

[1] In 1865 Grieg, Horneman (1840–1906), Louis Hornbeck (1840–1906), Gottfred Matthison-Hanson and Rikard Nordraak (1842–66) had established in Copenhagen a music association to which they gave the name "Euterpe". For further details see footnote 1 to Grieg's letter to Horneman of November 21, 1866.

[2] Carl Warmuth (1844–95) was a music publisher and proprietor of a music store in Christiania.

this capacity to feel—greatly and deeply, as only a true artist can, without boasting about it and showing it off. I will never forget the day when Nordraak[3]—our unforgettable friend—played and sang *Sigurd Slembe*[4] for you. That was the day that I began to regard you as a friend. I saw the struggle that you experienced between mind and heart—and mind had to yield, for only through the heart can one find the key to the new world into which he leads us in that piece. I will never forget that day. That moment was one of the greatest moments of my life. And the person who created that great situation was not Nordraak with his music: It was you with your singular, eloquent silence. That is why ever since that day you have been, so to speak, part and parcel of my thinking and my ideal world.

Surely I don't have to tell you that both you and various other people have the capacity to awaken my longing for Denmark, and hopefully the time is not too far off when we will see each other again. After a *happily concluded* winter I will come down to the green forests happier than ever before. Yes, down there under the canopy of heaven I will meet my little sweetheart,[5] go hand-in-hand with her into the church, and from there head homeward with her toward Norway's coast—Norway, where I shall live and work. Yes, it is a strange thought, a strange mixture of delight and wistfulness.

It is my enthusiasm for the national idea that leads me to reconcile myself with my native land as a place for an artist to make his home—but in dark moments my future is nonetheless covered with clouds because of the total isolation and lack of outside influences up here. Still, if I have no individuality, nothing is lost; and if I do, it will surely survive in spite of everything. That is my consolation.

As for how things are going for me, it is hardly possible to report anything. As things stand at the moment I am perpetually anxious about what is really going to happen. I have secured the position of conductor of "The Philharmonic Society"[6] (which gives symphony concerts) here. If I can handle this, everything will be fine. In today's issue of *Morgenbladet*[7] I and another Norwegian musician, [Otto] Winter-Hjelm, even invited people to participate in the establishment of a Music Academy[8] that will start up after New Year's Day if a sufficient number of students show an interest. If this also goes well, I hope that by spring—or, more correctly, by summer—I can go to Denmark for the purpose mentioned earlier. I currently have eight or nine pupils to whom I give private lessons and probably

---

[3] Grieg's friend and fellow composer Rikard Nordraak, who died of tuberculosis at age 23 on March 20, 1866.

[4] Rikard Nordraak had written incidental music for the historical drama *Sigurd Slembe* by Norwegian author Bjørnstjerne Bjørnson (1832–1910).

[5] The previous year Grieg had become engaged to his cousin, Nina Hagerup (1845–1935).

[6] Grieg's first concert as conductor of "Det Philharmoniske Selskab" ("The Philharmonic Society") was given on February 2, 1867, with Beethoven's *Fifth Symphony* as the main item on the program. Grieg had been selected for the position following the resignation of his predecessor, Otto Winter-Hjelm (1837–1931).

[7] *Morgenbladet* was a leading Christiania newspaper.

[8] Grieg and Winter-Hjelm outlined their plans for a Norwegian music academy in a long article in *Morgenbladet* on December 12, 1866. For the complete article see Benestad & Halverson (eds.), *Edvard Grieg: Diaries, Articles, Speeches* (Columbus, Ohio, 2001). The academy began operation in January, 1867, but did not survive for long. When Grieg went abroad in the autumn of 1869 it faded into oblivion.

won't get many more now, since most will prefer to take their lessons in connection with the much cheaper Music Academy! Just for the fun of it, read today's issue of *Morgenbladet.* I think you can find a copy at *Madsens Restauration paa Kongens Nytorv.*[9] It will amuse you to see such a grand article here in our little city.

Since we last saw each other I have written various little things. I finished two pieces for piano and cello in Bergen, and right now I'm stuck in the middle of the first movement of a symphony. I have also finished a volume of songs that will be published by Erslev before Christmas.[10]

If I dared to ask for yet another favor, it would be to request that you ask Erslev to send the free copies he has set aside for me to Warmuth in Christiania —NB, with the exception of two copies, of which I would ask you to take one for yourself and send the other to Miss [Nina] Hagerup. Don't be angry with me for bothering you with so many things. This summer I hopefully can be of service to you—maybe in the church. Yes, who knows if bygone days might not come back again.

My relationship with Nina's parents, as you know, is *lousy,* so don't go there —though I think it is better of late because of a very successful concert that I gave here with the assistance of Mrs. Norman and my fiancee, who was in Norway some time ago. You should have heard Mrs. Norman play the *Violin Sonata*! Why, I hardly knew what I should do—play, or just sit there and listen to her! The same concert included nothing but Norwegian music (!) and netted me about 150 *spesidalers* (!), and this good beginning has basically given me courage and confidence for the future.[11]

And now many thanks for the little song. It's just as it ought to be, I think. Can you expect a better critique? When I see Mrs. Thoresen,[12] may I give it to her? (r.s.v.p.)

---

[9] A restaurant in Copenhagen where current issues of various newspapers were available for customers to read.

[10] Nothing is known of the symphony to which Grieg is referring unless he means the first movement of the so-called "forbidden" symphony (EG 119) that he wrote in Copenhagen in 1863–64. This symphony, which he declared in 1869 "must never be performed", was published for the first time in *Edvard Grieg. Complete Works,* vol. 11 (1984). Movements 2–4 of this symphony were premiered under the baton of Danish composer and conductor H. C. Lumbye (1810–74) in Copenhagen's Tivoli on May 4, 1864. Grieg himself conducted the two inner movements in Copenhagen on April 1, 1865, and movements 2–4 on March 23, 1867, in Christiania. The songs to which he refers are *Songs and Ballads* op. 9, to texts by Norwegian poet Andreas Munch (1811–84). They were published by Horneman & Erslev in 1866. The two works for cello and piano have been found in a manuscript, where they appear to be two movements of an intended suite. One piece, "Intermezzo" (EG 115), is printed in *Edvard Grieg. Complete Works,* vol. 8 (1979). The other, "Humoresque", contains a version in E major of the beginning of the last movement of Grieg's *Violin Sonata No. 2* in G major, which was written in 1867.

[11] At the concert on October 15, 1866, Grieg played his *Violin Sonata No. 1* in F major with the Czech-born violinist Wilhelmina Neruda (1838–1911), who at that time was married to the Swedish conductor Ludvig Norman (1831–85). Nina Hagerup sang songs by Norwegian composers Halfdan Kjerulf (1815–68), Nordraak and Grieg, and Grieg himself played several of his own works including *Humoresques* and *Piano Sonata in E Minor.*

[12] The Danish-Norwegian author Magdalene Thoresen (1819–1903), Henrik Ibsen's mother-in-law and a close friend of Bjørnstjerne Bjørnson. It was Mrs. Thoresen who introduced Grieg to Nordraak in Copenhagen in 1863.

Get yourself a copy of a new collection of poems that came out up here a few days ago: *Norske Dikt* [*Norwegian Poems*], by Kristofer Janson. You will find something there that is both new and beautiful. Don't worry about the language: It will give you a little trouble at first, but it will get easier as you go along.[13]

Goodbye for now. Warm greetings to your loved ones down there, especially your wife and family. My address is: Kirkegaden No. 13, Uhrmager Smits Gaard, Christiania. Now in plain Danish: Write soon again to

Your devoted friend,
EDVARD GRIEG

2

Christiania, July 30, 1867

Dear friend!
Having now enjoyed the joys of honeymooning[14] for a suitable period of time, I am finally returning to matters of friendship—and business. This time I will begin with the business matters. I have learned from Fries,[15] to whom I wrote immediately after coming here—also sending him your letter—that early this spring he sent several borrowed items, including your *Folkedans*,[16] to Horneman[17] with a request that they be returned to their various owners as quickly as possible. When one is dealing with people like that one has to put up with quite a bit, though I grant that this is nothing but sheer carelessness. Will you now please fetch *Folkedans* from Horneman and send it to me C.O.D. at music dealer Warmuth's address—or better yet, if you think you can count on him to do it, ask Horneman to include it in his package to Warmuth at his earliest opportunity. (. . .)

As of today I have had three weeks of vacation, and during these three weeks I have written a new *Violin Sonata*[18] that I look forward to hearing soon when my compatriot Svendsen[19] comes here. He is the only one to whom I dare to give it. All of the other violinists here hate me, probably out of envy. They are like the people Andersen[20] describes somewhere or other: They focus on the weaknesses

---

[13] Kristofer Janson (1841–1917) wrote in *landsmål* (later called *nynorsk*, "New Norwegian"), a form of the language created by combining elements derived from several rural dialects.

[14] Edvard and Nina were married on June 11, 1867, in Johanneskirken (St. John's Church) in Copenhagen.

[15] The German-born violinist and conductor August Fries (1821–1913) was leader of Bergen's Music Society Harmonien, predecessor of the modern Bergen Philharmonic Orchestra, during the years 1864–73.

[16] Matthison-Hansen's *Folkedans* (*Folk Dance*) for orchestra. The piano version of the same piece, published by Wilhelm Hansen, is called "Fest-Polonaise".

[17] Danish music publisher Johan Ole Emil Horneman (1809–70), father of Grieg's friend Christian Frederik Emil Horneman.

[18] *Violin Sonata No. 2* in G major.

[19] Grieg's close friend and colleague Johan Svendsen (1840–1911), who was just completing his studies at the Leipzig Conservatory at this time. The sonata was dedicated to Svendsen.

[20] Danish writer of children's stories Hans Christian Andersen (1805–75).

and fail to see the good, or don't want to see it. It might look as if fortune were smiling upon me in the new circumstances that surround me, but in reality that is not the case. Most people hate my compositions, even the musicians. For some, to be sure, they are a closed book, and in such cases the dislike is forgivable. But there are others who understand them, and who express their admiration to my face, but who never have a good word to say about them to others. Kjerulf is one who does the latter, and it is less honorable than open criticism.

Well, never mind. In art, one city is like another, one human being is like the next—equally envious, petty and personal. The only thing to do is to hold fast to Goethe's words, "Let everyone take heed how he lives, and let him who stands take care lest he fall."[21] One doesn't understand that sort of thing until one becomes a man, but then one grasps its significance in all of its profound seriousness.

Enough for now. Write soon, and accept the warmest greetings from my wife and me.

Sincerely yours,
EDVARD GRIEG

P.S. Will you please see to it that the enclosure gets to Horneman senior?!

3

Christiania, October 8, 1867

Dear friend!
It seems like a long time since I last wrote to you, but it's even longer since I have heard anything from you. And that notwithstanding the fact that my last letter contained some important questions. There was one in particular[22] regarding which Fries wrote me that he had sent both it (the orchestral parts) and everything else he had borrowed (therefore *Folkedansen* as well) back to Horneman with a request that the latter see to it that all the items were returned to their respective owners. Thus you must have received the things belonging to you.

I assume that you are now sitting at home in your cozy sitting room reworking *Folkedansen*, and if so, for heaven's sake send me the score as quickly as possible—and what is even more important, let me know immediately whether I can expect to get the music to *Folkedansen* at all. If not, I must choose something else as soon as possible.

Today I attended a rehearsal for Johan Svendsen's concert and heard his symphony. That was really something! The most scintillating genius, boldest national flavor, and truly brilliant handling of the orchestra. Where he has gotten this from

---

[21] Grieg's German quotation is from Goethe's poem *Beherzigung* (*Reflection*): "Siehe Jeder wie er's treibe, und wer steht, dass er nicht fälle!" Cf. I Corinthians 10:12.

[22] Regarding Matthison-Hansen's *Drapa* op. 9.

the gods only know, but I think it is from Berlioz, about whom I unfortunately know too little to venture to affirm a strong influence here. But be that as it may, when I heard the symphony I was completely jolted. Everything had my fullest approval and forced itself upon me with irresistible power.

We're making progress up here now. Next month I'm giving a concert consisting entirely of my own compositions, and this Saturday Svendsen is conducting a concert consisting exclusively of his own works.[23] In my mind's eye I can already see my esteemed countrymen stare like cows at a red door. But let them do that to begin with. When several work together, recognition will soon follow.

Next month the concerts of The Philharmonic Society begin. For the first concert I have decided on the music to [Beethoven's] *Egmont* and ensembles from [Mozart's] *Don Giovanni.* I especially wanted to do the sextette. I have to start with the classics in order not to offend the musical congregation.

Enough for now. In due course you will hear much more news from me. You must not wait for it, however, before you let me hear both recent and old news from you. And about the orchestral parts for *Drapa* as well as all the music for *Folkedansen.* Those are the most important business items. Until these items are taken care of I am strictly a businessman, but thereafter I am

Your devoted friend,
EDVARD GRIEG

P.S. Warm greetings to your wife.
Please be so kind as to relay the enclosure to Erslev.[24]

4

Christiania, December 23, 1867

Dear friend!
It is a long time since I received your welcome letter, but I don't have time to make excuses, nor will this letter be very long. I am so involved in all kinds of busywork that I wish the day had 48 hours—or at least that the 24 it does have could all be used for work. Thanks for the information about *Folkedansen.* I have decided to include it and *Drapa* in my third subscription concert. That will take place around the middle of February, so it would be great if you would send *Folkedansen* by the end of January.

Have you heard about Emil and his *Aladdin* overture?[25] It strikes me that he

[23] Johan Svendsen's concert took place on October 12, 1867. See Grieg's review of this concert in Benestad & Halverson (eds.), *Edvard Grieg: Diaries, Articles, Speeches* (Columbus, Ohio, 2001).

[24] Danish music publisher Emil Erslev (1817–82).

[25] Christian F. E. Horneman's overture to the opera *Aladdin* was composed in 1864 and performed for the first time in "Euterpe" in Copenhagen in 1865. The opera was not completed until 1888. It was performed on

himself is an Aladdin who, without realizing it himself, is approaching fortune's highest peaks. But where is the lamp? Well, if I am going to be honest I must say that it is his childlikeness and fearlessness—yes, his impudence—in addition, of course, to his great talent, which we acknowledge. But diligence and hard work are not the things that have led him to this achievement.

But back to myself. Of late, as the tailors say, I have schooled myself in my field such that I now perform as a conductor *par excellence*. The Philharmonic Society, which I conducted last year, has given up and I myself have announced four subscription concerts. The first of these took place eight days ago. The program consisted of my *Funeral March for Rikard Nordraak* for large wind ensemble (a wonderful sound), Mozart's *Symphony* in G minor, songs by Kjerulf (sung by my wife), and Beethoven's *Egmont* music. The last-named was the most enjoyable. Our best tragic actress, Mrs. Gundersen[26] (talk to Bjørnson—he can tell you all about her), handled the speaking parts and my wife sang *Clärchen's Lieder*. In the next concert, which will also include a mixed chorus, I am giving the march from *Tannhäuser*, a scene from Spontini's *La Vestale* [*The Vestal Virgin*], and Schumann's B-flat major symphony.[27] I won't earn a penny from it—don't even think of such a thing—but I have to do that sort of stuff in order to survive here. Just think, I spend the rest of the day giving lessons so that my wife and I won't croak in this place. It's like Ibsen says in *Peer Gynt*: Everyone here is "to himself enough".[28] So it's every man for himself.

I never do any composing; I have neither time nor inclination. I am completely unmusical. During the summer vacations I did write a *Violin Sonata* [op. 13]. Did I tell you that? I look forward to showing it to you. You'll get a copy when it has been printed.

Now I have filled the pages with me and mine. Please, now you come with thee and thine. But soon. Warm greetings!

Sincerely yours,
EDVARD GRIEG

P.S. Greet your dear father when you see him, also your wife.

November 18 of the same year at The Royal Theater in Copenhagen, with Johan Svendsen conducting, as part of the jubilee celebrating the 25th anniversary of King Christian IX's ascension to the Danish throne.

[26] Laura Gundersen (1832–98), the leading actress at the Christiania Theater. Grieg later dedicated the melodrama *Bergliot*—a setting of a text by Bjørnstjerne Bjørnson—to her.

[27] The compositions listed by Grieg for the two concerts are as follows:
Grieg: *Funeral March for Rikard Nordraak* EG 107.
Mozart: *Symphony No. 40* in G minor, K. 550.
Beethoven: Incidental music to Goethe's play *Egmont* op. 84.
Wagner: Grand March from Act II of *Tannhäuser*.
Spontini: The opera *La Vestale* [*The Vestal Virgin*]
Schumann: *Symphony No. 1* in B-flat major (the "Spring Symphony") op. 38.

[28] The allusion is to *Peer Gynt* Act 2, scene 6, where the Troll King says, "Here, among us trolls, we say: 'Troll, to yourself be—enough!'"

5

Christiania, April 10, 1869

Dear friend!

I am writing to you on what for me is a day of celebration. My little daughter is marking her first birthday.[29] It is so nice to see this happiness around me. Yesterday was no less a day of celebration, albeit in quite another way: I received five different letters from dear Denmark telling about art and friendship down there. Yours was one of them. A friendly greeting such as that is like a ray of sunshine flooding into my lonely home. For I lack anything like that here in Norway, and you know very well that the ideal life requires it. For that reason I thank God for my kinship with the Danes, as a result of which my music is understood down there. Here there is coldness and harshness both in nature and in the minds of people. Oh yes, there is in many respects an underlying warmth of heart as well, but the artist needs to see some evidence of it. He can't use his gifts constantly searching the remotest corners in hope of finding some scrap of understanding. And that's how it is up here.

I was glad to hear about your *Trio*. I only wish I had heard it performed![30] I often read *Berlingske*,[31] and there I read about your involvement in the Easter concert. How I wished I could just fly down to hear one of the chamber-music evenings you talk about. I miss very much a flight of vision up here. Just think: This entire winter I have had no opportunity to hear any music except that in which I myself have been involved. I've gotten into a conflict with the orchestra because some first violinists demanded five *spesidalers* each for a concert plus three rehearsals. The result was that I couldn't assemble an orchestra, as I wasn't inclined to go to debtors' prison over such a matter. These gentlemen give chamber-music soirees, so it's easy to see why they would prefer to have my concerts "go to the dogs". But—it didn't work. I decided I wasn't going to let them trick me out of my work. I altered or, more correctly, discarded the lovely program that I had planned last summer in Denmark—and that cost plenty of hard cash, because last summer I had also copied some music from The Music Society in Copenhagen—and then I planned a new program consisting of works for choir, choir and piano, etc. NB no arrangements, so the whole concert had an artistic *raison d'être* even though it was not as satisfying to me as works for choir and orchestra.

But I wanted—somehow or other, I didn't care how—to make those concerts happen. And I did! I have now given two such concerts, both to a full house. On Thursday the 13th I am giving a commemorative concert for Halfdan Kjerulf

---

[29] Grieg's daughter Alexandra was born April 10, 1868.

[30] Matthison-Hansen's *Trio in F Major* op. 5.

[31] *Berlingske Tidende*, a Copenhagen newspaper.

consisting entirely of works by the deceased. The income will go toward a planned monument to mark his grave.[32]

This summer I will go home to Bergen in order to work in peace and quiet in the country (Landås!)[33] and in the fall we will go to Denmark, where we hope to spend some pleasant days if all goes well.

This has been a lot about myself, but to tell the truth I am thinking very much these days about what is going to become of me, and of course you have a friend's interest. I feel that I am living in an important period of my life and I ought not to let it just slip away.

[Bjørnstjerne] Bjørnson has written a fine article about me in today's issue of *Norsk Folkeblad*. You should read it. He says there that I am a painter of landscapes. That's right on target, for my life's dream is to be able to express Nordic nature in music.

Greet your wife, your father and your mother-in-law, and let me soon hear a bit from you again. Believe me, you are doing a good work, even if you don't have enough time.

Yours truly,
EDVARD GRIEG

April 18

It took this long before I got these lines in the mail. I don't understand myself what delayed their being sent. But now I can report right away that during the past week I have given two concerts, one in memory of the late Kjerulf (it brought in 220 *spesidalers* toward a monument for Kjerulf) and last evening a farewell concert for myself. I now have reason to hope that we can see each other this fall.

How nice: Each time I plan a trip to Denmark I always look forward to it more than before! Why? The answer is simple: I and my work are understood there.

If you see the Windings, greet them from me.[34]

Yours truly,
E. G.

---

[32] Halfdan Kjerulf (1815–68) was one of Grieg's predecessors as a composer of songs. He died on August 11, 1868, and Grieg took the lead in collecting funds for a monument. The monument was unveiled in Christiania on September 23, 1874. For the latter occasion Grieg wrote the choral piece, *At the Halfdan Kjerulf Statue*, to a text by Andreas Munch (1811–84).

[33] The Grieg family had a summer home at the foot of Mt. Ulriken in Landås, which is now a part of Bergen. Grieg had spent his summers there ever since childhood.

[34] Danish composer August Winding (1835–99) and his wife Clara (1838–1925).

6

Rome, March 1, 1870

Dear friend!

(. . .) From the eternal city my thoughts turn restlessly homeward toward that land in which I have been called to do my work. My first trip to southern Europe[35] was a dream, and it was precisely as a dream that it had value for me at that time. Now things are different. I have become more Nordic since then.

Last fall I didn't get to say goodbye to you, and it annoyed me. Now I look forward to seeing you again soon. I will be home in Denmark again in May, and then I hope that the summer will see our happy faces.

What greatly accelerated the writing of these lines and made me lonesome for you was Winding's report of a wonderful letter your wife had sent. I hope she is better than *my* wife at the moment: Today my room is a storage site for salammoniac mixture, camphor etc. (. . .)

The news about myself is also quickly told. I recently had the pleasure of having my *Violin Sonata* in F major played at a concert here by the Italians Sgambati and Pinelli,[36] and rather well at that. I have been to see Liszt on two occasions. The first visit was one of the most interesting experiences I have ever had. As an incredible favor I was asked to visit him, and he played—I tell you, I don't care if I ever hear anyone else play the piano. The point is that this is not piano playing. One forgets the pianist, the instrument, and all that trash; one is alone with a giant who marshals a legion of spirits in headlong flight with all of his unbridled fancy. In a moment of cool reflection this is a reproach I could make, that he has no 'bridle'. I wish you had heard him play my latest violin sonata, sight-reading it from beginning to end. Yes, you should have heard it—and the brilliance of his interpretation! I left convinced that he can do the impossible.[37]

Is your lovely *Trio* going to be played in the Music Association this winter? I hope you are more sure of that than I am of my sonata, about which Gade[38]—to my surprise, and of course without any urging from me—said, "It's going to be performed this winter—either the first sonata or the second, whichever you wish." He takes a strange delight in regarding people as fools!

---

[35] Grieg's first trip to Italy occurred in the winter of 1865–66. During this stay he kept a detailed diary which will be printed in its entirety in English translation in Benestad & Halverson (eds.), *Edvard Grieg: Diaries, Articles, Speeches* (Columbus, Ohio, 2001).

[36] Italian musicians Giovanni Sgambati (1843–1914) was a pianist and composer, Ettore Pinelli (1843–1915) a violinist.

[37] For a detailed report of Grieg's meetings with Franz Liszt see his letters to his parents on pp. 271–278.

[38] Danish composer Niels Wilhelm Gade (1817–90), who played an important role in Grieg's development as a composer during the latter's first year in Copenhagen.

Goodbye for now to you and your wife. Warm greetings from both of us.

Sincerely yours,
Edvard Grieg

P.S. Greet Neupert[39] and Horneman!

7

Børve, Hardanger, August 13, 1877

Dear friend!
Now I'm not going to continue any longer being ashamed of my behavior; I'm going to get right down to business. So: Forgive my long silence, and thank you so much for your letter—or, if I'm not mistaken, for your letters.

It makes me very happy that you are always the old one—and always the young one. Your trip to Hanover[40] now is certainly behind you and has won you a heap of laurels. I'd like to hear more of the details about them. And you must not return evil for evil, but give me soon a long account of your trip. You must also not forget those new compositions that you have promised to send me. I had thought that we would be seeing each other this fall, but unfortunately my plan went down the drain. I didn't get the grant[41] I applied for and without which I dare not go abroad with my better half. This development is all the more annoying in that Wieniawski,[42] with whom I performed in Christiania a couple of months ago, has urged me to go to London this winter, where he will arrange opportunities for the two of us to perform sonatas together. But—now that's all up in smoke.

As you see, at the moment I am living in beautiful Hardanger, where we have secured lodging from a farmer and are getting along splendidly. I have recently formed a plan that I may implement, namely, to stay at Ullensvang—half a mile from here—this winter in order to be able to work undisturbed. I hope it becomes a reality. There is something that I must do for the sake of my art. Day by day I am becoming more dissatisfied with myself. Nothing that I do satisfies me, and although I think I still have some ideas, I can give neither flow nor form to my ideas when I proceed to the working out of some larger project. It's enough

---

[39] Norwegian pianist Edmund Neupert (1842–88), who on April 3, 1869, had premiered Grig's *Piano Concerto* in Copenhagen.

[40] Matthison-Hansen had performed as an organ virtuoso at a music festival in Hanover sponsored by *Allgemeiner deutscher Musikverein.*

[41] In April, 1877, Grieg had applied for a grant of 500 *spesidalers*, but despite the unanimous recommendation of the appropriate committee his application was turned down. The following year he applied again, and this time he was successful.

[42] Polish violinist Henri Wieniawski (1835–80) and Grieg performed the latter's *F-major Sonata* op. 8 at a concert in Christiania on June 2, 1877.

to make one lose one's mind—but I know perfectly well what the problem is. It's lack of practice, thus lack of technique, because I have never gotten beyond composing by fits and starts. But that is going to end. I am going to fight my way through the large musical forms, cost what it may. If I go mad in the process, now you know why. I tell you this because I know and feel that you have been more supportive of my art than most people.

The next composition that you will see from me will be a work for string instruments. I'm in the middle of it, but God knows when I will finish.[43] Just now I am once again experiencing a numbing incompetence that must be violently attacked.

Perhaps you will be out in the country when you receive these lines. In Roskilde? Greet your father[44] warmly from me. And similar greetings also to you and your dear wife.

Yours truly,
EDVARD GRIEG

8

Bergen, October 17, 1877

My dear friend!
Your warm, beautiful letter! How I enjoyed it! And how much there is in it about which you are right! How often I have felt exactly the same way! But you are not right about everything! For you must not say that since the old masters did not use national themes except now and then, therefore we should not do so either —in other words, that we should not relate differently and more closely to the national folk tunes than they did—for *that's what we are doing*. I do not think, as Gade said, that one gets tired of national music, for if that were possible it would not be an idea worth fighting for. But regarding myself, I think that I have been stagnating because of a lack of technical compositional skill, the lack of routine in general—and insufficient experience with the larger musical forms. But I can take a hint, and in one thing you are right: I won't go hunting for national themes. I intend to discard all reflection and write from the heart, whether it turns out to be Norwegian or Chinese. It is for this reason—in order to have peace and quiet to do this—that I have chosen a place like Ullensvang. In Leipzig or anyplace else down there I wouldn't get this peace and quiet. I know how, the last time I was down there, I was made unsure of myself by what I heard around me. The fact is, I dare not and will not go to Germany without having something "in my portfolio". I think that at a certain stage in one's development one must regard musical impressions just as one regards impressions of

---

43 Grieg is referring to the *String Quartet* in G minor.
44 Hans Matthison-Hansen (1807–90), organist in Roskilde cathedral.

nature: One lives on them, but one must not go searching for them and *simultaneously* try to use them in one's creative endeavors. For my experience has been that this doesn't work. Nor is it for the sake of the impressions of nature that I have chosen Hardanger. All I need is peace and quiet—but *concentrated* peace and quiet. Even if one isn't giving lessons, in a city there are parties and distractions of all kinds that would encourage indolence etc. But you must remember: It is not my intention always to isolate myself, but only at a moment that is as critical as the present moment is for me. With you it is a different matter. You live in a city that has a rich cultural life, so you don't need these endless changes. You can take everything harmoniously, peacefully.

You could have sent me a program of your provincial concerts.[45] Enclosed you will find one from me. I need money for the winter, so I'm scraping up as much as I can here in Bergen. In a few days I'll be giving a second concert, and then I will go to Lofthus (near Ullensvang), where I will spend the winter. Believe me, I have rehearsed an outstanding choir here. 120 voices, rehearsals every evening of the week. The result is spontaneity. I evoked all the nuances I was trying to get.

Now let me hear from you again soon. In any case: steady correspondence this winter. Greetings to both of you from Nina and from

Your devoted friend,
EDVARD GRIEG

9

Lofthus, February 10, 1878

My dear friend!
Yes, "this Lofthus" as you so scornfully say. But you should see "this Lofthus", see the sky-high mountains covered with snow all the way down to the fjord, see these millions of picturesque things, see and speak with the handsome, noble and enlightened farmers here. I think that then, if you could, you would transport the whole of "this Lofthus" over onto Danish soil. Still, what use could you have for "this Lofthus"—you who just travel around, play 32 public concerts and are successful? Performing in public and being successful have become so unfamiliar to me that your report comes to me as if from another world. Yes, things have been going well for you, and I am glad to hear that Tappert[46] for once has allowed the truth to be heard. And now have you also become a piano "virtuoso"? Well, then, maybe I should get to work on another piano concerto. At least one person would play it. (. . .)

---

[45] During the years 1874–77 Gottfred Matthison-Hansen had given about a hundred organ concerts at various locations throughout Denmark.

[46] German music critic Wilhelm Tappert (1830–1907), who was editor of *Allgemeine deutsche Musikzeitung* during the years 1876–80.

If I were now to tell you a little about myself I would say that I needed this bath in solitude and nature that I have gotten here. I needed an opportunity to work without interruption, and I have gotten it—more, perhaps, than is good for me. I recently finished a *String Quartet* which I still have not heard. It is in G minor and is not intended to deal in trivialities for petty minds. It aims at breadth, flight of imagination, and above all sonority for the instruments for which it is written. I needed to do this as a study. Now I will get to work on another piece of chamber music.[47] I think it is in this way that I am going to find myself again. You have no idea how much trouble I am having with the forms, but that, too, is because I was on the point of stagnating—partly as a result of spending my time on too many occasional works (*Peer Gynt, Sigurd Jorsalfar* and other disgusting things),[48] partly from altogether too much folkishness. I intend to say "Farewell, shadow" to this if I am able to. Nonetheless, just now for a change and rest after the quartet I have made some free arrangements of a few folk songs and folk dances for male voices (soloists and men's chorus)—an interesting task[49]. I need some things like that for concerts.

If only I could continue working here without interruption through the summer. But unfortunately: There is going to be a big song festival in Trondheim, with choirs from all over the country, and I have been told privately that I am going to be asked to conduct the Bergen choir for this occasion. If only I could get away to Paris to hear Berlioz's *Requiem*. That would really be something! If I knew that I could get, say, Gottfred Matthison-Hansen to go with me, I think I would burn my ships—or, more correctly, sell my shirts—to get away. No doubt you have read about all the things by Berlioz that are going to be performed. It will be totally unique.[50] But it's not worth thinking about that. Life is something other than pleasure. Still, let me not be ungrateful. There is so much that is beautiful all the same.

When shall we see each other? Do you have plans for the summer? Let me hear from you soon.

This fall I absolutely must go abroad again. We must get together then, if not before.[51]

Warm greetings to both of you from Nina and from

Yours truly,
Edvard Grieg

---

[47] In 1878 Grieg wrote a work for violin, cello and piano marked *Andante con moto* (EG 116). It was probably intended as one movement of a piano trio which, however, was never finished. The piece was printed for the first time in *Edvard Grieg: Complete Works*, vol. 9 (1978).

[48] *Peer Gynt* (Ibsen) op. 23; *Sigurd Jorsalfar* (Bjørnson) op. 22. What Grieg means by the words "and other disgusting things" is uncertain.

[49] Grieg is referring to *Album for Male Voices*.

[50] Édouard Colonne (1838–1910), conductor of the Colonne Orchestra in Paris, had taken the initiative in arranging for a Berlioz festival in the French capital. All of Berlioz's large works for choir and orchestra were performed including *Requiem* and *The Damnation of Faust*.

[51] Grieg had received a travel grant from the government that enabled him to make plans for a trip abroad.

10

Bergen, March 7, 1878

Dear friend!

I am sending these lines to ask you to do me a favor. In connection therewith I must tell you a secret, but it's a long story, so you must be patient.

In 1874 I received a request from Mr. Eduard Wagner, operator of a music store in Copenhagen, to collect and arrange *Norges Melodier* (*Norway's Melodies*) for publication by his firm.[52] The whole project had nothing to do with art. From the publisher's perspective it was purely and simply a money-making venture, and when he insisted that the collection be developed according to the "vox populi" it goes without saying that it became for me a project without any artistic interest whatsoever. I would, therefore, have pulled out of the whole mess except for the fact that I had planned a trip abroad for which I needed the money. So I went along with his proposal on the express condition that my name would not be mentioned either publicly or privately in connection with the publication. Wagner didn't want to do this, but when I told him in no uncertain terms that either I would remain anonymous or I would have nothing to do with the whole affair, he chose to go along with my demand.

I noted more than once in the course of this project what a slipshod workman I was dealing with, and I was glad when my work was finished. But what happened? Wagner went bankrupt, and just this past January I got a letter from him telling me that *Norges Melodier* had been sold by his estate in bankruptcy to Mr. S. Tachau,[53] who returned it to Mr. Wagner as part of the final settlement. These gentlemen have now come up with the clever idea of publishing a new edition "adorned with my name". Wagner writes to me in this connection that "although he has done me a favor" (!), Mr. Tachau "does not intend to let his right be curtailed;" further, that the same gentleman "forbade him to write to me, as he didn't want to request a right that he already possesses."

It's a royal mess I've gotten myself into, isn't it? Now these people think they have the law on their side, but that's an impossibility. I have spoken with attorneys here who say that the case for those fellows is so weak that the letter certainly must have been sent to me simply as an empty threat. The letter includes (unbounded depravity) a request that "for a quite sizable honorarium" I "write a Foreword of just 8–10 lines for the new edition." Isn't that the limit, to want to buy me in this way? I immediately wrote to Mr. Wagner that, in accordance with our agreement (which his letter to me dating from the time of the original contract adequately proves), I explicitly rejected his or anyone else's right to use my name in connection with the specified work and warned him that if he nonetheless chose to try the above-mentioned experiment I would be obliged to prove my right in a court of law.

---

[52] See Grieg's letter to Eduard Wagner (1846–?) of October 27, 1874.

[53] Danish businessman Sophus Tachau (?–1911).

You can see with half an eye that morally the conduct of these fellows could almost be described as villainy; I can only assume that Danish law forbids such behavior.

Now you see, then, how the matter stands. The favor that I am requesting of you is twofold: 1) to keep an eye on what these fellows do—in other words, if you see or hear of any publication of my name in connection with this matter, let me know of it at once; and 2) talk with some attorney known to you (NB in strict confidence) and find out how Danish law stands with respect to this question.

It is my hope that after receiving my letter Wagner and his friend will realize that they can't stick me in their pocket and that, accordingly, they will refrain from acting as planned. If not—if the publication of my name occurs—I will be forced first to publish a protest in the Danish press and secondly to refer the matter to an attorney.

From one point of view, namely the artistic, this is certainly more than the whole affair is worth, for I am neither worse nor better because I, like many people more important than myself, have worked for money. (You undoubtedly know about the Alberti firm in Hamburg, for which Brahms did a lot of work in his youth.) But if morality can win a victory here, then it is my duty in the interest of artists as well as that of morality to spare no expense to reach the goal. I see clearly that I will draw much more public attention to the matter than is desirable for me personally. Obviously I will get plenty of dirt on myself from the rotten company I have kept, but I don't see any other solution.

Please let me hear from you soon.

Horneman certainly knows more about Wagner's affairs than you do, but there's a possibility that he is still on friendly terms with him. In that case, to approach him about the matter would be to go straight into the lion's den. I really didn't know anyone better than you to approach, and I think you understand fully how distressing the whole case must be for me. (The Wagner letters are packed away in boxes in Christiania. Just think if I had to take a trip there on account of this matter!) Now I take a vow of silence from you, and beyond that I know that you will handle the matter as if it were your own.[54]

And with that, farewell. Greet your wife!

Yours truly,
EDVARD GRIEG

P.S. Which attorney would you recommend for this matter in case the worst occurs?

I am in the city these days to hear my *String Quartet.* I have had a caterwauling rehearsal, but I hope it will go better tomorrow.

---

[54] The issue was resolved to Grieg's satisfaction. His name did not appear on the publication until the edition of 1910—three years after Grieg's death—and even then it appeared only on the back cover.

Are you familiar with Svendsen's wonderful *Symphony* in B-flat major? You must get it—at least the version for piano four hands. It has been published by Fritzsch.[55]

11

Bergen, November 14, 1880
Sunday

Dear friend!
Thank you for your letter and because you heap coals of fire upon my head! I should have written and would have done so long ago, but to give you some idea of how busy I have been I can just mention that I have not had time to give one single lesson—which is something I had absolutely counted on. (. . .)

Now you have gotten rid of Neupert![56] I think more than one Copenhagen musician has privately rejoiced! All things considered, he has been simultaneously both underrated and overrated in your fair city. It is difficult to distinguish the artist from the person. My opinion is that where there is a human weakness, there, too, is an artistic one—in other words, the two hang together *in the highest degree.* Only when you look deeply into the matter does this hold true; for superficialities, on the other hand, absolutely not. That is why there is so much talk about the artist and the person being two different things. When I say that it is difficult to distinguish the two I mean, then, that one often fails to see the *good* sides of the artist because of the *bad* things in the human being—and vice versa. But look at Neupert. See if his lack of serenity, lack of philosophy, is not true of both the person and the artist. And see if the same is not true of his strong feeling, his passions. I prefer to dwell on the good features of both artist and man, and fortunately there are many of these features—yes, in Neupert as a human being, despite the outward appearance. He is one of those people who are *hardest on themselves*—and as everyone knows, they are *not* the *worst* people. To the contrary.

My biography is quickly told. I gave two concerts and enjoyed them immensely.[57] The same goes for Harmonien's first concert. Mrs. Erika Lie Nissen performed in Beethoven's *Fantasia* (choir of 100, orchestra 40) and played Bach's

---

[55] Johan Svendsen's *Symphony No. 2* in B-flat major was published by E. W. Fritzsch, Leipzig, in 1877.

[56] In 1868 Norwegian pianist Edmund Neupert had been engaged as a piano teacher at the newly established Music Conservatory in Copenhagen, where he remained until 1880. He then took a professorial position at the Moscow Conservatory, but remained there for only two years. He returned to Norway for about a year, then gave a long series of successful concerts in the United States in 1882 and 1883. In April 1883 he was offered a professorship in piano at the new Conservatory of Music in New York City, which he accepted. He died in New York on June 22, 1888.

[57] These two concerts took place in Bergen on September 30 and October 3, 1880. The Harmonien concerts that followed were given on October 22, November 18 and December 9, 1880. The Music Society Harmonien was the predecessor of the modern Bergen Philharmonic Orchestra.

Fantasia and Fugue in G minor. In addition to that we did Haydn's *Symphony in D Major* and Mozart's *Ave Verum*. So: a classical program. Still, the program opener showed its trend in the form of Svendsen's [*Norwegian*] *Rhapsody* in C major. The second concert (chamber music) is next Thursday and will be an evening devoted to Schumann. I will play the A-minor *Sonata* with Fries, and with John[58] I will play the *Phantasiestücke* for cello (or the clarinet pieces). Nina will sing songs, and a good amateur will perform *Die Löwenbraut*. The program will conclude with the *String Quartet* in A minor (op. 41). For the third concert (December 9th) I am working like a horse on Schubert's *Symphony* in C major, Gade's *Agnete og Havfruerne* [*Agnete and the Mermaids*] and Beethoven's *Violin Concerto*. A serious undertaking, as you can see. Thanks to my daily exercises, I've been able to manage it so far.

I have all of your things except the *Violin Sonata* and the *Cello Fantasia*, which I would be grateful to receive at your convenience.

Erika Lie Nissen will be paying you a visit after New Year's Day. If only she does not play my *Ballade*, as she hinted she might; for that she lacks many things, above all passion and—stateliness.

Goodbye for now, my very dear friend. Let me hear from you again soon.

Yours truly,
Edvard Grieg

12

Bergen, April 29, 1881

Dear friend!

Well, finally I've gotten to this point. I haven't written a friend's letter to you for three months. You have no idea what I am going through. But even if I had had time to write a letter, where should I have sent it? Because obviously you don't live on Slotsgade any more. Is it not true that you have become organist at Trinity Church?[59] Yes, you are getting higher and higher positions. You'll eventually end up on top of Rundetårn [The Round Tower]![60] Let me know where you are now and where you are planning to be—and do it soon. You should come up here this summer. Then we could go to the mountains together. For I have now decided to stay where I am, since my health could not tolerate a trip abroad. I am very happy that your stay in Hardanger has had good results, so now I can relax about that matter. Truly, that did not happen to me.

[58] Edvard's brother, John Grieg (1840–1901).

[59] Matthison-Hansen was appointed organist at Trinitatis Church in Copenhagen in 1881.

[60] The Round Tower is a tourist attraction in Copenhagen. It was built in 1637–42, partly as an astronomical observatory and partly as a tower marking the location of Trinitatis Church. It is 117 feet high and consists of two concentric masonry walls. People can climb to the top on a spiral stairway built between the two cylindrical walls. Grieg is drawing an analogy between his friend's upward progress professionally and the course of someone climbing to the top of the tower.

I don't remember if I told you in my last letter that my little hut[61] has been sold and will be moved to the mountains to be used as a hunters' cabin. So Lofthus, for me, is a thing of the past.

Yes, time passes and it yields but meager results. Would to God that this observation were the fruit of a bad stomach and nothing more, but I know full well that there is more to it than that. Now I have another 3–4 months of slave work behind me. Ten concerts since New Year's: three Harmonien concerts, two repeat concerts, three chamber-music evenings and the rest ditto for various benevolent causes. For up here an artist is used to raise the money that it is the goddam duty of every merchant to shell out. We have done some things that you would have enjoyed, though. We concluded with Mozart's *Requiem.* I began rehearsing the choir in January, and we performed it in a very respectable way three times in a row. I told myself that, when I finally was going to offer a winter to my hometown, I would do everything in my power to push the appreciation of art a step forward while I was at it. And I don't think my work has been in vain. But *I* can't take this any longer. Now somebody else will have to carry on the work.

I have not given a lesson this winter, nor have I composed a single note, so you can imagine the rest. I must admit, however, that the public has been gracious and obliging. It is only prophets who are not always honored in their own country. Other mortals do not enjoy this dubious honor. Thus the concluding concert of the season was an absolute triumph. I was greeted with an orchestral fanfare, received laurel wreaths, and flowers—and when I got home, a pretty silver vase from the women's chorus. As a result of all this I have now become so cocky that nobody can stand me. It's a good thing, therefore, that you won't see me this summer. There really was a time when I had thought of spending the summer in Denmark, but it would have had to be out in the country near Øresund.[62] And a place like that isn't available when one needs it.

I have a little attic where I am now writing these lines, and this is where I will try to do some work. Have you composed anything new? Let me hear from you soon. I am thirsting for letters from friends. Tell me about Danish artistic life, for I hear almost nothing.

Did you hear Svendsen's prelude to *Sigurd Slembe*[63] in the Music Association? It is a brilliantly powerful piece, but I miss the Nordic element.

With that, goodbye for now. Many greetings to both of you from Nina and from

Yours truly,
EDVARD GRIEG

---

[61] Grieg is referring to the little composer's hut that he used in Hardanger in 1877–78. He wrote an amusing article about it that will be printed in Benestad & Halverson (eds.), *Edvard Grieg: Diaries, Articles, Speeches* (Columbus, Ohio, 2001).

[62] Øresund is the sound between Denmark and Sweden.

[63] Johan Svendsen's *Sigurd Slembe.* Symphonic Prelude to Bjørnstjerne Bjørnson's Play.

13

Bergen, December 20, 1882

My dear friend!

I just received your letter! You sentence me to writing immediately! Truly a light sentence! Lucky the man who is always judged so mildly! Still, what can I say: My misfortune is precisely that I have been judged *too* mildly by my friends. But I won't talk about that now.

I did not enjoy my stay in Copenhagen very much this summer, not least because we didn't spend any time talking with each other. As a matter of fact, I didn't even get to say goodbye to you and to thank you for the music. My biography since then is quickly or slowly told, whichever you wish. To outward appearances my life has been as tranquil as ever, but in reality it has been a life filled with inner struggle. I have no official duties. I give a few lessons, that is all. But I am both mentally and physically ill. Every other day I decide that I will not compose another note, because I am less and less satisfied with myself. When one must struggle for technique as I must do—more and more, strangely enough—in the end the births become so difficult that they totally consume my strength. Just lately I have come to understand better than ever what it is that I am lacking. But I still have the feeling that I could overcome it if this damn stomach of mine weren't so . . .[64]

This might be a suitable occasion to say something about my great countryman, who has everything that I lack. He is in my opinion the greatest *artist* (in contrast to *poet*) in all Scandinavia—and one of the few great spirits in Europe. That is why I am surprised that you say so little about something so significant. Was Svendsen really lauded most as a conductor? If so, one can only say that the Danish musicians have let themselves be fooled by the brilliance of his conducting skills. For he is just as brilliant a composer (inventor, master of form and orchestration) as he is a conductor—indeed, even more so. But to be sure, to see this requires a somewhat broader vision. There is something that makes this Danish opinion understandable, though, and that is that Denmark has had such a complete lack of capable conductors. This has always been obvious to me; it has long been one of the main factors in keeping new currents out of Denmark. Promise me that next time you write you will tell me about *your own* impressions of Svendsen. The judgment of the general public may be interesting enough, but you surely do not pretend to anything so titanic as to represent the public.[65]

---

[64] Grieg leaves the sentence unfinished.

[65] Johan Svendsen, who conducted the orchestra of the Music Association in Christiania until 1883, had been invited to Copenhagen in 1882 to demonstrate his skills as a composer and conductor. He gave two highly successful concerts and soon thereafter was offered the position of musical director at the Royal Theater in Copenhagen. He accepted, and from 1883 until the end of his career made a brilliant contribution to Danish music life.

While I am still talking about music, I must ask you to greet Franz Neruda from me and thank him most warmly for his brilliant orchestral pieces, which, however, I know only in arrangements for piano four hands. If the instrumental versions are as good as those for piano, they are some of the most splendid pieces in this genre that one can hear. I have not had so genuine a musical delight and surprise for a long time. The themes presumably are Slavic, but that is beside the point. One thing, in general, is more and more certain: The motives are nothing, how they are handled is everything! And the way in which Neruda *lives* in his motives, how they have become his own flesh and blood—that is precisely what I admire.[66]

You certainly are wide-ranging in the programs for your organ concerts. The idea of playing Handel is excellent. It is almost at the point where Handel has to be rescued from becoming an archived relic. I wish I could have the opportunity to hear a little Bach and Handel! Yes, indeed!

Just think, I am now studying French for one hour each day. I have thought of spending next winter in Paris if nothing unforeseen comes in the way. If that idea can't be realized, I am seriously considering Copenhagen. And I am serious! For I have no desire to stay home any longer. I get altogether too melancholy and philosophical here at home! It would be wonderful to live where you do and from there look in on the rest of Europe now and then. For from here that is not possible.

It makes me very happy to hear that you like *The Mountain Thrall*, for—as I once told you—there are some drops of my heart's blood in that piece. And no one can feel this better than you, either. That is why I am so happy and proud that it bears your name.[67]

And with this, warm greetings from home to home. Merry Christmas!

Yours truly,
EDVARD GRIEG

P.S. The news of Melbye's[68] death shook me deeply. I learned of it via the newspapers.

Greet your sister most warmly from both Nina and me.

---

66 Franz Neruda (1843–1915) was a Czech cellist, conductor and composer who had made his home in Copenhagen. He was a brother of the violinist Wilhelmina Norman-Neruda. The composition to which Grieg is referring is *Aus dem Böhmerwald* (*From the Bohemian Forest*).

67 Grieg composed *The Mountain Thrall* in 1877–78. The original manuscript is preserved in Det kgl. Bibliotek (Royal Library), Copenhagen. The title page bears the following inscription in Grieg's hand: "To my friend Gottfred Matthison-Hansen in Copenhagen." The work was published by Wilhelm Hansens Musikforlag in 1882 and carries the following dedication: "Seinem Freunde Gottfred Matthison-Hansen."

68 Danish painter Vilhelm Melbye (1824–82), who is best known for his dramatic depictions of storms at sea.

14

Bergen, March 27, 1885

Dear old friend!

Yes, you are right! The intermission was indeed long. It was almost "Beethovenian!" And now, therefore, I am going to give you the pleasure of setting myself down right away and telling about my long trip. Yes, that is what I would like to do, but let me rather *stand* here by my desk, which is more to my taste.

It was in July *1883* that I disappeared from home and headed for Bayreuth to hear *Parsifal.*[69] *July 1883*! It's a long story. I advise you not to do as I am doing; just sit quietly on your sofa. My first stop en route to Bayreuth was at Rudolstadt in Thüringen, where a young Belgian friend and brilliant musician by the name of Van der Stucken[70] was staying. We traveled together to Bayreuth and back again. I then stayed in Rudolstadt for a couple of months, where I mainly spent my time practicing the piano.

In September I went to Leipzig and then to Weimar, where I started my concert tour with a subscription concert on October 1. The program included my *Piano Concerto*, solo pieces, and some short pieces for string orchestra. It was a marvelous beginning, and for that I can certainly thank Liszt more than anyone. I tell you, his attitude toward me was incomparably nice.

Then back to Leipzig, which was the central point from which, like a spider, I surveyed my whole web. There I joined [Julius] Klengel in a performance of my *Cello Sonata* at a Gewandhaus soiree; I had performed the same piece in Dresden with Grützmacher.[71] At the beginning of November I went to Meiningen, where I performed in an orchestra concert and also presented a program of chamber music. Here I was as snug as a bug in a rug, for Bülow[72] was all kindness, as was also his protector, the grand duke. Yes, before it was over the grand duke decorated me with the inevitable "Hausorden" First Class.[73]

Then came Breslau, where I again gave two concerts (with Bruch,[74] a boring

---

69 Wagner's music-drama *Parsifal.*

70 American-born conductor and composer Frank van der Stucken (1858–1929) had moved with his parents to Antwerp in 1865. In 1884, after studies in Antwerp and Leipzig and professional work in Breslau, he returned to the United States as conductor of the Arion Society of New York City and in 1895 became the first conductor of the Cincinnati Symphony Orchestra. He was an important link between the music life of Europe and that of the United States, conducting the American premieres of works by such composers as Johannes Brahms (1833–97) and Hector Berlioz (1803–69) and introducing European audiences to the compositions of Edward MacDowell (1860–1908) and other American composers. Grieg wrote an article about him that appeared in the Leipzig journal *Musikalisches Wochenblatt* in 1883. It will be printed in English translation in Benestad & Halverson (eds.), *Edvard Grieg: Diaries, Articles, Speeches* (Columbus, Ohio, 2001).

71 Grieg premiered his *Cello Sonata* in collaboration with the German cellist Friedrich Grützmacher (1832–1903) at the Tonkünstlerverein in Dresden on October 22, 1883. The performance in Leipzig with Julius Klengel (1859–1933) took place on October 27.

72 German conductor and pianist Hans von Bülow (1830–94), who was leader of the court orchestra in Meiningen at this time.

73 On November 12 in Meiningen Grieg was awarded *Der Herzoglich Sächsische Ernestinische Hausorden.*

74 German composer Max Bruch (1838–1920).

pendulum). In December I went to Cologne and Karlsruhe, then to Holland, where in the space of four days I "absolved" Arnheim, The Hague, Rotterdam and Amsterdam. That was strenuous: each day travel, rehearsal and concert! But then I was done, too. And that was bad. The thing is, I had applied for a grant at home to enable me to go to Paris. When I didn't get it, I became furious and swore that I would raise the money in some other way. That's why I took that concert tour. After the concert in Amsterdam was over I found myself in possession of 3,000 crowns in cash. But what good was this money to me now? I was so worn out that I had to say no to both Colonne in Paris and the Philharmonic Society in London.

So I spent Christmas in Amsterdam with my talented young friend Julius Röntgen.[75] After resting there for four weeks I sent a telegram to Nina, who met me in Leipzig.[76] We went together to Rome, where I spent the winter and spring. That was a wonderful time despite the fact that I, weakened as I was, absolutely could not tolerate the southern climate. I did, however, give a memorable concert at the Capitol which was attended by people of many nationalities and which I, too, enjoyed immensely.[77] What amiable, unbiased and gifted artists there are among the younger generation down here! Sgambati[78] is a talent of the first order. Boito, unfortunately, I did not meet.[79] But when Italy can boast two talents like that, one can certainly say that music is alive and well in young Italy.

In June I finally came home and hid myself away in Lofthus until November, when I came here to spend the winter months. First I had to rehearse and conduct a cantata in connection with the unveiling of the Holberg monument [EG 171]. Since Christmas, to tell the truth, I have been more of a construction engineer than a musician. I'm building a small villa on Nordåsvannet, about five miles from Bergen. It is supposed to be finished by the middle of April, at which time I intend to move up there. You can understand how much that gives me to do. All my ideas, musical and unmusical, now have to do with Troldhaugen (the name of the villa). Just yesterday I wrote to Peters in Leipzig telling him[80] that if he wanted anything from me he had better go there armed with pick and shovel and dig for scores.

There you have it—my biography in brief. Are you satisfied? I hope so. I'll save all the details until we meet personally. But when will that be? I have a secret

[75] Dutch composer, pianist and conductor Julius Röntgen (1855–1932) was Grieg's closest friend in The Netherlands.

[76] Edvard and Nina were having serious marital problems at this time, and it was only through the mediating efforts of their close friend Frants Beyer (1851–1919) that they were reconciled. Frants and Marie Beyer (1852–1929) celebrated the reconciliation with Edvard and Nina by taking a trip with them to Rome.

[77] The concert at the residence of the German ambassador on Capitoline Hill in Rome took place on March 15, 1884.

[78] Giovanni Sgambati, Italian pianist and composer.

[79] Arrigo Boito (1842–1918), Italian composer and author best known as the composer of the opera *Mefistofele*. Boito was also the librettist for Verdi's two last operas, *Otello* and *Falstaff*.

[80] Grieg is referring to Dr. Max Abraham (1831–1900), proprietor of C. F. Peters.

but weak hope of going south for the winter, in which case I would stop off in Copenhagen for a month en route. But it may be that Troldhaugen will devour all my resources this summer, and then I will have to be content to stay where I am for the winter.

If only you knew how strongly I often long for you, Horneman, Winding and the few friends from the old days. We must get together again! I will not lose sight of this idea.

Thanks for the message about *The Mountain Thrall*, which made me very happy—also with respect to the relationship with Gade, by whom I consider myself—unworthy person that I am—forgotten or repudiated.

Do you ever see Svendsen, or does he spend all his time with the royal court and people with silk gloves? It's a good thing that there are various tastes in the world. I think it is healthier to do as you do: to associate with Bach and Handel. Yes, they are people who become greater with each year that one lives. I recently heard the Bach motet *Jesu meine Freude* [BWV 227] performed up here in our "kennel"—but it was a good performance, and I was deeply moved by the magnificent art.

Last week, to find out if I was still a musician, I gave a concert. I'll enclose a copy of the program. As you will see, the *Holberg Suite* is a work for string orchestra.[81]

So much for this time. Let us now become more sedate!

Warm greetings to both of you from Nina and from

Yours truly,
EDVARD GRIEG

15

Troldhaugen, September 6, 1895

Dear friend!

We have been rather concerned about you, so your letter was doubly welcome. Neither Horneman nor Winding wrote anything about you. From that we merely concluded that you were in Jutland.[82] Poor you, who were confined to a sickroom in the interesting town of Kristiansand![83] Still, now all the misfortunes are behind you, and you two are once again back in your good old Denmark. I cannot tell you how happy I am to have had you up here—doubly so because with you there is no admixture of bitterness in the memory.[84]

---

81 The concert to which Grieg refers took place on March 12, 1885, in Bergen. *Holberg Suite* was originally written for piano, but the arrangement for strings was made almost simultaneously and was published before the piano version.

82 Jutland is the peninsula comprising the continental portion of Denmark.

83 Kristiansand is a seaport on the south coast of Norway.

84 Horneman, Matthison-Hansen and Winding and their wives all came to Troldhaugen as guests of the Griegs. Unfortunately, for reasons that Grieg was never able to understand, a feeling of ill will developed between him and Horneman in the course of the visit that permanently poisoned their friendship. See Grieg's letter to August Winding of August 16, 1895.

My travel report since we were last together is quickly told. We traveled via Voss, Stalheim, Gudvangen and Lærdal to Skjolden, which is situated at the end of the Lusterfjord. From there—sometimes walking, sometimes riding—we climbed 3,500 feet to Turtegrø, right below the Skagastøl peaks. Here we spent a day the likes of which has not occurred all summer—splendid weather and the view, indescribable. We had a good breakfast at twelve o'clock and then climbed a mountain called Helgedalsnåset. It was from here that we had a view such as one rarely sees. Then we came down and had a good dinner at seven o'clock in the evening. But by the next morning it was already raining, so I made a quick decision. Down to Skjolden again, board the steamship and head straight for home. A decision I have had no reason to regret, for the weather since then has been uniformly terrible. I daresay that today is the first real sunny day. And still I have been thriving up here. I have been busy with work, swimming and gathering nuts.

I have been pondering how I should organize my *Haugtussa* music, for the text unfortunately creates obstacles that I have not yet managed to overcome.[85] And there is nobody in the whole country of Norway that I know who understands these things.

I'll be leaving here at the end of this month. Unfortunately we won't see each other in the near future, as I won't be stopping in Copenhagen. I have to be in Leipzig at the beginning of October.

Nina sends warm greetings, as does also

Sincerely yours,
EDVARD GRIEG

16

Leipzig, November 25, 1895
Hotel Hauffe

Dear friend!
I have at this moment just returned from Dessau, where we went last evening to hear a religious work, *Todtenfeier,* by my friend Herzogenberg.[86] It is a very beautiful piece in the spirit of Bach and Brahms. I recommend it for performance in Copenhagen. A choir, orchestra, soloists and organ performed absolutely splendidly under Klughardt's[87] leadership in the little town of Dessau (ca. 18,000 people).

I daresay that I have rarely heard orchestral music performed as perfectly as this time in Leipzig. But then the brilliant conductor Nikisch has replaced the

---

[85] Grieg's *The Mountain Maid,* a song cycle based on texts by Norwegian author Arne Garborg (1851–1924). Garborg's *Haugtussa* was published in spring, 1895, and Grieg was completely enthralled with the *nynorsk* poetry of his countryman.

[86] German composer Heinrich von Herzogenberg (1853–1900). *Todtenfeier* was a cantata written in 1894.

[87] The German composer and conductor August Klughardt (1847–1902) began working in Dessau in 1882.

decidedly unbrilliant Reinecke.[88] And then the programs! Recently they did Tchaikovsky's last symphony, *Pathétique*, a piece with strange lines and enormous tragic power. It is definitely the greatest thing Tchaikovsky ever wrote.

Just the other day I heard a great work that affected me more than usual, even though the performance was not of top quality. The performance was by a military band. The work was the oratorio *Les Béatitudes*—or *Die Seligpreisungen*, as the Germans translate it—by César Franck.[89] Yes, it is without doubt written by a master so great that in my opinion there is not another man living who is his equal. It is impossible to compare him with Brahms, inasmuch as Brahms's church music is built on a Protestant foundation whereas Franck's is built on a Catholic one. *Les Béatitudes* is one single, unified inspiration that lasts for two and a half hours! That says something. I don't understand those Frenchmen with their Berlioz cult when they have César Franck, who has more genuine music in his little finger than Berlioz has in his whole body.

I have followed music developments in Copenhagen through *Politiken*.[90] In fact, I am longing to be there with you. That is, after all, my winter home, where I prefer to work in peace and quiet and where I have the deepest personal connections. My hope is that fate will bring us to you around New Year's. In the meantime England remains a possibility, but my preference is not to go there.

Norway will reign in the Gewandhaus on December 19, when Nikisch will perform Svendsen's *Symphony* in B-flat major and my *Peer Gynt Suite*.[91] Send us a friendly thought on that date. Other times as well!! Yes, I know you do that, you dear, old friend.

Warmest greetings to the two of you both from Nina and from

Yours truly,
Edvard Grieg

17

Troldhaugen, October 25, 1901

Dear friend!
I should have written earlier, but I haven't been able to. I have lived through a sad time. My brother John died suddenly fourteen days ago. And the worst thing is that they found him in his woodshed with a bullet in his head. Why make a secret of it? So says his admirable wife, and I agree. In any case I will leave it to

---

[88] In 1895 the Hungarian-German conductor Arthur Nikisch (1855–1922) had replaced Grieg's old teacher at the Leipzig conservatory, Carl Reinecke (1824–1910), as conductor of the Gewandhaus orchestra.

[89] Belgian-French composer César Franck (1822–90).

[90] *Politiken* is a Copenhagen newspaper.

[91] Johan Svendsen's *Symphony No. 2* in B-flat major and Grieg's *Peer Gynt Suite No. 1*. The concert proved to be a disappointment for Grieg, however, for Nikisch fell ill and the concert was conducted instead by Hans Sitt (1850–1922), a conductor whom Grieg once described as a man possessing "respectable proficiency without a trace of brilliance."

the fat clergymen to judge and condemn. John had been very melancholy and downcast of late, felt tired and overworked, but would not go to the doctor despite all the entreaties. But what happened came, nonetheless, like a bolt out of the blue. The autopsy showed severe calcification in the heart, brain and arteries, which in the doctors' opinion explains everything. Poor fellow! How he must have suffered before he made this decision!

But I am such a heathen that after a death such as this he is more significant in my eyes than he was when he was alive. I can't fully understand it, but that's the way it is. When a life is over it acquires a character that makes it more sterling and consistent for me than before. How strange! One does not understand the living. One judges a living person on the basis of one's own presuppositions —and of course one is always wrong. Then comes death. And one understands. It is an understanding that costs dearly. It tells us that we must use the time we have left—use it to judge gently, gently, gently!

Dear friend, it is so good to have someone with whom to talk. And you are the only one. Yesterday I was given some letters that I had written to John, and I find that in those dating from my early youth (1864–65) your name is frequently mentioned. That is what led me at this very moment to sit down at my writing table. You and John had common acquaintances in Dresden. Once you urgently wanted to know the address of the Heinke girls. (That whole family is now gone.) It appears that you knew John, and as a matter of fact he was also in Copenhagen for a short time—I think it was in 1864, when we lived in Larslejstrædet.[92]

We have decided, Nina and I, to stay home until after Christmas in order to be of some help to John's poor survivors. Then we will go to Christiania and hopefully on to Copenhagen. It is only since the day before yesterday that I have begun to recover my old self, which has been absent. Sleepless nights and physical and mental suffering have rendered existence up here between the mountains more than crushing. Fortunately we are having the most marvelous autumn—glorious weather with colors that defy any attempt to describe them.

Just before the catastrophe I gave two concerts. The first was a Grieg concert in which just Nina and I made music. Then we did a Nordraak concert to raise money for his monument. I greatly enjoyed both concerts in every way.[93]

Then came the blow, and in the fourteen days since then I have scarcely touched the instrument. Like a restless spirit I have gone back and forth by train to see my poor sister-in-law and the children. But now I must try to get a little peace and quiet up in the attic room (the one where the Windings stayed).[94] I

---

[92] Larslejstrædet is a street in Copenhagen.

[93] Grieg's friend and fellow composer Rikard Nordraak had died of tuberculosis in 1866. The concerts to which Grieg refers took place in Bergen on October 1 and 5, 1901.

[94] Grieg is referring to the visit in the summer of 1895 by August Winding, Emil Horneman and Gottfred Matthison-Hansen and their wives.

have moved the piano, the music scores and all the other stuff up there from my hut down in Trolddalen.

Well, that's the news about me and mine. I know that you and [your wife] Helga are vitally interested in our welfare; that is why I did not hesitate to go into detail when it had to do with the serious side of life.

Yes, that was a *memento mori.*[95] The ring is broken. I will soon follow. I definitely feel it. But I would have to have lost my mind if it were to happen in the way John chose. It is true, I cannot endure *physical* suffering. May it be bearable when it comes!

If I get to Copenhagen again, I will look forward more than ever to sitting with you and talking about things both old and new.

But—I can say with Holberg[96]—there I see her coming! Nina is going to take the train, and I am going with her and shall hope to come upon some "motive" or other out in the glorious out-of-doors!

Warmest greetings to both of you, also from Nina!

Your old
EDVARD GRIEG

18

Christiania, December 14, 1902
Hotel Victoria

Dear friend!
Yes, here you have the traitor who was not present for your 70th.[97] That was a shame, but there was nothing I could do about it. Many things came together to prevent me from going. I gave two concerts in Bergen and had to wait for the hall.[98] By the time I finally came here the day was long past. Naturally I caught a cold on the trip—we came by way of Fagernes—so by the time we got to Christiania I was sick. Fortunately I didn't have a hard bronchitis attack, but nonetheless I had to postpone an announced concert for almost fourteen days. Now I have given two concerts.[99] Nina sang at the second of these. In the first one the singer was Marta Sandal, whom you may have heard in Copenhagen.[100] She is a singular and gifted phenomenon.

Yesterday we were at a Bjørnson festival in the Student Association, where Nina also sang my Bjørnson songs, and Tuesday we collaborated in a program

[95] *Memento mori*: "remember that you shall die".
[96] Norwegian playwright Ludvig Holberg (1684–1754).
[97] Matthison-Hansen celebrated his 70th birthday on November 1, 1902.
[98] The concerts in Bergen took place on October 24 and 26, 1902.
[99] The concerts in Christiania took place on November 23 and December 5, 1902.
[100] Grieg had heard the Norwegian singer Marta Sandal Bransen (1878–1931) in Copenhagen and had been so impressed that he engaged her for a concert in Christiania.

for an audience of 5,000 to raise money for the unemployed, whose number this year is greater than ever.

These Bjørnson festival days have been incomparably wonderful and grandiose.[101] All the political parties have come together to honor the dear, great author and patriot—and that is significant for us up here, believe me. We need a symbol of unity. How great it is that now in his old age *he* has become that symbol—he who has so often been a symbol of division among us. That is a good outcome of a life!

I forgot to reserve our old rooms in Hotel Phoenix[102] in time—especially my work room—and now everything has been rented out. That's how it is. I simply can't risk going to Copenhagen at this time of year without the prospect of a modest home. We will stay here through Christmas and then we'll see what fate has in store for us.

In March I will be conducting in Prague, in April in Warsaw and Paris. I hope to be able to spend February in Denmark. (. . .)

Your devoted
EDVARD AND NINA GRIEG

19

Troldhaugen, June 29, 1904

Dear friend!
(. . .) I have done absolutely nothing for you. I have now and then given myself pleasure. That is all. For that matter, I totally disagree with Georg Brandes, who says that love is "to make another happy!" Hell, no! Love is to make oneself happy.[103] That is the big secret that Christianity will not admit: that egoism lurks even within love—insofar as it produces contentment and a feeling of happiness. For that reason, however, egoism is also, ideally, a genuine article when it is expressed sincerely and not—like margarine! You cannot imagine how grateful I have felt toward you ever since my youth! I have you to thank for so many good and fortunate impulses. And you, dear friend, have a quite distinctively private chamber in my heart. It seems to me as if our art has been interwoven in appreciation and understanding in quite a rare way. Sacred feelings such as that are the most beautiful things life has to offer.

And there is one thing more. The few friends I have had are falling away like

---

[101] Christiania celebrated "Bjørnson Festival Days" in honor of the 70th birthday of Norwegian author Bjørnstjerne Bjørnson.

[102] Hotel Phoenix was in Copenhagen.

[103] Danish scholar and literary critic Georg Brandes (1842–1927). Matthison-Hansen had thanked Grieg for an invitation to him and his wife to come to Lofthus as guests of the Griegs. The visit occurred in July–August, 1904.

leaves in autumn. Either they die or—they desert me. All the more ardently do I cling to the best ones I have left! (. . .)

Yours truly,
EDVARD GRIEG

20

Troldhaugen, August 29, 1905

Dear friend! Dear friends!
I am a scum-bag. No excuses will help. Your dear postcard has been lying here for a long time accusing me. But the problem is that I am so busy with business letters—appeals and requests that must be answered—that to tell the truth I, with the limited strength that remains, totally lose the desire to write any more letters, because the job requires such enormous effort. That was not the case in the past. The influenza that I had this winter was, for me, a bad guest—yes, worse than any I have ever had before. We have both been spared any real sickness this summer, but I can't seem to get my strength back, and I feel a hundred years old—at the very least! Nonetheless, I have tugged and jerked at the bit in Pegasus's mouth for so long that he had to get moving. But it went for me as Emil Horneman once said regarding Johan Selmer[104] after a performance of the choral piece *Nordens Ånd* [*The Nordic Spirit*]. He said, "The mountains tremble, a mouse is born!" And my mouse is so tiny that one needs glasses to see it. It is just a volume of piano pieces to throw into the jaws of Mammon. It is bait for Peters in Leipzig to get him to print two orchestral scores without complaint. But with this "mouse" I have realized for the first time that I have aged. Pegasus had to be handled in a quite peculiar way just to get him to obey sufficiently to make any progress at all. There are some two-year-old Norwegian pieces that I like, but it is not my heart's blood that has flowed in the rest of these pieces.[105]

Well, the blood does flow elsewhere in the body—for example, in the place where Homer, Hæmor, Horace and other poets hang out! Ow![106]

(. . .) Here in Norway we are living in a great, rich time and I am happy that I have survived to experience it.[107] If I were just ten years younger I'm sure it would have found expression in a composition! But I cannot find tones to express what I feel, and chauvinistic art is something I hate like the plague. So it's better to remain silent. I hope there may be young people among us who understand

---

[104] Norwegian composer Johan Selmer (1844–1910).

[105] The little "mouse" is *Moods*, which proved to be Grieg's last composition for piano. The volume includes seven pieces. The orchestral works which Grieg hoped to get Peters to publish—and which were, in fact, published in 1905—were *Old Norwegian Melody with Variations*, which was originally written in 1890 for two pianos, and *Lyric Suite*, which is an orchestral version of four of the pieces in *Lyric Pieces V* from 1891.

[106] This is a play on words. What Grieg is saying is that he is bothered by hemorrhoids.

[107] Grieg is alluding to the fact that Norway was on the verge of winning its independence from the Swedish crown.

that a time such as this creates a responsibility to perform great spiritual exploits also in the realm of art!

In the middle of October we will go to Christiania, where we will stay for awhile. I have had to decline an invitation to conduct two concerts in Helsinki in the middle of September, as I cannot travel through Sweden without risking mistreatment and expulsion. Isn't that incredible? They won't perform [Bjørnstjerne] Bjørnson's dramas, and when my music is played they hiss and demonstrate against it. Norway treats all Swedes with the greatest courtesy. I think this contrast shows clearly who has the bad and who the good conscience!

No, enough for now. Many greetings to both of you from both of us.

Yours truly,
EDVARD GRIEG

21

Christiania, December 12, 1905
Hotel Westminster

Dear friend!
In front of me, despite all my effort, lies a whole stack of still unanswered business letters. That friendly letters have for that reason been postponed is shameful, so now I am going to forget about business and write to my friends. I don't understand how other people manage. I do almost nothing except write letters, and still my stack of unanswered letters is much greater than I can handle—despite the fact that I leave many letters unanswered. What, for example, shall one do with something like this: A Danish composer sends me a volume of songs and requests that I give him a statement for publication to the effect that he is "one of the real composers, such as one seldom meets." What, then, if I find that he is in fact "one of those who has only the tiniest shred of talent, of whom there are dozens?" In truth, it is a confounded task. Here the songs lie week after week, and I can't formulate an answer. I should be much more thick-skinned than I am.

Yes, the older I get the stranger life seems to me! Presumably the same is true for you. One must decrease the demands on one's own talents and above all on others! One should become more and more liberal, more and more empathetic, otherwise life would be incomprehensible and intolerable. But then the thick skin I talked about wouldn't be appropriate. No, let us be glad for the thin skin we have nonetheless!

I was sorry to learn from Helga's letter to Nina that you can't expect to receive the 800.[108] I hope you can manage without them! I know well enough that there are many ways to cut down. For example: You can get along without

---

[108] Matthison-Hansen had hoped to receive a pension of 800 Danish crowns annually from the Conservatory in Copenhagen.

parties; the theater and concerts can be dispensed with as well. After all, these things live in our imagination, and besides, we need peace and quiet in the evening. I once asked Brahms if he wasn't interested in hearing an excellent performance of his *Ernste Lieder*,[109] which he himself had never heard. This was in Vienna. But he answered, "No, it is enough for me to think to myself how Stockhausen[110] would have sung them." How characteristic! That was the satisfied old man speaking. And it's good that things are the way they are. There is something for each stage of life. Nature's wisdom is impressive in its versatility.

And now Norway can thank Denmark for a royal couple who are the soul of amiability, tranquility and directness. If we ourselves don't corrupt them, they will become precisely what we need: a *modern* royal couple[111] who will be no more than the symbol of the people's freedom and unity. Yes, how luck has been with us through this whole process! It is phenomenal.

Now, dear friends, live as well as your age permits and let us, if possible, soon hear from you, even if it be only a few lines!

Your devoted friend,
EDVARD GRIEG

22

Christiania, December 19, 1906
Hotel Westminster

Dear friend!
Thank you because you are a little lonesome for your old friend! The same is true with me. During recent days I have written to you in my thoughts each day. But now you beat me to it. When one gets old, I don't think it is as important to create as to live. Therefore I am glad that you have lived and heard so much that is excellent. To let that which is great affect one as in days gone by, to feel that it does that—therein is a blessedness that reconciles one with old age. That is what I miss up here, the opportunity to hear repeated everything from the great period. We are good at following that which is new: We hear Richard Strausss, Weingartner, Hugo Wolf—yes, even the Frenchman Debussy (a notable brilliance and boldness in the handling of harmony), not to mention the beautiful music of Finnish composer Sibelius.[112]

---

[109] Johannes Brahms's *Vier ernste Gesänge* op. 121.

[110] German baritone Julius Stockhausen (1826–1906), to whom Brahms dedicated his *Magelone-Lieder*, sang the baritone solo at the world premiere of Brahms's *Ein deutsches Requiem* in 1868.

[111] King Haakon VII (1872–1957) and Queen Maud (1869–1938) came to Norway on November 25, 1905. The grandiose welcome culminated with a festival event at the National Theater three days later that featured a performance of Bjørnson's drama *Sigurd Jorsalfar* with incidental music by Grieg. After the performance, Bjørnson and Grieg were called up to the royal box.

[112] Richard Strausss (1864–1949), Felix Weingartner (1863–1942), Hugo Wolf (1860–1903), Claude Debussy (1862–1918), Jean Sibelius (1865–1957).

What I miss, first of all, is chamber music, for which there is no feeling up here. And then the great choral works! But of course, one cannot have everything. I am grateful that I can keep going as well as I do here in Norway as long as I exercise great care. I have completed some *Psalms* for mixed chorus *a cappella* and [baritone] solo; they are free arrangements of old Norwegian religious tunes.[113] Would that I could find time one day to copy one of them for you. There is a moving depth and sincerity in these old melodies that tempted me to make love to them. It was an enjoyable project.

Our provisional plan is to leave here in March. I have invitations from Berlin, Munich, Paris, Prague, Budapest, Bucharest, Graz and Kiel. But how many of these I can manage is known only to the gods. I will probably give up on the most distant cities. Berlin, Munich and Prague are definite, and perhaps I will also go to Paris. It is on the way home from these places that I hope to make a stop in Copenhagen to greet old friends.[114]

Yes, now it is you and Steenberg[115] who are left from the beautiful time of youth, when the air and the sea and the beech forest on lovely Zealand were filled with music and beauty. How strange! Presumably they were no more beautiful than they are now. But we made everything beautiful because we ourselves read all our striving for beauty into the landscape and the folk life, into the saga and the history. The fact that we ourselves were so full of beauty—that was the secret! And this has been enough to live on for an entire lifetime. Shame on us if we are not filled with gratitude for that!

Farewell, then, you two dear ones! A merry Christmas, albeit with the gentle wistfulness of old age, is wished for you by Nina and

Your faithful friend,
EDVARD GRIEG

---

[113] *Four Psalms,* Grieg's last composition.

[114] Grieg's final concert tour in 1907 included the following cities: Christiania, January 12; Copenhagen, March 21 and 26; Munich, April 6; Berlin, April 12 and 14; and Kiel, April 26—his last public concert.

[115] Danish singer Julius Steenberg (1830–1911), a friend from Grieg's youth.

To Willem Mengelberg

The Dutch conductor Willem Mengelberg (1871–1951), after a brief stint as musical director of the municipal orchestra in Lucerne, Switzerland, returned to his homeland in 1895 to become conductor of the Concertgebouw Orchestra of Amsterdam, which had been established in 1888. Mengelberg continued in this position until 1945. He succeeded in making the Concertgebouw one of the finest orchestras on the continent and was sought out as a guest conductor by orchestras all over the world.

While giving concerts in Amsterdam in 1897, Grieg was astounded at the quality of Mengelberg's orchestra and eventually arranged for the group to perform as the featured ensemble at the Norwegian music festival in Bergen in the summer of 1898.

The German originals of Grieg's two extant letters to Mengelberg (one of which is included here) are preserved in 'collection Haags Gemeentemuseum, The Hague.

Copenhagen, April 28, 1898
Hotel King of Denmark

Dear Maestro!
On behalf of the Norwegian composers, I wish to express my deepest gratitude for the interest and appreciation you show them when rehearsing their works. We are all happy to know that our compositions are in your hands.[1]

As regards the music for both piano concertos,[2] *Olav Trygvason* and the songs with orchestra [EG 177], I am still awaiting word from Mr. Hutschenruyter.[3] With *Variasjoner for Orkester*, the composition by Catharinus Elling[4] sent to you most recently, the program is complete. Hopefully everything is in order.

I greatly look forward to the pleasure of welcoming you to Norway! Then we must *really* get to know each other—something that, to my regret, we did not have an opportunity to do in Amsterdam. Yes, it surely *will* be wonderful. I bid you a warm, warm welcome!

With sincere greetings, I am

Yours truly,
EDVARD GRIEG

---

[1] Grieg is speaking here of the Norwegian music festival held in Bergen June 26–July 3, 1898, in which the Concertgebouw Orchestra had responsibility for the orchestral works. During the festival, with few exceptions the Norwegian composers conducted their own works.

[2] Piano concertos by Grieg and Christian Sinding (1856–1941).

[3] Willem Hutschenruyter (1859–1943) was the administrator of the Concertgebouw Orchestra.

[4] Norwegian composer Catharinus Elling (1858–1942).

To Johannes Messchaert

The Dutch baritone and singing teacher Johannes Messchaert (1857–1922) was very highly regarded as a concert and oratorio singer. In 1911 he became professor of singing at the Königlische Hochschule für Musik in Berlin. In 1920 he moved to Zurich, Switzerland, where he taught at the conservatory.

Grieg had an exceptionally high opinion of Messchaert as a singer but rarely had an opportunity to use him at his own concerts. Messchaert did, however, perform frequently in collaboration with their mutual friend Julius Röntgen (1855–1932).

Grieg's letters to Messchaert, which were written in German, are preserved in Archiefdienst Westfriese Gemeenten, Hoorn, The Netherlands.

1

Lofthus, August 26, 1884

My dear and esteemed Mr. Messchaert!

Thank you so much for your letter. I am very happy that you have taken home with you such a good impression of Norway. I always say that anyone who has a heart that is open to beauty and grandeur must find this country surpassingly beautiful.

I have not yet heard anything from Röntgen, but I hope he is of the same opinion as you and that things are going well for him.

You probably received a picture of me some time ago. Now you are going to hear the funny story about this picture. I got a package from Bergen, opened it and found a lithograph of me without an explanation of any kind. "Ha, ha," I thought, "that's the picture that belongs to Mr. Messchaert." I immediately packed it back up, attached your address and dispatched it to Holland. The following day I got a letter from Mr. Musin,[1] a Belgian violinist who was traveling through Bergen. He had sent me the lithograph—which I had mailed off to Holland—in order that I might sign it! Now it was hard to know what to do. Fortunately I went in to Bergen a few days later, apologized to Mr. Musin for the theft and straightened things out.

Believe me, we have often spoken of you and your beautiful singing! Come back soon![2] In so doing you would please both my wife and

Your devoted colleague and friend,
EDVARD GRIEG

---

[1] Ovide Musin (1854–1929).

[2] Johannes Messchaert and Julius Röntgen had visited Grieg together in Lofthus, Hardanger, in the summer of 1884. Thereafter they traveled around in West Norway, venturing as far north as Trondheim. They returned to Holland by way of Christiania and Copenhagen. On September 8 Röntgen wrote Grieg a twelve-page thank-you letter describing in glowing terms what they had experienced on the trip.

2

Odnes Hotel, October 29, 1898

My dear mastersinger and friend!
I have become older—and wiser. In other words: In the face of a mastersinger such as you, I cannot under any circumstances remain "untransposed". Knowing that some of my songs are to be sung by you is such happy news that as far as I am concerned you may sing all my songs in P minor! I had secretly hoped that something from this cycle might fit your voice, and I have on several occasions expressed that very hope to my wife.[3]

Maybe we can meet in Copenhagen and come to some agreement about the selection. I also advise you to sing in German.

We are very happy that all is going well for you and that things seem to be improving for your wife.

Yes, in life it is exactly as in music: major—and minor. I for my part am living at the moment in a minor mood.

On October 12 we left Bergen to go to Copenhagen by way of Christiania. On the very first day of the trip I got chilled on the steamship, and after three days of carriage travel I got so sick (bronchitis) that I had to interrupt the trip and have been in bed here for ten days.

For a couple of days now I have been able to breathe fresh air for half an hour at a time. If I continue to improve, we hope to be able to continue our journey on November 1. After a few days' stay in Christiania we plan to go on to Copenhagen, and we look forward like children to the days we hope to spend there with you and Julius.[4]

Now I am sweating from the exertion. I haven't improved beyond that. So I must conclude. Cordial greetings to you, your wife and the child. I ask you also to greet Julius and his wife.

A happy reunion is anticipated by

Yours truly,
EDVARD GRIEG

P.S. My wife sends her warmest greetings!

How thankful I would be if you could show the people of Copenhagen how Munch's "Cradle Song" (in G-sharp minor) ought to be sung.[5] They don't have the slightest idea!

---

[3] Grieg is probably referring here to *Five Songs by Vilhelm Krag* op. 60, which he had dedicated to Messchaert. He usually did not like it when singers transposed his songs.

[4] In November, 1898, Messchaert and Röntgen gave concerts in Copenhagen for the first time. Grieg had earlier written a laudatory article in the Copenhagen press and the concerts were sell-outs.

[5] Grieg is referring to "Cradle Song" op. 9 no. 2, a setting of a text by the Norwegian poet Andreas Munch (1811–84).

3

Copenhagen, March 2, 1901
Hotel Phoenix

Dear Messchaert!
How wonderful it was to hear directly from you again! I knew through Julius that you had been sick but that you were well again. If only I could have taken a little trip to Berlin and met you at the Bach festival. Unfortunately, my health is not good. I have had to stay in my room for eight days because of the damned bronchitis.

We had a nice time at Voksenkollen Sanatorium near Christiania—1600 feet above sea level, with a marvelous view and light, clean air in the middle of a pine forest. But since coming here, everything has changed. I am constantly obliged to postpone my concert and have had to decline invitations to England and Holland. When will it come about that I shall be sitting at the piano while you sing? Ah well, I live in the constant hope.

How comical that the songs you have selected from among the new ones are the two little ones, "To My Son" and "At Mother's Grave". I had thought that the ones that I consider the most important of the lot—"Eros", "A Life of Longing" and "A Poet's Song"—were as if written for your voice.[6] Nina was of the same opinion. But perhaps you no longer sing the more flamboyant songs with as much interest as you do the more delicate, intimate ones. It is far too long since I have heard you sing. When will you be touring Norway again?

I am very much enjoying some of Posa's[7] songs. They have something very different from the empty, reflected artificiality of Richard Strauss's[8] songs, which are now being so ridiculously touted. In general: the young Germany and advertisements! I'm glad not to be a part of it.

Warm greetings, also to your dear wife and child, from Nina and from

Your friend and admirer,
EDVARD GRIEG

---

6 Grieg is referring to *Five Songs* op. 69 nos. 2 and 3 and *Five Songs* op. 70 nos. 1, 2 and 5. Both opuses were settings of texts by Otto Benzon.

7 Austrian composer Oscar C. Posa (1873–1951).

8 German composer Richard Strauss (1864–1949). Grieg admired his technique but by and large did not think well of his compositions, which he found artificial and ponderous.

To Oscar Meyer

The German pianist and composer Oscar Meyer (1865–1935) played Grieg's *Piano Concerto* for the first time, with Grieg conducting, at a concert in Munich on March 9, 1894, and was in contact with Grieg by letter during the years 1894–1907. They also met a few times in London, where Meyer lived for a number years. Among other things, he helped Grieg with some English translations of song texts.

Grieg addresses Meyer as "Court Pianist" ("Hofpianist"), but the reason for this is unknown. He uses the same title when referring to Meyer in his letters to Max Abraham (1831–1900). Meyer usually signed his letters using that title as well; indeed, on one occasion he went so far as to write "Executive Court Pianist" ("Oberhofpianist"). The correspondence is often quite jovial in tone.

Grieg's letters to Meyer are in German. The translation that follows is derived from the original letters as printed in *Die Musik*, Berlin 1908/09, vol. 12, pp. 330–41. It presumably was Meyer himself who provided the letters to *Die Musik*.

1

Copenhagen, November 9, 1894

Dear Mr. Court Pianist!

It was a great pleasure to hear from you. You are, as always, the spiritual son of Heine[1] through and through. You will end up doing like Cowen, who has abandoned the career of musician to become a poet.[2] Hopefully not, however. That would be a sad development for your beautiful talent. My only fear is that this talent will not be especially nurtured in London. The air there, for an artist blessed by God, is not healthy. I would never be able to compose a single note in that city.

Thank you so much for the picture, which is not at all bad. The second "picture"—the songs—is even better, however. They appear to be faithful imprints of their creator. Thus far I have only had time to read through them hurriedly, but I will study them more carefully as soon as I have an evening to myself.

The memories from Menton were very moving.[3] My wife sends her heartfelt thanks for the printed materials. I will send the manuscripts and the gilt-edged copy (for which sweetheart?) before long.[4]

We began an extended stay here eight days ago.

---

[1] German poet Heinrich Heine (1797–1856).

[2] The English composer, pianist and conductor Frederic Hymen Cowen was appointed conductor of The Philharmonic Society in London in 1888, but in 1892 he resigned over a disagreement with the directors of the Society. What Grieg means by the appellation "poet" is unclear. Cowen did write several books on music, but they were published many years after this letter was written.

[3] The Griegs stayed in Menton for a few weeks in March and April, 1894, together with their friends Max Abraham and Oscar Meyer. The picture mentioned earlier in Grieg's letter may have been a group photo of Abraham, Meyer, Nina and himself.

[4] Grieg is referring to some manuscripts of Meyer's own songs.

The fourth violin sonata is a canard.[5] Who is the violinist Adorjan?[6] Moreover, it is nice and most generous of the newspapers that they let me compose when in reality, unfortunately, I do not do so. My health was poor this summer, and I have to decline all invitations to conduct. Life's second half ought not to exist at all. That it does is another of nature's blunders.

Kindly greet the ugly Englishwoman (I do not dare to associate with the dazzlingly beautiful one[7]), and accept our warmest greetings yourself!

Yours truly,
EDVARD GRIEG

2

Troldhaugen at Bergen, June 7, 1898

Dear Mr. Court Pianist!
I just got a letter from Mr. Wolfson, to whose inquiry I unfortunately had to give a negative reply.[8] Everything that you write is very tempting, but my health is certainly not up to such a trip. To be sure, the honorariums being offered are good, but of course that cannot have any bearing on my decision. I must, therefore, reject the whole idea. The biggest triumph that remains to be seen would have to be the one you mentioned: that someone would come all the way from Australia to London to ask you if I prefer to eat ham raw rather than cooked! That must indeed be the highest form of popularity! The day this happens I will go to America with you to eat "cooked" ham!

But now a totally different matter. In the hope that you have retained your old appreciation for my muse, I enclose herewith a proof copy of my new Garborg songs,[9] which have been translated from Norwegian into German by Mr. von Enzberg in Berlin and into English by Mr. L.[10] There are many places in the English translation where I cannot accept the wording. I have underlined in

---

[5] Grieg wrote just three violin sonatas: F major op. 8, G major op. 13 and C minor op. 45.

[6] Hungarian violinist Jenö Adorjan (1874–1903).

[7] Grieg is referring to Mr. Meyer's fiancée.

[8] The American concert agent Wolfson had also approached Oscar Meyer to inquire about the possibility of a Grieg tour in America. The suggested honorarium was 100 English pounds for each of the 30 concerts that would be given in the space of two months.

[9] *The Mountain Maid*, which Grieg had composed in 1895 but which was not published until 1898. The texts were by the Norwegian poet Arne Garborg (1851–1924).

[10] When C. F. Peters Musikverlag published *The Mountain Maid* in 1898 with German and English (in addition to the original Norwegian) texts, the German translator was identified as Eugen von Enzberg. The name of the English translator was not given, however. The reason was that the English text was a synthesis of the work of several translators, one of whom was Oscar Meyer. A letter to Grieg dated May 25, 1898, from Henri Hinrichsen (1868–1942) of C. F. Peters, shows clearly that the first version of the English translation was executed by the English singer and author, Lady Natalia MacFarren (1828–1916). Grieg's letter to Henri Hinrichsen of August 9, 1898, also makes it clear that Meyer had made major improvements to the MacFarren translation, but Grieg then added that "at the right moment" he had been visited at Troldhaugen by an unnamed Englishman who was a poet with an intimate knowledge of the Norwegian language. "He

pencil the places in question which either distort the meaning of the original or result in poor musical declamation. Would you do me the great favor of giving these places some thought and then discussing them with L.? I would be eternally grateful to you if you would do that. Please tell L. that it is about a farm girl and that the tone of the original is folkish.

It's a pity that you can't understand Garborg's beautiful, versified story, *Haugtussa* (*The Mountain Maid*), from which the song texts are taken. It is a masterwork, full of originality, simplicity and depth and possessing a quite indescribable richness of color. Therefore, it will not escape your fine expert eye that these songs are profoundly different from my earlier ones. When the necessary changes have been made, please return the proof copies as quickly as possible.

The music festival was outstanding![11] You should have been there! It would certainly have captured your interest.

Hearty greetings, also from my wife, to Mr. and Mrs. Franz von Katzenmeyer (ow!).[12]

Yours truly,
EDVARD GRIEG

3

Troldhaugen, August 18, 1898

Dear Mr. Court Pianist!
Finally, finally, after the most unbelievable hindrances, I am getting around to expressing my most heartfelt thanks to you for the great kindness you showed me regarding the songs. But it was by no means my immodest intention to turn over this exacting job to you alone! As you will have seen from my last letter, my proposal was that you in conference with L. should get him to undertake the necessary changes. Nonetheless, I now say: Thank God that you, like a brilliant general, have acted contrary to the government's order! Only thus could the battle be won. For only now do I understand, albeit too late, that L. was absolutely incapable of performing this task.

As for your changes, I say as Clara Schumann[13] once wrote to me after I had

---

worked with me for two days," Grieg wrote, "and the result is what you now see. I daresay it is as good as I can ask for."

These statements undeniably set "Mr. L." in a strange light. It seems likely that the explanation is that when he published his letters from Grieg (see Introduction, paragraph 3), Meyer preserved Lady MacFarren's anonymity by referring to her as "Mr. L.". Since she had not been named as the translator in the Peters edition of the songs, perhaps it seemed inappropriate to use her name in 1908, when Grieg's letters to Meyer were published. By 1908, Lady MacFarren was 80 years old. As is evident from the letters, Grieg was very critical of her translations.

[11] Grieg is referring to the Norwegian music festival held in Bergen June 26–July 3, 1898.

[12] It seems likely from other letters to Meyer (not included here) that "Katzenmeyer" is a play on words involving the name "Meyer" and the maiden name of his fiancée, but the correspondence does not reveal the latter name.

[13] German pianist Clara Schumann (1819–69), wife of Robert Schumann (1810–56).

sent her my article on Schumann:[14] "In much I agreed, in much I did not." Still, I am not for that reason any less grateful.

As I studied your translation I became more and more astonished at the remarkable suppleness that you, a foreigner, show in using expressions from English poetry.

Thanks so much for your friendly offer to read the second proofs. But the matter has been delayed, and besides, you have already done much more than I dared to expect. Thus you will not be bothered any further with this boring story. Just come to Troldhaugen some day so that I can give you a hug for your kindness. If, as I hope, you take along your wife, I cannot swear that I will not also hug *her*! "Terrible, but onward!"[15] sings Don Ottavio, and I, too, shall leave this difficult subject.

The music festival [in Bergen] was quite simply colossal. I will not talk about the fact that in Norway—yes, in all Scandinavia—there had never been anything like it and that such a thing will never occur again in our lifetime. But some performances were in fact so good that I *never* and *nowhere else* have heard better ones. It's a pity that you weren't there. Now, though, I am totally exhausted and am going to the mountains for a few weeks.

With the warmest greetings, also to your little lady, I am

Yours truly,
EDVARD GRIEG

4

Christiania, February 12, 1906

Dear Mr. Court Pianist!
Or more correctly: Dear graybeard. I—a youngster of 72½ years[16]—must soon come to Wiesbaden[17] to console you! According to what I hear, Wiesbaden should be just the place for people with poor nerves[18] and bronchial trouble. And since it is also a place where one can hear a lot of excellent music, it is not impossible that you will see me there sometime if it is granted me to be numbered among the living for a few more years. For that matter, I very often say with the prophet Elijah: "It is enough!"[19]

---

[14] In 1893, in response to an invitation from the American journal *The Century Illustrated Monthly Magazine*, Grieg had written a long article on Robert Schumann. It was printed in the January 1894 issue of the magazine. See Benestad & Halverson (eds.), *Edvard Grieg: Diaries, Articles, Speeches* (Columbus, Ohio, 2001).

[15] "Schrecklich, doch weiter!" From Mozart's opera *Don Giovanni*.

[16] Grieg is claiming to be ten years older than he actually is. Meyer goes along with the joke in his reply of February 15, 1906: "I would never have believed that you are already 82½ years old. I thought I should be able to congratulate you on your 90th birthday in June!"

[17] In ca. 1901, after spending several years in London, Meyer had returned to his native Germany.

[18] Meyer had just had a visit from Grieg's German publisher, Henri Hinrichsen, director of C. F. Peters Musikverlag, who suffered from a nerve ailment.

[19] Grieg is alluding to I Kings 19:4, where it is written concerning the prophet Elijah: "But he himself went a day's journey into the wilderness, and came and sat down under a broom tree; and he asked that he might die, saying, 'It is enough; now, O Lord, take away my life; for I am no better than my fathers.'"

You are absolutely right to be amazed that I am still giving concerts. But the fact is that people beguile me into it and I, unfortunately, am not sufficiently principled to decline. To perform in public is the most frightening thing I know. And yet, to hear my works brought to life in a wonderful performance in accordance with my intentions—that I cannot resist.

That *you* have stopped giving concerts is, frankly speaking, unbelievable. *I* am the one who is "dead tired" and ought to quit doing it, but *you* absolutely should not.

You mention those beautiful days in Menton.[20] That's something one could do over again. If you have anything to do in Leipzig, plan in such a way that you—like me—will be there in the middle of April. We have so much to talk about.

Farewell, and write again—but not in two years!

With warm greetings from house to house,

Cordially,
EDVARD GRIEG

5

Christiania, February 26, 1907

Dear Mr. Court Pianist!
Happy married man!
Ditto father!
Ditto song composer!
What more can I say? That I don't have five minutes to spare, and nonetheless I must thank you for your delightful and humorous letter.[21]

My concert in Berlin is the 12th of April. It has been sold out for a long time and likely will be repeated as a matinee on the 14th. But it is equally likely that I will have to cancel it because of illness. I am in bad shape. But I must grin and bear it and see if I can manage the four concerts in Germany that I have promised to give. *But that will be the end of my giving concerts.*[22]

Not long ago someone from Germany addressed me like this: "Most esteemed old Graybeard!" The time has come that I am deserving of this title of honor.

How I would have enjoyed visiting you in your home! But it doesn't look like that will be possible. You, the younger of us, must, together with your wife, take the famous trip to the North country—and then you will come past our door. In this hope I send greetings to both of you from my wife and myself.

Yours truly,
EDVARD GRIEG

---

[20] See Grieg's letter of November 9, 1894.

[21] The letter to which Grieg refers is not extant.

[22] Grieg did manage to complete the concert tour to Germany. The first concert was given in Munich on April 4. Then followed Berlin on April 12 and 14 and Kiel on April 26—Grieg's last public concert.

To Christian Michelsen

Grieg's fellow townsman Christian Michelsen (1857–1925) was elected to the Norwegian Parliament (Stortinget) in 1891 at the age of 24 and quickly became one of the most influential representatives of the Liberal party. He was respected for his personal integrity by both his political friends and his adversaries. In 1894 he left the political arena for a time, partly owing to poor health but also to give more time to his business as a shipowner in his native city. In 1903 he was again elected to Parliament and quickly emerged as one of the country's most prominent political leaders. He became a strong and fearless spokesman for a united front in support of the Norwegian demand for freedom from the union with Sweden. On February 21, 1905, the Norwegian Parliament appointed a special committee to draft a law to establish an independent Norwegian consular service. This bill, which Michelsen supported but which was rejected by the government, led to the government's fall. On March 11 a coalition government was seated with Michelsen as the prime minister. Events thereafter moved very quickly toward the dissolution of the union with Sweden by action of the Norwegian Parliament on June 7, 1905.

Michelsen was perceived as the leader who made the dream of Norwegian independence a reality. From June 7 onward he was hailed as the liberator of the Norwegian people. During the negotiations in Karlstad that followed the declaration of June 7, it was thanks in considerable measure to Michelsen's diplomatic skills that the union was dissolved without bloodshed.

Grieg's letter to Michelsen is derived from a copy preserved in the University of Bergen library.

Christiania, September 23, 1905
Hotel Westminster

Dear Mr. Prime Minister Michelsen!
Let me be one of the first to congratulate you and thank you as warmly as any Norwegian can! You know better than I how much work and self-sacrifice have been invested in this Karlstad convention—but as a modern person I want only to say that twice as many border fortifications would not have been too much to sacrifice for Norway's independence. My ideal instinct rejoices, for the spirit of the future and of progress hovers over this work.

Warm greetings and sleep well!

Yours truly,
EDVARD GRIEG

To Louis Monastier-Schroeder

The Swiss theologian Louis Monastier-Schroeder wrote to Grieg in 1895 seeking information for an article he was writing about the Norwegian composer. This letter became the beginning of some interesting correspondence that was, in fact, continued by Nina Grieg after Edvard's death in 1907. Monastier-Schroeder's lengthy article, "Edvard Grieg. Essai de portrait d'un musicien", was published in *Bibliothèque universelle et Revue suisse* nos. 7 and 8, 1897.

Grieg's last letter to Monastier-Schroeder, which is dated August 28, 1907, is preserved in Nasjonalbiblioteket, Oslo (National Library of Norway, Oslo Division). The others are taken from Edvard Platzhoff-Lejeune's article, "Aus Briefen Edvard Griegs an einen Schweizer" in *Die Musik*, Berlin 1907–08. Platzhoff-Lejeune published the letters without giving Monastier-Schroeder's name.

1

Copenhagen, April 1, 1895

[Dear Pastor]:

It is unfortunately impossible for me to answer your letter in the way you wish. I have neither time nor strength for that. I am still very weak following a serious illness. But I will in any case try to answer some of your questions as well as I can. Fortunately I have the Reclam edition of *Peer Gynt* before me.[1] Ibsen's play is a masterwork of the highest order—which, unfortunately, you cannot understand from the wretched translation. This is the first thing that I must tell you. The only thing of interest on the part of the translator is the preface, to which I call your special attention. . . .

Aimar Grønvold's *Norske Musikere* (Christiania)[2] contains much correct information about the external influences, about collaboration with poets, and about Nordraak[3] as an artist. I was with Bjørnson[4] daily in the late 1860's and early 1870's, and it was during this time that I wrote most of my music based on his poetry. With respect to *Arnljot Gelline*, it would certainly have been easier for you to assess the convent scene if you had been familiar with the work in its entirety. Unfortunately, I do not know of any translation of it.[5]

The four songs [op. 21] from *Fiskerjenten* [*The Fisher Maiden*] are the only texts I have set from this novel. I have written no music for Bjørnson's play *Sigurd*

---

1 Grieg is referring to a reprint of Ibsen's play *Peer Gynt* in the German Reclams Universal-Bibliothek. The score of Grieg's *Peer Gynt* music was not published until after his death.

2 The book *Norske Musikere*, 1. Række [*Norwegian Musicians*, vol. 1], by Norwegian writer Aimar Grønvold (1846–1926), was published in Christiania in 1883. One long chapter was devoted to Grieg.

3 Grieg's friend and fellow composer Rikard Nordraak (1842–66).

4 Norwegian author Bjørnstjerne Bjørnson (1832–1910).

5 In 1871 Grieg had composed *Before a Southern Convent*, the text of which consists of a section of Bjørnson's poem *Arnljot Gelline*.

Jorsalfar except the pieces that have been published by Peters (op. 22 songs; op. 56 orchestra).[6]

The texts of op. 33 do not constitute a unified whole but are part of a larger collection of poems by Vinje.[7]

You are quite right: The music to *Peer Gynt* was conceptualized during the years 1874–75 at the request of the author. It was in connection with a staged performance of the work in Christiania that took place in 1876.[8] In the middle of the 1880's the work was produced on the Danish stage in Copenhagen, and a few years ago it was repeated in Christiania. The success was always very substantial.

I will now point out the places with music with reference to the Reclam edition [of the play]:

1. Before the first act, a prelude called "At the Wedding". In op. 23 it is printed for piano four hands.
2. Page 25, where Peer Gynt says, "The dancing's begun!"[9] one hears from backstage a *halling*[10] (dance) from the prelude.
3. Page 26: Here a fiddler, a peasant fiddler, sits on the stage and plays a *halling* and then a *springdans*[11] (not printed).
4. Page 34, before the beginning of the second act: Interlude music called "Peer Gynt and Ingrid". Printed as "Ingrid's Lament" in *Peer Gynt Suite No. 2.*
5. Pages 38–39: Three herd girls, a complete movement. The girls sing, Peer Gynt talks here and there (not printed).
6. Page 42 at the bottom: Peer Gynt hops up onto the boar; as he rides away, a short piece of music (not printed).
7. Page 43: "In the Hall of the Mountain King". Printed in *Peer Gynt Suite No. 1.* In the stage production the music begins as a prelude, and at the big *ff* the curtain rises as the troll courtiers' lines are sung. (The vocal parts are not printed in the score.)
8. Page 46: Playing and dancing. Printed for piano four hands in op. 23.
9. Pages 49–50 after the troll king says, "I'm vexed and sleepy. Good night!" A melodramatic scene with chorus (not printed).
10. Pages 50–52: Melodramatic scene between Peer Gynt and "the Voice" (not printed).

---

[6] Grieg is a little too modest here. He also wrote a prelude and two interludes to Bjørnson's play. These pieces were published for the first time in *Edvard Grieg: Complete Works*, vol. 19 (1988).

[7] Norwegian poet Aasmund Olavsson Vinje (1818–70).

[8] The world premiere of *Peer Gynt* took place at the Christiania Theater on February 24, 1876.

[9] This and subsequent quotations from *Peer Gynt* follow the translation by Rolf Fjelde (1980).

[10] A *halling* is a lively Norwegian folk-dance tune in 2/4 time.

[11] A *springdans* (also called a *springar*) is a lively folk-dance tune in 3/4 time.

11. Before Act 3: "The Death of Åse" is played as a prelude (printed in *Peer Gynt Suite No. 1* op. 46).
12. Page 63: At Peer Gynt's lines:

> Mother, let's talk, you and I—
> But only of this and that.
> Things that are twisted and wry,
> That rankle and hurt, let's forget—

one hears "The Death of Åse" being played backstage *pp*—so softly, in fact, that one is only vaguely aware of the music as a muffled sound that does not disturb the dialogue. The music lasts until page 67, where it stops at Peer's words, "An end to this fuss and bother—Mother Aase can come in free!" It can be handled in such a way that the piece ends at precisely this point.

13. Before Act 4 there is a short prelude (not printed). Instead of this, "Morning Mood" (first suite) is played here at performances, but this piece was really composed for page 83 ("Early Morning").
14. Page 83: A thief and a receiver, scene for two solo voices and orchestra (not printed).
15. Page 87: Girls' chorus. Printed as "Arabian Dance" in the second suite, but without voices. The middle movement, in A minor, is to be sung by Anitra.
16. Page 89: The girls dance. Here "Anitra's Dance" is played. Printed in the first suite. The music was conceived as an accompaniment to Peer Gynt's monologue, "Her legs go like drumsticks; faster still", and it should, therefore, be played backstage *pp*.
17. Page 91: "Peer Gynt's Serenade". Printed only in the piano reduction by Wilhelm Hansen in Denmark.
18. Page 101: A summer day in the far north. "Solveig's Song". Printed with piano accompaniment among my songs. Also as an orchestral piece in the second suite.
19. Page 113: Prelude to the fifth act. Printed in the second suite. The transition to "Solveig's Song" with woodwinds appears only in the suite.
20. Pages 133–35: Night, a forest that has been burnt out by a forest fire: a melodramatic scene with chorus (backstage). Not printed.
21. "Churchgoers singing on the forest path" (not printed).
22. Page 154: "Solveig's Cradle Song". Printed with piano accompaniment among my songs.[12]

[12] Grieg's list of the numbers composed for *Peer Gynt* is not complete. He actually wrote a total of 26 pieces. The complete music for *Peer Gynt* was printed for the first time in *Edvard Grieg: Complete Works*, vol. 18 (1988).

I hope the time is not too far distant when a complete piano reduction—yes, a complete orchestral score—of all the *Peer Gynt* music can be printed, perhaps with associated text.

As for *The Mountain Thrall,* Gade[13] has not composed a work with this title. He has, indeed, composed a large work entitled *Elverskud* [*Elf-king's Daughter*], and one can say that the subjects of the two works are related. But in composing our works we have drawn on different resources. Gade's composition is a large work—a ballad—for chorus, solo voices and orchestra. My piece was composed on the model of Old Norse folk songs. It is for just one voice and is quite short and decidedly lyrical, whereas Gade's work has a dramatic flavor.

The poem *Bergliot,*[14] which I have handled as a melodrama, is the same text that Danish composer [Peter] Heise[15] has set for solo voice and orchestra.

The *Holberg Suite*[16] was written for the jubilee in 1884. The song "Autumn Storm"[17] was written in Denmark in the summer of 1865, the overture the following winter in Rome. The poetic and musical contrasts in the overture are derived from the song, which describes the autumn storm, and the farmers' merry song of the harvest. In the overture there is no hint of the coming spring but rather a union of the serious and the light-hearted elements that characterize autumn.

The *Funeral March for Rikard Nordraak* was written in Rome in the spring of 1866 the same day I received word of Nordraak's death, and it has been printed only in a piano version. The piece has been performed by wind instruments in Christiania. I hope the composition can be published both in this form and in a version for full orchestra.[18]

... Perhaps we will see each other next winter in Leipzig, where I would be pleased to supply you with all kinds of details, but not—in writing!

With warm greetings from

Sincerely yours,
EDVARD GRIEG

---

13 Danish composer Niels Wilhelm Gade (1817–90).

14 *Bergliot,* a setting of a text by Bjørnson, was composed as a melodrama (with piano) in 1871 and revised and orchestrated in 1885.

15 Peter Heise (1830–79).

16 *Holberg Suite,* written for the bicentennial celebration of the birth of Ludvig Holberg.

17 "Autumn Storm" is a setting of a text by Danish poet Christian Richardt (1831–92). Motives from this song were used in the concert overture *In Autumn.*

18 Grieg's arrangement for winds has been published in *Edvard Grieg: Complete Works* vol. 13 (1983). Grieg never arranged the piece for full orchestra, but such an arrangement was made by Johan Halvorsen (1864–1935) in 1907 in connection with Grieg's funeral.

2

Troldhaugen at Bergen, Norway, August 23, 1903

[Dear Pastor]:

A lengthy, serious illness is to blame for the fact that I have not been able to answer your letter until today. You may be right in saying that I was not fully aware of the great contrast between Bjørnson and Ibsen's respective perceptions of the Norwegian national character at that time. Nonetheless, I could shout out with Holberg: "Gentlemen, you are both right!" In other words: Bjørnson and Ibsen complement each other with their respective perceptions. The Norwegian people, above all the peasantry, have sharply contrasting characteristics. It is clear that Bjørnson, the optimist, glorifies the common people whereas Ibsen, the pessimist, cracks the whip over them. A composer can certainly assimilate both terms of the contrast without losing his integrity. It is true that I did not take part in Ibsen's anniversary celebration, but I am an enthusiastic admirer of many of his writings—and very especially of *Peer Gynt.* My relationship to Bjørnson is different. In addition to the great affection and high regard I have for him as an author, we are close friends.

I cannot, then, share your opinions about the artist's task. The artist is *elastic.* His task is to give artistic expression to *contrasting* views, whether he applauds them or not. It is his *imagination,* not his *moral sense,* that must be set in motion.

You are absolutely right: It is sad that the complete *Peer Gynt* score has not been published. But the publisher has given out the two suites and the songs and doesn't want to compete with himself! . . . Many Norwegians used to believe, as I did, that *Peer Gynt* represented only an altogether exceptional case. Only in recent years, unfortunately, has it become clear how frightfully accurate the poet's depiction is as a portrait of the national character. Ibsen, in a shocking way, has revealed a dangerous side of all of our people. That is why political affairs here are in such a bad state.

With this depressing message I must close.

Sincerely yours,
EDVARD GRIEG

3

Christiania, October 15, 1905

[Dear Pastor]:

Forgive me that my answer. . . has been so long in coming. Often I wanted to write, but always there were harrowing days and illnesses in between. . . .

Like you, I am a republican and have always been so. But to proclaim a republic in Norway at this moment would be a dangerous and short-sighted beginning. Our enemies want that and often openly express this wish, and that is the best proof that we must be on guard. It is most important to Sweden—and also to Russia—to see us as a republic. Our friendly neighbors—above all England, a country we probably (we don't yet know for sure) have to thank for the peace—do not in any way want a republic. Moreover, Norway's constitution assures more freedom than do those of most republics, and the constantly recurring presidential elections might be the occasion for inter-party conflicts that could be dangerous. For when it comes to pugnacity, our people constantly exhibit a residuum of barbarism. It is still not unthinkable that the plebiscite will require a republic. The Parliament and the government, both official bodies that to a large extent—yes, perhaps predominantly—consist of republicans, neither anticipate nor desire this result, and this in itself is significant.

What do you say about our two great days: June 7, when we declared our independence from Sweden, and August 13, when the plebiscite demanded by Sweden, instead of becoming the fiasco they hoped for, became instead an enormous triumph for Norway? And also the convention in Karlstad? This convention has a foreseeable significance for the spiritual progress of all countries. Yes, indeed. But it is above all an *ethical* achievement. The basic concepts of honor and love of one's country generated there have now become part of a process of change that will create better human beings! Is that utopia? I believe wholeheartedly in this, and it fills me with joy and gratitude that my homeland has been called to lead the way.

Unfortunately, I must conclude . . .

4

Troldhaugen, July 3, 1906

[Dear Pastor]:

I will make no attempt whatsoever to excuse my long silence. I can only say that I have become a poor letter-writer. Letter-writing and creative work used to go quickly and easily. I moved like a fish in the water. Physical ailments and the press of the years have changed all this. The blood flows heavily and slowly, and the mind, too, unfortunately moves in the same slow tempo. So please excuse me!

Fortunately, my interest in life's big questions is as vivid as it was in my youth. . . . I am completely of the opinion that the church must be separated from the state and that such a separation will occur here in the not too distant future. I think I can foresee that fortunately the separation will not occur in so violent a way as it did in France. Rather, it will come about almost as a matter of course, without lasting animosities. The big event occurred here last year as something natural, obvious. The separation of the church from the state will occur in the same way.[19]

---

[19] Grieg was badly mistaken on this point. The Norwegian church remains to this day a so-called state church as provided in the constitution of 1814.

I had to smile at your fear that I might perhaps write a coronation cantata. No, and again no: I would never do that sort of thing, and I rejected out of hand the request that I do so on this occasion. A few years ago I was offered a commission from England to write a coronation march for the English king, and I also declined that unconditionally.[20]

When it comes to poetry it is a different matter.

I enjoyed composing incidental music for *Sigurd Jorsalfar*,[21] and I wish you could have been present at the Norwegian National Theater last fall for the celebration (the coronation festivities for King Haakon VII in Christiania). You would undoubtedly have enjoyed it, for the play—excellently staged by theater director Bjørn Bjørnson[22]—is, as an exception, ideally suited for national festival days.

One can argue about the various forms of government as long as the world exists. But I am convinced that you—if you, like me, are a republican, and if you were in a position to consider the matter at close quarters—would admit that the Norwegian king is a king only on paper. Just as our early history exhibited many small kingdoms—a circumstance resulting from the Norwegian geography—so our nation always remains a divided people, despite the great unification that occurred in 1905. Unfortunately, our political history since 1814[23] has in reality not altered this fact. We *must* wrangle! A republic with its unavoidable election conflicts would, therefore, only be a thing of evil.

This, then, is *one* side of the matter. As for the other side, i.e., the position of the great powers, it is an open secret in Norway that Sweden wanted nothing more than to attack us but that Germany and chiefly England sounded some serious warnings to prevent war from occurring. I say *chiefly* England, because this country was interested in seeing an English princess as a Norwegian queen. As matters unfolded, we would have liked to see something ideal and significant for the future. But unfortunately, egoism is the basic motive. And one more thing: We have been lucky.... Our present king ... belongs to a royal line that is mentally and physically sound. Moreover, he has grown up as a simple seaman and exhibits a simplicity and ingenuousness that are just right for us. It is as if he were created for precisely this task. The main thing is that it will enable the government, during the election that will now take place, to defeat the radical party of destruction that threatens to topple it. Michelsen[24] is still the man of the hour. He is in my opinion the greatest champion because he is an independent spirit,

---

20 See Grieg's letter of February, 1902 to George Augener (1830–1915).

21 The new Norwegian king, Haakon VII (1872–1957), was honored at a gala performance at the National Theater in Christiania on November 28, 1905. Bjørnson's play *Sigurd Jorsalfar* with Grieg's incidental music op. 22 was performed.

22 Bjørn Bjørnson (1859–1942) was the son of Bjørnstjerne Bjørnson.

23 Danish rule over Norway was terminated in 1814 by the Treaty of Kiel that marked the end of the Napoleonic wars.

24 Christian Michelsen (1857–1925), Norway's prime minister from 1905 to 1907.

a man with a clear vision and without the slightest vanity or desire for personal power. Quite the contrary: He desires nothing more than to withdraw from the publica arena. He loves his hometown of Bergen, where he operates a very thriving business as a shipowner.

Well, enough about politics. I learned of Ibsen's death in London, just before a concert that I was to conduct. I cannot say that I was deeply moved, because for me Ibsen had already been dead for many years, and because we expected word of his death with each passing day. Later it was different for me. The emptiness resulting from the absence of his eminent personality is increasingly painful to me. . . .

It is a long time since the *Peer Gynt* music and the Ibsen songs were written. So long that I now conduct and play these works as if they had not been written by me. I wanted to develop further. And I have done so—far enough, in any case, so that I now feel different. How I wish that I could have found an expression in music for my spiritual development right down to the present time! Physical ailments have been insurmountable obstacles. And now the end is near. But I am reconciled. Our peasant poet Vinje says in his marvelous poem "Våren" ("Spring"):[25]

> "More I've received than I ever have deserved,
> And all—all must vanish."

The poet Nordahl Rolfsen[26] lives in Christiania. To be sure, his dramatic works have no significance, but he has a great lyric talent. When his imagination focuses on childhood he always writes well.

I must conclude. . . . I have the feeling that we still have much to say to each other. . . .

5

Bergen Hospital, August 28, 1907

Dear Pastor:

I have been sick and am so still. The past days I have suffered so much from insomnia and shortness of breath that I had to come here. For that reason, both pen and ink have had to wait.

There is much that I would like to have written to you, and I also wanted to thank you for your last letter. But my strength prohibits it. These lines just to tell

---

[25] Grieg set Vinje's poem "Våren" ("Spring") as op. 33 no. 2. Later he created a setting for string orchestra of this song in op. 34 no. 2. He found, however, that audiences were confused by the title: They assumed that the music was intended to depict the glories of spring in all its splendor. But Vinje's poem is in fact a wistful reflection on the brevity of human life, which is also the background for the solemn character of Grieg's music. Therefore, in foreign editions of opp. 33 and 34, Grieg directed that the piece be given a new title more expressive of the content: "Last Spring", "Letzter Frühling" etc.

[26] Norwegian author and educator Nordahl Rolfsen (1848–1928).

you that, in accordance with your wish that I should put you in contact with a Norwegian clergyman, I have written to pastor Carl Konow of this city.[27] He has just replied that he will soon write to you and that it would be of interest to him to establish contact with a Swiss clergyman. Mr. Konow is a young man who has recently made himself heard because of his view of the dogmas. This view is anything but that prevailing in the state church, and the clergy are now demanding that he submit his resignation. But he refuses to do this. According to what I have heard today, the bishop and the Ministry of Church and Education have decided that he will be permitted to remain in his position after all and that an assistant pastor will be brought in. In other words: The clergy has difficulties because popular opinion dares to stir. Mr. Konow is said to be a very upright person who has won the hearts of the congregation. For the truth's sake, it is a good thing that it precisely such a man who represents the cause of liberalism. I hope that you will hear from him soon. I sent him your letter so that he could get a direct impression of your personality.

The Bojer book has also aroused attention. To my shame I must confess that I have not read it, so I cannot say anything about it.[28]

Nothing would please me more than telling you my views regarding religious questions. But to do that I need better health than I have at present. And yet—this does not require many words. During a visit to England in 1888 I was attracted to the Unitarian views, and in the nineteen years that have passed since then I have held to them. All the sectarian forms of religion that I have been exposed to since have not succeeded in making any impression on me. Pure science? As a means it is excellent, but as an end—at least for me—it is completely unsatisfying. I must retain the concept of God, even if this altogether too often comes in conflict with the concept of prayer.

But now I am beginning to get into details. And I am obliged, unfortunately, to conclude after I have conveyed to you my deepest gratitude for the beautiful translations.[29]

With warmest greetings from

Respectfully,
EDVARD GRIEG

---

27 The liberal clergyman Carl Konow (1863–1923) was parish pastor of the Sandviken congregation in Bergen. In autumn 1906 he gave a lecture on the subject, "Jesus in the present day". The bishop of Bergen gave a rebuttal lecture to which Konow replied in another lecture that was highly critical of the church's dogmas. After complaints from members of the congregation to the governmental office responsible for church affairs, Konow was relieved of most of his duties in the congregation but was allowed to continue leading worship services.

28 Grieg is referring to *Troens Magt* (1903, published in English in 1920 with the title *The Power of a Lie*) by Norwegian author Johan Bojer (1872–1959).

29 The translations to which Grieg is referring have not been identified.

To Fridtjof Nansen

The famous polar explorer, oceanographer, zoologist and statesman Fridtjof Nansen (1861–1930) played an important role during the dissolution of the union between Norway and Sweden in 1905. His worldwide fame gave him access to newspapers all over the world, and he used this access and his considerable skill as a writer to argue the case for Norwegian independence. Once independence was secured, he was also personally involved in the negotiations that were undertaken with Prince Carl of Denmark to become the first king of free Norway. These negotiations were successful, and in November, 1905, Prince Carl became King Haakon VII (1872–1957) of Norway. Nansen also served in 1906–08 as Norway's first ambassador to England.

Grieg was with Nansen on several occasions during his last concert tour to England. On May 17, 1906—the first observance of Norway's constitution day since the winning of independence—he conducted an orchestra concert in Queen's Hall in London. On May 24 he participated in a chamber-music concert at the same venue.

Grieg's letter to Nansen is preserved in Nasjonalbiblioteket, Oslo (National Library of Norway, Oslo Division).

[London], May 16, 1906
46 Grosvenor Street

Dear Fridtjof Nansen!
Thanks so much! May we then come to lunch on Saturday the 19th? Unfortunately, I can't talk with the English politicians[1] despite my great interest in their work. All in all, I would much prefer to be in a little Norway[2] (with exceptions, of course) with you, Brækstad and Consul Ottesen.[3]

Whether there are any Norwegians here interested in *art*, I do not know. But if you want to do something to please me, invite Mr. Percy Grainger,[4] a *brilliant* young musician from Australia (14, Upper Cheyne Row, Chelsea S.W.) with whom I became acquainted yesterday. He is crazy about Norway, *speaks* Norwegian (Danish!), and knows everything—the sagas, Faroese literature, Bjørnson, Ibsen[5] etc. He would be happy to shake your hand.

That you will invite our host and hostess is most kind of you. Moreover, they are amiable people in their own way—and liberal.[6]

So: We shall hope to see you on the 19th—at 1:30, shall we say?

With warm greetings,

Yours,
EDVARD GRIEG

---

1 Grieg was well aware that he was not able either to write or to speak English very well.

2 I.e., a gathering of Norwegians.

3 Norwegian vice-consul Hans Lien Brækstad (1845–1915) lived for extended periods of time in London. Peter Martin Ragnar Ottesen (1857–1927) was a Norwegian career diplomat serving in London at this time.

4 Grieg came to regard the Australian-born pianist and composer Percy Grainger (1882–1961), who later became an American citizen, as the foremost interpreter of his piano works, especially *Norwegian Peasant Dances*.

5 Norwegian authors Bjørnstjerne Bjørnson (1832–1910) and Henrik Ibsen (1828–1906).

6 Grieg's host in London was German-born businessman and impresario Eduard Speyer (1839–1934).

To Edvard Neovius

Edvard Neovius (1851–1917) was a Finnish mathematician and politician. In 1905 he held a high position in the Finnish department of the treasury, but after a general strike in that year he was forced to resign, whereupon he left Finland and thereafter made his home in Copenhagen. Grieg came in contact with Neovius and his wife Thyra through their mutual friends Bodil (1867–1959) and Rolf Viggo de Neergaard (1837–1916) at the Neergaards' estate "Fuglsang" ("Birdsong") on the Danish island of Lolland. The two men developed a warm friendship, and Neovius was especially helpful to Grieg in 1907, when he unselfishly accompanied him from Copenhagen to Troldhaugen. See Grieg's diary entry for June 28, 1907. Thyra Neovius had been in contact with Grieg as early as 1881, when she had written to him urging him to seek the position of Director of the music conservatory in Helsinki and conductor of the city's symphony orchestra—a proposal that Grieg declined.

All of the letters to Neovius included here are preserved in Bergen Offentlige Bibliotek (Bergen Public Library).

1

Voksenkollen Sanatorium at Christiania
February 10, 1903

Dear Neovius!

Well, for once it was a pleasant surprise! Thank you for your letter, and excuse my "idiocy" in sending a postcard to Helsinki when I should have known very well that you were in Merano. If only we could meet! But I'm afraid it now looks very doubtful, for as far as I can understand Prague is not going to work out. If something should still come of it, I will let you know. But Finland? No, that's out of the question.

I don't know what in the world Cesar Cui[1] is ranting about. He has written that I should include Finland when I visit St. Petersburg, and that's all there is to it. In my reply to him I have not so much as mentioned Finland, so it's unbelievable when he informs the newspapers that I am going there. Moreover, I won't be going to Russia this year, since the days that were proposed were not acceptable to me. In the meantime my old friend from Leipzig, the pianist Alexander Siloti,[2] who is conductor of the Philharmonic Society in Moscow, has invited me to give two concerts (one in St. Petersburg and one in Moscow) in the spring of *1904*, and I have accepted this invitation. Should it be possible for you to fulfill your old promise to be in St. Petersburg when I arrive—how exciting that would be for both Nina and me! But, I'll worry about that when the time comes. I have written to Siloti that by that time I probably will be telephoning him with further details from Mars or Saturn, for it's likely that I will have left this planet for good! Yes, one certainly does grow old! This summer I will go home and turn sixty.

---

[1] Russian composer César Cui (1835–1919).

[2] Russian pianist and conductor Alexander Siloti (1865–1945).

Naturally I have been well aware that you belonged to the national party—NB to the group that understands the situation and doesn't want to go around butting its head against a stone wall—and that for that reason you have been subjected to the severest unpleasantries from the chauvinists' camp. If I were Finnish, I would belong to the same party. I have always loved Finland and the Finns, and now I admire you as well. But I find that the language issue, which you dwell on, is of less significance. The national distinctiveness exists at a deeper level than that of language. If that were not the case, Norway would no longer be Norwegian. But it *is* Norwegian despite the Danish language—both written and spoken—that holds sway in the cities. Norway does not become Norwegian, nor does Finland become Finnish, through the efforts of the language partisans—unfortunately!—even if Russia were to allow the Finnish language to be used throughout the country but continued to suppress it in other respects.

I have the greatest affection for the indigenous languages, but I worry about the sentimentality in the understanding of the concept of nationality that often follows. Just as we speak Danish with a Norwegian accent, so you will speak Russian with a Finnish accent. The accent is the national element. No despotism can root it out, because it is intertwined with the temperament and the nature of the people. I think, in other words, that Russia will not be able to root out the soul of the Finnish people so long as the people have such a soul. And if it is once there, it will take centuries to kill it—and before these centuries have passed, new movements may have arisen to benefit the struggle for Finnish nationality.

One cannot write or speak about anything more interesting than this—but I must end for today. May you soon be perfectly healthy again! Nina has almost completely recovered during the stay here.

Warm greetings from both of us to both of you!

Sincerely yours,
EDVARD GRIEG

2

Aulestad via Christiania, January 17, 1904

Dear Neovius!
Thank you for the telegram and the letter! And thank you for all the kindness toward me expressed in both of them. But—nothing is coming of all those plans! Since I last wrote to you I have again had a bad spell, with symptoms that indicate that I have other things to think about than concert trips. Yesterday I sent a telegram to St. Petersburg withdrawing from that commitment, after having done the same thing regarding Vienna. Still on the schedule is Sweden, where I have been invited to give four concerts.

Tomorrow we go to Christiania, where I intend to subject myself to various kinds of cures. I am hoping that massage therapy will be the most helpful. My nervous system, which was supposed to have some good days here, has absolutely fallen apart, and my recent breathing difficulties have now increased to such an extent that for the time being I must give up any thought of conducting or playing. If the end is near, I hope it will come quickly—and if not, I must do everything to make the rest of my life bearable. You, too, have had to think about your health of late, so I hope you will be an indulgent and patient reader of this "patient letter".

Bjørnson is in bed with a stubborn but not severe case of bronchitis. But he has an inexhaustible store of vitality. He emits both oral and written thunder and lightning in his bedroom to such an extent that it is a great joy to listen to. You must understand that we have also been talking a lot about Finland and about the strange articles in Bobrikov's[3] paper—articles in which he accuses Bjørnson of agitating for the Finnish cause against Russia. Yes, I think it is even intimated that the Nobel prize is being used in support of this cause.[4] Greater madness or more atrocious rubbish cannot be imagined. Must one really resort to such means! Bjørnson holds the same view as everyone else in Europe. He is part of the great heart of the people—the same heart that beats also in Russia, and that Mr. Bobrikoff or his successors had better respect. For that heart belongs to the future.

And now farewell! Warmest greetings to all three of you, also from Nina.

Sincerely yours,
EDVARD GRIEG

P.S. Yes, thanks! We got the Lahmann[5] New Year's card!
Address: Hotel Westminster, Christiania.

3

Troldhaugen, July 17, 1907

Dear friend!
Here I sit and shall answer your letter with your "fountain pen". But the ink is running all over and the "graybeard" has forgotten how to refill it—so I better put it aside until I have acquired the necessary information. We have been anxiously

---

[3] Nikolai I. Bobrikov (1839–1904) was the Russian Governor General in Finland. His principal task was to implement the russification and unification of Finland with Russia, both of which were contrary to Finland's constitution. The freedom of the press was restricted, letters were censored, and freedom of assembly was suspended. Russian became the official language of the Finnish senate, higher government officials who did not speak Russian were removed and replaced with Russians. In 1903, when Bobrikov was given almost dictatorial power, deportations began. Bobrikov's brutality aroused reactions throughout the civilized world. On June 16, 1904, he was assassinated by a young Finn, who then committed suicide.

[4] Norwegian author Bjørnstjerne Bjørnson (1832–1910) had been awarded the Nobel prize for literature in 1903.

[5] A German physician, director of a sanatorium near Dresden, Germany.

awaiting news from you and were very happy to get your nice letter. We followed you on the trip in our thoughts and soon realized that you didn't get by without "rocking".[6]

Here we have been having absolutely devilish weather: cold, rain and strong wind until 3–4 days ago, and now suddenly full summer with 18 degrees Réaumur[7] in the shade. Believe me, it's wonderful here now.

Perhaps it won't make much of an impression on your pampered temperament when I confide that we missed you greatly after you left. Not only because you, despite your younger years, were the one among us with the greatest "life experience" but also because there was a unique warmth and an aura of elevation around you that did me good, and that I now long to meet again.

I deeply regret that we were not able to continue that last afternoon's contemplation of life's big issues: death and eternity. This mathematician-imagination has greatly interested me. In my masseur, with whom I wanted to discuss the subject, I found your complete opposite. He was totally earth-bound and had no desire to think about anything beyond the things belonging to this earth. Moreover, I have suspected you of being more earth-bound in your relation to the concept of eternity than your mathematical imagination let on. My masseur also gave me the brand new information that Christ was the son of the Virgin Mary and—a Roman general! That, he thought, was a clear finding of the most recent research. I took the liberty only of injecting that perhaps the general had been—a carpenter. And he was not totally unreceptive to this idea. That masseur concluded his work at Troldhaugen yesterday, because he needs his summer vacation. The result is that the hip is as before, but my general condition is somewhat improved.

Now you must be so kind as to write soon again and tell us how Thyra and Saima are getting along.[8] Your refusal of Consul Mohr's[9] invitation gave us the hopefully mistaken idea that things may be going badly for Saima. In declining the invitation, in any case, you certainly have chosen the right course. What Saima needs now is to *get back* her strength, not *squander* it.

Warmest greetings to all three of you from Nina and her sister[10] and from

Sincerely yours,
EDVARD GRIEG

Greetings to the medical director, also Miss Rask and Miss Hjorth. You may tell the last-named that each day we eat self-ground granulate with nuts.

---

[6] Because of Grieg's precarious health at this time, Neovius had generously accompanied Nina and Edvard from Copenhagen all the way to Troldhaugen.

[7] "Réaumur" denotes a temperature scale in which 0° represents the freezing point and 80° the boiling point of water. Thus 18° Réaumur equals 23° Celsius and 73° Fahrenheit.

[8] Thyra and Saima, Neovius's wife and daughter.

[9] Norwegian merchant Conrad Mohr (1849–1926) was the German consul in Bergen.

[10] Nina's sister, Tonny Hagerup (1844–1939), was living with the Griegs at this time.

To Wilhelmina Neruda

Wilhelmina (Vilemina, Wilma) Neruda (1838–1911), who was born in Czechoslovakia, was one of Europe's leading violin virtuosos in the latter half of the nineteenth century. In 1864, after marrying the Swedish composer Ludvig Norman (1831–85), she made her home in Stockholm and used the name Norman-Neruda. She and her husband separated in 1869, and in 1870 she moved to England. In 1888, three years after Norman's death, she married Sir Charles Hallé (1819–95), founder of the Hallé orchestra in Manchester, and thereafter was known as Lady Hallé.

At Grieg's first concert in Christiania on October 15, 1866, Wilhelmina Neruda collaborated with the composer in a performance of his *Violin Sonata No. 1* in F major, and in 1888, when Grieg was to give concerts in England, he again availed himself of her talents. On May 16, in St. James's Hall in London, they performed the *Violin Sonata No. 1* in F major and also played the last two movements of *Violin Sonata No. 3* in C minor. Later they also performed together at several concerts in Manchester, London and Copenhagen.

A copy of Grieg's letter to Wilhelmina Neruda has been provided by Ladislav Reznicek. It has also been published both in the original German and in Czech and Norwegian-Danish translation in Reznicek's book, *Edvard Grieg og tsjekkisk kultur* [*Edvard Grieg and Czech Culture*], Oslo 1975.

Leipzig, February 6, 1888

Dear madam!
Do you still remember that a few years ago, in the Casino auditorium in Copenhagen—in reply to my question as to when I might again have the pleasure of performing with you—you were so incautious as to reply, "Well, if you come to London". That's where I am heading! I am coming in the middle of March and will be unhappy if you escape me! For your incomparable mastery as shown in your performance of Brahms's *G-major Sonata* at that time shines even more brightly in my mind today than it did earlier. I didn't think such a thing was possible.

Enough about that! Kindly send me a few lines about how we might arrange to make music together! I have a commitment at The Philharmonic Society on March 22, but so far I am free except for that date. I ask only that you bear in mind the following: I am only a composer. You must, therefore, be satisfied with the name Grieg![1]

With the warmest greetings, also from my wife, I remain

Your devoted admirer,
EDVARD GRIEG

Address: C. F. Peters Musikverlag, Leipzig

---

[1] On February 18 Wilhelmina Neruda sent a positive reply to Grieg's letter. However, she advised him to get the concerts in London postponed because the period just before and after Easter was unlikely to draw the desired audiences.

To Carl Nielsen

Carl Nielsen (1865–1931) initiated a new epoch in Danish music. He broke away from the Nordic-tinged Romanticism of Niels W. Gade (1817–90) and created his own elegant style. Nielsen was trained as a violinist and played for many years under Johan Svendsen (1840–1911) in the Royal Theater Orchestra in Copenhagen. Later he himself became conductor of that orchestra. Grieg did not have extensive contact with the younger Danish master but had a high opinion of several of his compositions.

The letters from Grieg to Carl Nielsen are preserved in Det kgl. Bibliotek (The Royal Library), Copenhagen.

1

Copenhagen, January 18, 1894

Dear Mr. Nielsen!

Thank you for your compositions, which I have greatly enjoyed getting acquainted with—especially the *String Quartet* and several of the songs, for example "Genre-billede" ("Genre Picture") and "Det bødes der for" ("Sin in haste, repent at leisure").[1] These works bear witness to a spirit of such nobility that they certainly will bring honor both to you and to your homeland if you have an opportunity to develop your talent freely and unhindered by external pressure. I take it for granted that you will receive all the recognition and encouragement that you so richly deserve. I will therefore merely add my personal best wishes for a bright artistic future.

With friendly greetings,

Sincerely yours,
EDVARD GRIEG

2

[Copenhagen], April 18, 1905
Hotel Phoenix

Dear Carl Nielsen!

When you have read this letter I will exact from you a solemn promise that *without delay* you will take pen, ink and paper in hand and write the requested page of music in honor of Röntgen's 50th birthday on May 9. Send the page to me at

---

[1] The *String Quartet* to which Grieg refers presumably is the *G-minor Quartet* op. 13 (1887–88) or the *F-minor Quartet* op. 5 (1890). The songs are from the collection *Fem Sange* (*Five Songs*) op. 4 (1891), which are settings of texts by the Danish poet Jens Peter Jacobsen (1847–85).

Hotel Phoenix; Bodil Neergaard and I have agreed that this is the best way to handle it.[2]

Cordial greetings!

Sincerely yours,
EDVARD GRIEG

3

Holmenkollen Sanatorium at Christiania, March 7, 1907

Dear Carl Nielsen!
Thank you for Mozart![3] You make many telling observations—indeed, so many that it is a pity that you go chasing for even more. The statement that Mozart's symphonies will live after Beethoven's are forgotten is the kind of *parforce*-chase[4] from which you will not escape unscathed. Because it's not so. Remember that subjectivity and objectivity will continue until the end of time. Pessimism and optimism as well. Through the ages, both members of the pair will with equal justification find their representatives. For Mozart's symphonies to overshadow Beethoven's, pessimism in the world would have to decrease. Do you think it will? I do not. The opposite is more likely.

In your perception of Mozart as a personality, however, we are in complete agreement.

Warm greetings.

Sincerely yours,
EDVARD GRIEG

P.S. When will your opera be performed?[5]

---

[2] Grieg had taken the initiative in collecting greetings—in the form of musical compositions, drawings or poems—for the 50th birthday of his Dutch friend Julius Röntgen (1855–1932). Bodil Neergaard (1867–1959), granddaughter of Danish composer J. P. E. Hartmann (1805–1900), was a member of Grieg's circle of friends in Denmark.

[3] In 1906 Carl Nielsen wrote his first major essay, "Mozart and Our Time". It was included in its entirety in Nielsen's book, *Levende Musik*, published in 1925 (and in English in 1968 as *Living Music*).

[4] An expression derived from hunting life: a chase on horseback and with hunting dogs that continues until the prey collapses (from the French *par force*, by force).

[5] Grieg is referring to Carl Nielsen's opera *Masquerade*, which had its world premiere in Copenhagen on November 11, 1906.

4

Copenhagen, March 20, 1907
Hotel Bristol

Dear Carl Nielsen!

Thank you for last evening! It is an enjoyable and witty composition that you have created![6] I got the hang of the first act right away, I had some trouble understanding the second, and in the third I was once again able to follow the main lines. I do not doubt that as a whole it is a work by a new master who is saying: Here am *I*! What fine, humorous art and what wise economy in the technical treatment!

I was totally exhausted by the end of the opera, otherwise I would have used the opportunity to get together with you for awhile. But—we'll have to do that some other time!

With warm greetings, admiration and thanks—also to the *excellent* conductor.

Sincerely yours,
EDVARD GRIEG

---

[6] Grieg had been with Carl Nielsen at a dinner party hosted by Bodil and Rolf Viggo de Neergaard (1837–1916) preceding a performance of *Masquerade* at the Royal Theater. Nielsen himself was on the podium thanks to the generosity of Norwegian composer and conductor Johan Svendsen, musical director of the Royal Theater Orchestra, who yielded the baton to the young composer in order to advance his career. See also Grieg's diary entry for March 20, 1907, for some further comments on Nielsen's opera.

To Walter Niemann

The German composer and musicologist Walter Niemann (1876–1953) wrote several books on Scandinavian music: *Die Musik Skandinaviens*, 1906; *Edvard Grieg. Biographie und Würdigung seiner Werke*, which was co-authored by Norwegian composer and writer Gerhard Schjelderup (1859–1933), 1908; *Jean Sibelius*, 1917; and *Die nordische Klavier-Musik*, 1918. He was also editor of *Neue Zeitschrift für Musik* for a short time.

Grieg's letter to Niemann, written in German, is preserved in Universitätsbibliothek Leipzig (University of Leipzig Library).

Troldhaugen, Hop at Bergen, Norway
August 5, 1906

Dear Sir!

Your letter, in which you express appreciation for my art, has given me much pleasure. Your intention to dedicate your book on Scandinavian music[1] to me is exceptionally kind. I feel it with satisfaction as a sign of the times that just now—when Norway has at last achieved the long-desired goal of taking its place as an independent land among the nations of the world[2]—our music, too, will be appreciated. And especially by the German periodical in which Robert Schumann wrote so energetically and enthusiastically in support of Scandinavian music.[3]

It really is about time that Norwegian art at least be treated with understanding in Germany as well. And to put it bluntly: quite especially *my* art. How often I have had to tolerate criticisms of my compositions in German newspapers in the form of superficial banalities such as *Norwegerei, Er norwegert,*[4] etc. How devoid of understanding! No one would allow himself to insult a German composer by using such terms as *Deutschtum* or *Deutscherei.* And yet, it is in fact the case that German music critics adopt a mistrustful and unappreciative attitude not only toward Norwegian manifestations of national characteristics—no, toward all manifestations of national identity in music *outside Germany.* How petty and one-sided this is! I hope that in your book you will include a bold, serious word about this unfortunate situation! In so doing you would be performing a deed both good and *just.*

Forgive me: I'm getting completely off the subject! Back to the main theme. You have chosen as a title for your work *Die Musik Skandinaviens.* Allow me to note that this expression can easily be misunderstood. In my experience, people in Germany understand "Scandinavia" to include just Norway and Sweden. But

---

1 Grieg's music is given a prominent place in Walter Niemann's book *Die Musik Skandinaviens*, 1906.

2 Norway gained its independence from Sweden in 1905.

3 *Neue Zeitschrift für Musik*, published in Leipzig.

4 *Norwegerei*, a pejorative German word for "Norwegianness", i.e., an exaggerated and conscious use of Norwegian characteristics. *Er norwegert*: "He Norwegianizes".

among the Nordic countries, Denmark must also be included in the designation "Scandinavia". Since you have also dealt with Danish music in your book, it might be a good idea to add: (Dänemark, Norwegen, Schweden) under the title itself.

To what extent I will like the content of your book I must, naturally enough, wait to say anything about. But I hope I will like it, and on that assumption I accept your dedication with gratitude. I am also prepared to read through a proof copy in case you would appreciate hearing my views on matters where there might be some doubt. I am altogether at your service in word and deed and greet you with great respect as

Yours truly,
EDVARD GRIEG

To Georg Marcus Nordraach

Georg Marcus Nordraach (1811–90), a building contractor, was the father of Grieg's close friend and fellow composer, Rikard Nordraak (1842–66), who changed the spelling of his name out of a desire to "Norwegianize" it. Grieg and Nordraak had planned to go to Italy together in the fall of 1865, but when Grieg came to Berlin (where Nordraak was studying) he found that his friend had become so ill that he could not make the trip. In November Grieg had to go to Leipzig, where he had contracted to give two concerts. Upon his departure on November 2 he promised Nordraak that he would come back and wait for his health to improve so that they could proceed to Italy as planned. Despite his promise, however, Grieg did not return to Berlin but instead went directly from Leipzig to Italy—an act that was bitterly denounced by Nordraak.

After arriving in Rome, Grieg received a letter from Nordraak's father dated December 27, 1865. The letter was written in Berlin, where the elder Nordraach, at the insistent urging of the doctors, had gone to be at the bedside of his dying son. In his letter to Grieg, Nordraach tells Grieg of Rikard's despair upon learning that his friend had gone to Italy without him and his anger over "the enormous treachery he thought you had committed by leaving him without telling him of your plans."

Nordraak died on March 20, 1866, and was buried in Berlin. En route home from Italy in May, 1866, Grieg visited his late friend's grave. Upon leaving he took with him an oak leaf, which to this day is preserved in the beautiful letter that he sent to Nordraak's grieving father on May 7, 1866.

Grieg's letter to Georg Marcus Nordraach is preserved in Nasjonalbiblioteket, Oslo (National Library of Norway, Oslo Division).

Berlin, May 7, 1866

Mr. Nordraach, Christiania.

It is with a heavy heart that I take pen in hand today to send you a few lines from this city of sorrow. Even while I was in Italy I could have answered your kind letter, but I am convinced that it is best that I did not. Why should I, in the first, overwhelming time of sorrow, add more wormwood to the bitter cup that you had to drink?

What I could have written earlier would only have been an echo of the darkness and desolation that surrounded me. I do not know how a father's love differs from that of a true friend; I only know that I loved Rikard with all my heart. I know what I have had to suffer in leaving him, my best friend, lying on his sickbed; in seeing my concern and love misunderstood; in having to live in uncertainty and concern for five long months in southern Europe; and then at last, when hope once again began to stir in me, in receiving the bitter news that our young national art must fade in death because its champion was no more! I know what I have lived through in those days down there in Italy, when I didn't dare to confide in anyone because no one understood my sorrow. Only music felt compassion. I turned to the mournful tones that never fail in time of sorrow, and from them I received consolation. They whispered to me that Rikard Nordraak's name will live on in our Nordic art. His great, beautiful idea will carry it far beyond the grave and its oblivion—for that idea bears the stamp of truth and of eternity.[1]

"He who has something to live for cannot die," he once said to me in an intimate, happy moment. This certainly did not prove to be the case in the ordinary meaning of those words, but only now do I clearly understand their deep significance. And perhaps he uttered them in the consciousness of the triumph of the idea, even if the body should perish before the idea has been realized. But it will be realized, for it shall be my life's mission to carry it forward in his spirit. I feel the responsibility, but I feel that my strength and confidence have now also been doubled. Yes, it is as if he had given me this as a bequest—as if upon his death the vigorous, fighting spirit of his youth had flown to me and made its home in my soul.

We had both hoped that we could work together for the advancement of our national art. Since this was not granted to us, I simply have to hold loyally to the promise I gave him that his cause would be my cause, his goal mine. Do not think that what he aspired to will be forgotten. It will be my great mission to bring his few brilliant works to the people—our Norwegian people—to fight for their recognition, and to build further on their proud foundation. What he wanted was still too new to take root among the people, but the time will come when the national consciousness will be clearer, the need to assert it greater, and the name of each and every person who in his life work has struggled for it will be indelibly inscribed in our history. And among these, as surely as art has deep national significance, the name of Rikard Nordraak will be listed as one of the first!

Therefore, be comforted. Just let him rest serenely here in the foreign land. His spirit will hover over the homeland, where his cause will live and triumph!

May you not misunderstand these lines. They express the deepest feelings of my heart for the friend and for the artist. Both the friend and the artist have been of equally great significance for me and will be cherished in my memory with a veil of wistful love.

And now I bid you farewell. In the hope that some day in Christiania I may get acquainted with you personally, I am

Sincerely yours,
EDVARD GRIEG

The enclosed oak leaf is from Rikard's grave in the Jerusalemer Kirchhof cemetery. It is beautifully situated with an unobstructed view of the city.

---

[1] On April 6, 1866, when Grieg learned of Nordraaks's death, he wrote in his diary: "The saddest news that could strike me—Nordraak is dead! He, my only friend, my only great hope for our Norwegian art! And I do not have a single person here who can truly understand my sorrow. Let me, then, flee to the tones that never fail in time of sorrow! Composed a funeral march in honor of Nordraak!" (EG 107).

To John Paulsen

The Bergen author John Paulsen (1851–1924) was very productive as a writer, producing novels, plays, poems and volumes of memoirs in the course of his career.

In 1876 he went with Grieg to Bayreuth to attend the first Wagner festival, and following the festival the two friends visited Henrik Ibsen (1828–1906) at Gossensass. Paulsen later wrote two books about Ibsen—*Samliv med Ibsen* (*Life with Ibsen*) *I* (1906) and *II* (1913).

Three of Grieg's song opuses are settings of poems by Paulsen: *Five Songs* op. 26 (1876), *Five Songs* op. 58 (1894) and *Six Elegiac Songs* op. 59 (1894).

The location of the originals of the letters that follow is not known. Our source is Gunnar Hauch (ed.), *Breve fra Grieg* (*Letters from Grieg*), Copenhagen 1922.

1

Bergen, June 27, 1876

Dear Paulsen!
Thanks so very much for your letter! In reply I send you these few lines written in great haste. I am very busy, endlessly indisposed—and besides, we will see each other soon. That is really what this letter is written to tell you. I am leaving here in mid-July at the latest and will no doubt be in Copenhagen a week thereafter. Tell Feddersen[1] that he must have lodging for me, and give him warm greetings and thanks for his latest letter, to which I would prefer to reply orally.

I am glad to hear that you have started associating with people, but don't let yourself be flirted with—and especially, steer clear of the female writers,[2] because I don't think they will be good for you. You will have to put up with hearing that precisely because you and I are on a first-name basis.

Farewell, then, until we meet. Get ready to head south with me.[3]

Sincerely yours,
EDVARD GRIEG

P.S. Nina sends greetings! She now sings five of your poems to my music [op. 26].

Later in the evening

This [empty] page is strongly inviting me to tell you that I have become very fond of you and that I think you will understand me when I say this without further comments. In you I see much of myself as I was in former days. Therefore I can tell you: Get steel, steel, steel! And when you ask, "Where do I get it?" there is only

---

[1] Danish author Benjamin Feddersen (1823–1902) had been a close friend of Grieg since his youth.

[2] Grieg is referring here to Norwegian author Camilla Collett (1813–95) and Danish-born Magdalene Thoresen (1819–1903), both of whom were living in Copenhagen at this time.

[3] Grieg is referring to a trip to Bayreuth, where he would write a series of articles on the Wagner festival for the Bergen newspaper *Bergensposten*. The complete articles will be published in English translation in Benestad & Halverson (eds.), *Edvard Grieg: Diaries, Articles, Speeches* (Columbus, Ohio, 2001).

this one, terrible answer: You buy it with your heart's blood! God knows I speak from experience. Believe me, my friend, I am not sure that I should wish steel for you, it is so costly!! May God give you strength!

2

Børve, Hardanger, August 19, 1877

My dear Paulsen!

It is a beautiful Sunday morning. I am sitting in the schoolhouse, where I have taken over a little studio, and I see the church-goers as they pass by out on Sørfjorden. They are going to Ullensvang. Meanwhile, I am entering into another church— the great church that exists in memory—there to let my thoughts rise like pillars high up toward beauty and light. From that lofty place I then have a lovely panorama, and as I gaze toward distant coasts I see so much of what I have experienced that I feel that it alone was worth living for, even if I were to die today. And then I also see you, my friend—you, who with your childlike nature have touched me emotionally as have few others. Enjoy life to the full down there. What you are now experiencing will never come again. And even if it does so in a literal sense, you will never feel as you do now, you will never be receptive in precisely the same way as you are now. But do not do as some artists whom I know have done down there. Don't overdo the life of pleasure, for that leads to a cynicism that affects one's whole life and robs it of its freshness and its fragrance. Still: Your character will triumph, apart from all reflection. That's what I expect from you!

Thank you for your kind letter and for your birthday greeting! But listen: I don't want you to call me Norway's first 'skald of music'! I don't ever want to hear it again, because it is a lie. I could have become that—but I didn't. However, it is my intention to challenge fate to a duel. I still have enough strength to give it a try, and then we will see if I win. To that end I have given up all activity in Christiania and probably will stay someplace around here for the winter in order to work without interruption. Perhaps I will choose Ullensvang, three miles from here. I had thought of going abroad and applied for a grant for that purpose. But—we are in the same boat—my application was turned down![4] You can understand that after this experience I have, if possible, even less liking for Christiania than before. It would be best if I never had to set foot there again.

Still, I'm certainly "getting along" in a way, but can you say the same, poor fellow? If you have been irritated, Ibsen certainly has been no less so. Yes, conditions are wonderful in Christiania: The vilest cliques befoul the air there. [Some words are missing at this point.]

---

[4] Neither Grieg nor Paulsen received grants in 1877, but Paulsen—on Ibsen's recommendation—received a grant in 1878. For a full account of Grieg's varying fortunes as a grant applicant see his letters to the Ministry of Church and Education in Benestad & Halverson (eds.), *Edvard Grieg: Diaries, Articles, Speeches* (Columbus, Ohio, 2001).

This brings me to a related idea. My dear Paulsen! Never become a slave of *Morgenbladet* except out of conviction![5] I mean: Don't look to that clique to feather your own nest. Indeed, that would severely backfire. Perhaps you will not even achieve what you wish, but it is quite certain that you will lose some of that which you wish to keep: the integrity of your art. Whatever the future may bring you, remember what I have said to you here. These are not mere phrases, for I am speaking on the basis of actual experiences. I, too, have been captured from that quarter, unawares. But never have I regretted anything less than this, that after a brief acquaintance I told the whole lot of them to go to hell. Lies and slander are now being flung at me—but they can't reach me. If you come to Christiania you will first encounter a courtesy and friendliness that will surprise you so much that you will say: Surely there cannot be anything lurking here! But—the sly old fox is on the prowl.

Yet, what am I talking about, really? Well, it can only be intimated. If you pursue your own ideals, sooner or later you will run into this monster of prejudice, of half-this-and-half-that, of flabbiness, of egoism, of hate, of envy—yes, of bestiality, of low slavery. Only your own good genius can advise you how to escape it, but a warning from someone who wishes you well can also be a good thing.

So: These were the beautiful thoughts I wanted to bathe in, thoughts to which I tuned the strings in the first part of my letter. Yes, one can say with Kierkegaard:[6] "What is all human resolve!" Not even able to hold on to a thought for ten minutes!

Now I will tell you that next month I am giving a concert in Bergen, and then Nina will sing your songs. Perhaps "I Walked One Balmy Summer Eve" and "The First Primrose".

You mention *Ejvind Bolt*. But Welhaven's treatment is utterly impossible musically, although I grant that the subject matter has outstanding qualities. One couldn't even do something "based on" Welhaven. And to give a poet suggestions would be of almost no value if he didn't find the right solution on his own.[7]

So: According to *Bergensposten* you are working on *Dyveke*.[8] That's right, go ahead, go to the heart of the matter. That will give you steel. Unfortunately I don't

---

[5] The editor of the Christiania newspaper *Morgenbladet* at this time was Christian Fredrik Gotfried Friele (1821–99), under whose leadership it became an influential, arch-conservative organ.

[6] Danish philosopher Søren Kierkegaard (1813–55).

[7] In 1876 Grieg had abandoned work on *Olav Trygvason*, which was to have been a national opera with a libretto—never completed—by Norwegian author Bjørnstjerne Bjørnson (1832–1910). Grieg continued, however, to seek a suitable subject for an opera in the writings of Henrik Ibsen and elsewhere, but without success. The epic poem *Ejvind Bolt*, by Norwegian author J. S. Welhaven (1807–73), dealt with the Black Death and did not, in Grieg's opinion, lend itself to a musical treatment.

[8] Dyveke (?–1547) was the mistress of the Danish King Christian II (1481–1559), whom she met in Bergen. Later she returned with him to Copenhagen, and even after the king was married in 1515 he refused to end his relationship with her. Her death two years later was by poisoning—an act perpetrated by one of the King's subordinates. Several Norwegian and Danish poets have written about her life and sad fate.

have your short poems here, but I often remember the little poem *Dyveke.* For it contains music. I must make it into a *ballade.* I received your *Sjødronning* (*Ocean Queen*) from a bookstore in Christiania. It was from you, I suppose?! I have greatly enjoyed many things in it.

The Borch family[9] has come to Christiania now. That is to say, they did so at least several months ago. They were there already before I left, but strangely enough it didn't occur to them to look me up. Now I probably won't see them for years.

Whether you and I shall meet abroad again? My guess is that we won't see each other for a long time! Next winter (1878–79) I will be going abroad and then, I think, you will be coming home. And then? I will not live to be old, as far as I can understand. Lately I have often thought that there will be a catastrophe that just says, "Stop: thus far and no farther". It may be that it is called forth merely by the fact that I am stepping on an ant, or it may be that the cause lies deeper. Yes, who knows? Write soon to

Yours truly,
EDVARD GRIEG

P.S. Temporary address: Consul John Grieg, Jr. Bergen

I think I have not thanked you for your translation of Goethe's poem,[10] which was not used. The performance encountered obstacles.

3

Leipzig, September 8, 1879

My dear friend!
It is early morning, and I have just emerged from the blankets after an unforgivable night of carousing. As a result I have such a pervasive physical and moral hangover that I don't dare to promise you an "elevated" mood. But even so—I have just received your kind letter and must write. Thank you for all of your reports, and thank you most of all for those in which you show me a little of your inner life, of your struggle, your hopes and your disappointments. When I have become fond of someone, I can't be satisfied without getting at least a little peek behind the scenes. During the long hiatus in our correspondence I have, so far as possible, followed your career and rejoiced in all the recognition you have received. You say that you had dreamt of more! Yes, but who can have his dreams realized *at your age*? Believe me, you have already achieved much. And if you want to hear some good advice, don't try to achieve too much *outwardly* (NB, when

---

[9] The Norwegian sculptor Christopher Borch (1807–96), who had lived in Rome for eight years, returned to Christiania in 1877.

[10] Goethe's poem *Gesang der Geister über den Wassern,* which Schubert set for male chorus and strings, D 714.

material conditions don't compel you to do so). There is nothing that hinders the progress of one's ideals more than premature fame. I will say nothing about the fact that the joy you feel when your works establish themselves—albeit later, but, on the other hand, *on their own*, without your help—is genuine and substantial in a quite different way.

Lost illusions! It would not be good if one did not lose them. Remember that for each one you lose you take a step forward toward truth. And surely we can agree that however beautiful the illusions may be, the truth is still more beautiful—although, to be sure, it is often unpleasant. As for myself, I cannot speak of one lost illusion at a time. No, in my case they have showered down by the hundreds like rotten fruit in the gusty wind.

Indeed, I have been out in the gusty wind. Perhaps a little of the good fruit has been blown away too—unfortunately. But I still have some left, and that of the best—of the kind that does not fall to the ground in stormy weather. It is absolutely terrible how much an artist sees around him that is bad, low and stupid. It is a matter of seeing and not seeing! And I constantly say to myself: I *will* not see, I *will* rejoice in all the beauty, goodness and truth and move forward confidently, without letting myself be forced into sympathies and antipathies. Let criticism and meanness carry on their own business. One is happiest when one sticks to the eternal world of nature—or, more correctly, to that which one confidently feels is the best part of one's own nature. In your letter you have set certain strings in my soul vibrating, so excuse me for falling into contemplation.

Yes, that Molbech![11] He is one of the genuine ones—genuine preceded by *un*. I hate him, although I scarcely know him. And what is even better: I also hate his *Ambrosius*, which I do not know at all. But I can't help it. A half personality cannot ever create something whole.

Thank you so much for the planned dedication! I would like to read the stories. It is absolutely damnable that Molbech really should have it in his power to prevent the publication by Hegel.[12] Don't you know Munch?[13] To be sure, he is a friend of Molbech (!) but he would certainly be of much help to you. You should write to him (with milk and honey—he needs sweet stuff like that, poor fellow!) and you will see: It will work out.

Thanks for the photo! It's good, but you certainly have gotten thin! You should not worry too much about the world! Especially not about women! I think

---

[11] Danish author and critic Chr. K. F. Molbech (1821–88), whose best-known work is the play *Ambrosius* (1878). Molbech was the so-called "censor" at the Royal Theater in Copenhagen, i.e., the person who read through all the new plays submitted to the theater and made recommendations as to which of them should be performed.

[12] Fredrik Vilhelm Hegel (1817–87) and his son Jacob Hegel (1858–1918) were the owners of the Gyldendal Publishing Company in Copenhagen, the firm that published the works of all of the major Norwegian authors of the day.

[13] Norwegian poet Andreas Munch (1811–84).

I can read a "love story" between the lines of your letter. Remember: Women *want to play* and that is all! That sounds hard and materialistic, but there is some truth in it all the same. No woman has ever comprehended or ever will comprehend that which is great, that which is wild, that which is boundless in a man's—an artist's—love. And if I am right in this, I have at the same time proved that an artist should not marry. I don't dare to maintain that that was what I intended to prove, but it flowed so naturally from my pen.

I have recently had my picture taken but have still not received any prints. I will send you one as soon as I get them. Now we will really exchange letters again! There is indeed nothing nicer than friendly letters! My imagination is rarely as active as when I am writing to a friend! And you are a friend to me: I feel it as I sit here writing. Not because I begin the letter with "Dear friend!"—but because you are the person you are. But one promise I demand from you: I do not want to hear all your words of praise about *my* art. I do not deserve them. And you do not thereby do me any favor, for it is not good for me to hear that sort of thing.

Now the sun is breaking through, and I will go out and catch a breath of fresh air. Therefore, goodbye for now! Write soon to

Yours truly,
EDVARD GRIEG

P.S. Can you read my scribbling? If not, tell me and I will try to do better.

4

Bergen, April 28, 1881

Dear friend!

(. . .) Let me first of all thank you for your many proofs of my having been in your thoughts. In truth, I have not deserved all these manifestations of friendship. How often I have wanted to thank you—but then I didn't know your address at the moment. So what happened? Other thoughts swept away both the impulse and the duty. I found so many beautiful things in your *Margaritha*, especially in the descriptive passages. For the domestic mercenary types it was, as you know, altogether too realistic. For that reason I was doubly inclined to defend it. And now to the most recent joy you have given me: the joy over your triumphs and your progress in general. Soon you can speak of Berlin and Hamburg like Napoleon did of Wagram and Austerlitz! Is not the play that was performed in these cities the same one that you once sent to me under the name *Et Ungdoms-feiltrinn* [*A Youthful Lapse*]? And has this not helped you achieve a more independent existence? It has often awakened my highest admiration that you have had sufficient toughness and strength to endure in foreign countries, struggling to exist both physically and spiritually. Therefore I am doubly happy over this breakthrough.[14] Your feeling was certainly correct: It was a matter of staying outside Norway until *either/or* occurred. If you had come home before that time, you would have been done for. Just stay on where you are. It is still too soon for you to encounter the cold shoulder from Scandinavia. You will catch spiritual pneumonia if you don't wait.

And now you are in Sorrento (?) writing a novel? What a fabulously productive person you are! In any case you are living in a productive period, something that occurs in the life of every true artist. Yes, it is a delightful time. *My* productive period was so short. I have waited and am still waiting for it to return. But the fine web of circumstances must be in order before this can happen.

Recently I have just completed a long and strenuous undertaking here in the city, the goal of which was to elevate the cultural life of old Bergen.[15] But the result exacted too great a price. In any case, I have had enough of it. It is going as Bjørnson once said: Among us, no man of spirit can hold out for more than a short period at a time. A spurt now, a spurt then. But the sad thing is that a Norwegian artist's creative work also becomes erratic and discordant because of the adverse conditions. Therefore I can, in a way, understand those who have sufficient insight to turn their back on Norway and become European. But I could not do that. No, never! I, unfortunately, have a heart! I wish I had some of the modern Frenchmen's heartlessness. Damn this confounded subjectivity: It is life's most beautiful blessing—and it is the fountain of misfortune!

What are you doing this summer? I will stay where I am. Just think if we could meet somewhere next winter. Write to me soon. I will not bother to ask you to temper justice with mercy. Besides, the concept of mercy is old-fashioned.

Warm greetings from both of us.

Yours truly,
EDVARD GRIEG

5

Karlsbad, June 3, 1881

Dear friend!
No, I have neither forgotten nor half-forgotten you. But you know that in music there are rests and that these can sometimes be long. Beethoven made absolutely uncanny use of them in his *adagios*—but there they cannot be misunderstood. Unfortunately it is different with interruptions in correspondence. Therefore I

---

[14] Grieg is referring to Paulsen's play *Falkenstrøm & Søn,* which had been successfully performed in several places abroad.

[15] Grieg served as conductor of the Music Society Harmonien, predecessor of the modern Bergen Philharmonic Orchestra, in 1880–82.

will pull you out of your delusion immediately. Look carefully at where I am. It really is Karlsbad.[16] I have been plagued by a stomach problem for a long time, and now the doctor ordered me to go. And I had to obey, reluctant though I was to have my only, longingly anticipated work time spoiled. So I came here along with a traveling companion, Lieutenant Hans Christie,[17] and started the cure three days ago. The gods know what good it will do. I am feeble and incapacitated in soul and body. Just think of getting up at 5 A.M. each morning, drinking four large glasses of warm water and walking in between, not getting breakfast until sometime during the forenoon, keeping to the strictest diet consisting mainly of eggs, milk and bread! Yes, it produces a wonderful human being. But it's a passing phase, said the fox.[18]

And now to you, my dear friend! How do things really stand? Are you the same old Paulsen? I don't think so. It is as if I read between the lines much that is not good. If you have confidence in me, tell me a little of everything. However —I really don't deserve it, since I myself am responsible for the gap in the history of your development which I now want filled in. You are living in Rome! Yes, I can understand your reason for that. I, too, hope very much to spend a winter down there sometime soon. But the association with Ibsen is not giving you what you had expected. I can understand that. A person who has concerned himself so much with the concept of suspicion cannot come across as warm and pleasant in his personal contacts, even if he is genuine. The same goes for Mrs. Collett. I met her in Copenhagen, and what she offered me was *not cakes* but cloying stories. Bjørnson is supposed to have said, when Mrs. Collett's article on him was published: "Poor thing, she is such a liar!" And I must admit that the reported incidents with Hegel are indicative of a poor memory—to use a polite expression regarding a woman. Bjørnson and I have been on the outs since 1875, i.e., to speak very personally, so you must not think I am inclined to side with him for the sake of anything other than the truth.[19]

As for Ibsen, moreover, it surprises me greatly to hear of his conservatism. For Kr. Janson[20] wrote some time ago in a letter to Norway from Rome that if Ibsen's recipe were to be followed we would have complete anarchy. All farmers are stupid, he is alleged to have said to Janson, "but especially the Norwegian

---

[16] Karlsbad was a health spa in Germany. The town of Karlsbad now lies in the Czech Republic and has been renamed Karlovy Vary.

[17] Norwegian career officer Hans Christie (1843–1920).

[18] This is an abbreviated version of a saying well-known in Norway: "'It's just a passing phase' said the fox as he was being skinned."

[19] An interruption of Grieg and Bjørnson's collaboration on *Olav Trygvason* in 1876 led also to an interruption in their friendship that lasted until 1889.

[20] Kristofer Janson (1841–1917), a Norwegian poet who wrote in *landsmål* (later called *nynorsk,* "New Norwegian"), an indigenous form of the Norwegian language created by combining elements taken from various Norwegian dialects. Grieg's first song to a "New Norwegian" text—"Little Lad"—was a setting of a poem by Janson.

ones". Some divine words indeed—NB, to Janson. But to harshly criticize Norway nowadays is fully justified. Think of the Wergeland nonsense.[21] Christiania is nothing but one big insane asylum. And then all the party-puffery in Norway! No, the older I get the more I say to myself: Not conservative, not liberal—but both. Not subjective, not objective, but both. Not realist, not idealist, but both. The one must be fused with the other.

But now farewell and to hell with all philosophy—for it is not "kurgemäß".[22] Greet friends and acquaintances and send a few lines to

Yours truly,
Edvard Grieg

6

Karlsbad, May 28, 1882
Stadt Baden, Parkstrasse

Dear friend!
Your letter went to Karlsbad via Bergen, which is why you are not getting these lines until today. It made me very happy yesterday to see your well-known handwriting. Here in the world of loneliness, boredom and sadness your lines were doubly welcome. I had to give up my planned stop in Copenhagen, for otherwise I would have gotten here too late. But I hope to even things up on my way back. It would be great to see you again, but you must remember that a Karlsbad patient is a frightfully boring character with whom to associate. Not a penny's worth of youthful outlook or zest for life. Just today I said to Nina that I wish to God I had you here. You surely would have made me come to life!

I greatly look forward to your book, whatever may be the case regarding who is indebted to whom. If only you would let Denmark be Scandinavia and avoid getting mixed up in our [Norwegian] clammy fog-banks! For it is easier to get into them than to get out of them again. Do everything you can to avoid coming home yet. I assure you that what I am giving you is a good piece of advice. I have the feeling that it would destroy you if you settled down at home now. However—now comes the egoist—if you came home this winter we could have it really nice! I have resigned from Harmonien so as to be able to do my own work in complete peace and quiet. So we could go on hikes in the mountains and talk about everything that is noble and beautiful! But fortunately the temptation would not be very great for you, for you would certainly feel that you had a better option than to wall yourself in among philistines.

I am seeking seclusion, so I will stay at home. I just want to be free of all kinds

---

[21] Grieg is alluding to the discussion in Christiania's literary circles as to whether Bjørnson should be the principal speaker at the unveiling of the statue of Norwegian poet Henrik Wergeland (1808–45).

[22] "kurgemäß": compatible with the "cure" Grieg was undergoing at Karlsbad.

of significant outward impressions. If I were looking for these, then I certainly would go abroad. If everything goes as I hope, I will indeed head south next fall—1883. And then? Well, I'll worry about that when the time comes! In the meantime it is my intention to visit Copenhagen at the end of June, when it would be a great pleasure to see you. Also greet all other friends and acquaintances—and you yourself must live better than

Yours truly,
EDVARD GRIEG

7

Bergen, April 3, 1883

Dear Paulsen!
No, now it is getting too crazy! God knows how many letters I have to thank you for! And in addition your beautiful book, better than all the letters! Yes, I got a lot of pleasure from it. I have the definite feeling that it must signify a big step forward for you.[23] I should have told you this long, long ago, and I freely admit that I have never been a more unforgivable letter-writer than I have been this winter. I have at least fifty letters from all corners of the world lying unanswered. But now spring is coming and the annual scrubbing of ceilings and walls. I assure you that I am going around here like a person in need of a thorough cleaning. Would that I could, mentally speaking, take a steam bath and emerge from it twenty pounds lighter! One's soul becomes as heavy as lead here. For that reason I shall, must and will go abroad again, even though I don't know how. I would like so much to stay in Paris for one winter. If I can manage that this fall, I will do it. Come along! Yes, do it! Tell me what you intend to do. Maybe we could meet again as young and happy men. But that will certainly not be in Christiania. What do you really want to do there? It's really a big den of philistines. For it is philistinism to concentrate on being a conservative or a liberal instead of being a human being.

It would amuse me to know what is your real impression of the people of Christiania. It is possible that I take altogether too dim a view of them. And this boring terrain with these long ridges. No, either mountains or the sea! When I take my usual stroll on the mountain path "Fjeldveien"—with that glorious view that lets one's thoughts soar far away—and then think of Karl Johan Street and the park,[24] I am overcome by a sudden feeling of gratitude to fate, which has thrown me here instead of there. But home, of course, is where one's sense of beauty lies, so away, away! Yes, a Norwegian artist is a strange bird, with his monotonous song: "away, away!" and "home, home!" With this song life passes by!

---

[23] Grieg is probably referring to Paulsen's novel *Moderne Damer* (*Modern Ladies*).

[24] Karl Johan is the main street in downtown Christiania/Oslo. The park to which Grieg is referring is the one surrounding the royal palace.

Woops, somebody is knocking! So long, then! I'll write more when I can. This was just to tell you that I exist and that you are remembered by

Yours truly,
EDVARD GRIEG

P.S. Nina sends greetings!

8

Troldhaugen at Bergen, April 30, 1885

Dear Paulsen!
Here I sit in my Troldhaugen,[25] buffeted by the Bergen winds, and I would like to send you a few words in reply to your kind letter. But as a poet you know as well as I what it means to be "up" and to be "down". The former I am not, so don't expect anything that foams or crackles. There are times when I feel that it is the most beautiful thing in the world to be precisely a *Norwegian* artist. At other times—today, for example—it seems to me like an absolute damnation. And then the envy stirs within me when I think about the fact that you, lucky fellow that you are, are down there in a country where you can bathe in impressions of beauty of all kinds. No, there will not be a happy Norwegian artist—NB: *with* a love of the homeland—until everyone can spread his wings and fly like the birds, in *presto* tempo, wherever he wishes. *Without* a love of the homeland—this strange characteristic which several other artists are so fortunate (or unfortunate) as to lack—it is just fine to be a Norwegian, live abroad, and be ashamed of one's own country. Yes, today I envy such people!

This fall I must invent some deviltry to get away again. Let us plan to meet someplace. Thanks for your portrait! There is no doubt that it looks like you. Other than that, the bald pate indicates that one can also fret abroad—unless heredity's consuming demands have come into play here.

What you say about the fate of your play at Bergen's theater is just what could be anticipated here. One can't expect anything other than such treatment at home. So you see, you belong to the ranks of the prophets.[26] What more can you wish for? Yesterday I saw Mrs. Edgren's *Hvorledes man gjør godt* [*How One Does Well*], a boldly limned work that they weren't willing to perform in the playwright's homeland.[27] You see, this must be a consolation to you. [Some text is missing at this point.]

One thing you do not have down there, however: the fragrance of the world

---

25 Grieg had moved into his new villa, Troldhaugen, in the spring of 1885.

26 Grieg is alluding to Matthew 13:57, "A prophet is not without honor except in his own country and in his own house." (RSV)

27 The play by Anne Charlotte Edgren-Leffler (1849–92) was a protest against social conditions in her native Sweden.

of nature, of birch and chokecherry, which in all humility and virginal innocence are asking permission these days to burst forth. It is a glorious sight, which in spite of everything still engenders faith in that which is pure and genuine.

Farewell, dear friend, and write again soon to

Yours truly,
EDVARD GRIEG

My address: Hop Station at Bergen.

9

Troldhaugen, January 21, 1887

Dear Paulsen!

I remember that one time in a letter to me you expressed the wish for a whole lot of opposition so that you wouldn't get too cocky. But that was a long time ago—so long, unfortunately, that you probably don't remember it any more. But in any case, after what you wrote to me most recently, it is appropriate to remind you of it now. We all think that the characters in *Gaffelen* [*The Fork*] were some numbskulls, some extremely short-sighted blockheads—and we are not a whit different ourselves, when you get right down to it. No, if we are going to wish for something let us wish in rosy colors, for existence provides plenty of the dark colors. Fate sees to that. Between the lines of your letter I think I catch a glimpse of the real secret of your despondency: You can't get yourself into shape. That is the worst battle an artist can wage, but it is also the one that makes him the strongest—if he does not give in. I think it is the time in which you are living that is nudging you. It goads you and leads you to think that you belong to it. But neither you nor I belong to this time, my friend. We are Romanticists, both of us, and if at the moment the world doesn't seem to have use for Romanticism in literature, it is weak or cowardly to use that as a reason to renounce Romanticism. It brings its own severe punishment, too, for one messes up one's natural bent in the process. Romanticism will return before anyone realizes it. I believe that in your heart of hearts you are one of its men. If this is the case, then be a man and don't hesitate to be one of its messengers. If one should end up in the mill pond,[28] then our literature will have done its duty and a new Romanticism, one that stands on the shoulders of that which we have now experienced, will burst forth. Yes, be on the alert! If we are living twenty years from now, we will talk about this. Do you remember that I once told you that I thought the fairytale was the world of your future? But one must be a child, or something of a child, to understand what I mean.

---

[28] Grieg is alluding to the concluding scene in Ibsen's play *Rosmersholm* (1886), where the main characters Rebecca West and Johannes Rosmer leap to their deaths in the mill pond. The play had had its Norwegian premiere at The National Stage in Bergen on January 17, 1887.

Lastly, I cannot deny myself the enjoyment of consoling you with something that I found recently in Jacobsen's posthumous papers.[29] In any case it did me good as it applies to my own case. Jacobsen writes that Thorvaldsen[30] is supposed to have said one day, "Now I'm beginning to decline, for I'm beginning to think well of my own works." So: When you do not think well of your own works you are living in a period in which you are advancing and developing. Be sure of that. I have felt exactly the same way.

Damn, damn, damn! Almost four pages of philosophizing! But if you sat here at Troldhaugen this evening you would not be surprised. Outside it is trickling and pouring, howling and blowing. The conditions for walking are impossible: enough patches of ice and slush to break your arms and legs. As a result, we sit holed up in our loneliness, and not a living soul dares to come to see us. So of course the philosophy must flourish. All the more in that these days I am in the middle of—yes, what shall I call it?—a composition holiday.

I have just written a *Violin Sonata* [op. 45], which I shall now have the pleasure of having lie on my desk until autumn before I get a chance to hear it. For in the autumn I *will* get away. If I can keep going that long here at home during this "time of decadence and decline". Politics has poisoned everything, everything. NB: not the great politics, which has vision and enthusiasm, but the politics of hypocrisy, pettiness and egoism. Indeed, that is the only kind to be found in this country at present.

Have you read Christian Krohg's book?[31] It certainly is genuine art, for behind everything there lurks the deep feeling. But that a confused society doesn't know what to do about such a book is understandable. Be that as it may, today Krohg is Norway's—not to say Scandinavia's—most popular man. And for that he can thank the Norwegian government. For despite its free outlook and the provocative character of the subject, the book would not have stirred up so many dregs but for the official morality that is now at the helm, and that for me is worse than if the whole city of Christiania consisted of only [some words are missing at this point].

No, enough for now—before I jump out of my skin. Write again soon!
Warm greetings from

Yours truly,
Edvard Grieg

---

[29] The posthumous writings of Danish author Jens Peter Jacobsen (1847–85) had recently been published by Vilhelm Møller (1846–1904) and Edvard Brandes (1847–1931).

[30] Danish sculptor Bertel Thorvaldsen (1770–1844).

[31] The distinguished Norwegian painter Christian Krohg (1852–1925) was also a writer. In 1886 his novel *Albertine*, which was an attack on the hypocritical morality of the time, was published. On December 21, 1886, by order of the Ministry of Justice, the book was banned and all available copies were impounded. Moreover, Krohg was indicted for "violation of public standards of decency and morality" and was fined.

10

Troldhaugen, July 15, 1898

Dear Paulsen!
Thanks for your letter and for the translations![32] Since the music festival[33] I have been sick. Naturally it is the old gut[34] that is acting up again. Yesterday I was in bed all day. I have now lived for 3–4 days on crackers and milk. You understand.

Well: I have had to make a few changes in the translations, partly out of regard for the spirit of the music, partly for the sake of the declamation. And lastly, I have kept the original where that was possible in order not to lose the flavor. In that respect I have been bolder than you, who in my opinion have been very cautious. Is that also my belly that is at work? Yes, it is versatile, that jackass. Now go to Wilhelm Hansen[35] and read through my changes—and remember that it is the Danes brought up on Norwegian literature that I have in mind, not the uppity Copenhageners. Pure, out-and-out Danish would, in my opinion, completely destroy Garborg. It won't hurt the people down there to stretch their imaginations a little. I understand full well that the task has been difficult—and doubly so for you in this case, when the words must be adapted to the music rather than the reverse. This has given first you and then me a lot to pay attention to. I would not have recommended that you undertake this task if I did not assume that it interested you.

I was very glad that I could be one of those who got you a "stipend". May both your soul and your body get some benefit from the trip. What a pity that you were not here during the music festival! It was simply unique. Indeed, people here have no idea of what they have had. They enjoyed themselves. Period. But that the festival—as a Norwegian who is living abroad put it[36]—"is one of the most important events in our cultural life in this century"—nobody realizes that. To curry favor with the press is not my style. For that reason you will find little or nothing in the newspapers. That, too, is unique. A unique proof of the press standard in this country. Something should be written about that by an unbiased person. But—where shall we find one? I myself am quite certainly such a person, and if I have lived my life until now without the Norwegian press I can surely get along without it for the days that are left to me. But frankly speaking, if I can avoid it

---

[32] Grieg is referring here to Paulsen's translation into Danish of *Haugtussa* by Norwegian author Arne Garborg (1851–1924). Grieg had set selected poems from Garborg's book in the song cycle *The Mountain Maid* op. 67. The eight songs comprising the cycle were composed in the summer of 1895 as settings of the original "New Norwegian" texts, but not until 1898 were they printed in Copenhagen by Wilhelm Hansen in an edition containing the original text plus a Danish translation and in Leipzig by C. F. Peters Musikverlag in a German translation.

[33] The Norwegian music festival held in Bergen in the summer of 1898.

[34] Grieg uses the word *kakkelovn*, literally "heating stove", but the context makes it clear that he is referring to his digestive system.

[35] The Wilhelm Hansen Music Publishing Company in Copenhagen.

[36] Grieg is referring to the Norwegian journalist and vice-consul Hans Lien Brækstad (1845–1915), who lived in London.

I would rather not touch the press—not even with a ten-foot pole and a handkerchief full of eau de Cologne.

Farewell, dear Paulsen, and write soon!

Sincerely,
EDVARD GRIEG

11

Voksenkollen Sanatorium,[37] *December 29, 1900*

Dear John Paulsen!
Fortunately silence is not the same as forgetfulness. But illness has prevented me from doing any letter-writing of late. But now, before the year ends, I will spite fate and pretend that nothing is wrong with me just to thank you for the book.[38] You can well understand that it had to be especially interesting to me, for whom it awakened memories from a long-vanished, rich and happy time. It was a time with *Sturm und Drang*—but there was *life* in it. Otherwise I think that the best chapter in the book is the one on Camilla Collett. Here you have created both a source document and a beautiful and empathetic portrayal. You will be glad to hear, if you don't know it already, that old Ibsen and his wife have read the book with great enjoyment. This I learned from Sigurd Ibsen, who is staying here at the moment, as is also his wife.[39]

If I were a clever journalist I would sing the praises of this place for all the world to hear. It is a little fairytale world: It is with good reason that people have dubbed the sanatorium "Soria-Moria Castle".[40] But it is not just the fairytale's gentle side that one gets to know here: You also get a good dose of its gruff wildness. Today a snowstorm is raging around us, so everything is enveloped in whiteness, and it is pretty much impossible for anyone to get here. The fact is that we live 1600 feet above sea level, and today we have the feeling of being in the wild mountains.

Warm greetings, dear Paulsen, and accept the most cordial New Year's wishes both from my wife and from

Yours truly,
EDVARD GRIEG

---

[37] Voksenkollen Sanatorium was located on the outskirts of Christiania, near Holmenkollen.

[38] In 1900 Paulsen had published the book *Erindringer* (*Memoirs*), which, among other things, contains descriptions of his encounters with some of the leading figures in the world of literature and the arts.

[39] The Norwegian statesman Sigurd Ibsen (1859–1930), son of Henrik Ibsen, was married to the singer Bergliot Bjørnson (1869–1953), daughter of Bjørnstjerne Bjørnson.

[40] "Soria-Moria Castle" is the castle in a fairytale that is well-known to all Norwegians. In 1901 Grieg wrote an effusively positive article about Voksenkollen Sanatorium entitled "The Soria-Moria Castle". It will be printed in translation in Benestad & Halverson (eds.), *Edvard Grieg: Diaries, Articles, Speeches* (Columbus, Ohio, 2001).

P.S. I suppose you have heard about Dr. Abraham's sudden death.[41] A hard blow for me. He was truly a fatherly friend to me.

12

Troldhaugen, November 6, 1901

Dear Paulsen!
Of course I should have thanked you for the book long ago. But I haven't been able to, haven't been up to it. I am simply not a human being. [Some words are missing here.]

The leaves are falling, sometimes gently, sometimes like here—in a storm. I could wish that I were a Buddhist, the better to understand and sympathize with the idea of annihilation. The concepts of peace and rest should, indeed, be something beautiful. But the Christianity in which we were brought up has nothing left but a sympathetic shrug of the shoulders for the seeking souls whose pathway through life it has made difficult. It will take hundreds of generations to free us from the yoke of Christianity. [Some words are missing here.]

Warm greetings from Nina and from

Yours truly,
EDVARD GRIEG

P.S. The letter became as it had to be. Forgive me!

13

Christiania, June 4, 1905
Hotel Westminster

Dear Paulsen!
Thank you for your letter and for your article in *Verdens Gang*. It reflects warm appreciation. But since an article like that could easily be used later as a source, it should not contain factual errors. "The Old Mother" was not written "when my mother had recently died". She was still living in Sandviken at that time. I brought her the song, which had arisen from thoughts of her who with boundless energy and an unceasing sense of duty toiled and suffered until she dropped. I wish that at some time or other you would get this corrected.[42]

The English lady about whom you speak in connection with "Last Spring"

---

[41] Dr. Max Abraham (1831–1900) had been the owner of the C. F. Peters Musikverlag in Leipzig, the firm that published most of Grieg's compositions. He had committed suicide on December 8, 1900.

[42] *Verdens Gang* was the leading Liberal newspaper in Christiania. Paulsen's article, entitled "Regarding Grieg and the Vinje Songs", was later reprinted in his book *The Trip to Monaco*, Christiania 1909, pp. 135–46. *Twelve Songs to Poems by A. O. Vinje* is op. 33, published in 1881. All of the songs mentioned in this letter are from op. 33. "The Old Mother" (no. 7) was composed in 1873, two years before Grieg's mother's death.

was an Austrian. She was the great violinist Mrs. Wilhelmina Norman-Neruda, later called Lady Hallé after the German pianist and conductor whom she married.[43] "Beside the Stream" was composed at Børve in Hardanger, not at Lofthus, in 1877. "The Old Mother" was earlier—yes, it was the very first of the Vinje songs: It dates from 1872 or '73. All the others were written one after the other in my childhood home on Strand Street in the spring of 1880.

It is quite certain, as you say, that in addition to the purely spiritual element, the mountainous terrain of Hardanger also lies hidden in these songs. It totally captivated me for a couple of years and put its stamp on everything I wrote at that time. Moreover, its influence has extended right down to the present day.

This, then, has been confidential information—a rarity for me—occasioned by your article.

We leave for Bergen this evening. See you at home!

Warm greetings from

Yours truly,
EDVARD GRIEG

---

[43] Grieg is referring to the Czech (not Austrian) violinist Wilhelmina Neruda (1838–1911).

To Carl Rabe

The German violinist Carl Rabe (1829–97) came to Norway in 1851 as a member of the Schwarzenbacher Orchestra. He settled in Bergen, where in 1858 he established a music store and publishing company. Little by little the business expanded to include also a concert bureau and a lending library. Rabe also continued to perform as a violinist in the Music Society Harmonien, the predecessor of the modern Bergen Philharmonic Orchestra. The correspondence between Grieg and Rabe shows that Grieg often made use of the services of Rabe's firm.

Grieg's Letter 1 to Rabe is preserved in Nasjonalbiblioteket, Oslo (National Library of Norway, Oslo Division), Letter 2 in Bergen Offentlige Bibliotek (Bergen Public Library).

1

Grefsen Baths, Christiania, June 5, 1894

Dear Rabe!
Enclosed you will find a document regarding a chest that is being sent to me from Paris in care of your address, and I am sending it to you to keep the record straight as I do not know if it is needed when the shipment arrives. Moreover, the chest does not contain *musical instruments* but printed music and a glass jar.

My wife asks me to tell you that if a box comes from Leipzig containing a cotton dress, you can confidently swear that it is used since she has worn it at concerts for several years.

It's worse with a Bechstein concert grand piano that will be coming to me in Bergen in care of your address at the end of this month. It is a present from Bechstein, and I have asked that it be played both privately and publicly in London before it is sent so that it can enter Bergen duty-free. Give me your good advice, and if you fear difficulties kindly let me hear from you as soon as possible. Other than that the big question is: Where shall the piano be put? For I don't have room for it at Troldhaugen. Can you not find some place for it during the summer months? For—just between us!—it is my intention to move to Bergen for a few months in the fall in order finally to give the much-discussed concerts. And then I will take the piano with me to my living quarters. But it would be very strange if some music-lover or other wouldn't be interested in having a Bechstein standing in his living room with the understanding that he could make use of it. To be sure, it would have to be someone to whom one could *safely* entrust it. Hopefully you will come up with some brilliant idea.[1]

We are staying here so that, if possible, I can become healthier before I head homeward. They are plying me with baths and massages, so I hope to be happy

---

[1] The piano was placed in the home of Johan Halvorsen (1864–1935) in Bergen.

and healthy when we see each other at the end of the month at the latest. If the longing for home becomes too strong, I will cut short the cure.

Warm greetings to your son. I hope he enjoyed the concert that I saw in the newspapers he was going to give.

And with that, farewell for today! Warm greetings to all! Also from my wife.

Sincerely yours,
EDVARD GRIEG

P.S. Should any other boxes come for me, please hold them for me until my arrival.

2

Copenhagen, December 29, 1894
Hotel King of Denmark

Dear Rabe!
Before the year goes to rest I want, in a few words, to send you hearty thanks for it—thanks for all the friendship and the kindness you have shown me, and not least, thanks for the memorable October days with *your* invaluable contribution to the fact that I managed them and carried them off.[2]

Please let me keep your friendship also in the new year, be it with or without concerts. Besides, I don't think you have to worry. This time it was ten years since I last gave concerts in Bergen, and next time it will certainly not be less. If I should die in the meantime, I want to be buried at home and to have my *Funeral March in Memory of Rikard Nordraak*—the score of which always accompanies me on my travels—played *as well as possible* over my grave. You must see to that. That is the friendly favor I ask of you in the new year—should it be required.

Warmest greetings to you and all of yours, also the best wishes for the new year both from my wife and from

Yours truly,
EDVARD GRIEG

---

[2] Grieg had given concerts in Bergen on October 16, 18, 20 and 21, performing *Bergliot* and *Scenes from Olav Trygvason*. He was so pleased with the musicians' performances that he wrote an open letter of thanks to them that appeared in *Bergens Tidende*, the city's principal newspaper, on October 22. Grieg did not perform in Bergen again until the Norwegian music festival that took place in the summer of 1898.

To Alexander Rajchmann

Grieg's correspondence with Alexander Rajchmann, administrative director of the Warsaw Philharmonic, deals almost exclusively with details concerning Grieg's participation in various proposed concerts in Warsaw. The first such concert took place on April 22, 1902, with Venezuelan pianist Teresa Carreño (1853–1917) as soloist in the *Piano Concerto* and Norwegian soprano Elisa Wiborg (1862–1938) in selected songs. The concert was an enormous success, and Grieg returned to Warsaw for concerts on April 14 and 15 of the following year, this time with French pianist Raoul Pugno (1852–1914) as soloist in the *Piano Concerto* and Finnish singer Ida Ekmann (1875–1942) performing a group of songs. A large women's chorus sang in *Before a Southern Convent* and an even larger men's chorus in *Land-sighting.* Grieg had also planned to conduct yet another concert in Warsaw in the spring of 1906 but had to cancel both for reasons of illness and because of the uncertain political situation in Poland.

The Grieg collection in Bergen Offentlige Bibliotek (Bergen Public Library) includes seventeen letters to Grieg from the Warsaw Philharmonic. Fifteen of them are in Rajchmann's hand, the other two are typewritten. All are in German. The Bergen collection also has drafts of Grieg's letters of reply; these, too, are in German. Some of the latter are so complete that they could almost be described as copies. The one included here in translation is a draft of Grieg's last letter to Rajchmann.

[Troldhaugen, July 31, 1905]

Dear Mr. Rajchmann!
I can only regret that under no circumstances will it be possible for me to conduct in Warsaw on March 16 [1906].[1] The only possible time for me would be the middle of April. Nor is my health good enough to allow me at this early date to make a firm commitment. But I would be very happy if by January it might be possible for me to give a definitive answer.

I take the liberty of noting also that when you wish to have me participate both as a performer in the *Violin Sonata* and as conductor, I must demand a double honorarium.[2]

Lastly I must express my sincerest thanks to you for your good wishes in connection with the national independence that we have achieved. I am happy to have lived through this great and deeply longed-for time, and together with my countrymen I harbor the optimistic hope that what has been achieved can also be of significance for other nations that strive toward the same goal.

With respectful greetings I am,

Sincerely yours,
EDVARD GRIEG

---

[1] In a letter dated July 19, 1905, Rajchmann had expressed his pleasure both regarding Grieg's willingness to participate in another concert in Warsaw and over Norway's having gained its independence from Sweden. His letter concluded as follows: "A Pole sends these sincere, warm wishes with a feeling of envy and with a hope that the example of Scandinavia's valiant sons will also instill new courage in nations that are less fortunate."

[2] The plan was that Grieg should play his *Violin Sonata No. 3* with the Polish violinist Stanislaw Barcewicz (1858–1929). Rajchmann accepted Grieg's demand for a double honorarium.

To Harry Randall

Harry Randall (1858–1955) was born in Christiania. As a young boy he studied piano with Edvard Grieg and harmony with Johan Svendsen (1840–1911), and he retained a love for music throughout his life. In 1878 he emigrated to the United States, where for three decades he led an active and varied life as a merchant, insurance agent, leader of an opera company, orchestra conductor and impresario. He was one of the founders of what is now the Minnesota Orchestra and was instrumental in bringing the first symphonic band from St. Olaf College to Norway. In 1908 he returned to Norway, where he became director of the Tivoli Amusement Park in Christiania.

During the 1890's Randall served as secretary of The United Scandinavian Singers of America and in this capacity was actively involved in planning and promoting big song festivals in Minneapolis (1891) and Chicago (1893). Randall had written to Grieg inquiring about the possibility of the famous composer coming to the Chicago festival. The letter that follows is Grieg's answer to Randall's inquiry. Grieg received many invitations to visit the United States but his answer, in the end, was always negative. The biggest obstacle to such a visit was his fear of sea-sickness, which was so great that on one occasion he reportedly said, "I would not go to America even if I were offered a million dollars!"

Grieg's letter to Randall is owned by Mrs. Vera Vea, Oslo.

Leipzig, February 9, 1893
C. F. Peters, Thalstrasse 10

Mr. Harry Randall
New York

It is true that the exposition committee in Chicago has asked me to conduct some concerts this summer, but no contract has been signed yet and unfortunately it is very uncertain whether my health will allow me to undertake the long sea voyage. In any case I will not come before the beginning of September, so unfortunately I will not be there for the song festival to which you refer. As stated, however, I still have not concluded anything with the Board of the Exposition and cannot, therefore, provide you with more detailed information.

Respectfully yours,
EDVARD GRIEG

To Niels Ravnkilde

Grieg met Danish composer Niels Ravnkilde (1823–90) on his first visit to Rome in 1865. They were often together on Grieg's subsequent visits to the city, and the two men eventually became close friends. Ravnkilde had studied at the Leipzig Conservatory, then had settled permanently in Rome. He made his living as a music teacher and became a central figure among the Scandinavians living in the Italian capital as well as others who came to stay for shorter periods of time. He was an ardent supporter of the Scandinavian Society, which was for many years the principal common meeting place for Scandinavians in Rome.

All of Grieg's letters to Ravnkilde included here are preserved in Det kgl. Bibliotek (The Royal Library), Copenhagen.

1

Christiania, November 2, 1868

Dear Ravnkilde!

Now, after a strenuous day, I am sitting here at home with your letter before me, and I will do my best to send you a sensible letter. Thank you for writing. (. . .)

The breeze from Rome does me good, believe me—yes, even if it comes in the form of a letter from Sgambati[1] of which I can't understand a word. Even so, there is truth and interest in the mere thought of his writing to me. But just this evening I have sent it to a gentleman who has promised to translate it for me.

Your words awaken longing for southern Europe, a longing that becomes stronger day by day, and with God's help I will succeed in overcoming all the obstacles. Remember that I am married, so there are a lot of details that have to be taken into consideration. But: I will do it—that's the watchword.

As you will see from the enclosed letter, I am already trying to assemble the resources needed for the realization of my plan. I am applying for a grant for next spring and am now asking Liszt for a recommendation. Don't you think he will give me one? Encouraged by your report in your last letter about his having played my *Violin Sonata* [op. 8], I have confidently taken this step and hope that you will use whatever method seems best to get the letter into Liszt's hands.[2]

---

[1] Italian pianist and composer Giovanni Sgambati (1843–1914).

[2] Ravnkilde relayed Grieg's letter to Liszt, who on December 29, 1868, wrote a strong recommendation for Grieg. On January 10, 1869, Grieg included Liszt's letter in his application for a study grant. After a six-month wait he received a grant of 500 *spesidalers*. Liszt's letter, which was written in French, reads as follows:

Monsieur:

It is with the greatest pleasure that I express to you the sincere joy that I felt upon reading through your sonata, opus 8. The sonata bears witness to a great talent for composition and shows a well-conceived, inventive and excellent treatment of the material; it demonstrates a talent that needs only to follow its natural bent in order to attain to a high level. I hope and trust that in your homeland you will receive the success and the encouragement that you deserve; surely that is not asking too much. If you should come to Germany this winter, I cordially invite you to make a visit to Weimar so that we could meet.

Receive, monsieur, the assurance of my deepest regard.

FRANZ LISZT

I see that you have really been at work creating new compositions: two volumes for piano, a serenade for strings, and now you probably are in the middle of something for orchestra. That's the right way to do it—always more, always bigger and better. I constantly think of doing that, but for me the outlook is not good: seven lessons each day plus choir rehearsals and orchestra rehearsals and concerts—and worries, although the rehearsals have not yet begun. As for creative work, I have produced *nothing* so far this winter.

How can I get copies of your works? Send them to Erslev.[3] He knows my address. Bohlmann[4] got your "March" in C major. I haven't seen him for a long time, but I think he is a decent man; I say this for your solace. As for the other things about which you write, I can only answer with a sigh that contains a longing to see your dear face again, to get to know you better than the last time we were together, and to enter more deeply into life in Italy than I did last time. As you can see, this is the theme to which I always return. I must force myself to banish these thoughts.

I received your letter in Denmark, where I spent the summer. My wife lived with her parents in Copenhagen, and I moved out with Emil Horneman[5] and Edmund Neupert (a Norwegian pianist) to Søllerud, a small town with which you no doubt are familiar. The heat was unbearable, but nonetheless I think about this time with pleasure. To be sure, I felt lethargic because of the temperature, but I also felt that now I had to get down to business. So I have written a concerto for piano and orchestra that I think contains some good things. I had hoped to get time now during the autumn evenings to orchestrate the first movement, but—time. The evenings, too, are taken from me. Neupert is scheduled to play it in the Musicians' Association in Copenhagen after Christmas.[6]

You certainly know from an earlier letter that last year I wrote a new *Violin Sonata* which I expect to receive any day now from Breitkopf & Härtel.[7] Before Christmas, Erslev is releasing a volume of songs and a volume of pieces for piano four hands that I have written.[8]

Why didn't you get a copy of *Songs and Ballads* op. 9 during your stay in Denmark? They were published by Erslev and are the best things I have written. I plan

---

3 Emil Erslev (1817–82), a music publisher in Copenhagen.

4 The Danish composer Georg C. Bohlmann (1838–1920), whom Grieg had met in Rome, was known as an excellent arranger and orchestrator. Grieg used Bohlmann's orchestral version of "Bridal Procession" in the 1886 production of *Peer Gynt* at the Dagmar Theater in Copenhagen.

5 Danish composer Emil Horneman (1840–1906).

6 The premiere of Grieg's *Piano Concerto* in A minor, op. 16, actually took place on April 3, 1869, with Edmund Neupert (1842–88) as soloist. The Musicians' Association (Musikerforeningen) and the Music Association (Musikforeningen) were two different institutions in Copenhagen.

7 *Violin Sonata No. 2* in G major op. 13. Breitkopf & Härtel did not publish the sonata until 1871.

8 *Nine Songs* op. 18 and *Two Symphonic Pieces* op. 14. Both compositions were published by Horneman & Erslev in 1869. The latter consists of arrangements for piano four hands of the two inner movements of Grieg's *Symphony in C Minor*, which was written in 1863–64. Grieg later wrote the following inscription on the orchestral score: "Must never be performed".

to get my Roman overture[9] published in Stockholm. Last Christmas Horneman published a volume of easy pieces for piano—*Lyric Pieces* [op. 12], for piano students.

Excuse me, but when you praise *Poetic Tone Pictures* [op. 3] you are not being honest. Those pieces are nothing but immature rubbish that stinks to high heaven. It pains me to think that you have forgotten me so completely that you do not have better thoughts about me. Well, that was a joke, but in all seriousness: You will understand my thought when the principle is to be "oneself"—not *enough*, as Ibsen says.[10] Ibsen is not in Rome now, of course. If he comes back, greet him from me.

Munch[11] and his wife and whole household have left. Presumably you will see him in Rome. But Bjørnson[12] is here, thank God; where he is there is also life and imagination. Just recently I have made settings for men's voices of two of his poems. There is going to be a farewell greeting from Norwegian students to the poet Welhaven, who has retired from his position as professor at the university because of illness.[13]

Greet Sgambati. I will learn enough English that I can answer him in this language.

Just now I had a visit from my wife and my little daughter, a cute little Alexandra, both of whom send their greetings. Goodbye for now, and the warmest greetings from

Yours truly,
EDVARD GRIEG

P.S. The enclosed picture is for Miss Wrangel.[14]
Greet Hartmann[15] from me.

---

[9] *In Autumn* op. 11 for piano four hands was published by Abraham Hirsch, Stockholm, in 1867. The orchestral version was published as *In Autumn. Concert Overture* by C. F. Peters Musikverlag, Leipzig, in 1888.

[10] The allusion is to Act 2 of Ibsen's *Peer Gynt*, where the Troll King avers that the difference between human beings and trolls is that human beings say "Man, to yourself be true!" whereas trolls say "Troll, to yourself be—enough!"

[11] Norwegian author Andreas Munch (1811–84).

[12] Norwegian author Bjørnstjerne Bjørnson (1832–1910).

[13] Norwegian poet J. S. Welhaven (1807–73) was a prominent figure in literary circles. One of the two pieces for men's chorus that Grieg wrote on this occasion to texts by Bjørnson presumably was "Serenade to J. S. Welhaven", which the students sang during a torchlight parade for the honoree. The other piece has not been identified. "Serenade to Welhaven" was later arranged as a song for solo voice and piano and included in *Nine Songs* op. 18.

[14] Grieg mentions the Wrangel family several times in the diary he kept during his visit to Italy in 1865–66. He never says who they were, however, and nothing is known about them except that the family included at least three daughters of whom one was named Elisabeth.

[15] Danish sculptor Carl Christian Hartmann (1837–1901), son of the composer J. P. E. Hartmann (1805–1900), had made a bust of Grieg in Rome in 1866.

2

Landås at Bergen, June 29, 1869

Dear Ravnkilde!

It was shortly after Christmas that I received your welcome letter, which is still unanswered. The reason is that I wanted so much to wait for word regarding my grant so that I could tell you how likely it is that we might meet this winter. Unfortunately, the only answer I can give you today is the same unsatisfactory one I could have given you earlier. The grant issue has still not been decided. To be sure, I have every reason to hope for the best—but one can't be sure of anything in this world. I learned this the hard way recently: We had just come here to visit my parents when my little girl, our only child, came down with brain fever and—died.[16] My joy in being a father is now but a dream. You can understand that this has been a difficult time for me. It is hard to watch the hope of one's life lowered into the earth, and it took time and quiet to recover from the pain. But thank God, if one has something to live for one does not easily fall apart; and surely art has—more than anything—this soothing power that allays all sorrow!

Your last letter included, as I recall, enthusiastic words in praise of marriage, and certainly marriage can harbor a peace and a truth that one might seek in vain elsewhere; but perhaps the other side of the scale—the side that contains affliction—is as full as the side that contains all of life's joys. In that respect you are the enviable one. But the secret is really to find the right glasses—the optimistic and bold ones—with which to look at life. He who does this is equally happy whether he be a married man or a bachelor.

Since I last wrote I have been working and slaving in Norway's capital for food and drink, for money, and—perhaps I have sacrificed a mite for a crumb of honor as well. Seven lessons per day and four concerts, that is all. The four concerts have been so well attended that my wife and I hope to be able to greet you in Rome—if I get the grant. She looks forward to meeting you; she is very fond of your *Album Leaves*. But if this comes about, we must spend more time together than we did last time. In fact, I did not know at all how to make use of my stay in Rome last time, and I promise myself to do better this time.

In September I will go to Copenhagen, where it is my intention to arrange to give a concert, and from there to Leipzig, Dresden etc. You no doubt know that the Windings[17] are going to Italy for the winter. We may make the journey together.

If you see Liszt you must convey to him my sincerest thanks for the altogether too kind letter of recommendation that he wrote for me—and not least, thanks to you for doing me the great favor of providing it.

---

16 Grieg's daughter Alexandra, born April 10, 1868, died on May 21, 1869.

17 Grieg's Danish friends August Winding (1835–99) and his wife Clara (1839–1925). August Winding was a pianist and composer. See Grieg's letters to him.

Greet Wrangels when you write, also Sgambati and Pinelli.[18] I should write to Sgambati. If I still write an enclosure in Norwegian, will you please translate it and give it to him?

Farewell for now. Warmest greetings from

Yours truly,
EDVARD GRIEG

P.S. Greetings to Carl Hartmann and Swedes, Danes and Norwegians [in Rome] whom I know.

3

Lofthus, Hardanger, July 21, 1884

Dear friend Ravnkilde!
Almost two months have passed since we parted, and only today do you hear from me with a word of thanks. Yes, I am an unforgivable blockhead—and I won't besmirch the page with lame excuses. Let me rather get straight to the point and thank you with all my heart for the beautiful time in Rome. Yes, it was beautiful despite all the unpleasantry that afflicted me. How I would love to go there again soon if I knew that I could be healthy down there. You wouldn't recognize me if you saw me now—round, corpulent, chubby and fat as a stuffed pig. This weight gain began the moment I left Rome. By the time we got to Lake Como I already began to feel like a new man.

In Munich we parted ways with Auberto,[19] whom we had met in Bellagio, and headed for home *prestissimo*. Upon arriving in Norway I spent fourteen lovely days with Frants Beyer at his new little country home[20] near Bergen, then came here, where it is more beautiful than beauty itself.

Before leaving, however, I made preparations for a new opus, the best one I have ever produced: I bought a plot of land a few miles from Bergen, and this fall I intend to realize my old dream to build my own cabin and get my own home.[21] It may look like madness from an artistic standpoint. But now the die is cast, and so far, at least, I do not regret it. To the contrary: I am as happy as a child about it. No opus has filled me with more enthusiasm than this one. I spend half the day painting and drawing: rooms, basements, attic rooms—including one in which you shall rest on soft cushions when you come. For you must come, be it

---

[18] Italian violinist Ettore Pinelli (1843–1915).

[19] Presumably a friend of Grieg's from Rome.

[20] In 1884 the Bergen attorney Frants Beyer (1851–1919), Grieg's closest friend, had built the villa "Næsset" on *Nordåsvannet*, a salt-water inlet about six miles south of Bergen.

[21] Grieg is alluding to Troldhaugen, which was designed by his cousin Schak Bull (1858–1956), an architect. The villa was completed in the spring of 1885. It was situated near Næsset.

incognito or officially. It would be fun to draw you a picture of the house here. But I won't: I don't dare to assume your interest in my opus at this stage. And yet it is, unfortunately, the only opus concerning which I can generate any enthusiasm at the moment. What I have produced in the way of compositions of late isn't worth many pipefuls of tobacco. I have started several different things concerning which I myself cannot, for the moment, express any opinion.

I have now had a week-long visit from Julius Röntgen[22] of Amsterdam, about whom I no doubt have spoken with you. A fine person and an equally fine artist. He brought with him an unusually gifted singer, a baritone, who is also from Amsterdam. His name is Messchaert,[23] and during the Easter season he sang in Bach's *St. Matthew Passion* in Leipzig. Believe me, we made music. He and Nina had a veritable singing contest. He is a Brahms singer *par excellence*, and I really got my eyes opened about how important Brahms is also as a composer of songs—despite the fact that I find him too much the musician and too little the poet. A symphonic composer is a musician and nothing else. But if one is going to include words, one really should be faithful to the words. This is an opinion from which I don't think I shall ever depart.

I will be anxious to find out where these lines have reached you. Hopefully you are in Gossensass and have peace and quiet—and a desire to work. For peace and quiet by themselves are really not sufficient; that is what I have sometimes experienced. How choosy one becomes in this matter as one gets older. I now have the firm belief that when I own my own home I will be able to get seriously to work. Perhaps that is how one deceives oneself until one fine day one stands at the end of one's career. Well, things will have to take their course. The main point, after all, is to live, not to write.

And now it is possible to live happily in Norway. It is a wonderful time for those who believe, as I do, that what has happened is a step forward. Hopefully the struggle will continue, for without the struggle for freedom life isn't worth a plugged nickel. But the hate and pettiness will recede, and that will make room for other interests. What has been unhealthy about politics in Norway is that it has destroyed interest in anything that didn't fall in line under the banner of this or that political party. It must be a proud moment for Johan Sverdrup,[24] to witness in his old age the fruit of all his work. You surely can learn about Sverdrup's life via German or Italian newspapers, and you should not fail to take advantage of such opportunities. The air is so full of happiness and jubilation over what has happened here—over the unexpected resolution of the long, bitter strife—that

---

[22] Julius Röntgen (1855–1932) was Grieg's closest friend in The Netherlands.

[23] Johannes Messchaert (1857–1927), who in the years that followed became one of Grieg's favorite singers.

[24] Johan Sverdrup (1816–92) was a champion of Norwegian independence and democratic constitutional reforms who played a pivotal role in Norwegian politics during much of the latter half of the nineteenth century.

nobody from these parts writes a letter that doesn't reflect the jubilant mood. For that reason you must excuse the fact that even a musician's letter includes a bit of politics. But what am I saying: politics? No, it is nothing more nor less than love of the homeland, and I know that you understand and treasure that fully as much as I do. May Denmark have as bright a future as I and many with me believe that Norway is now about to enter; then it will be wonderful to be a Scandinavian.[25]

I must not forget to tell you that the last evening in Rome proved to be fateful for Lenbach's picture of Nina. You remember that it was taken out of the packing that Lenbach himself had prepared so that it could be admired—or more correctly, vilified—by the Scandinavians gathered at Hotel Anglo-Americain. Afterward, little Hansen was so kind as to arrange for a new kind of packing material that was supposed to be even sturdier, but alas! Upon arriving in Bergen it was discovered that the paints had run and gotten smudged at several places in the face. The picture is now enclosed in glass and frame and from now on, fortunately, will not incur any further damage. But the damage is done and cannot be undone. He had promised to send us the oil painting, but whether he will do so is another question.[26]

It's 11 P.M. Nina, who is sitting here reading newspapers, asks me to greet you warmly. When you add to that my equally warm greetings, you will be well taken care of in that respect. If you are in Rome, please greet friends. If you are in Gossensass, greet the scenic nature—and above all, good luck with your work! I say that every day to the farmer in his meadow here at home and honestly confess that I often wish I were in his place. For he knows nothing of the artist's insatiable longing for—yes, for what? If you can tell me that I will cover you with gold.

Farewell, then, old friend. Write soon!

Yours truly,
EDVARD GRIEG

---

[25] The situation that Grieg is discussing here is the struggle over parliamentarianism in Norway. The struggle, which pitted the power of a democratically elected parliament of Norwegian citizens against that of cabinet members and other administrative officials who served at the pleasure of the Swedish king, had been fought ever since 1821 with neither side being able to win a definitive victory. In 1883, under the leadership of Johan Sverdrup, whose Liberal Party dominated the Norwegian Parliament (Stortinget), the Parliament voted to impeach Conservative Prime Minister Christian A. Selmer (1816–89) for abuse of the royal veto and sentenced him to forfeit his office. The sentence was handed down on February 27, 1884, and Selmer was forced to resign. On June 27, after an unsuccessful attempt to install another Conservative government, King Oscar II capitulated and called upon Johan Sverdrup to form a new government. This act signified the triumph of parliamentarianism in Norway.

[26] The portraits of Nina and Edvard Grieg by Franz von Lenbach (1836–1904) today hang at Troldhaugen. The portrait of Nina to which Grieg refers is reproduced on p. 326.

4

Bergen, December 17, 1884

Dear Ravnkilde!
Never before have you written anything for piano as beautiful as the pieces you sent me. It was a real joy to play through them. It was as if I were in your immediate presence. Your amiable, generous nature comes through clearly in these pieces. One feels that one shares this mind's happy equanimity that is more precious than property, money, honors and fame combined. A gentle warmth permeates the whole work; that is what makes it so alluring. Your performance indications strike me as a bit comical, but perhaps that is my fault. When you write "happily and sadly", one cannot help but think of "exulting to heaven—deathly sad".[27] And if so you miss both of these totalities, for your joy is a calm happiness and your sorrow a gentle wistfulness. But again: Considered simply as music it is so noble and beautiful that one forgets the performance indication and enjoys it apart from that. Thank you so much for those pieces. I will not fail to make use of them when I have a suitable opportunity. You understand that I also am referring to pupils, in which case the performance is not first-rate, but rest assured that I will preach understanding in such a way that you will be well served by the result.

I can easily understand that you feel an urge to get moving in the large forms. If you didn't, you would not be the serious, genuine artistic nature that you are. But still, you are first and foremost a highly sensitive person, and as such you are equipped to give your best in the smaller forms. No reflection that one might set up can outweigh such a fact; that is my scrap of experience. You will not misunderstand that I, the younger of us, speak in this way right from the heart. I would never do it either if I didn't know you well enough to dare to say it. And if I dare to do it, it would be wrong of me not to. What does the difference in our ages have to do with the matter! Understanding is a better guide than all formalities.

You would have heard from me long ago if the Holberg festival[28] had not given me so much to do. Father Holberg cost me two months of strenuous work. But he deserves it, too, splendid fellow that he is—he more than any other Norwegian, I say in this moment. The truth is that I really haven't known him until now. His views on history, on morality, on life's biggest questions were foreign to me. Now I have learned that his horizon was one of the widest we have

---

27 Grieg wrote these phrases in German: "freudvoll und leidvoll" and "Himmelhoch jauchzend—zum Tode betrübt". In Goethe's *Egmont* 3,2 ("Clara's Love-song"), from which the latter phrase is taken, the line continues: "—glücklich allein ist die Seele, die liebt" ("happy alone is the soul that loves").

28 In September, 1884, in connection with the observance of the bicentennial of the birth of Norwegian playwright Ludvig Holberg (1684–1754), Grieg was commissioned to write a cantata for male chorus *a cappella* to a text by Norwegian author Nordahl Rolfsen (1848–1928), EG 171. It was sung on Holberg's birthday December 3, 1884, at a gala program that also included the unveiling of a statue of the playwright by Swedish sculptor Johan Börjeson (1835–1910). *Holberg Suite* op. 40 was completed in August of the same year.

encountered in all history. For the unveiling I conducted a cantata for men's voices *a cappella*—unfortunately, in view of the time of year. The chorus consisted of 250 men. I conducted wearing a fur coat and fur boots, so you can imagine the situation! But the effect was not bad, and they sang with enthusiasm.

I will send you a copy of my *Holberg Suite* in olden style when I have an opportunity. Hopefully your songs will also appear in print soon, and then I will send both items at the same time.

Have you read Ibsen's *The Wild Duck*? It neither moves me nor entrances me, and it seems to me—despite a few masterfully limned figures—to be lacking in inspiration.

And now I want to wish you a merry Christmas in old Rome! Happy is he who could be with you down there!

Cordial greetings from Nina and from

Yours truly,
EDVARD GRIEG

P.S. Greet friends!

5

Copenhagen, February 14, 1886

Dear Ravnkilde!

(. . .) When I shall now report to you my latest biographical data, I don't know where to begin since I don't remember when I last wrote to you. Unfortunately it was an eternity ago, that's for sure, and you have every reason to complain, for last summer I could have had time. Last winter I was totally occupied with my new opus: the villa near Bergen, which now is standing in all its glory. We moved there in April and stayed until early October except that I made a trip to the Jotunheimen mountains in August, at which time Nina went back to our old home at Lofthus in Hardanger.

In September I finished a melodrama with orchestra for which I have had some sketches stored away for a long time. Then I went to Christiania, where I first gave two concerts, then conducted in the Music Association[29] and in the theater. The program at the theater included the aforementioned melodrama, which was superbly declaimed by our excellent dramatic actress Mrs. Gundersen. The melodrama is called *Bergliot* and is a setting of the wonderful poem by Bjørnson with which you are undoubtedly familiar.[30] It has always annoyed me that

---

29 Grieg's first two concerts took place on October 17 and 21. On October 24 he shared conducting duties with Johan Svendsen (1840–1911) in an orchestral concert by the Music Association orchestra.

30 The setting for speaker and piano of Norwegian author Bjørnstjerne Bjørnson's dramatic poem *Bergliot* was written in 1871. The orchestral version was premiered on November 3, 1885. "Mrs. Gundersen" is the Norwegian dramatic actress Laura Gundersen (1832–98), to whom the composition was dedicated.

Heise[31] could dream of setting this piece for solo voice, for in this way the whole thing becomes, in my opinion, ridiculously weak and unnatural. Certainly [in this way] he has the advantage of being able to keep the whole thing nicely musical whereas I, in order to achieve a realistic effect, often was obliged to forsake the musical domain and write things that get their value only in the dramatic situation. Be that as it may, I would be the last one to defend the melodrama as an art form; but if this poem *Bergliot* is going to be set at all it just *has* to be melodramatic. There is no other choice. My piece has many weak points, that is only too clear; but on one point I will insist as along as I live: The basic idea is right.

I came here from Christiania in November, whereupon I gave two concerts and conducted in the Concert Association, the Music Association and at a philharmonic concert, where I also played my *Piano Concerto*.[32] As you can understand, this was a lot for a weak body, but the worst thing was that I had to re-orchestrate the *Peer Gynt* music so that it would be suitably garbed for the performance at the Dagmar Theater.[33]

Finally, during the last few days, I have gotten to the point where I can look around me and find some enjoyment in existence, the most beautiful manifestation of which I find in nature. The first day that I had free—and fortunately, after a long period of cloudy weather it was a sunny day—I headed out to Charlottenlund Forest, where I spent more or less the whole day. That was medicine! I could just feel the strength returning!

Both Nina and I are feeling such an enormous wanderlust that if it weren't the height of irresponsibility we would hop on a ship and head straight for old Rome and shake your hand in person. This is not mere fantasy, for there is rarely a day when we do not talk about it. Unfortunately, there are so many reasons not to do it. The money that we would spend on travel must be used to pay for the villa, and Nina's throat is in such bad shape that she can hardly talk. Nonetheless, we hope that she will be well by the end of March in order to accompany me on a short concert tour to some towns in Jutland—Ålborg, Århus, etc. etc. The whole thing stinks from afar for me, but—O, thou damned Mammon![34]

---

31 Danish composer Peter Heise (1830–79).

32 Nina Grieg also participated in Grieg's concerts given in Copenhagen on November 23 and 27, 1885. The Concert Association concert took place on November 14, the one in the Music Association on December 10. Edvard and Nina also took part in a concert by the Student Choral Society on December 18. On January 30, 1886, Grieg was soloist in the *A-minor Concerto* at the first philharmonic concert of the season. The conductor was Johan Svendsen who, in addition to serving as musical director of the Royal Theater Orchestra, each year gave a series of philharmonic concerts in Copenhagen.

33 The Danish premiere of *Peer Gynt* op. 23 took place at the Dagmar Theater in Copenhagen on January 15, 1886—nearly ten years after the world premiere in Christiania. Grieg re-orchestrated some of the music for the Danish production and also inserted some pieces that had not been written specifically for Ibsen's play—for example, three of the *Norwegian Dances* op. 35 as orchestrated by Danish composer Robert Henriques (1858–1914) and "Bridal Procession" as orchestrated by Georg Bohlmann (1838–1920). See Grieg's letters to Robert Henriques of December 21, 1885 and January 16, 1886.

34 Grieg did take this concert tour, giving concerts in Århus, Ålborg, Randers, Horsens, Vejle and Ribe.

Your dear niece has been up to visit us twice, but I think she is too self-conscious to sing as she has not mentioned anything about it. She looks very sweet and nice.

And now I'd better stop. Greet friends and acquaintances. And write again soon—I will be here until spring—to your old friend,

EDVARD GRIEG

P.S. Nina asks me to greet you warmly.

6

Troldhaugen, December 5, 1886

Dear Ravnkilde!
It was no longer ago than this Sunday afternoon that I was wandering up and down in my lovely, big living room, and when the conversation turned to Italy I said, "That dear old Ravn,[35] how much fun it would be to have him here at Troldhaugen today. Sure, I could just send a telegram to Rome: Will you have dinner with us tomorrow? But with that I was up against a (still) insoluble problem." Well, that is more or less what went through my mind, and then, after we had enjoyed our quiet evening meal, I asked for paper and ink and pen—and here I am.

Have you really been home this summer? Yes, so I heard from Winding and later from several others. But even if, in so doing, you came within a thousand kilometers of Norway, did that help us to catch a glimpse of you? No, it appears that for Norway you are lost forever. We must go to old Rome again if we are to meet. And in fact I really do think so often of going there again. I have been thinking that next year I might get serious about my soon old plan to visit Paris. And if that happens I think that Rome, too, will not be beyond the realm of possibility.

I have discussed with Drachmann,[36] who visited us here this summer, the possibility of a trip to southern Europe this coming winter. So you see, the idea is being approached from several angles.

We heard a little about you from Fanny Riis,[37] but far too little. And now it is so very long since we heard from you. The last communication was a letter from Rome with passions and dagger thrusts from, as I recall, June or July. We were sitting here with the Beyers[38] when the letter arrived. I read it aloud—with the result

[35] This is a play on words: "Ravn", in Danish, means "raven".
[36] Danish author Holger Drachmann (1846–1908).
[37] Fanny Riis (1834–1924)was Grieg's cousin. During the 1880's she was librarian at The Scandinavian Society in Rome.
[38] Frants and Marie Beyer, Edvard and Nina's neighbors and very close friends.

that the mood became high Roman. Yes, it even brought Frants Beyer, who is easily moved, to the verge of tears behind the smile. That I have not answered such a charming letter earlier is a crying shame, but—no! There is no "but". You will have to be content with all the good thoughts that constantly follow you.

I heard from Winding that one enjoyable aspect of your visit home was that Gade[39] firmly promised you that he would perform some movements of your symphony. Well, that's good as far as it goes, but—I'll believe it when it really happens. But how about the other possibilities? How did it go with them? You must tell me that when you write—soon.

And Liszt!![40] Yes, it often seems to me that now the musical world has become empty. One no longer sees anything new from Rubinstein[41]—and Brahms has become so doctrinaire that, spirit notwithstanding, it often is difficult to find the fresh, pulsating life. I believe deeply in people like Sgambati. You must tell me about him. The so-called Wagnerites and Lisztians are too blindly one-sided to be able to contribute anything of their own. No, what is needed is something that they sorely lack, notwithstanding all their admiration for these masters. That is to say, one must vaguely discern their dedication, but not a speck more.

Don't forget to give Mrs. Bretschneider my warmest greetings when you see her. The same goes for von Kendell.[42] Yes, those were the days! If only I had been healthier. Shouldn't it be possible to live in a more healthful and reasonable way down there? A pleasant little sun-drenched flat, a little household help, and only dinner out. That sounds ideal to me. And then, most important of all—a private workroom. For I should be whipped if I spend my time in a disgraceful, immoral *dolce far niente*[43] like I did last time.

This afternoon I read Ibsen's new play *Rosmersholm*. Powerful, brilliant! But liberating? No! And I place the biggest question mark over the last act. From a man like Ibsen I expect the strictest logic—something that he himself quite rightly regards as the alpha and omega. But if the motivation for the action in the last act makes sense, then my name is Peder Madsen—or else I will keep my name but be an idiot by profession! His depiction of the depressing view of life here is indeed true! But the implications—these Ibsen deduces in a way that fits neatly into his play. Thus, despite the masterful writing, one feels a certain artificiality.

Well, so it is: Even the greatest among us are tempted to strive for the great—and for so many, unattainable—techniques in art. Nothing is perfect! And yet—

---

[39] Danish composer and conductor Niels W. Gade (1817–90).

[40] Franz Liszt died in Bayreuth on July 31, 1886.

[41] Anton Rubinstein (1829–94), Russian composer and pianist.

[42] The Bretschneider and von Kendell families were acquaintances from Grieg's earlier visits to Rome. He had met the Bretschneiders during his stay there in 1865–66. On March 15, 1884, he had given a concert in von Kendell's residence on the Capitoline Hill.

[43] "dolce far niente": pleasant indolence.

a few days ago I heard Mozart's little E-flat major symphony. One is inclined to say: Behold, it was very good![44]

Now I am going to stop for the very selfish reason that I want to be able to sleep tonight and I will not be able to do so if I continue writing right up to my bedtime.

Farewell for now, then, dear Ravn. Write soon and tell me about this and that—all about yourself. Everything falls into the best soil, and up here between the snow-drifts secrets are not bandied about. But of course you are one of these lucky paragons of piety who have no secrets!

Warm greetings from Nina and from

Yours truly,
EDVARD GRIEG

7

Karlsbad, October 17, 1887

Dear Ravnkilde!
Yes, just think: I—no, not just I!—Nina and I have now been here for four weeks on account of our sins. But however enormous they may be, I will not add to them the sin of not writing to you from this place. For here one cannot complain about lack of time. To be deported to Karlsbad[45] in October is a torture that I would not wish on my worst enemies. It's actually enough to kill you. Everything that could take one's mind away from one's own infirmities is gone: the teeming life, the beautiful paintings and orchestra concerts, the sparkling boutiques, nature in its summer garb—everything, everything! But thank God, tomorrow we leave for Leipzig and then, hopefully, the seven years of plenty will begin.[46]

You remember, of course, that I am a stomach patient from way back; but you do not know that in recent years Nina has had worrisome tendencies toward kidney stones. You understand, however, that this is a serious condition that cannot be taken lightly. We plan to spend the winter on the continent, and perhaps next summer we will have to go through Purgatory here again.

Oh! If Rome weren't so far south of here we could get together. Presumably there is no possibility of your coming to the music festival in Copenhagen next summer.[47] I am considering a visit to Vienna, but from Vienna to Rome—no, I can't even think of it.

It is indeed a long time since you heard from me, but my life in the last year

---

[44] Grieg is alluding to Genesis 1:31: "And God saw everything that he had made, and behold, it was very good." (RSV)

[45] Karlsbad was a health spa in Germany. The town of Karlsbad now lies in the Czech Republic and has been renamed Karlovy Vary.

[46] Grieg is alluding to the story of the seven years of plenty and the seven years of famine in Genesis 41.

[47] The first Nordic music festival took place in Copenhagen June 3–10, 1888.

has been so peaceful that there isn't much to tell. I lived at Troldhaugen all winter and most of the summer except for a trip to the mountains in West Norway—Jotunheimen, my passion, where for two weeks each summer I immerse myself in that which is timeless with my noble friend Frants Beyer. Yes, here one stands face to face with greatness: It is Shakespeare, Beethoven and whoever else you wish concentrated into a single pure extract! I wouldn't exchange this for a dozen Gewandhaus concerts!

I must tell you about a wonderful, sunny August day between the Skagastøl peaks. We were going to cross a mountain called "Friken", but we couldn't get a mountain guide, partly because it was Sunday and partly because the men were out hunting reindeer. Then two nice milkmaids from a mountain farm appeared, one older and one younger. The younger one, a gorgeous blonde, was named Susanne. These two offered to go with us over the mountain. So with singing and jollity we started out, and up at the top we sat down and made the best of what the knapsacks had to offer us. Cognac and glacial water helped elevate the mood to an absolutely ethereal height. But the most beautiful part was still to come, for Susanne had brought a little national instrument with her—a *bukkehorn*,[48] on which you can play just *three* tones. After the girls had said goodbye to us up there at the top—because they had to go back down to milk the cows—Frants and I stood entranced by the beautiful sight as they walked along the edge of the mountain: the girls fair, graceful and erect, with the blue horizon as background. All of a sudden they stood still, Susanne put the "bukkehorn" to her mouth—I will never forget the pose, the outline of her body against the sky—and then, as if it were coming from the mountain scenery around us, we heard the soft, melancholy sound:

When the final G had died away we looked at each other—and stood there in tears! For we had both felt the same way.

Yes, when I think of this—and then I think of Reinecke[49] standing on his podium beating one, two, one, two and turning Beethoven into an ordinary highway patrolman.

You see, this is the sort of thing that makes a Norwegian musician become bewitched. It's lovely—but whether it is something to wish for is another matter. For to be overwhelmed to the point of annihilation by that which is great in nature is a dangerous thing, and I know that there is something in my soul that

48 A "bukkehorn" is a primitive wind instrument made from a ram's horn.

49 Carl Reinecke (1824–1910), Grieg's composition teacher at the Leipzig conservatory, was conductor of the Gewandhaus orchestra in Leipzig.

suffers from this. But it cannot be otherwise when one does not choose to don kid gloves and settle down in one of Europe's capitals—as most of our great men, remarkably enough, do.

Yes, the world is strange, dear Ravnkilde, and not least your old friend with the bad stomach,

EDVARD GRIEG

P.S. Nina sends warm greetings! And both of us ask to be remembered to friends and acquaintances!

Address: C. F. Peters, Thalstrasse 10, Leipzig.

8

Troldhaugen at Bergen, August 13, 1888

Dear Ravnkilde!

You must not consider me as big an ass as I appear to be when it comes to letter-writing. But I have been traveling so much, have had so little peace and quiet, that my correspondence has been thoroughly disrupted.

In a few days I will be leaving again for England,[50] where I will conduct some of my compositions at the music festival in Birmingham, but I didn't want to do that in any case without having thanked you for what you sent me recently. There were many beautiful things there, in my opinion, and I think the most beautiful of them give evidence of all this poignant homesickness that constitutes your life's deepest poetry. If you were able to go home each year, you wouldn't have nearly so strong a feeling for Denmark and Danish art as you now do.

Moreover, you may rest assured that Danish art was brilliantly represented at the music festival[51] through Gade's *Elverskud* [*Elf-king's Daughter*][52] and Hartmann's *Vølvens Spådom* [*The Vølve's Prophecy*].[53] I have never heard so masterful a performance of *Elverskud*, and although Gade has received much honor in his life I heartily welcomed the unique joy he must have had from this composition. He surely has never heard it done like this himself, and the beauties of the piece have never before shone forth so clearly for me either. It is an excellent choice to represent Gade at a *Nordic* music festival. He has never exceeded the inspiration manifested in the second half of this work. It is movingly and lastingly beautiful. And the mastery exhibited in the handling of voices and orchestra! Yes, that is something we all could wish for!

---

[50] Grieg had spent three weeks in England and had given several concerts in May, 1888.

[51] Grieg had participated in "The First Nordic Music Festival" in Copenhagen June 3–10, 1888.

[52] *Elverskud* for choir, orchestra and solo voices is one of Niels W. Gade's most frequently performed works.

[53] Danish composer J. P. E. Hartmann (1805–1900) wrote *Vølvens Spådom* for male chorus and orchestra in 1872.

Nina is sitting downstairs and singing Nordraak's[54] songs. It sounds so melancholy that it makes me feel very strange. Yes, he also had something that all of us might desire. But it is good that he died because he was not a real musician, and when all is said and done a composer must be that to win complete victory.

And what do you say about Neupert,[55] who had to die in New York! He was indeed a great artist! Did you know him?

I really don't understand any more that I myself am still alive. One thing is certain and that is that when I start composing again it will be completely different from before—or so I hope. For so much has stormed in on me and made me older and, as it were, more clear-sighted. It is amazing how one alters one's feelings with respect to the national element in art. Still, at root it is not to be wondered at that *these feelings* undergo development when so many other things do so.

Regarding the representation of Nordic composers at the music festival, there was *so much* that absolutely was not as it should have been. Let that also be your consolation. But I admit that no matter how one arranges a program there will be those who feel offended.

Goodbye for now, dear Ravn, and be assured of the warmest greetings from both of us by

Your old friend,
EDVARD GRIEG

P.S. Frants Beyer sends greetings. He is going with me to Birmingham.

---

54 Grieg's friend and fellow composer Rikard Nordraak (1842–66), who died of tuberculosis at age 23 on March 20, 1866.

55 Norwegian pianist and composer Edmund Neupert had died in New York on June 22.

To Hans Richter

The Austro-Hungarian conductor Hans Richter (1843–1916) was one of the greatest orchestra conductors of his day. He was chosen by Richard Wagner to lead the first music festival in Bayreuth in 1876 and in the years that followed he held responsible positions in London, Birmingham, Manchester and Vienna.

Grieg's letters to Richter, one of which is included here, are preserved in Nasjonalbiblioteket, Oslo (National Library of Norway, Oslo Division).

Leipzig, January 20, 1893
Address: C. F. Peters, Thalstrasse 10

Dear Maestro!

I was very happy to get your exceptionally kind letter. According to information recently received from Cambridge, I will be occupied there between the 7th and the 14th of June.[1] Your proposal for the end of *the third week in June* would, therefore, fit my plans very nicely. I will be staying here for the time being but will leave at the end of February, probably for the Riviera—for reasons of health, unfortunately—but my address will continue to be as indicated above.

I have just one concern: to find a female singer who can sing the part of the vølve[2] (an alto part with great range). It would have to be somebody similar to Mrs. Moran-Olden;[3] the part has big, broad lines. Hopefully it will not be difficult for you to secure a well-qualified singer.

I thank you—and the gods—for the fact that *you* will be conducting my work. First, simply because you are Hans Richter! And secondly, because in my present state of health I could hardly tolerate the anguish in connection with the rehearsals and the actual conducting.

So, once again: my heartiest thanks!

Respectfully,
EDVARD GRIEG

---

1 Grieg was to have received an honorary doctorate from Cambridge University in 1893 but because of poor health had to postpone this trip to 1894. Thus the collaboration with Richter on concerts in England that summer also had to be abandoned.

2 In Old Norse mythology the "vølve" was a woman who practiced witchcraft and had the ability to foresee the future.

3 German singer Fanny Moran-Olden (1855–1905). The part of the vølve occurs in Grieg's opera torso, *Olav Trygvason*, libretto by Bjørnstjerne Bjørnson.

To George Riseley

The English organist, conductor and composer George Riseley (1845–1932) worked in Bristol, where he served as resident conductor of the Bristol Musical Festival from 1896 onward. He also conducted "The Riseley Male Voice Choir" and on June 21, 1902, at a coronation concert in Royal Albert Hall, he conducted a 400-voice male chorus in a performance of Grieg's *Land-sighting.*

In 1902 Riseley wrote to Grieg regarding the possibility of his participating in the Bristol Music Festival that autumn. Grieg initially accepted the invitation but later had to withdraw because of illness.

Drafts of three letters from Grieg to Riseley, all in somewhat clumsy English and all dating from 1902, are preserved in Bergen Offentlige Bibliotek (Bergen Public Library). The second of the three is given below as drafted by Grieg.

Copenhagen, March 12, 1902
Hotel Phoenix

Dear Sir!
I thank you for your kind letter of 3 March and accepting your engagement for 2 concerts on the terms I have mentioned (100 £ for both concerts) I am looking forward with great pleasure to visit Bristol at the festival October 8–11.

The works I spoke of were probably "Olav Trygvason", dramatic fragment by Bjørnson for chorus, solo voices and orchestra and "At the Cloister Gate" from Bjørnson's poem "Arnljot Gelline" for soprano and alto solo, female chorus, orchestra and organ.[1] Both works are edited by C. F. Peters, Leipzig, the first of them taking the time of ca. 40, the second of ca. 15 minutes.

Will you kindly tell me which solo voices you have to your disposition.

If you don't wish me to conduct the same works at both concerts I shall propose you some orchestral works.

Hoping soon to hear from you again,

Yours very faithfully,
EDVARD GRIEG

---

1 Grieg is referring to *Scenes from "Olav Trygvason"* and *Before a Southern Convent* to texts by Norwegian author Bjørnstjerne Bjørnson (1832–1910).

To Nordahl Rolfsen

The Norwegian writer Nordahl Rolfsen (1848–1928) was born in Bergen. In his younger years he was a teacher in Oslo and later in Bergen. As an author he achieved remarkable success with his fairytale comedy, *Svein Uræd* (*Svein the Intrepid*), for which Norwegian composer Ole Olsen (1850–1927) wrote incidental music. The play enjoyed no fewer than sixty performances at the Christiania Theater. Rolfsen also made an important contribution to Norwegian education with his children's books, not least those written for use in the schools. The latter constituted a dramatic departure from the somber, moralistic books that had been in use and entered like a fresh breeze into schools all over Norway.

Several of Grieg's songs are settings of poems by Rolfsen. Grieg also availed himself of Rolfsen's skills as a translator to create Norwegian versions of some of his German songs—for example, in *Six Songs* op. 48.

Grieg's letters to Nordahl Rolfsen, one of which is included here, are preserved in Nasjonalbiblioteket, Oslo (the National Library of Norway, Oslo Division).

Troldhaugen, August 17, 1894

Dear Rolfsen!

(...) I recently received from Mr. Grøndahl[1] a request to write two melodies to poems in your reader.[2] This led me to page through the book anew, this time with musical eyes. And thanks to your genius—perhaps also to the pen with which I wrote (it once belonged to Hans Christian Andersen[3])—the childlike voices awakened such a rich echo in my soul that I developed a desire to live in this world for awhile. As a result, before I knew what was happening eight songs had seen the light of day. What you have produced in your childlike poems and stories is really incredible. You have tapped some of that which is most genuine in yourself. This is yours and no one else's. I love and admire you for it, and I hereby express my sincerest thanks, not only for these poems but also and above all for the national spirit with which—throughout the book, and in an elegant and discreet and yet intensive way—you imbue the child. I realize more and more what a masterwork this book is—and that no one else could have done such a thing. When the above-mentioned songs are printed I intend to dedicate them to you. Among them are your poems "The Ocean" and "Good-night Song for Dobbin". Doesn't your daughter sing? These would be just the thing for her.

Alas, the dinner bell is ringing!

Warm greetings, also to your wife!

Yours truly,
EDVARD GRIEG

---

[1] Norwegian choral conductor Olaus Andreas Grøndahl (1847–1923).

[2] The publication of Rolfsen's *Læsebok for folkeskolen* (*Reader for the Grade School*), his most important pedagogical work, began in 1892 and the book was quickly adopted in most Norwegian schools. It differed radically from earlier readers in its freshness and objectivity, the distinctively Norwegian (as distinguished from Danish) tone of the language, and the singularly apt arrangement of the material for young learners. Seven of the eight songs Grieg wrote to poems from the reader were published as *Seven Children's Songs* op. 61, first in a version for voice and piano (1895), later in a three-part arrangement for children's choir (1901).

[3] Danish writer of children's stories Hans Christian Andersen (1805–70).

To Julius Röntgen

The Dutch pianist, conductor and composer Julius Röntgen (1855–1932) was one of Grieg's closest friends. Grieg visited the Röntgen family for the first time in December, 1883, and the two men quickly developed a friendship that lasted until Grieg's death in 1907. Röntgen visited Norway many times, and through the years the two friends exchanged more than 400 letters. This correspondence has been published in the original German by Finn Benestad and Hanna de Vries Stavland (eds.), *Edvard Grieg und Julius Röntgen. Briefwechsel 1883–1907*, Amsterdam 1997.

Grieg's letters to Röntgen are preserved in 'collection Haags Gemeentemuseum, The Hague, Röntgen's letters to Grieg in Bergen Offentlige Bibliotek (Bergen Public Library).

Included here are two representative samples of Grieg's letters to Röntgen.

1

Vienna, January 3, 1897
Hotel Kaiserin Elisabeth

Dear friend!
I was up at Semmering[1] for eight full days and found your welcome letter when I returned here on January 1. The day after tomorrow I am expecting Sistermans,[2] who will be joining me for a program at Bösendorfer[3] on Wednesday evening. Then I go to Leipzig, where, however, I can no longer expect to see you, for this evening or early tomorrow you will already be back in Amsterdam. Yes, we had bad luck with this story.[4] And even though in the end the visit here was an artistic success for me, too, just between us I can tell you that Vienna left me absolutely broke. I used up my entire honorarium, and if I had not had the 1,000 francs that I got for my Mozart article[5] I would have been forced to write to Dr. Abraham:[6]

Ge - ben Sie mir
Vor- schuß, Vor- schuß,
Vor- schuß,

All things considered, Vienna is Europe's most costly city—more costly, in any case, than Paris or London. And Hotel Kaiserin Elisabeth understands very

---

1 Semmering is a well-known resort area in the mountains south of Vienna.

2 The Dutch singer Anton Sistermans (1865–1920), who took part in Grieg's concert in the Bösendorfer auditorium in Vienna on January 6, 1897.

3 Bösendorfer, Austria's foremost manufacturer of pianos.

4 Röntgen had given concerts in Vienna in November, and the plan was for the two friends to meet there. By the time Grieg arrived on November 15, however, Röntgen had already left. They met again soon after this exchange of letters, however, as Grieg was in Holland in February and March to give a series of concerts in Amsterdam and The Hague.

5 Grieg's article *Mozart* was first published in the American journal *The Century Illustrated Monthly Magazine* in November, 1897. It will be printed in a new English translation in Benestad & Halverson (eds.), *Edvard Grieg: Diaries, Articles, Speeches* (Columbus, Ohio, 2001).

6 Max Abraham (1831–1900), Director of C. F. Peters Musikverlag in Leipzig, Grieg's principal publisher. "Geben Sie mir Vorschuß" means "Give me an advance".

well how to take advantage of foreigners. I will never stay here again. Would that I had just found some quiet place and concentrated on my own work! Vienna has robbed me of almost two whole months of my time.

But now to something happier. Above all, the warmest wishes for the new year that can be conveyed by the hand of a friend! Now if only we can meet in Amsterdam! Not another bout of influenza for all the world.

Regarding *The Mountain Thrall* [op. 32], I will not transpose it to D minor. That would create many difficulties, especially in the cello part, and—it would not sound good. What would Messchaert[7] say about 1) "Henrik Wergeland" and 2) "A Swan" with orchestra? Both songs would certainly be appropriate for a voice like his. Mrs. Gulbranson[8] could then sing "Solveig's Song" and "From Monte Pincio".[9] It is totally incomprehensible to me that Messchaert can't sing *The Mountain Thrall* in E minor. But this isn't open for discussion.

Unfortunately I was unable to spend New Year's Eve with Brahms and Joachim.[10] The reason was that because I was not feeling well I had to prolong my stay at Semmering by one day. Last evening, however, I heard the last Joachim concert at Bösendorfer and was overwhelmed by the interpretation of Beethoven's *F-major Quartet* ("Muß es sein?"). But I was not a whit less overwhelmed by Brahms's *G-major Quintet*, which—especially in the first three movements—is one of his most important compositions. Brahms stayed in the green room during the entire concert, but the applause was so enormous that in the end he was brought out along with the string players and four times in a row was showered with jubilation such as, according to Gutmann,[11] had never before been seen in Vienna. Brahms was so moved that he was on the verge of tears. Perhaps—who knows?—he was thinking something like this: "Yes, yes, now they all think for sure that they are seeing me for the last time."

One could in fact very well get that impression. I, for my part, have never experienced such an intense, enthusiastic tribute. It was quite simply overwhelming. Everything that could move was flying around in the air: handkerchiefs, hats, canes, programs. It must have made a peculiar impression on Brahms, for as far as I know, in this respect he is—fortunately for him—unspoiled. Afterward he could hardly say a word. Some think he is improving slightly. I would say the very opposite!

Have I already told you that Hanslick[12] has actually said a few laudatory

---

[7] The Dutch singer Johannes Messchaert (1857–1927).

[8] Swedish-born Norwegian singer Ellen Nordgren Gulbranson (1863–1947).

[9] In 1894–95 Grieg had arranged some of his songs for solo voice and orchestra. In addition to the songs mentioned in this letter, the collection—*Six Songs with Orchestra* (EG 177)—includes "Solveig's Cradle Song" from *Peer Gynt* op. 23 and "Last Spring" from op. 33.

[10] The Austro-Hungarian violinist and composer Joseph Joachim (1831–1907), one of the greatest violin virtuosos of the day.

[11] Albert Gutmann (1862–1915), an impresario in Vienna.

[12] Eduard Hanslick (1825–1904), conservative music critic in Vienna's *Neue Freie Presse*.

words about me? I must find the article and send it to you. Frants[13] has sent me a copy of my folk songs from Fossli,[14] of which I should like very much to hear your evaluation. But I don't dare to send a manuscript from here, as Vienna's postal system is frightfully disorganized.

Well, now I have done exactly enough prattling for today. Let me hear a bit from you soon!

Warm greetings, also from Nina.

Sincerely yours,
EDVARD GRIEG

2

Troldhaugen, October 2, 1897

Dear friend!
Today the sun is shining, but only outside. For Nina has been sick in bed for several days with her old kidney problem. It is a piece of bad luck, as we had planned to get out of here today. Now we hope that we can leave Troldhaugen on Monday and continue our journey on Wednesday. The bad part is that I must leave, with or without Nina.[15]

Many thanks for your welcome letter and for the folk songs, which I have just received.[16] I have only read through them, but it seems to me that you have hit the nail on the head. The conception must be simple and bold, and with this in mind you have also handled the piano part in a superb way. The many little imitations always come across well. It really is a contrast to my way of treating folk tunes. Who knows? Maybe you are right and I am wrong! But, away with pessimism: The fact is that we are both right. That, indeed, is the secret.

We were glad to hear that you think so highly of Neovius.[17] We have very high regard for him. And we are no less glad that things are going so well for Messchaert. Give him and his wife our warmest greetings.

Your idea that we might get together after the trip to England is very tempting. Thanks so much to you and your wife for the invitation![18] But at the moment I don't know how everything is going to develop. In any case you will hear further details regarding my plans as soon as possible. The latest word is that my wife will come along on the trip. But perhaps that will not be the case.

---

[13] Grieg's close friend and next-door neighbor, Bergen lawyer Frants Beyer (1851–1919).

[14] *Nineteen Norwegian Folk Songs* for piano op. 66. Fossli is a tourist hotel in West Norway where Grieg harmonized many of the folk tunes used in op. 66.

[15] Grieg, who was under contract to give a series of concerts in Great Britain in November and December, left Bergen by steamship on October 8.

[16] Röntgen's composition *Oud-Hollandse Boerenliedjes en Contradansen* for violin and piano.

[17] Finnish mathematician and politician Edvard Neovius (1851–1917). See Grieg's letters to him.

[18] Edvard and Nina ended up spending Christmas 1897 with the Röntgens in Amsterdam.

A few days ago I had a meeting in Bergen where some ideas were bandied about regarding the possibility of a Norwegian music festival to be held during the international exposition in Bergen next summer. During the discussion I got an idea that for the time being I am keeping to myself. Could you tell me in complete confidence whether and on what conditions it might be possible to engage the Concertgebouw orchestra?! The festival would take place in June or July and would involve two or three concerts, each with two or three rehearsals. The stay—in addition to the actual journey (Amsterdam–Rotterdam–Bergen and return) that would have to be compensated—would last about eight days. Such a visit would probably be too costly for us, but there's no harm in asking.[19]

Perhaps you are surprised by my idea of a Dutch orchestra at a Norwegian music festival. But in the first place the festival is Norwegian in that only Norwegian compositions will be played, and secondly, there are so many German players in Norwegian orchestras that the question of the performers' nationality is for that reason already problematic. So: If it would be possible for you to get some information by means of a confidential conversation with Mr. Hutschenruyter,[20] I would be much obliged. NB! As soon as possible. Address: Wilhelm Hansen,[21] Gothersgade 11, Copenhagen.

And with that I must already close because there are so many other letters that I must write. If only I could write them in Norwegian or German! But a letter to Colonne[22] declining an invitation to conduct his orchestra is no easy matter for one who is as clumsy in French as I am. And then all the English letters! No, I must stop doing this. The time that is left to me must be used in a different and better way. What Dr. Abraham has said is right: "You don't know how to live!" Well, few people do, that's some consolation!

Warm greetings, also to your wife, who has become so dear to us! To your children! To your friends! To everyone in dear Holland with—yes, even without—oysters![23]

Nina and your faithful
EDVARD GRIEG

---

19 This is the first inquiry Grieg made regarding the possibility of the Concertgebouw Orchestra participating in the Norwegian music festival that was held in Bergen from June 26 to July 3, 1898. After lengthy negotiations with the orchestra and many serious disagreements with Norwegian musicians—see, for example, Grieg's letters to Norwegian conductor Iver Holter (1850–1941) of December 25, 1897, and January 25, 1898—the arrangements were concluded and the Concertgebouw orchestra came to Bergen.

20 Villem Hutschenruyter (1859–1943) was the administrator of the Concertgebouw orchestra.

21 Wilhelm Hansen music publishing company. Grieg often used this publisher as a mailing address during his visits to Copenhagen.

22 The French conductor Édouard Colonne (1838–1910), leader of the famous Colonne concerts in the Châtelet Theater in Paris.

23 Oysters were Grieg's favorite dish.

To Gerhard Schjelderup

The Norwegian composer Gerhard Schjelderup (1859–1923), who was born in Kristiansand, composed a number of orchestral works but is best known as a composer of operas. He turned to opera at an early age. Several of his musical dramas were performed successfully in Germany, where he lived during much of his adult life, but his music was not well received in Norway. Schjelderup was also a fine cellist and a competent writer on musical subjects. He authored one book on Grieg and co-authored another with the German musicologist Walter Niemann (1876–1953). He also collaborated with the Norwegian music historian Ole Mørk Sandvik (1875–1976) in editing the two-volume *Norges Musikhistorie* (*Norway's Music History*), the first comprehensive work on this subject in Norway.

Most of Grieg's many letters to Schjelderup are preserved in Nasjonalbiblioteket, Oslo (National Library of Norway, Oslo Division). Of the ones included here, no. 3 is in Bergen Offentlige Bibliotek (Bergen Public Library) and no. 13 in The Pierpont Morgan Library, The Frederick R. Koch Foundation, New York.

1

Troldhaugen, August 20, 1898

Dear Mr. Schjelderup!

Incredible as it sounds, I still have not been able to have a look at *Astrid.*[1] I don't have to tell you that it is not lack of interest that has prevented me from getting seriously at it. It is—you will forgive me for it—pure egoism. For I have been sitting up to my ears in my own music. And all influences from without during such a period are for me, as perhaps for all older artists, out of the question. And then there is the music festival's[2] unavoidable aftermath: the newspaper squabbling. How chauvinism and jealousy render people stupid and narrow-minded!

I understand that you have written beautifully and well in *Morgenbladet.*[3] Unfortunately, I have not read it. I still hope to get hold of it, though.

I read yesterday about a philology meeting in Christiania. One of the speakers there stated that the saga poetry of the Middle Ages distinguishes the Norwegians from the Swedes and Danes by their penchant for the *colossal* and the *supernatural.* This strikes me as the truth to the extent that it applies even in our time: Our artists are so preoccupied with "the supernatural" that they lose the feeling for "the natural". What I mean is—in a social perspective—that they have lost the feeling for the special qualities that are so important, and rightly so, for the natural connections between people. For example: Of all the Norwegian composers whose causes I have worked for and whose interests I have advanced through the festival, you are the only one who has found it "natural" to send me

---

[1] *Astrid* was the working title of an opera that Schjelderup later decided to call *Østenfor Sol og Vestenfor Måne* (*East of the Sun and West of the Moon*).

[2] Grieg is referring to the Norwegian music festival held in Bergen in the summer of 1898.

[3] *Morgenbladet*: a conservative Christiania newspaper.

a word of thanks. You see, this is characteristic. In order to become a great author, as Gunnar Heiberg[4] rightly said to Ibsen, one must possess the right mixture of respect and disrespect. Mere disrespect—or let me call it impiety, or lack of a feeling of gratitude—cannot make an artist great be he ever so colossal in his attitude toward other people. Yes, indeed: Nature has united the colossal and the minute in the same individual—and not least in this country. That certainly is the secret.

A lucky star shone over the music festival. It was its own triumph because the cause was great and good. That your talent won adherents who can be of importance for your future is not the least of the benefits of the festival. Thank you for coming! Thank you for what you gave, and best wishes for your future!

Sincerely yours,
EDVARD GRIEG

2

Copenhagen, January 1, 1900
Hotel King of Denmark

Dear Mr. Schjelderup!
The first lines I write in the new century shall be dedicated to you. For I am ashamed of my long silence at the conclusion of the one just past. I had hoped to get some kind of word during November that your opera had been performed in Prague. But unfortunately it goes with you as with other mortals: They are stripped of their illusions, one by one! No one gains more bitter experiences of people's "deceitfulness" than the dramatist, and especially the music dramatist. You must cling to this realization, so that the idea that you personally are being treated unkindly by fate doesn't take hold of you. Don't lose your courage. I can tell you that the time of life when you are not famous is the happiest time. At that time one associates first and last with one's own ideals. Later one gets entangled in a web of preoccupation with all sorts of insignificant people and things that often make life a burden to Mrs. Musa[5] and in the end lead her to say farewell—and disappear. NB: when one doesn't have the ruthlessness to chop down everything that gets in the way and press resolutely forward over the dead bodies of others to reach one's goal. There are geniuses who have this callousness, but there are also those who do not have it. The latter group has included some of the noblest natures—a Mozart, a Schubert, a César Franck. What is to be preferred? I think each individual must follow his inner voice.

I know of nothing better to wish you for the new century than that the best

---

[4] Gunnar Heiberg (1857–1929), Norwegian journalist, author and theater director; Henrik Ibsen (1828–1906).

[5] Mrs. Musa: one of Grieg's favorite names for the goddess of inspiration.

that is in you may triumph, be it early or late. Everything else—getting recognition etc. etc.—will then follow as a matter of course. I know that so-called renown is a heavy suit of armor to carry. Many a time I have wished it would go to hell.

How are you getting along in Dresden? Let me hear a few lines when it is convenient.

With warm greetings to you and also to your wife—whom I do not know.

Sincerely yours,
EDVARD GRIEG

3

Troldhaugen, October 20, 1901

Dear Mr. Schjelderup!

You, as well as your Christiania plans, have been often in my thoughts, and I was just about to write to you when a tragic death in my family abruptly occupied all my thoughts. My only brother John died suddenly. He died by his own hand, which makes what happened so much sadder. Since you knew him, I want to tell you that the autopsy showed considerable calcification in the heart, brain and arteries—which in the doctors' opinion explains everything. Those who suffer from this condition become broken in body and mind and deathly tired. Neither he nor we had any inkling of this illness, so you can understand that the catastrophe came like a bolt of lightning from a clear sky. I feel totally worn out and am in no condition to recover my equilibrium. My nerves are shattered, and I feel that everything here at home has suddenly become leaden and empty and devoid of light. The doctor has wanted me to take a trip to Voss to strengthen my nerves, and I probably will do so one of these days. But otherwise, for the sake of the family, I have decided to stay home until after Christmas. Our planned meeting in Christiania, therefore, must unfortunately be abandoned for this time.

I hope that you are now in the middle of your orchestra rehearsals and that the performance will go well. Why, sure enough, it's today, the 19th![6] If only it in some degree could pave the way for a stage performance of one of your dramatic works. Then it would have served its purpose. That sort of thing is not easy to assess right away, but long live hope and faith! It surely will work out! Why do your wife and your sister not give concerts together? No illness, I hope?

Warm greetings!

Sincerely yours,
EDVARD GRIEG

---

[6] Schjelderup's wife, soprano Elsa Schjelderup, and his sister, the pianist Hanka Schjelderup (1865–1937), gave concerts in Christiania on October 15 and 17, and on October 27 there was an all-Schjelderup concert at the National Theater with Johan Halvorsen (1864–1935) as conductor. Schjelderup was present for the concert.

4

Bergen, January 13, 1902

Dear Mr. Schjelderup!

Yes, you are right! It turned into a long interruption. Altogether too long. And I am to blame. Or more correctly: my health. I cannot remember ever having been as far down as I have been during these months. When your sister was here I was a bronchitis patient as well and had to stay indoors in the evening. But I have been and still am thoroughly downcast and sad and unsociable. A week from now I hope to get out of here—the weather makes it absolutely impossible at the moment—and then I hope and believe that everything will instantly be different. Here at home it really seems as if there are no good forces that could give me a little protection from the endless rain and snow and stormy darkness, the endless illness and death and "misery of the world" that assault me from every quarter. I look forward more than I can say to getting down to Denmark and breathing easier.

And then the level of music here at home! It is beneath all criticism. Harmonien,[7] the only music society that is supposed to have true art as its goal, is lowering its standard more and more. Last evening I saw in the newspapers the program for a so-called "church concert" being given under Harmonien's auspices and it consisted of virtually nothing except—arranged works. It's just too bad. I wish that I were twenty years younger so that I could at least point out the right path.

Both through Halvorsen and in the newspapers I have heard of the success you had at your concert in Christiania. I knew in advance that Halvorsen would be interested. There are not many who conceal as much warmth and noble thought beneath an aloof exterior as he does. Moreover, I think you will come to the same conclusion as I: that the theater orchestra leaders are better than the theater directors, whose positions have made them hard, inconsiderate and "smart" men of the world. Bjørn,[8] in my opinion, should represent an exception because he is an artist through and through. His father has never compromised the demands of the ideal, and things like that are passed down from father to son.

And now the best wishes for the new year! Since fate has made you an opera composer, I wish for you above all: patience and—more patience!

Warm greetings from

Yours truly,
EDVARD GRIEG

---

[7] The music society Harmonien, predecessor of the modern Bergen Philharmonic Orchestra. Grieg served as conductor of the orchestra in 1880–82.

[8] Bjørn Bjørnson (1859–1942), theater director of the National Theater in Christiania.

5

Copenhagen, May 20, 1903

Dear Mr. Schjelderup!

Quite by accident I have received your letter here as I am passing through the city. When you hear my opinion about the biography question, you will again say: Oh, oh! For on this point I am a queer duck. It goes without saying that you have all the qualifications to fulfill such an assignment, but you must excuse me from having anything at all to do with the matter personally. Through C. F. Peters in Leipzig you will have access to my compositions as well as whatever has been written about me. But I do not want to influence your assessment in the slightest.

And then there is also the fact that I have been stupid enough to cooperate with another Norwegian, an organist by the name of Rojahn[9] in Tønsberg, who is writing something about me in connection with my sixtieth birthday in June. He has often visited me, and having once promised him information I couldn't refuse. But I have sworn: never again. Look at Garborg's work on Jonas Lie (when he turned sixty). Here you have a sympathetic and insightful account by an independent observer.

But I must take the liberty of saying how pleased I would be if your plan became a reality. For however well-intended Mr. Rojahn's book may be, it is precisely from someone of your unusual qualifications that I would expect something that goes beyond a routine biographical study. In other words: I think that you have the qualifications to be for me what Garborg was for Jonas Lie. Granted, I do not know how you view my art. I only know that thus far no one has written *truly* about it. What has been written has been wrong either from an artistic or from a national point of view. And it has often made me dispirited.[10]

And with that I send my best wishes for what lies ahead. We head north tomorrow and when I get home I hope to hear good things about *Offerildene* [*The Sacrificial Fires*].[11]

With warm greetings,

Sincerely yours,
EDVARD GRIEG

---

[9] The Norwegian educator and musician Ferdinand Rojahn (1860–1928), organist in Tønsberg 1887–1927. Rojahn's article "Edvard Grieg" was published in German in *Musik- und Theaterwelt*, Berlin, and in Norwegian as "Edvard Grieg som national Tonedigter" ("Edvard Grieg as a National Composer") in *Nordisk Musik-Revue* 3, pp. 89–93, both in 1903.

[10] Schjelderup's book *Edvard Grieg og hans Værker* (*Edvard Grieg and His Works*) was published in Copenhagen in 1903. The biography of Jonas Lie (1833–1908) to which Grieg refers was written by Arne Garborg (1851–1924) and published in 1893.

[11] *Offerildene*: a play by Danish playwright Karl Gjellerup (1857–1919) for which Schjelderup had written incidental music.

6

Troldhaugen, September 3, 1903

Dear Mr. Schjelderup!

This will be just a few lines, as I still do not dare to go ahead with anything at all. You apparently think I am healthy again, since you assault me anew. But that is so far from the case that you must now promise to go easy on me. To write down or dictate memories from childhood and early youth would be poison for my poor shattered nerves. Given my present condition, you must not try to get from us any information beyond that which you have already received. My wife cannot report anything without a conference with me, and that is the very thing I absolutely cannot tolerate. I must still strongly insist that private letters except for the ones I have mentioned (the letters in *Samtiden*[12] to my parents from Rome in 1870) must not be published. The letters to Feddersen[13]—about which, moreover, I can tell you that they do not contain anything of great artistic interest—also must not be published. In general it is my unalterable position that my private letters must not be published before I am gone, and even then the selection should be made with the very greatest discretion.

Thank you for your letter. I greatly regret that you cannot delay the publication by Hegel,[14] especially now, since there is a possibility that we could meet in Copenhagen before Christmas. Yes, if only I could get healthy enough to be artistic as well. Congratulations on the prospect of the performance of *The Sacrificial Fires* at the Royal Theater in Copenhagen. It looks as if you are finally beginning to prevail over the Boyg.[15]

To my surprise, I see from your letter that you refer to the book about me as a "Festschrift", whereas you previously called it a biography. This is fortunate, for a "Festschrift" does not require exhaustive biographical data.

I am also sending under separate cover a few photographs with a request that you kindly return them after you have used them. I hope that you will have an opportunity to get hold of my latest excellent photographs from the Royal Saxon court photographer N. Perscheid[16] in Leipzig. They were taken for the Leipzig sculptor Prof. Seffner,[17] who has made a bust of me. The marble bust is a gift from Edition Peters to the board of the Gewandhaus on the occasion of my 60th birthday. It will be installed in the foyer of the Gewandhaus this fall. I say with Oehlenschläger:[18] "Too much honor for the Norwegian skald." He, of course, said

---

12 *Samtiden*: a journal published in Bergen until 1899. It is still in existence but is now published in Oslo.

13 Danish writer Benjamin Feddersen (1823–1902), a long-time friend of Grieg in Copenhagen.

14 Danish book publisher Jacob Hegel (1851–1919), owner of the Gyldendal Publishing Company in Copenhagen.

15 "The Boyg": a reference to the mysterious creature by that name in Ibsen's *Peer Gynt*.

16 Liepzig photographer Nikolas Perscheid (1864–1913).

17 German sculptor Carl Seffner (1861–1932).

18 Danish writer Adam Oehlenschläger (1779–1850).

"Danish skald". Do you know the story? He (Oehlenschläger) came sailing into Christiania just as Akershus[19] was firing a salute in honor of a royal birthday. That is when the poor guy, misunderstanding the situation, uttered those famous words, "Too much honor for the Danish skald!" The story is divine and extremely characteristic of the vain Oehlenschläger.

Good wishes. The paper is finished and so am I.

Warm greetings from

Yours truly,
EDVARD GRIEG

P.S. I found a Perscheid photo, which will follow the other pictures. But you must request permission from Perscheid to reproduce it.

7

Bergen, September 18, 1903

Dear Mr. Schjelderup!
Thank you for your letter! I have had to delay my departure from here for eight days because of an indisposition which fortunately is now done with. I venture once again to take up pen and ink, and I will immediately use the opportunity to explain to you my position with respect to your biography. Basically, I have just kept the matter at arm's length and said "no" again and again because I needed quiet. But you must not consider me so doctrinaire as to insist that *none* of my private letters should be published until I am gone. It depends so much here on which letters are used and what the excerpt says. What I had to assume was that *I myself* would be the one to make the choice, or in any case that I would be given time to monitor (to read through, therefore) each detail. But all of this was made impossible by the *prestissimo* tempo with which you wanted to carry out the whole project. I understand, of course, that from your point of view, because of your financial situation, it could not be otherwise, but I greatly regret it for the sake of the project. There certainly is no Norwegian who is more qualified than you—yes, or even as well qualified—to do this job. It could have become a full-fledged biography, which is now an impossibility despite your sensitive appreciation for my art—which moves me all the more in that it is quite different from your own. Surely we can readily agree on that. There are certain basic views that we share. We are descended from the same family tree. But our branches have sprouted on different sides of the tree and have not grown up under the same climatic influences.

---

[18] Akershus: a fortress in Christiania overlooking the fjord.

Look carefully at my earlier letter and you will see that I specifically approved the word "Festschrift" instead of biography. But you wrote as if I preferred *biography*, which is not the case—given the way that your book is now shaping up.

I knew, to be sure, that you would be open to *The Mountain Thrall.* Between the Sørfjord mountains in winter garb, at the time I wrote this and much else of the best I've done (the *String Quartet*, for example), I also got hold of Landstad's[20] collection of folk poetry. I was looking for more material cut from the same cloth as that which I had used in *The Mountain Thrall.* I would then have included chorus and a bigger orchestra. But I didn't find the text I was looking for, so all that came of it was this fragment.[21] This was during the years 1877–78. It was an important period in my life, filled with significant events and emotional upheavals. I sought peace, insight and self-understanding, and I found all of this in the magnificent Hardanger district. The place became so dear to me that I built a little hut to work in, and for 4–5 years I returned there each summer. But finally I got the feeling that the mountains no longer had anything to tell me. I became stupid looking at them and decided that it was high time to get out of there.

From autumn 1880 to spring 1882, as you know, I conducted Harmonien in Bergen. That was a contrast to life at Lofthus! How un-ideal in comparison! But the resources—especially the winds—were terrible, and after two years I couldn't stand it any longer. Still, I wish you had heard what we achieved in Schubert's *Symphony in C Major* and Handel's *Anthem.* For I developed the choir to a level that was really something. But of course I got on the outs with the board, which neither could nor would understand me and waded in nonsense, anonymous filthiness and much more. No, sometime I must write about this and many other things myself.

You can tell from these lines that I am beginning to come back to life again—too late for you, unfortunately. It is dreadful, demonic, isn't it? I can just see you pounding your clenched fist on the table!

Now I will go out into the beautiful autumn sunshine and see if I can manage to reach "Fløyen".[22]

Warm greetings!

Sincerely yours,
EDVARD GRIEG

---

[20] Magnus Brostrup Landstad (1802–80), Norwegian clergyman, hymn-writer and collector of folklore.

[21] *The Mountain Thrall* is scored for baritone solo, string orchestra and two horns.

[22] Fløyen: one of the seven mountains overlooking the city of Bergen.

8

Christiania, April 11, 1904
The Deaconess Home's Hospital "Lovisenberg"

Dear Gerhard Schjelderup!
No, I did not know that you had lost your mother! It moved me, made me serious and melancholy such as a bit of one's own personal experience can do. I had great affection for her, and I know that for all of you she was a mother in the best sense of the word. What a piece of the world disappears with one's own mother! There is no other sorrow like it. Everything becomes so cold around one—despite all the sympathy. But time passes and the memories provide warmth. There is no more beautiful place for a mother to live than in the hearts of those who loved her!

Thank you for *The Sacrificial Fires*, which I have just read through. There is loftiness and noble architecture—yes, as noble as it is simple—in this work. With your sonorous and evocative music it cannot fail to have an impact also in the cold north. Unfortunately I will not be able to hear the performance in Copenhagen, as I clearly won't be going there in the near future.

As you see, at the moment I am in a hospital. I came here a few days ago to get the peace and quiet that my shattered nerves so sorely need. During my trip to Sweden my energy consumption was such that I was living "beyond human power"[23]—and now I am experiencing the reaction. But I hope that eight days here will at least bring me to the point where I can be with people again. In any case I will go into the city on the 16th to hear Brahms's *Requiem*—which, oddly enough, is being performed in the National Theater. We don't have a concert hall in this city at present, you know. (. . .)

It surprised me in your last letter to see you rate Humperdinck[24] so low. To be sure, *Hansel and Gretel* is not especially distinctive, and the instrumentation is often too dense—but the whole opera is infused with both poetry and a fairytale flavor. Thus it signifies a step—yes, a very big step—toward the embodiment of the folk fairytale in music, and since this has always been my ideal I am appreciative of every attempt that proves to be as successful as this one. It's not a good idea to criticize his use of Wagnerian *leitmotifs* too harshly, for where are they not present these days? When we look around we easily discover that the back side of the Wagner medallion is full of epidemic bacilli!

But now, finally, "No more these sounds continue . . ."[25] Thank you, however, for your kind invitation, which I shall look forward to accepting when times are better.

---

[23] An allusion to *Over Evne* (*Beyond Human Power*), a play by Norwegian author Bjørnstjerne Bjørnson (1832–1910) published in 1883. Bjørnson wrote another play by the same title that was published in 1895.

[24] German opera composer Engelbert Humperdinck (1854–1921), whose opera *Hansel and Gretel* was performed with great success at the National Theater in Christiania on December 2, 1903.

[25] Grieg often cited these words from Schiller's *Ode to Joy*, which Beethoven employed in the last movement of his *Ninth Symphony*: "nicht diese Töne. . . !!"

With the warmest greetings,

Sincerely yours,
EDVARD GRIEG

NB: not master!

P.S. Regarding your plan to publish the "Festschrift" in German: *It must not be done unless many errors are corrected.* It grieves me that you have detected "a disgusting fellow" in H.[26] You will understand that I, who know the whole firm and was a friend of the deceased, do not find much of "a disgusting fellow" in him. The old man was "significant" in several respects. He was forward-looking and had an understanding of the importance of mutuality in business life—qualities which one can seek in vain in nearly all other publishers. I am glad that you have found decent publishers for your smaller works. That is how one survives the seven lean years.[27] Since I am not an opera composer, they have not been as lean for me as they have for you. But believe me, there were years when I had to count my pennies and resign myself to giving lessons. You even have the advantage of being able to augment your income through your writing. And in so doing you also do much good, sow many a seed for the future here and there. You will see: Things will work out.

"The woods take revenge," it says in *The Wild Duck.*[28] I say: "Norway takes revenge." Norway is marvelous! But it takes revenge. Especially when the people bellow in chorus: "We're a-comin'—but it may take awhile." (Ivar Aasen[29]) These words make me furious!!!

9

Christiania, May 11, 1904
Hotel Westminster

Dear Schjelderup!
In great haste, some corrections to your book:

Page 5: "300-year night" should be "400-year night". The quotation from Ibsen should not be "the three-hundred-year night" etc. but "the four-hundred-year night" etc.

Page 6: It won't do to call Halfdan Kjerulf[30] a martyr. He enjoyed a lot of recognition among those who understood music, and it was only his ill health (tuberculosis) that slowly tortured him to death—if this expression is to be

---

[26] The reference is to music publisher Karl Hals (1822–98), founder of the firm Brødrene Hals (The Hals Brothers).
[27] An allusion to the "seven years of famine" described in Genesis 41:25 ff.
[28] The quotation is from Act Five of Ibsen's play.
[29] Norwegian linguist and writer Ivar Aasen (1813–96).
[30] Norwegian composer Halfdan Kjerulf (1815–68).

retained. Farther down on the same page it says, "The same miserable existence that led the sensitive Kjerulf to an early grave"!!! No, Kjerulf did not have a miserable existence. He enjoyed giving lessons, and he always had more offers than he could manage. Besides, he was probably not without means. He lived by and large a brilliant life at the top of the society of his day, quite especially in the Welhaven[31] circle.

Page 14: At my brother's funeral I did not play *Appassionata* but the *Sonata in C♯ Minor.*

Page 18: It is stated that in Leipzig I did not have an opportunity to become acquainted with Wagner's music. No, not the later Wagner, whom few if any were acquainted with at that time. But as early as 1858 *Tannhäuser* was performed, and it moved me so much that I heard it fourteen times in a row.

Page 19: What is termed "pneumonia" should be what the Germans call "Brustfellentzündung" (pleurisy).

Page 20: It was not the *Violin Sonata No. 1* in F—composed at Rungsted in 1865—that Gade characterized as being altogether too Norwegian. On the contrary, he spoke very favorably of this sonata (which, moreover, was not uninfluenced by him either). It was, rather, the second violin sonata, composed in Christiania in the summer of 1867. After its first performance in Copenhagen, Gade came down to the green room and said, "No, Grieg, you must not make your next sonata so Norwegian." I tasted blood at that moment and I answered, "Yes, Herr Professor, the next one will be even worse!" (As you know, however, it wasn't.)

Page 23: My wife was not born at Haukeland but in Bergen itself.

Page 28: *Fantasy Pieces* op. 3 should be *Poetic Tone Pictures.*

Page 33, near the bottom: You have "The Swan" instead of "A Swan".

Page 39: It says, "My mind is *like* a mountain steep." This *like* should be removed. Farther down on the same page you state that Nordraak went to Berlin in 1864. It should be 1865.

Page 44: You write, "He and his new wife gave lessons." It was just I who gave lessons, not my wife.

Page 46: You write that Grieg had some time previously sent Liszt his sonata. I never did that. He came upon it accidentally, probably through Sgambati or Ravnkilde.[32]

Page 60: It says here that the state never did anything for music until Svendsen and I received public grants in 1874 (that should be 1873).[33] This is incorrect,

---

[31] Norwegian author J. S. Welhaven (1807–73).

[32] Italian pianist and composer Giovanni Sgambati (1843–1914) and Danish composer Niels Ravnkilde (1823–90), both of whom lived in Rome.

[33] Grieg's memory is faulty here. He and Johan Svendsen (1840–1911) both began receiving annual grants in 1874. L. M. Linderman (1812–87) collected thousands of Norwegian folk melodies.

as before that L. M. Lindeman received for many years a similar amount to collect and arrange folk melodies.

Page 67 refers to fragments of a symphony that was never completed. The symphony was completed—indeed, it had already been completed when the two inner movements were performed in "Euterpe".[34] But I have never been satisfied with it and for that reason have never allowed it to be printed in its entirety or to be performed. Only the two inner movements have been published in a version for piano four hands, op. 14. The symphony corresponds to op. 3 and the *Poetic Tone Pictures* were published without an opus number.[35]

Page 73: Regarding "Autumn Storm" it is stated that "this poem is one of *Andersen's* best." The poem is by Christian Richardt.

Page 79: The words "It was a balmy" etc. should be "I walked one balmy" etc.

Page 84: Again "The Swan" is used instead of the poet's title, "A Swan". I spent most of 1876 not in Christiania but in Bergen, where in the spring I wrote the *Ballade* and the songs to texts by Ibsen and Paulsen. In July I went to Bayreuth. I did not come to Christiania until the end of September. Regarding the song "Fiddlers", which was written in Bergen in the spring of 1876, it may be mentioned that its opening measures constitute the principal motive in the *String Quartet* in G minor.

Page 85: The only winter I spent in Lofthus was in 1877–78, but I spent many of the following summers there.

Page 88: The Vinje songs were not written in Hardanger but in Bergen—in the spring of 1880. Also, op. 27 is the *String Quartet,* not the songs to Paulsen's poems. You call one of the latter "The Hope". It should be "Hope".

Page 89: You have P*o*ulsen instead of P*a*ulsen.

Page 92, at the top, you state "Grieg has employed Norwegian folk dances" [in op. 35]. This can be misunderstood, especially in Germany, to mean that I have used national folk dances, which is not the case. They are my own themes, and the Germans who are constantly sniffing around for evidences of "Norwegianizing"—a word that they use pejoratively—must not be given new ammunition.

Page 93: The four *Album Leaves* [op.28] date from the same period at Lofthus, likewise the *Improvisations on Two Norwegian Folk Songs,* which are occasional pieces, written for the fund for the Holberg monument in Bergen.[36]

Page 94: You have "The Greatest Fool" instead of "It Is the Greatest Foolishness" and "Young Ole" instead of "Ole".

---

[34] "Euterpe" was a music society established by Grieg and his friends in Copenhagen in 1864–65 to present performances by young Nordic composers.

[35] The symphony was never assigned an opus number. *Poetic Tone Pictures* was first designated op. 3 in an edition of 1876.

[36] Playwright Ludvig Holberg (1684–1754) was born in Bergen. In 1878 contributions were solicited for a fund to finance the creation and erection of a statue of Holberg in Bergen to mark the bicentennial of his birth. In 1884 Grieg also wrote the *Holberg Suite* op. 40 and the *Holberg Cantata* EG 171.

Page 95: It is quite true that *Land-sighting* was written in 1872. Both the text and the music were occasional works. Both came into existence in connection with a concert to raise money toward the restoration of the Trondheim cathedral. *Olav Trygvason* was conceptualized in 1873.

Page 102: Again you have *Appassionata* instead of the *Sonata in C♯ Minor.*

Page 108: It was indeed in Landstad's collection of folk songs that I found the words to *The Mountain Thrall* among the old texts.

Page 124: You write, "Some of the songs were composed several years earlier." No, they were written shortly before they were published.

Page 125: You have, "Of the works mentioned, *Bergliot* was written most recently." No, *Bergliot* was first conceptualized as early as 1871, when the only Wagner works I knew were *Tannhäuser* and *Lohengrin* (oh yes, also *The Flying Dutchman*). But the orchestration dates from the 1880's, when the score was published.

Page 137: The *Old Norwegian Melody With Variations* op. 51 was intended for orchestra but was first written down and published for two pianos. The orchestral score now exists in manuscript and was performed as an orchestral piece by Halvorsen at a National Theater concert here this winter. Hopefully it will soon be published. I say *hopefully*, for it is not so easy for me to get the scores that I want published either. If it were, the complete score of *Peer Gynt*, for example, would have been published long ago.

Well, these are the main points. After rereading your book, I again found so much that is true, felt and beautiful that had partly escaped me the first time—and that now moved and captivated me. You often find such vivid expressions for your thoughts. But I must insist that you are *too* harsh with respect to our homeland. You judge there like a *German,* not a Norwegian. God knows that we are still barbarians—yes, take it from me, I really think that we are more barbaric now than we were a generation ago. (That is the downside of democracy!!) But we should assess the motives of that which unfortunately is occurring just now and not just—cuss it out! The latter can be tempting, but it is absolutely futile. And it has no effect on a dyed-in-the-wool Norwegian.

I had a good laugh over your reflections regarding my family origin. They are absolutely priceless! Here you have written a "double counterpoint" that is elegant!

Now may you just succeed in getting Breitkopf & Härtel.[37]

I have toiled at a careful rereading of the book in order to be able to send this from here, as I see from your letter that the matter is urgent.

Warm greetings!

Sincerely yours,
EDVARD GRIEG

---

[37] The German music publishing company Breitkopf & Härtel.

10

Copenhagen, May 13, 1905
Hotel Phoenix

Dear Schjelderup!

Finally, finally! What must you think of me! But—there has been constant illness and more illness, and the only letters I have written have been those that were extremely urgent. I will tell you, though, that at the beginning of January, just as I was beginning a long period of illness, I dictated to my wife a letter to Arctander[38] regarding your application. So you see, I have thought of you. I did only what seemed natural to me, without hoping that it would do any good. So you got 1,000 crowns! A splendid herring salad: Sinding, Schjelderup and Haarklou![39] I simply cannot find words to express how much I think the whole business is inexpressibly miserable! But—you must look at it practically. It is a little support, and you now have a firm foothold in Norway, which indeed loves its sons—even if it loves the farmers most, especially when they are really shrewd.

Would you like to hear how a sick 62-year-old musician spends his day? On an empty stomach I go off to a stomach specialist, who employs all the tricks of the trade to pump me out and irrigate me. Believe me, it's quite a delightful feeling to have a rubber hose put in your mouth and down through the esophagus to the lower regions. When this is finished it's time for the intestines, which are taken care of in short order. Then I go home and drink more tea. Then I rest for half an hour, whereupon I go out to the Øresund hospital, where my wife is confined with erysipelas in her arm. Thereafter I go to town again for my second breakfast, then off to the dentist, who has tortured me every day *for a month* trying to kill some nerves. Then it's off for a massage. After this I come home dead tired, go to bed and rest until dinner at six. After this, if I am up to it, I go to the theater or a concert, but most often I am incapable of using my brain—so I just listen.

Isn't that an ideal life? But it will be over in about a fortnight, and then I will head home, come what may. This has been the most miserable, useless winter I have ever lived. May it go better with you, who still have so much to achieve!

Warm greetings from

Yours truly,
EDVARD GRIEG

---

[38] Sofus Arctander (1845–1924), chairman of the budget committee in the Norwegian Parliament.

[39] Norwegian composers Christian Sinding (1856–1941) and Johannes Haarklou (1847–1925).

11

Christiania, October 26, 1905
Hotel Westminster

Dear Schjelderup!
Unfortunately, you must no longer expect of me the "Leistungsfähigkeit"[40] that frequent letter-writing presupposes. The truth is that soon I will no longer be able to stand doing anything at all. No doubt you think that I could at least have found an occasion for you, and you may indeed be right about that. Forgive me for not having employed such an occasion. It is precisely this movement from thought to act that I call "Leistungsfähigkeit"—and that is what I, in fact, no longer have. Your letter has been lying here accusing me for a long time. But you must also admit that it is not easy to answer. It contains eight pages of jeremiads regarding matters the causes of which I can do nothing to remedy, not even with the best will in the world. (. . .)

And now to your folk-song project. "To handle them in such a way that they can even be used on the concert stage," as you say, is precisely what Johan Svendsen has done with such great mastery in his *Norwegian Rhapsodies* and what I have also attempted in my *Norwegian Dances.* In this way the folk song merges with one's own individuality and, after the process is complete, becomes a constituent of the work of art. I have also published folk songs in their original form but have harmonized them in accordance with my own inclination. Such treatment is only for musical "gourmets" and cannot count on appealing to a large audience. If, on the other hand, you want to harmonize or treat folk songs with the goal of getting them widely disseminated among the people, then you must put away your "oysters and caviar" and get out the "rye bread and butter". One must forget about heaven and remain on earth. Moreover, such publications are entirely justified if they are intelligently and carefully organized—not unwieldy and impractical like Lindeman's collection.[41]

Norges Melodier [*Norway's Melodies*], which you judge so harshly, is just such an unassuming collection. That it has served its purpose is evident from the fact that many thousands of copies have been sold in the space of a generation.[42] I had a good laugh over your criticism of it as "scandalously bad". For just between us I can tell you that it was the undersigned who, in his youth—NB! in response to a request—harmonized the whole thing from beginning to end! The requirements were that the harmonies be simple and that the pieces be as easy to play as possible. I needed money and for my part demanded only complete anonymity. Voila tout![43] I kept my promise except—as I recall—for five or six folk

---

40 Grieg often used this German word meaning "capacity for work".
41 Grieg is referring here to *Ældre og nyere norske Fjeldmelodier* [*Older and Newer Norwegian Mountain Melodies*], vols. 1–10, published seriatim 1853–67 by Ludvig M. Lindeman (1812–87).
42 *Norway's Melodies* was first published in 1875.
43 "Voila tout": That is all.

songs in which the harmonies were such that it might have been suspected that it was I who had written them. To these I attached my name as the arranger. Wasn't that clever? If you will take the trouble to look once again at *Norway's Melodies* and judge the treatment according to the premises appropriate to it, I am confident that you will take back the expression "scandalously bad". It makes no sense to try to shoot sparrows with cannons, just as it makes no sense to create idylls out of pastorales with pathos à la *Tristan and Isolde*.[44] But it is true: Norwegian folk music is so profound, so rich and infinitely pithy, that when, being the kind of person you are, you really immerse yourself in it for the first time, it will *completely* captivate you and tempt you to embrace it with all the fervor you can muster. Regarding this, I have just one thing to say: It is splendid that it is being done. Splendid to see various aspects highlighted by different individualities. But this concept absolutely must not be the basis for a publication intended for the general population. It would make the masses—for whom, when all is said and done, the collection is intended—both confused and bewildered. You see, I am right. That is the secret. One does not get to be 62 years old for nothing! Of course: From a purely artistic standpoint I would prefer to say about *Norway's Melodies* and that sort of thing in general what Wagner said of his American march: "The best thing about it is—the money!" And without this motto you will never get a Scandinavian publisher!! That's how wretched conditions are in Scandinavia.[45]

Toward the end of your letter you say, very movingly: "Now I have complained more than enough." But you must not be afraid to do that. I understand so well your need to unburden yourself to a sympathetic person. And I consider myself such a one, even if I am often in danger of having to contradict you.

You want to know my opinion about our politics? Well, then I will say that when you ask and then you still add a new question—"What does all that effusive love of the homeland really mean?"—I will just answer: It means June 7 and August 13.[46] Everything is now concentrated on the political enthusiasm. For offerings on the altar of art there is, therefore, less space than ever. But I think that what has been done is great. And I think that however much I may love the idea of a republic, I do not doubt for a moment that *at present* a monarchy is needed. Only that can save us from the inevitable economic and political failure. As you now know, on November 12 we presumably will have a plebiscite regarding this Parliament's right to select a king: yes or no. The government had no

---

[44] *Tristan and Isolde*: music-drama by Richard Wagner.

[45] Regarding Grieg's involvement with *Norway's Melodies*, see his letter of October 27, 1874, to Danish music publisher Eduard Wagner, who commissioned the collection. See also Grieg's letter to Gottfred Matthison-Hansen of March 7, 1878.

[46] Norway's long struggle for independence from Sweden was in its climactic phase as this letter was written. On June 7, 1905, the Norwegian Parliament had unanimously passed a resolution declaring Norway's independence. This action of the Norwegian Parliament was confirmed by a nearly unanimous vote of the people in a plebiscite held on August 13, 1905 (368,208 voted for, 184 against).

choice. For only on these conditions will the Danish prince become king of Norway.[47] There is an underground party here that can forge as well as any of their colleagues in *The Rhine Gold*.[48] Now, therefore, the government must act as quickly as it can. That is to say, as soon as the Karlstad agreement is ratified, which is to occur the day after tomorrow.[49] Hopefully, then, before the end of November we will have a king and queen and, with that, the peace that is so sorely needed in the land.

I could wish that you had spent this time at home. I am proud and happy to have experienced it. At your age, the strong national life that is now developing would have the most salutary influence on your mission if you had breathed Norwegian air during these great days. But also from afar you will feel what a joy it is to shake off the "fleas of dependency" and stand forth refreshed and renewed.

But finally I want to say one thing: I would not for anything have missed the longings for freedom and hope of my youth! These were the things that put steel in the task that Norway's intellectual leaders of the 1860's and 1870's had to carry out. Freedom is a risky thing. God knows if it is not Ibsen—yes, I think it is Stockmann[50] whom he has say that the *struggle for* freedom is what is important. Not freedom itself. That is a genuine Ibsenesque paradox. It remains for the youth of this time to prove that it can be a good thing to stand on one's own legs—if they are made of the right stuff. "The gods of the time are its men," said Wergeland.[51] We shall see!

I can conclude by telling you that no one has gotten twelve pages from me for a long time. But my wife is with friends, and solitude has *its* poetry!

Warm Greetings!

Yours truly,
EDVARD GRIEG

12

Troldhaugen, Hop Station at Bergen, July 4, 1906

Dear Schjelderup!
For many reasons that to me are sad, I am doing less and less letter-writing. Otherwise you would have heard from me long ago. Believe me, I thought about

---

[47] Prince Carl of Denmark stated that he would accept the throne only on condition that the people of Norway indicated by means of a plebiscite that they wished him to do so. The plebiscite was held on November 12 and 13, 1905, and Prince Carl became King Haakon VII (1872–1957).

[48] *The Rhine Gold*, the first of the four music-dramas in Richard Wagner's *Ring* series.

[49] The agreement certifying Norway's independence from Sweden was signed at Karlstad, Sweden on September 23, 1905. The agreement was ratified by the Norwegian and Swedish parliaments on October 9 and October 13, respectively, and was signed by the appropriate representatives of both countries in Stockholm on October 26.

[50] Dr. Stockmann is the leading character in Ibsen's play *En Folkefiende* (*An Enemy of the People*, 1882).

[51] Henrik Wergeland (1808–45), one of Norway's most distinguished poets.

you more than once when I was in Germany.[52] But my itinerary had to be arranged in such a way that a stop in Dresden was not possible. And now I am sitting once again on my hill[53] with gratitude and many beautiful memories behind me. That I was still able to do my artistic duty—that is what has strengthened me. It really is a wonderful thing with these big foreign orchestras that are so elastic that with one or two rehearsals they understand the most subtle intentions.

But to another matter. You mention that Ibsen wanted an interlude in *Peer Gynt* in which the folk melodies of various countries would be played in order to illustrate Peer Gynt's wandering around the earth.[54] This isn't what you actually wrote, but it is what happened. And I find this wish musically stupid, unrealistic and completely uncomprehending. Nor could anything else be expected of an Ibsen, whose wisdom lay in other areas. What in the world would one accomplish in Dresden by implementing this absurd idea at a performance of the work next year? Absolutely nothing, in my opinion. Well, yes, one would accomplish one thing: The performance, which currently lasts until almost midnight, would conclude even later. Still, it is of course possible that the younger generation has different nerves and different resources than those of my generation. I could be mistaken. But I am not mistaken in this: An interlude like the one requested would totally depart from the concept and style [of the existing *Peer Gynt* music], especially if it were written by any other composer. And that it would have to be, because I will not do it.

If it weren't precisely for the time question, I would find your idea of orchestrating my *Ballade* op. 24 for this purpose well worth undertaking. For then, in any case, the consistency of style would be preserved. But the deeper meaning of the *Ballade* and the deeper meaning of the desired interlude are about as different as can be imagined. Another possibility is that the *Ballade*, skillfully orchestrated by you, for example, could perhaps be used as a concert piece. It certainly would be an unanticipated dividend. But I can tell you in advance: It would not be to Peters'[55] liking. They are drowning in arrangements—orchestrations, which they reject as a matter of principle. So this cannot be recommended either. (...)

May you succeed in expressing clearly what moves you! I completely agree with you that Strauss[56] basically is nothing but a "re-hash of old stories". One can safely say that since his splendid *Death and Transfiguration* he has steered what for art is a fatal course. But I think it is a consequence of too little imagination, too much technique!

But when you, with your high goal in view, find fault with the Norwegian

---

[52] Grieg went to Germany on April 7, 1906, and did not return to Norway again until June 11. He gave concerts in Prague on April 16, in Amsterdam on April 26 and May 2, and in London on May 17 and 24.

[53] An allusion to Troldhaugen, which means "hill of the trolls".

[54] See Ibsen's letter to Grieg of January 23, 1874.

[55] C. F. Peters, Grieg's publisher in Leipzig.

[56] German composer Richard Strauss (1864–1949).

theater management—NB, on the basis of your principles—you now seem to be forgetting that whereas the creative spirit must pay attention *only* to ideals, a National Theater that is *not paid* by the state has to unite ideal and practical concerns. It has to pay attention to *everything*. This is about as difficult as it was for Oscar[57] to be king of Sweden and Norway—in other words, impossible.

Permit me as the older of us to tell you that you will live more happily if you do not let a bitterness toward Norway get the upper hand, for it begets a morbid fieriness and finds expression in an immodesty of which you certainly are not aware. You have been struck by "how much more positively" people treated Ibsen in his youth than they have treated you. You ought not to say such things. Have you gone around in sandals instead of boots because of your poverty? You think that Ibsen was more cunning than you: He let his friends pay. Add up, if you can, how much others have paid out for you and compare that with the amount paid out for others—to see for whom the larger sum has been paid. I think you will discover that you were completely wrong.

Regarding younger Bohemians perhaps one can justifiably make the accusations that you toss out against Ibsen. But he was not the kind of person who made it a practice to live at the expense of others. That at one time he *had to* do so was because he was starving—more than most people realize.

I regret that you have written to Bjørn Bjørnson.[58] I do not think it is from that source that help will come. The Norwegian Parliament is still negatively disposed toward culture, and as long as this tactic persists the Theater will get no support, and dramatic composers in Norway will have no hope for the future of their art in their home country. Still—I know now that it is to old Bjørnson[59] that you have written. About that there is indeed much to say. But you do not know his situation. Otherwise you would not have done it. He is as good as the day is long. And precisely for that reason—I do not want and am not able to say any more on this point. I only want you not to be disappointed.

Lastly, you speak of yourself in the following revealing words: "Thus far my thoughts about myself have been too small!" If this is true, I would only say: "Lucky you!" For it is not with excessively great thoughts about oneself that one achieves mastery. Moreover, your letters contain innumerable proofs of a self-confidence for which I have never reproached you—because it bears witness to a spirit that is permeated by the feeling of having a calling.

With that I shall conclude for today. Warm greetings from

Yours truly,
EDVARD GRIEG

---

57 Oscar II (1829–1907), king of Sweden and Norway 1872–1905; of Sweden alone from 1905 until his death.

58 Director of the National Theater in Christiania.

59 Norwegian author Bjørnstjerne Bjørnson.

13

Christiania, December 4, 1906
Hotel Westminster

Dear Schjelderup!

(...) What you write about *Peer Gynt* in Munich really is a quite a piece, but when on top of it all you suggest that it is Bjørn Bjørnson's fault that my music is mutilated there—well, this is even more unreasonable. The fact is, it is Bjørnson's duty to refuse to hand over a score of a piece owned by the National Theater that no one else has a right to perform without this score. This has to do with an autograph score. But since the materials needed for the performance (both the score and the parts) have been printed by Peters, it simply will not do—indeed, it is an impropriety—to say such things as that one does not know that "Solveig's Cradle Song" exists. Otherwise I think your "passing thought" about the two evening programs with the *Ballade* as the opening number of the second program has much to commend it. But I wouldn't dream of orchestrating it myself. The tiny bit of strength that I still have left for work I prefer to use in other ways.

I have just completed some hymns for mixed chorus based on Norwegian church melodies taken from Lindeman's collection. I may orchestrate them, but they are intended for *a cappella* chorus.[60]

I am only too willing to believe, unfortunately, that you have been treated badly by the Norwegian newspaper editors. And for you this is sad. I see now that I have only benefitted from the fact that I was at one time treated badly at home. It was the "bitter tonic" that I needed in order to develop.

That Svendsen[61] had to bury himself in Copenhagen—yes, it's true, that is also sad. It is quite a drama. That Sinding, as you say, "has to deliver manufactured goods"—that, to tell the truth, hits Sinding himself rather than Norway since he does not want to conduct, perform public concerts or give lessons as all the rest of us have had to do in order to live—or, more correctly, to avoid accumulating a crushing debt.

It is all well and good if one wants only to compose—provided one arranges things so as to be able to do that. But that the people who have the dubious fortune of possessing wealth exist for the sake of the artists—that I don't agree with. Let the honorable capitalists manage their affairs in their own way, and we will manage our affairs in ours. But this collusion with the rich, these superman tendencies—they evoke something in me that protests most strenuously. When the rich feel it as a relief to dish out money for the benefit of art and science—like Carnegie,[62] for example—my hat is off to them. But there is a pride in me

---

[60] Grieg is referring to *Four Psalms,* his last composition. "Lindeman's collection" is Ludvig M. Lindeman's *Ældre og nyere norske Fjeldmelodier* [*Older and Newer Norwegian Mountain Melodies*].

[61] Norwegian composer and conductor Johan Svendsen.

[62] The American manufacturing tycoon and philanthropist Andrew Carnegie (1835–1919) gave ca. 500 million dollars of his considerable fortune to various causes around the world.

that abhors applying to those who are sitting on their moneybags like a brooding hen. Believe me, I know the rumbling noise it creates, required as I am to play the middleman in season and out of season.

You are right in saying that artistically we are a highly "gifted people", we Norwegians, but we are also a people with an inordinate liking for life in the grand style. Sewage or cinnamon, as Alexander Kielland[63] said. We have a whole proletariat of artists in the younger generation who want at all costs to live a luxurious life, even if they have to borrow and beg every penny. I call that disgraceful—yes, "morally putrid", to use Ibsen's words. An artist here at home who does not mingle with highballs, champagne and libertines at the cafés is not an artist suitable for this clique, which would like to set the tone. Naturally the clique has taken possession of the press, so it leads a kind of seemingly successful gaudy existence. I can only say "Welcome to it!" and withdraw into my lair. For "I am longing for something much better!"[64]

I have gotten onto a subject that leads to many pages. I really wanted only to state my position, that I have still not gotten so far that I "would gladly live at others' expense and bring my works to completion"—NB, when these others are not Carnegies for whom it was an honor and a joy to support art. Of course you can assert: Theory is one thing, practice another. But to that I will say that had I not practiced "the theory of self-help" from my youth, I would not be as certain as I am now about the correctness of my view of this matter.

I look forward to hearing from you soon, hoping for some good news about yourself.

With warm greetings,

Yours truly,
EDVARD GRIEG

63 Norwegian author Alexander Kielland (1849–1906).

64 Grieg is quoting here from "Die beiden Grenadiere", a setting by Robert Schumann (1810–56) of a ballad by Heinrich Heine (1797–1856). Heine's line, which Grieg quotes in the original German, is: "Ich trage weit besseres Verlangen."

To Clara Schumann

The German pianist Clara Schumann (1819–96), who in 1840 married Robert Schumann (1810–56), was known as an outstanding pianist and succeeded in making her husband's compositions known and loved throughout Europe. As a student, Grieg heard her play Schumann's *Piano Concerto,* and as late as January 20, 1907, he made a diary entry regarding his memory of the event: See Benestad & Halverson (eds.), *Edvard Grieg: Diaries, Articles, Speeches* (Columbus, Ohio, 2001).

Grieg's letters to Clara Schumann are preserved in the Staatsbibliothek zu Berlin, Preussischer Kulturbesitz, Musikabteilung.

1

Copenhagen, December 2, 1879
Hotel King of Denmark

Dear Madam:
Encouraged by my friend Heinrich von Herzogenberg,[1] I take the liberty of respectfully directing a question to you regarding a matter that is of great importance to me.

I intend to go to England in the spring to perform some of my own compositions (a piano concerto, chamber-music works and songs). Would you be so exceptionally kind as to prepare the way for me with some recommendations? To whom? That you yourself certainly know best! Mr. von Herzogenberg, who will write further details to you regarding the matter, has informed me that you know something about me. Were that not the case, it would have been difficult for me to dare to address myself directly to you.

You will hopefully excuse my request and my poor German. Honored lady, it pains me to burden you with such things; indeed, I dare say that I am embarrassed even as I am writing these lines—all the more inasmuch as I myself am always annoyed by all forms of recommendations and therefore am acting most inconsistently. London, however, is a city where every artist is more or less inconsistent when he, in order to make progress with certain matters, must, so to speak, forget his principles.

Finally, begging once again that you not take my request amiss, I sign my name, with deep respect,

Edvard Grieg
Norwegian Musician

---

[1] German composer Heinrich von Herzogenberg (1843–1900).

Clara Schumann, from an engraving after a photograph. On January 20, 1907, Grieg wrote in his diary: "I came to Leipzig in 1858 and a few months after my arrival heard the bewitching Clara Schumann play [her husband's piano] concerto, and each tempo was indelibly impressed on my soul. Youthful impressions such as that do not lie." (PD)

2

Copenhagen, January 8, 1880
Hotel King of Denmark

Dear Madam:
Accept, dear Mrs. Dr. Clara Schumann, my sincerest thanks for your kind communication. If I should be so fortunate as to get engagements in London you may be assured that I will remember you and Professor Joachim[2] with gratitude. May I hope to meet you in London? I have heard that you have plans to go there.

In the hope that my lucky star will in the not too distant future lead me to where you live, I am,

With great esteem,
EDVARD GRIEG

---

[2] The same day that Grieg sent his first letter to Clara Schumann, he sent a similar request to the Austro-Hungarian violinist Joseph Joachim (831–1907), and Clara Schumann transmitted a recommendation from Joachim. Grieg's plans for concerts in London in 1880 did not work out, however, and it was not until 1888 that he made his first visit there.

3

Leipzig, February 12, 1894
c/o C. F. Peters, Thalstrasse 10

Dear Mrs. Dr. Clara Schumann:

At the request of the American periodical *The Century Monthly Magazine* I have undertaken to write an essay on Schumann.[3] Enclosed with these lines I take the liberty of sending you a copy of my work. From this you will understand my deep respect for the incomparable master; and even if I dare not expect that you will agree with all of my views, still I hope that you will be able to approve of other things in the essay as being current and correct—for example, my comments on the Schumann-Wagner question.[4]

I would be most happy if you would send me a few words to the effect that my essay has not displeased you from beginning to end. Although I am not an author, I daresay that my intentions have been the best and that my homage to the immortal hero is that of a true musician.

With great esteem,
EDVARD GRIEG

---

[3] Grieg's long and insightful article on Schumann was published in the January, 1894 issue of *The Century Illustrated Monthly Magazine.* The article, which was originally written in Norwegian, will be printed in a new translation in Benestad & Halverson (eds.), *Edvard Grieg: Diaries, Articles, Speeches* (Columbus, Ohio, 2001).

[4] In the article Grieg sharply attacked the so-called "Wagnerites", who belittled Schumann's contributions to the world of music.

To Johan Selmer

The Norwegian composer Johan Selmer (1844–1910) was the leading representative of program music in nineteenth-century Norway. He began receiving annual composer's grants from the Norwegian Parliament (Stortinget) in 1879. He served as conductor of the Music Association orchestra in Christiania from 1883 to 1886.

Grieg's letters to Selmer are preserved in Nasjonalbiblioteket, Oslo (National Library of Norway, Oslo Division).

1

Christiania, October [exact date unknown], 1871

Dear Mr. Selmer!
It is a pleasure for me to have an opportunity to express my judgment regarding your talent. That this is of the genuine sort is something that was clear to me as soon as I saw your first measures. I would especially mention your *Scène funèbre.*[1] I will not venture to express a decisive opinion about this work after having heard it just once, but it is certain that it bears witness to a vivid inventiveness and power of description, a feeling for interesting combinations and, in general, an urge to strive for the sublime in art. If you could have an opportunity to spend some time in Germany it would certainly be of the greatest significance for your future—and if these lines could contribute to the achievement of this goal, it would greatly please

Yours truly,
EDVARD GRIEG

2

Bergen, April 12, 1876

Dear Selmer!
I say like Bjørnson's[2] Brewmaster Jacobsen: "Yes, I'm a dirty dog, a big dirty dog." For your kind letter should have been answered long ago. This winter I have been living as if in a dream, and in a dreamy state one is not responsible. That is my excuse. This fall, when we meet, I promise that I will be fully awake, and then we will have a good time together if you stay in Norway.

But wait: It could happen that we will meet earlier, for I will certainly go through Christiania in June en route to Bayreuth. Yes, what do you say about a publisher like Dr. Abraham[3] (Peters), who without further ado sends me a ticket

---

1 *Scène funèbre* was composed in 1871.
2 Norwegian author Bjørnstjerne Bjørnson (1832–1910). Brewmaster Jacobsen is one of the principal characters in Bjørnson's play *En Fallit* (*The Bankrupt*) from 1875.
3 Dr. Max Abraham (1831–1900) was proprietor of the C. F. Peters Musikverlag in Leipzig.

as a gift—it is good for the entire series of second performances—and who even promises to get me access to the dress rehearsals. I can only conclude that the whole undertaking is one of the greatest—and in any case one of the most singular—events in the history of music. I only regret not being able to make a thorough study of the piano reductions here at home this winter. Will you do me a favor and tell me if any of them are in Warmuth's library,[4] for if so he must let me have them for a while. Ask him directly from me if he will do me the big favor of letting me borrow the piano reductions of the trilogy,[5] if they are in his possession, and if in this case he will immediately send them to me in Bergen. I will return them in June—or earlier, if he wishes. I will be most grateful if you will do this. (. . .)

I was pleased to hear about your successful concert in Christiania.[6] Yes, one can take satisfaction in acclaim when one has a good conscience in relation to one's artistic ideals. But that does not apply to me and that wretched *Peer Gynt* music, for every moment I had to banish my ideals in order to cover up for a poor orchestra and enhance the popular stage effects. If I had had the strength to be my better self, it goes without saying that I would have been there to see to it that my intentions were realized. But you can surely understand that under these circumstances I preferred to be elsewhere.[7]

Give Svendsen[8] my best regards and tell him that now he must not make me wait any longer for a few lines.

Warmest greetings also to you both from Nina and from

Yours truly,
EDVARD GRIEG

---

[4] Carl Warmuth Jr. (1844–95), a music publisher in Christiania, also operated a big lending library offering all kinds of printed music.

[5] Grieg is referring to Wagner's tetralogy, the four musical dramas of the so-called *Ring* series: *The Rhine Gold, The Valkyries, Siegfried* and *Twilight of the Gods.* Grieg regularly refers to this work as a trilogy, treating *The Rhine Gold* as a prologue to the three dramas comprising the trilogy. Grieg went to Leipzig at the invitation of his Leipzig publisher, Dr. Max Abraham, to attend the inauguration of the Wagner festivals in the summer of 1876. While there he wrote a series of articles for the Bergen newspaper *Bergensposten.* The complete articles will be printed in English translation in Benestad & Halverson (eds.), *Edvard Grieg: Diaries, Articles, Speeches* (Columbus, Ohio, 2001).

[6] Selmer had given a concert of original compositions on March 11, 1876.

[7] For further information regarding the premiere of *Peer Gynt* see the correspondence between Grieg and Ibsen.

[8] The Norwegian composer and conductor Johan Svendsen (1840–1911), who since 1874 had been conductor of the Music Association orchestra in Christiania.

3

Troldhaugen, Hop Station at Bergen, May 25, 1885

Dear Selmer!

Today I have written to Bentsen in Svendsen's interest.[9] Naturally I don't have to tell you that I am in complete agreement with your view. I find it to be a scandal that someone can think for a moment of taking away Svendsen's grant. I have also expressed this view as I have had opportunity and have secured partial agreement—but only partial, unfortunately. Might something be going on behind the scenes? I didn't think Svendsen had any enemies in the government, as he has managed so masterfully to conceal his political position with the cloak of diplomacy. I think, though, that despite his cultivation of the big-wigs he is a leftist through and through. But perhaps it is the feeling of this that the decision-makers do not like. Be that as it may, from a place so distant from the very "scene of the crime" I cannot determine exactly what is the real root of the matter and cannot, therefore, undertake anything directly. That you do so, however, is exactly what I would have done if I were in your place.

As for E,[10] you no doubt will remember that for good reasons I have not permitted myself to judge his character. It may have its faults—I don't know the man—but I think the same can be said of all of us and we should, therefore, speak gently about the character of others. As an artist, E. has my warmest appreciation, and I am all the happier to hear that he also has yours—for I know that within musical circles in Christiania there are perceptions of E. that have been written in mean, anonymous letters, one of which has been addressed to me. When a young artist in a setting as small as Christiania is subjected to such contemptible treatment, I can do nothing but think twice as well of him—despite his possible mistakes, even if they are as great as those of Atlas himself. I would be very sad if you do not agree with me on this, as from earlier days I have always known you as one who possesses a generous portion of high-mindedness and nobility.

---

9 Both Grieg and Svendsen had been awarded annual composer's grants in 1874 on the condition "that they dedicate their talents to the furtherance of music in the homeland." In 1883 Svendsen accepted the position of musical director at the Royal Theater in Copenhagen, and in 1885 the Norwegian government proposed to the Parliament that Svendsen not receive the grant as long as he continued to work abroad. In a letter dated May 25, 1885, to Halvor Andreas Bentsen (1825–91), president of the larger division of Parliament (*Odelstinget*), Grieg stated that he hoped conditions in Norway "in a not far distant future will become more favorable for the termination of his [Svendsen's] enforced exile. I think, in other words, that he, in common with the rest of us, the spokesmen for Norwegian art, looks forward with longing to the moment when the Parliament, through other protective measures and an art academy, will take the initiative in gathering Norwegian artists in the homeland." In his letter of May 30, 1885, to president Bentsen, Selmer also pointed out how unreasonable it was that Svendsen should be deprived of the grant. Action on the issue was postponed in 1885, but in 1886 the annual grants to Svendsen were terminated.

10 The "E" to whom Grieg is referring is the Norwegian composer Catharinus Elling (1858–1942). Grieg had written a very positive article about him that was published in *Bergens Tidende* on March 14, 1885. It will be printed in English translation in Benestad & Halverson (eds.), *Edvard Grieg: Diaries, Articles, Speeches* (Columbus, Ohio, 2001).

Still—such things are better discussed orally, and I hope very much that it might happen soon. I must get away this fall, in any case—I don't know how—and then I must try to stop off in Christiania on the way.

With warm greetings from

Yours truly,
EDVARD GRIEG

4

London, November 11, 1897
47 North Side, Clapham Common

Dear Selmer!
Thank you for your letter! It did me good—doubly good in the sad life I am leading for the time being. I am very despondent, for I am not able to regain my strength after the hard attack of bronchitis, and I am not likely to do so here in London. If only someone had told me that the climate here at this time of the year is poison for people like me. Up to the last moment I had hoped to be able to fulfill about half of my commitments here, but today it is clear to me that the only goal should be to get out of here alive.

Yesterday, for the first time, I went outdoors for half an hour, but then I had a bad night—and today the fog is so thick that I have to stay in my room. Meanwhile the doctor wants me to go down to the coastal city of Hastings the day after tomorrow in order to recover more quickly. I really don't know how that is supposed to happen, but I am now so depressed that I don't oppose anything. I just let myself be treated like a child. It's a good thing I got my wife to come here, for the loneliness at the beginning was crushing. I get tons of letters, but only from people who want to exploit me. Therefore your kind letter was doubly welcome.

The Delius story[11] seems to me to be a striking proof of the low level of music in Norway. People make a musical question out of something that in its

---

11 On October 18, 1897, the Christiania Theater had premiered *Folkeraadet* [*The People's Council*], a play by Norwegian author Gunnar Heiberg (1857–1929). The play was a satire on the Norwegian parliamentary system and Norwegian politicians. English composer Frederick Delius (1862–1934) had been commissioned to write incidental music. This he did in the form of an overture and three entr'actes. For one reason or another he used the melody to "Ja, vi elsker dette landet" ["Yes, we love this land, our country"]—the Norwegian national anthem—as part of the music. In the prelude to the third act the anthem was transposed into a minor key and played as a funeral march. Many listeners reacted angrily to such "sacrilegious" treatment of the national anthem, and a lively debate over the issue was waged in the newspapers. Delius was thrown out of his hotel, and after a few performances he withdrew his music. But after the students, following a debate in the University Student Association, asked him to send the music back to the theater, he did so. At one of the performances a young man from Flekkefjord drew a revolver, fired at the conductor, Per Winge (1858–1935)—with blank shells, fortunately—and then threw the revolver up to him. Performances of *The People's Council* continued until November 27, 1897. Grieg never heard Delius's incidental music to this play. For further information regarding this episode see Lionel Carley: *Grieg and Delius. A Chronicle of their Friendship in Letters*, London 1993, pp. 168–73.

essence has nothing to do with music, for no one can get me to believe that people were *musically* indignant. All of the conditions for such indignation are lacking. The breadth of the controversy demonstrates that chauvinism is its root cause. I regret that Delius has used his beautiful talent for this work. I am not familiar with it, but given the content of the play it is in my opinion a misunderstanding that he tackled it. To parody melodies, of course, is not new. Berlioz, as a matter of fact, has pushed it to an extreme without producing something that could be called unartistic, for the very idea forms the explanatory background.[12] But what is the idea behind "Yes, we love this land, our country" in minor? Wasn't that the situation? Well, this I don't understand. I wouldn't want to see Bjørnson to his grave to the tones of "Yes, we love this land, our contry"—in minor! I do not appreciate this idea at all, either musically or nationally. I have seen Ole Bull buried to the tones of "Sæterjentens Søndag" ("The Shepherd Girl's Sunday")[13]—in major, fortunately, as it was written—and the effect was gripping. The thought of playing it in minor on that occasion makes me more or less seasick!

Well, look at this, now I am sweating. To tell the truth, I have not been able to write such a long letter for quite some time. So I must conclude. Farewell to you and your wife, and be happy if you are on German soil. *I* will be happy the day I get there.

Warm greetings both from Nina and from

Yours truly,
Edvard Grieg

12 Grieg is referring here to *Symphonie phantastique* by Hector Berlioz (1803–69).
13 "The Shepherd Girl's Sunday" was composed by Norwegian virtuoso violinist Ole Bull (1810–80).

To Jean Sibelius

Jean Sibelius (1865–1957) remains to this day the greatest composer to come out of Finland. Grieg and Sibelius were not personal friends and it is not known which Sibelius compositions Grieg was familiar with. In his diary from 1906, however, Grieg expressed his admiration for the music of his Finnish colleague. See his diary entries for November 3 and 30. In a letter to Gottfred Matthison-Hansen (1832–1909) of December 19, 1906, he wrote of the "beautiful music of Finnish composer Sibelius."

The letter—a postcard—is reproduced in facsimile in Erik Tawaststjerna's biography, *Sibelius* (Helsinki, 1997).

Troldhaugen at Bergen, Norway
June 26, 1903

Dear Mr. Sibelius:
Hearty thanks to you and those who joined with you in sending the telegram in honor of my 60th birthday! I am proud and happy to have received this greeting, for which I still hope some day to have the opportunity to thank you in person. Thank you also for your beautiful music, which I greatly admire and love.

Very respectfully yours,
EDVARD GRIEG

To Alexander Siloti

Grieg first met the Russian pianist and conductor Alexander Siloti (1863–1945) during a stay in Leipzig in 1887–88. Siloti, a pupil of Franz Liszt (1811–86), had come to Leipzig to conduct a concert devoted to the works of his great teacher. Grieg visited him a short time later along with Tchaikovsky (1840–93), who had been Siloti's teacher in Moscow. Siloti himself was a teacher at the Moscow Conservatory in 1887–90, but he also concertized extensively. During the years 1890–1900 he lived for the most part in Western Europe. He was the soloist in Grieg's *Piano Concerto* in Leipzig on February 7, 1893, with the composer conducting. In 1901–02 he conducted a series of philharmonic concerts in Moscow, and in 1903 he established his own orchestra in St. Petersburg. After the Russian revolution he emigrated to England. In 1922 he moved to New York City, where he taught at the Juilliard School of Music from 1924 to 1942.

Siloti had an exceptionally high opinion of Grieg's music and also admired his stance on the burning political issues of the day. In an undated note to Grieg he thanked him, among other things, for his letter to the French conductor Édouard Colonne (1838–1910) in connection with the so-called "Dreyfus affair".[1]

Grieg's letters to Siloti are preserved in The Russian Institute of History of the Arts, St. Petersburg, Siloti's letters to Grieg in Bergen Offentlige Bibliotek (Bergen Public Library).

1

Troldhaugen at Bergen, Norway, July 10, 1902

Dear Mr. Siloti!

It really is very kind of you to take such a friendly interest in my concert appearance in Russia. But this possibility first came up after I had accepted an invitation from the Warsaw Philharmonic, and in the absence of some compelling reason I cannot withdraw from this commitment. Should the negotiations between the Warsaw Philharmonic and Russia encounter difficulties, I would of course be prepared to accept your invitation with thanks.

Moreover, *as a matter of principle* I do not give my own orchestral concerts but conduct only in response to invitations from the concert associations. César Cui[2] has invited me to St. Petersburg many times, but my poor health has always proven to be an insurmountable obstacle. After tolerating the trip to Warsaw so well this spring, I now have renewed hope that my long-standing desire to perform my works in Russia may be fulfilled after all.

Your *comme il faut* sounds very funny to me. Hopefully in German it means: the *best* orchestra![3]

---

[1] See Grieg's letters to Édouard Colonne.

[2] César Cui (1835–1918), a Russian, was by profession an engineer who specialized in military fortifications, but he was also very active in the music life of St. Petersburg both as a composer and as a writer on music. From about 1900 until his death he devoted himself entirely to music.

[3] In a letter of June 24 Siloti had mentioned that he himself wanted to arrange the concerts in such a way that they would be *comme il faut*, i.e., worthy of a master like Grieg.

With friendly greetings from house to house,

Very sincerely yours,
EDVARD GRIEG

2

Troldhaugen at Bergen, Norway, August 26, 1902

Dear Maestro Siloti!

I know from my own experience that certain composers who are even "amiable people" cannot stomach Tchaikovsky.[4] I know a very talented and honorable Danish composer for whom Tchaikovsky is abominable! Since in this case there are no personal motives involved, it must quite simply be explained as an abnormality in the construction of the man's brain. An artist to be pitied! In the instance you mention, in any case, it appears to be organs other than the brain that seem by nature to be inadequately equipped! In the years that have passed since the noble master Tchaikovsky died, I have come to love him even more dearly, and our old friendship—renewed by him—would be for me the best reason to prefer your invitation to St. Petersburg above all others. But then it would be necessary not only to appear under your auspices but also to perform the concert in St. Petersburg under your protection. In your absence I absolutely do not dare to take the risk of standing there alone and vulnerable—yes, without even being able to understand the language of the country, and perhaps becoming a victim of possible intrigues. You *must* be present in St. Petersburg. If not, it is completely out of the question for me to appear under your auspices. Apropos: Who is giving this concert? I take the liberty of asking this question since I myself absolutely do not want to appear as the one giving the concert. (. . .)

Then I have one more question: I am no longer so dumb as to play my own *Piano Concerto*! (I will, in general, only conduct and if necessary accompany my songs. That, unfortunately, is all my health will tolerate.) But of course I had hoped for a certain *Siloti* as pianist. Are you really serious about not playing? And why? No, that must just be a joke on your part!

So: The whole affair must be organized in such a way that *both of us* are satisfied. You can work it out, I'm sure.

There can be no thought of including a chamber-music work on the program at an orchestral concert (not even with an artist like Ysaÿe[5]).

And now you must give me an answer to the following question: Which orchestra will be available to me? Is it the best one? How many violins, violas,

---

[4] In a letter of August 12 Siloti had informed Grieg that César Cui opposed Tchaikovsky's music as vigorously as he could. Siloti also mentioned that he would not be able to attend Grieg's concert in St. Petersburg as he would be busy with his own concerts in Moscow.

[5] Belgian violinist, conductor and composer Eugène Ysaÿe (1858–1931) was one of the leading performing artists of his day.

cellos and double basses? How many rehearsals? Who is providing the printed orchestral material for the musicians? *I have to know all of this* before I can make a definitive decision.

For the program at St. Petersburg and Moscow I recommend the following:

1. "Homage March" from *Sigurd Jorsalfar*, [incidental music to] a play by Bjørnson.
2. Songs with orchestra: a) "Solveig's Cradle Song", b) "From Monte Pincio", c) "A Swan".
3. *Piano Concerto.*
4. *Two Elegiac Melodies* for string orchestra.
5. Songs with Piano.
6. *Ballade in the Form of Variations on a Norwegian Melody* (op. 24) for piano. (Can be omitted if it is not in Mr. Siloti's repertoire.)
7. *Peer Gynt Suite No. 1*, [incidental music to] a dramatic poem by Ibsen.

With respect to my songs I request that you please suggest a suitably qualified female singer.

As to dates for the St. Petersburg and Moscow concerts, it should be mentioned that the day for the Warsaw concert to which I am already committed—April 14—cannot be changed, as I am going directly from Warsaw to England.

Well, that's enough for today. I hope to hear soon that you have managed the impossible!

No doubt you already know that our dear Fritzsch[6] has passed away. He was a real idealist (what a rarity for a journalist!) and a good person. What an empty place Leipzig has gradually become!

With heart-felt greetings from house to house,

Sincerely yours,
EDVARD GRIEG

3

Troldhaugen at Bergen, Norway, September 25, 1902

Dear Maestro Siloti!
The decision is made. It will be as you wish. Now you can "dance with joy!" For I am not coming.[7] But I must smile sadly at your letter. You apparently think I am immortal when you invite me to come in 1904. Bear in mind that I am an old

---

6 E. W. Fritzsch (1840–1902), Leipzig music publisher and editor of the music journal *Musikalisches Wochenblatt.*

7 The dates recommended by Siloti in his letter of September 6 were unacceptable to Grieg because of his agreement with the Warsaw Philharmonic.

man. I am 59, and it is my firm intention to stop giving concerts abroad when I turn 60. I long for peace and quiet—for soul and body in equal measure.

Since I have now given up my Russian trip in 1903, I am relinquishing altogether the hope of personally presenting my works in Russia. Oh well, I can peacefully depart this world without having visited Russia. But Russian art, which, with its grand conception, richness of color and advanced technique has meant so much to me, cannot be taken from me. I carry it with me in my heart with infinite gratitude!

With that, let us let the matter lie. I am going to Warsaw as agreed; I have asked only that I might come 14 days earlier.[8] For Colonne[9] has recently invited me to conduct his orchestra. Mr. Henri Rochefort[10] and various other anonymous letter-writers have promised to give me a beating if I should ever dare to visit Paris! I have, therefore, expressed my misgivings to Colonne and am very anxious to see what he will answer.

And now, dear friend, may all be well with both you and your esteemed wife. Hearty thanks for the interest you have shown in me and my music, and accept, both of you, the warmest wishes from the inhabitants of Troldhaugen (i.e., the hill of the trolls).

Your devoted friend,
EDVARD GRIEG

4

Berlin, May 17, 1903

Dear Mr. Siloti!
(. . .) Today my wife and I came here en route to Copenhagen from Leipzig, where we spent eight days. I had not been there for five years. Such changes! All my dear, old friends were either dead or had left the city. But a new, fresh, broad-minded musical spirit is blowing over Leipzig, a spirit that I have always found lacking in this city. But it will never supplant the old friends or take the poetry from the past.

As I observed in an album in Hotel Hauffe, you have also been in Leipzig recently. But these albums! I hate them: Owners of albums, cyclists and automobiles are the modern plague. Where such people appear I immediately withdraw. Hopefully this plague has not become an epidemic in Russia as it has, for example, in France.

---

[8] Grieg conducted two concerts in Warsaw on April 14 and 15, 1903.

[9] Colonne had invited Grieg to conduct his orchestra. The concert was given in the Châtelet Theater in Paris on April 19, 1903.

[10] Henri Rochefort (1830–1913), French journalist and politician, who had promised to give Grieg a beating if he dared to show his face in Paris after his involvement in the Dreyfus affair in 1899.

Now the awful dinner music is beginning! I must close. Farewell for now, and let me hear from you soon (address Bergen, Norway). Receive the friendliest greetings from house to house!

Yours truly,
EDVARD GRIEG

5

Christiania, February 12, 1904
Hotel Westminster

Dear Mr. Siloti!
I should like very much to know what you must think of me. First I send you a telegram saying, "I agree", and then, two days later, "Russia impossible". But you see, I was already ill when the first telegram was sent. I didn't have the courage to decline the invitation. I kept hoping that my health would soon improve. But during the next days it got much worse, and I saw it as my duty to take the matter seriously. Now, to be sure, I am better, thank God, but it is more than doubtful that I will be in shape to give a concert in April.

And now to the main point: Under the present political conditions I couldn't think of going to Russia in any case.[11] I also assume that you and the Philharmonic Society will be best served by my not coming. People in St. Petersburg obviously have things other than art on their minds just now. I think it is terrible and sad that the many beautiful words about peace among men are only phrases and play-acting. The concept of honesty still appears to be nothing but a utopian dream. When will honesty become a reality? When will it be set forth as a program? The political concepts need to be cleaned up. Perhaps it will happen by means of great political upheavals such as can now be glimpsed on the horizon.

And we artists sit here and talk about culture, about civilization! How little we have accomplished! Battle songs and requiems can indeed be very beautiful—and yet, the duty of art is something much higher than this. Art should be so comprehensible to the nations of the world that, as the messenger of peace, it would make war feel impossible. Only then would we have become *human beings.* Now we stumble around like *barbarians.* Yes, in view of the latest political events I am *ashamed* to be a human being! We really have much to learn from animals! They don't *lie*!

Now I will conclude. And you surely agree with me in that. For my telegram today would have read like this: "Grieg impossible!"

---

[11] Grieg is referring to the unrest in Russia around the turn of the century as well as the Russian attack on Japan, and he reacted strongly against the tsar's tyranny and imperialism. See his letter to Adolf Brodsky (1851–1929) of April 26, 1905.

Heart-felt greetings from house to house!

Sincerely yours,
EDVARD GRIEG

P.S. I would be happy to hear from you soon that you say with Heine, "Ich grolle nicht!"[12]

6

Christiania, October 29, 1904
Address: Hals Brothers Piano Company

Dear Mr. Siloti!
Now you see how fate plays with us! If you had had any idea what was going to happen you would rather have let me come two years ago!

I have just received an invitation from the Music Teachers' Association in St. Petersburg to conduct two concerts of my own works. The invitation was signed by Rimsky-Korsakov, Glazunov, Lyadov and other well-known masters.[13] What was my answer? No, of course! First because I had already said yes to the Philharmonic Society, but also—and most importantly—because under the present political conditions I do not wish under any circumstances to go to Russia. It is a mystery to me how a country in which almost every family is grieving over someone who has fallen in battle can think of inviting an artist. Maybe this is just something I don't understand. I have only to act in accordance with my own feelings. And these feelings make it totally impossible for me to concertize in Russia at the present time. I am well aware that many artists have a more robust view of life. I am not one of them. I, therefore, regard it as my duty at precisely this time, when by virtue of a new invitation I have a double opportunity to do so, to tell you openly what I think.

It is a pity that it should end like this. One must *first* be a human being. All true art grows out of that which is distinctively human. Ah well, I am sure that you understand me even if with respect to politics you do not share my opinion.

With heartiest greetings from house to house,

Yours truly,
EDVARD GRIEG

P.S. Please forgive me for not writing earlier, but it couldn't occur to me in my wildest dreams that, under the current sad circumstances, concert life in St.

[12] Grieg is quoting the title of no. 7 of Robert Schumann's *Dichterliebe* op. 48, text by Heinrich Heine (1797–1856). It means, "I bear no grudge."

[13] The Russian composers Nicolai Rimsky-Korsakov (1844–1908), Alexander Glazunov (1865–1936) and Anatol Lyadov (1855–1914) were key figures in St. Petersburg's music life.

Petersburg is steadily continuing in peace and quiet, as if nothing had happened—which the invitation from the music teachers shows to be the case.

6

Troldhaugen at Bergen, August 16, 1907

Dear Mr. Siloti!

My telegram will have given you the bad word: *No*. Unfortunately, it was just out of the question.[14] I have to be in London at the end of September for rehearsals for the festival in Leeds, where I shall conduct some of my own works. Thereafter I have two concerts in London and perhaps one in Berlin. And then—I will be exhausted and not worth a penny, i.e., if it hasn't already happened long before that. It is likely that I will have to cancel everything, for my health is worse than it has ever been. And in addition to this comes the main point: Old age is there knocking on my door and shouting, *Here I am!* Then one must obey. Moreover, I could finally be killed by the Russians! And I much prefer a natural death!

But now to that which I really wanted to say: How wonderful is your faithfulness, and how much my wife and I have rejoiced in it! Yes, that's how it is. We should get together again and talk about the bygone glorious days with Tchaikovsky. And since you really are in a position to arrange an orchestral concert for the end of September (a time of the year when I still dare to travel), it is in fact a great pity that previous engagements prevent me from giving an affirmative answer to your tempting invitation.

Unfortunately, I can no longer count on any future. I am a sickly 64-year-old, and after this winter I will withdraw from all public appearances.

It's good that there is a younger generation. A short time ago I had a visit from a young Australian. His name is Percy Grainger[15] and he lives in London. But how he could play! I have never heard such an interpretation of Bach. And when he played my own works for me, the old Adam awoke and asked in amazement: But is it really so beautiful, what you once wrote? And besides: What a noble human being he is! Remember the name. You will undoubtedly hear about him. Moreover, he has the same absurd idea as you: He doesn't want to be a pianist, but—something else! In other words: "Where you are not, there is happiness."[16]

Heartiest greetings to you and your dear wife from the inhabitants of Troldhaugen.[17]

Very sincerely yours,
EDVARD GRIEG

---

[14] Grieg had been invited to come to Russia in 1907.

[15] Australian-American pianist and conductor Percy Grainger (1882–1961).

[16] "Dort wo Du nicht bist, dort ist das Glück!" The quotation is from *Der Wanderer*, a poem by German author and lawyer Schmidt von Lübeck (Georg Philipp Schmidt, 1766–1849) which Franz Schubert set in the song by the same title.

[17] Siloti answered Grieg's letter on August 25 and invited him to come to St. Petersburg in autumn 1908. He could also give his friend the happy news that on December 14, 1907, he would play his "wonderful *Piano Concerto*". These two letters mark the end of their correspondence. Grieg died on September 4, 1907.

To Christian Skredsvig

The Norwegian painter Christian Skredsvig (1854–1924) went abroad at the age of sixteen to receive advanced training in his chosen field. In 1885 he returned to Norway and in the years that followed produced a number of paintings that today are considered masterworks. In his later years he also wrote several autobiographical novels and some portrayals of folk life.

Grieg's letter to Skredsvig was printed in facsimile in Skredsvig's book *Dage og Nætter blandt Kunstnere* (*Days and Nights among Artists*), Christiania 1908.

Troldhaugen, July 14, 1907

Dear Skredsvig!
Your letter will stand out among my effects as one the most valuable contributions to the Bergen library.[1] Thus you are immortal, even if all of your paintings should burn up! It is only *Bergen*, of course—but after all, there is going to be a railroad to Christiania![2] Ow!

"Rheumatism in the right arm!" Hell and damnation! We can't afford to have you going around like that. Get well again soon and let me finally see how, in your "beautiful painting: Fantasy over *Last Spring*",[3] you have "released the mystery of spring in your child-soul". I am sure you could do this. You better than any other painter in Norway. You are a Romanticist of precisely the same breed as Vinje. Both of you have had your hearts torn to pieces by life's inexorability—and, no less, you both have an armor of great irony. I think there will be enough of it—of this Vinje/Ole Bullesque[4] devil-may-care attitude—in your book.

Enclosed you will find the first stanzas of Vinje's and my *Last Spring*. You have a touching blind faith in their effect. Thank you for everything, and thank you for the pleasure of meeting you again. Let it happen oftener. Life is so short. Soon you will look for me in vain: "So be it, then: I received many beautiful things to enjoy in life; more I've received than I ever have deserved, and all—all must vanish."[5]

Dear Skredsvig! Warm greetings from both of us: Nina and

Yours truly,
EDVARD GRIEG

---

[1] According to Edvard and Nina Grieg's wills their letters, manuscripts, sheet music and various other effects were to go to Bergen Offentlige Bibliotek (Bergen Public Library) after their deaths. The letter of conveyance to the Bergen Public Library of November 12, 1906, will be printed in translation in Benestad & Halverson (eds.), *Edvard Grieg: Diaries, Articles, Speeches* (Columbus, Ohio, 2001).

[2] Skredsvig lived in Bærum, a suburb of Christiania. The railroad line between Christiania and Bergen was opened on November 27, 1909.

[3] *Våren* (*Last Spring*): a poem by Norwegian poet Aasmund Olavsson Vinje (1818–70) which Grieg set as op. 33 no. 2.

[4] An allusion to Norwegian virtuoso violinist Ole Bull (1810–80).

[5] These are the concluding lines from Vinje's poem, *Last Spring*. The Norwegian text is:

> Låt det so vera: Eg mykje av Vent i Livet fekk njota;
> meire eg fekk, enn eg hadde fortent og Allting må trjota.

To Julius Steenberg

The Danish singer Julius Steenberg (1830–1911) was one of Grieg's close friends. In a letter of recommendation written on October 24, 1900, in support of Steenberg's candidacy for a state grant, Grieg wrote, "Once in describing Julius Steenberg I said that he is a song-poet and a poet-singer by the grace of God."

Grieg's letters to Julius Steenberg are preserved in Bergen Offentlige Bibliotek (Bergen Public Library).

1

Eidsvold, Railway Station Hotel, December 22, 1903

Dear old friend!
(...) It was my intention to write to you on one of our first days at Aulestad,[1] to where we are en route this evening. But as luck would have it, because of the holiday we can get only this far, so I will use this evening hour to have a little chat with you.

I have had a wretched time at Voksenkollen.[2] Before I went there I said to Nina: Just watch, I will get sick up there. And sure enough: After a few days I got a tenacious attack of bronchitis with shortness of breath, hallucinations and every devilish thing imaginable. I had a clever nurse who comforted me during my torments. And now I am far enough along on the road to recovery that we are venturing a visit to the Bjørnsons, who have invited us so insistently that it is not possible to turn them down. After an eight-day stay there we will spend a month in Christiania and then—ah, then at last it's on to dear old Denmark and our friends. Friends? Oh, that group has shrunk so grievously! But I still have you and Gottfred Hansen,[3] so I won't complain. You are of the genuine kind that neither moth nor rust consumes.[4] But things surely look bad for Gottfred Hansen. An illness such as that at his age is most serious.

And now about Schjelderup's book.[5] What do *I* think of it? Well, we are of the same opinion. I am happy for the warm, sympathetic tone, but the book suffers in every way from the fact that it was written in haste and published too soon because the poor author needed the money. I am happy, in any case, that for once the person writing about me is a real musician—indeed, one who even with respect to the national element must be presumed to have all the requirements to do the job right. I hope for his sake that the book will find many readers.

---

1 Aulestad was the estate, near Lillehammer, of Norwegian author Bjørnstjerne Bjørnson (1832–1910).

2 Voksenkollen Sanatorium was located on the outskirts of Christiania, near Holmenkollen.

3 Grieg's Danish friend from his earliest days in Copenhagen, Gottfred Matthison-Hansen (1832–1909).

4 The allusion is to Matthew 6:20, "But lay up for yourselves treasures in heaven, where neither moth nor rust consumes..."

5 The biography, *Edvard Grieg og hans Værker* (*Edvard Grieg and his Compositions*), by Norwegian composer Gerhard Schjelderup (1859–1933), was published in Copenhagen in 1903.

The contents of the letter to you, from which he has included a fragment, fortunately is of such a nature that it represents my view right down to the present day. Thanks for giving him precisely *that* and not more.

Feddersen's letters (I mean the letters *to* Feddersen[6]) contain absolutely nothing of interest. Of course, as an artist I couldn't completely confide in him, however much I might like him in other respects. As [here some words are obliterated] I must say, however, that I do not approve of the publication of the letters when they cannot be given *in extenso*, and for me that would be an impossibility. I myself was ill at the time, and to allow Schjelderup to select the passages to publish—that I wasn't willing to do. That is why I said what I did: no letters. I am sorry that my illness prevented me from helping him with his work. But committed to the task as he was, he proved to be so insistent that I had to give in. He approached everyone—Nina, my sisters, sisters-in-law etc., and when all of these came to me for material—well, in the end I didn't know where I could hide.

All things considered, *under the circumstances* he has done a good job. He did not have as thorough an insight as you, but of course no one does—with respect to the songs, in any case. You, therefore, have a right to be stern in your criticism. If he had found time to delve deeply into "Wergeland", "A Piece on Friendship", "Beside the Stream" and several others I think he would not have passed over them so lightly or dismissed them or ignored them altogether. In one respect he is a bit unfair, in my opinion. He talks about poor declamation—and I have, as you know, always stressed the importance of natural declamation. But these Wagner people, who put all the melody in the orchestra, have an easy time of it when it comes to declamation. The rest of us, who aren't so wild about hypermodernity as to apply this principle to a song—we try to unite a concern for melody with an equal concern for declamation. I strongly suspect that Schjelderup has had access only to the German edition of my songs. If this is the case he is only too right to censure the declamation, for in many places it is, to my despair, just bad. But of course that is not my fault. I think that in the songs in which the German text is the original one the declamation is good.

This book will suffer the same fate as all literature and music: That in it which is good will live and be used by others, the rest will die away.

Moreover, how can you say that it is inappropriate that your name is mentioned? It is done, after all, in a very nice way. You don't like the word "expert". Neither do I—because you are something better than that. You are a person who warms the very cockles of my heart. But of course Schjelderup, who does not know you, cannot be aware of that.

I think that what you say about the Jutland element in you contains a lot of

---

6 Danish author Benjamin Feddersen (1823–1902).

truth. Your feeling for that which is hard and grand comes from Jutland. And then I think that both you and I are right to think that if we had not met "her", we would in all likelihood have become totally different. Better? Worse? I don't know enough to answer that. I only know that I prize both "her" and "her" and prefer to think that we have been fortunate.[8]

Your diary is superb. I laughed harder than I have done for a long time. It felt so good. Yes, you have retained your sense of humor. And it must be "her" who is the cause of it.

Thanks to both of you for your good wishes. We return them a thousandfold. And Thora[9] has been discovered! Finally! By damn, all you have to do in this world is wait. How long did Bjørnson wait until *Over Evne*[10] was discovered! And it had even been published.

Warmest greetings to all three of you! Also to Oluf[11] and his "her" when you write.

Your old friend,
EDVARD GRIEG

P.S. Yes, yes: I *have* gotten old, really and truly. Only in music am I young—as young as ever, that is how I feel. No, even younger. It is as if all the beauties increase in intensity! (. . .)

2

Christiania, October 23, 1904
Hotel Westminster

Dear old friend!
It was awfully nice to hear from you again—and from the fleshpots of Egypt, no less. But now, please be so nice and so European and so Danish—and at the same time so Norwegian-minded—as to turn your nose toward Copenhagen when we arrive there at the end of November! You must promise me that you will do that, and you must write and tell me that you are doing it. Isn't Trine[12] coming home then? It would be too sad if we didn't get to see each other once more! It probably will be—yes, almost certainly will be—our last trip to Denmark. I can't tolerate the climate down there, and besides, I am getting so frail that like an animal I seek solitude when I understand that the end is near. But yet once

8 "her" and "her": Grieg's and Steenberg's wives.
9 Thora was Steenberg's daughter.
10 *Over Evne* (*Beyond Human Power*) was a play by Bjørnstjerne Bjørnson published in 1883. He wrote another play by the same title that was published in 1895.
11 Grieg's friend Oluf Hartmann (1879–1910), a painter, son of Danish composer J. P. E. Hartmann (1805–1900).
12 Cathrine [Trine], Steenberg's wife.

again I must "see winter's cloak fade with springtime advancing."[13] And then we must do something in the way of oysters, good wine and good friendship! (. . .)

What's this about Schade?[14] Listen now, dear Steenberg, I don't do that sort of thing any more. Once and for all I have had to say no, and I'll tell you why. Because everyone who is going to America wants to play for me in order to get a written recommendation. The fact is that my name is better known there than it is in Europe. But in the first place I can't stand to listen to all these people, and secondly, I must give recommendations either to all or to none. I cannot and will not offend one whom I cannot recommend only, in the next instant, to recommend someone else. Therefore, and because this business of playing and singing my compositions for me had gotten so out of hand that it began to put extreme demands on both my time and my health—for that reason I, with a sudden heartlessness, have had to stop the machine. To Schade I say "Schade!"[15] She is a sweet girl, I remember her clearly. Would that she were intelligent enough to understand how useless an exercise it would be for her to play for me. I cannot give her individuality if she doesn't have it in her nature. And I lack the energy to inject my own, for that requires more than merely listening to a single play-through and then saying a few words. When it is a matter of seriously trying to realize my intentions, I can sit for hours with sixteen measures. And I am too old and frail for that. *You* understand me, that I know. And I think Trine does too. I don't know if Thora does, but as her father's daughter it is her duty to do so as well.

You ask me to write about myself. Well, good God, when one has to take in one's oars at a time when one would still like to use them it's not pleasant to write about oneself. For the last couple of years (!) Pegasus has been standing in the stall. The only thing I have been able to produce is some orchestral arrangements of old compositions. My deepest wish is to create a home for myself up here in the spruce forest near Christiania. It has a climate that is quite unusually effective against bronchitis, asthma and things like that. The problem is that Nina's immortal mother and Tonny[16] are in Bergen. For their sake we have to go home every summer, and that is also the main reason why we keep Troldhaugen. But I can't afford *two* homes, for—just between us—I have a lot of poor family members whom I must help. The home, therefore, is the same as the "parsonage" was for Henrik Wergeland:[17] it is "nice clouds".

But I must be content if I *have* been able to accomplish something and to

---

[13] Quotation from the text of "Last Spring", a poem by Aasmund Olavson Vinje (1818–70) set by Grieg as op. 33, no. 2. Grieg uses the Danish version of Vinje's poem: ". . . jeg Vintren få se for Våren at rømme."

[14] Marie Schade, possibly a friend of Steenberg's daughter Thora.

[15] This is a play on words. "Schade" means "too bad!"

[16] Nina's sister, Tonny Hagerup (1844–1939).

[17] Norwegian patriot and national poet Henrik Wergeland (1808–45).

express *something* of what I wanted to say. For now I understand that so infinitely much—yes, the very best—of what I still have in my heart will remain unsaid. But that is the way things are in nature's household. And above all: The ideals should be held at a respectful distance. It is a blessed fact that they do not penetrate too deeply into our lives. If there really are aristocrats in the world, they are the ideals. Ibsen calls them "life's lies". That is the same as cutting off the head of the entire human race, and I will have no part of that since we are placed here for the purpose of making life as rich as possible. In the last analysis there is only *one* source of riches and that is the ideals—one's *own* ideals. It is a great mistake to think that one can use those of other people, as so many do. Even people like the two of us can have ideals that will be in agreement on many things and yet be radically different. Doesn't it say someplace in a wise book, "My thoughts are not your thoughts!"[18] That is excellently said. I know, of course, that the context is totally different, but the words can be used about the ideals.

All is well, I'm on the last page, for when I begin to prattle about philosophical matters it is for no other reason than to write "a little about myself"—but, to be sure, not what you would like to have.

How I wish that you were here today. We would have dinner together at Christophersen's, where you get a meal that is really something.[19]

Saturday the 29th I am giving an evening program of Grieg songs with Ellen Gulbranson.[20] We will perform many rarely heard songs that I consider some of my best. To this point Mrs. Gulbranson has been working on the songs with Nina's help. Tomorrow, though, *I* will start rehearsing with her.

And farewell for now! Send me a few lines soon with information about when you are returning home.

Sincerely yours,
Edvard Grieg

P.S. Nina sends warm greetings.

---

18 Grieg is quoting from Isaiah 55:8, "For my thoughts are not your thoughts, neither are my ways your ways, says the Lord." (RSV)

19 In 1857 Engebreth Christophersen (1828–1915) opened "Café Engebret" in Christiania. It was located close to the old Christiania Theater and the Freemasons' Hall.

20 Swedish-born soprano Ellen Nordgren Gulbranson (1863–1947).

To Johan Svendsen

The Norwegian composer and conductor Johan Svendsen (1840–1911) was second only to Grieg as the most important Nordic composer of the nineteenth century. His orchestral works were played all over the world with great success. Svendsen was also an outstanding conductor who devoted more than a decade of his life to raising the standard of orchestral music in his homeland—beginning in 1872, when he became co-conductor with Grieg of the Music Association orchestra in Christiania. In 1883 he was appointed musical director of the Royal Theater in Copenhagen, where he served with great distinction until his retirement in 1908.

Grieg and Svendsen first met in Leipzig in 1865 and initiated at that time a warm friendship that was to last throughout their lives. It is known that Grieg wrote a number of letters to Svendsen during the years 1868–72 that are no longer extant. The letters included here are preserved in the Musikhistorisk Museum Carl Claudius Samling (Museum of Music History, Carl Claudius Collection), Copenhagen.

1

Leipzig, November 19, 1895
Hotel Hauffe

Dear Svendsen!

It was *good* to see you again! *I* have gotten an idea that I think is good, but whether *you* will think so is another matter. Last evening Nikisch[1] gave me the happy news that on December 19th he will be performing your B-flat major *Symphony* and my *Peer Gynt Suite* [no. 1 op. 46] in the Gewandhaus. Just think if you could sneak away for two days! You could leave in the evening, be here by noon, leave for home during the night and be home again by the next evening—thus 48 hours. Remember, you only live once—and it would be very enjoyable. You might even be able to bring Alfred Hansen[2] along!

A Gewandhaus concert under Nikisch is an absolutely outstanding event. Unfortunately, I do not always agree with his tempos or what in my opinion is sometimes an inappropriate use of *rubato*, but he has an admirable ability to bring out light and shadow and to characterize. And then this sonorous orchestral sound such as people here have not heard for many years!

I have been so fortunate as to hear some exceptionally important new works. First Tchaikovsky's posthumous *Symphony* in B minor (Pathétique). A remarkable work! Weren't you planning to perform it next spring? And then last evening the big choral work by César Franck,[3] *Les béatitudes*. Brilliant from beginning to end, certainly his greatest composition. And that such a man dies without

---

[1] The German conductor Arthur Nikisch (1855–1922) had assumed the leadership of the Gewandhaus orchestra in Leipzig in 1895.

[2] Alfred Wilhelm Hansen (1854–23), one of the proprietors of Wilhelm Hansen's Music Publishing Company in Copenhagen.

[3] French composer of Belgian birth César Franck (1822–90).

recognition after a long life in Paris—spent, in fact, in a prominent position! I simply cannot understand it.

Send a few lines to cheer me up!

Your old friend and admirer,
EDVARD GRIEG

2

Leipzig, December 20, 1895
Hotel Hauffe

Dear Svendsen!

You will see in the enclosed program the bad news that Nikisch is ill and that Sitt conducted last evening.[4] In other words: Thank your lucky stars that let you stay where you are. Sitt is a first-class technician, but where he ends is the very place where Nikisch begins. Sitt has an incredible ability to lower the level, to make even the greatest into the ordinary. Everything suffered as a result, but most of all the symphony, I think. To sit there and hear this splendid work played by the Gewandhaus orchestra in such a way that every moment I wanted to run up and pull the baton out of the conductor's hand—it is too bad. When the "tempo rubato" sickness infects even the most important conductors, one can understand that a man like Sitt doesn't want to be the exception. The first movement was mutilated most horribly. Here there were the most absurd changes of tempo, with the second theme nearly fifty percent slower than it should have been, arbitrary *rubatos*, etc. The *Andante* and the *Scherzo* sustained the least damage.

Unfortunately I have been ill in recent days, so I wasn't able to attend any of the rehearsals, but one evening Sitt came into a café where he knew I usually went. He had both of our scores under his arm. We paged through the symphony, and I had an opportunity to indicate the correct main tempos. In the middle of the *Scherzo*, where you so beautifully let the motive sing out in augmentation, he said, "But I would take that significantly faster and then *ritardando* before the entrance of the main theme." I said, "For God's sake, it is just the opposite: The composer intends that this passage should be rather tranquil." He didn't like this, but fortunately he gave up his plan, so the movement was rescued to some extent.

So that you can understand what he can think up, I will just mention that the end of "Anitra's Dance" was performed with a big *ritardando* that ended in *andante*. A worse corrupter of rhythms I do not know. And yet, in a way the fellow is competent. But the architecture of the music—he doesn't have the slightest feeling for that.

There was plenty of applause, but if Nikisch had been on the podium the

[4] Hans Sitt (1850–1922) was assistant conductor of the Gewandhaus orchestra.

Johan Svendsen, with whom Grieg enjoyed a close friendship throughout his adult life. On April 25, 1881, Grieg wrote to Aimar Grønvold: "There are few artists to whom I owe as much as I owe to Svendsen." (Nasjonalbiblioteket, Oslo)

success would have been colossal. Fritzsch[5] was ecstatic. He is and always will be a big child with a questionable power of judgment. The three Dutch women sang enchantingly, as you see—Norwegian songs, too. I gave them a good tongue-lashing because they had not mentioned the composers' names. They excused themselves by saying that they hadn't known the names, but that in the future they would announce them.

The moral of the whole episode is: Never look forward to anything. Even here, where for once all the wheels really seemed to be turning together to produce a happy result—even here, big disappointment. Whether the honorable music critics will be in a good humor—I haven't the slightest idea and ought not to care in the least. We can both, in a way, thank our lucky stars that it was not new works that were played, for they would have been damned beforehand.

Unfortunately, Due's melody[6] for string orchestra still has not been published, as Abraham[7] thinks—perhaps correctly—that it is too short to be included in

---

[5] Leipzig music publisher E. W. Fritzsch (1840–1902).

[6] Grieg's orchestral arrangement of a melody by Fredrik Due (1833–1906), *Two Nordic Melodies* op. 63 no. 1, was given the title "In Folk Style".

[7] Max Abraham (1831–1900), proprietor of the C. F. Peters Musikverlag in Leipzig.

concert programs. I am now at work, therefore, arranging a Norwegian folk dance as a contrast.

How much I wish I could have a chat with you! But that's not possible for the time being. We will be here for some time into the new year. Nina asks me to greet you. She—I, too, for that matter—was often enchanted during the symphony despite its *crappy* performance. But I was not moved to tears, as she was. My imagination carried me back to the 1870's. How good Norway's air was for you at that time, despite all the obstacles! There is some of this, which is reflected in your symphony without sounding obtrusive, that for me is a bonus in addition to all the other beauty.[8]

Farewell for now, dear Svendsen, and accept my sincerest thanks for this illuminating emanation of your individuality!

Merry Christmas! And warmest greetings from

Yours truly,
EDVARD GRIEG

3

Troldhaugen at Bergen, June 26, 1903

Dear Svendsen!
Here you have me at last with thanks for your telegram of the 15th.[9] I wish you had been here, if for no other reason than to hear Bjørnson's[10] marvelous speeches. And then, of course, there was a week-long party that was carried off in true Bergen style. Everything went well; even the weather was good. But I especially missed you that forenoon up at Fløjen, where I had the orchestra up for a breakfast.[11] I daresay that there was jubilation. My speech in honor of you was good—if I do say so myself. In the course of the speech you became champagne whereas I was beer, brandy and red wine (which is what I was serving). You should have heard the hurrahs and the shouting for you! The tears streamed down old Jähnigen's[12] cheeks.

And then Bjørnson stood up and began like this: "I see that there is a plaque on the wall that says, 'Don't spit on the floor!' I will make that the text for the day. Because we *know how* to spit in Norway. And we can spit *far*. Don't spit on the floor! Don't spit on others, don't spit on the homeland, don't spit on art and science, don't spit on those who think differently—don't spit on the floor!" And he

---

[8] This paragraph has to do with Svendsen's *Symphony No. 2*, composed in 1876.

[9] Grieg's 60th birthday had been celebrated with pomp and circumstance on June 15, 1903.

[10] Norwegian author Bjørnstjerne Bjørnson (1832–1910), who was also known as a skillful orator.

[11] "Fløjen" is the name of one of the mountains overlooking the city of Bergen. Atop the mountain is a restaurant, also called "Fløjen", that has long been used as a venue for festive occasions.

[12] German-born musician Christian Jähnigen (1830–1910), who had played under Svendsen in Christiania.

continued in this way in a great crescendo, as only Bjørnson can, and then he concluded with a toast for tolerance. It was unforgettable. And you can imagine what these broad vistas meant to the orchestra.[13] Halvorsen, who is now staying at Troldhaugen with his wife after having completed the concert tour, says that the orchestra members became like children when they spoke about this time up on Fløjen. And then, of course, there was the fact that the trip up was easier than your famous one up "Løvstakken",[14] as we went both up and down in carriages.

I hope that you are now at Voksenkollen, and if so I request that you give cheery greetings to Dr. Holm and his family.[15]

Yes, dear Svendsen, in spirit I send you a telegram: Thank you for *your* great artistic achievement and for *your* faithful friendship through many years! Thank you for what you taught me, and thank you for the innumerable times you entranced me!

Yours truly,
EDVARD GRIEG

4

Göteborg, May 24, 1905
Grand Hotel

Dear Svendsen!
What happened last evening was the darndest thing. I had been looking forward so intensely to visiting with you! But my only choice was to go to bed and take some antipyrin powder.[16] And the result was that this morning I woke up with a more or less normal temperature, but I felt so weak that I had to send for the doctor, because I didn't dare to undertake the trip without his permission. It went as I thought it would: I had hardly left the island of Zealand[17] before I began to feel better, and now I think I am coming to life again. But—when will we meet again? There was so much for us to talk about—about the possibility of a music festival in Christiania, for example. I think that Halvorsen has a very fine sense of when the situation is ripe for such a thing, but he has to remember that we two—or, more correctly, *I* am getting so old and feeble that he had better not

---

[13] The National Theater orchestra and its conductor, Johan Halvorsen, had come to Bergen to participate in the festivities celebrating Grieg's 60th birthday. See Grieg's letter to Halvorsen (1864–1935) of May 30, 1903, regarding the invitation to Fløjen.

[14] "Løvstakken" is another of the mountains overlooking Bergen. After the music festival in Bergen in the summer of 1898, Grieg had taken several of his friends on a hike to the top of this mountain. For the corpulent Svendsen it had proved to be almost more than he could manage. He reached the top bathed in sweat—and the trip down was no less strenuous.

[15] Dr. Ingebrigt Chr. L. Holm (1844–1919), medical director of the Voksenkollen Sanatorium, which was located on the outskirts of Christiania, near Holmenkollen.

[16] An anti-fever medication.

[17] Zealand (Sjælland) is the largest island in Denmark. Copenhagen is situated on this island.

delay it too long. For the moment, of course, one cannot think of initiating anything. Now politics engulfs everything.[18]

Your friends tell me that you have become a new man out there in the country. That gives me a good idea: Take the third symphony[19] out again, pound the table a couple of times and say, "Damn it all!" Then you'll see that the new man is inspired to start anew! You may answer, "That's no concern of yours." But I protest. Nobody feels more strongly than I that you still have much to say. Moreover, I know from my own experience what music a Danish summer like that conceals in its bosom. If the new man even faintly resembles the old one from the 1870's, I know what he will do. I would be happy for a few lines telling me that you have taken out the folder with the sketches, that one thought gives wings to the next, and that you are composing as if your life depended on it!

And with that, farewell, dear friend! Now a piece of Swedish "smörgås" [a sandwich] and then to bed. Thank you for the far, far too rare visit we had last winter! It was almost *my* fault [that we did not see each other more frequently], unfortunately. Warmest greetings from

Your old friend and admirer,
EDVARD GRIEG

P.S. Greet all your dear ones, also from Nina!

5

Christiania, November 5, 1905
Hotel Westminster

Dear Svendsen!
So you have placed the variations on your program![20] I see in this a manifestation of your long-standing appreciation for me and my art. Thank you for that! It moves me and makes me happy. I hope that you have by now received the score which, in order not to waste time, I let Peters send to you directly. Since the printed material has never been used before, there could be some inaccuracies. If such is the case, you would be doing me a great favor if you would report them to me. It certainly is a difficult piece to make into a well-integrated whole. I have conceived of it as a kind of drama, and I wish you could share this concept,

---

18 Norway and Sweden were on the verge of war at this time because of Norway's demand for independence. The issue was resolved peacefully a few weeks after this letter was written.

19 Svendsen had completed his third symphony before taking the position of musical director at the Royal Theater in Copenhagen. In a fit of jealousy, however, his wife Bergliot (Sarah) had thrown the only copy of the manuscript into the fire. For further details of this episode see Finn Benestad & Dag Schjelderup-Ebbe, *Johan Svendsen: The Man, The Maestro, The Music*, Columbus 1995, pp. 206–07. After coming to Copenhagen in 1883, Svendsen tried to reconstruct the symphony but did not succeed in doing so.

20 Grieg is referring to his composition *Old Norwegian Melody with Variations.*

especially for the latter half of the work, for the result is a more subjective and freer handling of the tempo. Looked at simply as music, variations can easily fall apart in such a composition—but of course a certain Johan Svendsen will prevent that from happening. Toward the end, the section in F minor must rush past in a furious tempo like a raging storm. Right before that there is a big *fortissimo* (C major) where I have thought a cymbal tremolo (using wooden drumsticks) should, if possible, thunder through the whole orchestra. It should be, as it were, the apex of the jubilation, after which everything collapses. Under Halvorsen last year the piece lasted 23 minutes! That is too long. I myself didn't have the heart to cut anything out, but if you think it is advisable just omit what appears between the symbols—and, if you want more, the variation that follows.

I see that I am just sitting here and giving detailed instructions à la Selmer.[21] Forgive me! I think old age makes me nervous and uncertain. Only one thing is certain: my being vilified by Mr. Kjerulf[22] and his cronies. But fortunately it cannot make bitter the joy that I feel over the fact that *you* are performing my work. Unfortunately I am too fragile to come down and attend the performance. Moreover, I do not deny that being here at home at this significant time has its own poetry.[23] Yes, what do you say about this? Is it not a tremendous job that has been performed? It was done with national bear-paws (that's what the Swedes reproachfully call "the agreement"!)—but it is done, and with admirable strength and clarity. It is wonderful to experience it! There is, of course, a lot of mud in the offing. But—Michelsen[24] has the temperament of an Aladdin. He will manage it, as long as he doesn't get sick again. Recently everything came to a halt because he had eaten lobster! When I met him on the street I asked him how it went with "the lobster". "Well," he answered, "believe me, it came out rather quickly! And that was just wonderful." He has a dry, calm wit that enables him to conquer everything and everyone.

And now farewell! Warm greetings to you and yours both from Nina and from

Your old friend and admirer,
EDVARD GRIEG

---

[21] Norwegian composer Johan Selmer (1844–1910).

[22] Grieg is referring to Danish music critic Charles Kjerulf (1858–1919), who wrote for the Copenhagen newspaper *Politiken*.

[23] A plebiscite was about to be held confirming the wish of the overwhelming majority of Norwegian citizens that Prince Carl of Denmark accept the throne of the newly independent Norway.

[24] Christian Michelsen (1857–1925), Norwegian Prime Minister in 1905.

6

Christiania, November 20, 1905
Hotel Westminster

Dear Svendsen!

I hear via a letter that I have just received from Mr. Hinrichsen[24] that you recommend a deletion at the end of the *Variations.* I myself have wanted to consider such an idea but have not been able to bring myself to do it. But since you feel as I do, then it must be right. Do me the favor of marking in your copy of the score what you think should be cut, and also indicate which variations were omitted at the performance. Then have [Alfred] Hansen send me your score, and as soon as the piece is published you will get the first printed copy.

The reviews that were sent to me today—besides being thoroughly ill-tempered and uncomprehending—find the piece too long, and I think that for people like the honorable newspaper writers this criticism must be warranted, NB: after their having heard the piece for the first time.

You see, I am trying to save you from unnecessary scribbling! That you must acknowledge! And with that, once again my sincerest thanks, dear friend!

Yours truly,
EDVARD GRIEG

---

24 Henri Hinrichsen (1868–1942) had succeeded his late uncle, Max Abraham, as director of the C. F. Peters Musikverlag in 1901.

To Sedley Taylor

Grieg was to be awarded an honorary doctorate at Cambridge University on May 10, 1894, and it was in this connection that he came in contact with Sedley Taylor (1854–1920). Mr. Taylor, who headed the University's music association, wrote to Grieg on January 18, 1894, inviting him to participate in a chamber-music evening during his visit to Cambridge. The only concert Grieg was involved in on this visit to England, however, took place in London on May 24, when he conducted the Philharmonic Society orchestra in a performance of *Three Orchestral Pieces from "Sigurd Jorsalfar"*.

As for the awarding of the doctorate, Grieg found it hard to identify with the solemnity of the occasion. The whole affair was "enough to make you laugh yourself to death," he wrote to his friend Frederick Delius (1862–1934) on May 12. "I didn't laugh, though," he continued, "because I was already sick, and the first thing I had to do as a fresh-baked doctor was—go to a doctor."

Grieg's letter to Taylor, which was written in German, is preserved in the Cambridge University Library.

Leipzig, February 12, 1894
Address: C. F. Peters, Thalstrasse 10

Dear Sir!

In addition to extending warm greetings to Mr. Austen Leigh,[1] please tell him that I shall be very pleased to avail myself of his kind invitation to stay with him in King's College Lodge.

As for my participation in the festival concert, however, the prospects are not good if what you have in mind is chamber music and not an orchestral concert. For my health, unfortunately, compels me to perform as rarely as possible. I can, of course, allow myself to conduct a few pieces, but to play the piano is so frightfully agonizing for me that so far as possible I must avoid it so as not to get seriously ill during my short stay in Cambridge. How I wish it were possible for me to accommodate your wish! But unfortunately, in the form you have proposed it cannot be. Would it not be possible to arrange for an orchestral concert?[2]

I very much look forward to shaking hands with my English friends, among whom I also take the liberty of including the admirers of my art in Cambridge!

Respectfully,
EDVARD GRIEG

---

1 Augustus Austen Leigh (1840–1905) was Provost of King's College, Cambridge University, and in 1894 he was Vice Chancellor of the University. He also headed the University's music association for many years.

2 Although he himself did not participate, Grieg was present at a concert in Cambridge at which the English mezzo-soprano Marie Brema, whose real name was Minny Fehrmann (1856–1925), performed some of his songs.

Correspondence with Peter Tchaikovsky

Grieg met Russian composer Peter Tchaikovsky (1840–93) in Leipzig on New Year's Day, 1888, at the home of their mutual friend, Russian violinist Adolf Brodsky (1851–1929), who on December 10, 1887, had premiered Grieg's new *Violin Sonata in C Minor*—with Grieg himself at the piano. Johannes Brahms was also present at this New Year's Day party. Tchaikovsky described his first meeting with Grieg thus: "As they were playing through Brahms's new trio, a man walked into the room—very small of stature, middle aged, extremely sickly in appearance, shoulders of uneven height, head covered with large, blond, tousled locks. His beard and moustache were most unusual, indeed, almost youthful. The facial features of this man, whose appearance for some reason immediately appealed to me, are not especially noteworthy; one cannot call them either handsome or unusual. But on the other hand, he has exceptionally attractive, medium-sized, sky-blue eyes of an irresistibly charming character, eyes that remind one of an innocent, adorable child. I was glad in the very depths of my soul when, upon being introduced to each other, it was revealed that the bearer of this inexplicably attractive exterior was a musician whose deeply felt music had long since secured for him a place in my heart. It was Edvard Grieg."[1]

Peter Ilyich Tchaikovsky in 1891. On January 25, 1906, Grieg wrote to Adolf Brodsky: "Each evening Nina reads from Tchaikovsky's life and letters. You can't imagine how vividly I recognize myself in him!" (PD)

---

1 From Tchaikovsky's *Autobiographical Description of a Journey Abroad in 1888*. This English translation is derived from a Norwegian rendition of the Russian original by Jon-Roar Bjørkvold entitled "Peter Čajkovskij og Edvard Grieg—en kontakt mellom to åndsfrender" ("Peter Tchaikovsky and Edvard Grieg—A Meeting of Two Kindred Spirits"), in *Studia Musicologica Norvegica* 2, 1976, pp. 37–50.

Four weeks later Grieg and Tchaikovsky again visited the Brodsky's. On this occasion the guests included two other Norwegian musicians—Christian Sinding (1856–1941) and Johan Halvorsen (1864–1935), the latter of whom was at that time a violin student of Brodsky—as well as the Russian pianist, Vasilij Sapelnikov (1868–1940). In a letter to his Bergen friend Frants Beyer (1851–1918) dated January 29, 1888, Grieg wrote: "I have just come from Brodsky's, where we have been to dinner along with Tchaikovsky, who is still here with a young and *wonderfully brilliant* Russian pianist, Sapelnikov. Sinding and Halvorsen were also present, and we made music all the time. First, at Tchaikovsky's request, Brodsky and I played my new sonata. Then Sinding's quintet was tried out, with Sapelnikov at the piano, and lastly my *String Quartet.* Those fellows can really play! My God, what a sound! (. . .) In Tchaikovsky I have gained a warm friend for my music. He is as favorably disposed toward me as I am toward him, both as an artist and as a human being."

During the stay in Leipzig, Grieg was also with Tchaikovsky at the home of the Russian pianist Alexander Siloti (1865–1945), who had studied with Liszt. Grieg had come to know Siloti as conductor at a concert on December 12, 1887. In February, 1888, he was with Tchaikovsky again, this time at the home of the Belgian singer Désirée Artôt (1835–1907).

During the months that followed, Grieg and Tchaikovsky sent each other several works accompanied by personal greetings, and Tchaikovsky dedicated *Hamlet. Fantasy-overture* to his Norwegian friend.

The correspondence between Grieg and Tchaikovsky is in German. Grieg's letters to Tchaikovsky are preserved in the Tchaikovsky Museum in Klin, Russia, those from Tchaikovsky to Grieg in Bergen Offentlige Bibliotek (Bergen Public Library).

Grieg to Tchaikovsky 1

Leipzig, February 27, 1888

Dear Tchaikovsky!!

Your telegram has of course given me great pleasure, and quite especially because it came from *you! Hearty thanks!*

I got a letter from Svendsen today. He writes that by performing your works in both Copenhagen and Christiania he has expressed his high regard for you, also that he hopes for your participation at one of his philharmonic concerts next year.[2]

My first concert in London takes place on May 3. Where will you be then? And above all: How have things been going? Did you give your concert in Paris? It would be wonderful to have a postcard with a few words from you!

Warmest greetings, also from my wife. Please give my regards to Mr. Colonne.[3]

Sincerely yours,
EDVARD GRIEG

---

[2] In 1883, the Norwegian composer and conductor Johan Svendsen (1840–1911) had become artistic director of the Royal Theater Orchestra in Copenhagen. Each year he gave a series of philharmonic concerts in which, among other things, he presented a number of contemporary Russian works. His desire that Tchaikovsky might conduct at one of these concerts was never realized.

[3] The French conductor Édouard Colonne (1838–1910).

Tchaikovsky to Grieg 1

Paris, March 2, 1888

Dear, good friend!
I was very glad to receive your letter. I think so often of my dear "little son" and am so happy to have gotten to know both him and the lovable "little daughter".[4]

I don't have a thing to tell you about Prague, as I hope Siloti[5] has told you how great everything was. My concert in Paris is scheduled for Sunday, March 4. We have already had several rehearsals, and everything is going very well. Since the French are absolutely crazy about Russians just now, I am entertained so often and so warmly—indeed, I am so tired of visits, breakfasts, dinners, soirées etc. that now and then I am totally exhausted and feel very out of sorts.

Are you aware that you are very *popular* in Paris? Something by you is played at nearly every concert. Colonne was very glad when he heard from me that you yourself could play your concerto. You will certainly get an invitation from him; he likes you very much.

From Prague I sent a telegram to Francesco Berger[6] telling him that I would like to perform with *my friend Grieg* on March 22. But he replied that this was impossible, since you would not be playing until May 3. I will, however, conduct my *Serenade* and *Suite*[7] on March 22. It's very sad that we will not see each other in London.

Please write to Svendsen that I thank him heartily and certainly will be prepared to collaborate with him at his concerts next year.

Greet your wife, the Brodsky family and all my friends! How often I think of all of you! Until we meet again, my good, dear Grieg! I'll write to you once more after the concert.

P. TCHAIKOVSKY

P.S. Excuse my poor German!

Grieg to Tchaikovsky 2

Leipzig, April 12, 1888

Dear friend and maestro!
Before I leave Leipzig I must indeed thank you for the friendly letter from Paris. You have truly gladdened us, and I would have answered you long ago if only I had known where to send the letter. But I just heard from Brodsky that you are

4 Tchaikovsky is alluding to the fact that both Edvard and Nina were very short in stature—a little under five feet.
5 Russian pianist and conductor Alexander Siloti.
6 Francesco Berger (1834–1933) was Secretary of The Philharmonic Society in London.
7 Tchaikovsky presumably is referring to *Serenade in C Major for String Orchestra* op.48 and *Suite no. 3* op. 55.

full of triumphs and are once again back in Russia. So now I will use the address I was given and we'll see if I succeed in reaching you.

You can't imagine how much joy your company has given us. No, not joy; it is something far greater than that! For you as an artist and a human being have made such a deep impression on me that I feel that you have taught me much. And something like that is an event for someone who is 44 years old. Well, you'll see: If I can just find time to write music again I will certainly be so bold as to adorn one thing or another with your name!

At the end of next week we go to London, and I for my part must say that unfortunately I am not looking forward to it. I am very anxious to hear what kind of an impression you have gotten. Sometime when you are writing an *Adagio*—or better: a *Largo*—and include in it a genuine Beethovenian rest, preferably a whole measure with a *fermata*—then you must use the hiatus for a free fantasy on the theme: London. And if you should also write a quarter-note rest, then you must remember what you have promised me: first of all[8]

and then the *Piano Concerto* in B-flat minor, and then—yes, everything! No, of course, that's enough—I am satisfied. When my new scores (a *Peer Gynt Suite* and the concert overture *In Autumn)*[9] are published—I think it will be in September—I will take the liberty of sending them to you if you would like to have them.

I have just come from a visit to the Brodsky's; they are all fine and send their greetings. My wife does the same, as does also in true esteem and friendship,

Yours truly,
Edvard Grieg

P.S. My mail address is always: C. F. Peters, Thalstrasse 10, Leipzig.

Tchaikovsky to Grieg 2

Klin by Moscow, Frolowskoie
April 24/May 6, 1888[10]

My dear, good friend!
I was exceedingly happy when I received your letter! How good, amiable and friendly you are, and how proud I am to have gained your friendship! It's too bad

---

[8] Grieg is quoting—not quite correctly—the second theme from Tchaikovsky's *1812 Overture*.

[9] *Peer Gynt Suite no. 1* op. 46 and the concert overture *In Autumn* op. 11. On the title page of *Peer Gynt Suite No. 1* Grieg wrote, "To P. Tchaikovsky, the revered and beloved maestro—from Edvard Grieg. Bergen, Norway, October 1888."

[10] The earlier dates on Tchaikovsky's letters 2 and 3 refer to the Eastern (old) calendar, the later ones to the Gregorian calendar.

that it is so extremely difficult for me to write in German, otherwise I would have said much more about my love and esteem!

Have you received a few pages from me that I wrote to you from Vienna? Apparently my letters to you and Brodsky have gotten lost, for I haven't heard anything from the latter even though I asked him to write to me.

From London I went directly to Tiflis (Caucasus). This big trip took two long weeks, but you cannot imagine how beautiful and pleasant it was when, after an extended period of poor weather, I arrived at Tiflis and suddenly found summer, flowers and southern sunshine. I stayed there for three weeks.

Four days ago I came to Moscow, and today I arrived here. Now I want to live and work as peacefully as possible out in the *country.* I intend to write a symphony and want to dedicate it to my good friend *Grieg.*

When will I see you, my dear, good friend? Let us hope that I will have the joy of seeing you and your highly esteemed wife many times. I will never forget the beautiful days we spent together in Leipzig!

Yesterday I sent you the *1812 Overture* and the *Piano Concerto in B-flat Minor*,[11] and I shall impatiently await the scores you have promised me.

I should like very much to know if everything went fine in London, as I am sure it did. You are highly regarded and popular in London—indeed, everywhere.

Greet your dear and highly esteemed wife from me. I embrace *you!* Until we meet again!!

Your true friend,
P. Tchaikovsky

Grieg to Tchaikovsky 3

Brobyværk at Fyn, Denmark
May 26, 1888

Dear and esteemed friend!
How your letter has gladdened us! And especially me, as I had hoped for just such a meaningful dedication. Believe me when I say that I indeed appreciate how much you honor me by such recognition—and that I will demonstrate my gratitude for it if I ever get so far as to write something worthy of you. I look forward immensely to seeing your scores. I will study them in Norway, where they have been sent.

---

11 On the title page of the *Piano Concerto* Tchaikovsky wrote, "To Edvard Grieg from his greatest admirer, Peter Tchaikovsky, May 8, 1888." On the *1812 Overture* he wrote, "To my dear and highly esteemed friend Edvard Grieg as a reminder of P. Tchaikovsky. May 4, 1888."

My stay in London gave me more pleasure than I had ever dared to hope for. In addition to my appearance in The Philharmonic Society I also gave a concert of my own works in St. James's Hall, and in the latter the English—obviously to their great pleasure—were fed some of my shorter works. My wife sang (fortunately she was in very good voice), and Madame Norman-Neruda[12] charmed the audience with her beautiful violin-playing.

Today and tomorrow I am resting here in the country at the home of a brother-in-law,[13] and tomorrow I will go to Copenhagen to participate in the music festival.[14] It's a pity that you won't be there!

Is there anything to the rumor that you may come to Birmingham in August?[15] That would really be something! In any case, we must see each other again, be it in Russia, in Norway, or wherever. Kindred spirits do not grow on trees![16]

My wife sends her warmest greetings! So also does

Yours truly,
EDVARD GRIEG

Tchaikovsky to Grieg 3

Klin by Moscow, September 5 & 17, 1888

Dear esteemed friend!
"The Royal Russian Music Association" in Moscow recommends that you participate in one of the concerts of the Association by playing your *Piano Concerto* and conducting some of your compositions. Unfortunately the Association cannot offer a very large honorarium. They can only pay 600 rubles (about 1200 German marks at the current exchange rate) for your participation. That really is far too little, but hopefully you will do the Association the honor of promising your valuable participation. People would be very happy to see and hear you in Moscow! If you accept this proposal, it would be best if you could participate at the concert on November 28. Please send me your answer immediately!

---

12 In 1864 the Czech violinist Wilhelmina (Wilma) Neruda (1838–1911) married the Swedish composer Ludvig Norman and thereafter went by the name Norman-Neruda. Norman died in 1885, and in 1888 Wilhelmina married Sir Charles Hallé, founder of the Hallé Orchestra in Manchester, whereupon she became Lady Hallé.

13 Edvard and Nina were guests at the home of the Danish medical doctor Karl Nommels (1845–1912), whose late wife, Yelva (1847–86), was Nina Grieg's sister.

14 The first Scandinavian music festival took place in Copenhagen June 3–10, 1888. At the opening concert, Grieg conducted his *Piano Concerto* in A Minor with Norwegian pianist Erika Lie Nissen (1845–1903) as soloist.

15 Grieg took part in a music festival in Birmingham, England, in August, 1888. On the 29th he conducted the concert overture *In Autumn* and on the 30th the *Holberg Suite*. Tchaikovsky did not participate in the festival.

16 The two friends never saw each other again. It looked as if they might meet in the spring of 1893, when both were to receive honorary doctorates from Cambridge University, but because of illness Grieg had to postpone his visit to Cambridge until May 10, 1894.

How are things going, dear friend! I have written a new symphony and also a *Hamlet Overture* (which is not yet orchestrated).[17] This overture is dedicated to you.

I hope you are in good health!

Warm greetings to your dear wife!

It is so hard for me to write in German. There is so much I would like to have said to you, but I can't manage it.

Until we meet again, my dear, good, most esteemed friend!

P. Tchaikovsky

Grieg to Tchaikovsky 4

Bergen, September 27, 1888

Dear friend and maestro!

I am as happy as a child about the *Hamlet* overture. Heart-felt thanks for the dedication!

It is impossible for me to come to Moscow this winter! The invitation really is very flattering, and I shall hope to visit Moscow at some other time.[18] Now, however, I *must* work. I have only until the end of January, for then I have promised to be in London.[19]

I am working on a choral composition[20] that will keep me busy throughout the winter months. My overture *In Autumn* and the suite from *Peer Gynt* [op. 46] will be out very soon, and I will then take the liberty of immediately sending you both works.

My wife sends warm greetings. So also, in friendship and high esteem, does

Yours truly,
Edvard Grieg

---

17 *Symphony No. 5* and *Hamlet. Fantasy-Overture.*

18 During the years 1897–1903 Grieg received several letters from the Russian Music Association inviting him to give concerts in Russia. Invitations came also from a number of leading composers as well as from the St. Petersburg Philharmonic. Grieg had to decline all of the invitations, primarily because of poor health.

19 Grieg's first London concert in 1889 took place on February 23. During the next five weeks he gave a total of eight concerts in England.

20 Grieg is referring to the opera torso *Scenes from Olav Trygvason,* which was published by C. F. Peters in a piano reduction in 1888 and in an orchestral version in 1890. It was premiered in Christiania on October 19, 1889.

To Olav Anton Thommessen

Olav Anton Thommessen (1851–1942) assumed the editorship of *Verdens Gang*, a newspaper published in Christiania, in 1878. He quickly put his stamp on it and made it into one of the Liberal party's most influential organs. Grieg carried on an extensive correspondence with Thommessen and often used *Verdens Gang* to communicate his views.

Grieg's letters to Thommessen are preserved in Nasjonalbiblioteket, Oslo (National Library of Norway, Oslo Division).

1

Troldhaugen, March 21, 1892

Dear Mr. Thommessen!

I really am furiously angry with you. Because you have reportedly—I have not read it—ushered me into Paradise! To be sure, the main outlines of the story as you tell it are true,[1] but nonetheless: How can people who wish me well publish something like this? I must be permitted to say that advertising of this sort may be suitable for certain other Norwegian-salmon-fishing musicians, but not for me. My whole career is not of the kind that I deserve to be lumped together with people who seek fame by such means. You have an obligation to give me satisfaction in the form of a notice—perhaps it could be called "Bergensian Sense of Music"—in which, as a contrast to my popularity with the street urchins, it is made clear (albeit *not* on my behalf, of course) that, judging by all the signs, the popularity is not exactly part of the *adult* Bergensians' view of Norwegian art and Norwegian artists.

Yes, just listen to this. The fact is that those same Bergensians have let their only music association, which has been in existence for over 100 years, fold for lack of support. They have let their orchestra decline to such an extent that for now it is completely unusable for artistic purposes—and at the same time they have raked me over the coals in *Bergens Aftenblad*[2] (naturally!) because, among other things, I will not attempt the impossible by performing my works in Bergen with orchestral resources that are not there but that I nonetheless absolutely need for this purpose. And this unjust criticism is occurring NB without a single

---

[1] The "Paradise" to which Grieg refers is a district by this name south of Bergen. The popularity that he goes on to discuss somewhat condescendingly has to do with the song "Northland Folk" from his incidental music to the play *Sigurd Jorsalfar* by Norwegian author Bjørnstjerne Bjørnson (1832–1910). In an April 5, 1892, letter to Max Abraham (1831–1900) of C. F. Peters, Grieg wrote, "Here in Bergen, for example, 'Northland Folk' is so absurdly popular that after being performed at concerts in the park it is even being sung by street urchins. (. . .) More than once I have had to go another route to avoid hearing these stanzas, which are yelled with terrible coarseness." His letter to Abraham makes it clear, however, that in reality Grieg enjoyed the popularity, so his seemingly harsh words to Thommessen must be taken with a grain of salt.

[2] *Bergens Aftenblad*: an evening newspaper published in Bergen.

pen being lifted in my defense. This, together with the fact that I do not even have access to Bergen's theater (!!), casts such a glaring searchlight on this city's view of its artists that one should speak quite softly about the "Bergensian Sense of Music".

Try to enter into my train of thought and you will certainly understand that after such treatment the last thing I want is to be officially accused of being popular in my home town. You must admit that you have unintentionally done me a disservice, and if you don't admit it—well, you are nonetheless who you are, and I gladly forgive you for it, especially if you sometime find your way to Troldhaugen!

Warm greetings to you and your wife.

Sincerely yours,
EDVARD GRIEG

2

Copenhagen, December 28, 1893
Hotel King of Denmark

Dear Mr. Thommessen!
It would please me if the song[3] did some good. It is not one of the best I have written, but there is one thing I like and that is the contrast between the sharp, rhythmic middle section and the gentle conclusion. For that is something I have experienced.

The issue of an honorarium is unimportant. I sent the song to you because I have a positive view of your newspaper. Send the paper to me wherever I travel in the world, and this will be honorarium enough.

With warm greetings and a wish for a good new year—a big wish when we think about what it *now* signifies.[4]

Sincerely yours,
EDVARD GRIEG

P.S. Believe me, I have had a marvelous time down here the past month. For I have had a daily visit from a fine lady: Mrs. Musa.[5] She has ushered me into a whole world of lyric poetry and a multitude of new songs to texts by Norwegian poets

---

[3] "Election Song", a setting of a text by Norwegian author Bjørnstjerne Bjørnson (1832–1910).

[4] Grieg is alluding to the parliamentary election that was to take place in 1894. Although he himself was not a member of the Liberal party he, like Bjørnson and Thommessen, was strongly sympathetic to the Liberal movement. He hoped for a strong vote for the Liberals and he was not disappointed: The election produced a Liberal majority in the Norwegian Parliament.

[5] Mrs. Musa: a name Grieg often used for the goddess of inspiration.

now lie before me. Eroticism through and through, naturally! That is and always will be the beginning and the end![6]

3

Troldhaugen, September 30, 1898

Dear Mr. Thommessen!

I don't know whether you are in Amsterdam or at home, but in any case—thank you for being on the lookout in the music festival matter![7] But I think you took the brochure altogether too seriously. Either it belongs to *Vikingen* [*The Viking*][8] and should be laughed at—though God knows it isn't funny—or it should be rejected as a mixture of vulgarity and lies. I am now beginning to think that that fellow is doing me a bigger favor than he realizes. Yes, nemesis takes many forms!

If Christiania does not consider me a Dutchman, perhaps it will be of interest to readers of *Verdens Gang* that two new pieces of mine have recently been published in Leipzig by [C. F.] Peters:

1) *Symphonic Dances* for orchestra.

2) *The Mountain Maid*, a song cycle based on Arne Garborg's book. (German and English edition.) The Scandinavian edition is about to be published by Wilhelm Hansen in Copenhagen.

If you want to have Norwegian music well reviewed, I can most warmly recommend Mr. Gerhard Schjelderup[9] in Dresden, Franklinstrasse 18, III. Mark my words, you will hear about this man. He is a considerable talent.

Can't you strike a blow in support of bringing Svendsen[10] home again now that the new National Theater is about to open? Don't you think it would help? Or are we really not so broad-minded, and are we completely lacking in the

---

[6] Grieg is referring to *Five Songs* op. 58 and *Six Elegiac Songs* op. 59, both with texts by John Paulsen (1851–1924), and *Five Songs* op. 60, texts by Wilhelm Krag (1871–1933).

[7] Grieg is referring to the Norwegian music festival held in Bergen in the summer of 1898. He had incurred the anger of many Norwegian musicians by his decision to invite the Concertgebouw Orchestra of Amsterdam to play at the festival instead of a Norwegian orchestra. Some Norwegian composers were also unhappy with his choices of compositions to be performed at the festival. In a letter to Thommessen of August 21, 1898, Grieg had written: "I have still not read the attacks after the music festival from Johannes Haarklou [1874–1925] and Winter-Hjelm [1837–1931]. According to Bergen newspapers, they were 'vehement'. Please be on the lookout!" After the festival was over, the Christiania newspaper *Aftenposten* commissioned Johannes Haarklou to write an account of the controversies surrounding the festival. The result was a brochure entitled "The Music Festival in Bergen: Overture–Scherzo–Finale". It is a vitriolic, ironic tirade that takes Grieg seriously to task for the way he handled the festival. There had been no love lost between Grieg and Haarklou before this episode, and the brochure obviously did nothing to improve it.

[8] *Vikingen*: a Norwegian humor magazine.

[9] The Norwegian composer Gerhard Schjelderup (1859–1933) lived the greater part of his life in Dresden, Germany. Grieg carried on a voluminous correspondence with him over a period of many years. See Grieg's letters to him.

[10] The Norwegian composer and conductor Johan Svendsen (1840–1911) had been serving as musical director at the Royal Theater in Copenhagen since 1883.

feeling for what is best for our nation? Is it the case, then, that we have plenty of big words but we do not love to see such a brilliant maestro in this high position? Does the prevailing mediocrity really have the power to prevent this? Mr. Winge is capable enough and could continue as an assistant conductor with Svendsen as the chief musical director. I think Svendsen would not be unwilling if one approached him in the right way.[11]

I remember what old [Bjørnstjerne] Bjørnson wrote in 1873 in a letter that he asked me to give to Johan Sverdrup[12] at the time when Svendsen and I, with Bjørnson's help, applied for and received annual state grants. He wrote: "Let us know the time of our visitation!" Genuinely Bjørnsonian! But—how true! However: We have no idea of that in Norway. We squander like Peer Gynt, and in the end we sit empty-handed, without the fruit of all the rich life we own and could have had around us. And that for the sake of a few lousy crowns! It's enough to make you cry. Where among us is the understanding that wealth also creates obligations with respect to art? It does not exist. And without this understanding there is nothing of that level that elevates people above the daily grind. But this understanding can be awakened and nourished—precisely through the press. Think about this! You are the very man who can do some good here. Especially if you can get a conservative paper—*Morgenbladet*, for example—to join in so that we can avoid the small political reefs.

Hopefully we will see each other soon in Christiania, where we will arrive around the 16th of October en route [to Copenhagen].

Warm greetings.

Sincerely yours,
EDVARD GRIEG

4

Troldhaugen, June 21, 1901

Dear Thommessen!
Instead of pouting I prefer to show the other side of the Norwegian national character: to be coarse. So: What in hell ever became of "The Battalion"?[13] The

---

[11] Grieg was deeply engaged in the question as to who should become musical director of the new National Theater in Christiania, which opened in 1899. His first choice was Johan Svendsen, with Per Winge (1858–1935), who was musical director at the Christiania Theater, serving as his assistant. If this arrangement could not be worked out, Grieg thought the only truly qualified applicant was Johan Halvorsen (1864–1935). It was Halvorsen who got the appointment. See Grieg's letter to Aimar Grønvold (1846–1926) of February 3, 1899.

[12] Johan Sverdrup (1816–92): Norwegian politician, president of the Norwegian Parliament from 1871 to 1884.

[13] Grieg is alluding to "Gentlemen-Rankers", a poem by Rudyard Kipling (1865–1936), which to date he had seen only in a Norwegian translation by Norwegian author and journalist Rosenkrantz Johnsen (1857–1929). Impressed with its "underlying hatred of war, not to mention hatred of chauvinism" (letter to Thommessen of December 18, 1900), he had set it to music. He wanted to see the English original, and Thommessen had

famous battalion that was solemnly promised via handshake, letter and telegram! If I don't get it immediately you are a scoundrel whom I will bawl out in *Verdens Gang*! So now you know. I have been miserable for the last month, and now the battalion could make me into a new and better person. Therefore: Send it! You're not a fellow from Sogn who says, "We could promise it all right, but we couldn't keep the promise!"

Well, that was that. Regarding the Nordraak matter,[14] I would prefer not to write anything in order to avoid a paroxysm of hemorrhaging and irritation over those damned *baglers*,[15] who have also been at work here. And I don't have any talent for irritation today, for I am happy and grateful. Last evening I received an essay on my art that appeared in a German music journal. It was written by a Norwegian (I think) whom I do not know, a man by the name of Rojahn who lives in Tønsberg. This is so exceptionally well written, so sensitively observant and with such an appreciative view of my relationship to Norway, that I wish Norwegians could get an opportunity to read it. I will write to the author today and urge him to send you his article.[16] If you are able to commit space to it, do so. It is precisely a clear understanding of my relationship to the national element that is lacking—in Norway. Many good things are said abroad, but at home people only throw mud at me when in one way or another I beat the drum for Norway and that which is Norwegian.

Believe me, it is beautiful here now! What a pleasure it would be to see you—preferably both of you—here! A little Roman celebration at Troldhaugen! I heard today that Ross[17] is here too. But you will live and die at your "Jelø" or whatever it is called.[18]

Warm greetings to you and your wife from Nina and me.

Sincerely yours,
EDVARD GRIEG

---

promised to send it to him. When he finally received it, however, he was so dismayed to see that the translator had omitted several important passages that he decided not to publish the piece. It was printed for the first time in 1991 as EG 156 in *Edvard Grieg: Complete Works*, vol. 15, p. 270.

[14] At the very time when Grieg was trying to gather money for a monument to Rikard Nordraak (1842–66) to be erected in Christiania, another group in Christiania launched an effort to raise money for a "Nordraach fund". Grieg took a dim view of this undertaking, as it appeared to him to be in competition with his own effort—which it was. The end result was two monuments, one at Nordraak's grave in Berlin and a huge statue of Nordraak designed by Gustav Vigeland (1869–1943) and erected in Nordraak Square in Christiania.

[15] The *baglers* were members of a political movement led by the bishops in opposition to King Sverre Sigurdson (1150–1202), who had reaffirmed the supremacy of the king over the church. Grieg is using the term derisively to denote the ultra-conservatives who had been so brazen as to launch a competing fund to honor his late friend.

[16] Grieg is referring to the article "Edvard Grieg. Eine biographische Skizze", by Norwegian educator and musician Ferdinand Rojahn (1860–1928). The article had been published in *Musik- und Theaterwelt*, Berlin, vol. 4, nos. 22–23.

[17] The Norwegian painter Christian Meyer Ross (1843–1909).

[18] "Jeløya" is an island in the Oslofjord near Moss, some forty miles south of Oslo.

5

Berlin, March 28, 1903
Continental Hotel

Dear Thommessen!
You asked about news from Prague.[19] Today I have sent you a whole bundle of reviews, but they are all in Czech—of which neither you nor I understand a word. There were only two in German, which I also sent along with the others. It might facilitate the understanding of a dark point in both reviews to know that the Germans in Prague are offended—or half offended and somewhat "aggrieved"—about the fact that it is not *they* who had invited me! I tell you, the language controversy is more furious here than anything imaginable at home.[20] How marvelous, then, to be able as a musician to gather the contending parties in the same auditorium and subject them to the power of music.

You ought to see how Norway and Norwegianness have filled the ears of people in the Bohemian countries these days. When I was in Prague, my works were being performed in all the larger cities to demonstrate their joy over my presence among them. And then my reception at the concert—yes, Mr. Helliesen,[21] who was there, can tell about that. (Unfortunately I did not get to see him.) The laurel wreaths were as big as millwheels, and if they come to Troldhaugen you will see a beautiful silver wreath that was given to me.

We will remain in Berlin until April 10. We will then go to Warsaw, where I will conduct on the 14th. From this city I assume that Mr. Fischer[22] will send you the necessary information.

It was wonderful that agreement was reached regarding the consular question—on the main issue, in any case. That Sigurd Ibsen has combed out the snarls recently created by leading politicians is admirable and proves which responsible tasks he may be called to perform in the future.[23]

And now, dear Thommessen: Thanks for the whiting and the red beefsteak! Warmest greetings to you and your wife from Nina and me.

Sincerely yours,
EDVARD GRIEG

P.S. Greet Sindings![24]

---

19 Grieg gave a concert in Prague on March 25, 1903.

20 The language controversy in Norway was between those who wished to preserve the Dano-Norwegian form of the language spoken and written by virtually all urban Norwegians and those who wished to adopt "new Norwegian", a form of the language derived from the dialects of rural Norway.

21 Norwegian attorney Henrik Michael Helliesen (1856–1933).

22 Grieg's Norwegian impresario Peter Vogt Fischer (1863–1938).

23 The so-called "consular question" was a major bone of contention between Norway and Sweden during the years 1892–1905. In 1892 the Norwegian Parliament had passed a resolution establishing an independent consular service, which they insisted Norway had a right to do. But the Swedish king had refused to approve the resolution on the grounds that Norway had no right to take such action without prior authorization from Sweden. Sigurd Ibsen (1859–1930), son of the famous playwright, was a member of the consular committee appointed in 1902 and played an important role in the negotiations with Sweden.

24 Norwegian composer Christian Sinding (1856–1941) and his wife.

6

Copenhagen, March 1, 1905

Dear Thommessen!

If you should see that some Norwegian newspaper carries a mendacious interview to which I was subjected by the Copenhagen newspaper *Ekstrabladet*, I urgently request that you do me the personal favor of communicating to the Norwegian newspapers in question the correction that the paper itself was obliged to carry the following day. It has to do with an outright swindle. I crossed out most of the interviewer's beastly draft in the proof copy, which I had reserved the right to do, and wrote in what had been my meaning and what I had said. And then the fellow played me for a fool in that his own draft had already been sent to the printer when he sent me the proof! These are noble colleagues that you have, you journalists. If the interview gets into Norwegian or Swedish papers without the correction, I will be disgraced. It's scandalous that there is no punishment for such conduct. The correction, which the newspaper of course wants to be construed as an inadvertent mistake, reads as follows: "We should report that in the interesting interview with Edvard Grieg that we carried yesterday a number of statements were included that Mr. Grieg cannot acknowledge and that he had corrected in a proof copy which, as agreed, he had submitted but which mistakenly did not reach the composing room before the paper went to press."

It is cunningly contrived, but the rascal wanted to stick with his own *long* article, by which he *earned more*. That is the high level [of the press]! I hope that no one in Norway reprints what a worthless rag like *Ekstrabladet* writes. But as I said: If you will keep your eyes open and, if necessary, rescue me, I will be grateful.

These are indeed desperate times. And that Michelsen should be ill![25] That is the worst of all. By the way, I am surprised at you during this time. I am a great admirer of Nansen.[26] But I would rather have prime minister Thommessen than prime minister Nansen! Yes, 1,000 times rather. And if dilettantism is really going to be the order of the day in Norway, why not prime minister Grieg? He isn't as stupid as you think.

But enough for now. Warm greetings!

Sincerely yours,
EDVARD GRIEG

---

[25] "Desperate times" is an allusion to the fact that negotiations between Norway and Sweden regarding Norway's demand for independence were at a critical stage at this time. Christian Michelsen (1856–1925) was Norway's prime minister in 1905.

[26] The famous polar explorer Fridtjof Nansen (1861–1930), who was later appointed Norway's first ambassador to England.

7

London, May 18, 1906
46 Grosvenor Street

Dear Thommessen!

Since I have not acceded to the requests of any of the many interviewers who have sent me their cards, the press is a little surly after the first concert compared with my previous visit, when it was effusively warm. It is very important to me that the *surliest* reviews not be the very ones that are reprinted in Norway, so I am sending you clippings from *Daily News* and *Evening Standard*, which are better. I have sent *The Morning Post* to Vogt Fischer, but I would nonetheless be grateful if you would see to it that excerpts from the two enclosed reviews get into *several* of the best newspapers in Christiania.

I wish you had been here on the 17th.[27] It was deeply moving. And then the party at the Norwegian Club in the evening. Nansen gave a splendid speech in honor of the day, and I spoke in honor of Bjørnson, Norway's "conscience" for nearly fifty years. Nansen is loved by all. He is solid gold for Norway, most of all just now.

On the 22nd I will go to Oxford to receive an honorary doctorate at the university. I am very busy, but fortunately I'm feeling better than I have for a long time.

Warm greetings.

Sincerely yours,
EDVARD GRIEG

---

[27] May 17 is Norway's Constitution Day.

To Mojmir Urbánek

Mojmir Urbánek (1873–1919) was a Czech music publisher. In 1900, after a period of apprenticeship with his father, František A. Urbánek (1842–1919), a music publisher and impresario, and after travels abroad, he established his own music publishing company in Prague. At that time he also began publishing the journal *Dalibor* and started an impresario business. Grieg had been invited to Prague as early as 1889 by Mojmir Urbánek's uncle, Velebín Urbánek (1853–92), but plans for some concerts in the early 1890's did not work out and Grieg did not give his first concert there until 1903.

A copy of Grieg's letter to Urbánek (in the original German) has been provided by Ladislav Reznicek. Portions of it and three additional letters not included here have also been published in Czech and Norwegian-Danish translation in Reznicek's book, *Edvard Grieg og tsjekkisk kultur* [*Edvard Grieg and Czech Culture*], Oslo 1975.

Bergen, Norway, October 29, 1902

Dear Mr. Urbánek

As far as I can recall, we had talked about the 23rd [of March]. But I am also willing to accept the 25th and shall regard this date as firm.[1] I must unfortunately exclude the possibility of a second concert, as I must now give definite responses to other invitations.

You ask me to give you a free hand in the choice of soloists. Unfortunately I must tell you that this is impossible for me to do. I have had some altogether too bitter experiences along this line. But let us hope that in the end we will be in agreement. I for my part will do everything in my power to be cooperative.

I wish it might be possible for me to stay in Prague for a few days after the concert in order to get acquainted with that interesting city. It is most likely, however, that I will have to leave immediately for Paris.[2] And with regard to your kind invitation to spend an evening with your esteemed family, I must, unfortunately, speak plainly: My health can tolerate absolutely no socializing when I am going to conduct. I need to rest as much as possible when I am not busy with rehearsals and concert. Only in this way is it possible for me to do my artistic duty. It was the same way in Warsaw[3] last winter: I declined all invitations and spent all the evenings in the hotel or at most at the theater or a concert. You understand, Mr. Urbánek, what a difficult person you unfortunately have gotten involved with! But that's the way things are now. I have no choice.

We will certainly get together on the choice of a program. I hope you can inform me soon as to what kind of orchestral resources—especially the number of strings—you can have available.

Lastly, I thank you for the appreciation you express in your letter. I will do my very best to truly deserve this appreciation.

Respectfully,
EDVARD GRIEG

---

1 Grieg's concert in Prague took place March 25, 1903.

2 Grieg did not go directly to Paris. After a stop in Berlin he went to Warsaw, where he conducted his own compositions on April 14 and 15, 1903. In Paris he conducted the Colonne Orchestra at the Châtelet Theater on April 19 and participated in a chamber-music concert on April 27 in Salle Pleyel.

3 Grieg had given a concert in Warsaw on April 22, 1902.

To Eduard Wagner

Eduard Wagner (1846–?) was a music dealer and publisher in Copenhagen. In 1874 he hit upon the idea of publishing a collection of simple piano arrangements of Norwegian melodies with Grieg as the arranger. As the letter indicates, Grieg did not think much of the idea but went along with it for financial reasons on the condition that his name would not be publicly associated with the project in any way. The result of the collaboration with Wagner was a volume entitled *Norges Melodier* (*Norway's Melodies*), which was published in 1875 and became a big and lasting success. See also Grieg's letter to Matthison-Hansen (1832–1909) of March 7, 1878, and to Gerhard Schjelderup (1859–1933) of October 26, 1905.

Grieg's letter to Eduard Wagner is preserved in Bergen Offentlige Bibliotek (Bergen Public Library).

Christiania, October 27, 1874

Music dealer Wagner, Copenhagen:

I received your letter yesterday. Regarding the opera text,[1] I cannot embark upon it inasmuch as my available time is occupied with other compositions. As for the collection of folk melodies, you can understand that from an artistic standpoint I cannot derive any enjoyment from such a project. However, since I am desperately in need of money it is my duty to do it. I will, therefore, take on the job for 125 *spesidalers.*

Before I begin, however, I want to give you one thing to consider: Do you think it will pay? I am not a practical man, but to me this project appears highly problematic. It can be a good collection; I will spare no trouble to make it accessible, inviting and yet dignified. Naturally I do not want my name to appear as editor, for in that case I would owe it to Norway and Norwegian publishers to let the collection come out in my home country. But you must consider the fact that quite a few things in this genre have been produced by *Norwegian* publishers. You might reasonably expect, therefore, that they will suppress the collection and conspire against it in every conceivable way so that it would not enjoy many sales in Norway. (Here, in addition to Lindeman's big collection, there are published arrangements by Kjerulf, Winter-Hjelm and me and undoubtedly others.)[2] Of these collections I know that Kjerulf's and mine have enjoyed very good sales. If, then, you must look mainly to Denmark for your market, what would be the

[1] Wagner had proposed that Grieg write an opera based on the play *Fjeld-Luren* (*The Mountain Horn*) by Danish author Camillo Bruun (1818–80).

[2] The collections Grieg has in mind are presumably the following:

1) Ludvig Mathias Lindeman: *Norske Fjeld-Melodier* (*Norwegian Mountain Melodies*) from 1841 and *Ældre og nyere norske Fjeldmelodier* (*Older and Newer Norwegian Mountain Melodies*), which came out in ten volumes during the years 1853–67.

result? Still—this collection would have one advantage over the others: It would be unique in that it would consist of easy arrangements of the Norwegian song literature. I don't know anything about the Norwegian copyright law, but I will get hold of it and send a copy to you. To tell the truth, I didn't think we had anything like that up here.

I must tell you that I find the error in Miss Andrée's sonata[3] inexcusable.

One thing you must tell me: Precisely when do you intend that these melodies shall be published? For it is impossible for me to get seriously to work on the project right away. For the time being I can only start collecting and doing some preliminary work.

Respectfully yours,
EDVARD GRIEG

---

2) Halfdan Kjerulf: *25 udvalgte norske Folkedandse for Piano udsatte* (*25 Selected Norwegian Folk Dances Arranged for Piano*) from 1861 and *Norske Folkeviser satte for Pianoforte* (*Norwegian Folk Songs Arranged for Piano*) from 1867.
3) Otto Winter-Hjelm: *Norske Fjeldmelodier for Pianoforte* (*Norwegian Mountain Melodies for Piano*) from 1869.
4) Edvard Grieg: *25 norske Folkeviser og Danse* (*Twenty-five Norwegian Folk Songs and Dances*) from 1870.

[3] Swedish organist and composer Elfrida Andrée (1841–1929). Grieg probably is alluding to her *Piano Sonata* in A major op. 3 published in 1873. It is not known to what mistake he is referring.

To Carl Warmuth Jr.

The music publisher Carl Warmuth Jr. (1844–95) was the son of German-born hornist Carl Warmuth Sr. (1811–92), who came to Norway in 1840 with the "Harz-Verein" orchestra. Soon thereafter Warmuth Sr. opened a small music and instrument store in Christiania and in 1851 a music publishing company. In 1874 Warmuth Jr. assumed the leadership of the firm and developed it into the country's leading music business. Its activities included a retail music store, a music publishing house, a rental library and a concert booking agency.

Grieg's letters to Carl Warmuth Jr. are preserved in Nasjonalbiblioteket, Oslo (National Library of Norway, Oslo Division).

1

Rome, February 8, 1870

Dear Warmuth!
Thank you for your letter. The questions you have raised can be quickly answered. I was born on June 15, 1843. In autumn 1858 I went to Leipzig, studied there (albeit with an interruption owing to a long illness) until 1862 and from 1863 onward continued my studies in Copenhagen. I received my first instruction from my mother, who in her youth studied in Germany herself under Methfessel.[1]

You presumably are familiar with most of my published compositions, and I do not want the unpublished ones to be mentioned. Moreover, *Folkebladet* once carried something about me, although, it is true, no data. In any case I think my date of birth was not given.[2] Since we last met, sorrow and joy have taken their turns as always. This fall I hope to be in my homeland again and to be able to work for Norwegian art.

Life down here is extremely interesting. It cannot be described or painted, it can only be seen and felt. It is just a pity that my stay here will be so brief. In April I am thinking of going to Naples, in May northward through Germany to Copenhagen, and in June to my parents in Bergen.

Perhaps it would be of interest to you to hear a little about Liszt, but unfortunately I still have not met him. The fact is that he does not live in Rome but in Tivoli, a small town out in the country. He is expected here today or tomorrow, though, to attend some concerts by his students.[3] I have, however, become acquainted with one of these students—Sgambati,[4] a uniquely gifted artist. It is just a pity that I cannot converse with him: He speaks only Italian and French and I

---

[1] The German composer Albert Methfessel (1785–1869), who also gave instruction in piano, singing and music theory.

[2] Grieg's reference is to *Norsk Folkeblad*, an illustrated weekly magazine in Christiania owned and edited by Bjørnstjerne Bjørnson (1832–1910) during the years 1869–71. He presumably is referring to Bjørnson's article "Edvard Grieg", which appeared in 1869.

[3] Grieg met Liszt a few days later. See his letters to his parents of February 17 and April 9, 1870.

[4] Italian pianist and composer Giovanni Sgambati (1843–1914).

speak only German and a little English. On Saturday he is playing my *Violin Sonata No. 1* in F at a concert with an Italian violinist named Pinelli,[5] and he really handles the sonata exceptionally well.

Be sure to greet Cappelen[6] when you write. Cordial greetings to you as well as your father and the family.

Sincerely yours,
EDVARD GRIEG

2

Amsterdam, January 10, 1884

Dear Warmuth!
Believe me, I have indeed heard everything that you have gone through, and in that connection I have more than once wanted to write to you—but I have always decided not to do so, because such matters seem to me to be too serious for outsiders to meddle with. What others can try to say by way of comfort based on their own life experience is worth nothing. One must live through both this and that.

As you see, I am in Amsterdam. Yes, it is not, in fact, by choice. I was so totally exhausted when I came here that I had to withdraw from concerts in both Paris and London, where I had been engaged to perform. I now intend to go to Rome in order, if possible, to regain my strength in southern Europe.

By the way, it was a curious story. I applied for a travel grant in order to go to Paris, but I did not get it. So I wanted to try to earn the means in another way and decided, therefore, on a concert tour. Now that the means are finally there, I have to give up going to Paris. Isn't that the limit! I am telling you this because Fritzsch,[7] in all naiveté, has peddled the inelegant untruth via his *Wochenblatt* that I gave concerts in order to make my compositions known.

Otherwise, believe me, it has been an interesting trip. Never before have I experienced so much understanding and recognition. Holland, especially, was moving. It is not so easy for me to send newspapers from here now, since I do not remember which issues they were—and besides, I am staying indoors these days because of endemic fever—but I thought you could get along with clippings from the daily papers, since yours is a monthly publication.[8]

The last thing I can tell you is that last Sunday I was in the audience at a matinee where the first part of the program consisted of Brahms's E-minor symphony and the second part included my *Norwegian Dances* op. 35 in an orchestral

[5] Ettore Pinelli (1843–1915).
[6] Norwegian organist and composer Christian Cappelen (1845–1919).
[7] Music publisher Ernst Wilhelm Fritzsch (1840–1902) was also editor of *Musikalisches Wochenblatt* in Leipzig.
[8] In 1880 Warmuth had taken the initiative in establishing *Nordisk Musik-Tidende*, a Norwegian music journal that was published monthly until 1892.

arrangement by Mann,[9] the musical director who was also conducting the concert. After the last piece there was such a racket in the audience that it had to be played *da capo*, and when the racket continued unabated I was fetched by a deputation and escorted up to the orchestra, where I was greeted with a triple fanfare accompanied by applause from the large audience—as if I were one of their own.

I have unfortunately promised to play my *Cello Sonata* next Saturday at one of the chamber-music evenings being given by the "Maatschappij tot Bevordering der Toonkunst" ["Society for the Promotion of Music"]. I don't know how in the world I can do it, for I am sitting here with a fever and headache, and I lie awake at night bathed in sweat. If all goes well, I will leave here for Leipzig on Sunday to meet my wife, with whom I am traveling to Italy.

And now thank you so much for what you sent me. I have still not been able to study it thoroughly but hope to do so soon. As glad as I would have been to write about Cappelen, I would rather have done it on my own initiative. I myself have literally nothing at the moment. But I will not forget your publication whenever I may have something. Recently I have unfortunately not been able to read it, but naturally as a patriot I am greatly interested in its continued existence.

I recently sent to *Dagbladet*[10] a Dutch journal, *De Portefeuille*, that contained a well-written article about my art which you could use—omitting, of course, the biographical information. When you ask *Dagbladet* for it on my behalf, you will certainly get it. The article appeared in installments in two numbers of the journal.[11]

And with that, farewell! Happy new year and continued good luck with your work!

Warm greetings!

Sincerely yours,
EDVARD GRIEG

P.S. My address remains: Peters.

3

Bergen, November 19, 1884

Dear Mr. Warmuth!
No, that's a bit thick! You are not going to get out of it so easily! You print the conclusion of Dr. Kretzschmar's article and not the main body dealing with my

[9] Dutch conductor Johan Gottfried Hendrik Mann (1858–1904). The concert took place on January 6, 1884.
[10] *Dagbladet*: a Christiania newspaper.
[11] Grieg is referring to "Edvard Grieg", an article by one J. de Jong in *De Portefeuille*, Amsterdam, 1883.

position as an artist and the statement about my *String Quartet.*[12] That will not do. In the next number you must make up for the blunder. Remember, you yourself have repeatedly asked me for information, and you have not carried anything from the issue that I gave you but only something from a later one. Right is right. Either nothing or everything. Your publication is, after all, a professional journal. If it were a daily paper the use of the fragments could be justified, though I see that certain dailies, too, have printed the whole article. I hope that there has just been a misunderstanding.

Respectfully yours,
EDVARD GRIEG

P.S. I always receive your paper long after others have gotten it. Why does this happen?

[12] In October, 1884, the German musicologist and conductor Hermann Kretzschmar (1848–1924) had written a long article, "Neue Compositionen von Edvard Grieg" ("New Compositions by Edvard Grieg"), which appeared serially in two numbers of *Musikalisches Wochenblatt* in Leipzig. Kretzschmar gave an unusually laudatory account of Grieg's works. The bulk of the first installment consisted of a thorough analysis of the *String Quartet* in G minor. Regarding this composition he wrote, for example, "In Scandinavian music it is of monumental value. It is the most outstanding and mature work that Grieg has yet produced. (...) The handling of the musical thoughts reminds us more than once of the late Beethoven." In the second installment of the article Kretzschmar discussed Grieg's shorter works, and it was only this part of the article that was carried in Norwegian translation in the October number of *Nordisk Musik-Tidende.*

To August Winding

The Danish pianist and composer August Winding (1835–99) was one of Grieg's closest Danish friends. At times Grieg lived in his home at Fredensborg. On June 22, 1899, upon learning of Winding's death just six days earlier, Grieg wrote to their mutual friend Gottfred Matthison-Hansen (1832–1909) as follows: "When I search my memory I cannot remember (. . .) anything that has affected me as deeply as this. I am sitting here and literally gulping down my sobs like a child. (. . .) I see—perhaps all the more clearly because I am not Danish—a big chunk of Danish nature in Winding. There was something pastoral about him that made him appear almost like a stranger amidst the buzzing confusion of city life. This noble, retiring nature—who has it still?"

Grieg's letters to Winding are preserved in Det kgl. Bibliotek (The Royal Library), Copenhagen.

1

Christiania, October 26, 1872

Dear friend!
If I could have taken up pen and ink each time you have been in my thoughts you would have received a flood of letters from me, but believe you me it has been a busy time—so Denmark has had to wait.

But now I send my sincerest thanks to you and your *matchless* wife for your friendship. I long to be able to show both of you here in Norway how I feel about you, and I am hoping you might come next summer. I first ask you to promise me that you will reply soon to these lines and tell me if your health is such that we can entertain the hope of seeing you. I have often feared a bit for you when I think of how busy you are these days, and for that reason I am anxious to hear from you.

I wish you were here this evening and could go with me to Svendsen's concert, which includes some truly brilliant works.[1] I enclose a copy of the program, which will be of interest to you. It shows that we have some talent up here. *Carnival in Paris* is the best. Here rhythm and harmony vie with an orchestration that is not only masterful but often entirely new. For this occasion Svendsen has managed to put together an enormous orchestra (and for once the musicians are donating their services; the Music Association, which has to pay its musicians, simply can't compete). He conducts splendidly, so I finally am in a position to

---

[1] Grieg had founded the Music Association orchestra in Christiania in 1871. During the first year he was the sole conductor, but in 1872 Johan Svendsen (1840–1911) returned to Norway and for a time thereafter shared the conducting duties with Grieg. The October 26 concert to which Grieg is referring included a new composition by Svendsen—*Carnival in Paris,* an orchestral work—as well as Liszt's *Hungarian Rhapsody No. 6* in an orchestral arrangement by Svendsen, and *Nordens Aand* (*The Nordic Spirit*) by Norwegian composer Johan Selmer (1844–1910), a composition for choir and orchestra based on a text by Danish author and politician Carl Ploug (1813–94).

give myself completely to the enjoyment of the music. You should hear his orchestration of Liszt's *Rhapsody*! In his arrangement, the piano passages turn into the most original and imaginative orchestral sounds, pizzicato strings and piccolos whip around your ears, not to mention the dynamic level. Here it is as it should be, but sometimes in the other pieces it assumes such dimensions that I—once the initial surprise is over—become almost numb and then weak, unreceptive to everything, no matter how wonderful it may be.

Another Norwegian musician—Johan Selmer, whose name you see on the program—is also talented but a bit murky in comparison with Svendsen. In his music he, like Svendsen, displays what could almost be called revolutionary tendencies. In his setting of Ploug's poem there are some things that completely carry me along. It is as if the powers of nature were set in motion: Thor comes charging so the sparks fly, but Loki comes along. Yes, that's it: Loki comes along! I think I have found the expression: Loki comes along. It's just that there is altogether too much of him, and that, naturally, is a result of the French influence—all this preoccupation with the demonic, which, to be sure, has its place in life and in art, just as Loki drives beside Thor, but, but—but it should also be possible for him to be away once in awhile.

But as I said, we have talent up here—and better to have something demonic when talent keeps it under control than that German morbidity that isn't capable of vigorous development. (. . .)

Farewell for now! Greet your wife and Ingeborg,[2] who must learn to remember us.

Sincerely yours,
Edvard Grieg

P.S. I have recently re-orchestrated *Before a Southern Convent* and now expect a much greater effect.

2

Leipzig, February 4, 1875

Dear Winding!
(. . .) I don't know if you read *Musikalisches Wochenblatt*, and that is why I am writing today. For there, among new works performed, it says "Winding: *Piano Quartet* in D major (Wurzen, Concert zum Besten des Frauenvereins)." There you see, now it begins. One more signal is needed; when and from whence it will come is strictly a matter of chance.

You would be most astonished if you knew what a tremendous amount of

[2] Winding's daughter Ingeborg (1871–1921).

music I have listened to during the three weeks that I have been here.[3] Almost every day a concert and frequently rehearsals in the forenoon. How it has gone with my own work under such circumstances you can well understand, but I really look upon it as a kind of duty to gather as much honey as I possibly can while I am here. To be sure, one often gets poor honey. But recently in St. Thomas Church I heard the first concert by a Bach Association under the leadership of Volkland, von Holstein and Spitta[4] (the author of an excellent book on Bach). The concert included three cantatas by Bach that had not been performed publicly before. I have never heard anything so beautiful by Bach; they are marvelous, great, profound, childlike and fervent. (. . .)

The public view here nowadays regarding such composers as Mendelssohn is ridiculous. If at one time he was overrated, then, by God, the opposite is true today. It seems to me to bespeak a period that has no feeling for the purity and beauty that stream from Mendelssohn. The more's the pity, since what one calls spirit and originality does not exist here any more. Mendelssohn, however, was himself, but now, to the most unbelievable degree, one sees only copies wherever one turns.

Neupert has been engaged to play in Euterpe on the 16th; he will play my *Piano Concerto* and some pieces for solo piano.[5]

I will be here at least until April. I hope you might be well enough to be able to send me a few lines. That would be good both for you and for me.

Warm greetings to your wife—and to Ingeborg if she is in a mood to remember me.

Sincerely yours,
EDVARD GRIEG

P.S. Address: Fritzsch, Königstrasse 24.

---

[3] In early January, 1875, Grieg went to Leipzig, where he remained until early May. Then, traveling by way of Munich and Weimar, he went to the Windings' home in Fredensborg.

[4] German pianist and conductor Alfred Volkland (1841–1905), German composer and author Franz von Holstein (1826–78), and German musicologist Philipp Spitta (1841–94), all of whom were active in Leipzig's music life at this time.

[5] "Euterpe" was a concert association in Leipzig that featured contemporary music in deliberate competition with the well-established and more conservative Gewandhaus concerts. Edmund Neupert (1842–88) was a Norwegian pianist and friend of Grieg who, among other things, had been the soloist in the world premiere of Grieg's *Piano Concerto* in Copenhagen on April 3, 1869.

3

Leipzig, April 5, 1875

Dear Winding!

(. . .) I have your letter in front of me, but I don't know if I have written since I received it. We were very glad to get it but, as I have said before, think it over very carefully if you are planning to choose Gastein.[6]

You want me to tell you what I am working on and about conditions in Leipzig. As for the first, unfortunately there is nothing to tell. I am still plugging away at the music to *Peer Gynt*, and it doesn't interest me. I am also collecting all of my best songs, which are going to be published here this fall. Von Holstein has been so kind as to make German translations of most of the texts.

Now that the concert season is over, Leipzig is a dreadfully boring place to live—which, to be sure, has the advantage that it allows time to get some work done. We have had tropical weather here for the past few days. I sit with open windows, and of course I hear Moscheles'[7] *G-minor Concerto* sounding forth from one of the nearby buildings.

Farewell for now. Warmest greetings to you and your wife and little one from Nina and from

Your friend,
EDVARD GRIEG

P.S. NB: My name is not *Eduard!*

4

Bergen, September 28, 1875

Dear friend!

Of course I remember the agreement. It was to the effect that so long as you do not write it is a sign that everything is just the way it has been. And that certainly is sad. But that certainly cannot prevent me from writing. If you have recovered sufficiently to do so, ask your wife to read; it would make me very happy if a moment of mountain air could cheer you up a little. Unfortunately I am not in as good a mood as you might imagine me to be up here in the mountain air. Here, too, one encounters the human, the transitory, in its endlessly recurring forms.

Last week I attended my father's funeral, and my mother will not survive the winter. As you can see, that is a lot at one time. For now, life has lost its fragrance for me, and I do not wish to talk about art. I think that one can speak in music about the sorrow of others, but when it touches one's own life too closely, then it is impossible.

---

[6] Gastein was the site of a health spa in Austria.

[7] Austrian pianist Ignaz Moscheles (1794–1870) had been one of Grieg's teachers at the Leipzig conservatory.

I hope this lethargy is only a temporary condition, for such a condition must be unhealthy for both soul and body. You have also lost your dear parents, so you know how one becomes small, how everything decreases in value—yes, how one feels an inexpressible longing to go with them.

For the near future I will stay here; I cannot leave mother in her present condition. My income situation is very problematic, but good God! One must first deal with the strong and deep feelings and only then with life's other demands, isn't that right?

Yes, this is something I feel—that when one stands face to face with the deepest thoughts, all lesser interests must rest. Moreover, I think that such periods in life store up material that later, in the moment of beauty, can be put to use. Thus, when all is said and done, it is good for us to see the eternal law fulfilled in those whom we love most. It is inexpressibly hard, but it is good. And the hardest part of all is the doubt and struggle to which one is subjected.

Recently I spent some time with one of my nearest relatives, and to him it was such a comforting thought that the dead now had "eternal" peace and had entered the eternal rest. In other words, that everything was past. Most appalling was the fact that for a time this thought totally filled me, but afterward it left me empty to the very depths of my soul. No, you can have all the dogmas, but the belief in immortality I must have. Without that everything comes to nothing. You must assure me so that I can know that you also believe this, for it still strikes me as humbug when I fall back into these doubts. My perception is that you are beyond these religious torments—otherwise you would not be so full of confidence. May God grant that you have that kind of medicine when all the physical ones do not help.

Nina says she wants to write, so I will conclude with the best wishes and warmest greetings to all three of you. If you can let us hear from you, the address is still *Bergen.*

Sincerely yours,
EDVARD GRIEG

5

Bergen, December 17, 1875

Dear friend!
Your last letter, which was infinitely dear, has lain unanswered for a long time, and your hope that you might soon hear from me from Christiania came, as you see, to nothing.

I now sit here unspeakably lonely and forlorn. Perhaps you know that I also had to see my mother to her final resting place a scant six weeks after father's death, and since then I have not been able to pull myself together to do a single thing. Life and death and eternity, religion and art—everything creates hazy pictures in my mind that I still have not been able to clarify.

I have thought that I would compose a lot, but as strongly as my feelings overwhelm me these days, reflection is equally strong—yes, even stronger. I live in a constant struggle with these elements and cannot find clarity. I hope this transitional life will soon come to an end, for there is something agonizing about it even if it eventually bears fruit.

I will stay here through the winter and live at the home of my brother, Consul John Grieg.[8] I give a few lessons; other than that I live in total seclusion and am glad to be out of the public eye. You will understand this all the better when I tell you that just before father's death I had advertised and made preparations for a concert—which, of course, was suddenly canceled. Then, one month later, at mother's insistent urging, I got it ready again, advertised it anew—and once again had to cancel it. Any thought of a concert is now loathsome to me. But sometime next spring I must do it anyway to get money to go down and see you again at unforgettable Fredensborg.

Have you decided anything for the summer? I would like to know of your plans in order to plan my trip to Germany accordingly. For I continue to entertain the hope of going to Bayreuth this summer, and I won't give up until I have exhausted all the possibilities.[9] According to *Wochenblatt* the performances will take place in August.

When I mention *Wochenblatt* I must not forget to tell you something that you may already know, namely that your overture was performed in Hamburg and your quartet in St. Petersburg. Earlier I saw the clarinet pieces mentioned among new works that had been performed, but I have now forgotten where the performance took place.

And that will have to be enough for today. Merry Christmas to all of you, and warm greetings from Nina and from

Yours truly,
EDVARD GRIEG

P.S. *Peer Gynt* will be performed at the Christiania Theater in January, and yesterday in that connection I had to send a *28-page* letter to the conductor.[10]

---

8 Edvard's brother John Grieg (1840–1901).

9 The big event in Grieg's life in the summer of 1876 was his encounter with Wagner's art during the opening of the first festival in Bayreuth with the opera cycle *The Ring of the Nibelung*. Grieg's publisher in Leipzig, Max Abraham (1831–1900), had gotten tickets for him, and he was commissioned by the Norwegian newspaper *Bergensposten* to write about the event. Grieg sent eight long articles to the paper, and his evaluations provide interesting evidence of his ability to enter into the Wagnerian world of sound, which both attracted and repelled him. These articles will be printed in their entirety in English translation in Benestad & Halverson (eds.), *Edvard Grieg: Diaries, Articles, Speeches* (Columbus, Ohio, 2001). After the visit to Bayreuth, Grieg and his traveling companion John Paulsen (1851–1924) went to Tyrol, where they visited Henrik Ibsen (1828–1906) at Gossensass.

10 See Grieg's letter of December 14, 1875, to Johan Hennum (1836–94). The premiere of *Peer Gynt* took place at the Christiania Theater on February 24, 1876.

6

Lofthus, November 28, 1877

My dear friend!
I don't have to tell you how happy your last letter made me. When I had read it I was transported into the middle of the region of "fertility". Yes, that Fredensborg! There are composed quintets, "Sommerminder",[11] Pentecost hymns and little boys lacking only orchestration—or does this apply only to the Pentecost hymn? I hope, in any case, that the little boy[12] is perfect in every way—also with respect to orchestration! If there should be some hidden fifths, just let them be; that's less of a problem in our day and age. The point of the whole story is: You have my respect—yes, I am tempted to say with Mantzius:[13] my *complete respect!* (. . .)

You ask why I am leaving Christiania and what it is that is drawing me to spend the winter at Ullensvang. Well, the point is just this: It had to be done if I am to survive as an artist. Perhaps it surprises you, but if you only knew what an inner struggle I have been waging these last years you would understand me. Every possible outward circumstance has prevented me from following my calling, and certainly no one has been more dissatisfied with what I have achieved than I myself. There have been bits and pieces, to be sure, in which aspiration has now and then been present, but the integrated whole that I began to grasp when I was twenty-five—and for a few years thereafter—has since, year by year, slipped away from me. I have lost the ability to handle the larger musical forms—and if one loses that, after once having had it, which I really did at one time, then it is farewell to the future! In a word, I felt that things were beginning to go awry, the ideal picture was becoming stunted. That is why something had to be done. And I have not been as happy as I am now for a long time—yes, as grateful, as innocently happy. I am again busy immersing myself in my art, and with God's help something will come of it.[14] Things are very tight financially, for I'm not earning a penny—but even so, it's better this way.

We have rented lodging from Mr. Utne,[15] a storekeeper, and are very comfortable. Not far from our quarters—on a small plot of ground near a rushing mountain stream—I have built myself a little hut where I am working. Nothing is perfect in this world, and that is true also in this case, for the people of the neighborhood occasionally have the bad habit of sneaking up to listen. But so what? I am as free as a bird.[16]

When I got your last letter I was just about to leave on a trip. I went to

---

11 "Sommerminder" ("Summer Memories") was a composition by Winding.

12 Winding's wife Clara (1839–1925) had just give birth to their son Poul (1877–1966).

13 Kristian Mantzius (1819–79), a well-known Danish actor.

14 The most important artistic result of Grieg's stay in Hardanger in 1877–78 was the *String Quartet* in G minor op. 27.

15 Hans Utne (1827–95), Grieg's sometime landlord in Ullensvang, Hardanger.

16 Grieg eventually found it advisable to have his hut moved to a location where he was less likely to be

Bergen, where I gave two concerts—primarily to raise money for the winter stay in Ullensvang. That is why these lines have been delayed.

And with that I think you have gotten a kind of overview regarding me and mine.

You ask about the Music Association in Christiania. It is led now by a young man by the name of Ole Olsen.[17] The name is ordinary enough but the fellow has talent, that's for sure.

In addition to your own family, you must first and foremost greet Hartmann and his family.[18] Is he not writing anything? Let me hear from you soon if you are well enough to tolerate writing. And in any case do not forget that you have a faithful friend, namely

Yours truly,
EDVARD GRIEG

7

Bergen, December 27, 1880

Dear friend!
Thank you for your letter as well as the enclosure from Clara. It was a double joy, first as a Christmas greeting and secondly because we hadn't heard from you for such a long time. We were very happy to get the picture, and in order to demonstrate the resemblance to her father we made the most careful comparisons with the bust by Bissen,[19] which holds sway in the corner of the living room. But we couldn't make up our minds. From your letter, however, I got the very happy news that you are feeling better than you have for a long, long time. The Copenhagen air must have been especially invigorating for musicians these past few months, for Gottfred Matthison-Hansen has also become a new man.

Believe me, there were many times when I wanted to come down to see you. But I am walled in for the winter, and perhaps for the summer too. It's a huge clearing job that I have launched here at home, trust me, for when one clears things out one bumps into unpleasantries with which one would prefer not to deal. Just now I am being attacked—not only in the newspapers but in private letters, some signed and some anonymous—because I have tried to uphold the artistic standard of the Music Society, of which I am conductor this winter.[20] There was a whole group of chorus members who, after we had rehearsed a

disturbed. See his humorous account of the moving of the hut in his article, "The Compost", in Benestad and Halverson (eds.), *Edvard Grieg: Diaries, Articles, Speeches* (Peer Gynt Press, 2000).

17 Norwegian composer and conductor Ole Olsen (1850–1927).

18 Danish composer J. P. E. Hartmann (1805–1900), Winding's father-in-law.

19 Grieg had in his home a plaster-of-Paris cast of a bust of J. P. E. Hartmann. The bust had been sculpted by Danish sculptor Herman Vilhelm Bissen (1798–1868).

20 Grieg was conductor of the Music Society Harmonien, predecessor of the modern Bergen Philharmonic Orchestra, during the years 1880–82.

large, difficult work, decided to miss the dress rehearsal and concert because a public dance was being held at the same time. The people involved had signed pledges committing themselves to participation in the chorus. I, therefore, used my authority and informed the deserters that I regretfully found it necessary to prohibit their future participation. But then people began to attack me like mad dogs. I could send you a whole packet of newspaper clippings. But now, after the basic concepts have been clarified, I am gaining more and more supporters for my way of handling the matter. Yesterday I even received a statement signed by the women's chorus (about sixty members) in which they frankly sided with me. That was a nice gesture—in contrast to the city gossips and the press, all of whom have branded my course of action as *rude.*

Well, believe me, the artistic conditions here are primitive. There is no idea of a feeling of responsibility anywhere. But—there is at least one good thing about people up here and that is their receptivity. Once the initial surprise at that which is new and unfamiliar is over, there is the richest soil for everything great and noble. For that reason it is more satisfying to work here than in over-cultivated circumstances. (. . .)

8

Troldhaugen, September 3, 1886

Dear Winding!

A moment ago I jumped up from the piano, where I was about to go mad over *Tristan and Isolde*—mad over both Wagner's genius and my own idiocy as a piano player—and shouted: "No, damn it all, now I am going to write to Winding!" Nina seconded the idea: "Yes, do that," she said—so here I am. Actually I would like to say as little about the matter as possible—i.e., the matter of my being a great sinner for not having written sooner. To my credit it should be said that many good thoughts have been just as good as letters. I constantly say to myself: Why will not one of my few—ah, so very few!—genuine Danish friends from a vanished glorious time come up and enjoy a little of all this beauty? I think especially of you and Emil Horneman.[21] I regard the latter, despite all the discord, as the genuine, good old Horneman whose noble heart and deep musical feeling I have to thank for several of the most significant influences of my youth. I have received the same from you, but with the difference that the form has been calmer, milder, more subdued, as your nature requires. Therefore it will always remain as one of my most precious dreams to get you up here sometime.

My Troldhaugen has now become so dear to me that I hope to be able to keep it. If this happens, I obviously will not give up the hope of seeing at least you

[21] Danish composer Emil Horneman (1840–1906).

and Clara. Next year I hope to see Julius Röntgen and his wife.[22] Do you know them? They are quite unusual, wonderful people—and very talented and capable artists. But first—fortunately—comes a long, long winter during which I hope to get a lot done. I plan to spend the entire winter here on my hillock, where I am now making such preparations as I can to cope with that harsh season of the year. You can understand that making preparations for winter is no joke here in the countryside, but once it is done we also enjoy a peaceful working situation that you would envy.

As Nina no doubt wrote, we have had Holger Drachmann[23] up here for a time. He and I took a trip through West Norway that ended up in the mountains and did much to inject new life into both body and soul. He wrote poems for which I wrote music, and for once life was the way it ought to be. This Drachmann of yours is a strange fellow. There is something of the troubadour— or the "minnesinger," or whatever I should call it—about him, and it seems to me that he stands out so oddly in contrast to our reality-afflicted time. In the poems he wrote for me I got him to be concise, which he admittedly sometimes is not.[24] Have you never set any of his texts?

The talented Norwegian composer Christian Sinding[25] recently sent me a four-movement setting that he has made of one of Drachmann's longer poems. He calls it *Et Efterår* [*One Autumn*] (en modo d'una sonata), for voice and piano. It is a bold piece to which you would object in more than one place, but the idea is good and, most important of all, he shows how the genre called "song" can be expanded into larger forms. And Drachmann is just the poet for that sort of thing. In the same collection of poems there is a similar cycle called "One Spring" that I would like to try my hand at.

From what I have just heard, Drachmann has begun a series of articles in *Berlingste Tidende* about his trip to Norway. You must be sure to get a copy.

Well, that will be enough for today. I will expect soon to see your familiar handwriting, and remember: When I open the letter, I am to receive definite word about how things are going. With warmest greetings to all of you, including Professor Hartmann,

Sincerely yours,
EDVARD GRIEG

---

22 Dutch composer, pianist and conductor Julius Röntgen (1855–1932) and his Swedish-born wife, Amanda (Maier) Röntgen (1843–94).

23 Danish author Holger Drachmann (1846–1908).

24 The songs Grieg wrote to Danish poet Holger Drachmann's texts consititute *Reminiscences from Mountain and Fjord.* Drachmann's account of his trip to the mountains with Grieg appeared in the Copenhagen newspaper *Berlingske Tidende* in August–September, 1886.

25 Sinding's dates are 1856–1941.

9

Troldhaugen, August 16, 1895

Dear friend!
I have just finished the very difficult task of writing to Emil Horneman and now, after having removed a heavy stone from my mind, I come to a task that is no work at all: to tell you and Clara how much we enjoyed seeing you recently and to thank you for your letter.

Yes, it was a beautiful time, even if it could and should have been much more beautiful.[26] Emil Horneman does not mention a single thing in his letter that could have been different. But I think that old friendship is an altogether too precious wine to be poured out in such a cavalier way and I, therefore, decided to address the matter, naturally without any bitterness. Regarding his taking offense from me in connection with the travel arrangements on the way back, I have used your own expression: that it was practically as if he almost felt "declared incompetent" as a result of my not having explicitly told him that you and I were sharing the same carriage. So on this point, anyway, no distortion or misunderstanding is possible. I have tried to convince him as to how "illogical" it would be for me to invite an old friend up here in order to hurt him. Well, sure enough, the saying is true in this case also—unfortunately: He who seeks will find. Emil must almost have *sought* grievances against me, otherwise his way of thinking would be absolutely and unbelievably absurd. But I continue to believe that there was something sick about him. And to tell the truth, I think the same would have been true of any of us if we had divided ourselves into several portions and devoted the largest portion to our mental work—as he did on this trip. Because that sort of thing doesn't work, and it was a big blunder that it was tried. You were smarter: You put your manuscript aside until you got home. You must send me a copy of the piano piece or whatever it was you were working on.

Let me now not forget to beg your pardon for giving you the name of the wrong hotel in Dalen. I didn't mean "Hotel Bandak" but "Hotel Dalen"—the big, new building—as you no doubt noticed. (. . .)

I haven't heard anything from the Gottfred Matthison-Hansens. You know that we left Lofthus before they did, so I can only hope that everything went as it was supposed to and that they finished their trip as planned.

We traveled to the Sognefjord by way of Stalheim and Gudvangen, then to Skjolden via the Lusterfjord, and from there up to a mountain plateau called "Turtagrø", directly below the Skagastøl peaks. Here we all spent an absolutely wonderful day together with Beyer.[27] We let our horses take us much of the way

---

26 Winding, Horneman, and Matthison-Hansen and their wives had all visited Troldhaugen as guests of the Griegs. Unfortunately, for reasons that Grieg was never able to understand, a feeling of ill will developed between him and Horneman in the course of the visit that permanently poisoned their friendship.

27 Grieg's close friend, Frants Beyer (1851–1918) .

up, then relied on our legs to carry us the rest of the way to the top of the mountain: Helgedalsnåset. What a view! Yes, you still have the best to look forward to!

Last evening I was up on Fløjen[28] with several relatives and a man from Germany. We saw next to nothing, and I couldn't help but think how fortunate we had been that other evening when we saw that beautiful sunset.

Well, all things considered it could have been worse. After all, nothing can be perfect, for as it is written: "Therefore it has been decreed that no tree shall grow up into heaven."[29] And further: Whosoever sees Jehovah shall die![30] However: We did not see Jehovah, so we get to live for awhile on the happy memories! Hopefully—yes, definitely—we will forget the things that are less happy.

I am glad to know that you are safely home, for I had a terrible dream about Clara and Gottfred Matthison-Hansen falling out of the train during the trip!

As to whether we will see each other this fall, who knows? Now there is work to be done, thereafter everything will fall into place of its own accord!

Farewell, dear friends! Warm greetings to you and the children from

Yours truly,
EDVARD GRIEG

10

Leipzig, December 13, 1895
Hotel Hauffe

Dear friend!
Thank you for the letter! I was just about to write when I received it, and here you have me—not, unfortunately, as a precursor of myself in the flesh, for we will not be spending Christmas in Copenhagen as I had hoped. Since I may be conducting someplace or other at the beginning of the new year, it would be impractical not to stay here for the time being. Unfortunately my health is so poor that one fine day—if a change doesn't occur soon—I will just have to give up all public appearances and head north. In that case you will see me, but it is not something to wish for.

And you have had another visit from Mrs. Musa[31] on a grand scale! Good luck! You deserve that she should become a true friend of yours, for it is incredible how much you have grown in recent years. It is as if you have tapped an inner youth; that must be what one gets from happiness and contentment with one's lot in life.

---

[28] Fløjen is one of the mountains overlooking Bergen.

[29] These words appear as a motto at the beginning of Goethe's great work *Dichtung und Wahrheit*: "Es ist dafür gesorgt, dass die Bäume nicht in den Himmel wachsen."

[30] Exodus 33:20, "But," he said, "you cannot see my face; for man shall not see me and live."

[31] "Mrs. Musa": the muse of inspiration.

I am unfortunately not so harmonious, so I'll have to put up with the fact that Mrs. Musa rarely does me the honor of visiting me. I don't think I have ever been more unmusical than during these last months, but then my health has also been worse than usual. Moreover, I am in complete agreement with Mrs. Musa in her dislike for people with bad stomachs, for they are absolutely the most boring creatures on the face of the earth. I have had to get along without her help because I *had to* write a piece for men's chorus[32] for a song festival to be held in Christiania this summer. But in my own opinion, what I have written is just a piece of trash.

"Rather let us sing something more pleasant and more joyful!"[33] Last evening the Gewandhaus orchestra, with Nikisch[34] conducting, gave an absolutely colossal performance of Beethoven's *Seventh Symphony* and [Weber's] *Oberon* overture, and Mrs. Carreño[35] gave a brilliant performance of Chopin's *Piano Concerto* in E minor and Liszt's *Hungarian Fantasy* with orchestra.[36]

But damn these virtuosos with their *Bessermachen*.[37] In the first part of the concerto she decided to play slower in the brilliant passages, thus disrupting the flow, and in the Finale she suddenly decided to take the second theme much slower. There should be punishment for things like that. And the worst part of it was that she bragged about doing it. But then I told her what I thought and added, "Well, at least Chopin is dead so he didn't hear it!" What Weingartner[38] says about *tempo-rubato* conductors applies with equal force to the performing artists: They all suffer from virtuoso- or inflated-ego sickness. And still, Mrs. Carreño is such a sweet person that it irritates me that she is also infected. We had supper with her and Fritzsch[39] in Hotel de Prusse, where she is staying, and then we got a true impression of an unusual and perceptive lady. You know what she has gone through. Now she travels and plays the piano as if the devil were nipping at her heels. We parted at 12 o'clock last night, and at 5:00 this morning she left for Cassel, where she was to have a rehearsal with the orchestra at noon and a concert this evening. Enviable vitality!

Thursday evening you must think of us. Svendsen's B-flat-major symphony[40] will be played in the Gewandhaus as well as my *Peer Gynt Suite No. 1*. I am really

---

[32] Grieg is alluding to *Greetings from Christiania Singers* for baritone solo and male chorus a cappella, text by Norwegian author Jonas Lie.

[33] A passage from Friedrich von Schiller's "Ode to Joy" that Beethoven used in the last movement of his *Ninth Symphony*: "Aber—lasst uns angenehmere Töne anstimmen—und freudenvollere."

[34] Arthur Nikisch (1855–1922) had recently become conductor of the Gewandhaus orchestra in Leipzig.

[35] Venezuelan pianist Teresa Carreño (1853–1917).

[36] Presumably *Fantasie über ungarische Volksmelodien* (1853).

[37] "Bessermachen": attempt to improve on what the composer has written.

[38] German conductor Felix Weingartner (1863–1942).

[39] Leipzig music publisher E W. Fritzsch (1840–1902), who among other things had published the first edition of Grieg's *Piano Concerto* and *String Quartet*.

[40] *Symphony No. 2* in B-flat major.

quite anxious about how it will go, for as brilliant as Nikisch is as a conductor he is not totally free of the *tempo-rubato* nuisance.[41] That is to say, obviously both you and I want some *rubato*, but we want it in the *right* places, not inappropriate ones. That is precisely the point. Beethoven is dangerous in this respect because it is easy to use *rubato* in such a way as to destroy the beautiful architecture.

You talk about Tchaikovsky's *Symphony Pathétique.* And God help you if you had not loved it! Isn't it remarkable! Despite the fact that I must use reflection to understand the unity in the whole work, still all four movements are brilliant. It is so thoroughly Tchaikovsky and so thoroughly masterful. You mention the last movement. Yes, indeed! But how about the first, then? Take it home, study it, and you will be crazy about it.

How splendid it will be to get together in your new flat! Yes, if it doesn't happen sooner we will see you in February in any case. Thank you for the past year and for all your friendship!

Warm greetings to all, also from Nina.

Yours truly,
EDVARD GRIEG

---

[41] Unfortunately, Arthur Nikisch fell ill and the concert was instead conducted by Hans Sitt (1850–1922). See Grieg's letter to Svendsen of December 20, 1895.

Chronological List of Grieg Letters in the Present Volume

Abbreviations: A (Australia), Au (Austria), B (Belgium), (C) Czechoslovakia, D (Denmark), E (England), F (Finland), Fr (France), G (Germany), H (Holland), Hu (Hungary), N (Norway), P (Poland), R (Russia), S (Sweden), Swi (Switzerland), US (United States).

1863

Bergen	Feb 23	Nina Hagerup (D)
Copenhagen	July 14	Nina Hagerup and sisters (D)

1865

Berlin	Oct 22	Louis Hornbeck (D)
Leipzig	Dec 2	Breitkopf & Härtel (G)

1866

Berlin	May 7	Georg Marcus Nordraach (N)
Copenhagen	June 10	Henrik Ibsen (N)
Frascati	Aug 24	Ibsen to Grieg (N)
Christiania	Nov 5	Emil Erslev (D)
Christiania	Nov 21	Chr. F. E. Horneman (D)
Christiania	Dec 12	Gottfred Matthison-Hansen (D)

1867

Christiania	May 5	Chr. F. E. Horneman (D)
Christiania	July 30	Gottfred Matthison-Hansen (D)
Christiania	Oct 8	Gottfred Matthison-Hansen (D)
Christiania	Dec 23	Gottfred Matthison-Hansen (D)
Christiania	Dec 29	Emil Erslev (D)

1868

Christiania	May 4	Breitkopf & Härtel (G)
Christiania	Nov 2	Niels Ravnkilde (D)

1869

Christiania	April 10	Gottfred Matthison-Hansen (D)
Christiania	April 18	Gottfred Matthison-Hansen (D)
Christiania	April 24	Chr. F. E. Horneman (D)
Landås	June 29	Niels Ravnkilde (D)

1870

Rome	Feb 8	Carl Warmuth (N)
Rome	Feb 17	Alexander and Gesine Grieg (N)
Rome	March 1	Gottfred Matthison-Hansen (D)
Rome	April 9	Alexander and Gesine Grieg (N)

1871

Christiania	Oct 12	J. P. E. Hartmann (D)
Christiania	Oct [?]	Johan Selmer (N)

1872

Christiania	April 18	Frants Beyer (N)
Copenhagen	June 17	Bjørnstjerne Bjørnson (N)
Christiania	Oct 26	August Winding (D)

1874

Dresden	Jan 23	Ibsen to Grieg (N)
Dresden	Feb 8	Ibsen to Grieg (N)
Bergen	June 7	Edward Dannreuther (E)
Bergen	July 5	Bjørnstjerne Bjørnson (N)
Bergen	Aug 27	Frants Beyer (N)
Bergen	Aug 28	Ludvig Oscar Josephson (S)
Kristiansand	Sept 12	Bjørnstjerne Bjørnson (N)
Copenhagen	Oct 1	Bjørnstjerne Bjørnson (N)
Christiania	Oct 27	Eduard Wagner (D)

1875

Brobyværk	Jan 2	Bjørnstjerne Bjørnson (N)
Leipzig	Feb 4	August Winding (D)
Leipzig	Feb 21	Bjørnstjerne Bjørnson (N)
Dresden	March 3	Ibsen to Grieg (N)
Leipzig	March 17	Bjørnstjerne Bjørnson (N)
Leipzig	April 5	August Winding (D)
Fredensborg	July 25	Henrik Ibsen (N)
Kitzbühel	Aug 20	Ibsen to Grieg (N)
Bergen	Sept 2	Ludvig Oscar Josephson (S)
Bergen	Sept 28	Ludvig Oscar Josephson (S)
Bergen	Sept 28	August Winding (D)
Bergen	Dec 14	Johan Hennum (N)
Bergen	Dec 17	August Winding (D)

1876

Bergen	March 15	Henrik Ibsen (N)
Munich	March 30	Ibsen to Grieg (N)
Bergen	April 12	Johan Selmer (N)
Bergen	May 2	Bjørnstjerne Bjørnson (N)
Bergen	June 27	John Paulsen (N)

1877

Børve	Aug 13	Gottfred Matthison-Hansen (D)
Børve	Aug 19	John Paulsen (N)

Børve	Sept 2	Frants Beyer (N)
Bergen	Oct 17	Gottfred Matthison-Hansen (D)
Lofthus	Nov 28	August Winding (D)

1878

Lofthus	Feb 10	Gottfred Matthison-Hansen (D)
Bergen	March 7	Gottfred Matthison-Hansen (D)
Lofthus	July 4	Robert Heckmann (G)
Lofthus	July 22	Robert Heckmann (G)
Leipzig	Dec 16	Robert Heckmann (G)

1879

Leipzig	Jan 3	Brahms to Grieg (G)
Lofthus	Aug 9	Modesta Grieg (N)
Leipzig	Sept 8	John Paulsen (N)
Copenhagen	Dec 2	Edward Dannreuther (E)
Copenhagen	Dec 2	Joseph Joachim (Hu)
Copenhagen	Dec 2	Clara Schumann (G)
Copenhagen	Dec 10	Johan A. Budtz Christie (N)

1880

Copenhagen	Jan 4	Francesco Berger (E)
Copenhagen	Jan 8	Clara Schumann (G)
Copenhagen	Jan 16	Francesco Berger (E)
Copenhagen	Jan 27	Johan A. Budtz Christie (N)
Bergen	Nov 14	Gottfred Matthison-Hansen (D)
Bergen	Dec 27	August Winding (D)

1881

Bergen	April 25	Aimar Grønvold (N)
Bergen	April 28	John Paulsen (N)
Bergen	April 29	Gottfred Matthison-Hansen (D)
Karlsbad	June 3	John Paulsen (N)
Bergen	Nov 12	Johan Hennum (N)
Bergen	Dec 8	Angul Hammerich (D)
Bergen	Dec 19	Johan A. Budtz Christie (N)

1882

Karlsbad	May 28	John Paulsen (N)
Christiania	Aug 31	Breitkopf & Härtel (G)
Bergen	Dec 20	Gottfred Matthison-Hansen (D)

1883

Bergen	March 18	Aimar Grønvold (N)
Bergen	April 3	John Paulsen (N)
Bergen	May 23	Max Abraham (G)
Rudolstadt	July 29	Frants Beyer (N)
Leipzig	Oct 17	Frants Beyer (N)
Leipzig	Nov 15	Frants Beyer (N)
Leipzig	Dec 1	Frants Beyer (N)
Amsterdam	Dec 28	Johan A. Budtz Christie (N)
Amsterdam	Dec 29	Frants Beyer (N)

1884

Amsterdam	Jan 10	Carl Warmuth (N)
Rome	Feb 15	Frants Beyer (N)
Rome	Feb 22	Ernst Wilhelm Fritzsch (G)
Rome	March 16	Frants Beyer (N)
Lofthus	July 21	Niels Ravnkilde (D)
Lofthus	Aug 5	Schak Bull (N)
Lofthus	Aug 23	Louis Hornbeck (D)
Lofthus	Aug 26	Charles Harding (E)
Lofthus	Aug 26	Johannes Messchaert (H)
Lofthus	Aug 29	Schak Bull (N)
Lofthus	Sept 28	Agathe Backer Grøndahl (N)
Bergen	Nov 19	Carl Warmuth (N)
Bergen	Dec 17	Niels Ravnkilde (D)

1885

Bergen	March 27	Gottfred Matthison-Hansen (D)
Troldhaugen	April 30	John Paulsen (N)
Bergen	May 10	Breitkopf & Härtel (G)
Troldhaugen	May 25	Johan Selmer (N)
Copenhagen	Nov 14	Sigurd Hals (N)
Copenhagen	Nov 26	John and Marie Grieg (N)
Copenhagen	Dec 21	Robert Henriques (D)

1886

Copenhagen	Jan 5	Frants Beyer (N)
Copenhagen	Jan 16	Robert Henriques (D)
Copenhagen	Feb 14	Niels Ravnkilde (D)
Copenhagen	April 26	Frants Beyer (N)
Troldhaugen	Aug 27	Frants Beyer (N)
Troldhaugen	Sept 3	August Winding (D)
Troldhaugen	Dec 5	Niels Ravnkilde (D)

1887

Troldhaugen	Jan 21	John Paulsen (N)
Troldhaugen	April 24	Robert Henriques (D)
Troldhaugen	Aug 28	Jonas Lie (N)
Karlsbad	Oct 8	Frants Beyer (N)
Karlsbad	Oct 17	Niels Ravnkilde (D)
Leipzig	Nov 22	Frants Beyer (N)
Leipzig	Dec 21	Charles Harding (E)
Leipzig	Dec 25	Frants Beyer (N)

1888

Leipzig	Jan 29	Frants Beyer (N)
Leipzig	Jan 30	Johan A. Budtz Christie (N)
Leipzig	Feb 28	Frederick Delius (E)
Leipzig	Feb 6	Wilhelmina Neruda (C)
Leipzig	Feb 13	Frants Beyer (N)
Leipzig	Feb 20	Jonas Lie (N)
Leipzig	Feb 27	Peter Tchaikovsky (R)
Paris	March 2	Tchaikovsky to Grieg (R)
Leipzig	April 12	Peter Tchaikovsky (R)
Leipzig	April 16	Frederick Delius (E)
London	May 1	Edward Dannreuther (E)
London	May 4	Frants Beyer (N)
London	May 5	Edward Dannreuther (E)

Klin	May 6	Tchaikovsky to Grieg (R)
London	May 10	Adolf Brodsky (R)
London	May 21	Francesco Berger (E)
Brobyværk	May 26	Peter Tchaikovsky (R)
Bergen	July 7	Charles Harding (E)
Hop Station	July 28	Charles Harding (E)
Bergen	Aug 5	Charles Harding (E)
Troldhaugen	Aug 13	Niels Ravnkilde (D)
Klin	Sept 17	Tchaikovsky to Grieg (R)
Bergen	Sept 27	Peter Tchaikovsky (R)
Troldhaugen	Oct 18	Jonas Lie (N)
Bergen	Oct 23	Charles Harding (E)

1889

Bergen	Jan 1	Alexander Bull (N)
Leipzig	Feb 13	Charles Hallé (E)
London	Feb 20	Charles Hallé (E)
London	March 16	Frants Beyer (N)
London	March 22	Hans Lien Brækstad (N)
London	March 23	Hans Lien Brækstad (N)
London	April 1	Alexander Bull (N)
Paris	April 12	Hans Lien Brækstad (N)
Bergen	Sept 14	Paul Klengel (G)
Bergen	Sept 24	Iver Holter (N)
Christiania	Oct 6	Bjørnstjerne Bjørnson (N)
Christiania	Oct 15	Bjørnstjerne Bjørnson (N)
Christiania	Oct 31	Frants Beyer (N)
Christiania	Oct 31	Hans Lien Brækstad (N)
Copenhagen	Nov 21	Angul Hammerich (D)
Brussels	Dec 6	Sigurd Hals (N)
Brussels	Dec 9	Sigurd Hals (N)
Paris	Dec 14	Frants Beyer (N)
Paris	Dec 17	Sigurd Hals (N)

1890

Paris	Jan 11	Frants Beyer (N)
Paris	Jan 15	Vincent d'Indy (Fr)
Leipzig	March 10	Frants Beyer (N)
Bergen	Aug 25	Bjørnstjerne Bjørnson (N)
Copenhagen	Dec 10	Bjørnstjerne Bjørnson (N)
Copenhagen	Dec 25	Bjørnstjerne Bjørnson (N)
Copenhagen	Dec 26	Sigurd Hals (N)
Copenhagen	Dec 29	Arthur de Greef (B)
Copenhagen	Dec 29	Hedwig von Holstein (G)

1891

Copenhagen	Jan 13	Alexander Bull (N)
Copenhagen	Jan 18	Sigurd Hals (N)
Copenhagen	Feb 9	Frants Beyer (N)
Copenhagen	March 15	Ernst Wilhelm Fritzsch (G)
Troldhaugen	June 2	Bjørnstjerne Bjørnson (N)
Troldhaugen	June 17	Iver Holter (N)
Troldhaugen	July 23	Bjørnstjerne Bjørnson (N)
Troldhaugen	Sept 5	Iver Holter (N)
Christiania	Nov 6	Bjørnstjerne Bjørnson (N)

1892

Troldhaugen	Jan 20	Alexander Bull (N)
Troldhaugen	Feb 7	Bjørn Bjørnson (N)
Troldhaugen	Feb 16	Johan Hennum (N)
Troldhaugen	Feb 26	Hedwig von Holstein (G)
Troldhaugen	March 21	Olav Anton Thommessen (N)
Bergen	May 5	Albert Gutmann (Au)
Troldhaugen	June 25	Chr. F. E. Horneman (D)
Troldhaugen	Aug 3	Jonas Lie (N)
Christiania	Oct 27	Hans Lien Brækstad (N)

1893

Leipzig	Jan 20	Hans Richter (Au)
Leipzig	Feb 2	Charles Hallé (E)
Leipzig	Feb 8	J. P. E. Hartmann (D)
Leipzig	Feb 8	Johan Hennum (N)
Leipzig	Feb 9	Harry Randall (N)
Menton	April 4	Robert U. Johnson (US)
Grefsen Baths	June 7	Robert U. Johnson (US)
Troldhaugen	July 15	Arthur de Greef (B)
Bergen	July 18	Robert U. Johnson (US)
Christiania	Oct 4	Robert U. Johnson (US)
Copenhagen	Dec 28	Olav Anton Thommessen (N)

1894

Copenhagen	Jan 18	Carl Nielsen (D)
Copenhagen	Feb 12	Clara Schumann (G)
Leipzig	Feb 12	Sedley Taylor (E)
Geneva	March 16	Iver Holter (N)
Menton	March 21	Jonas Lie (N)
Menton	April 4	Alexander Bull (N)
London	May 6	Frants Beyer (N)
Grefsen Baths	June 5	Carl Rabe (N)
Troldhaugen	July 28	Ellen Gulbranson (S/N)
Troldhaugen	Aug 17	Nordahl Rolfsen (N)
Copenhagen	Nov 9	Oscar Meyer (G)
Copenhagen	Nov 28	Albert Gutmann (Au)
Copenhagen	Dec 29	Frants Beyer (N)
Copenhagen	Dec 29	Carl Rabe (N)

1895

Copenhagen	Feb 12	Johan Halvorsen (N)
Copenhagen	Feb 22	Albert Gutmann (Au)
Copenhagen	March 2	Albert Gutmann (Au)
Copenhagen	March 14	Bjørn Bjørnson (N)
Copenhagen	March 23	Albert Gutmann (Au)
Copenhagen	March 25	Johan Halvorsen (N)
Copenhagen	April 1	Monastier-Schroeder (Swi)
Troldhaugen	June 3	Chr. F. E. Horneman (D)
Troldhaugen	Aug 16	August Winding (D)
Troldhaugen	Sept 9	Louis Hornbeck (D)
Troldhaugen	Sept 11	Ellen Gulbranson (S/N)
Leipzig	Oct 27	Frants Beyer (N)
Leipzig	Nov 6	Bella Edwards (D)
Leipzig	Nov 15	Bella Edwards (D)
Leipzig	Nov 16	Adolf Brodsky (R)

Leipzig	Nov 19	Johan Svendsen (N)
Leipzig	Nov 25	Gottfred Matthison-Hansen (D)
Leipzig	Dec 5	Bella Edwards (D)
Leipzig	Dec 9	Adolf Brodsky (R)
Leipzig	Dec 13	August Winding (D)
Leipzig	Dec 20	Johan Svendsen (N)
Leipzig	Dec 24	Bella Edwards (D)
Leipzig	Dec 25	Adolf Brodsky (R)
Leipzig	Dec 30	Bella Edwards (D)
1896		
Leipzig	Jan 12	Iver Holter (N)
Leipzig	Jan 19	Gerhard Armauer Hansen (N)
Leipzig	Jan 24	Frants Beyer (N)
Leipzig	Jan 27	Bella Edwards (D)
Leipzig	March 5	Bjørnstjerne Bjørnson (N)
Leipzig	March 28	Iver Holter (N)
Leipzig	April 1	Johannes Brahms (G)
Leipzig	April 2	Johan Halvorsen (N)
Vienna	April 4	Brahms to Grieg (G)
Leipzig	April 9	Johannes Brahms (G)
Vienna	April 17	Brahms to Grieg (G)
Troldhaugen	July 1	Bjørnstjerne Bjørnson (N)
Troldhaugen	July 15	Bjørnstjerne Bjørnson (N)
Fossli	Aug 8	Robert U. Johnson (US)
Troldhaugen	Sept 15	Chr. F. E. Horneman (D)
Christiania	Oct 17	Ellen Gulbranson (S/N)
Christiania	Nov 5	Frants Beyer (N)
Vienna	Nov 18	Robert U. Johnson (US)
Vienna	Dec 23	Ernst Wilhelm Fritzsch (G)
Semmering	Dec 27	Frants Beyer (N)
1897		
Vienna	Jan 3	Julius Röntgen (H)
Vienna	Jan 8	Iver Holter (N)
Leipzig	Jan 14	Sigurd Hals (N)
Leipzig	Jan 26	Johan Halvorsen (N)
Amsterdam	Feb 9	Iver Holter (N)
Amsterdam	Feb 27	Ernst Wilhelm Fritzsch (G)
Amsterdam	March 4	Frants Beyer (N)
Copenhagen	March 21	John Theodor Lund (N)
Copenhagen	April 4	Iver Holter (N)
Troldhaugen	May 28	Agathe Backer Grøndahl (N)
Troldhaugen	July 10	Bjørnstjerne Bjørnson (N)
Bergen	July 13	Francesco Berger (E)
Troldhaugen	Sept 3	Adolf Brodsky (R)
Troldhaugen	Oct 2	Julius Röntgen (H)
Copenhagen	Oct 10	Iver Holter (N)
London	Nov 8	Joachim Grieg (N)
London	Nov 11	Johan Selmer (N)
London	Dec 6	Hans Lien Brækstad (N)
London	Dec 8	Hans Lien Brækstad (N)
London	Dec 10	Frants Beyer (N)
London	Dec 16	Joachim Grieg (N)
Amsterdam	Dec 25	Iver Holter (N)
1898		
Amsterdam	Jan 1	Iver Holter (N)
Leipzig	Jan 13	Arne Garborg (N)
Leipzig	Jan 25	Iver Holter (N)
Leipzig	Feb 4	Frants Beyer (N)
Leipzig	Feb 6	Hans Lien Brækstad (N)
Leipzig	Feb 18	Agathe Backer Grøndahl (N)
Leipzig	Feb 23	Hans Lien Brækstad (N)
Leipzig	Feb 25	Thorvald Lammers (N)
Leipzig	March 10	Thorvald Lammers (N)
Leipzig	March 27	Frants Beyer (N)
Copenhagen	April 28	Willem Mengelberg (H)
Troldhaugen	June 2	Iver Holter (N)
Troldhaugen	June 7	Oscar Meyer (G)
Troldhaugen	July 15	John Paulsen (N)
Troldhaugen	July 26	Robert Henriques (D)
Troldhaugen	July 27	Adolf Brodsky (R)
Troldhaugen	Aug 9	Hans Lien Brækstad (N)
Troldhaugen	Aug 18	Hulda Garborg (N)
Troldhaugen	Aug 18	Oscar Meyer (G)
Troldhaugen	Aug 20	Gerhard Schjelderup (N)
Troldhaugen	Sept 30	Hans Lien Brækstad (N)
Troldhaugen	Sept 30	Olav Anton Thommessen (N)
Odnes	Oct 28	John and Marie Grieg (N)
Odnes	Oct 29	Johannes Messchaert (H)
Fuglsang	Dec 25	Henrik Ibsen (N)
1899		
Copenhagen	Jan 10	Henrik Ibsen (N)
Christiania	Jan 13	Ibsen to Grieg (N)
Copenhagen	Jan 16	Henrik Ibsen (N)
Copenhagen	Feb 3	Aimar Grønvold (N)
Rome	March 31	Johan Halvorsen (N)
Christiania	Sept 7	Tor Aulin (S)
Aulestad	Sept 12	Édouard Colonne (Fr)
Christiania	Sept 14	Bjørnstjerne Bjørnson (N)
Copenhagen	Oct 2	Bjørnstjerne Bjørnson (N)
Copenhagen	Oct 4	Édouard Colonne (Fr)
Copenhagen	Oct 5	Édouard Colonne (Fr)
Copenhagen	Oct 26	Edward MacDowell (US)
Stockholm	Nov 9	Arne Garborg (N)
Copenhagen	Nov 25	Frants Beyer (N)
1900		
Copenhagen	Jan 1	Gerhard Schjelderup (N)
Copenhagen	Jan 16	Bjørnstjerne Bjørnson (N)
Copenhagen	Jan 16	Olaus Andreas Grøndahl (N)
Copenhagen	Feb 23	Henry T. Finck (US)
Copenhagen	March 26	Robert Henriques (D)
Copenhagen	April 13	Henry T. Finck (US)

Troldhaugen	May 19	Otto Benzon (D)
Troldhaugen	June 4	Otto Benzon (D)
Troldhaugen	June 21	Olav Anton Thommessen (N)
Troldhaugen	June 30	Edward MacDowell (US)
Troldhaugen	July 17	Henry T. Finck (US)
Troldhaugen	Aug 22	Otto Benzon (D)
Troldhaugen	Sept 1	Otto Benzon (D)
Hop	Sept [?]	Lymon Judson Gage (US)
Troldhaugen	Sept 24	Henry T. Finck (US)
Voksenkollen	Dec 5	Max Abraham (G)
Voksenkollen	Dec 9	Henri Hinrichsen (G)
Christiania	Dec 21	Henry T. Finck (US)
Voksenkollen	Dec 29	John Paulsen (N)

1901

Voksenkollen	Jan 2	Børre Giertsen (N)
Copenhagen	Feb 13	Jonas Lie (N)
Copenhagen	March 2	Thorvald Lammers (N)
Copenhagen	March 2	Johannes Messchaert (H)
Copenhagen	March 11	John Theodor Lund (N)
Copenhagen	April 1	John Theodor Lund (N)
Copenhagen	April 8	Edward MacDowell (US)
Troldhaugen	June 14	Henry T. Finck (US)
Troldhaugen	Sept 30	Henry T. Finck (US)
Troldhaugen	Oct 18	Knut Dahle (N)
Troldhaugen	Oct 18	Johan Halvorsen (N)
Troldhaugen	Oct 20	Gerhard Schjelderup (N)
Troldhaugen	Oct 25	Knut Dahle (N)
Troldhaugen	Oct 25	Gottfred Matthison-Hansen (D)
Troldhaugen	Nov 4	Knut Dahle (N)
Troldhaugen	Nov 4	Johan Halvorsen (N)
Troldhaugen	Nov 6	John Paulsen (N)
Troldhaugen	Nov 23	Johan Halvorsen (N)
Troldhaugen	Dec 6	Johan Halvorsen (N)

1902

Bergen	Jan 11	Edward MacDowell (US)
Bergen	Jan 13	Gerhard Schjelderup (N)
Copenhagen	Feb [?]	George Augener (E)
Copenhagen	March 1	Frants Beyer (N)
Copenhagen	March 12	George Riseley (E)
Copenhagen	April 30	Sigurd Hals (N)
Troldhaugen	July 10	Alexander Siloti (R)
Troldhaugen	Aug 26	Alexander Siloti (R)
Troldhaugen	Aug 28	Albert Langen (G)
Troldhaugen	Sept 15	Iver Holter (N)
Troldhaugen	Sept 22	Édouard Colonne (Fr)
Troldhaugen	Sept 25	Alexander Siloti (R)
Troldhaugen	Oct [?]	Édouard Colonne (Fr)
Bergen	Oct 29	Mojmir Urbánek (C)
Christiania	Dec 14	Gottfred Matthison-Hansen (D)

1903

Christiania	Jan 16	Henry T. Finck (US)
Voksenkollen	Feb 10	Edvard Neovius (F)
Berlin	March 27	Édouard Colonne (Fr)
Berlin	March 28	Olav Anton Thommessen (N)
Berlin	April 1	Børre Giertsen (N)
Berlin	April 16	Johan Halvorsen (N)
Paris	April 20	John Grieg (publisher) (N)
Paris	April 21	Frants Beyer (N)
Paris	April 23	Johan Halvorsen (N)
Paris	May 2	M.-D. Calvocoressi (Fr)
Berlin	May 17	Alexander Siloti (R)
Copenhagen	May 20	Gerhard Schjelderup (N)
Bergen	May 30	Johan Halvorsen (N)
Troldhaugen	June 26	Georg Brandes (D)
Troldhaugen	June 26	Jean Sibelius (F)
Troldhaugen	June 26	Johan Svendsen (N)
Troldhaugen	Aug 23	Monastier-Schroeder (Swi)
Troldhaugen	Aug 25	Paul Klengel (G)
Troldhaugen	Aug 28	Charles Harding (E)
Troldhaugen	Sept 3	Gerhard Schjelderup (N)
Bergen	Sept 16	Albert Langen (G)
Bergen	Sept 18	Gerhard Schjelderup (N)
Christiania	Nov 16	Hakon Børresen (D)
Eidsvoll	Dec 22	Julius Steenberg (D)

1904

Aulestad	Jan 2	Albert Gutmann (Au)
Aulestad	Jan 17	Edvard Neovius (F)
Christiania	Feb 12	Alexander Siloti (R)
Christiania	April 11	Gerhard Schjelderup (N)
Christiania	May 11	Gerhard Schjelderup (N)
Troldhaugen	June 29	Gottfred Matthison-Hansen (D)
Troldhaugen	July 21	Tor Aulin (S)
Troldhaugen	Aug 14	Johan A. Budtz Christie (N)
Troldhaugen	Aug 16	Albert Langen (G)
Christiania	Oct 23	Julius Steenberg (D)
Christiania	Oct 29	Alexander Siloti (R)
Christiania	Nov 17	Frants Beyer (N)
Christiania	Dec 7	Bjørnstjerne Bjørnson (N)
Christiania	Dec 20	Bjørnstjerne Bjørnson (N)

1905

Copenhagen	Feb 22	Bjørnstjerne Bjørnson (N)
Copenhagen	Feb 28	Johan Halvorsen (N)
Copenhagen	March 1	Olav Anton Thommessen (N)
Copenhagen	March 6	Bjørnstjerne Bjørnson (N)
Copenhagen	March 9	Albert Langen (G)
Copenhagen	April 2	Georg Brandes (D)
Copenhagen	April 4	Joachim Grieg (N)
Copenhagen	April 18	Carl Nielsen (D)
Copenhagen	April 26	Adolf Brodsky (R)
Copenhagen	May 2	Henry T. Finck (US)
Copenhagen	May 13	Bjørnstjerne Bjørnson (N)
Copenhagen	May 13	Gerhard Schjelderup (N)
Copenhagen	May 17	Thomas B. Barratt (N)

Gothenburg	May 24	Johan Svendsen (N)
Christiania	May 29	Adolf Brodsky (R)
Christiania	June 4	John Paulsen (N)
Troldhaugen	June 22	Henry T. Finck (US)
Troldhaugen	June 29	Tor Aulin (S)
Troldhaugen	July 30	Henry T. Finck (US)
Troldhaugen	July 31	Alexander Rajchmann (P)
Troldhaugen	Aug 4	Frants Beyer (N)
Troldhaugen	Aug 4	Sigurd Hals (N)
Troldhaugen	Aug 7	Albert Langen (G)
Troldhaugen	Aug 29	Gottfred Matthison-Hansen (D)
Troldhaugen	Sept 2	Henrik Hennings (D)
Troldhaugen	Sept 4	Henry T. Finck (US)
Christiania	Sept 23	Christian Michelsen (N)
Christiania	Sept 29	Henry T. Finck (US)
Christiania	Oct 8	Henry T. Finck (US)
Christiania	Oct 9	Tor Aulin (S)
Christiania	Oct 15	Monastier-Schroeder (Swi)
Christiania	Oct 25	Frants Beyer (N)
Christiania	Oct 26	Gerhard Schjelderup (N)
Christiania	Nov 5	Johan Svendsen (N)
Christiania	Nov 12	Agathe Backer Grøndahl (N)
Christiania	Nov 17	Agathe Backer Grøndahl (N)
Christiania	Nov 20	Johan Svendsen (N)
Christiania	Dec 7	Iver Holter (N)
Christiania	Dec 11	Henri Hinrichsen (G)
Christiania	Dec 12	Frants Beyer (N)
Christiania	Dec 12	Gottfred Matthison-Hansen (D)
Christiania	Dec 14	Marian MacDowell (US)
Christiania	Dec 20	Frants Beyer (N)
Christiania	Dec 30	Henry T. Finck (US)
1906		
Christiania	Jan 6	Frants Beyer (N)
Christiania	Jan 8	Ernst von Dohnányi (Hu)
Christiania	Jan 14	Frants Beyer (N)
Christiania	Jan 25	Adolf Brodsky (R)
Christiania	Feb 5	Tor Aulin (S)
Christiania	Feb 12	Oscar Meyer (G)
London	May 16	Fridtjof Nansen (N)
London	May 18	Olav Anton Thommessen (N)
London	May 23	Sigurd Hals (N)
London	May 26	Agathe Backer Grøndahl (N)
Troldhaugen	June 30	Percy Grainger (A/US)
Troldhaugen	July 3	Monastier-Schroeder (Swi)
Troldhaugen	July 4	Gerhard Schjelderup (N)
Troldhaugen	Aug 5	Walter Niemann (G)
Troldhaugen	Aug 20	Adolf Brodsky (R)
Christiania	Oct 20	Robert Henriques (D)
Christiania	Nov 12	Bergen Public Library (N)
Christiania	Nov 27	Percy Grainger (A/US)
Christiania	Dec 4	Gerhard Schjelderup (N)
Christiania	Dec 6	Albert Gutmann (Au)
Christiania	Dec 10	Johan Halvorsen (N)
Christiania	Dec 14	Adolf Brodsky (R)
Christiania	Dec 19	Frants Beyer (N)
Christiania	Dec 19	Gottfred Matthison-Hansen (D)
Christiania	Dec 23	Albert Gutmann (Au)
1907		
Christiania	Jan 17	Percy Grainger (A/US)
Christiania	Feb 26	Percy Grainger (A/US)
Christiania	Feb 26	Oscar Meyer (G)
Christiania	Feb 27	Agathe Backer Grøndahl (N)
Holmenkollen	March 7	Carl Nielsen (D)
Christiania	March 10	Percy Grainger (A/US)
Copenhagen	March 20	Carl Nielsen (D)
Leipzig	April 19	Frants Beyer (N)
Copenhagen	May 3	Frants Beyer (N)
Copenhagen	May 15	Agathe Backer Grøndahl (N)
Copenhagen	May 16	Bjørnstjerne Bjørnson (N)
Skodsborg	May 28	Percy Grainger (A/US)
Skodsborg	May 29	Frants Beyer (N)
Skodsborg	June 1	Fridtjof Backer-Grøndahl (N)
Skodsborg	June 7	Peter Vogt Fischer (N)
Troldhaugen	June 30	Percy Grainger (A/US)
Troldhaugen	July 17	Edvard Neovius (F)
Troldhaugen	Aug 5	Hakon Børresen (D)
Troldhaugen	Aug 11	Percy Grainger (A/US)
Troldhaugen	Aug 16	Alexander Siloti (R)
Bergen	Aug 28	Monastier-Schroeder (Swi)

List of Compositions

This list consists of two parts. The first part comprises the compositions with opus numbers as assigned by Grieg himself. The second part lists the remaining compositions with the "EG" numbers assigned in Vol. 20 of *Edvard Grieg: Complete Works.* Titles in the language used in the original composition are given in parentheses following the corresponding English titles. The entry "*GGA* vol. *n*, 19xx" signifies that the composition was printed for the first time in *Edvard Grieg: Complete Works* vol. *n*, published in the year indicated. Numbers in brackets refer to the List of Compositions in Finn Benestad and Dag Schjelderup-Ebbe, *Edvard Grieg: The Man and the Artist,* University of Nebraska Press, 1988.

All of Grieg's compositions are printed in *Edvard Grieg: Complete Works* vols. 1–20, C. F. Peters Musikverlag, Frankfurt/Leipzig/London/New York 1977–95, published under the auspices of the Edvard Grieg Committee, Oslo, Norway. The English titles employed below (and throughout the present volume) are the ones used in the C. F. Peters edition of Grieg's works.

A. Compositions with Opus Numbers

Op. 1. Four Piano Pieces (*Vier Stücke für das Pianoforte*)
1861.

Op. 2. Four Songs (*Vier Lieder*)
Voice/piano, 1861.
1. The Maid of the Mill (*Die Müllerin*) (Chamisso)
2. Closely Wrapped in Misty Billows (*Eingehüllt in graue Wolken*) (Heine)
3. I Stood Before Her Portrait (*Ich stand in dunkeln Träumen*) (Heine)
4. What Shall I Say (*Was soll ich sagen?*) (Chamisso)

Op. 3. Poetic Tone Pictures (*Poetiske tonebilder*)
(1–6) Piano, 1863.

Op. 4. Six Songs. (*Sechs Lieder*)
Voice/piano, 1863–64.
1. The Orphan (*Die Waise*) (Chamisso)
2. Morning Dew (*Morgentau*) (Chamisso)
3. Parting (*Abschied*) (Heine)
4. Hunting Song (*Jägerlied*) (Uhland)
5. The Old Song (*Das alte Lied*) (Heine)
6. Where Have They Gone? (*Wo sind sie hin?*)(Heine)

Op. 5. Melodies of the Heart (*Hjertets Melodier*)
(H. C. Andersen). Voice/piano, 1864–65.
1. Two Brown Eyes (*To brune Øjne*)
2. The Poet's Heart (*Du fatter ej Bølgernes evige Gang*)
3. I Love But Thee (*Jeg elsker dig*)
4. My Mind is Like a Mountain Steep (*Min Tanke er et mægtigt Fjeld*)

Op. 6. Humoresques (*Humoresker*)
(1–4). Piano, 1865.

Op. 7. Piano Sonata in E Minor (*Klaversonate i e-moll*)
Four movements, 1865.

Op. 8. Violin Sonata No. 1 in F Major (*Fiolinsonate nr. 1 i F-dur*)
Three movements. Violin/piano, 1865.

Op. 9. Songs and Ballads (*Romancer og Ballader*)
(Andreas Munch). Voice/piano, 1863–66.
1. The Harp (*Harpen*)
2. Cradle Song (*Vuggesang*)
3. Sunset (*Solnedgang*)
4. Outward Bound (*Udfarten*)

Op. 10. Four Songs (*Fire Romancer*)
(Christian Winther). Voice/piano, 1864–66.
1. Thanks (*Taksigelse*)
2. Woodland Song (*Skovsang*)
3. Song of the Flowers (*Blomsterne tale*)
4. Song on the Mountain (*Sang på Fjeldet*)

Op. 11. In Autumn (*I Høst*)
A Fantasy for piano four hands, 1866.

Revised and arranged for symphony orchestra 1887 with the title: In Autumn. Concert Overture (*I Høst. Koncertouverture*).

Op. 12. Lyric Pieces I (*Lyriske stykker I*)
Piano, 1864(?)–67.
1. Arietta (*Arietta*)
2. Waltz (*Vals*)
3. Watchman's Song (*Vektersang*)
4. Fairy Dance (*Alfedans*)
5. Folk song (*Folkevise*)
6. Norwegian (*Norsk*)
7. Album Leaf (*Albumblad*)
8. National Song (*Fædrelandssang*)

Op. 13. Violin Sonata No. 2 in G Major (*Fiolinsonate nr. 2 i G-dur*)
Three movements. Violin/piano, 1867.

Op. 14. Two Symphonic Pieces (*To symfoniske stykker*)
(*Deux pièces symphoniques*), 1869.
Arrangement for piano four hands of the 2nd and 3rd movements from Symphony in C Minor, EG 119.

Op. 15. Four Songs (*Romancer*)
Voice/piano, 1864–68.
1. Margaret's Cradle Song (*Margretes Vuggesang*) (Henrik Ibsen)
2. Love (*Kjærlighed*) (H. C. Andersen)
3. Folk Song from Langeland (*Langelandsk Folkemelodi*) (H. C. Andersen)
4. A Mother's Grief (*Modersorg*) (Christian Richardt)

Op. 16. Piano Concerto in A Minor (*Klaverkonsert i a-moll*)
Three movements, 1868.

Op. 17. Twenty-five Norwegian Folk Songs and Dances (*25 Norske folkeviser og danser*)
Piano, 1870.
1. Springdans (*Springdans*)
2. The Swain (*Ungersvennen*)
3. Springdans (*Springdans*)
4. Nils Tallefjorden (*Nils Tallefjorden*)
5. Dance from Jølster (*Jølstring*)
6. Wedding Tune (*Brurelåt*)
7. Halling (*Halling*)
8. The Pig (*Grisen*)
9. Religious Song (*Når mit øye*)
10. The Wooer's Song (*Friervise*)
11. Heroic Ballad (*Kjempevise*)
12. Solfager and the Snake King (*Solfager og Ormekongen*)
13. Wedding March (*Reiselåt*)
14. I Sing with a Sorrowful Heart (*Jeg sjunger med sorrigfuldt hjerte*)
15. Last Saturday Evening (*Den siste lørdagskvelden*)
16. I Know a Little Maiden (*Eg veit ei lita jente*)
17. The Gadfly and the Fly (*Kleggen og fluga*)
18. Peasant Dance (*Stabbelåten*)
19. Hølje Dale (*Hølje Dale*)
20. Halling (*Halling*)
21. The Woman from Setesdal (*Sæbygga*)
22. Cow Call (*So lokka me over den myra*)
23. Peasant Song (*Så du nokke kjerringa mi*)
24. Wedding Tune (*Brurelåt*)
25. The Ravens' Wedding (*Rabnabryllaup i Kråkelund*)

Op. 18. Nine Songs (*Romancer og Sange*)
Voice/piano, 1865–69.
1. Moonlit Forest (*Vandring i Skoven*) (H. C. Andersen)
2. My Darling is as White as Snow (*Hun er så hvid*) (H. C. Andersen)
3. The Poet's Farewell (*En Digters sidste Sang*) (H. C. Andersen)
4. Autumn Storm (*Efteraarsstormen*) (Christian Richardt)
5. Poesy (*Poesien*) (H. C. Andersen)
6. The Young Birch Tree (*Ungbirken*) (Jørgen Moe)
7. The Cottage (*Hytten*) (H. C. Andersen)
8. The Rosebud (*Rosenknoppen*) (H. C. Andersen)
9. Serenade for Welhaven (*Serenade til J. S. Welhaven*) (Bjørnstjerne Bjørnson)

Op. 19. Pictures from Folk Life (*Folkelivsbilder*)
Piano, 1869–71.
1. In the Mountains (*Fjellslått*)
2. Bridal Procession (*Brudefølget drar forbi*)
3. From the Carnival (*Fra karnevalet*)

Op. 20. Before a Southern Convent (*Foran Sydens Kloster*)
Two pieces from B. Bjørnson's *Arnljot Gelline.* Soprano and alto soloists/women's chorus/

piano, 1871. For soprano and alto soloists/ women's chorus/orchestra, 1890.

1. Who Knocks so Late at the Cloister Door? (*Hvem banker så silde på klosterets port?*)
2. From Guilt, from Sin, to God Come In (*Kom barn, kom brud*)

Op. 21. Four Songs from B. Bjørnson's "Fisher Maiden" (*Fire Digte fra Bjørnsons "Fiskerjenten"*)

Voice/piano, 1870–72.

1. The First meeting (*Det første møde*)
2. Good Morning (*God morgen*)
3. To Springtime My Song I'm Singing (*Jeg giver mit digt til våren*)
4. Say What You Will (*Tak for dit råd*)

Op. 22. Sigurd the Crusader (*Sigurd Jorsalfar*)

Incidental music to B. Bjørnson's play, 1872. Complete score printed in *GGA* 19, 1988. See also op. 56.

1. Prelude to Act 1. (*Forspill til 1. akt*) Orchestra
2. Borghild's Dream (*Borghilds drøm*) (Act 1). Orchestra
3. At the Matching Game (*Ved mannjevningen*). March (Introduction to Act 2). Orchestra
4. Northland Folk (*Kvad*) (End of Act 2). Tenor solo/male chorus/orchestra
5. Homage March (*Hyldningsmarsj*) (Act 3). Orchestra
6. Interlude I (*Mellomspill I*) (Act 3). Orchestra
7. Interlude II (*Mellomspill II*) (Act 3). Orchestra
8. The King's Song (*Kongekvadet*) (Act 3). Tenor solo/male chorus/orchestra

Op. 23. Peer Gynt (*Peer Gynt*)

Incidental music to H. Ibsen's play. Comp. 1874–75, rev. 1885, 1887–88, 1890–92 and 1901–02. Complete score printed in *GGA* 18, 1988. See also opp. 46 and 55.

Act I

1. Prelude. At the Wedding (*Forspill. I bryllupsgården*). Orchestra
2. Halling (*Halling*). Violin solo
3. Springdans (*Springdans*). Violin solo

Act II

4. Prelude. The Abduction of the Bride. Ingrid's Lament (*Forspill. Bruderovet. Ingrids klage*). Orchestra
5. Peer Gynt and the Herd Girls (*Peer Gynt og seterjentene*). Voice/melodrama
6. Peer Gynt and the Woman in Green (*Peer Gynt og Den Grønnkledte*). Orchestra
7. Peer Gynt: "You can tell great men by the style of their mounts" (*Peer Gynt: "På ridestellet skal storfolk kjennes."*) Orchestra
8. In the Hall of the Mountain King (*I Dovregubbens hall*). Orchestra and chorus
9. Dance of the Mountain King's Daughter (*Dans av Dovregubbens datter*). Orchestra
10. Peer Gynt Hunted by the Trolls (*Peer Gynt jages av troll*). Melodrama
11. Peer Gynt and the Bøyg (*Scene med Bøygen*). Melodrama and chorus

Act III

12. The Death of Åse (*Åses død*). Orchestra

Act IV

13. Prelude. Morning Mood (*Forspill. Morgenstemning*). Orchestra
14. The Thief and the Receiver (*Tyven og heleren*). Two bass voices/orchestra
15. Arabian Dance (*Arabisk dans*). Soprano solo/women's chorus/orchestra
16. Anitra's Dance (*Anitras dans*). Orchestra
17. Peer Gynt's Serenade (*Peer Gynts serenade*). Baritone solo/orchestra
18. Peer Gynt and Anitra (*Peer Gynt og Anitra*). Melodrama
19. Solveig's Song (*Solveigs sang*). Soprano solo/orchestra
20. Peer Gynt at the Statue of Memnon (*Peer Gynt ved Memnonstatuen*). Orchestra

Act V

21. Prelude. Peer Gynt's Homecoming. [Stormy Evening on the Sea]. (*Forspill. Peer Gynts hjemfart. [Stormfull aften på havet]*). Orchestra
22. The Shipwreck (*Skipsforliset*). Orchestra
23. Solveig Sings in the Hut (*Solveigs sang i hytten*). Soprano solo/mixed chorus/ string orchestra
24. Night Scene (*Nattscene*). Melodrama
25. Whitsun Hymn: "Oh Blessed Morning" (*Kirkefolk synger på skogstien*). Mixed chorus
26. Solveig's Cradle Song (*Solveigs vuggevise*). Soprano solo/mixed choir/orchestra

Op. 24. Ballade in G Minor (*Ballade i g-moll*)
(Ballade in the Form of Variations on a Norwegian Melody). Piano, 1875–76.

Op. 25. Six Songs (*Sex Digte af Henrik Ibsen*)
(Henrik Ibsen). Voice/piano, 1876.
1. Fiddlers (*Spillemænd*)
2. A Swan (*En Svane*)
3. Album Lines (*Stambogsrim*)
4. With a Water Lily (*Med en vandlilje*)
5. Departed! (*Borte*)
6. A Bird-Song (*En fuglevise*)

Op. 26. Five Songs (*Fem Digte af John Paulsen*)
(John Paulsen). Voice/piano, 1876.
1. Hope (*Et Håb*)
2. I Walked One Balmy Summer Eve (*Jeg reiste en deilig Sommerkvæld*)
3. You Whispered That You Loved Me (*Den Ærgjerrige*)
4. The First Primrose (*Med en Primula veris*)
5. Autumn Thoughts (*På Skogstien*)

Op. 27. String Quartet No. 1 in G Minor (*Strykekvartett nr. 1, g-moll*)
Four movements, 1877–78.

Op. 28. Album Leaves (*Fire albumblad*)
1–4, piano, 1864–78.

Op. 29. Improvisations on Two Norwegian Folk Songs (*Improvisata over to norske folkeviser*)
Piano, 1878.

Op. 30. Album for Male Voices (*Album for mannssang*)
Male chorus/soloists, "freely adapted from Norwegian folk songs", 1877–78.
1. I Lay Down So Late (*Jeg lagde mig så sildig*)
2. Children's Song (*Bådn-låt*). Humoresque.
3. Little Torø (*Torø liti*)
4. Kvålin's Halling (*Kvålins halling*)
5. It Is the Greatest Foolishness (*Dæ æ den største Dårleheit*)
6. Springdans (*Går e ut ein Kveld. Springdans*)
7. Young Ole (*Han Ole*)
8. Halling (*Halling*)
9. Fairest Among Women (*Dejligste blandt Kvinder*)
10. The Great White Host (*Den store, hvite flokk*)
11. The Gypsy Lad (*Fantegutten*)
12. Røtnams-Knut (*Røtnams-Knut*)

Op. 31. Land-sighting (*Landkjenning*)
(Bjørnstjerne Bjørnson). Baritone solo/male chorus/harmonium, 1872. Rev. and arr. for baritone solo/male chorus/orchestra, 1881.

Op. 32. The Mountain Thrall (*Den Bergtekne*)
(Text from Landstad's *Norwegian Folk Ballads* [*Norske Folkeviser*], 1853). Baritone solo/string orchestra/two horns, 1877–78.

Op. 33. Twelve Songs to Poems by A. O. Vinje (*12 Melodier til Digte af A. O. Vinje*)
Voice/piano, 1873–80.
1. The Youth (*Guten*)
2. Last Spring (*Våren*)
3. The Wounded Heart (*Den Særde*)
4. The Berry (*Tytebæret*)
5. Beside the Stream (*Langs ei Å*)
6. A Vision (*Eit Syn*)
7. The Old Mother (*Gamle Mor*)
8. The First Thing (*Det Første*)
9. At Rondane (*Ved Rondane*)
10. A Piece on Friendship (*Eit vennestykke*)
11. Faith (*Trudom*)
12. The Goal (*Fyremål*)

Op. 34. Two Elegiac Melodies (*To elegiske melodier*)
String orchestra, 1880.
1. The Wounded Heart (*Hjertesår* ["*Den Særde*"])
2. Last Spring (*Våren*)

Op. 35. Norwegian Dances (*Norske danser*)
Four pieces for piano four hands, 1880.

Op. 36. Cello Sonata in A Minor (*Cellosonate i a-moll*)
Three movements. Cello/piano, 1883.

Op. 37. Waltz Caprices (*Valse-kapriser*)
Two pieces for piano four hands, 1883.

Op. 38. Lyric Pieces II (*Lyriske stykker II*)
Piano, 1883.
1. Cradle Song (*Berceuse*)

2. Folk Song (*Folkevise*)
3. Melody (*Melodi*)
4. Halling (*Halling*)
5. Springdans (*Springdans*)
6. Elegy (*Elegi*)
7. Waltz (*Vals*)
8. Canon (*Kanon*)

Op. 39. Six Songs [Older and Newer] (*Romancer [ældre og nyere]*)
Voice/piano, 1869–84.
1. From Monte Pincio (*Fra Monte Pincio*) (B. Bjørnson)
2. Hidden Love (*Dulgt Kjærlighed*) (B. Bjørnson)
3. Upon a Grassy Hillside (*I Liden højt deroppe*) (Jonas Lie)
4. Among Roses (*Millom Rosor*) (Kristofer Janson)
5. At the Grave of a Young Wife (*Ved en ung Hustrus Båre*) (O. P. Monrad)
6. Hearing a Song or Carol (*Hører jeg Sangen klinge*) (Heine, trans. Nordahl Rolfsen)

Op. 40. From Holberg's Time [Holberg Suite] (*Fra Holberge tid [Holberg-suiten]*)
Suite in Olden Style. Piano, 1884. Arr. for string orchestra, 1885.
1. Preludium (*Preludium*)
2. Sarabande (*Sarabande*)
3. Gavotte (*Gavotte*)
4. Air (*Air*)
5. Rigaudon (*Rigaudon*)

Op. 41. Transcriptions of Original Songs I (*Klaverstykker etter egne sanger I*)
Piano, 1884.
1. Cradle Song (*Vuggesang*) (op. 9, no. 2)
2. Little Håkon [Margaret's Cradle Song] (*Lille Håkon [Margretes vuggesang]*) (op. 15, no. 1)
3. I Love But Thee (*Jeg elsker dig*) (op. 5, no. 1)
4. She Is So White (*Hun er så hvid*) (op. 18, no. 2)
5. The Princess (*Prinsessen*) (EG 133)
6. To Springtime My Song I'm Singing (*Til våren [Jeg giver mit digt til våren]*) (op. 21, no. 3)

Op. 42. Bergliot (*Bergliot*) (B. Bjørnson). Melodrama/piano, 1871. Rev. and arr. for orchestra, 1885.

Op. 43. Lyric Pieces III (*Lyriske stykker III*)
Piano, 1886.
1. Butterfly (*Sommerfugl*)
2. Solitary Traveler (*Ensom vandrer*)
3. In My Native Country (*I hjemmet*)
4. Little Bird (*Småfugl*)
5. Erotikon (*Erotik*)
6. To Spring (*Til våren*)

Op. 44. Reminiscences from Mountain and Fjord (*Rejseminder fra Fjeld og Fjord*)
(Holger Drachmann). Voice/piano, 1886.
1. Prologue (*Prolog*)
2. Johanne (*Johanne*)
3. Ragnhild (*Ragnhild*)
4. Ingeborg (*Ingeborg*)
5. Ragna (*Ragna*)
6. Epilogue (*Epilog*)

Op. 45. Violin Sonata No. 3 in C Minor (*Fiolinsonate nr. 3 i c-moll*)
Three movements. Violin/piano, 1886–87.

Op. 46. Peer Gynt Suite No. 1. (*Peer Gynt Suite nr. 1*)
Orchestra, 1887–88.
1. Morning Mood (*Morgenstemning*)
2. The Death of Åse (*Åses død*)
3. Anitra's Dance (*Anitras dans*)
4. In the Hall of the Mountain King (*I Dovregubbens hall*)

Op. 47. Lyric Pieces IV (*Lyriske stykker IV*)
Piano, 1885–88.
1. Waltz-Impromptu (*Valse-Impromptu*)
2. Album Leaf (*Albumblad*)
3. Melody (*Melodi*)
4. Halling (*Halling*)
5. Melancholy (*Melankoli*)
6. Springdans (*Springdans*)
7. Elegy (*Elegi*)

Op. 48. Six Songs (*Seks Sange*)
(Norwegian trans. by Nordahl Rolfsen) Voice/piano, 1884 and 1889.
1. Greeting (*Gruss/Hilsen*) (Heine)
2. One Day, O Heart of Mine (*Dereinst, Gedanke mein/Jeg ved, min Tanke, ved*) (Geibel)
3. The Way of the World (*Lauf der Welt/ Verdens Gang*)(Uhland)
4. The Nightingale's Secret (*Die verschwiegene*

Nachtigall/Nattergalen) (W. von der Vogelweide)
5. The Time of Roses (*Zur Rosenzeit/I Rosentiden*) (Goethe)
6. A Dream (*Ein Traum/En Drøm*) (Bodenstedt)

Op. 49. Six Songs (*Seks Digte af Holger Drachmann*) (Holger Drachmann). Voice/piano, 1886 and 1889.
1. Tell Me Now, Did You See the Lad (*Saa du Knøsen?*)
2. Rocking, Rocking on Gentle Waves (*Vug, • Vove*)
3. Kind Greetings, Fair Ladies (*Vær hilset, I Damer*)
4. Now Is Evening Light and Long (*Nu er Aftnen lys og lang*)
5. Christmas Snow (*Julesne*)
6. Spring Showers (*Foraarsregn*)

Op. 50. Scenes from "Olav Trygvason" (*Scener fra Olav Trygvason*) (B. Bjørnson). Unfinished opera. Comp. 1873, rev. and arr. for orchestra 1888.

Op. 51. Old Norwegian Melody with Variations (*Gammelnorsk romanse med variasjoner*)
Two pianos, 1890. Rev. and arr. for orchestra, 1900–05.

Op. 52. Transcriptions of Original Songs II (*Klaverstykker etter egne sanger II*)
Piano, 1890.
1. A Mother's Grieg (*Modersorg*) (op. 15, no. 4)
2. The First Meeting (*Det første møde*) (op. 21, no. 1)
3. The Poet's Heart (*Du fatter ej Bølgernes evige Gang*) (op. 5, no. 2)
4. Solveig's Song (*Solveigs sang*) (op. 23, no. 19)
5. Love (*Kjærlighed*) (op. 15, no. 2)
6. The Old Mother (*Gamle mor*) (op. 33, no. 7)

Op. 53. Two Melodies for String Orchestra (*To melodier for strykeorkester*). 1890
1. Norwegian ["The Goal"] (*Norsk* ["*Fyremål*"]) (op. 33, no. 12)
2. The First Meeting (*Det første møde*) (op. 21, no. 1)

Op. 54. Lyric Pieces V (*Lyriske stykker V*)
Piano, 1891.
1. Shepherd's Boy (*Gjetergutt*)
2. Gangar (*Gangar*)
3. March of the Dwarfs (*Trolltog*)
4. Nocturne (*Notturno*)
5. Scherzo (*Scherzo*)
6. Bell Ringing (*Klokkeklang*)

Op. 55. Peer Gynt Suite No. 2 (*Peer Gynt Suite nr. 2*) Orchestra, 1890–92.
1. The Abduction of the Bride. Ingrid's Lament (*Bruderovet. Ingrids klage*)
2. Arabian Dance (*Arabisk dans*)
3. Peer Gynt's Homecoming. Stormy Evening on the Sea (*Peer Gynts hjemfart. Stormfull aften på havet*)
4. Solveig's Song (*Solveigs sang*)

Op. 56. Three Orchestral Pieces from "Sigurd the Crusader" (*Tre orkesterstykker fra "Sigurd Jorsalfar"*), 1892.
1. Prelude ("At the Matching Game") (*Forspill* ["*Ved mannjevningen*"])
2. Intermezzo ("Borghild's Dream") (*Intermezzo* ["*Borghilds drøm*"])
3. Homage March (*Hyldningsmarsj*)

Op. 57. Lyric Pieces VI (*Lyriske stykker VI*)
Piano, 1893.
1. Vanished Days (*Svunne dager*)
2. Gade (*Gade*)
3. Illusion (*Illusjon*)
4. Secret (*Hemmelighet*)
5. She Dances (*Hun danser*)
6. Homesickness (*Hjemve*)

Op. 58. Five Songs (*Norge* ["*Digte af John Paulsen*"])
(John Paulsen). Voice/piano, 1893–94.
1. Homeward (*Hjemkomst*)
2. To the Motherland (*Til Norge*)
3. Henrik Wergeland (*Henrik Wergeland*)
4. The Shepherdess (*Turisten*)
5. The Emigrant (*Udvandreren*)

Op. 59. Six Elegiac Songs (*Elegiske Digte af John Paulsen*)
(John Paulsen). Voice/piano, 1893–94.
1. Autumn Farewell (*Når jeg vil dø*)
2. The Pine Tree (*På Norges nøgne fjelde*)
3. To Her (I) (*Til Én I*)
4. To Her (II) (*Til Én II*)

5. Good-bye (*Farvel*)
6. Your Eyes Are Closed Forever (*Nu hviler du i jorden*)

Op. 60. Five Songs (*Digte af Vilhelm Krag*)
(Vilhelm Krag). Voice/piano, 1893–94.
1. Little Kirsten (*Liden Kirsten*)
2. The Mother's Lament (*Moderen synger*)
3. On The Water (*Mens jeg venter*)
4. A Bird Cried Out (*Der skreg en Fugl*)
5. Midsummer Eve (*Og jeg vil ha mig en Hjertenskjær*)

Op. 61. Seven Children's Songs (*Barnlige Sange*)
Voice/piano, 1894. All arr. for 3-part chorus, 1901.
1. The Ocean (*Havet*) (Nordahl Rolfsen)
2. The Christmas Tree (*Sang til juletræet*) (Johan Krohn)
3. Farmyard Song (*Lok*) (B. Bjørnson)
4. Fisherman's Song (*Fiskervise*) (Petter Dass)
5. Good-night Song for Dobbin (*Kveldssang for Blakken*) (Nordahl Rolfsen)
6. The Norwegian Mountains (*De norske fjelde*) (Nordahl Rolfsen)
7. Hymn of the Fatherland (*Fædrelandssalme*) (Johan Ludvig Runeberg, trans. by Nordahl Rolfsen)

Op. 62. Lyric Pieces VII (*Lyriske stykker VII*)
Piano, 1895.
1. Sylph (*Sylfide*)
2. Gratitude (*Takk*)
3. French Serenade (*Fransk serenade*)
4. Brooklet (*Bekken*)
5. Phantom (*Drømmesyn*)
6. Homeward (*Hjemad*)

Op. 63. Two Nordic Melodies (*To nordiske melodier*)
String orchestra, 1895.
1. In Folk Style (*I folketonestil*) [melody by Fredrik Due]
2. Cow Call and Peasant Dance (*Kulokk & Stabbelåten*)

Op. 64. Symphonic Dances (*Symfoniske danser*) 1–4.
Orchestra, 1896–98.

Op. 65. Lyric Pieces VIII (*Lyriske stykker VIII*)
Piano, 1896.
1. From Early Years (*Fra ungdomsdagene*)
2. Peasant's Song (*Bondens sang*)
3. Melancholy (*Tungsinn*)
4. Salon (*Salong*)
5. Ballad (*I balladetone*)
6. Wedding Day at Troldhaugen (*Bryllupsdag på Troldhaugen*)

Op. 66. Nineteen Norwegian Folk Songs (*Nitten norske folkeviser*)
Piano, 1896.
1. Cow-Call (*Kulokk*)
2. It Is the Greatest Foolishness (*Det er den største dårlighed*)
3. A King Ruled in the East (*En konge hersket i Østerland*)
4. The Siri Dale Song (*Siri Dale-visen*)
5. It Was in My Youth (*Det var i min ungdom*)
6. Cow-Call and Lullaby (*Lokk og bådnlåt*)
7. Lullaby (*Bådnlåt*)
8. Cow-Call (*Lokk*)
9. Small Was the Lad (*Liten va guten*)
10. Tomorrow You Shall Marry Her (*Morgo ska du få gifta deg*)
11. There Stood Two Girls (*Der stander to piger*)
12. Ranveig (*Ranveig*)
13. A Little Grey Man (*En liten grå mann*)
14. In Ola Valley, in Ola Lake (*I Ola-dalom, i Ola-tjønn*)
15. Lullaby (*Bådnlåt*)
16. Little Astrid (*Ho vesle Astrid vår*)
17. Lullaby (*Bådnlåt*)
18. I Wander Deep in Thought (*Jeg går i tusen tanker*)
19. Gjendine's Lullaby (*Gjendines bådnlåt*)

Op. 67. The Mountain Maid (*Haugtussa*) ("Song Cycle from Arne Garborg's Story")
Voice/piano, 1895–98.
1. The Enticement (*Det syng*)
2. Veslemøy. The Young Maiden (*Veslemøy*)
3. Blueberry Slope (*Blåbær-Li*)
4. The Tryst (*Møte*)
5. Love (*Elsk*)
6. Kidlings' Dance (*Killingdans*)
7. Hurtful Day (*Vond Dag*)
8. At the Brook (*Ved Gjætle-Bekken*)

Op. 68. Lyric Pieces IX (*Lyriske stykker IX*)
Piano, 1898–99.

1. Sailors' Song (*Matrosenes oppsang*)
2. Grandmother's Minuet (*Bestemors menuett*)
3. At Your Feet (*For dine føtter*)
4. Evening in the Mountains (*Aften på høyfjellet*)
5. At the Cradle (*Bådnlåt*)
6. Valse Mélancholique (*Valse mélancholique*)

Op. 69. Five Songs (*Fem Digte af Otto Benzon*)
(Otto Benzon). Voice/piano, 1900.

1. A Boat on the Waves Is Rocking (*Der gynger en Båd på Bølge*)
2. To My Son (*Til min Dreng*)
3. At Mother's Grave (*Ved Moders Grav*)
4. Snail, Snail! (*Snegl, Snegl!*)
5. Dreams (*Drømme*)

Op. 70. Five Songs (*Fem Digte af Otto Benzon*)
(Otto Benzon). Voice/piano, 1900.

1. Eros (*Eros*)
2. A Life of Longing (*Jeg lever et Liv i Længsel*)
3. Summer Night (*Lys Nat*)
4. Walk With Care (*Se dig for*)
5. A Poet's Song (*Digtervise*)

Op. 71. Lyric Pieces X (*Lyriske stykker X*)
Piano, 1901.

1. Once Upon a Time (*Det var engang*)
2. Summer's Eve (*Sommeraften*)
3. Puck (*Småtroll*)
4. Peace of the Woods (*Skogstillhet*)
5. Halling (*Halling*)
6. Gone (*Forbi*)
7. Remembrances (*Efterklang*)

Op. 72. Norwegian Peasant Dances (*Slåtter*)
Arrangements for piano of Hardanger-fiddle dance tunes; based on Johan Halvorsen's transcriptions of the tunes as played by Knut Dahle, 1902–03.

1. Gibøen's Bridal March (*Gibøens bruremarsj*)
2. John Vestafæ's Springdans (*John Vestafæs springdans*)
3. Bridal March from Telemark (*Bruremarsj fra Telemark*)
4. Halling from the Fairy Hill (*Haugelåt*)
5. The Prillar from Os Parish (*Prillaren fra Os prestegjeld*)
6. Myllarguten's Gangar (*Gangar etter Myllarguten*)
7. Røtnams-Knut (*Røtnams-Knut*). Halling
8. Myllarguten's Bridal March (*Bruremarsj etter Myllarguten*)
9. Nils Rekve's Halling (*Nils Rekves halling*)
10. Knut Luråsen's Halling I (*Knut Luråsens halling I*)
11. Knut Luråsen's Halling II (*Knut Luråsens halling II*)
12. Myllarguten's Springdans (*Springdans etter Myllarguten*)
13. Håvar Gibøen's Dream at the Oterholt Bridge (*Håvar Gibøens draum ved Oterholtsbrua*). Springdans
14. The Goblins' Bridal Procession at Vossevangen (*Tussebrureferda på Vossevangen*). Gangar
15. The Skuldal Bride (*Skuldalsbrura*). Gangar
16. The Maidens from Kivledal (*Kivlemøyane*). Springdans from Seljord
17. The Maidens from Kivledal (*Kivlemøyane*). Gangar

Op. 73. Moods (*Stemninger*)
Piano, 1901–05.

1. Resignation (*Resignasjon*)
2. Scherzo-Impromptu (*Scherzo-Impromptu*)
3. A Ride at Night (*Nattlig ritt*)
4. Folk Melody(*Folketone*)
5. Study (*Studie*) ("Hommage à Chopin")
6. Students' Serenade (*Studentenes serenade*)
7. The Mountaineer's Song (*Lualåt*)

Op. 74. Four Psalms (*Fire salmer*)
Mixed chorus a cappella with baritone solo, 1906.

1. How Fair is Thy Face (*Hvad est du dog skjøn*) (H. A. Brorson)
2. God's Son Hath Set Me Free (*Guds Søn har gjort mig fri*) (Brorson)
3. Jesus Christ Our Lord is Risen (*Jesus Kristus er opfaren*) (Thomissøn)
4. In Heav'n Above (*I himmelen*) (Laurentii)

B. Compositions with EG Numbers

EG 101. Larvik Polka (*Larvikspolka*)
Piano, 1858. *GGA* 20, 1995 [B & Sch 102].

EG 102. Three Piano Pieces (*Tre klaverstykker*)
1858–59 [= 104, nos. 2, 6, 5]. *GGA* 20, 1995 [B & Sch 103].

EG 103. Nine Children's Pieces (*Ni barnestykker*)
Piano [= EG 104, nos. 4, 9, 10, 19, 21, 18, 13, 16, 7]. *GGA* 20, 1995 [B & Sch 104].

EG 104. 23 Short Pieces for Piano (*23 småstykker for klaver*)
Piano, 1858–59. *GGA* 20, 1995. (Cf. EG 102–103.) [B & Sch 105].

EG 105. Three Piano Pieces (*Tre klaverstykker*)
1860 [B & Sch 107].

EG 106. Agitato (*Agitato*)
Piano, 1865. *GGA* 20, 1995 [B & Sch 116].

EG 107. Funeral March for Rikard Nordraak (*Sørgemarsj over Rikard Nordraak*)
Piano, 1866. Also arr. for large wind ensemble with percussion, 1867 [B & Sch 117].

EG 108. Norway's Melodies (*Norges Melodier*)
("Norway's Melodies arranged for piano with accompanying texts"—a total of 154 numbers.) 1874–75 [B & Sch 133].

a. Six Norwegian mountain melodies. Piano, 1866. A revised edition of six numbers from EG 108 [B & Sch 134].
b. 10 original compositions.
c. 36 folk melodies.
d. 102 melodies by other composers.

EG 109. Album Leaf (*Albumblad*)
Piano, 1878 [B & Sch 136B].

EG 110. White Clouds (*Hvide Skyer*)
Piano, 1898 [B & Sch 154, no. 1].

EG 111. Procession of Gnomes (*Tusseslåt*)
Piano, 1898 [B & Sch 154, no. 2].

EG 112. In the Whirl of the Dance (*Dansen går*)
Piano, 1898 [B & Sch 154, no. 3].

EG 113. Mozart Piano Sonatas with a Freely Composed Second Piano Part (*Klaver II til fire sonater av Mozart*)
1877 [B & Sch 135].

EG 114. Fugue in F Minor (*Fuge i f-moll*)
String quartet, 1861. *GGA* 9, 1978 [B & Sch 109].

EG 115. Intermezzo (*Intermezzo*)
Cello/piano, 1866. *GGA* 8, 1979. [B & Sch 118].

EG 116. Andante con moto (*Andante con moto*)
Piano/violin/cello, 1878. *GGA* 9, 1978 [B & Sch 137].

EG 117. String Quartet No. 2 in F Major (*Strykekvartett nr. 2 i F-dur*)
Unfinished, 1891 [B & Sch 146].

EG 118. Fragments of a Piano Quintet (*Fragmenter av en klaverkvintett*)
Year of composition unknown. *GGA* 20, 1995 [B & Sch 162].

EG 119. Symphony in C Minor (*Symfoni i c-moll*)
1864. *GGA* 11, 1984 [B & Sch 112].

EG 120. Fragments of a Piano Concerto in B Minor (*Fragmenter til en klaverkonsert i h-moll*)
1883. *GGA* 20, 1995 [B & Sch 142].

EG 121. Look to the Sea (*Siehst du das Meer*)
(Geibel). Voice/piano, 1859. *GGA* 15, 1991 [B & Sch 106].

EG 122. The Singing Congregation (*Den syngende Menighed*)
(Grundtvig). Voice/piano, 1860. *GGA* 15, 1991 [B & Sch 108].

EG 123. Devoutest of Maidens (*Til Kirken hun vandrer*)
(Benjamin Feddersen). Voice/piano, 1864. *GGA* 15, 1991 [B & Sch 114].

EG 124. Clara's Song (*Claras Sang*)
From the light opera *Courting on Helgoland* (*Frieriet på Helgoland*) (Benjamin Feddersen). Voice/piano, 1864. *GGA* 15, 1991 [B & Sch 115].

EG 125. The Soldier (*Soldaten*)
(H. C. Andersen). Voice/piano 1865 [B & Sch 100, no. 5].

EG 126. My Little Bird (*Min lille Fugl*)
(H. C. Andersen). Voice/piano 1865 [B & Sch 100, no. 2].

EG 127. I Love You, Dear (*Dig elsker jeg!*) (Caralis = Caspara Preetzmann). Voice/piano, 1865 [B & Sch 100, no. 3].

EG 128. Tears (*Tåren*) (H. C. Andersen). Voice/piano, 1865 [B & Sch 100, no. 4].

EG 129. Little Lad (*Vesle gut*) (Kristofer Janson). Voice/piano, 1866. *GGA* 15, 1991 [B & Sch 119].

EG 130. The Fair-haired Maid (I) (*Den blonde Pige [I]*) (B. Bjørnson). Voice/piano, 1867 [B & Sch 100, no. 1].

EG 131. The Odalisque (*Odalisken synger*) (Carl Bruun). Voice/piano, 1870 [B & Sch 125].

EG 132. The Miner (*Bergmanden*) (Ibsen). Voice/piano, 1870 (?). *GGA* 15, 1991.

EG 133. The Princess (*Prinsessen*) (B. Bjørnson). Voice/piano, 1871 [B & Sch 126].

EG 134. Sighs (*Suk*) (B. Bjørnson). Voice/piano, 1873 [B & Sch 101, no. 4].

EG 135. For L. M. Lindeman's Silver Wedding Anniversary (*Til L. M. Lindemans Sølvbryllup*) (V. Nikolajsen).Voice/piano, 1873. 1873. *GGA* 15, 1991 [B & Sch 129, no. 2].

EG 136. To Christian Tønsberg (*Til Generalkonsul Christian Tønsberg*) (Johan Bøgh). Voice/piano, 1873. *GGA* 15, 1991 [B & Sch 129, no. 2].

EG 137. The White and Red, Red Roses (*Den hvide, røde Rose*) (B. Bjørnson). Voice/piano, 1873. *GGA* 15, 1991 [B & Sch 128].

EG 138. The Fair-haired Maid (II) (*Den blonde Pige [II]*) (B. Bjørnson). Voice/piano, 1874. *GGA* 15, 1991.

EG 139. Morning Prayer at School (*Morgenbøn på skolen*) (Fredrik Gjertsen). Voice/piano, 1875 [B & Sch 129, no. 3].

EG 140. On the Ruins of Hamar Cathedral (*På Hamars Ruiner*) (Vinje). Voice/piano, 1880 [B & Sch 101, no.1].

EG 141. The Young Woman (*Jenta*) (Vinje). Voice/piano, 1880. *GGA* 15, 1991 [B & Sch 138, no. 2].

EG 142. The Forgotten Maid (*Attegløyma*) (Vinje). Voice/piano, 1880. *GGA* 15, 1991 [B & Sch 138, no. 1].

EG 143. Dyre Vaa (*Dyre Vaa*) (Welhaven). Voice/piano, 1880. *GGA* 15, 1991.

EG 144. Beneath the Christmas Tree (*Under Juletræet*) (Nordahl Rolfsen). Voice/piano, 1885 [B & Sch 129, no. 4].

EG 145. The Blueberry (*Blåbæret*) (Didrik Grønvold). Voice/piano, 1896. *GGA* 15, 1991 [B & Sch 153].

EG 146. Easter Song (*Osterlied*) (A Böttger). Voice/piano, 1889 [B & Sch 144].

EG 147. A Simple Song (*Simpel Sang*) (Holger Drachmann). Voice/piano, 1889 [B & Sch 101, no.3].

EG 148. You Often Fix Your Gaze (*Du retter tidt dit Øyepar*) (Holger Drachmann). Voice/piano, 1889. *GGA* 15, 1991 [B & Sch 145].

EG 149. Election Song (*Valgsang*) (B. Bjørnson). Men's chorus, 1893 [B & Sch 122].

EG 150. Ave maris stella (*Ave maris stella*) (Thor Lange). Voice/piano, 1893. Mixed chorus, 1899 [B & Sch 155 & 156, no. 2].

EG 151. National Song (*Fædrelandssang*) (John Paulsen). Voice/piano, 1894. *GGA* 15, 1991 [B & Sch 160].

EG 152. Garborg Songs (*Haugtussa-sanger*) (Songs from The Mountain Maid not included in op. 67). Voice/piano, 1895. *GGA* 15, 1991 [B & Sch 149].

1. Prologue (*Prolog*)
2. Veslemøy at the Spinning Wheel (*Veslemøy ved rokken*)
3. Dusk (*Kvelding*)
4. The Sparrow (*Sporven*) arr. for 3-part

women's chorus/piano 1895, *GGA* 17, 1995 [B & Sch 150].
5. Warning (*Fyrevarsel*)
6. In the Hayfield (*I slåtten*)
7. Veslemøy Wondering (*Veslemøy undrast*)
8. Doomed (*Dømd*)
9. The Nice Boy (*Den snille guten*)
10. Veslemøy Longing (*Veslemøy lengtar*)
11. Forest Joy (*Skog-glad*)
12. Cow-call (*Ku-Lok*)

EG 153. I Loved Him (*Jeg elsket*)
From the unfinished "Peace Oratorio" (*oratoriet Fred*)(B. Bjørnson). Voice/piano, 1891 [B & Sch 101, no. 2].

EG 154. To a Devil
(English text was the original) (Otto Benzon). Voice/piano, 1900. *GGA* 15, 1901 [B & Sch 157].

EG 155. Yuletide Cradle Song (*Julens Vuggesang*)
(Adolf Langsted). Voice/piano, 1900 [B & Sch 101, no. 5].

EG 156. Gentlemen Rankers (*Gentlemen-menige*)
(Norw. trans. Rosenkrantz Johnsen) (R. Kipling). Voice/piano, 1900. *GGA* 15, 1901 [B & Sch 158].

EG 157. The Hunter (*Der Jäger*)
(W. Schultz). Voice/piano, 1905 [B & Sch 101, no. 6].

EG 158. Cantata for the Unveiling of the W. F. K. Christie Monument (*Christie-kantate*)
(Andreas Munch). Male chorus/wind instruments, 1868. *GGA* 16, 1986 [B & Sch 123].

EG 159. Dona nobis pacem (*Dona nobis pacem*)
Mixed chorus, 1862. *GGA* 17, 1985 [B & Sch 110].

EG 160. Four Songs for Male Chorus (*Fire mannskorsanger*)
1863. *GGA* 17, 1985 [B & Sch 111].
1. Norwegian War Song (*Norsk krigssang*) (Wergeland)
2. Fredriksborg (*Fredriksborg*) (Chr. Richardt)
3. Student Life (*Studereliv*) (Chr. Richardt)
4. The Late Rose (*Den sildige rose*) (A. Munch)

EG 161. Denmark (*Danmark*)
(H. C. Andersen). Mixed chorus/piano, 1864. *GGA* 17, 1985 [B & Sch 113].

EG 162. Two Songs for Male Chorus (*To sanger for mannskor*)
(Jørgen Moe). 1867.
1. Evening Mood (*Aftenstemning*) [B & Sch 121]
2. The Bear Hunter (*Bjørneskytten*) [B & Sch 120]

EG 163. Norwegian Sailors' Song (*Sjømandssang*)
(B. Bjørnson). Male chorus, 1869–70 [B & Sch 124].

EG 164. Cantata for Karl Hals (*Kantate til Karl Hals*)
(B. Bjørnson). Tenor/women's chorus/mixed chorus/piano, 1873. *GGA* 17, 1985 [B & Sch 130].

EG 165. At J. S. Welhaven's Grave (*Ved J. S. Welhavens Grav*)
(Jørgen Moe). Male chorus, 1873 [B & Sch 127].

EG 166. Chorus for the Supporters of Freedom in Scandinavia (*Opsang for Frihedsfolket i Norden*)
(B. Bjørnson). Male chorus, 1874 [B & Sch 131].

EG 167. At the Halfdan Kjerulf Statue (*Ved Halfdan Kjerulfs Mindestøtte*)
(Andreas Munch). Tenor/male chorus, 1874 [B & Sch 132]. Also arr. for piano solo.

EG 168. Inga Litamor (*Inga Litamor*)
Baritone/male chorus, 1901. *GGA* 17, 1985 [B & Sch 136A].

EG 169. Two Songs for Male Chorus (*To mannskorsanger av Olav Lofthus*)
(Olaf Lofthus). 1881.
1. My Finest Thought (*Min deiligste tanke*) [B & Sch 139].
2. Our Watchword (*Vårt løsen*) [B & Sch 140].

EG 170. A Greeting to the Singers (*Sangerhilsen*)
(Sigvald Skavlan). Male chorus, 1883 [B & Sch 141].

EG 171. Holberg Cantata (*Holberg-kantate*)
(Nordahl Rolfsen). Baritone/male chorus, 1884 [B & Sch 143].

EG 172. Song of the Flag (*Flagvise*)
(Johan Brun). Male chorus, 1893. *GGA* 17, 1985 [B & Sch 147].

EG 173. Greetings from Christiania Singers (*Kristianiensernes Sangerhilsen*)
(Jonas Lie). Baritone/male chorus, 1896 [B & Sch 151].

EG 174. Westerly Wind (*Jædervise*)
(Jonas Dahl). Male chorus, 1896 [B & Sch 161].

EG 175. Impromptu (*Impromptu*)
(B. Bjørnson). Male chorus, 1896 [B & Sch 152].

EG 176. To Ole Bull (*Til Ole Bull*)
(Welhaven). Male chorus, 1901. *GGA* 17, 1985. Voice/piano, 1901. *GGA* 17, 1985 [B & Sch 159].

EG 177. Six Songs with Orchestra (*Seks sanger med orkester*)
Orchestrated 1894–95 [B & Sch 148].

1. Solveig's Song (*Solveigs sang*) (op. 23, no. 19)
2. Solveig's Cradle Song (*Solveigs vuggevise*) (op. 23, no. 26)
3. From Monte Pincio (*Fra Monte Pincio*) (op. 39, no. 1)
4. A Swan (*En Svane*) (op. 25, no. 2)
5. Last Spring (*Våren*) (op. 33, no. 2)
6. Henrik Wergeland (*Henrik Wergeland*) (op. 58, no. 3)

EG 178. Halling (*Halling*)
Transcription for Hardanger fiddle. *GGA* 20, 1995.

EG 179. Canon a 4 voci (*Kanon*)
Piano, 1862–62. *GGA* 20, 1995.

EG 180. Andante (*Andante*)
Introduction to "The Mountain Maid" (*Innledning til "Haugtussa"*) [?]. Piano, 1895. *GGA* 20, 1995.

EG 181. Ragnhild. (*Ragnhild*)
(Drachmann). Voice/piano, 1886, The original version of op. 44 no. 3. *GGA* 20, 1995.

EG 182. Resignation (*Resignasjon*)
Grieg's orchestration of Edmund Neupert's piano piece, 1895.

EG 183. Entry of the Boyars (*Bojarernes Indtogsmarsch*)
Grieg's piano arrangement of Johan Halvorsen's orchestral work, 1895.

EG 184. Pieces from exercise books at the Leipzig Conservatory of Music.

Bibliography

A Chronological List of the Most Important Published Editions of Grieg's Letters

Platzhoff-Lejeune, Edvard: "Aus Briefen Edvard Griegs an einem Schweizer," in *Die Musik*. Berlin, 1907–08.

Hauch, Gunnar: *Breve fra Grieg*. Copenhagen, 1922.

Beyer, Marie: *Breve fra Edvard Grieg til Frants Beyer 1872–1907*. Oslo, 1923.

Röntgen, Julius: *Edvard Grieg*. The Hague, 1930.

Zschinsky-Troxler, Elsa von: *Edvard Grieg. Briefe an die Verleger der Edition Peters 1886–1907*. Leipzig, 1932.

Röntgen, des Amorie van der Hoeven: *Brieven van Julius Röntgen*. Amsterdam, 1934.

Anker, Øyvind: "Knut Dahle—Edvard Grieg—Johan Halvorsen. En brevveksling," in *Norsk Musikkgranskning. Årbok 1943–46*. Oslo, 1947.

Berg, Sigurd: "Edvard Grieg. Brev til Niels Ravnkilde," in *Ord och Bild*. Stockholm, 1947.

Wallner, Bo: "Edvard Griegs brev til Tor Aulin," in *Ord och Bild*. Stockholm, 1952.

Gaukstad, Øystein: "Edvard Grieg og Adolf Brodsky," in *Norsk Musikktidsskrift*. Oslo, 1967, nos. 1 og 2.

Kortsen, Bjarne: *Grieg the Writer. Vol. 2: Letters to Frants Beyer*. Bergen, 1973.

Reznicek, Ladislav: *Edvard Grieg og tsjekkisk kultur*. Oslo, 1975.

Bjørkvold, Jon-Roar: "Peter Čajkovskij og Edvard Grieg—en kontakt mellom to åndsfrender," in *Studia Musicologica Norvegica 2*. Oslo, 1976.

Huys, Bernhard: Onuitgegeven autographische brieven van Edvard en Nina Grieg en Alexander Bull aan Arthur de Greef, bewaard in de Koninklijke Bibliotheek Albert I te Brussel," in *Academiae Analecta*, Jahrgang 49, No. 1. Brussels, 1988.

Benestad, Finn & Bjarne Kortsen: *Edvard Grieg. Brev til Frants Beyer 1872–1907*. Oslo, 1993.

Carley, Lionel: *Grieg and Delius. A Chronicle of Their Friendship in Letters*. London & New York, 1993.

Stavland, Hanna de Vries: *Julius Röntgen og Edvard Grieg. Et musikalsk vennskap*. Bergen, 1994.

Huys, Bernhard & Eivind A. C. Eikenes: *Arthur de Greef— en venn av Edvard Grieg*. Stavanger, 1994.

Oelmann, Klaus Henning: *Edvard Griegs Briefwechsel. Bd 2: Der Briefwechsel mit dem Hause Breitkopf & Härtel, die Briefe von Frederick Delius an Nina und Edvard Grieg und andere ausgewählte Schreiben*. Egelsbach/Frankfurt/St. Peter Port, 1997.

Benestad, Finn & Hella Brock: *Edvard Grieg. Briefwechsel mit dem Musikverlag C. F. Peters 1863–1907*. Frankfurt am Main, 1997.

Benestad, Finn & Hanna de Vries Stavland: *Edvard Grieg und Julius Röntgen. Briefwechsel 1883–1907*. Amsterdam, 1997.

Benestad, Finn: *Edvard Grieg: Brev i utvalg 1862–1907*. 2 vols. Oslo, 1998.

• • •

A detailed account of Grieg's life and work will be found in Finn Benestad & Dag Schjelderup-Ebbe: *Edvard Grieg: The Man and the Artist*. Lincoln, 1988.

All of Grieg's extant compositions are printed in *Edvard Grieg: Complete Works*, vols. 1–20. C. F. Peters Musikverlag, Frankfurt/Leipzig/London/New York, 1977–95.

Index of Compositions

Compositions by Grieg mentioned in the introductions or footnotes are indicated by, respectively, a lower-case "i" or "n" following the page number. All other page numbers indicate references by Grieg to the compositions in question. Extensive works and works comprising more than one item or movement are italicized. The opus numbers are those assigned by Grieg himself. Compositions without opus numbers are listed with the "EG" numbers assigned in Vol. 20 of *Edvard Grieg: Complete Works.* When a composition is mentioned both in a letter and in a footnote keyed to that occurrence, only the former is indexed.

General Index

This index includes names and topics in a single alphabetical list. Grieg's compositions are not included here but are listed in a separate Index of Compositions on pp. 707–710. Compositions by other composers will be found here as sub-entries under the names of the respective composers, with longer works in italics, shorter works in quotation marks. Cities are indexed when mentioned by Grieg in connection with his travel or concert plans but not when they are merely identified as the place where a given letter was written. For information regarding the latter, see "Chronological List of Grieg Letters in the Present Volume" on pp. 687–692. When an item occurs both in a letter and in a footnote keyed to that occurrence, only the former is indexed.

Bold numbers indicate the page(s) containing Grieg's letter(s) to the person named or an extended discussion of the individual or topic identified. Numbers followed by "i", "n" or "p" denote, respectively, an editor's introduction, a footnote, or a picture caption.

The letter "æ" is alphabetized as "ae", "ø" and "ö" as "o", "å"and "ä" as "a", "ü" as "u".

C

D

O

P

T